YOWAMUSHI PEDAL

WATARU WATANABE

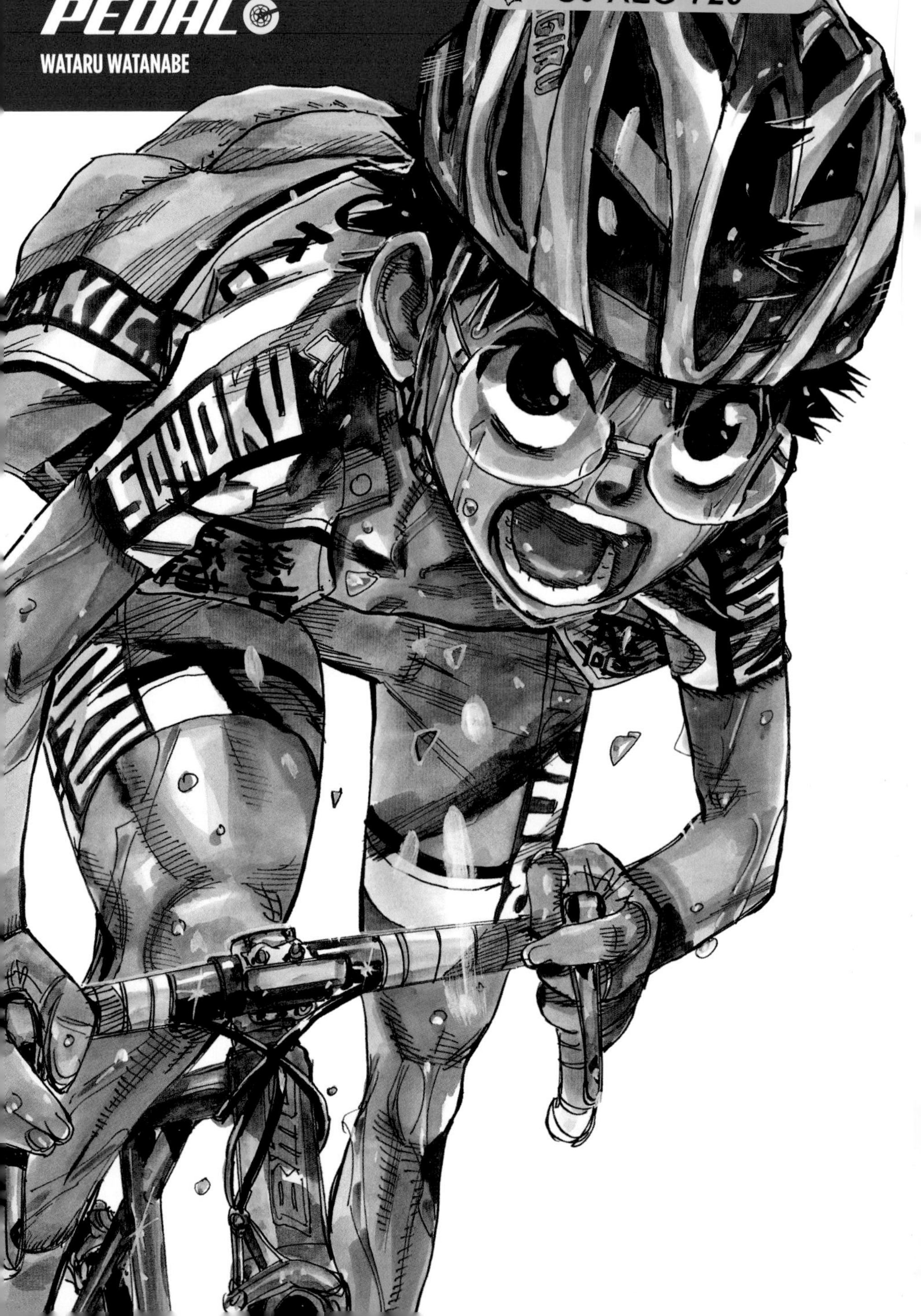
SOHOKU

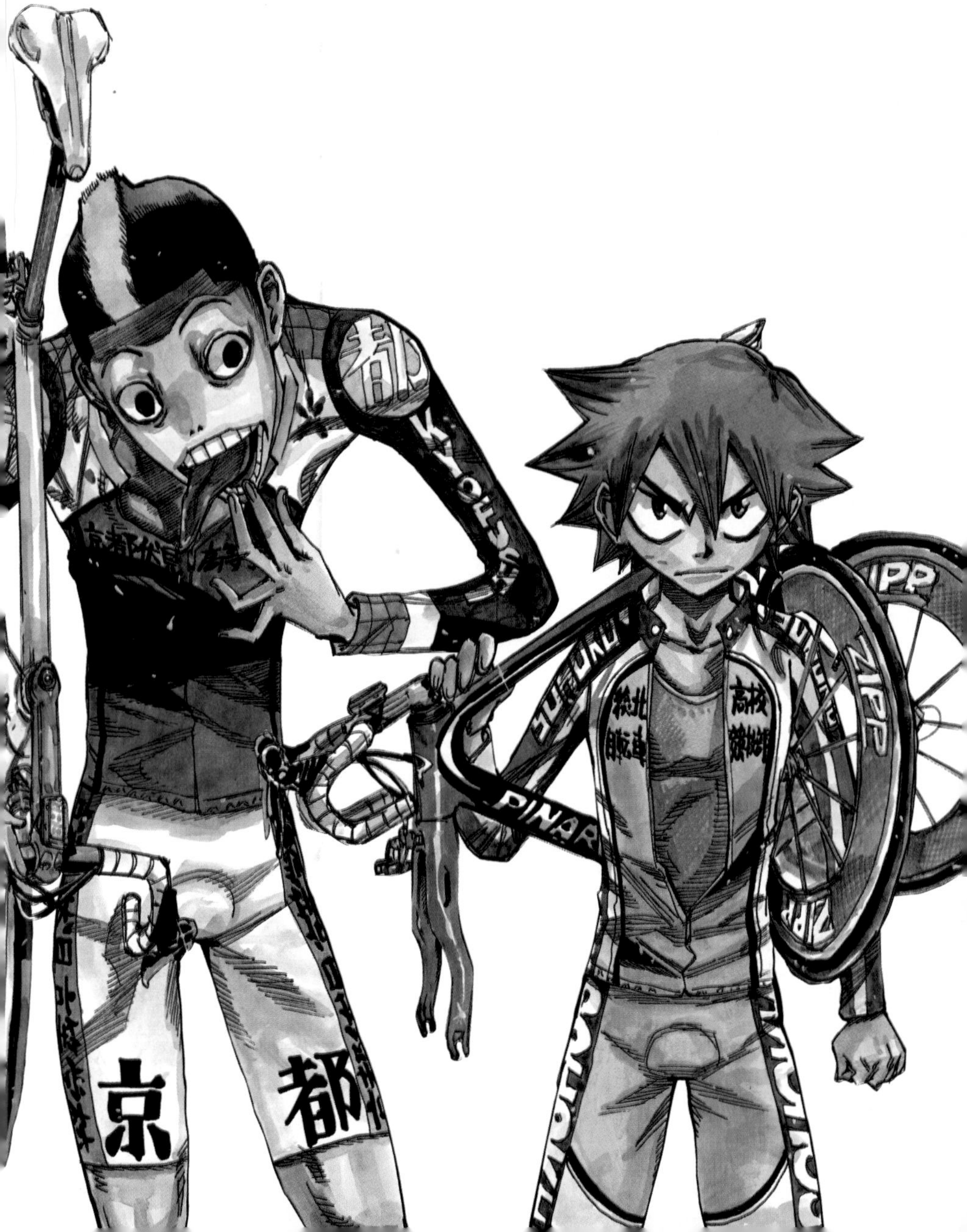
京
都
ZIPP
PINAR

YOWAMUSHI PEDAL

WATARU WATANABE

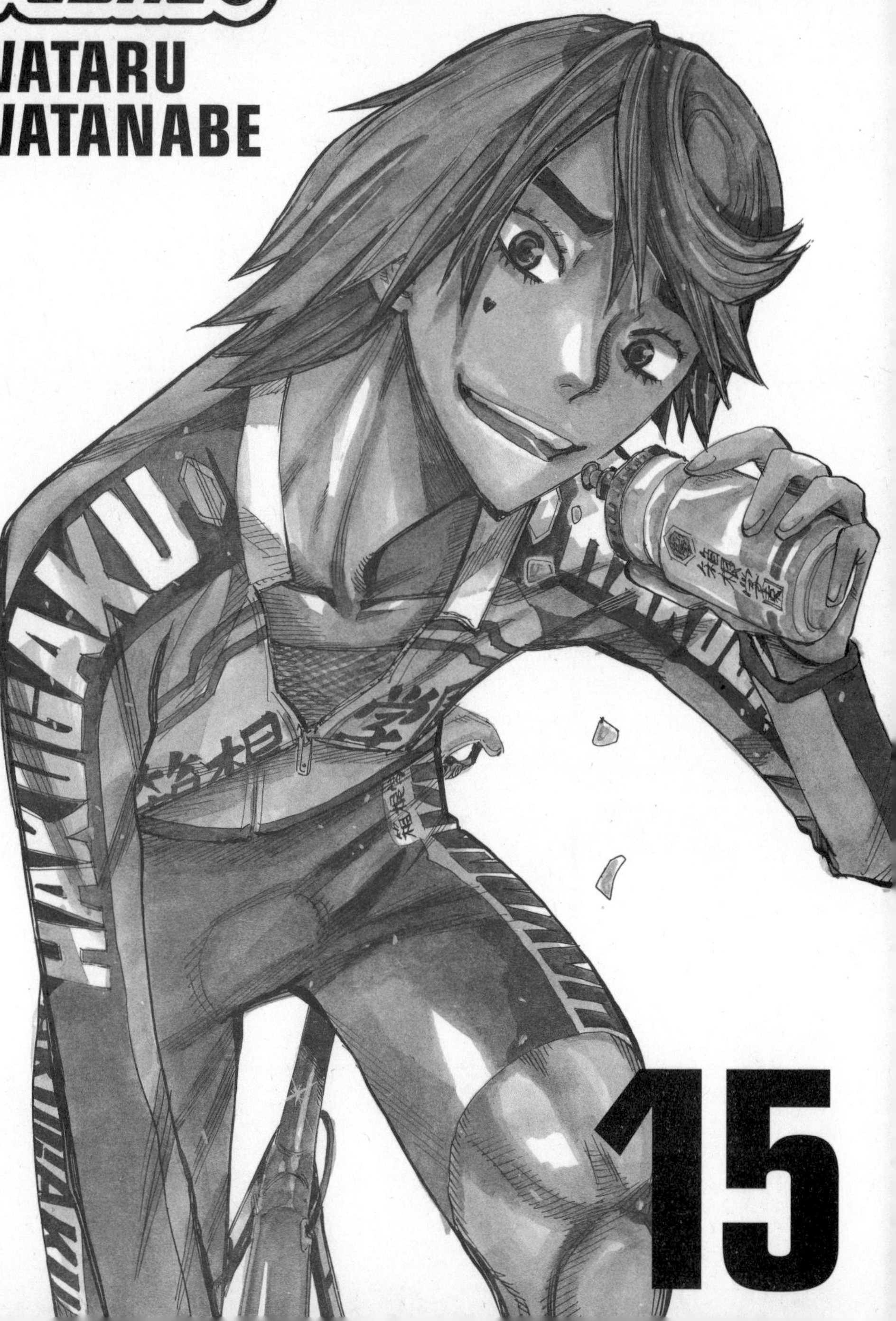

15

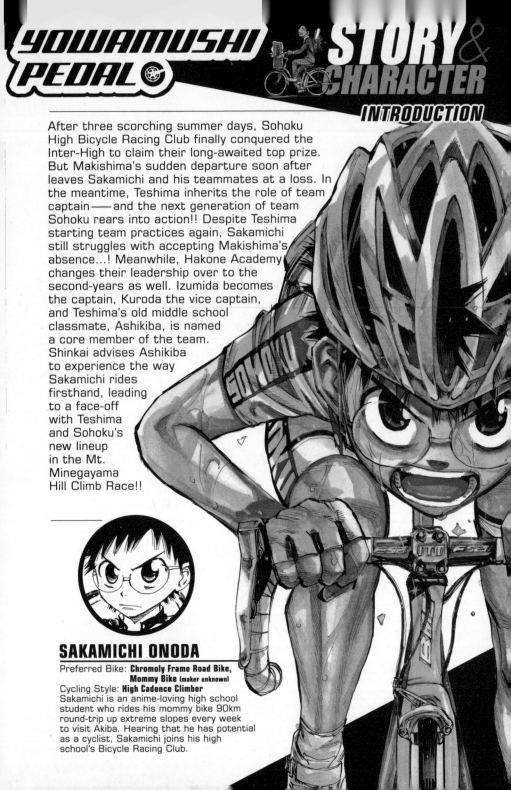

YOWAMUSHI PEDAL

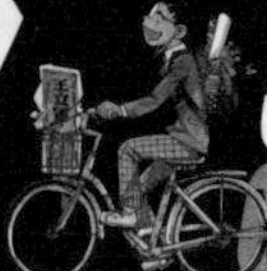

STORY & CHARACTER

INTRODUCTION

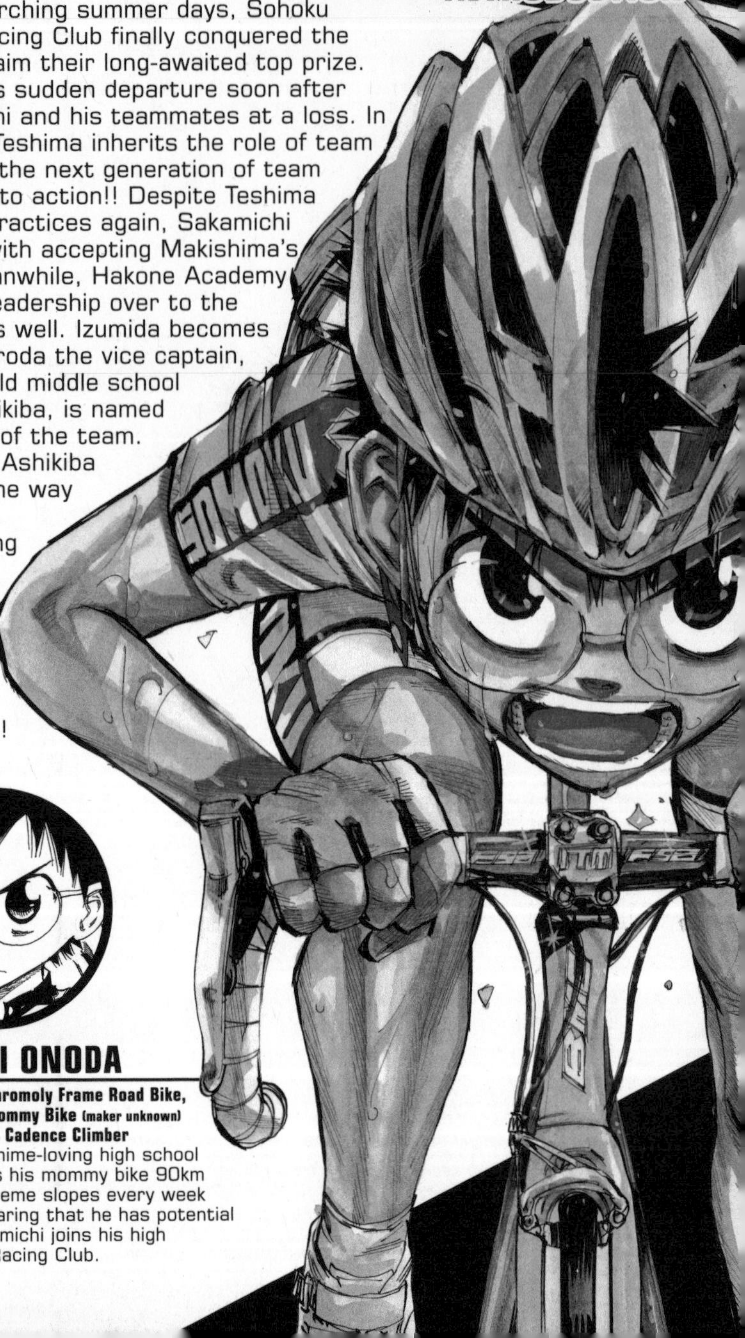

After three scorching summer days, Sohoku High Bicycle Racing Club finally conquered the Inter-High to claim their long-awaited top prize. But Makishima's sudden departure soon after leaves Sakamichi and his teammates at a loss. In the meantime, Teshima inherits the role of team captain——and the next generation of team Sohoku rears into action!! Despite Teshima starting team practices again, Sakamichi still struggles with accepting Makishima's absence...! Meanwhile, Hakone Academy changes their leadership over to the second-years as well. Izumida becomes the captain, Kuroda the vice captain, and Teshima's old middle school classmate, Ashikiba, is named a core member of the team. Shinkai advises Ashikiba to experience the way Sakamichi rides firsthand, leading to a face-off with Teshima and Sohoku's new lineup in the Mt. Minegayama Hill Climb Race!!

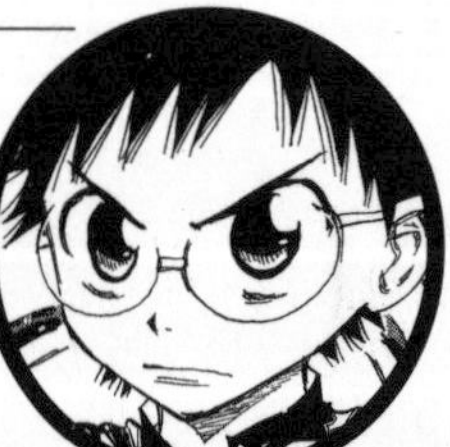

SAKAMICHI ONODA

Preferred Bike: **Chromoly Frame Road Bike, Mommy Bike (maker unknown)**

Cycling Style: **High Cadence Climber**

Sakamichi is an anime-loving high school student who rides his mommy bike 90km round-trip up extreme slopes every week to visit Akiba. Hearing that he has potential as a cyclist, Sakamichi joins his high school's Bicycle Racing Club.

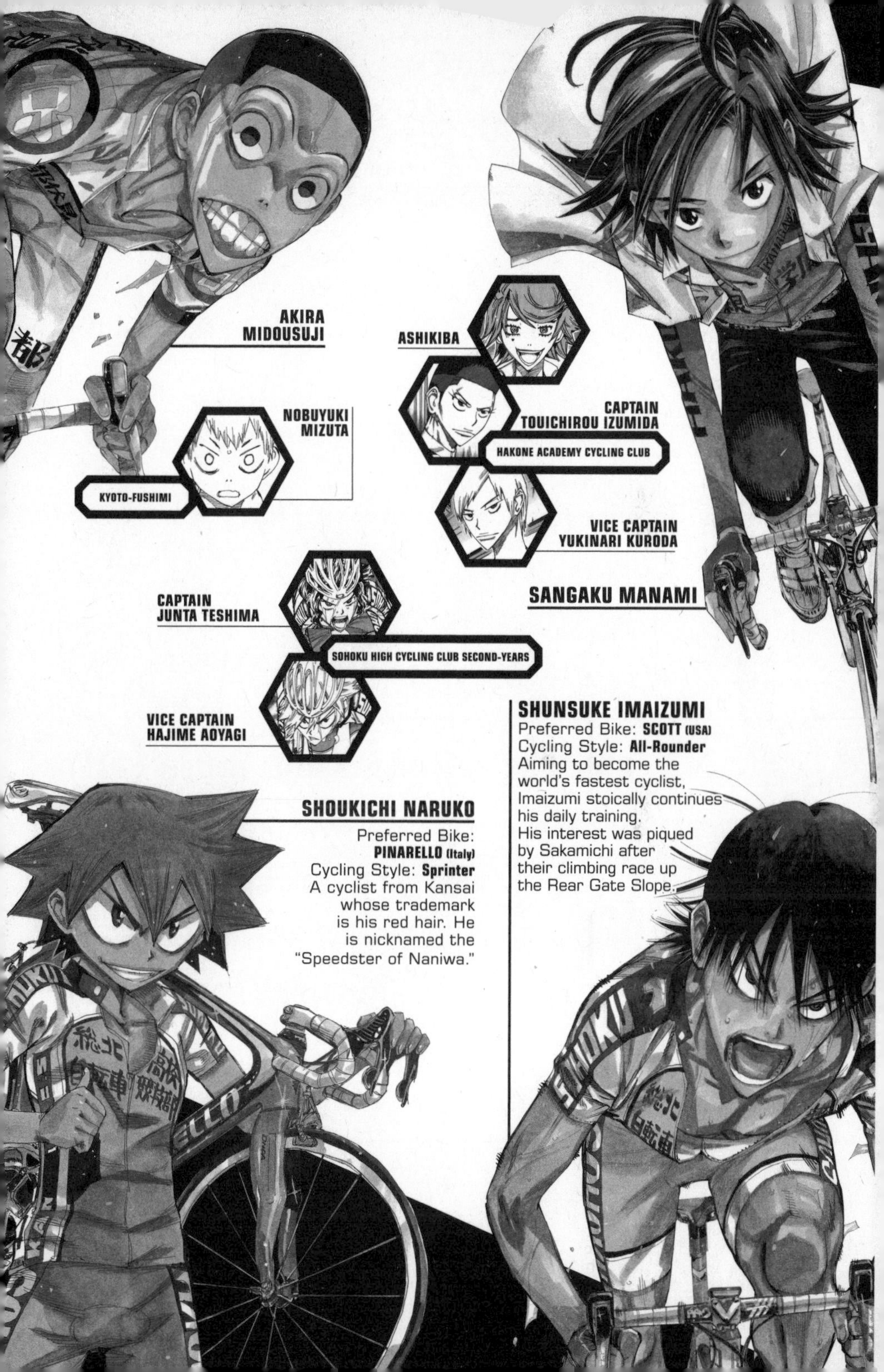
SANGAKU MANAMI
HAKONE ACADEMY CYCLING CLUB
ASHIKIBA
CAPTAIN
TOUICHIROU IZUMIDA
VICE CAPTAIN
YUKINARI KURODA
AKIRA
MIDOUSUJI
KYOTO-FUSHIMI
NOBUYUKI
MIZUTA
SOHOKU HIGH CYCLING CLUB SECOND-YEARS
CAPTAIN
JUNTA TESHIMA
VICE CAPTAIN
HAJIME AOYAGI
SHUNSUKE IMAIZUMI
Preferred Bike: SCOTT (USA)
Cycling Style: All-Rounder
Aiming to become the world's fastest cyclist, Imaizumi stoically continues his daily training.
His interest was piqued by Sakamichi after their climbing race up the Rear Gate Slope.
SHOUKICHI NARUKO
Preferred Bike: PINARELLO (Italy)
Cycling Style: Sprinter
A cyclist from Kansai whose trademark is his red hair. He is nicknamed the "Speedster of Naniwa."

VOL.15 YOWAMUSHI PEDAL CONTENTS

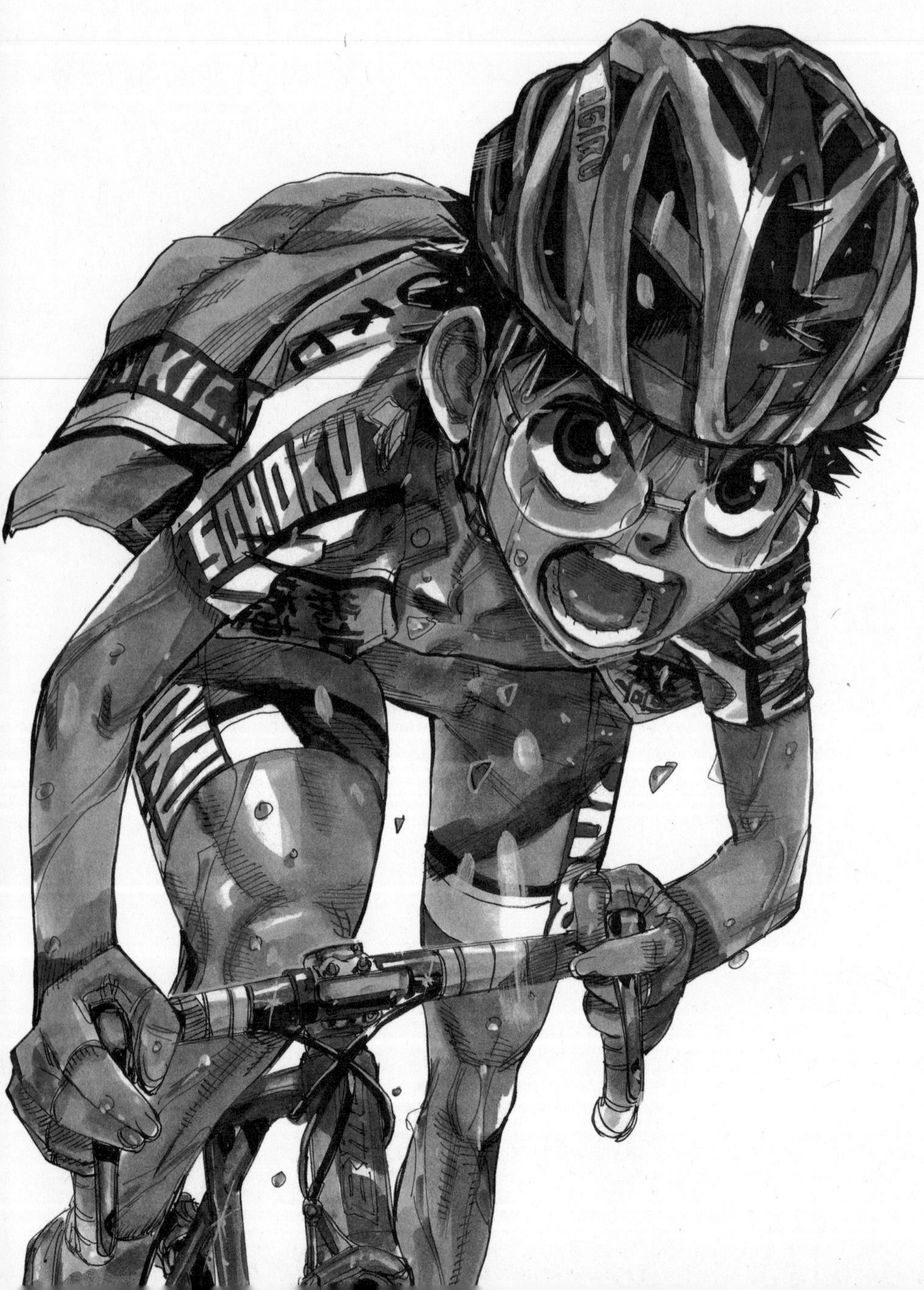
SOHOKU

RIDE.244 THE FASTEST MAN ON MINEGAYAMA

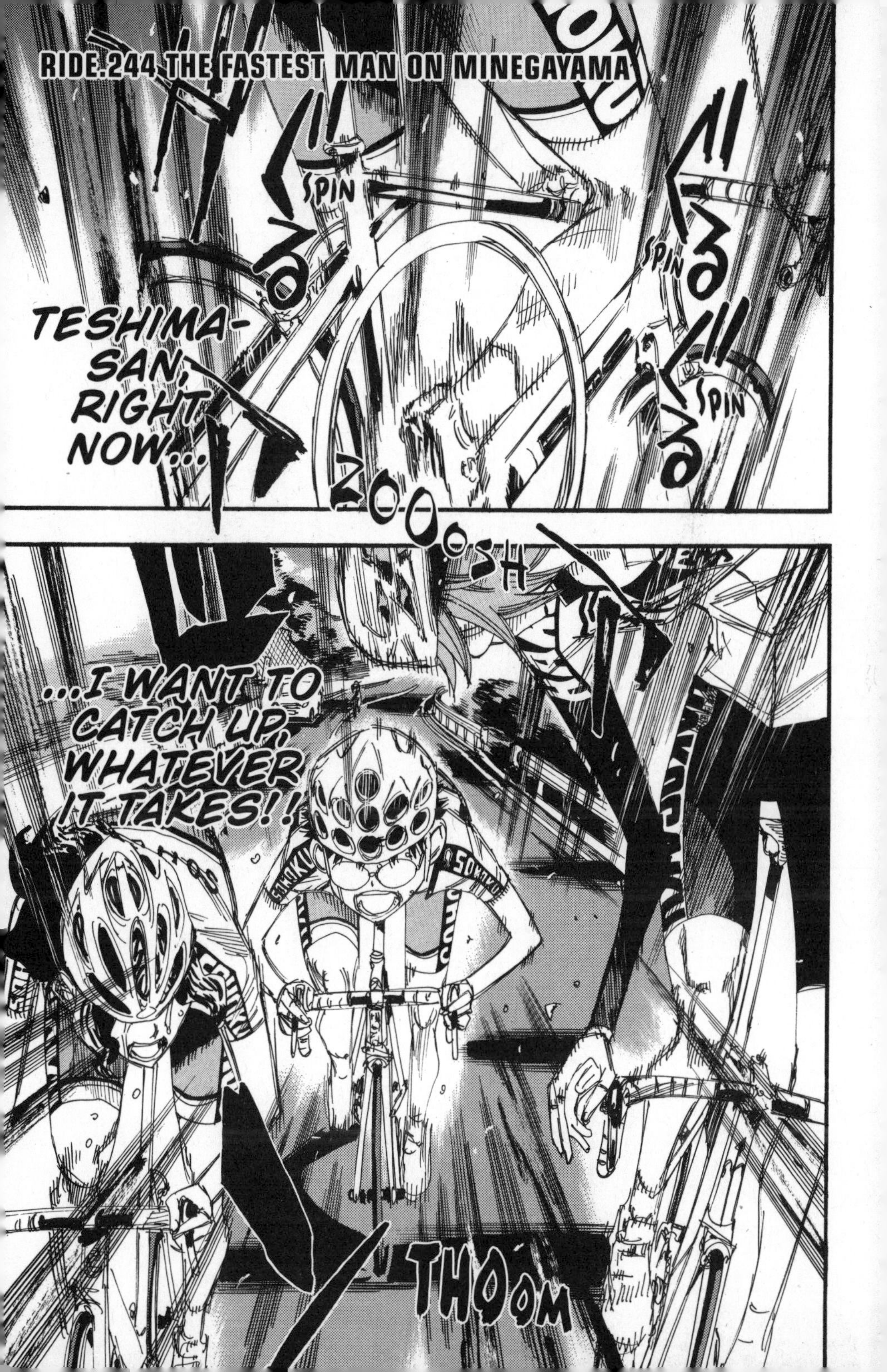

SPIN
SPIN
SPIN
TESHIMA-SAN, RIGHT NOW...
ZOOOOSH
...I WANT TO CATCH UP, WHATEVER IT TAKES!!
THOOM

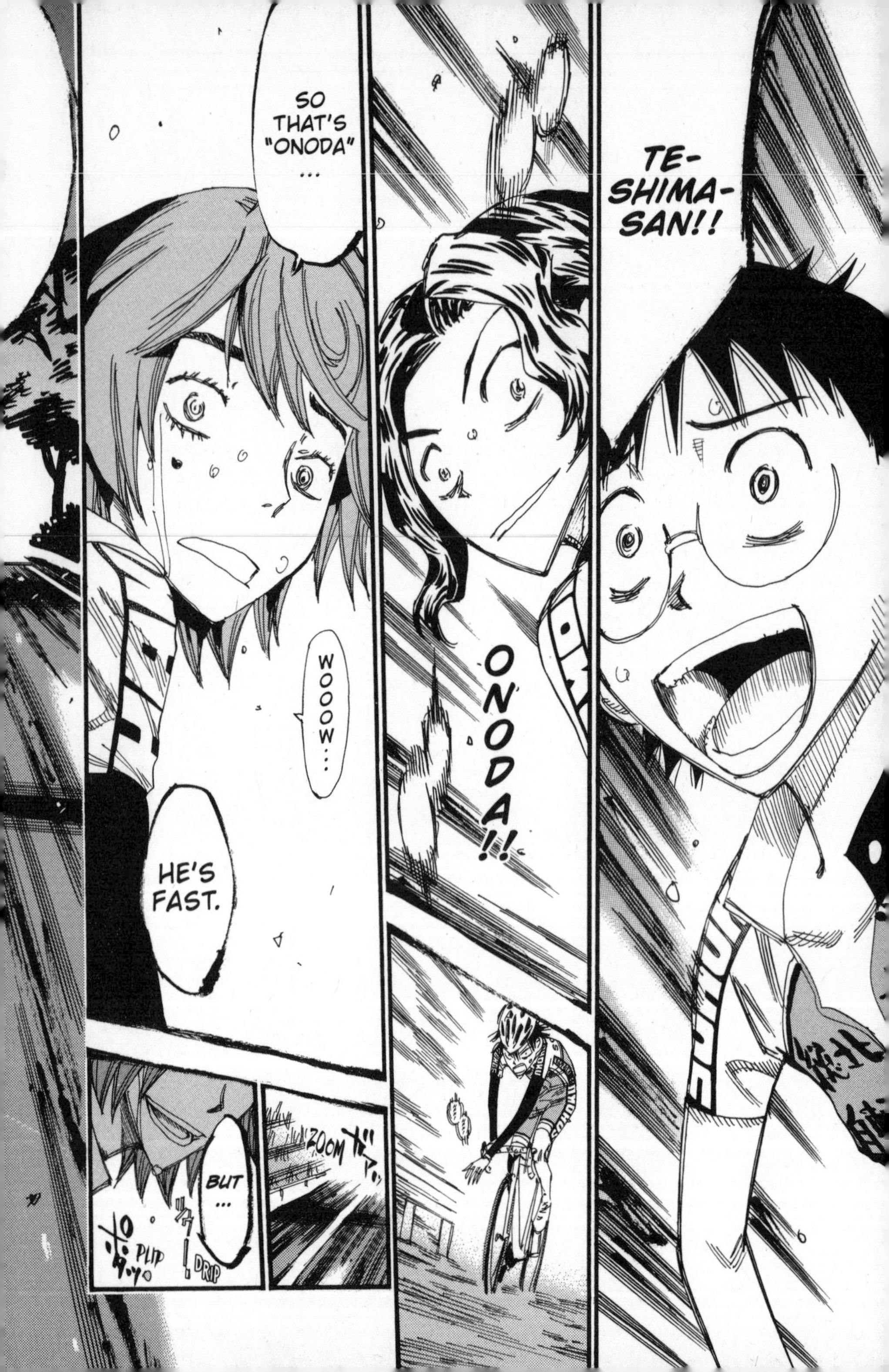
TE-SHIMA-SAN!!
ONODA!!
SO THAT'S "ONODA" ...
WOOOW...
HE'S FAST.
ZOOM
BUT ...
DRIP
PLIP

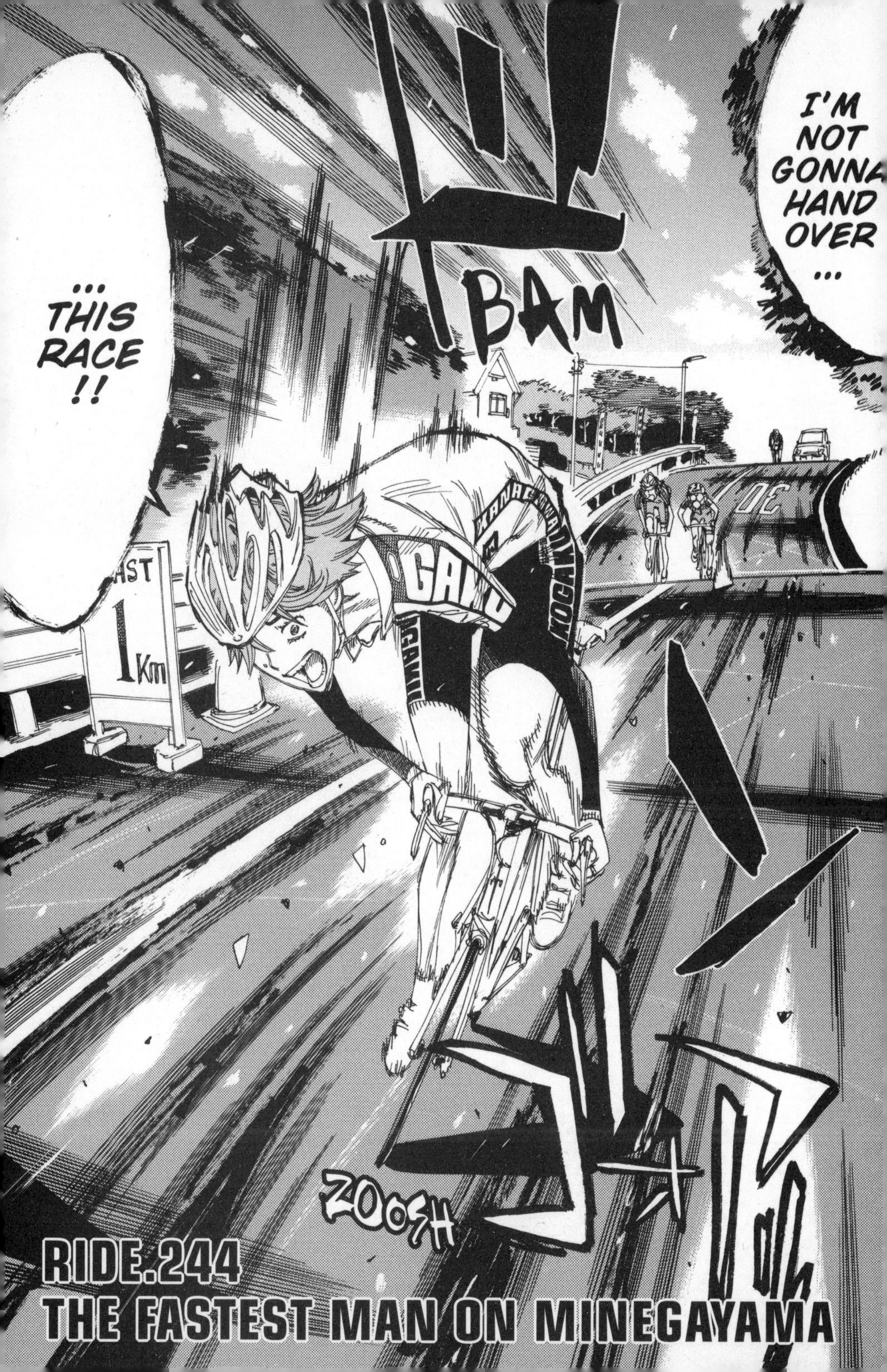
I'M NOT GONNA HAND OVER ...
BAM
... THIS RACE !!
ZOOSH

RIDE.244
THE FASTEST MAN ON MINEGAYAMA

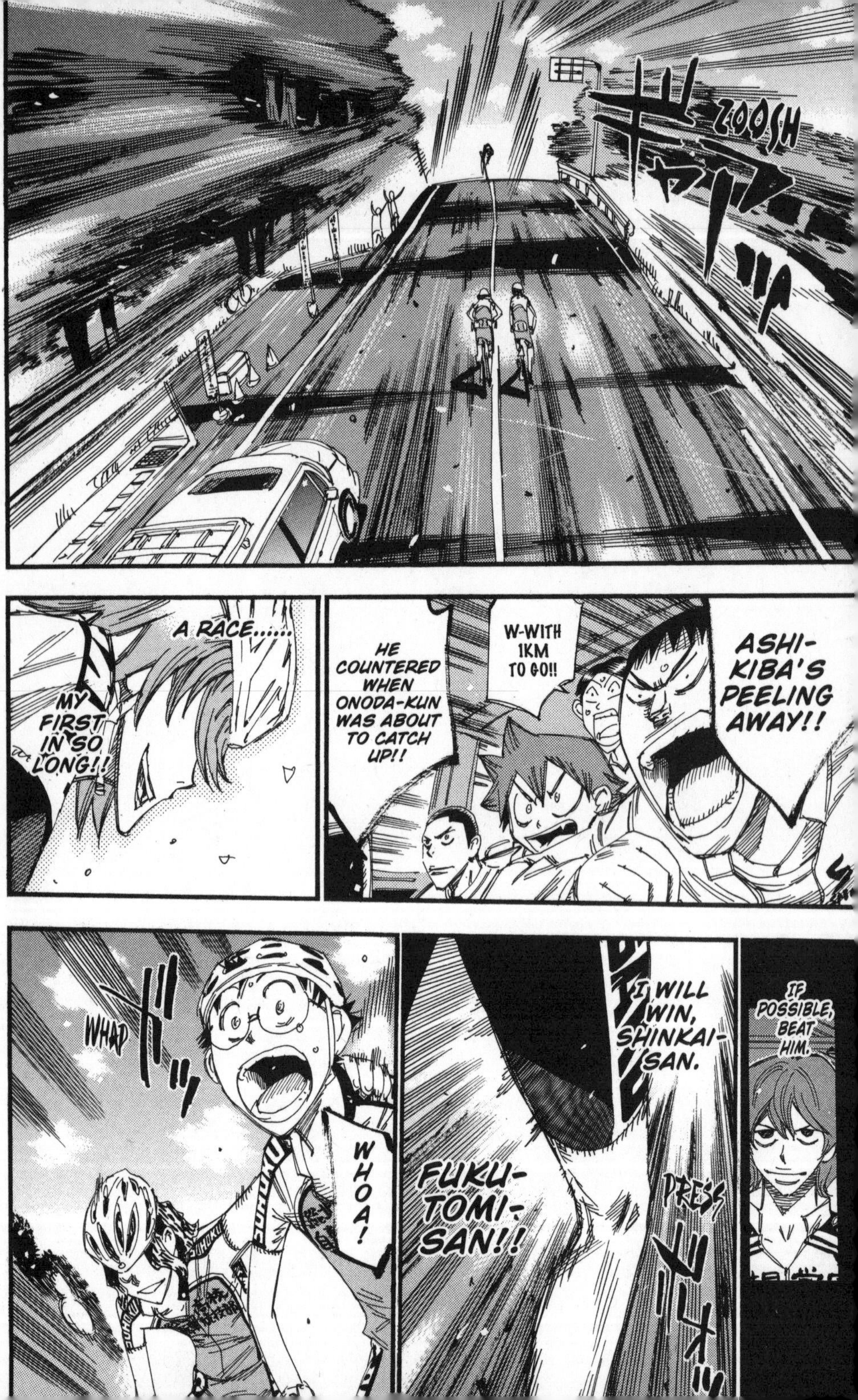
ZOOSH
ASHI-KIBA'S PEELING AWAY!!
W-WITH 1KM TO GO!!
HE COUNTERED WHEN ONODA-KUN WAS ABOUT TO CATCH UP!!
A RACE......
MY FIRST IN SO LONG!!
IF POSSIBLE, BEAT HIM.
I WILL WIN, SHINKAI-SAN.
FUKU-TOMI-SAN!!
PRESS
WHAD
WHOA!

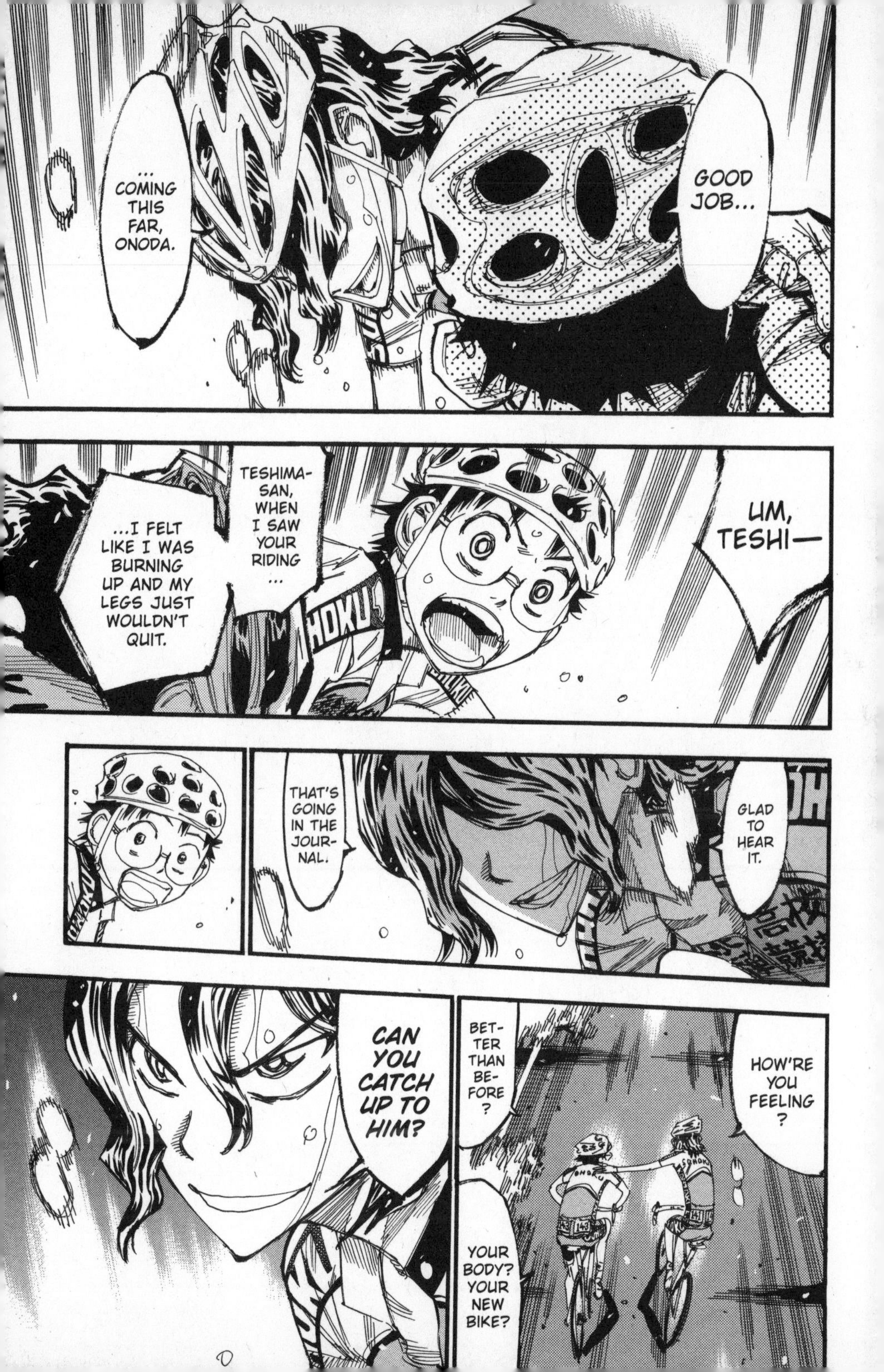
GOOD JOB...
...COMING THIS FAR, ONODA.
UM, TESHI—
TESHIMA-SAN, WHEN I SAW YOUR RIDING...
...I FELT LIKE I WAS BURNING UP AND MY LEGS JUST WOULDN'T QUIT.
GLAD TO HEAR IT.
THAT'S GOING IN THE JOURNAL.
HOW'RE YOU FEELING?
BETTER THAN BEFORE?
YOUR BODY? YOUR NEW BIKE?
CAN YOU CATCH UP TO HIM?

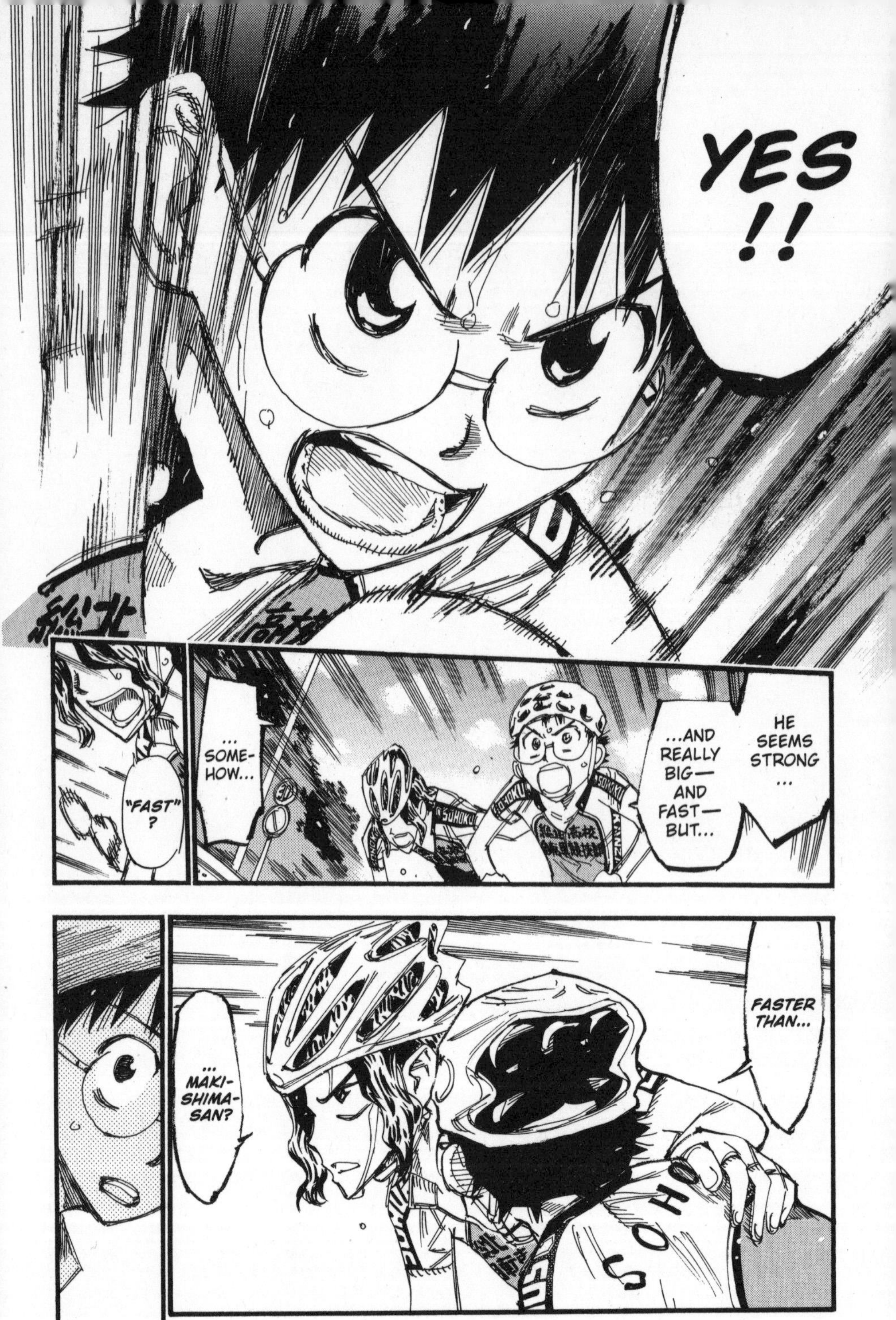
YES !!
HE SEEMS STRONG ...
...AND REALLY BIG— AND FAST— BUT...
... SOME- HOW...
"FAST" ?
FASTER THAN...
... MAKI- SHIMA- SAN?

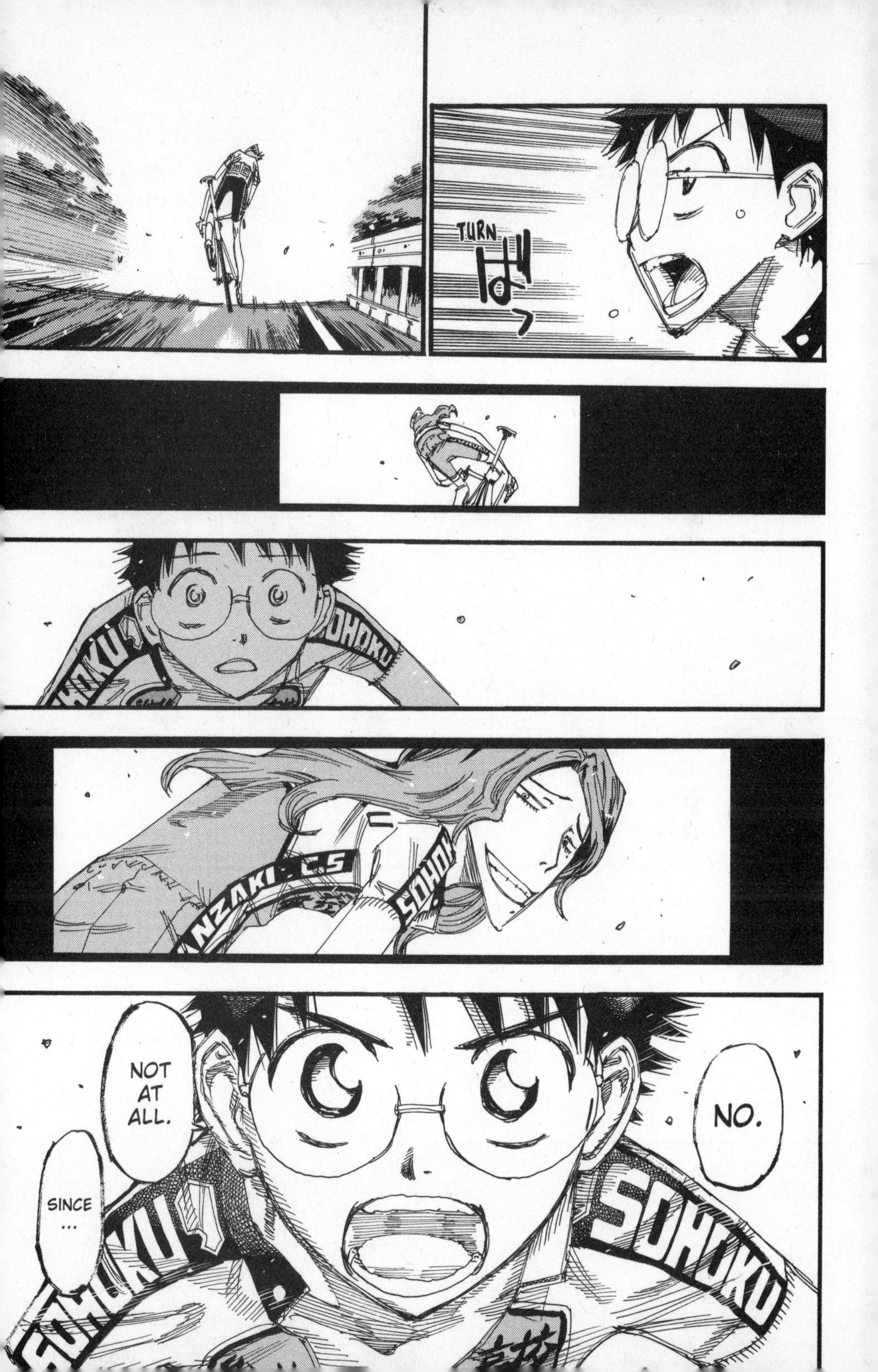
TURN
はっ
NO.
NOT AT ALL.
SINCE ...

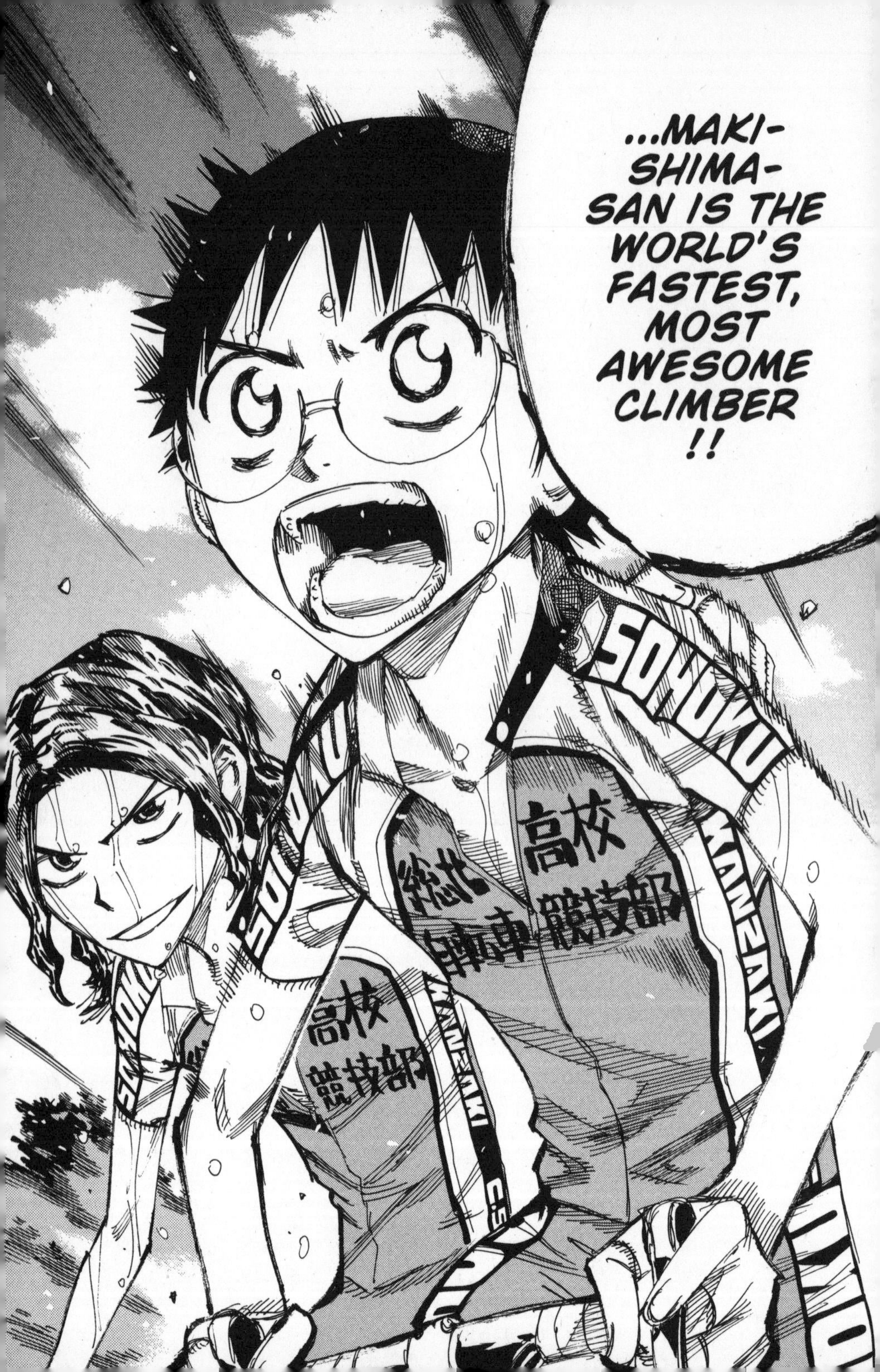
...MAKI-SHIMA-SAN IS THE WORLD'S FASTEST, MOST AWESOME CLIMBER !!

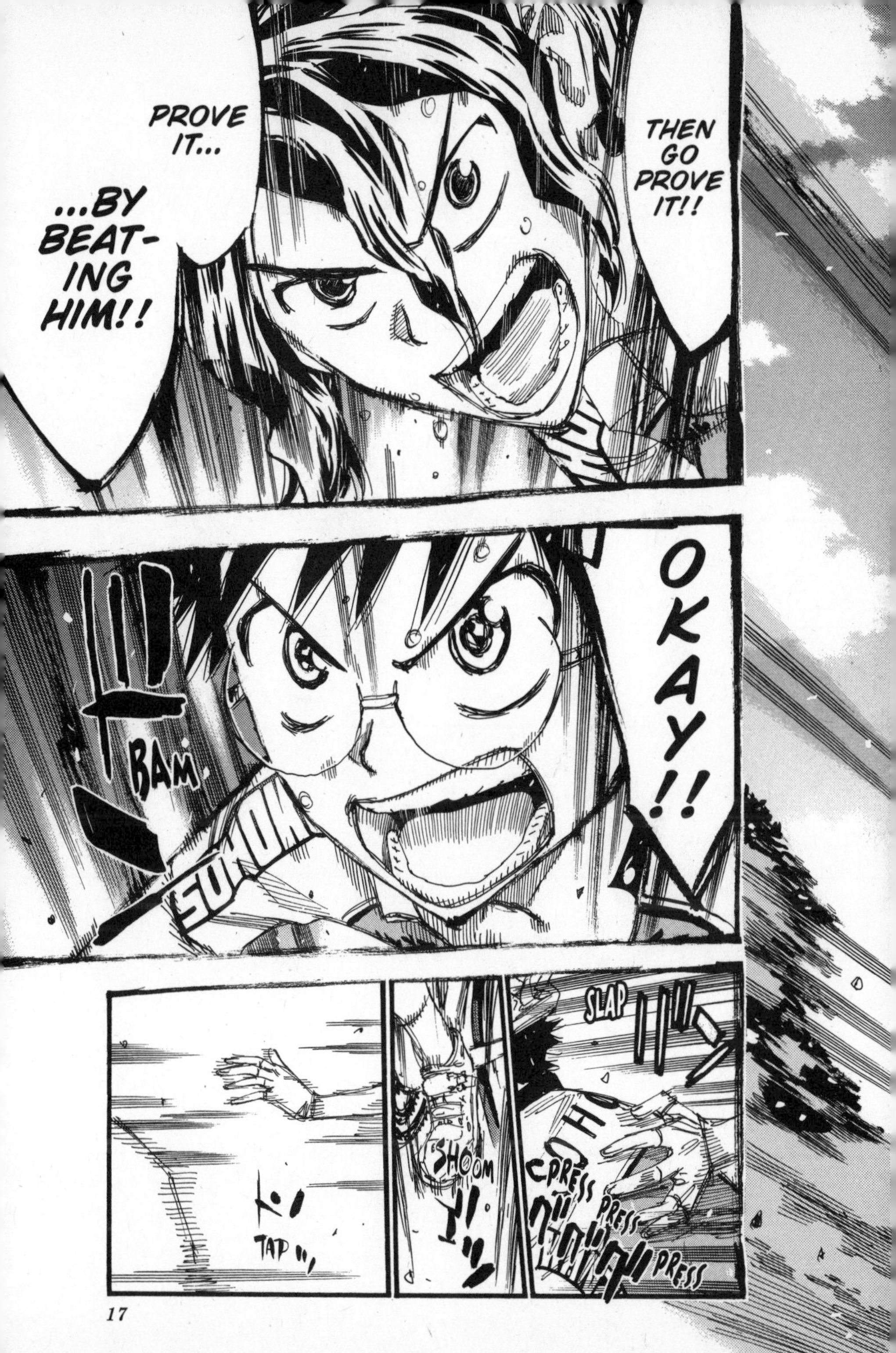
THEN GO PROVE IT!!
PROVE IT...
...BY BEATING HIM!!
OKAY!!
BAM
SLAP
PRESS PRESS PRESS
SHOOM
TAP

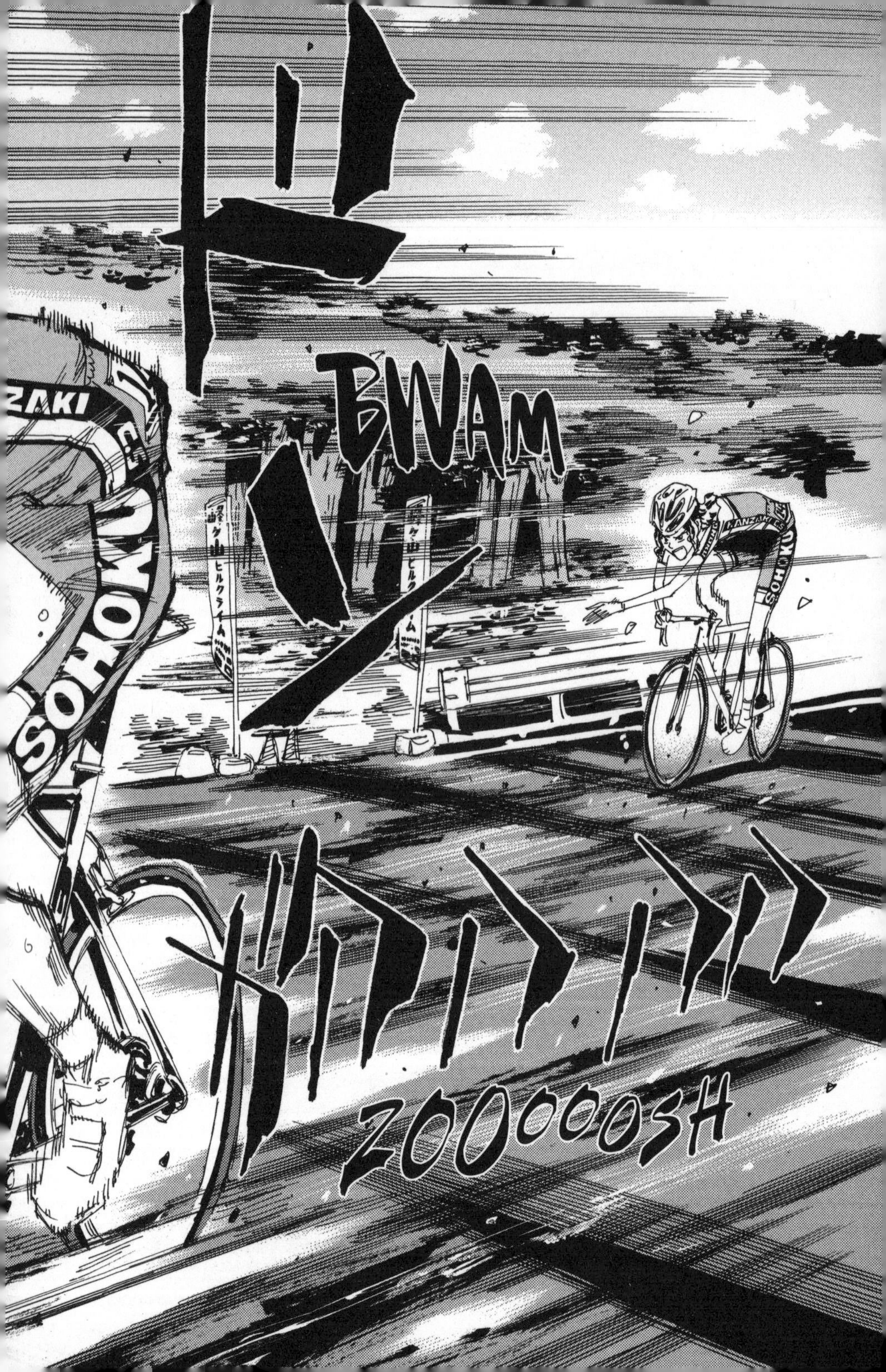
BWAM
SOHOKU
ZOOOOOSH

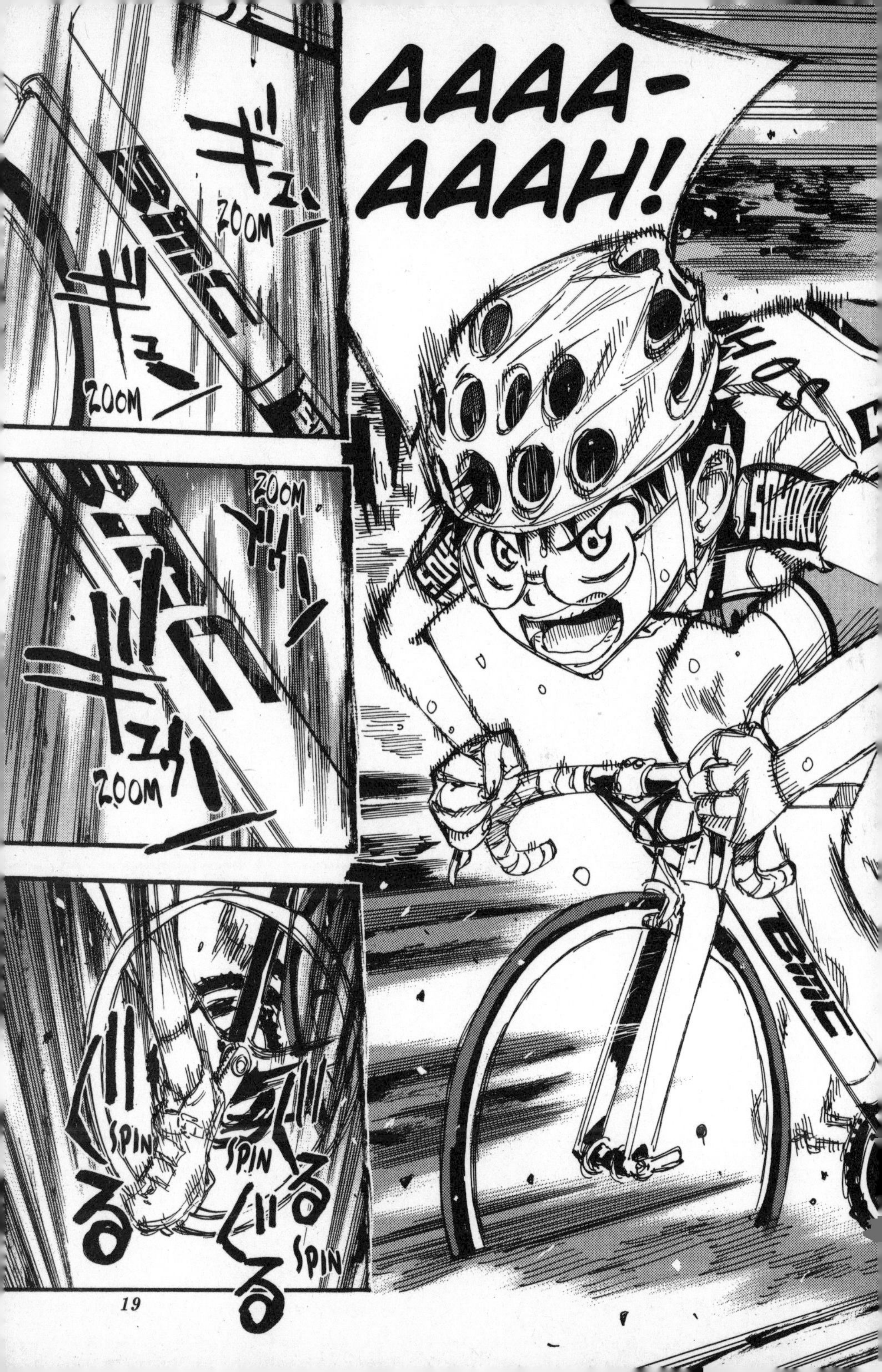
AAAA-
AAAAH!
ZOOM
ZOOM
ZOOM
ZOOM
SPIN
SPIN
SPIN

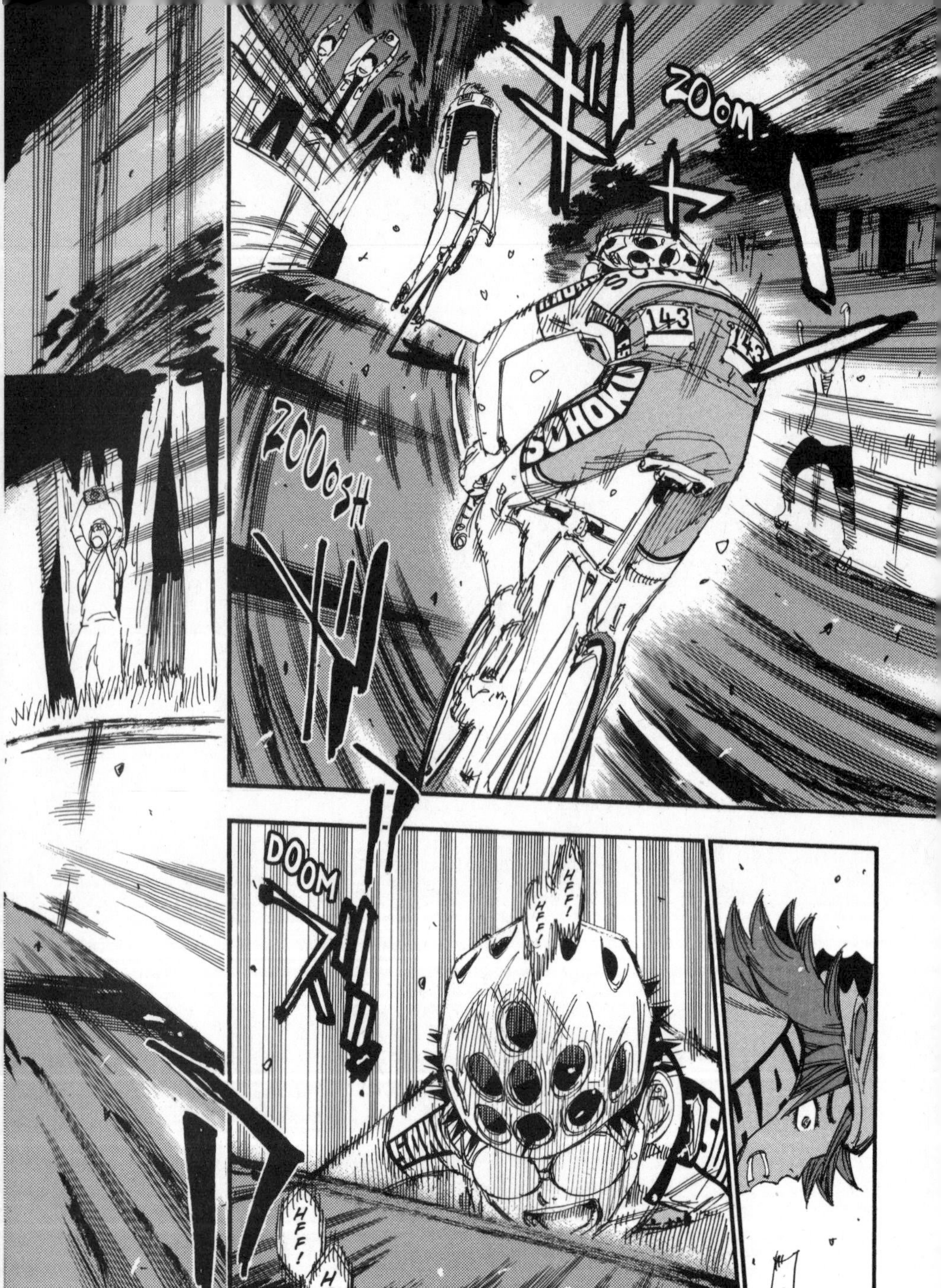
ZOOM
ZOOOSH
HFF! HFF!
DOOM
HFF! HFF!
!

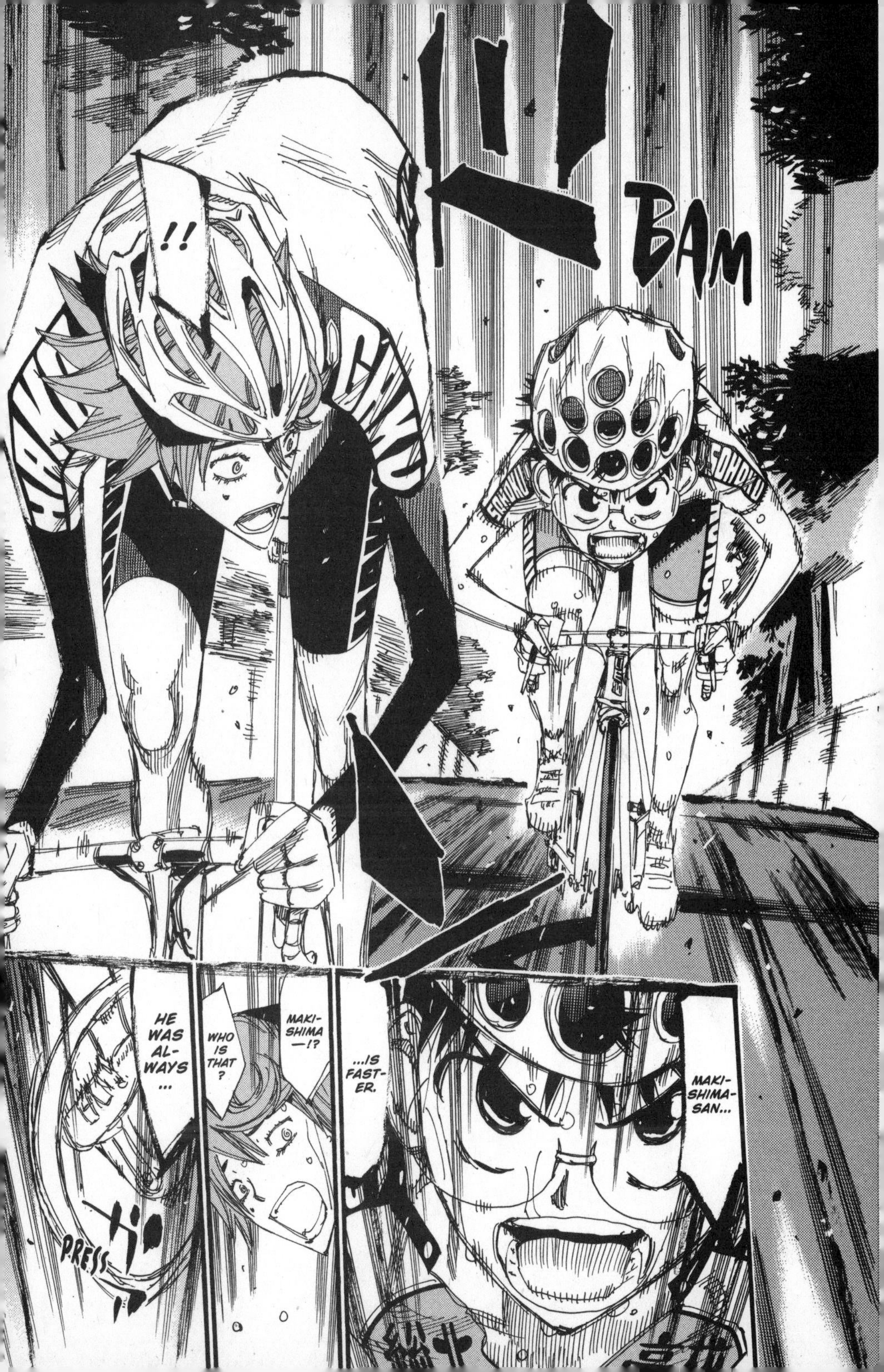
BAM
!!
MAKI-SHIMA-SAN...
...IS FASTER.
MAKI-SHIMA—!?
WHO IS THAT?
HE WAS AL-WAYS...
PRESS

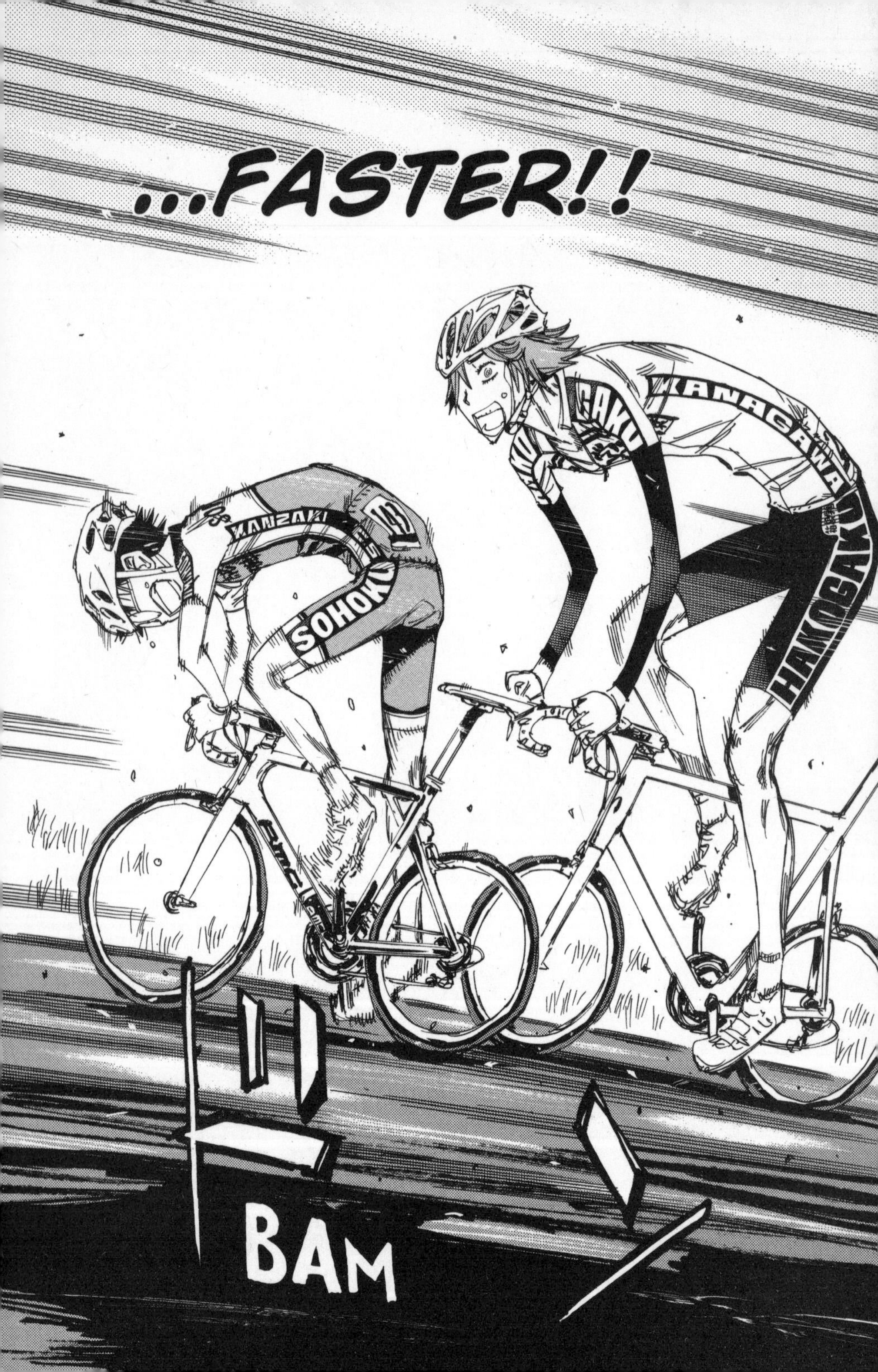
...FASTER!!
BAM

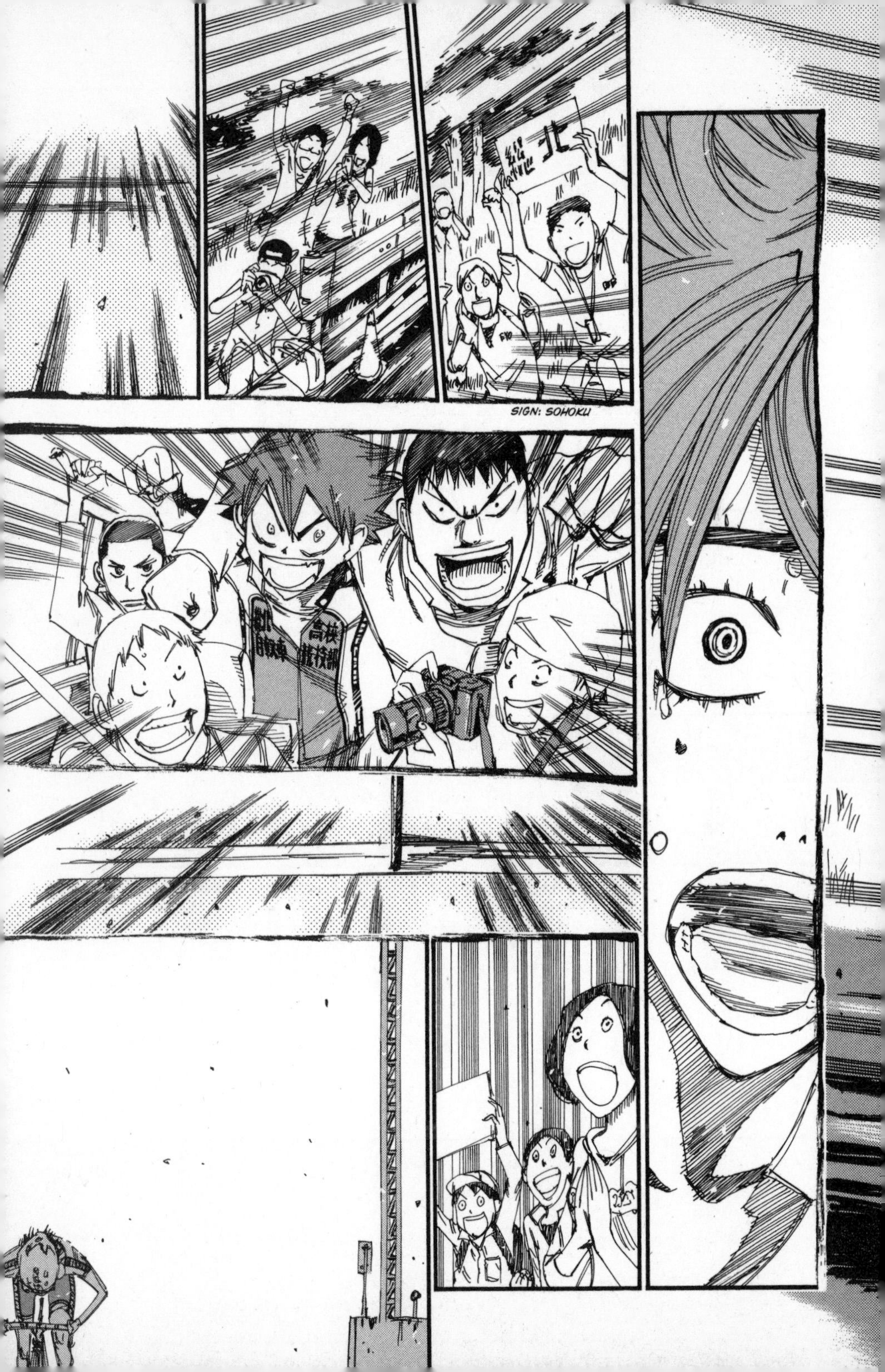
SIGN: SOHOKU

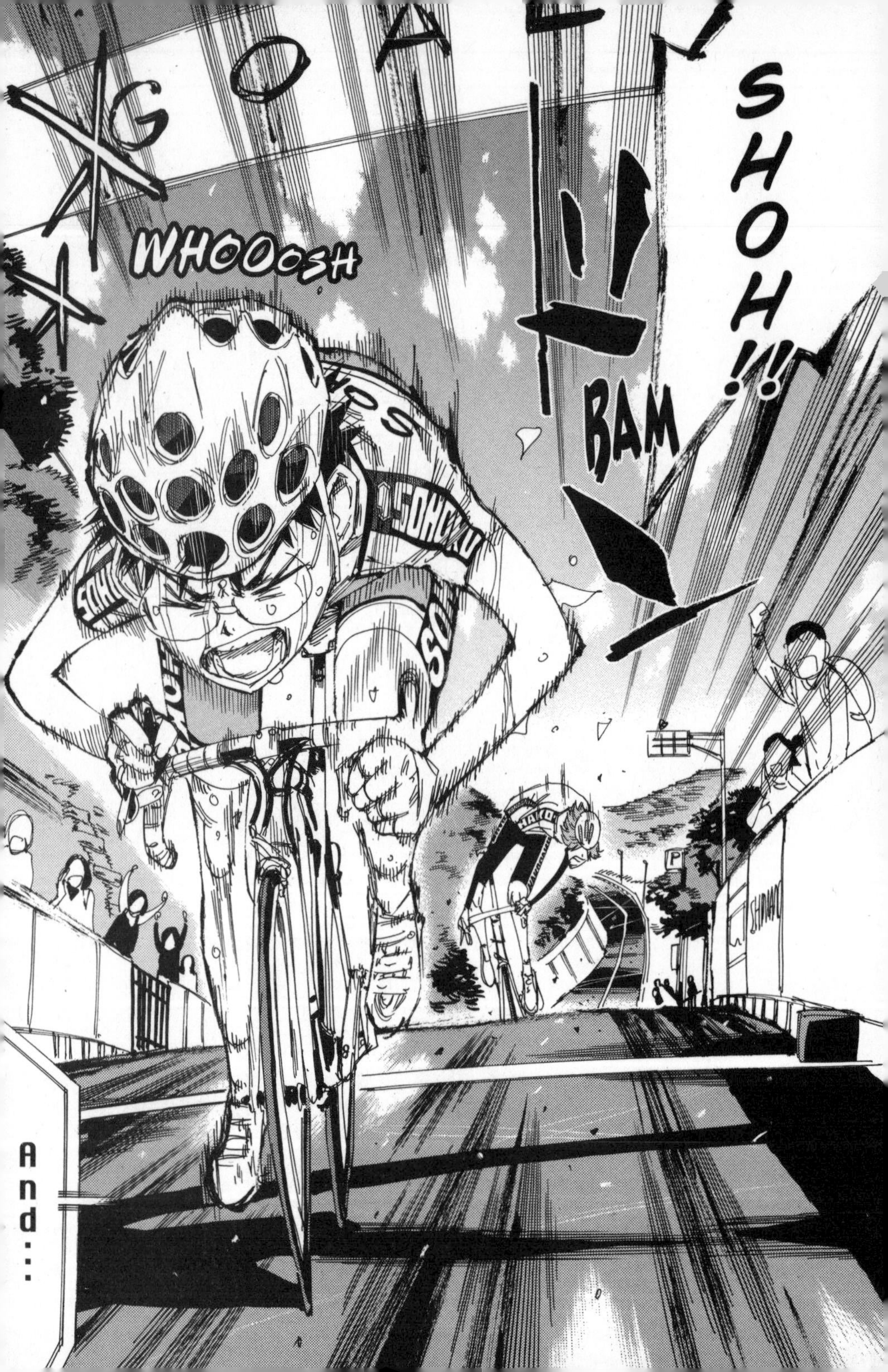
SHOH!!
GOAL
BAM
WHOOOOSH
And...

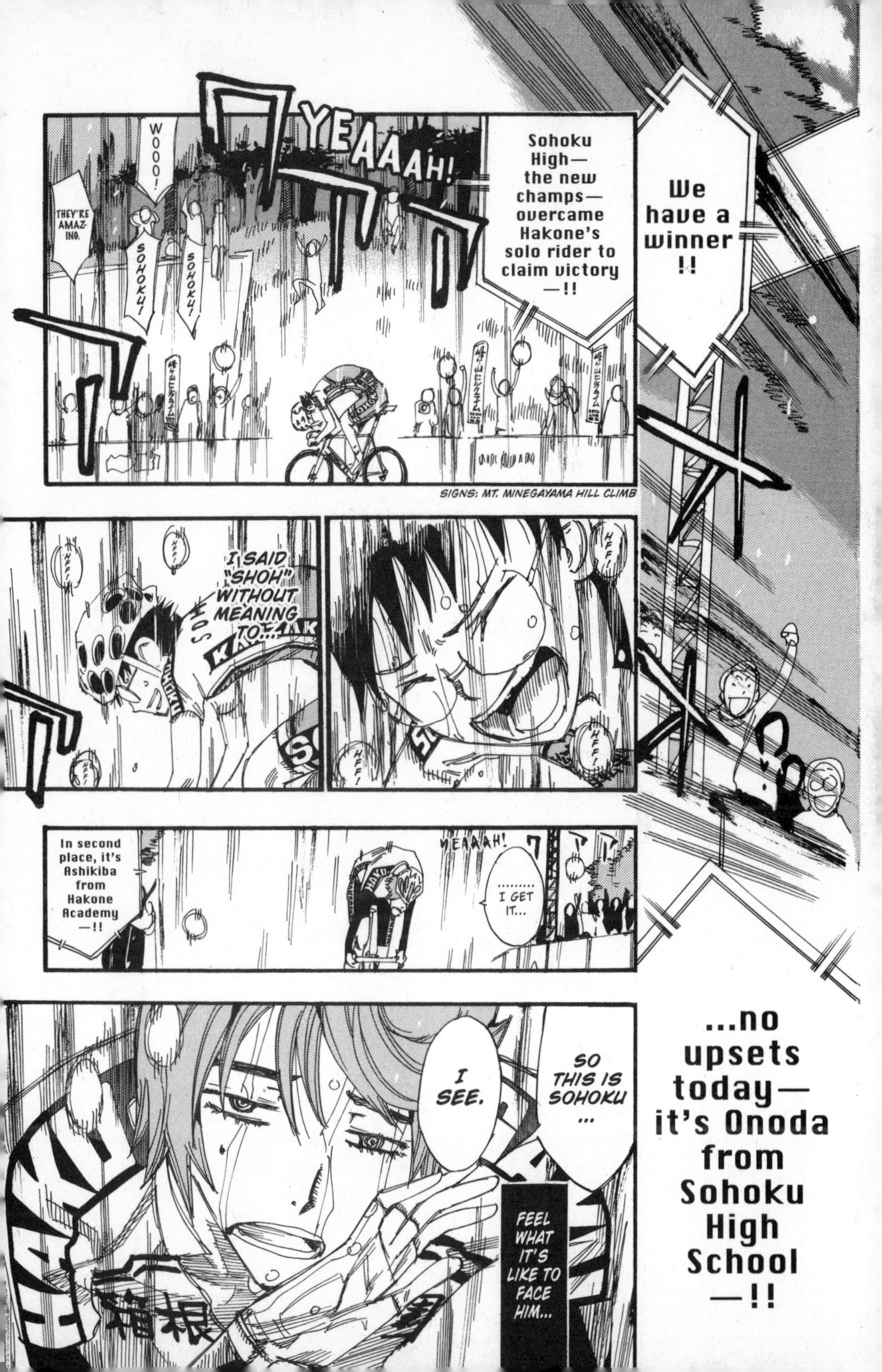
We have a winner!!
Sohoku High—the new champs—overcame Hakone's solo rider to claim victory—!!
YEAAAH!
WOOO!
SOHOKU!
SOHOKU!
THEY'RE AMAZING.
SIGNS: MT. MINEGAYAMA HILL CLIMB
HFF!
HFF!
HFF!
I SAID "SHOH" WITHOUT MEANING TO...
HFF!
HFF!
HFF!
YEAAAH!
.... I GET IT...
In second place, it's Ashikiba from Hakone Academy—!!
...no upsets today—it's Onoda from Sohoku High School—!!
SO THIS IS SOHOKU...
I SEE.
FEEL WHAT IT'S LIKE TO FACE HIM...

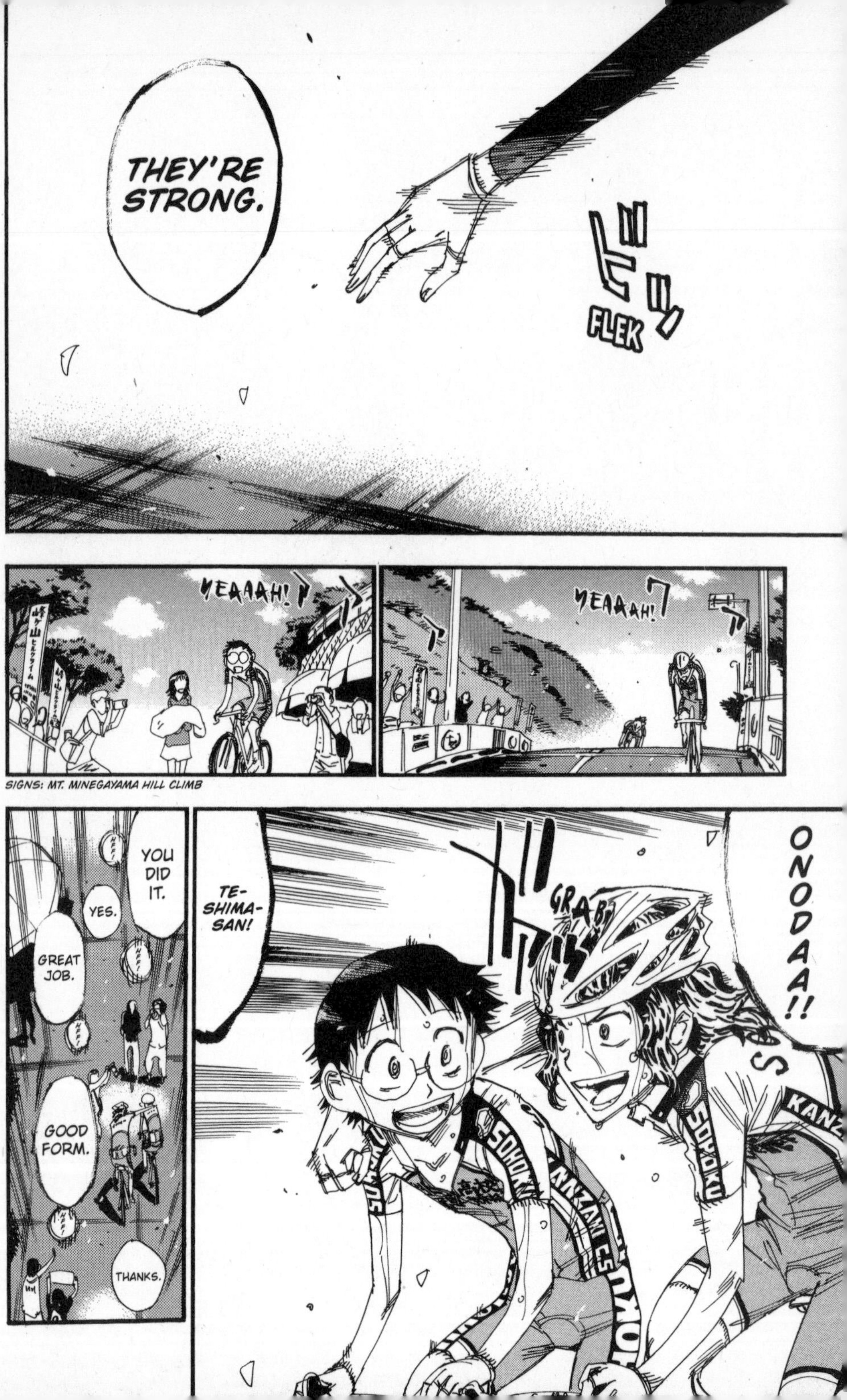
THEY'RE STRONG.
FLEK
YEAAAH!
YEAAAH!
ONODAA!!
GRAB
TE-SHIMA-SAN!
YOU DID IT.
YES.
GREAT JOB.
GOOD FORM.
THANKS.
SIGNS: MT. MINEGAYAMA HILL CLIMB

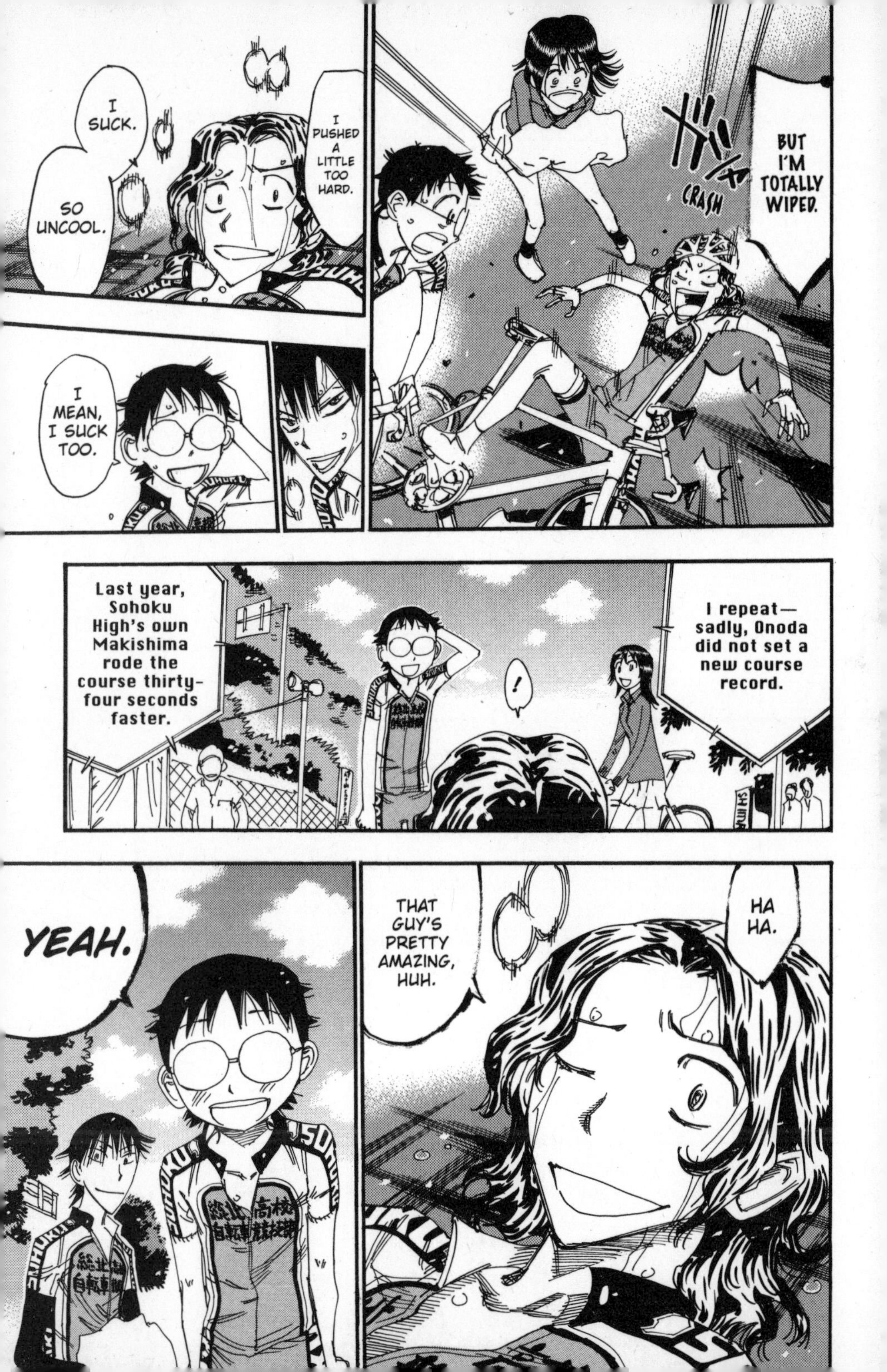
BUT I'M TOTALLY WIPED.
CRASH
I PUSHED A LITTLE TOO HARD.
I SUCK.
SO UNCOOL.
I MEAN, I SUCK TOO.
I repeat—sadly, Onoda did not set a new course record.
!
Last year, Sohoku High's own Makishima rode the course thirty-four seconds faster.
HA HA.
THAT GUY'S PRETTY AMAZING, HUH.
YEAH.

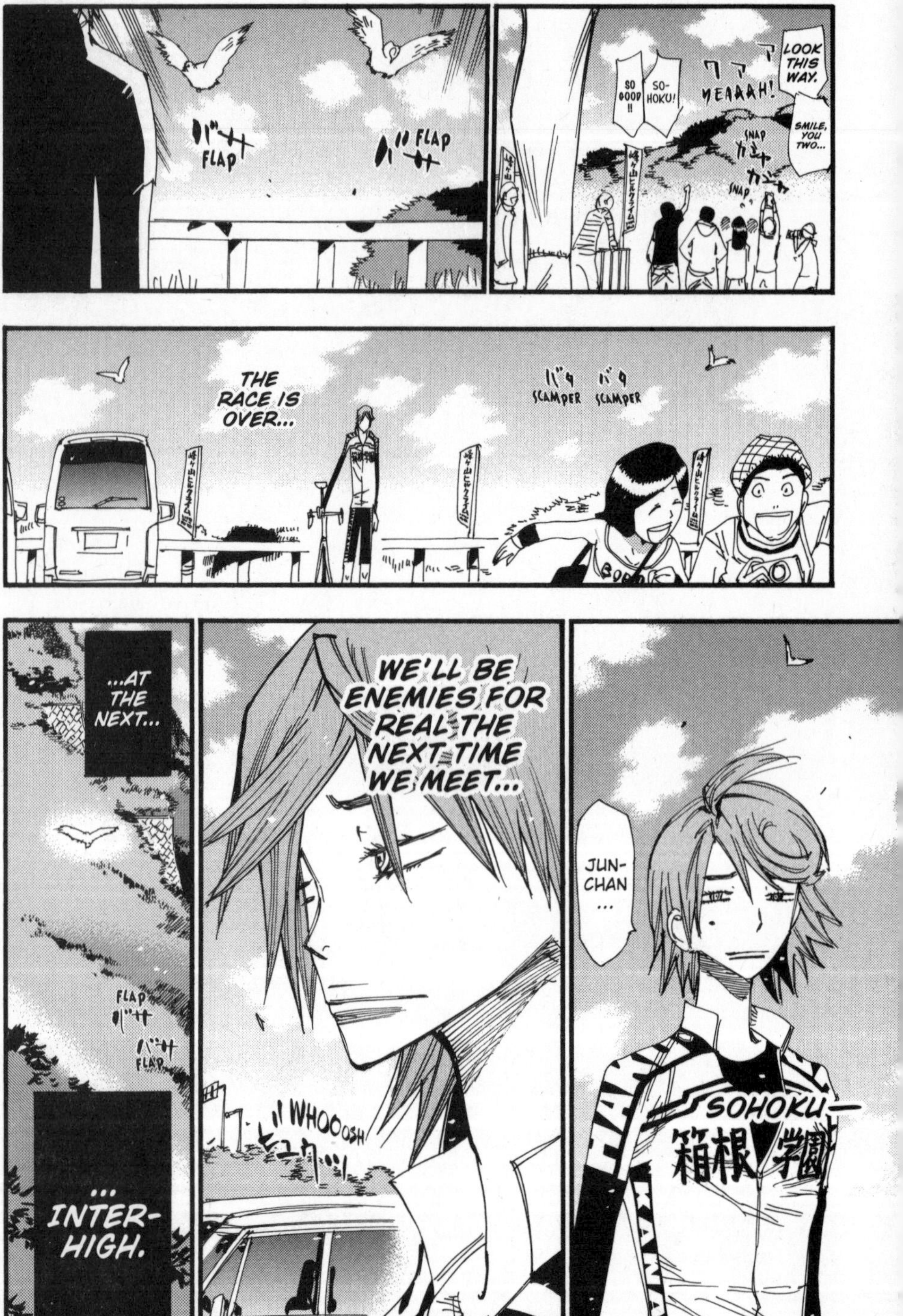
LOOK THIS WAY.
SMILE, YOU TWO...
YEAAAH!
SO-HOKU!
SO GOOD!!
SNAP
SNAP
FLAP
FLAP
THE RACE IS OVER...
SCAMPER SCAMPER
JUN-CHAN...
SOHOKU—
WE'LL BE ENEMIES FOR REAL THE NEXT TIME WE MEET...
WHOOOSH
...AT THE NEXT...
FLAP
FLAP
...INTER-HIGH.

RIDE.245 ASHIKIBA'S PATH

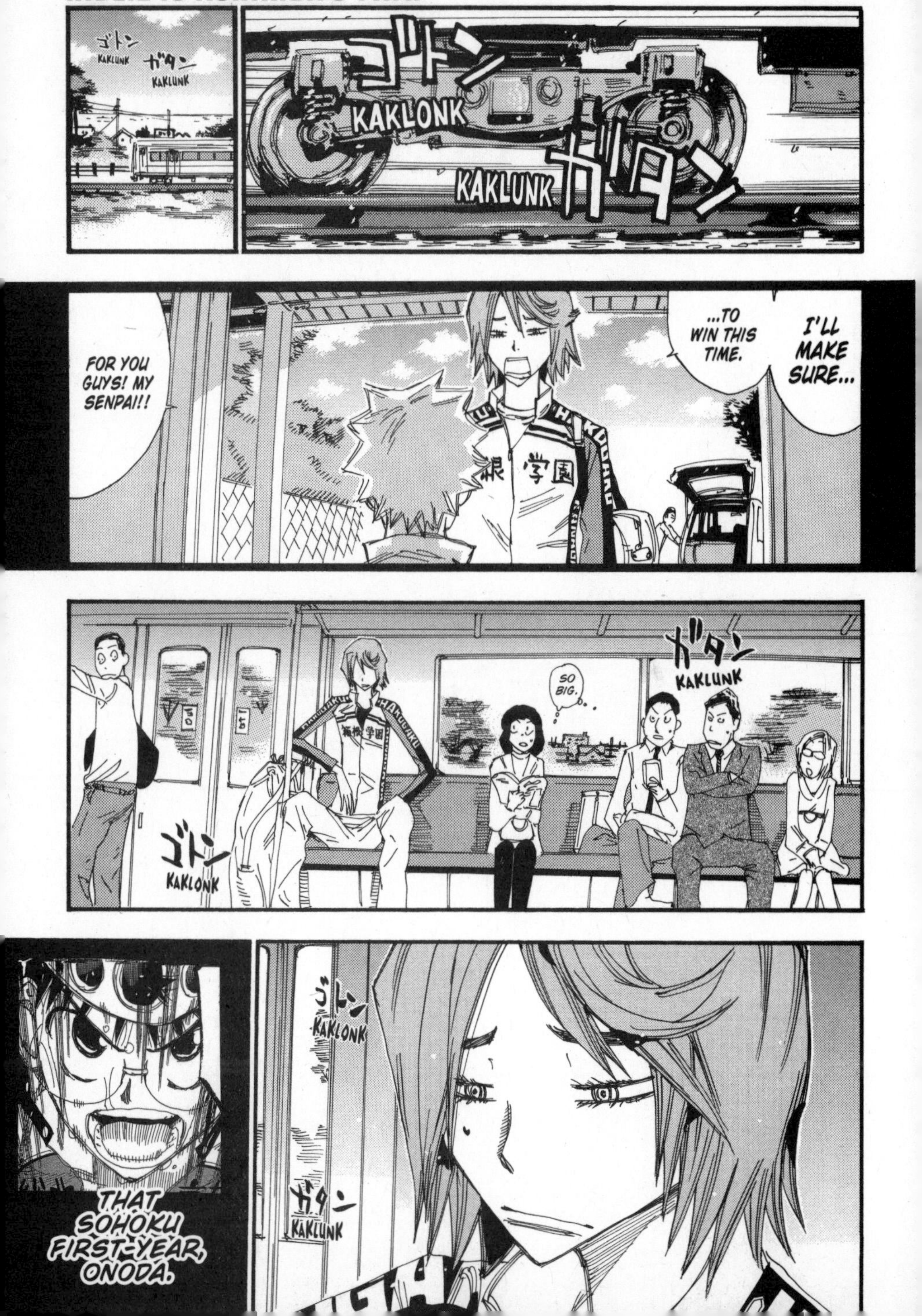
ゴトン
KAKLONK
ガタン
KAKLUNK
ゴトン
KAKLUNK
ガタン
KAKLUNK
I'LL MAKE SURE...
...TO WIN THIS TIME.
FOR YOU GUYS! MY SENPAI!!
ガタン
KAKLUNK
SO BIG.
ゴトン
KAKLONK
ゴトン
KAKLONK
ガタン
KAKLUNK
THAT SOHOKU FIRST-YEAR, ONODA.

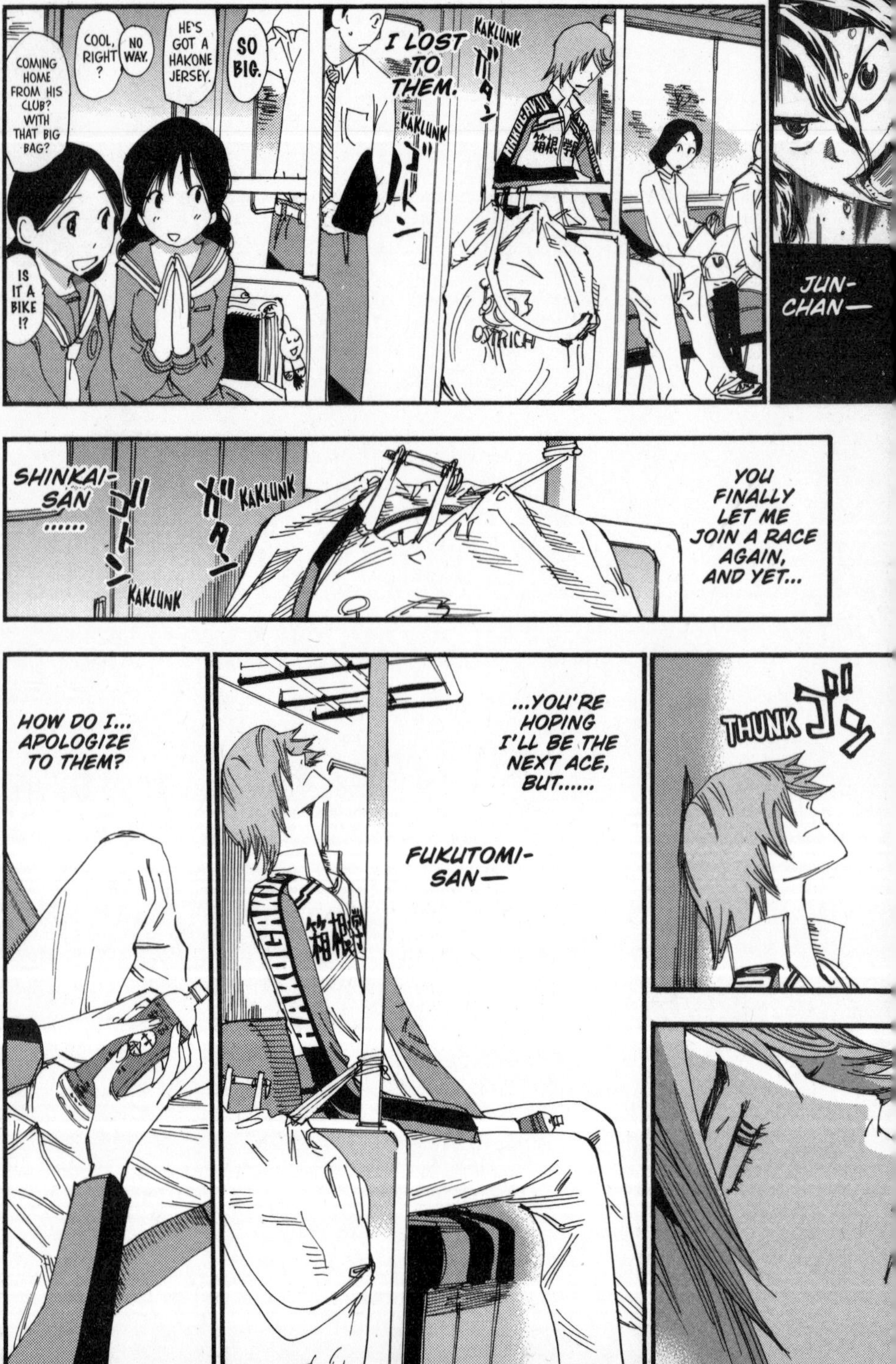
JUN-CHAN—
KAKLUNK ガタン
I LOST TO THEM.
KAKLUNK ゴトン
SO BIG.
HE'S GOT A HAKONE JERSEY.
NO WAY.
COOL, RIGHT?
COMING HOME FROM HIS CLUB? WITH THAT BIG BAG?
IS IT A BIKE!?
YOU FINALLY LET ME JOIN A RACE AGAIN, AND YET...
KAKLUNK ガタン
ゴトン KAKLUNK
SHINKAI-SAN......
THUNK ゴッ
...YOU'RE HOPING I'LL BE THE NEXT ACE, BUT......
FUKUTOMI-SAN—
HOW DO I... APOLOGIZE TO THEM?

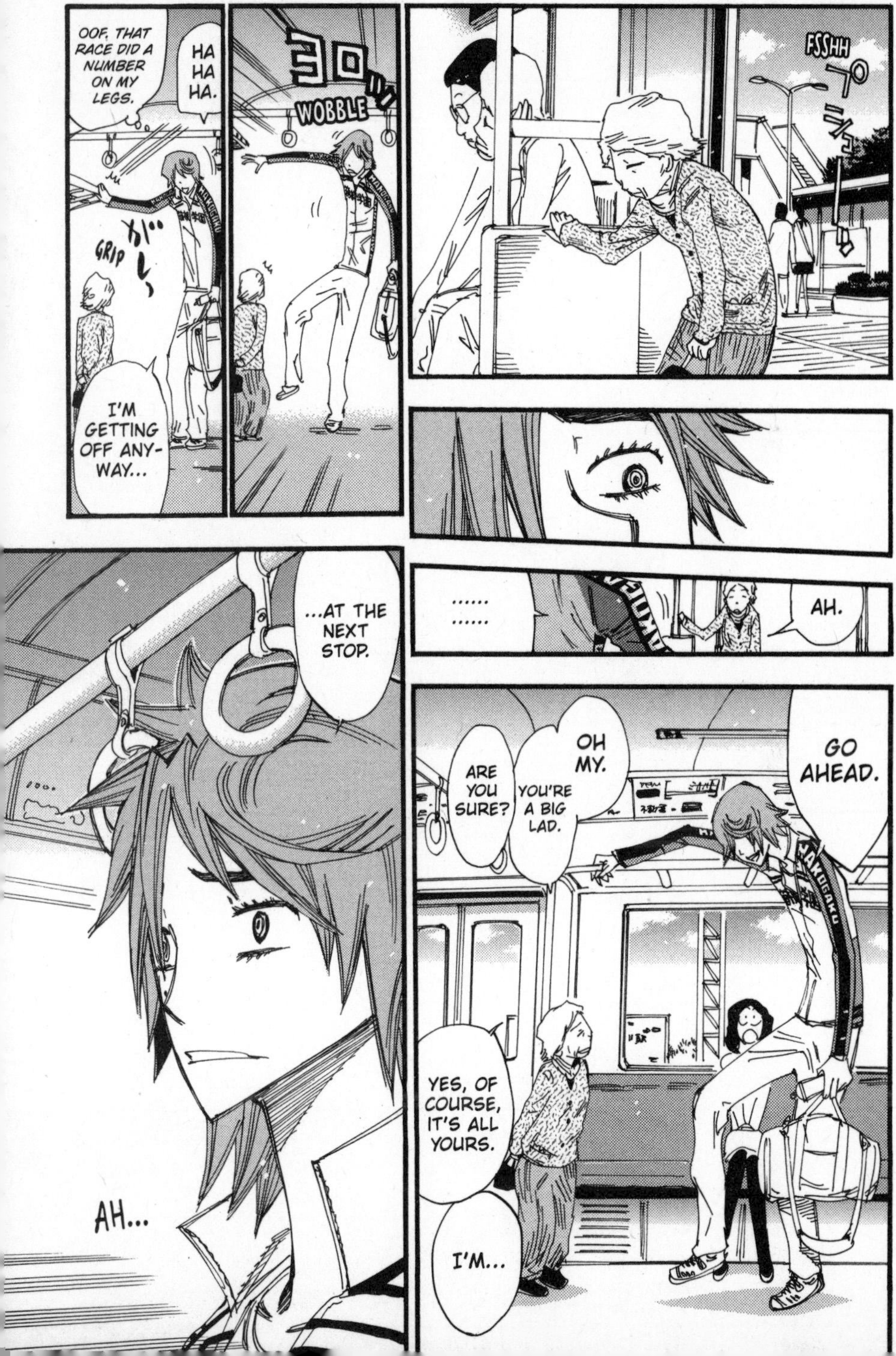

FSSHH
WOBBLE
OOF, THAT RACE DID A NUMBER ON MY LEGS.
HA HA HA.
GRIP
I'M GETTING OFF ANYWAY...
AH.
....
GO AHEAD.
OH MY.
YOU'RE A BIG LAD.
ARE YOU SURE?
YES, OF COURSE, IT'S ALL YOURS.
I'M...
...AT THE NEXT STOP.
AH...

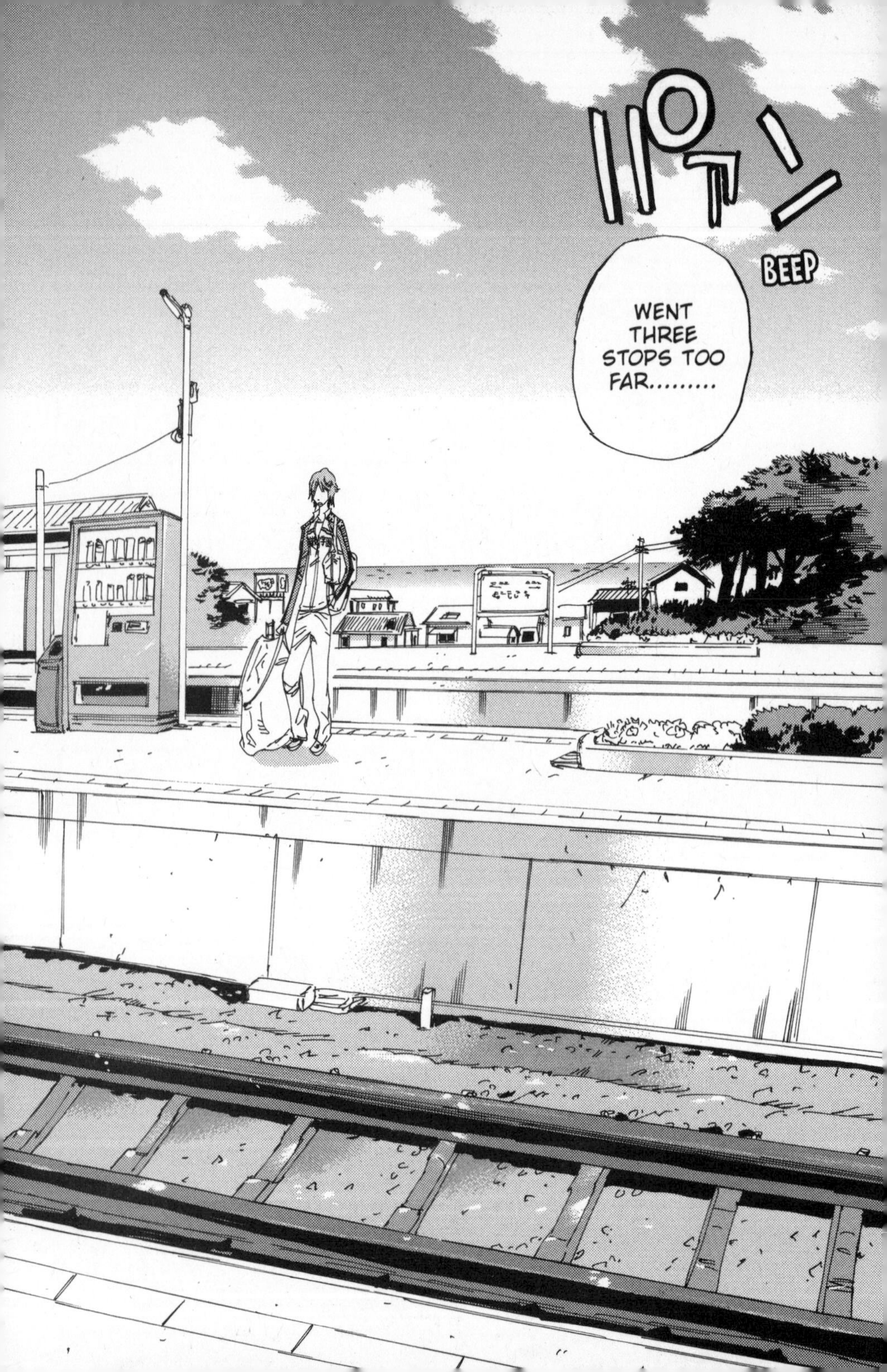
パァン
BEEP
WENT THREE STOPS TOO FAR.........

RIDE.245 ASHIKIBA'S PATH

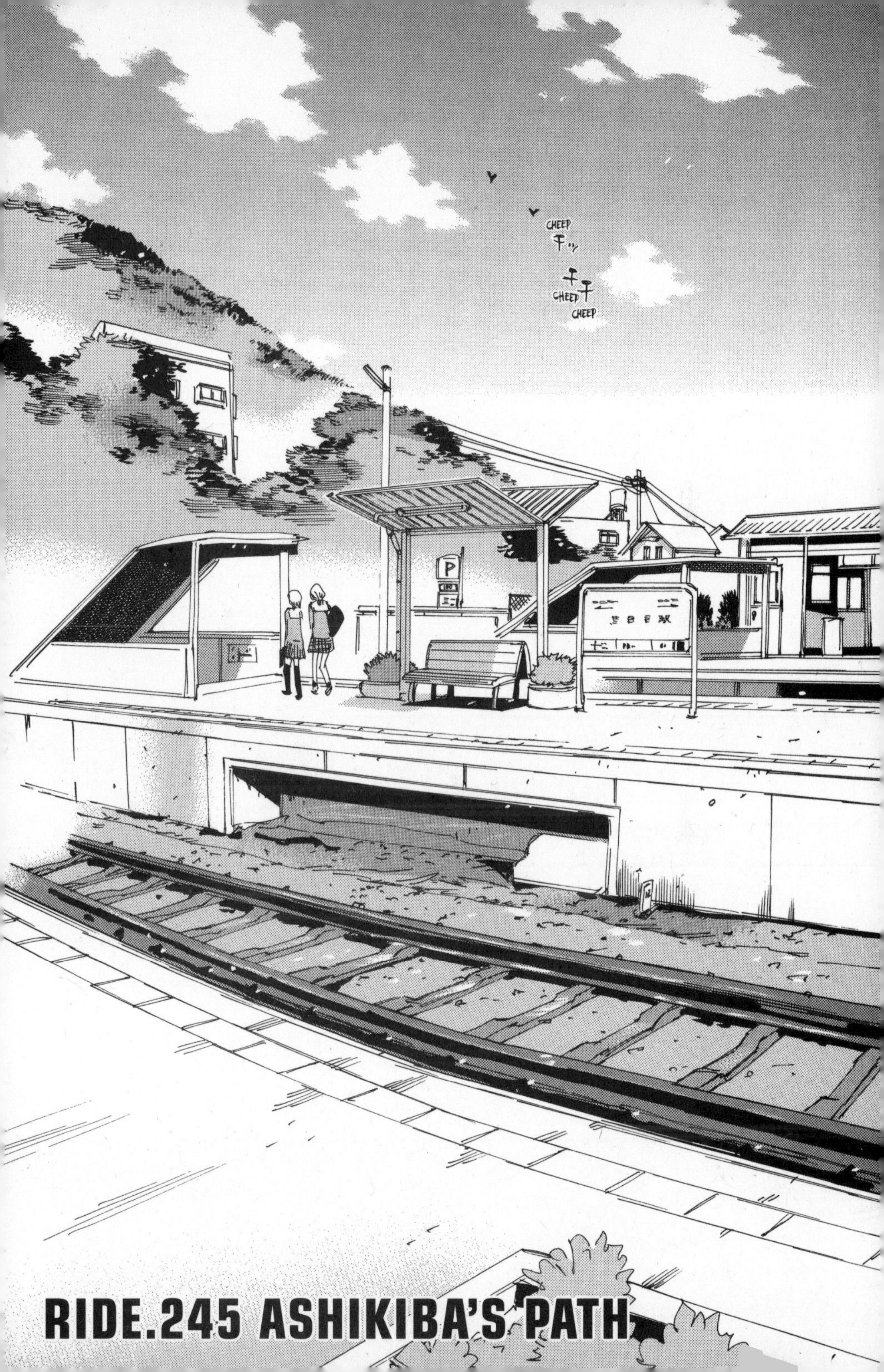
CHEEP
チッ
チチ
CHEEP
CHEEP

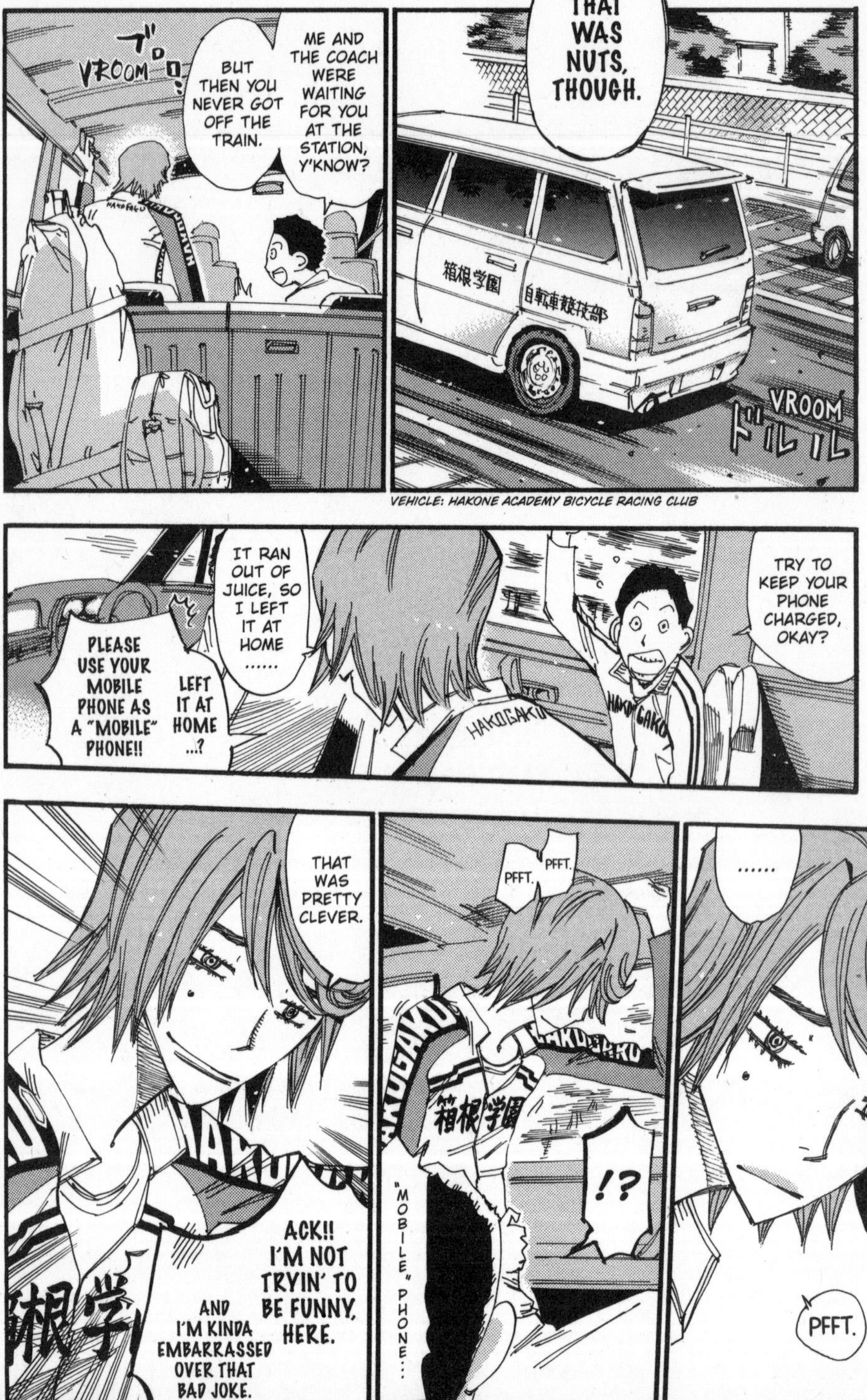
THAT WAS NUTS, THOUGH.
箱根学園
自転車競技部
VROOM
VEHICLE: HAKONE ACADEMY BICYCLE RACING CLUB
ME AND THE COACH WERE WAITING FOR YOU AT THE STATION, Y'KNOW?
BUT THEN YOU NEVER GOT OFF THE TRAIN.
VROOM
TRY TO KEEP YOUR PHONE CHARGED, OKAY?
IT RAN OUT OF JUICE, SO I LEFT IT AT HOME ......
LEFT IT AT HOME ...?
PLEASE USE YOUR MOBILE PHONE AS A "MOBILE" PHONE!!
......
PFFT.
PFFT.
PFFT.
!?
"MOBILE" PHONE...
THAT WAS PRETTY CLEVER.
ACK!! I'M NOT TRYIN' TO BE FUNNY, HERE.
AND I'M KINDA EMBARRASSED OVER THAT BAD JOKE.

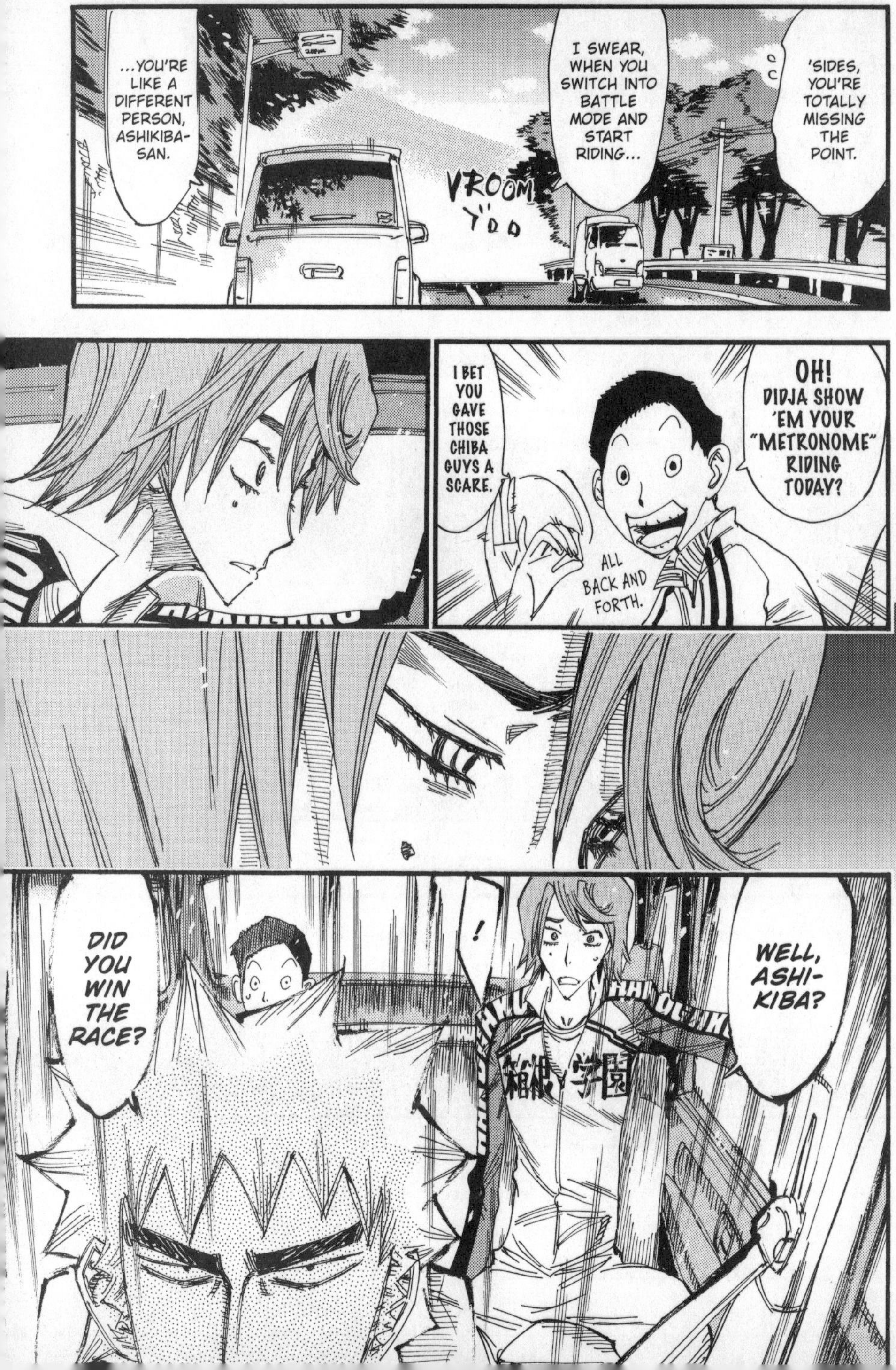
'SIDES, YOU'RE TOTALLY MISSING THE POINT.
I SWEAR, WHEN YOU SWITCH INTO BATTLE MODE AND START RIDING...
VROOM
...YOU'RE LIKE A DIFFERENT PERSON, ASHIKIBA-SAN.
OH! DIDJA SHOW 'EM YOUR "METRONOME" RIDING TODAY?
I BET YOU GAVE THOSE CHIBA GUYS A SCARE.
ALL BACK AND FORTH.
WELL, ASHI-KIBA?
!
DID YOU WIN THE RACE?

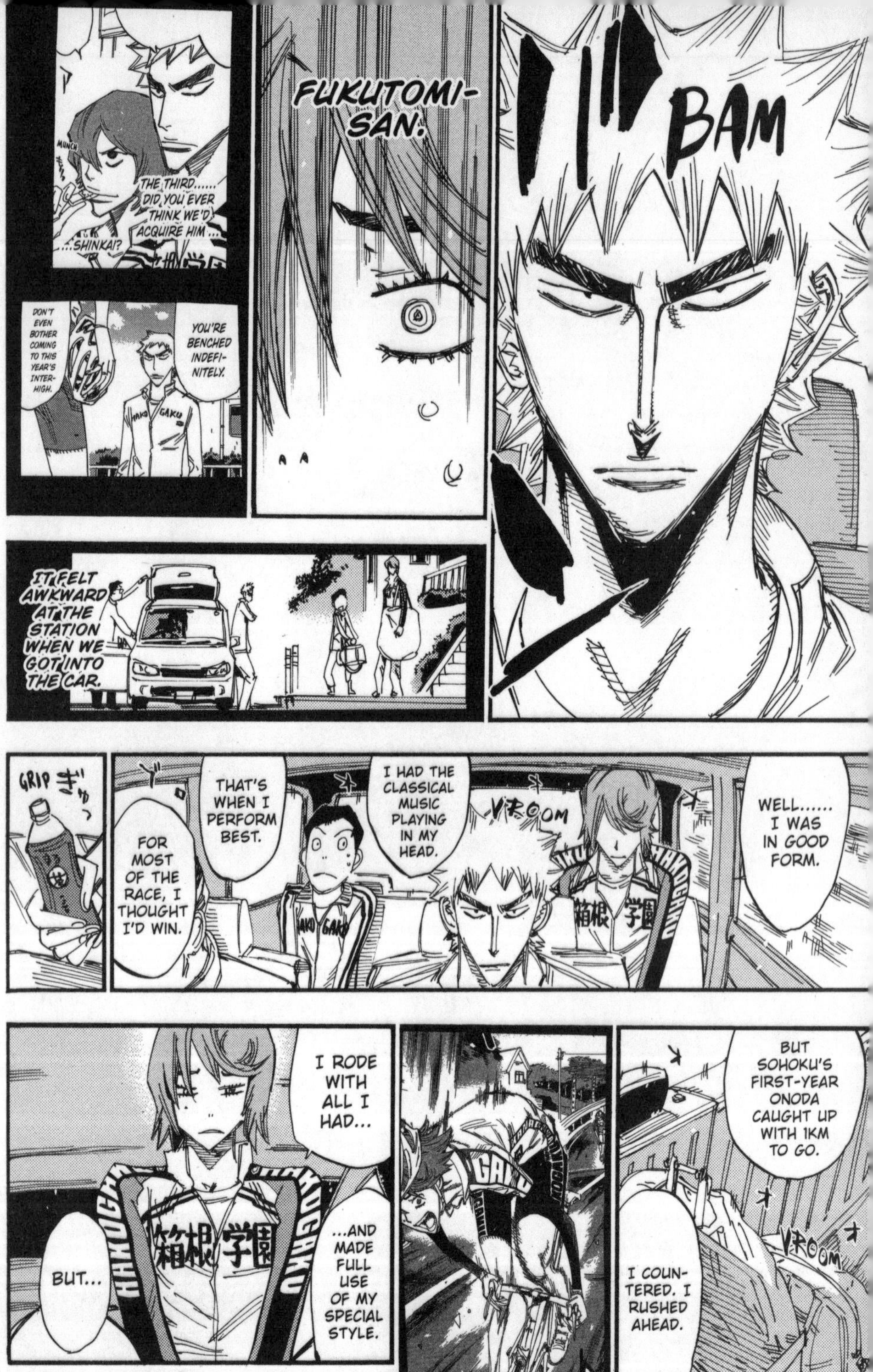
BAM
FUKUTOMI-SAN!
MUNCH
THE THIRD...... DID YOU EVER THINK WE'D ACQUIRE HIM ...
...SHINKAI?
YOU'RE BENCHED INDEFINITELY.
DON'T EVEN BOTHER COMING TO THIS YEAR'S INTER-HIGH.
IT FELT AWKWARD AT THE STATION WHEN WE GOT INTO THE CAR.
WELL...... I WAS IN GOOD FORM.
VROOM
I HAD THE CLASSICAL MUSIC PLAYING IN MY HEAD.
THAT'S WHEN I PERFORM BEST.
FOR MOST OF THE RACE, I THOUGHT I'D WIN.
GRIP ぎゅっ
BUT SOHOKU'S FIRST-YEAR ONODA CAUGHT UP WITH 1KM TO GO.
VROOM
I COUNTERED. I RUSHED AHEAD.
I RODE WITH ALL I HAD...
...AND MADE FULL USE OF MY SPECIAL STYLE.
BUT...

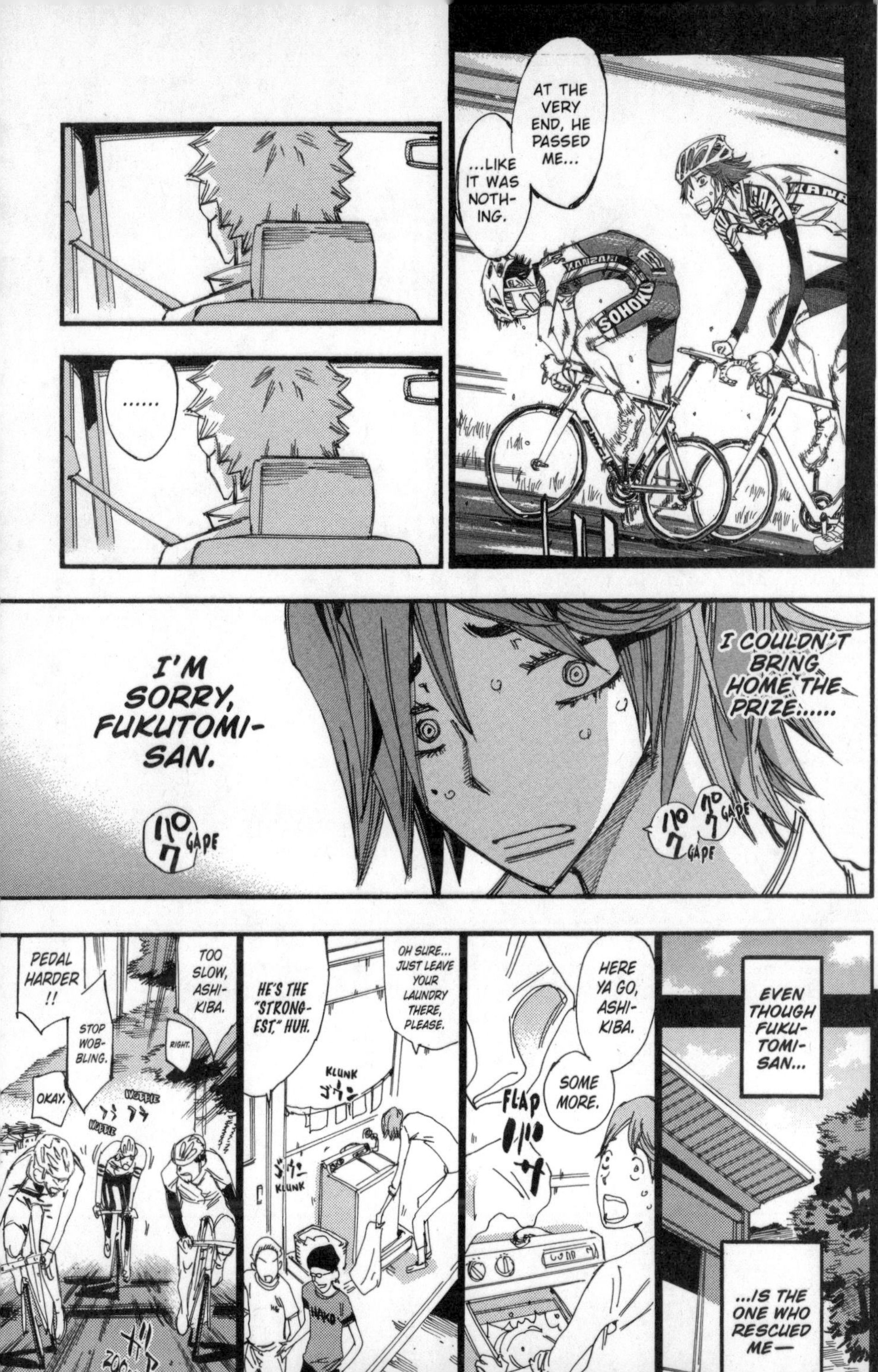
AT THE VERY END, HE PASSED ME...
...LIKE IT WAS NOTHING.
......
I COULDN'T BRING HOME THE PRIZE......
GAPE
GAPE
I'M SORRY, FUKUTOMI-SAN.
GAPE
EVEN THOUGH FUKUTOMI-SAN...
...IS THE ONE WHO RESCUED ME—
HERE YA GO, ASHIKIBA.
SOME MORE.
FLAP
OH SURE... JUST LEAVE YOUR LAUNDRY THERE, PLEASE.
HE'S THE "STRONGEST," HUH.
KLUNK
KLUNK
TOO SLOW, ASHIKIBA.
PEDAL HARDER !!
RIGHT.
STOP WOBBLING.
WOBBLE
OKAY.
WOBBLE

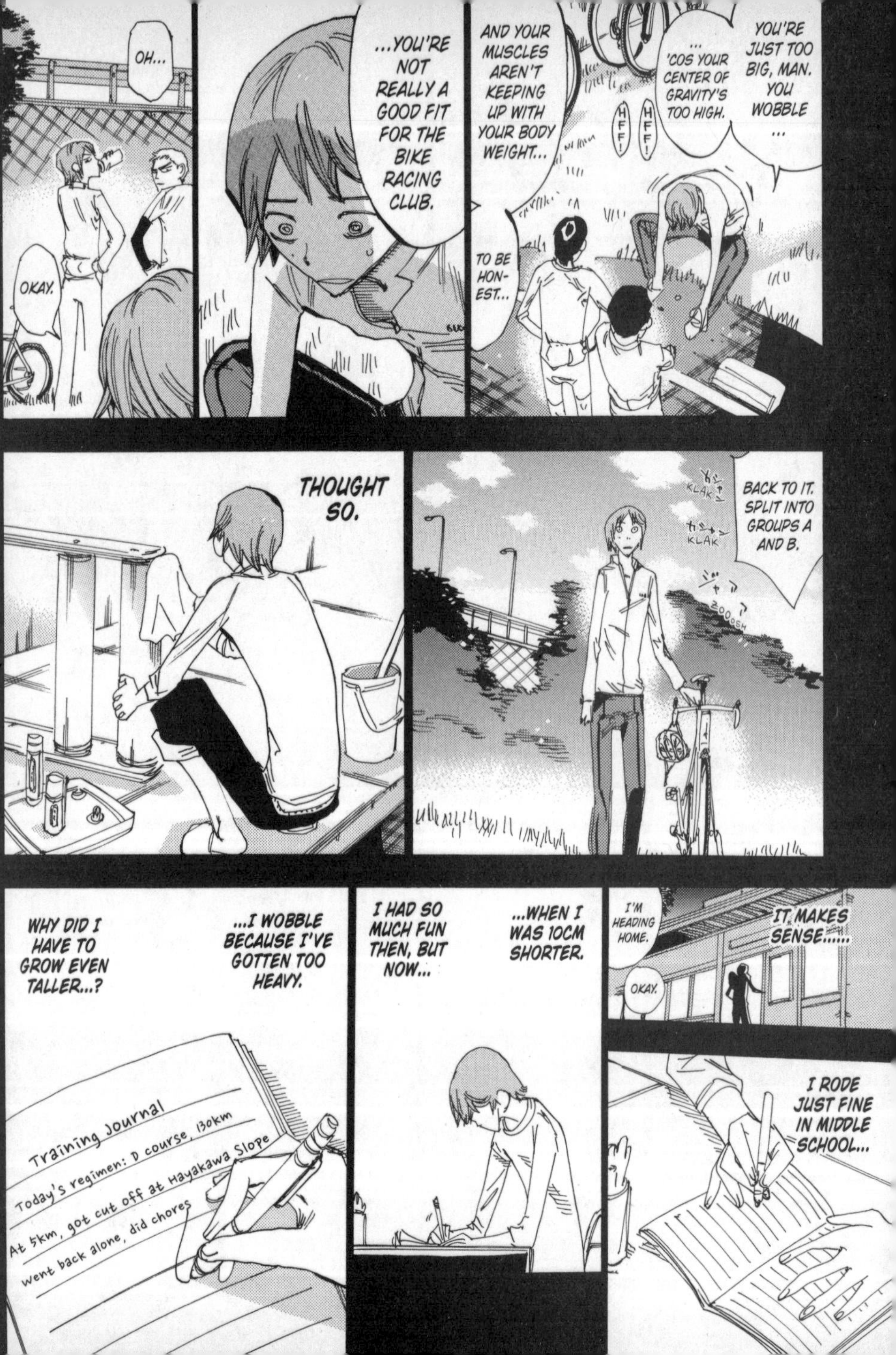
YOU'RE JUST TOO BIG, MAN. YOU WOBBLE ...
... 'COS YOUR CENTER OF GRAVITY'S TOO HIGH.
HFF!
HFF!
AND YOUR MUSCLES AREN'T KEEPING UP WITH YOUR BODY WEIGHT...
TO BE HONEST...
...YOU'RE NOT REALLY A GOOD FIT FOR THE BIKE RACING CLUB.
OH...
OKAY.
BACK TO IT. SPLIT INTO GROUPS A AND B.
KLAK
KLAK
ZOOOSH
THOUGHT SO.
IT MAKES SENSE......
I'M HEADING HOME.
OKAY.
I RODE JUST FINE IN MIDDLE SCHOOL...
...WHEN I WAS 10CM SHORTER.
I HAD SO MUCH FUN THEN, BUT NOW...
...I WOBBLE BECAUSE I'VE GOTTEN TOO HEAVY.
WHY DID I HAVE TO GROW EVEN TALLER...?
Training Journal
Today's regimen: D course, 130km
At 5km, got cut off at Hayakawa Slope
went back alone, did chores

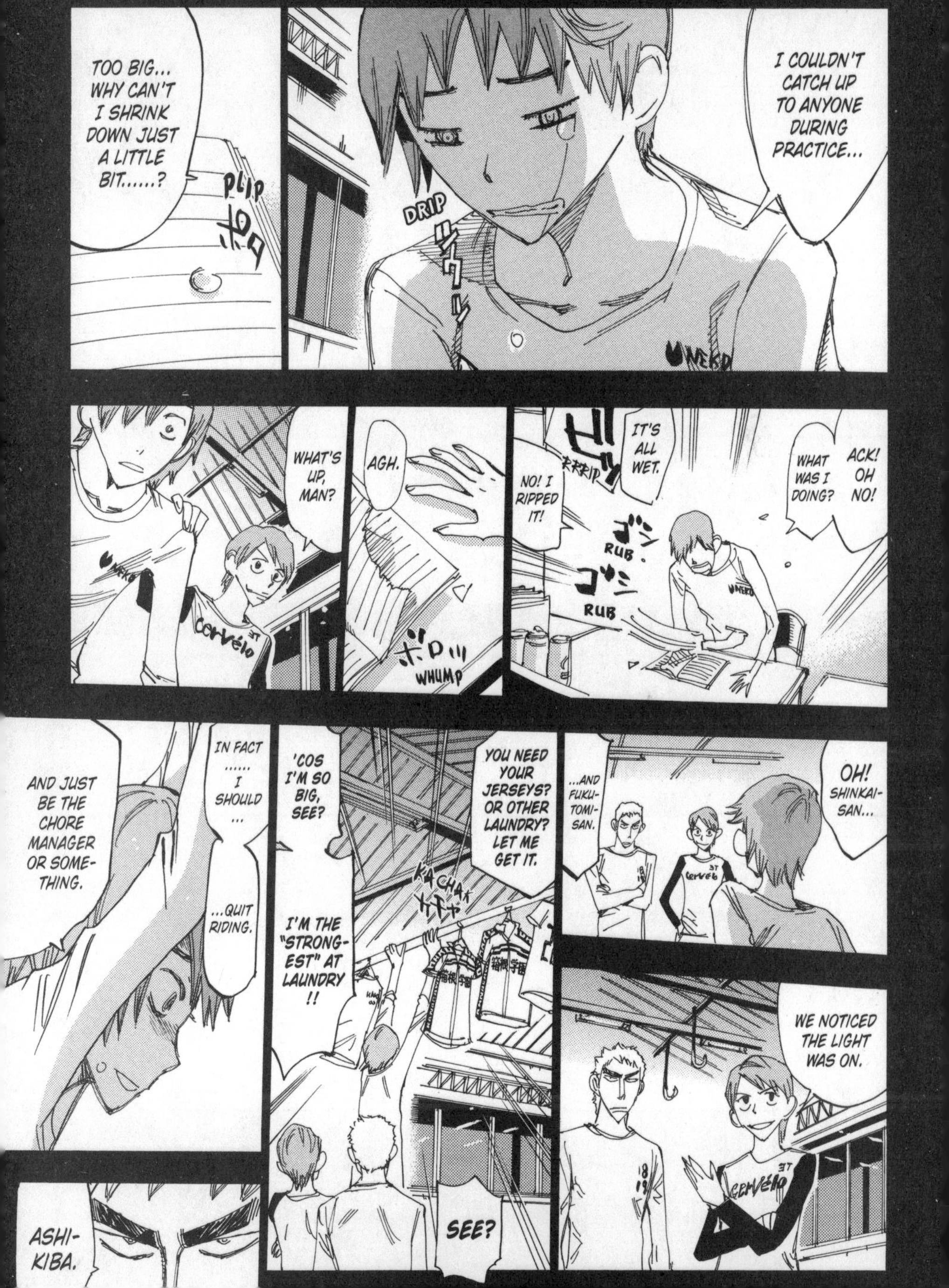
I COULDN'T CATCH UP TO ANYONE DURING PRACTICE...
DRIP
TOO BIG... WHY CAN'T I SHRINK DOWN JUST A LITTLE BIT......?
PLIP
ACK! OH NO!
WHAT WAS I DOING?
IT'S ALL WET.
SKRRIP
NO! I RIPPED IT!
RUB
RUB
AGH.
WHUMP
WHAT'S UP, MAN?
OH! SHINKAI-SAN...
...AND FUKU-TOMI-SAN.
WE NOTICED THE LIGHT WAS ON.
YOU NEED YOUR JERSEYS? OR OTHER LAUNDRY? LET ME GET IT.
'COS I'M SO BIG, SEE?
KACHAK
I'M THE "STRONG-EST" AT LAUNDRY !!
SEE?
IN FACT ...... I SHOULD ...
...QUIT RIDING.
AND JUST BE THE CHORE MANAGER OR SOME-THING.
ASHI-KIBA.

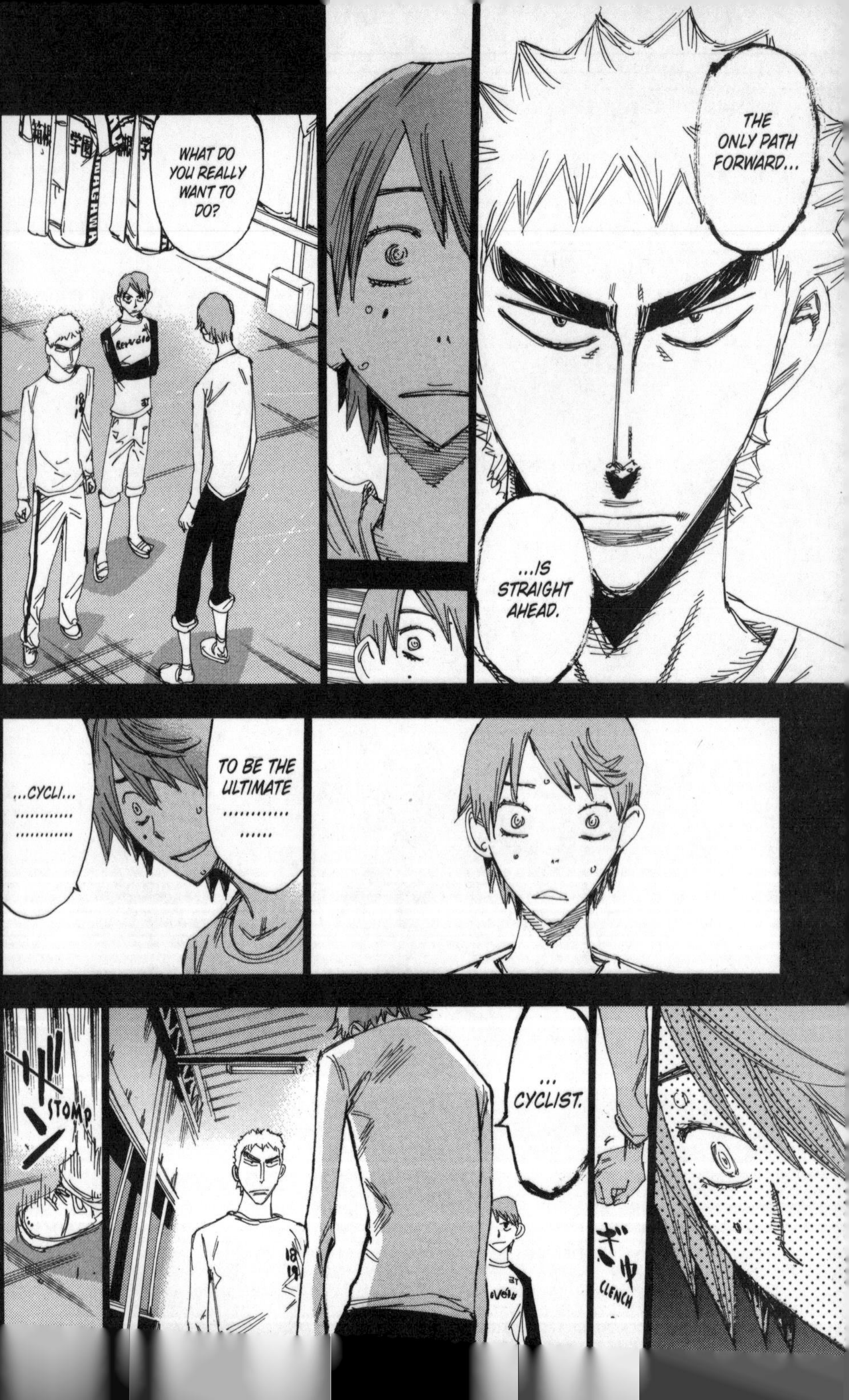
THE ONLY PATH FORWARD...
...IS STRAIGHT AHEAD.
WHAT DO YOU REALLY WANT TO DO?
TO BE THE ULTIMATE ....
...CYCLI... ....
... CYCLIST.
ギュ
CLENCH
STOMP

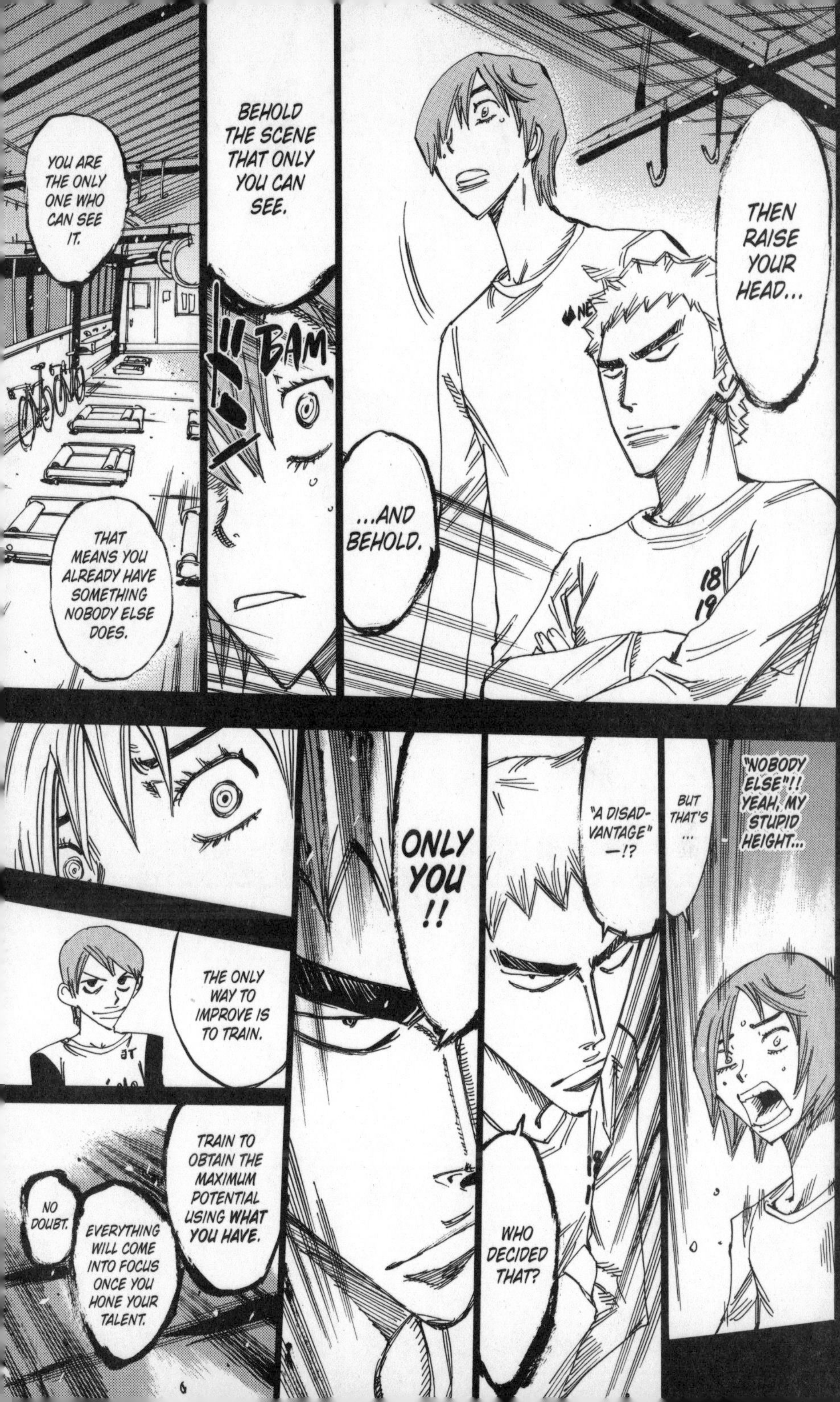
THEN RAISE YOUR HEAD...
...AND BEHOLD.
BEHOLD THE SCENE THAT ONLY YOU CAN SEE.
BAM
YOU ARE THE ONLY ONE WHO CAN SEE IT.
THAT MEANS YOU ALREADY HAVE SOMETHING NOBODY ELSE DOES.
"NOBODY ELSE"!! YEAH, MY STUPID HEIGHT...
BUT THAT'S...
"A DISAD-VANTAGE"—!?
WHO DECIDED THAT?
ONLY YOU!!
THE ONLY WAY TO IMPROVE IS TO TRAIN.
TRAIN TO OBTAIN THE MAXIMUM POTENTIAL USING WHAT YOU HAVE.
EVERYTHING WILL COME INTO FOCUS ONCE YOU HONE YOUR TALENT.
NO DOUBT.

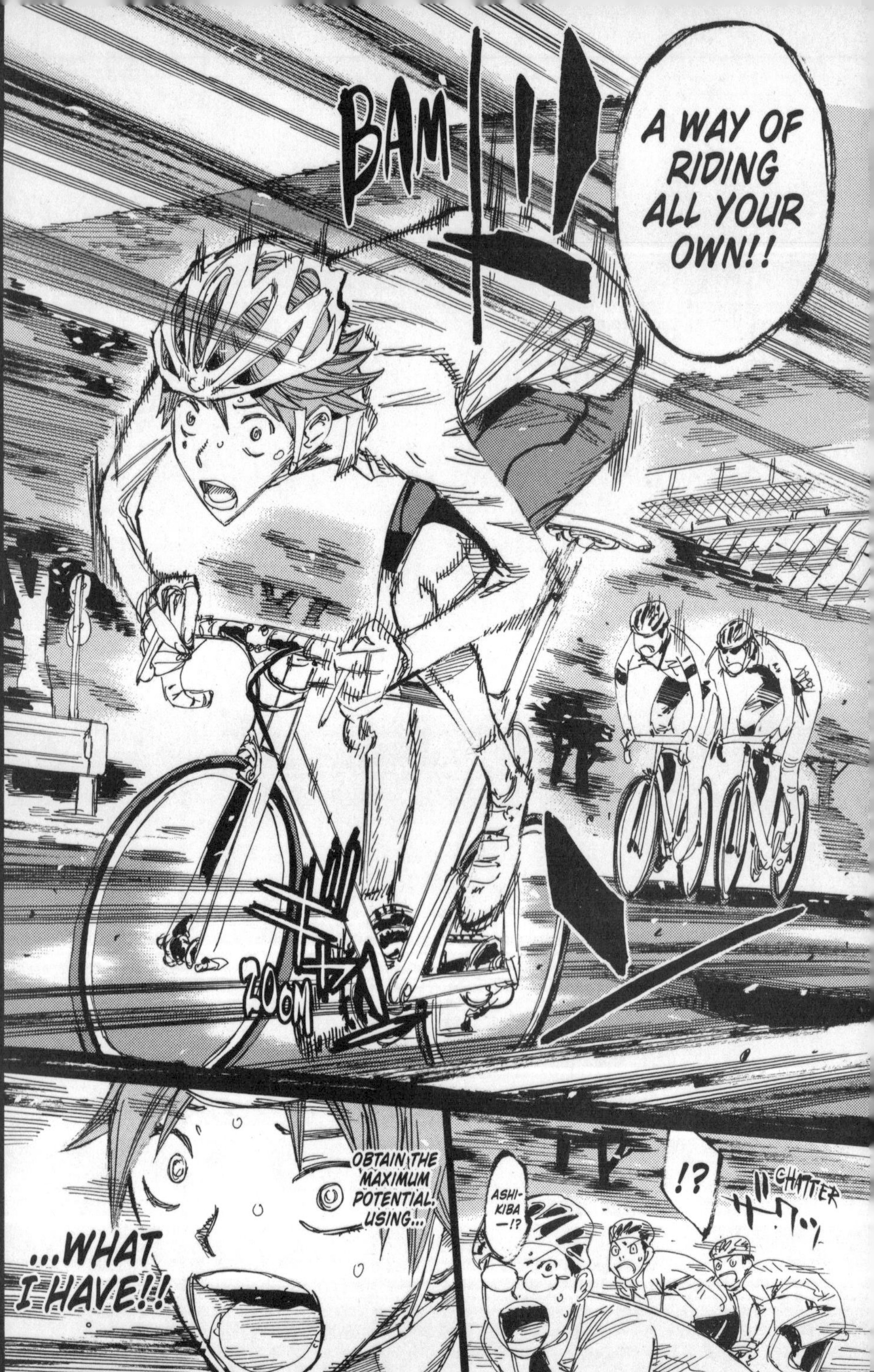
A WAY OF RIDING ALL YOUR OWN!!
BAM
ZOOM
!?
ASHI-KIBA—!?
CHATTER
OBTAIN THE MAXIMUM POTENTIAL USING...
...WHAT I HAVE!!

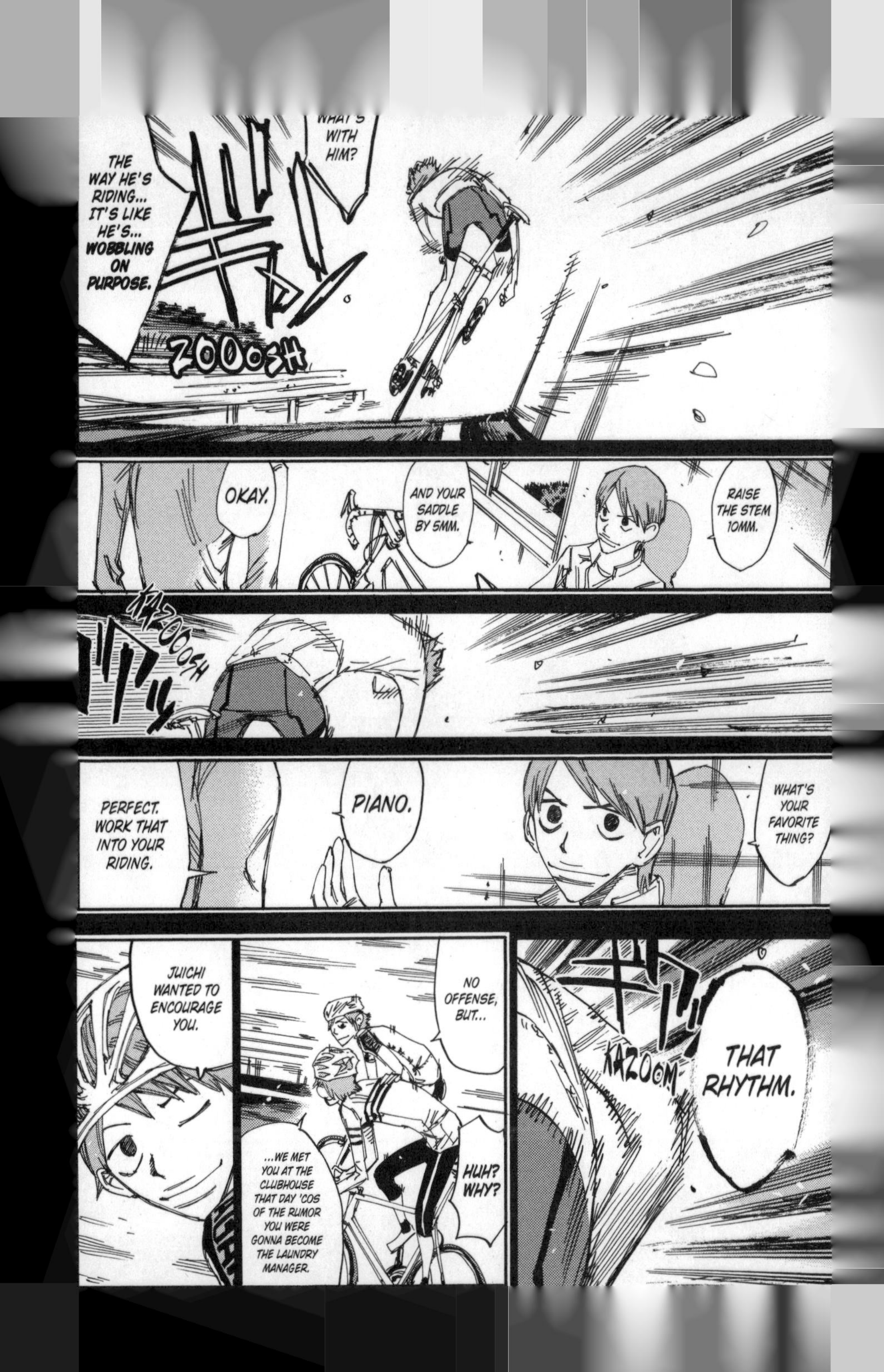
WHAT'S WITH HIM?
THE WAY HE'S RIDING... IT'S LIKE HE'S... WOBBLING ON PURPOSE.
ZOOOSH
RAISE THE STEM 10MM.
AND YOUR SADDLE BY 5MM.
OKAY.
KAZOOOSH
WHAT'S YOUR FAVORITE THING?
PIANO.
PERFECT. WORK THAT INTO YOUR RIDING.
THAT RHYTHM.
KAZOOM
NO OFFENSE, BUT...
...WE MET YOU AT THE CLUBHOUSE THAT DAY 'COS OF THE RUMOR YOU WERE GONNA BECOME THE LAUNDRY MANAGER.
HUH? WHY?
JUICHI WANTED TO ENCOURAGE YOU.

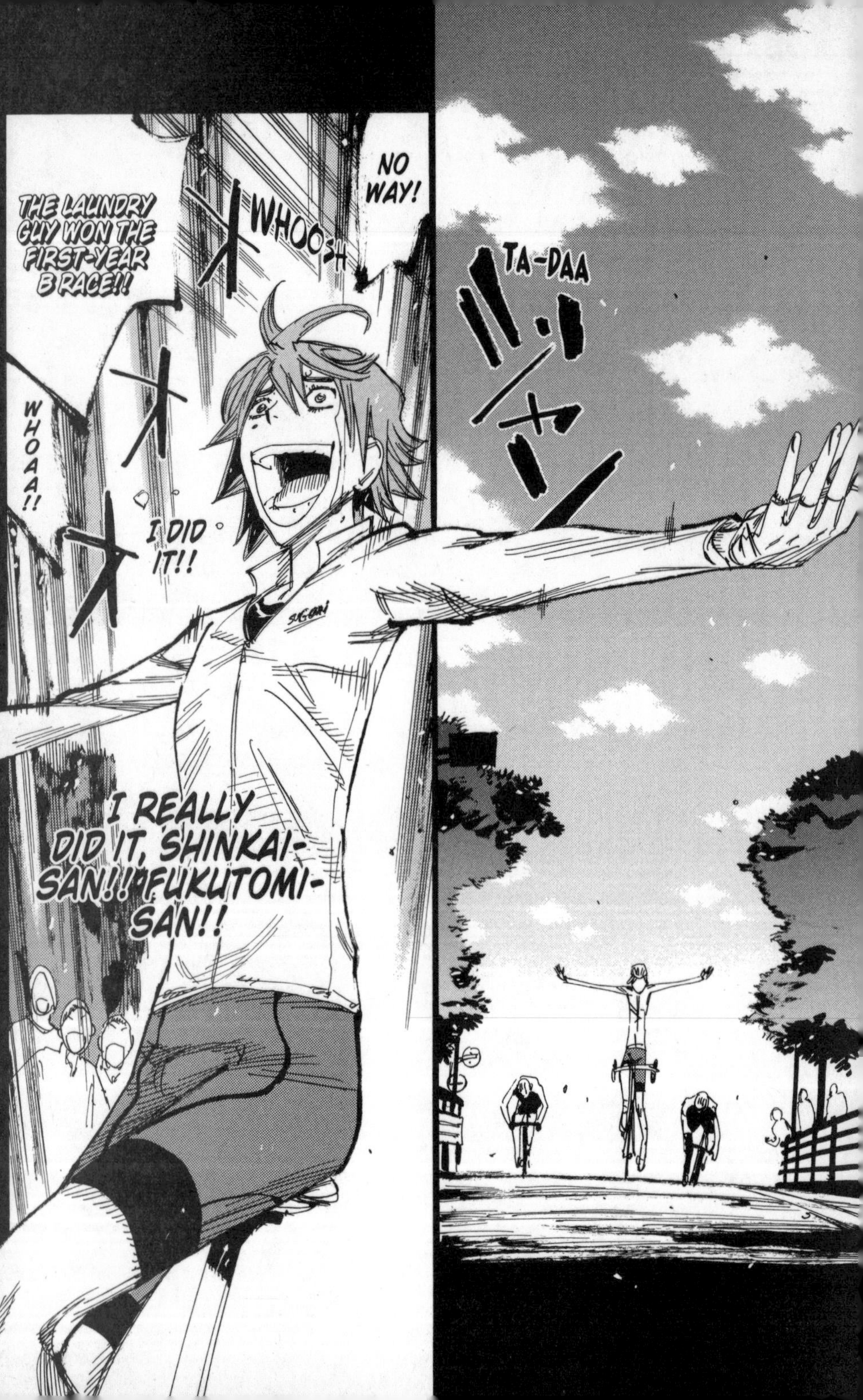
TA-DAA
NO WAY!
WHOOSH
THE LAUNDRY GUY WON THE FIRST-YEAR B RACE!!
WHOAAA!!
I DID IT!!
I REALLY DID IT, SHINKAI-SAN!! FUKUTOMI-SAN!!

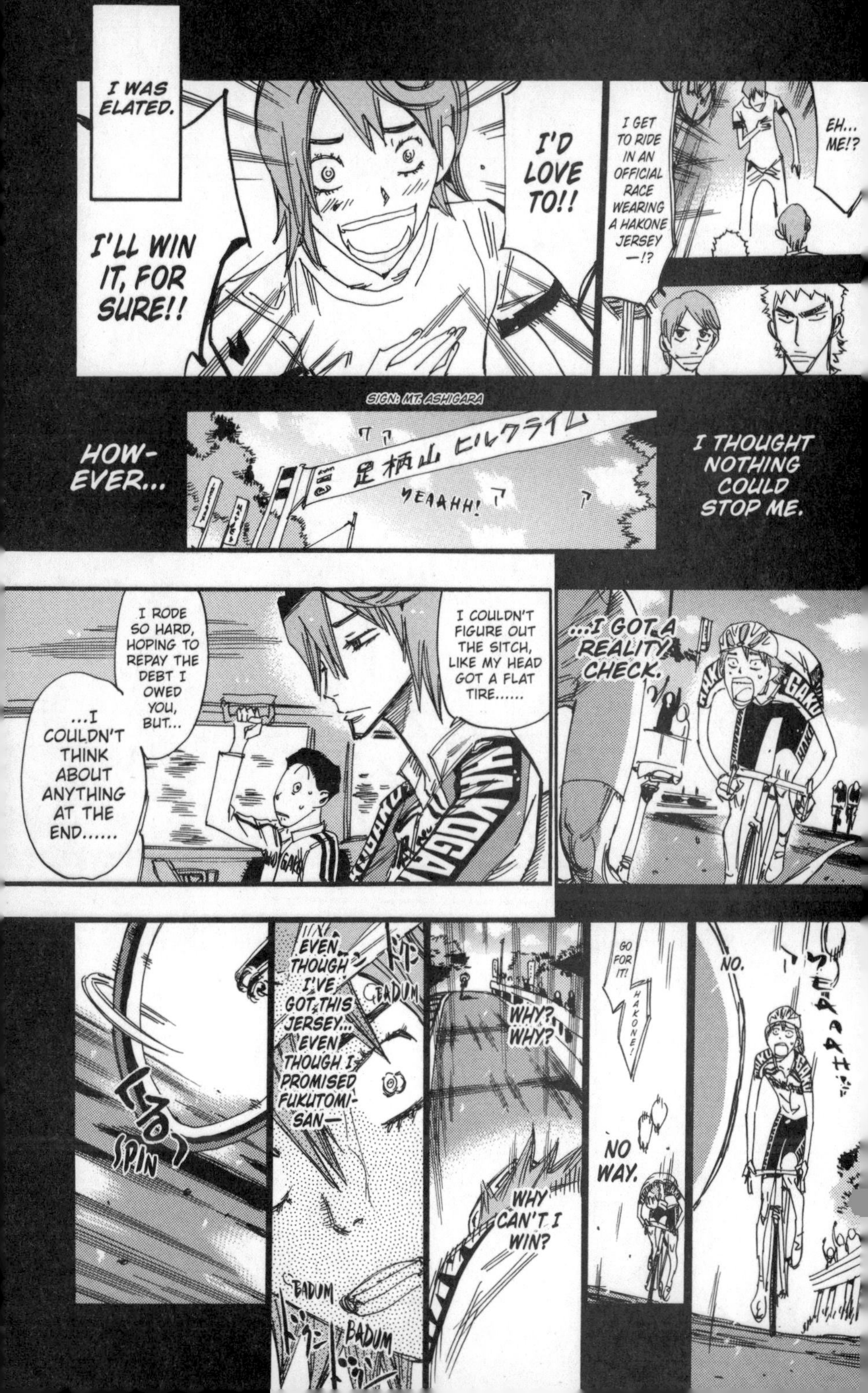
EH... ME!?
I GET TO RIDE IN AN OFFICIAL RACE WEARING A HAKONE JERSEY—!?
I'D LOVE TO!!
I WAS ELATED.
I'LL WIN IT, FOR SURE!!
I THOUGHT NOTHING COULD STOP ME.
SIGN: MT. ASHIGARA
足柄山 ヒルクライム
YEAAHH!
HOW-EVER...
...I GOT A REALITY CHECK.
I COULDN'T FIGURE OUT THE SITCH, LIKE MY HEAD GOT A FLAT TIRE......
I RODE SO HARD, HOPING TO REPAY THE DEBT I OWED YOU, BUT...
...I COULDN'T THINK ABOUT ANYTHING AT THE END......
NO.
GO FOR IT!
HAKONE!
NO WAY.
WHY? WHY?
WHY CAN'T I WIN?
EVEN THOUGH I'VE GOT THIS JERSEY... EVEN THOUGH I PROMISED FUKUTOMI-SAN—
BADUM
BADUM
BADUM
SPIN

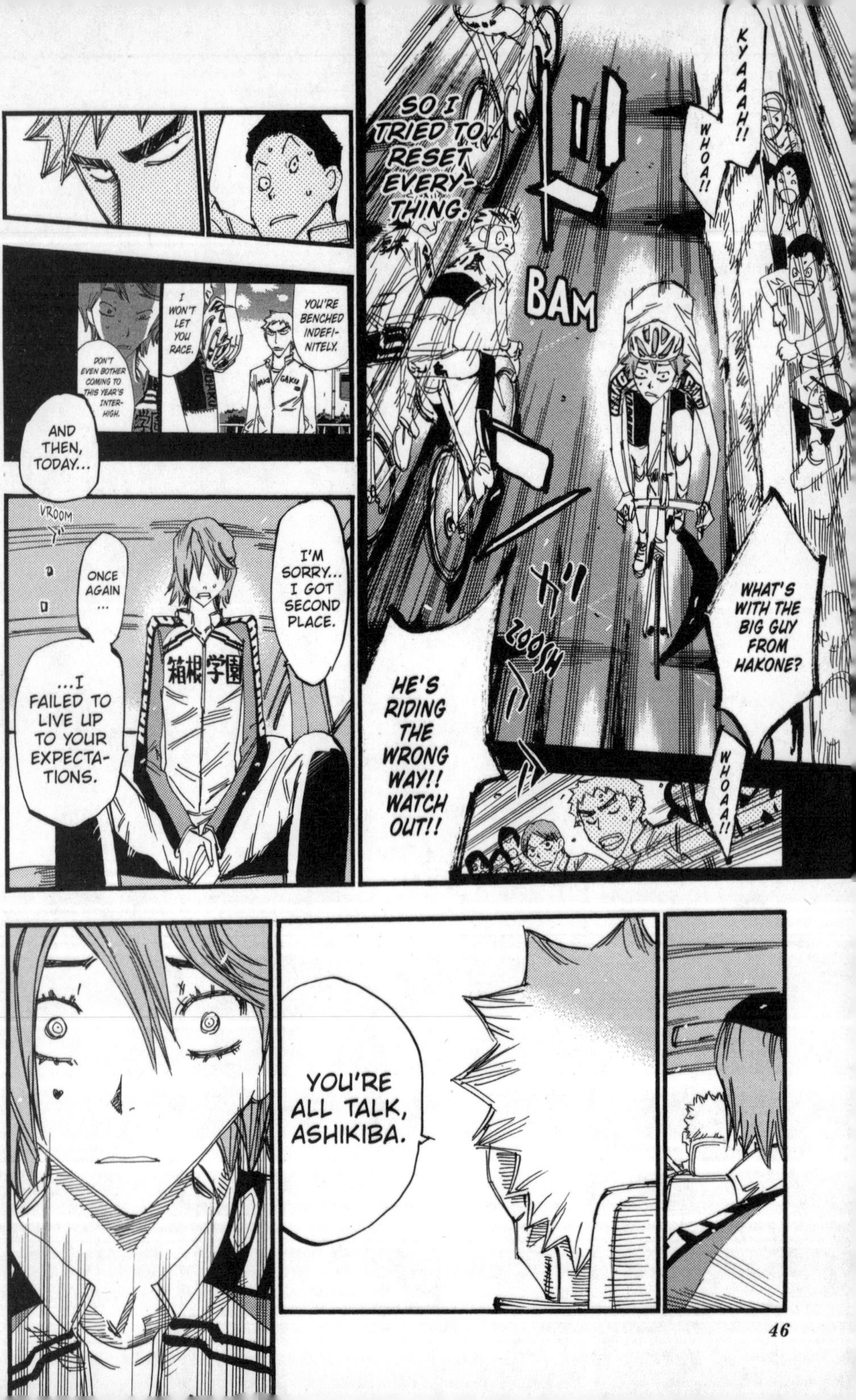
KYAAAAH!!
WHOA!!
SO I TRIED TO RESET EVERY-THING.
BAM
WHAT'S WITH THE BIG GUY FROM HAKONE?
HE'S RIDING THE WRONG WAY!! WATCH OUT!!
ZOOSH
WHOAA!!
YOU'RE BENCHED INDEFINITELY.
I WON'T LET YOU RACE.
DON'T EVEN BOTHER COMING TO THIS YEAR'S INTER-HIGH.
AND THEN, TODAY...
VROOM
I'M SORRY... I GOT SECOND PLACE.
ONCE AGAIN...
箱根学園
...I FAILED TO LIVE UP TO YOUR EXPECTA-TIONS.
YOU'RE ALL TALK, ASHIKIBA.

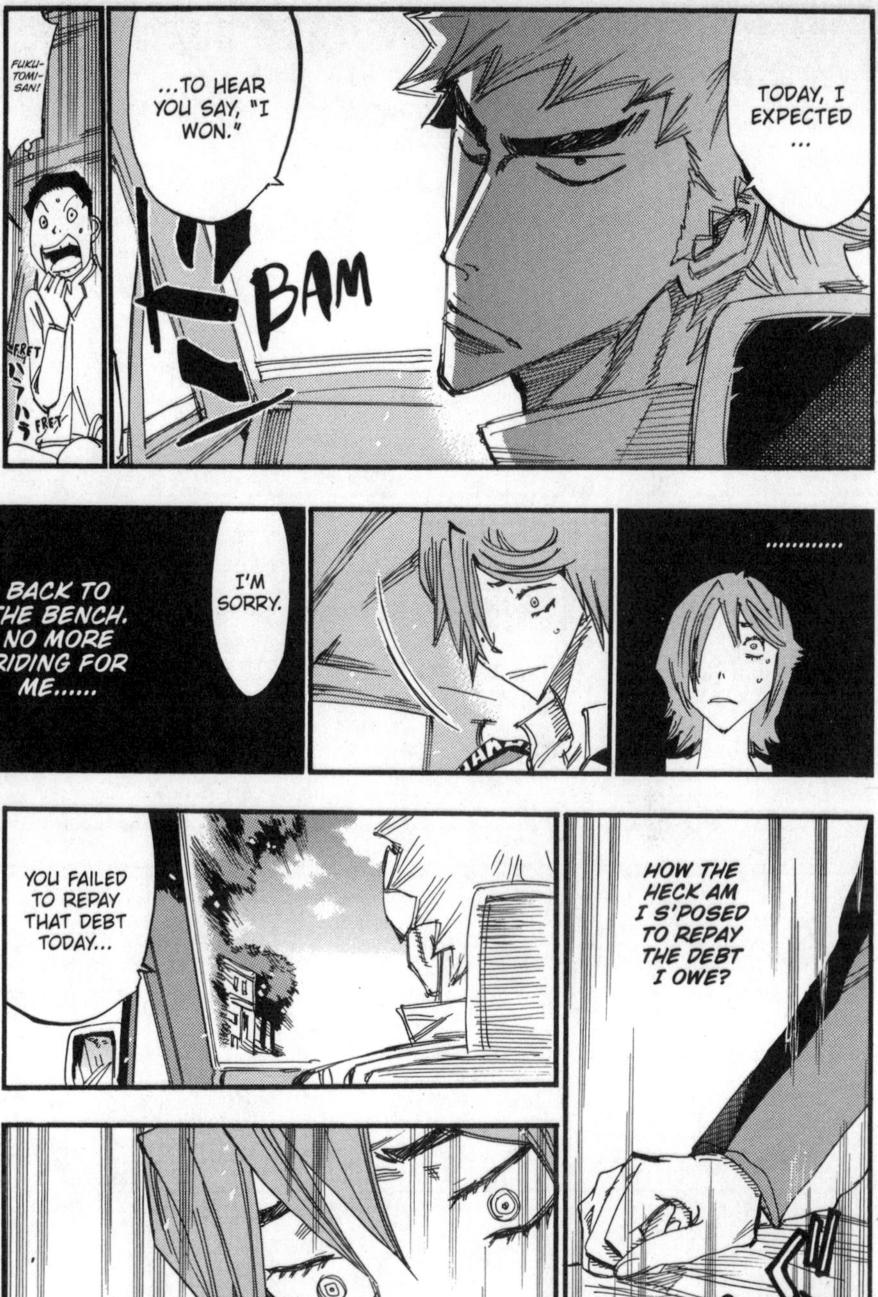
TODAY, I EXPECTED ...
...TO HEAR YOU SAY, "I WON."
BAM
FUKU-TOMI-SAN!
FRET
FRET
....
I'M SORRY.
BACK TO THE BENCH. NO MORE RIDING FOR ME......
HOW THE HECK AM I S'POSED TO REPAY THE DEBT I OWE?
CLENCH
YOU FAILED TO REPAY THAT DEBT TODAY...

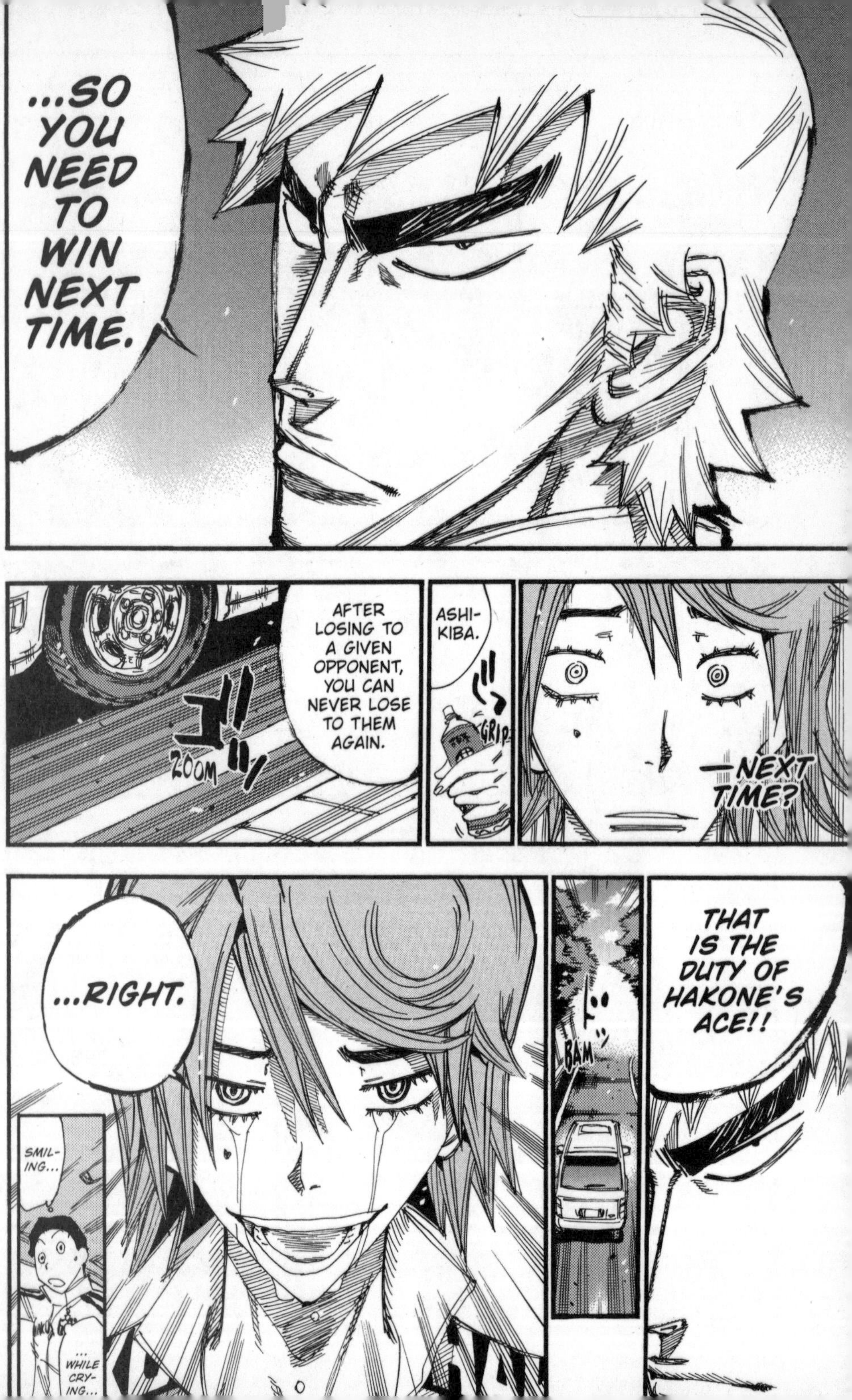
...SO YOU NEED TO WIN NEXT TIME.
—NEXT TIME?
ASHI-KIBA.
GRIP
AFTER LOSING TO A GIVEN OPPONENT, YOU CAN NEVER LOSE TO THEM AGAIN.
ZOOM
THAT IS THE DUTY OF HAKONE'S ACE!!
BAM
...RIGHT.
SMIL-ING...
...WHILE CRY-ING...

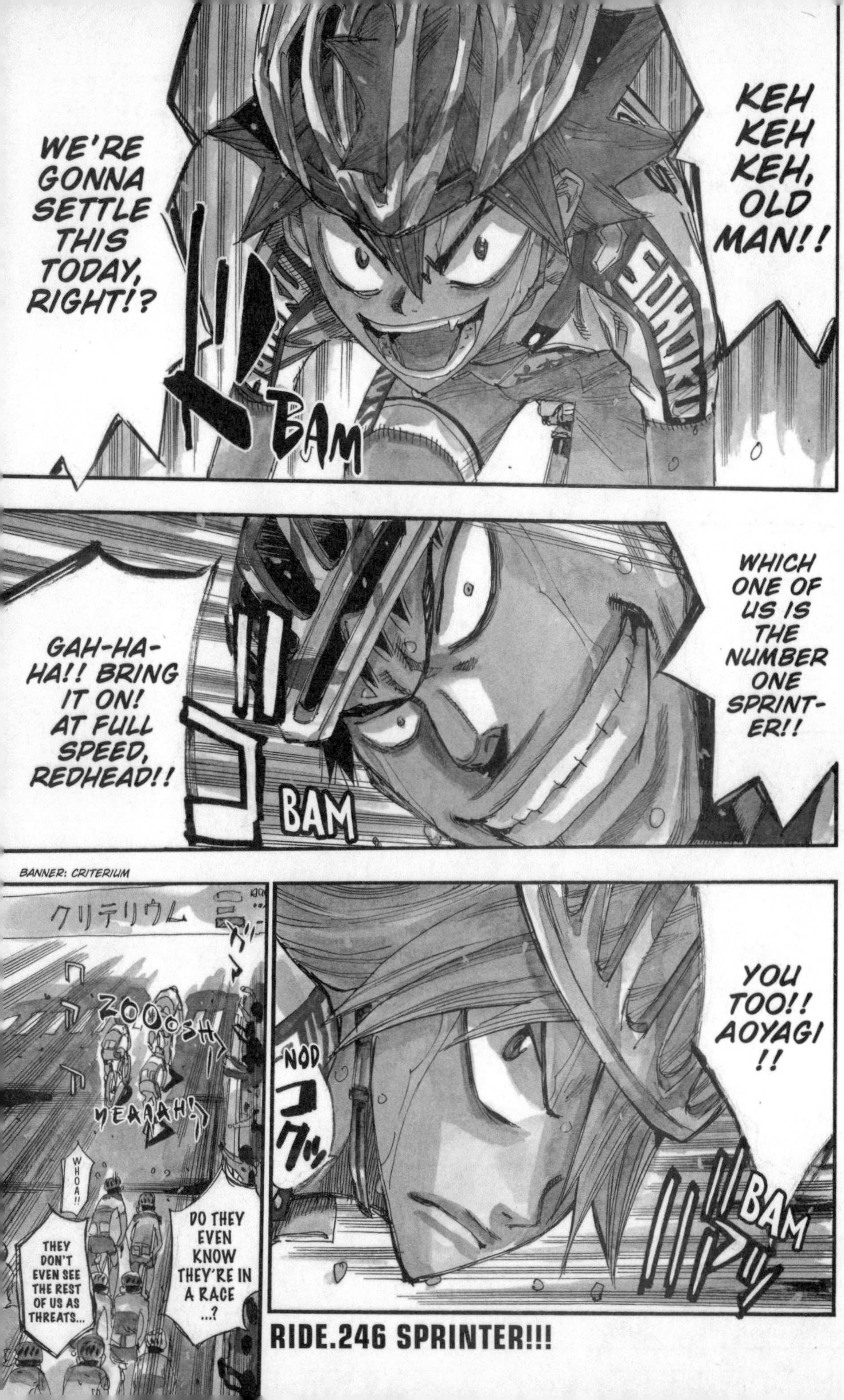
KEH KEH KEH, OLD MAN!!
WE'RE GONNA SETTLE THIS TODAY, RIGHT!?
BAM
WHICH ONE OF US IS THE NUMBER ONE SPRINTER!!
GAH-HA-HA!! BRING IT ON! AT FULL SPEED, REDHEAD!!
BAM
BANNER: CRITERIUM
YOU TOO!! AOYAGI!!
NOD
BAM
ZOOOOSH
YEAAAH!
WHOA!!
DO THEY EVEN KNOW THEY'RE IN A RACE ...?
THEY DON'T EVEN SEE THE REST OF US AS THREATS...

RIDE.246 SPRINTER!!!

RIDE.246 SPRINTER!!!

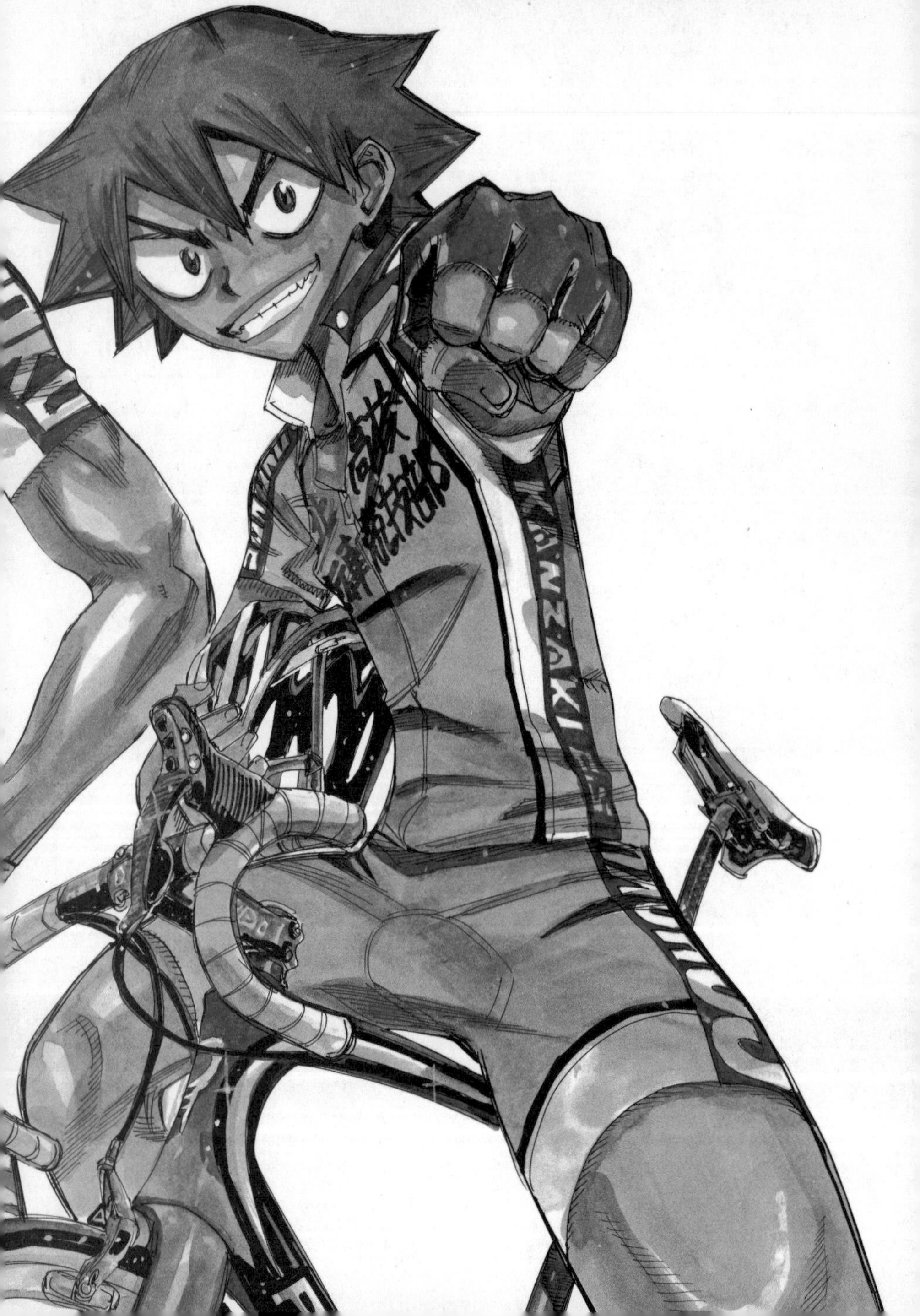

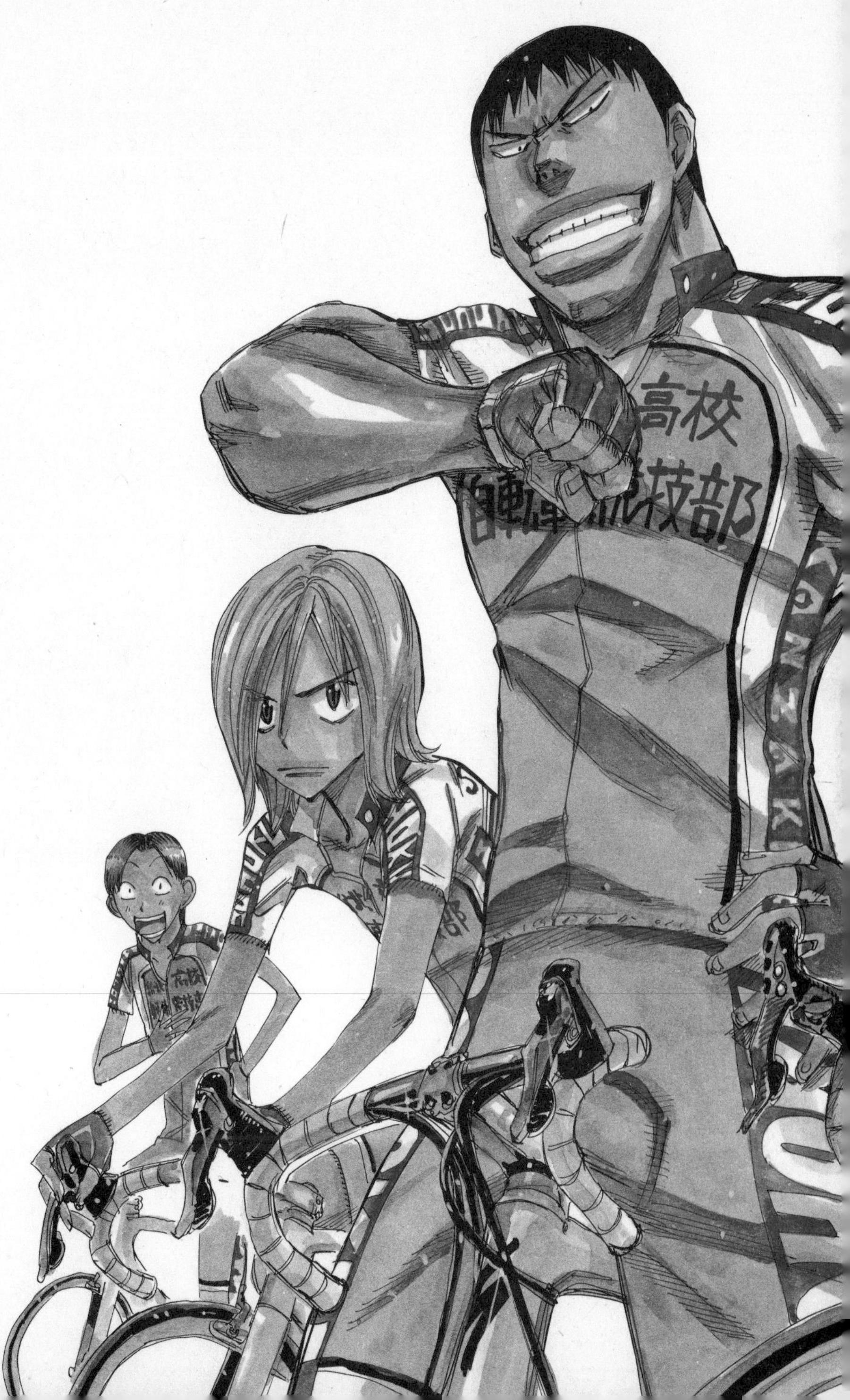
高校

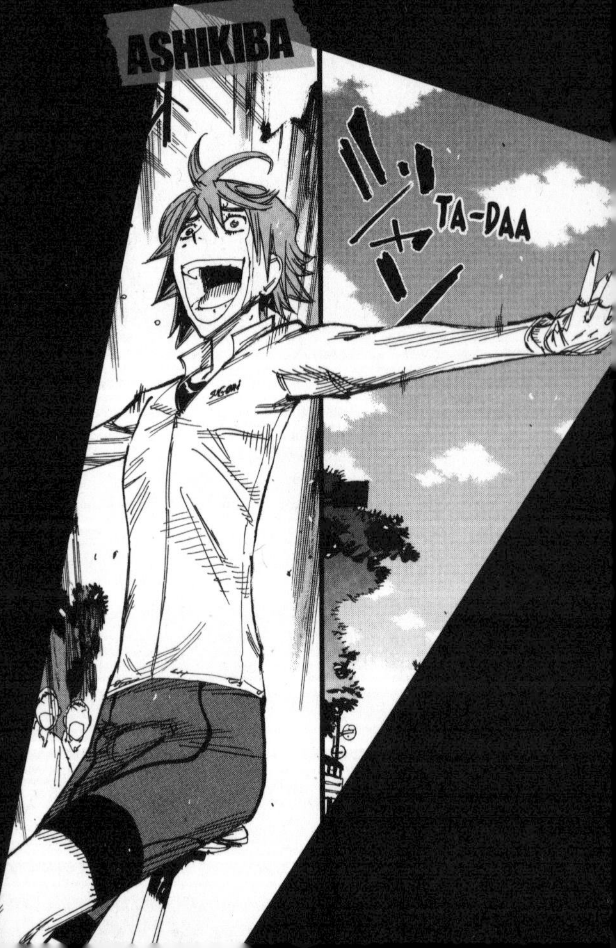
ASHIKIBA
TA-DAA

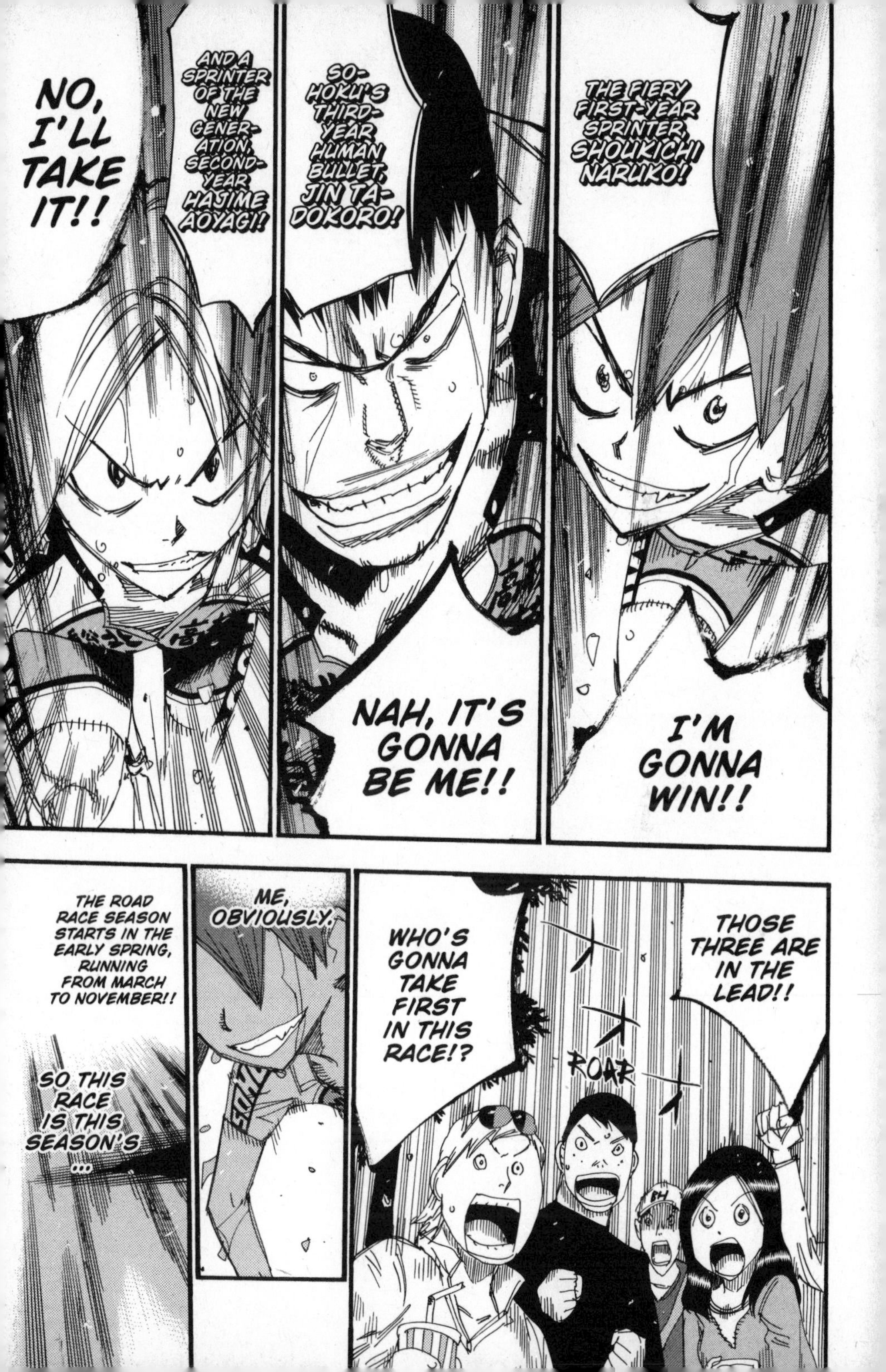
THE FIERY FIRST-YEAR SPRINTER, SHOUKICHI NARUKO!
I'M GONNA WIN!!
SO-HOKU'S THIRD-YEAR HUMAN BULLET, JIN TA-DOKORO!
NAH, IT'S GONNA BE ME!!
AND A SPRINTER OF THE NEW GENER-ATION, SECOND-YEAR HAJIME AOYAGI!
NO, I'LL TAKE IT!!
THOSE THREE ARE IN THE LEAD!!
WHO'S GONNA TAKE FIRST IN THIS RACE!?
ROAR
ME, OBVIOUSLY.
THE ROAD RACE SEASON STARTS IN THE EARLY SPRING, RUNNING FROM MARCH TO NOVEMBER!!
SO THIS RACE IS THIS SEASON'S ...

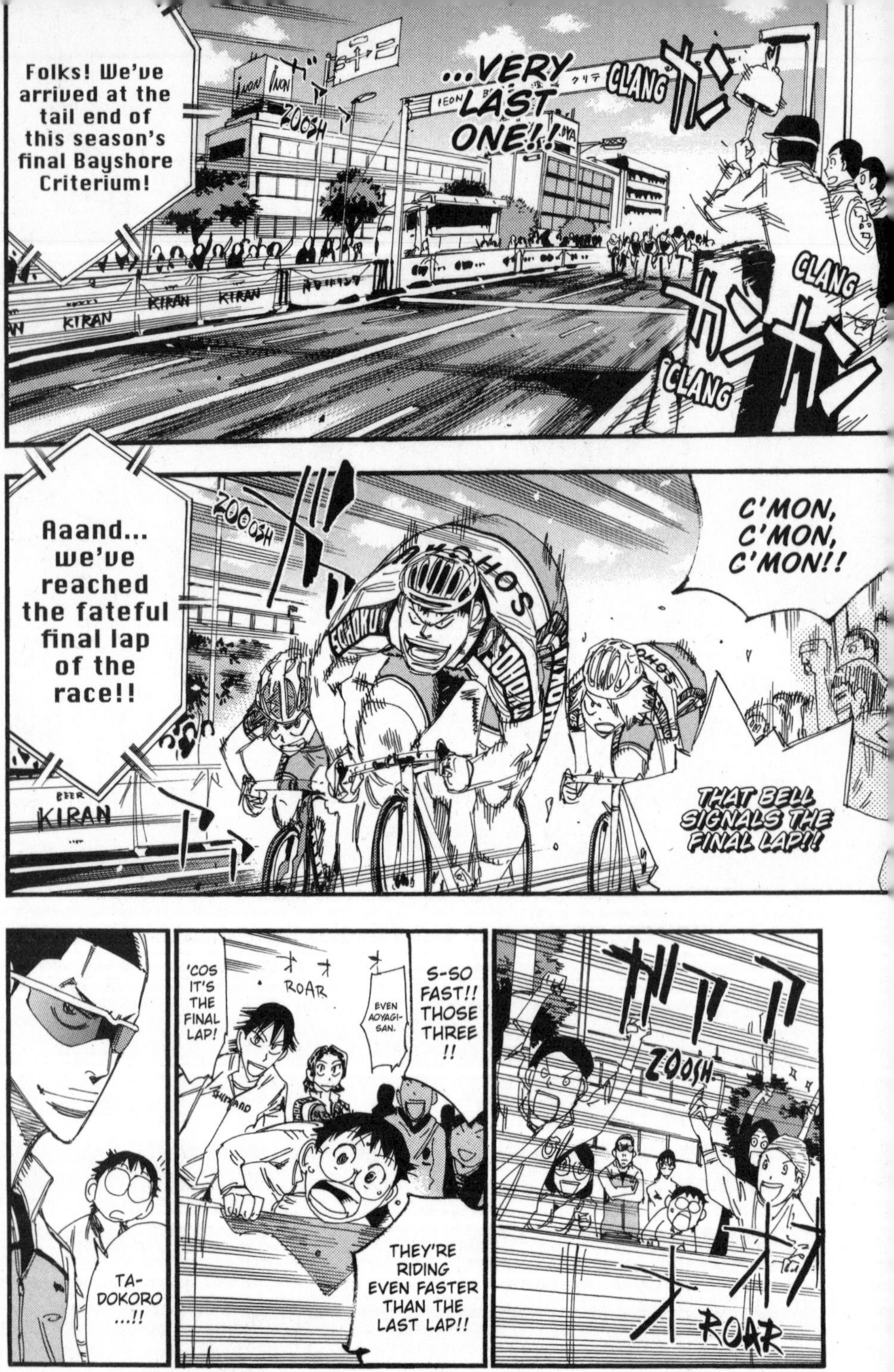
CLANG
...VERY LAST ONE!!
Folks! We've arrived at the tail end of this season's final Bayshore Criterium!
ZOOSH
KIRAN
CLANG
CLANG
C'MON, C'MON, C'MON!!
Aaand... we've reached the fateful final lap of the race!!
ZOOSH
THAT BELL SIGNALS THE FINAL LAP!!
KIRAN
ZOOSH
ROAR
S-SO FAST!! THOSE THREE!!
EVEN AOYAGI-SAN.
ROAR
'COS IT'S THE FINAL LAP!
THEY'RE RIDING EVEN FASTER THAN THE LAST LAP!!
TA-DOKORO...!!

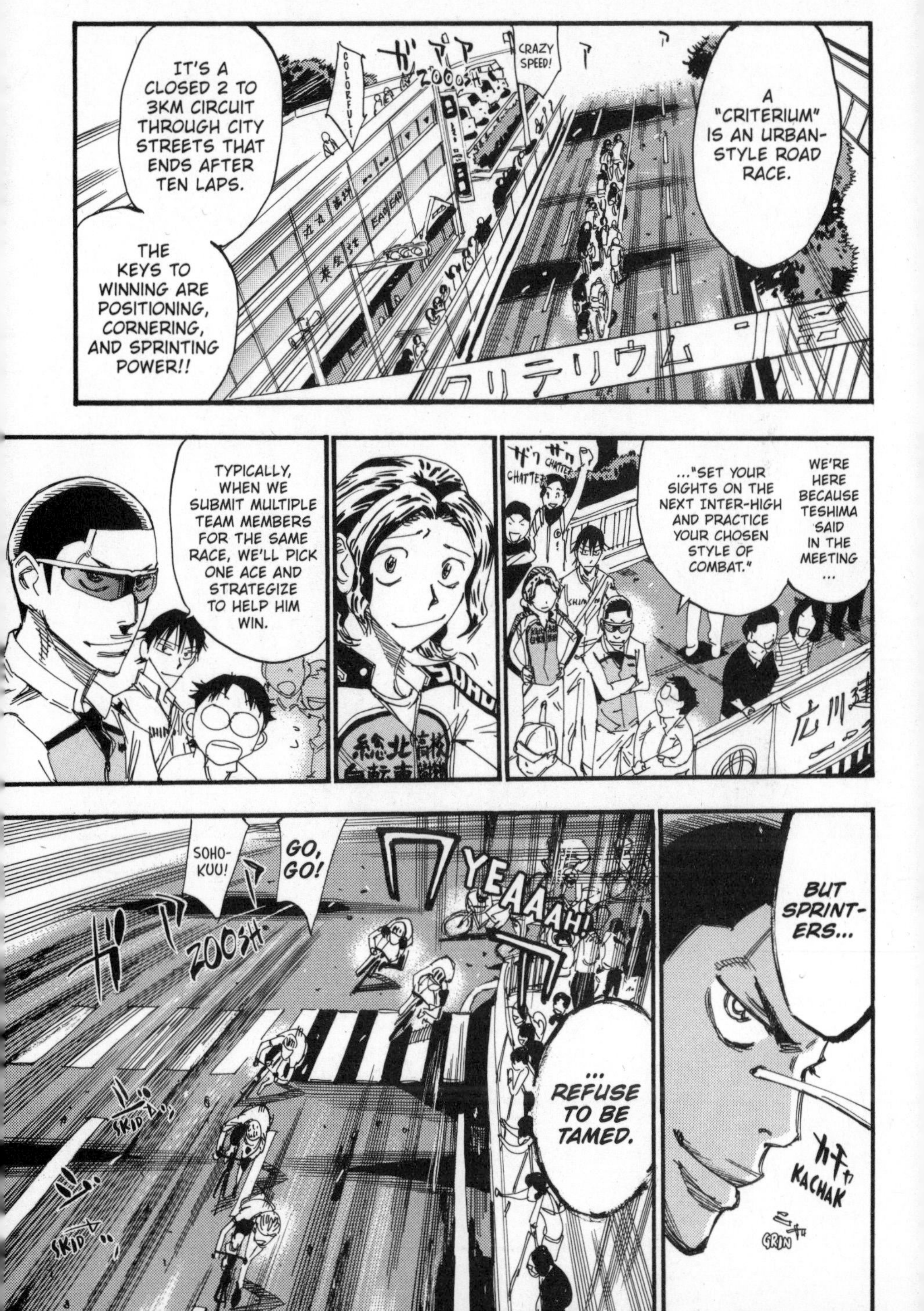
A "CRITERIUM" IS AN URBAN-STYLE ROAD RACE.
CRAZY SPEED!
ZOOOSH
COLORFUL!
IT'S A CLOSED 2 TO 3KM CIRCUIT THROUGH CITY STREETS THAT ENDS AFTER TEN LAPS.
THE KEYS TO WINNING ARE POSITIONING, CORNERING, AND SPRINTING POWER!!
クリテリウム
WE'RE HERE BECAUSE TESHIMA SAID IN THE MEETING ...
..."SET YOUR SIGHTS ON THE NEXT INTER-HIGH AND PRACTICE YOUR CHOSEN STYLE OF COMBAT."
CHATTER CHATTER
TYPICALLY, WHEN WE SUBMIT MULTIPLE TEAM MEMBERS FOR THE SAME RACE, WE'LL PICK ONE ACE AND STRATEGIZE TO HELP HIM WIN.
BUT SPRINTERS...
... REFUSE TO BE TAMED.
KACHAK
GRIN
YEAAAAH!
GO, GO!
SOHO-KUU!
ZOOSH
SKID
SKID

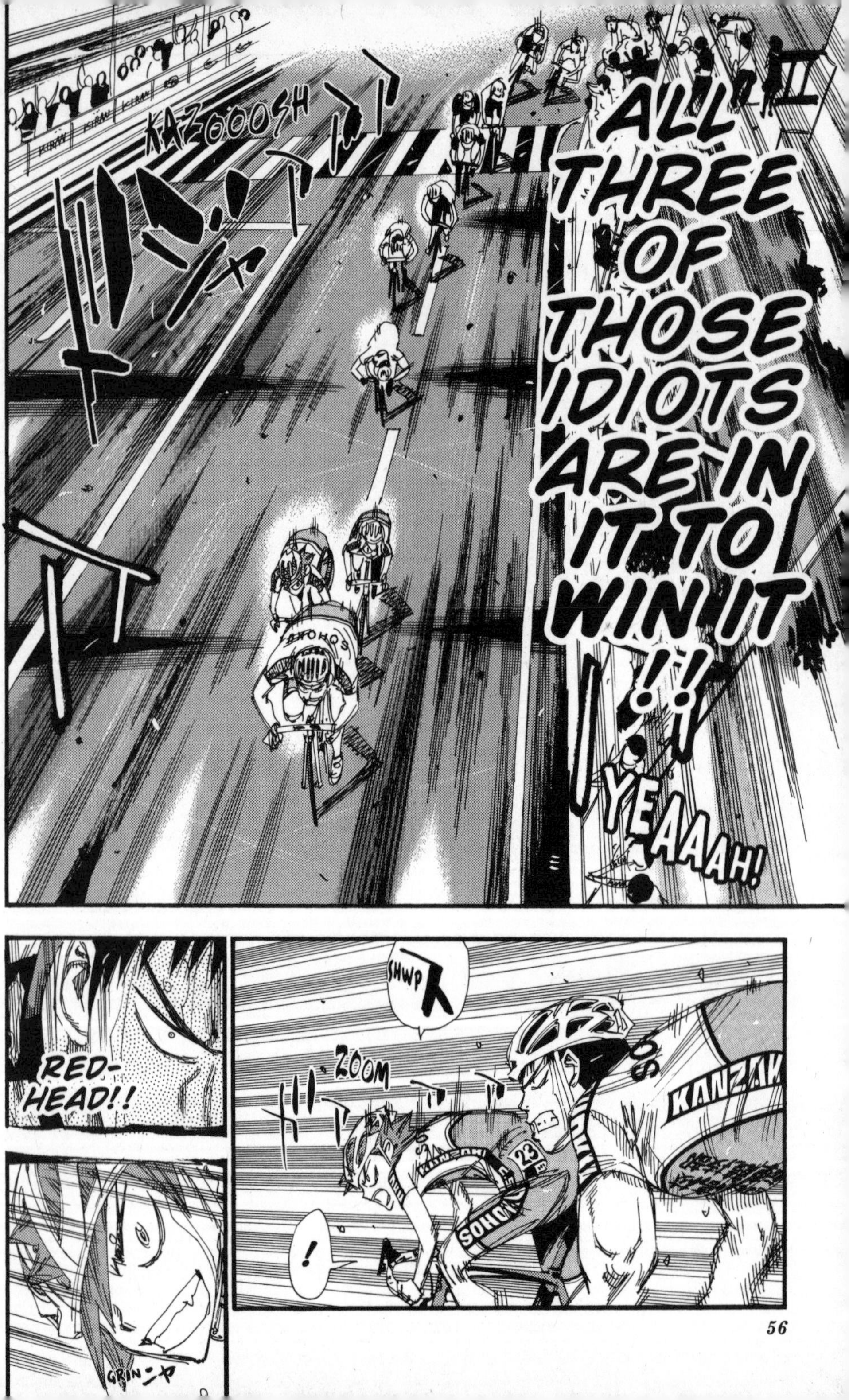
KAZOOOSH
ALL THREE OF THOSE IDIOTS ARE IN IT TO WIN IT!!
YEAAAAH!
SHWP
ZOOM
!
RED-HEAD!!
GRIN

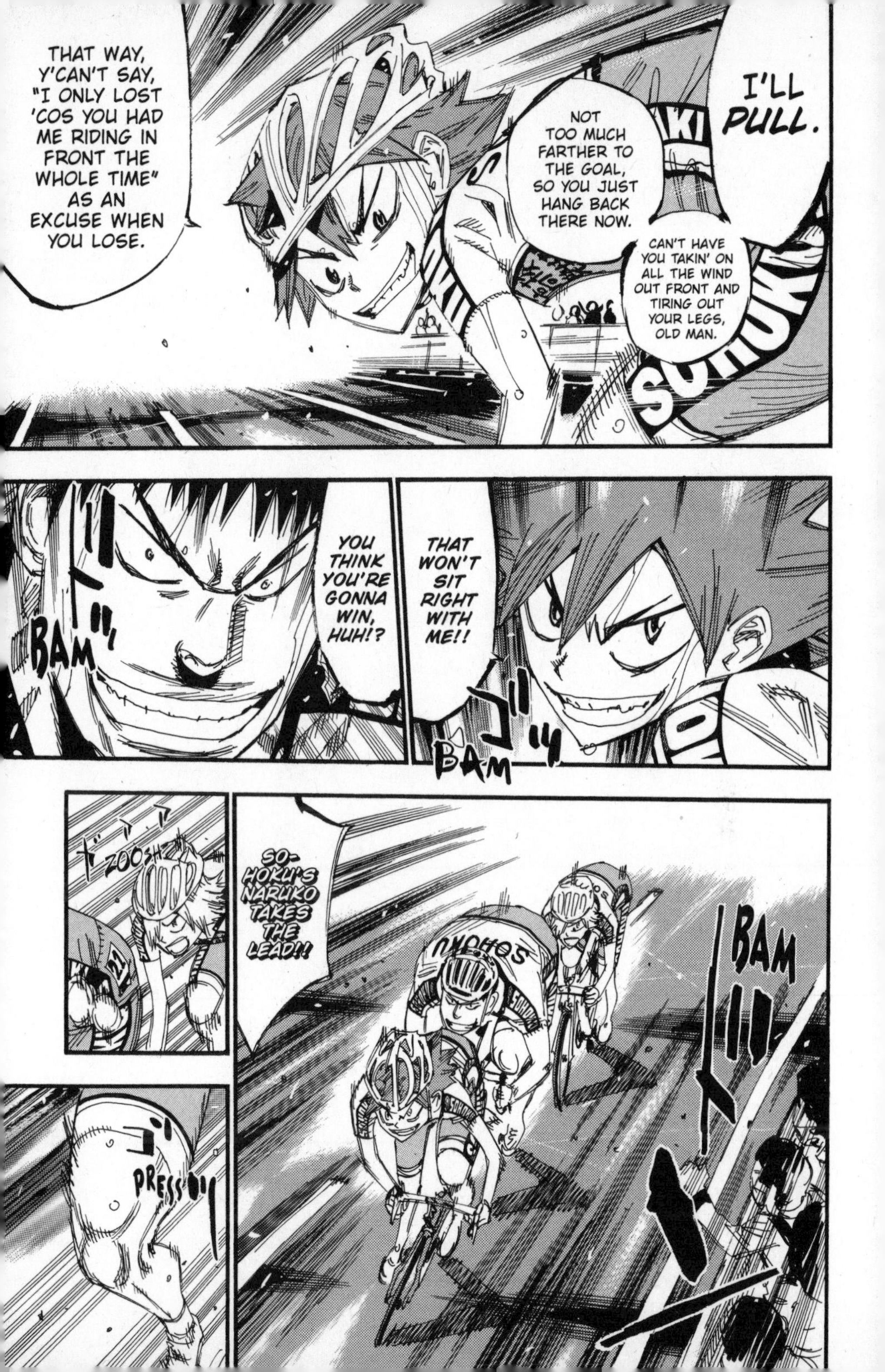
I'LL PULL.
NOT TOO MUCH FARTHER TO THE GOAL, SO YOU JUST HANG BACK THERE NOW.
CAN'T HAVE YOU TAKIN' ON ALL THE WIND OUT FRONT AND TIRING OUT YOUR LEGS, OLD MAN.
THAT WAY, Y'CAN'T SAY, "I ONLY LOST 'COS YOU HAD ME RIDING IN FRONT THE WHOLE TIME" AS AN EXCUSE WHEN YOU LOSE.
THAT WON'T SIT RIGHT WITH ME!!
BAM
YOU THINK YOU'RE GONNA WIN, HUH!?
BAM
BAM
SO-HOKU'S NARUKO TAKES THE LEAD!!
ZOOSH
PRESS

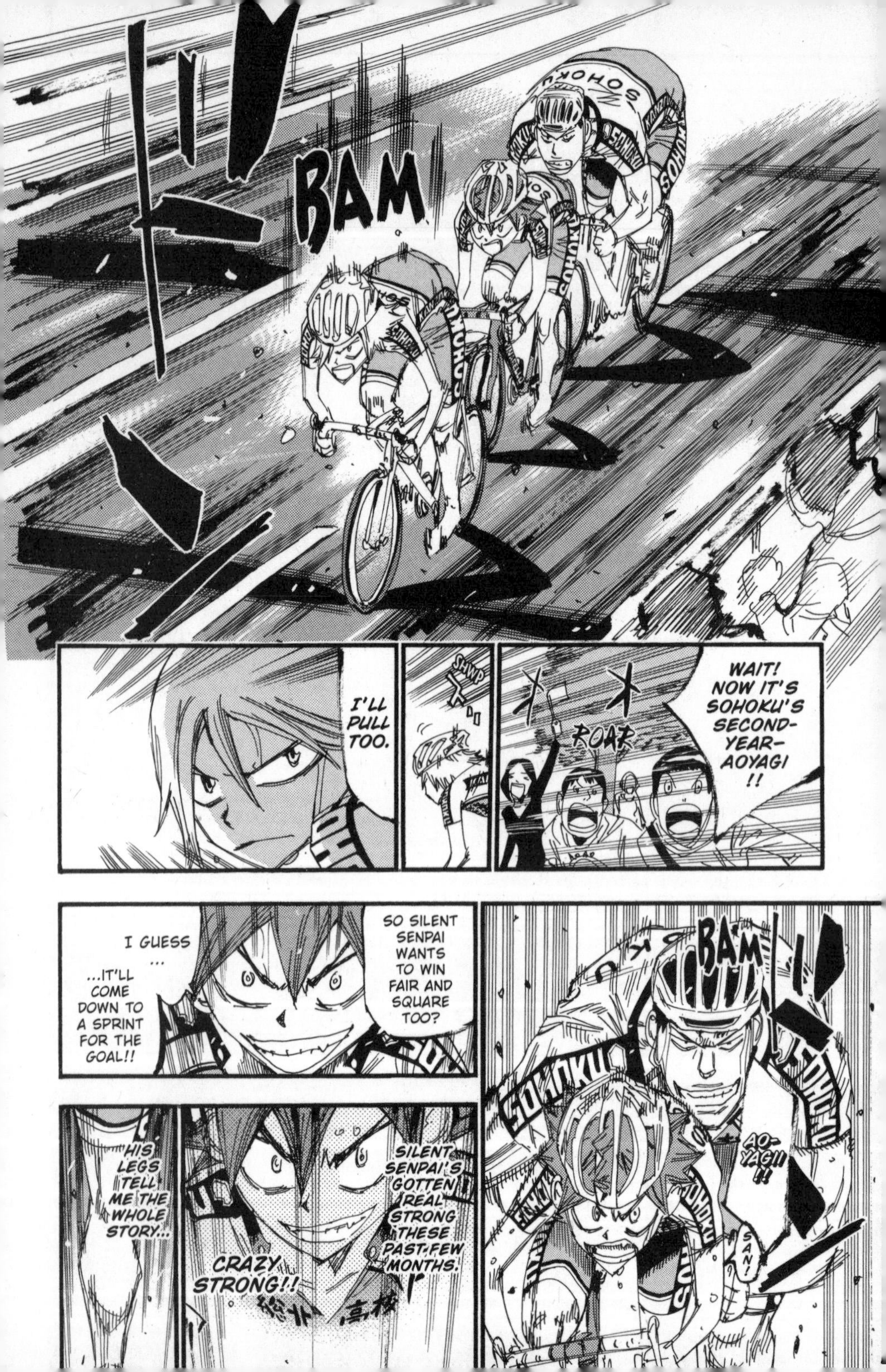
BAM
WAIT! NOW IT'S SOHOKU'S SECOND-YEAR-AOYAGI!!
ROAR
SHWP
I'LL PULL TOO.
BAM!!
AO-YAGI!!
SAN!
SO SILENT SENPAI WANTS TO WIN FAIR AND SQUARE TOO?
I GUESS...
...IT'LL COME DOWN TO A SPRINT FOR THE GOAL!!
SILENT SENPAI'S GOTTEN REAL STRONG THESE PAST FEW MONTHS.
CRAZY STRONG!!
HIS LEGS TELL ME THE WHOLE STORY...

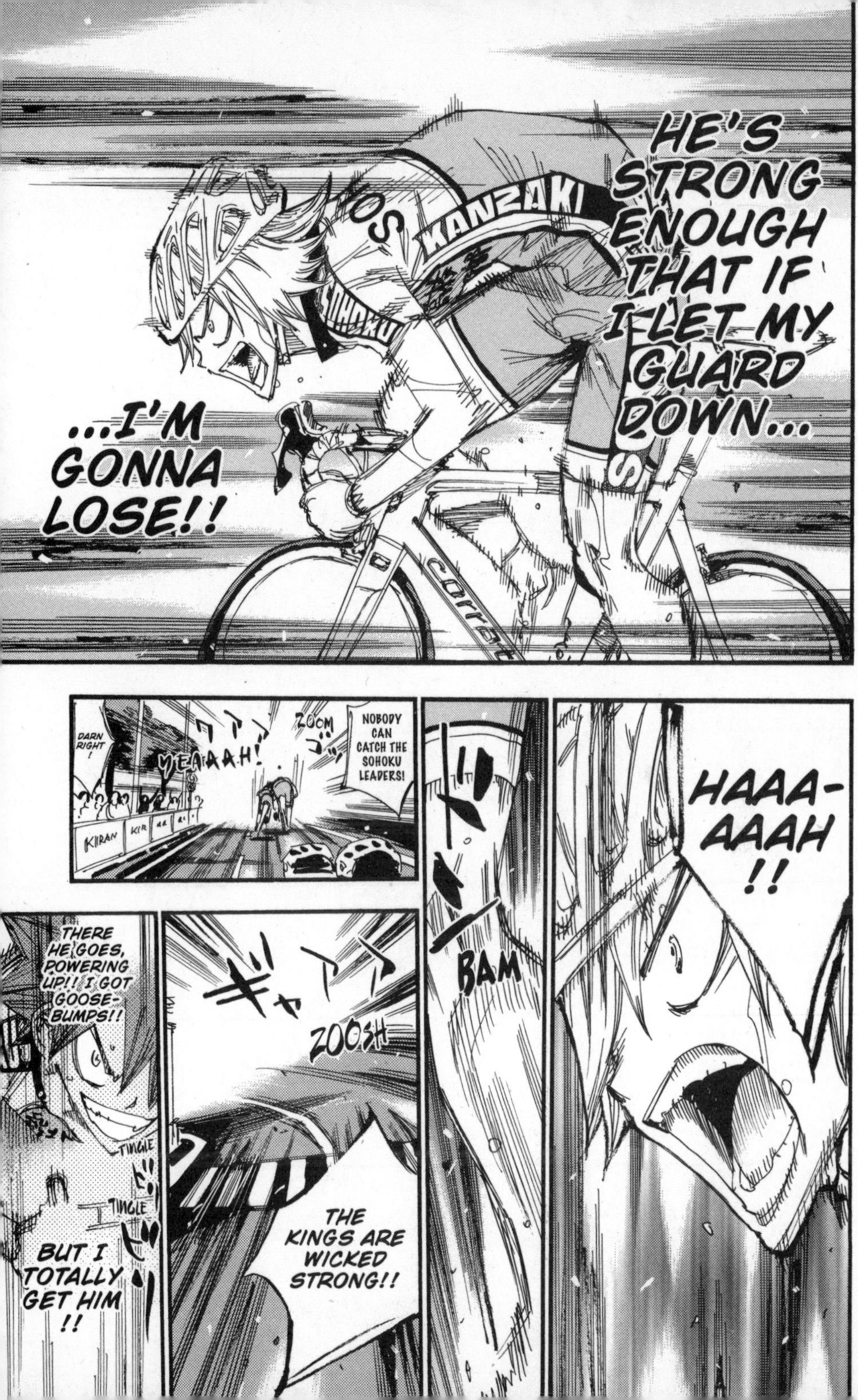
HE'S STRONG ENOUGH THAT IF I LET MY GUARD DOWN...
...I'M GONNA LOSE!!
HAAAA-AAAH!!
BAM
NOBODY CAN CATCH THE SOHOKU LEADERS!
ZOOM
YEAAAAH!
DARN RIGHT!
ZOOSH
THE KINGS ARE WICKED STRONG!!
THERE HE GOES, POWERING UP!! I GOT GOOSE-BUMPS!!
TINGLE
TINGLE
BUT I TOTALLY GET HIM!!

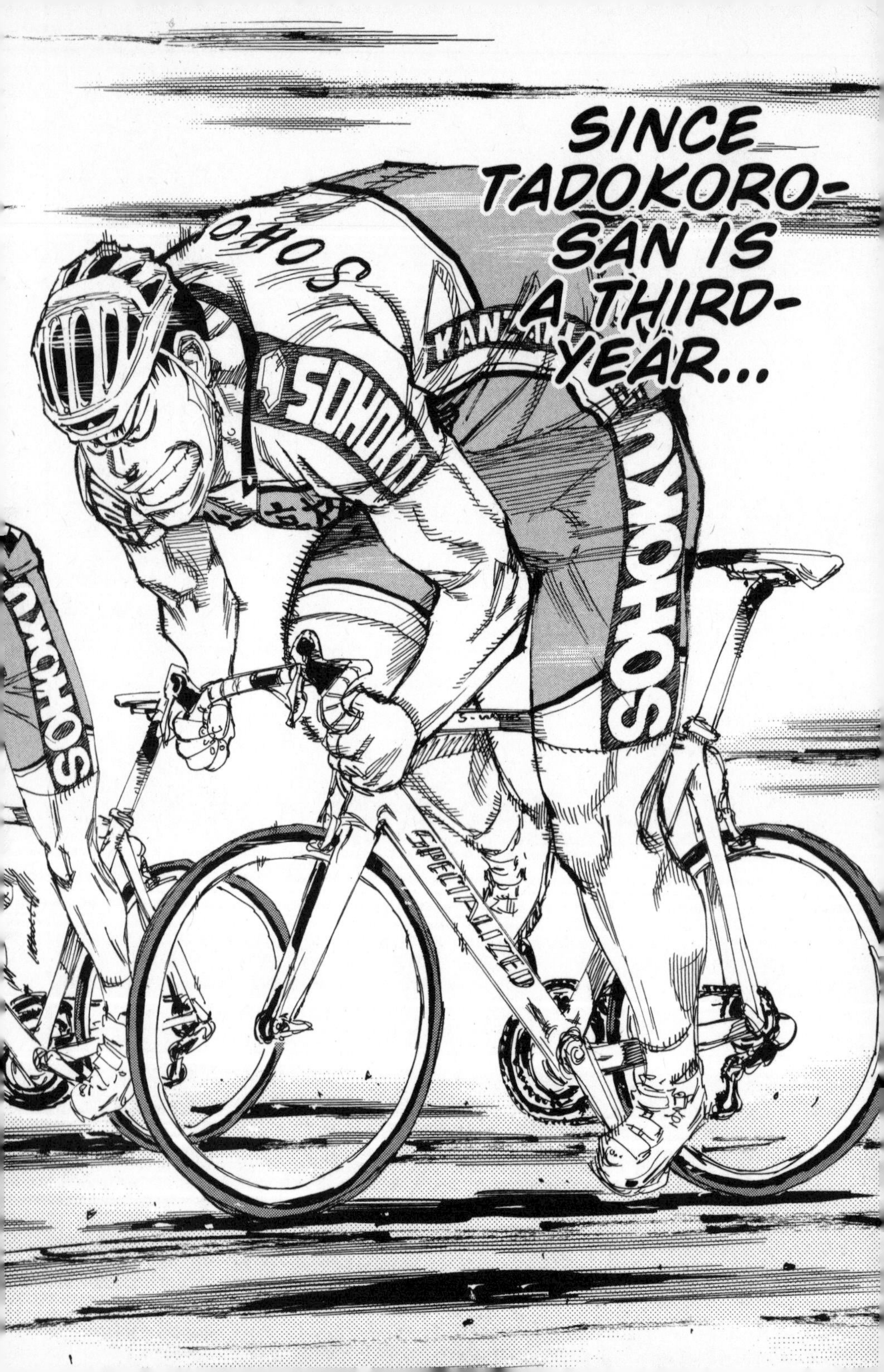
SINCE TADOKORO-SAN IS A THIRD-YEAR...

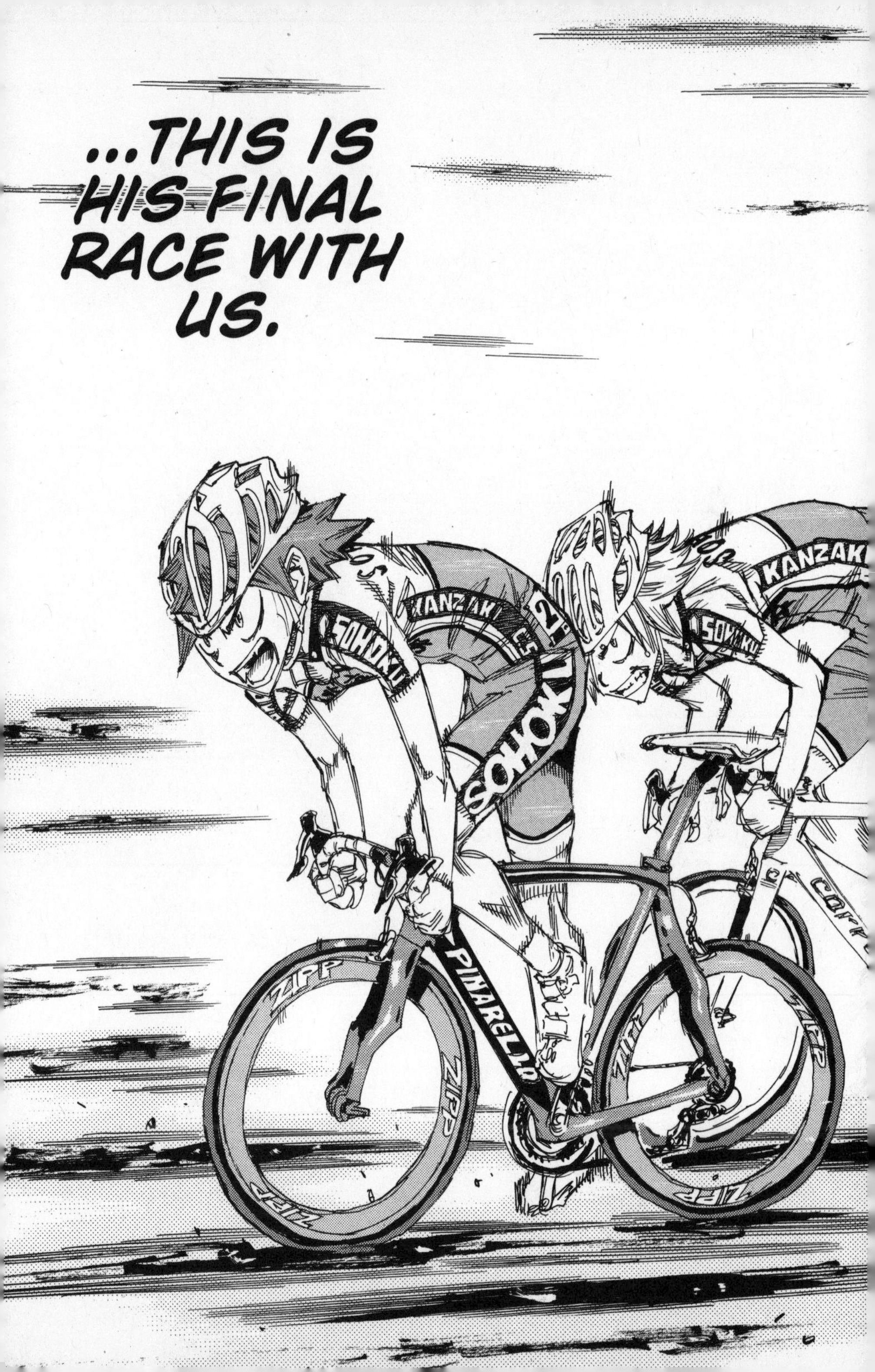
...THIS IS HIS FINAL RACE WITH US.

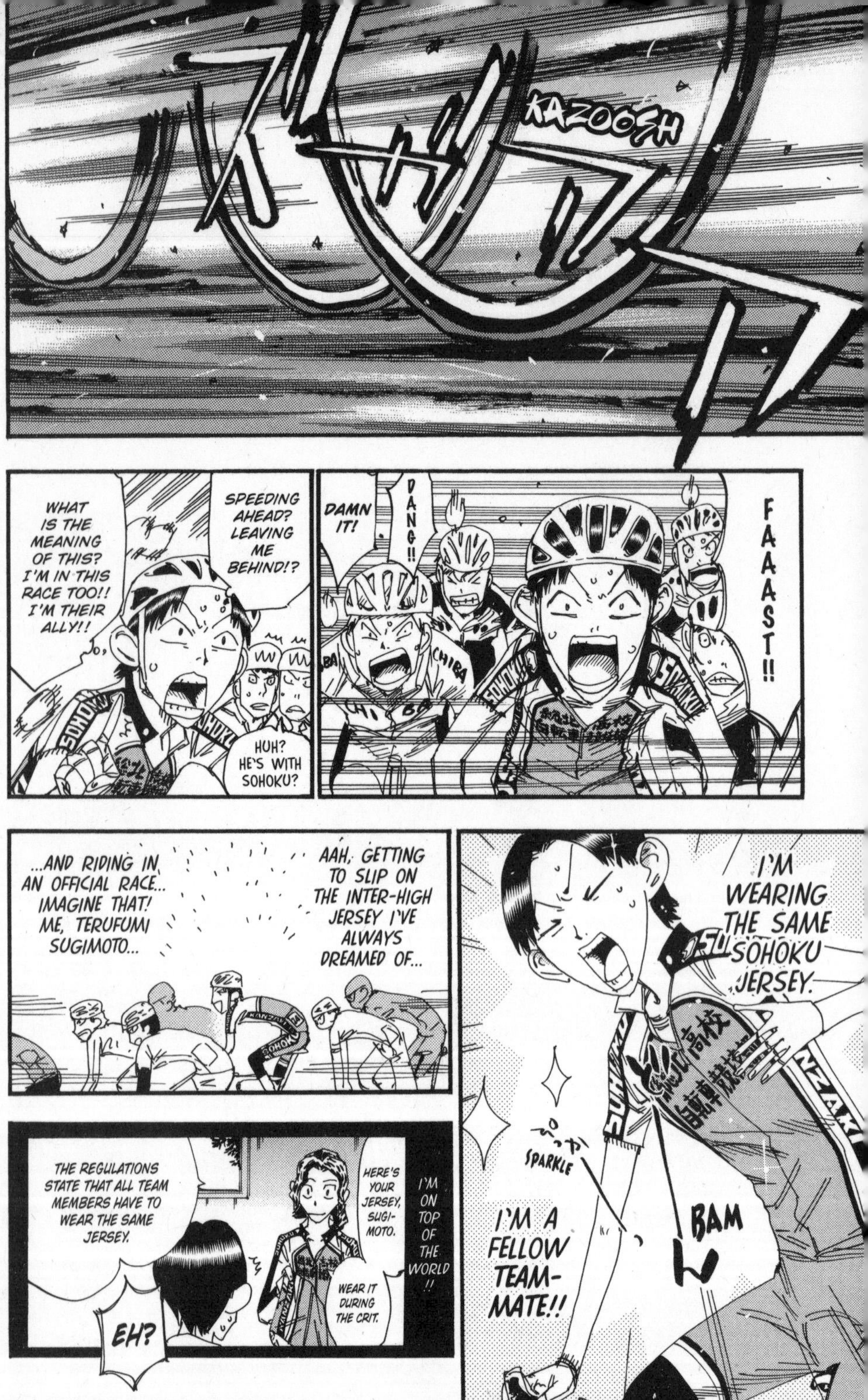
KAZOOSH
FAAAST!!
DANG!!
DAMN IT!
SPEEDING AHEAD? LEAVING ME BEHIND!?
WHAT IS THE MEANING OF THIS? I'M IN THIS RACE TOO!! I'M THEIR ALLY!!
HUH? HE'S WITH SOHOKU?
I'M WEARING THE SAME SOHOKU JERSEY.
SPARKLE
BAM
I'M A FELLOW TEAM-MATE!!
AAH, GETTING TO SLIP ON THE INTER-HIGH JERSEY I'VE ALWAYS DREAMED OF...
...AND RIDING IN AN OFFICIAL RACE... IMAGINE THAT! ME, TERUFUMI SUGIMOTO...
I'M ON TOP OF THE WORLD!!
HERE'S YOUR JERSEY, SUGIMOTO.
WEAR IT DURING THE CRIT.
THE REGULATIONS STATE THAT ALL TEAM MEMBERS HAVE TO WEAR THE SAME JERSEY.
EH?

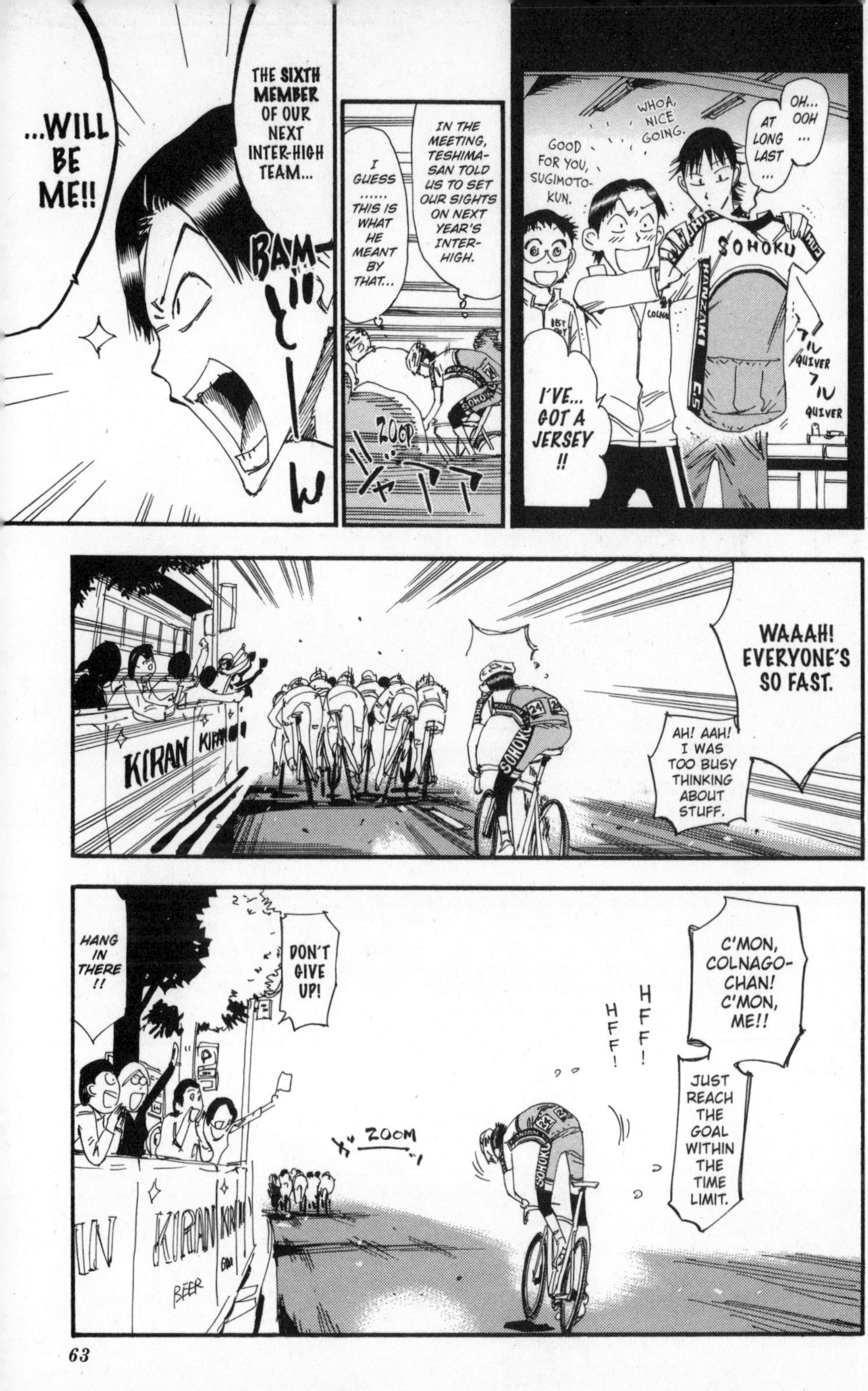
OH... OOH ... AT LONG LAST ...
WHOA, NICE GOING.
GOOD FOR YOU, SUGIMOTO-KUN.
SOHOKU
I'VE... GOT A JERSEY !!
QUIVER
QUIVER
IN THE MEETING, TESHIMA-SAN TOLD US TO SET OUR SIGHTS ON NEXT YEAR'S INTER-HIGH.
I GUESS ...... THIS IS WHAT HE MEANT BY THAT...
ZOOP
THE SIXTH MEMBER OF OUR NEXT INTER-HIGH TEAM...
...WILL BE ME!!
BAM
WAAAH! EVERYONE'S SO FAST.
AH! AAH! I WAS TOO BUSY THINKING ABOUT STUFF.
KIRAN
C'MON, COLNAGO-CHAN! C'MON, ME!!
JUST REACH THE GOAL WITHIN THE TIME LIMIT.
HFF!
HFF!
DON'T GIVE UP!
HANG IN THERE !!
ZOOM
KIRAN
BEER

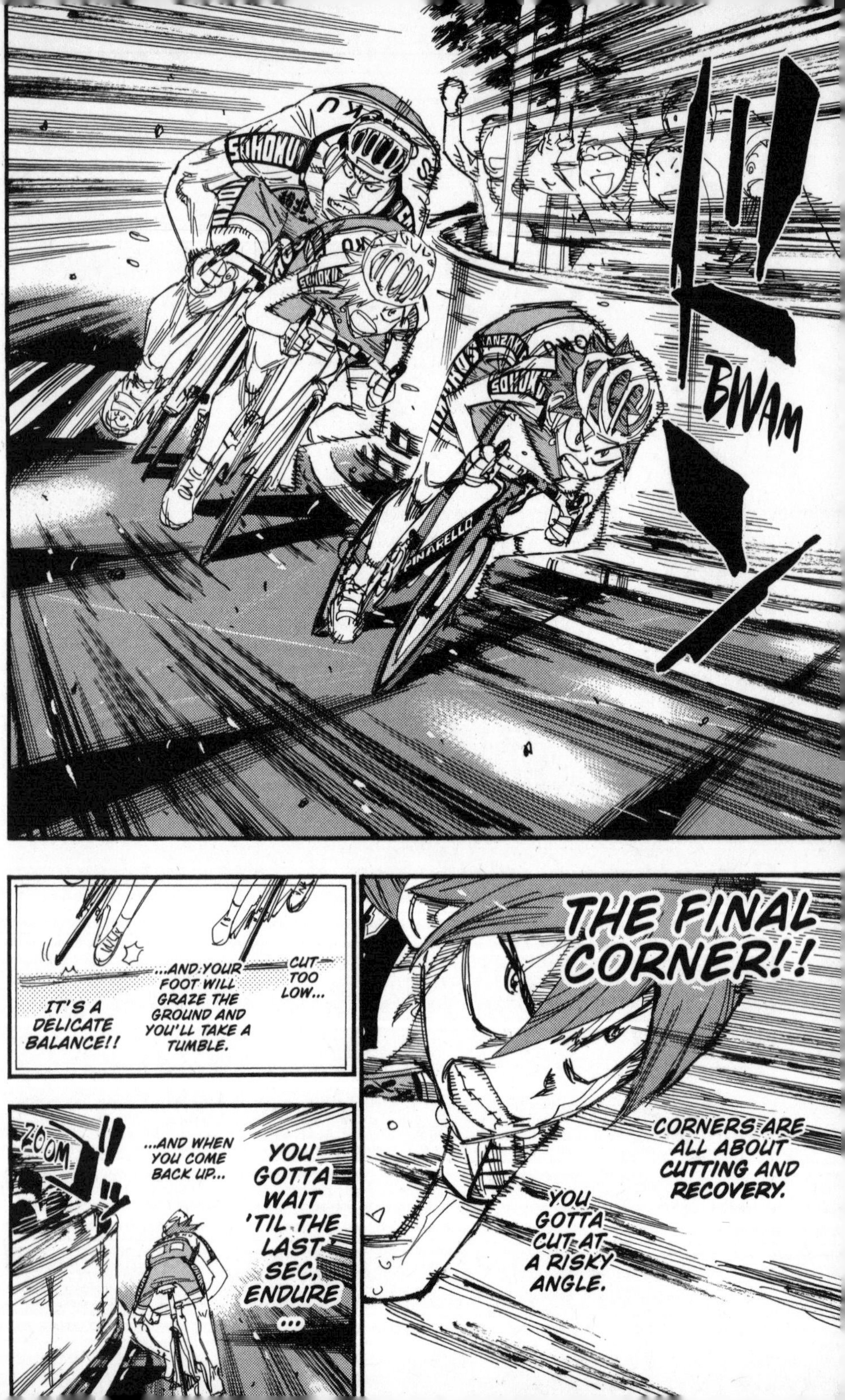
BWAM
THE FINAL CORNER!!
CORNERS ARE ALL ABOUT CUTTING AND RECOVERY.
YOU GOTTA CUT AT A RISKY ANGLE.
CUT TOO LOW...
...AND YOUR FOOT WILL GRAZE THE GROUND AND YOU'LL TAKE A TUMBLE.
IT'S A DELICATE BALANCE!!
...AND WHEN YOU COME BACK UP...
YOU GOTTA WAIT 'TIL THE LAST SEC, ENDURE ...
ZOOM

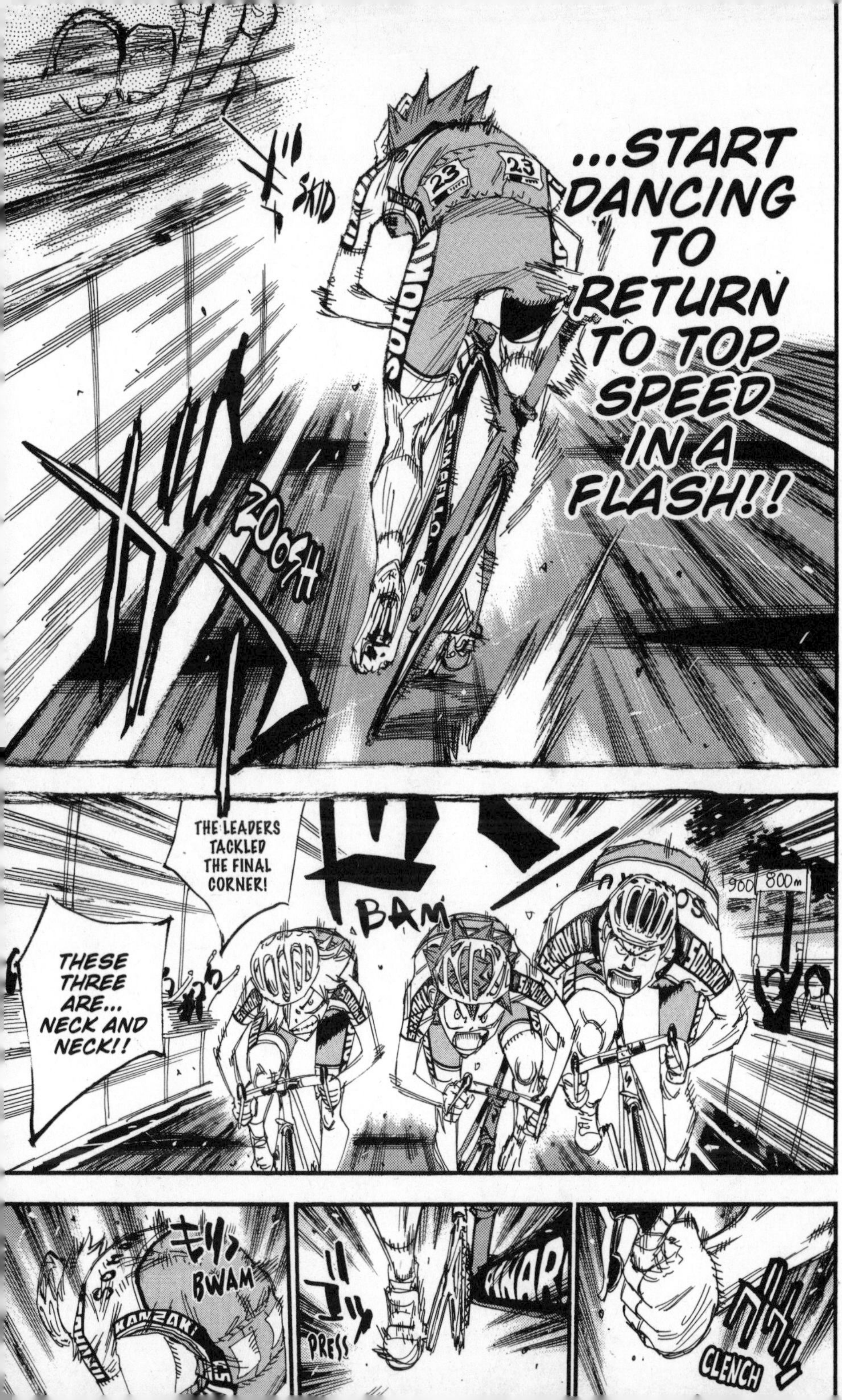
...START DANCING TO RETURN TO TOP SPEED IN A FLASH!!
SKID
ZOOSH
900 800m
BAM
THE LEADERS TACKLED THE FINAL CORNER!
THESE THREE ARE... NECK AND NECK!!
CLENCH
PRESS
BWAM
KANZAKI

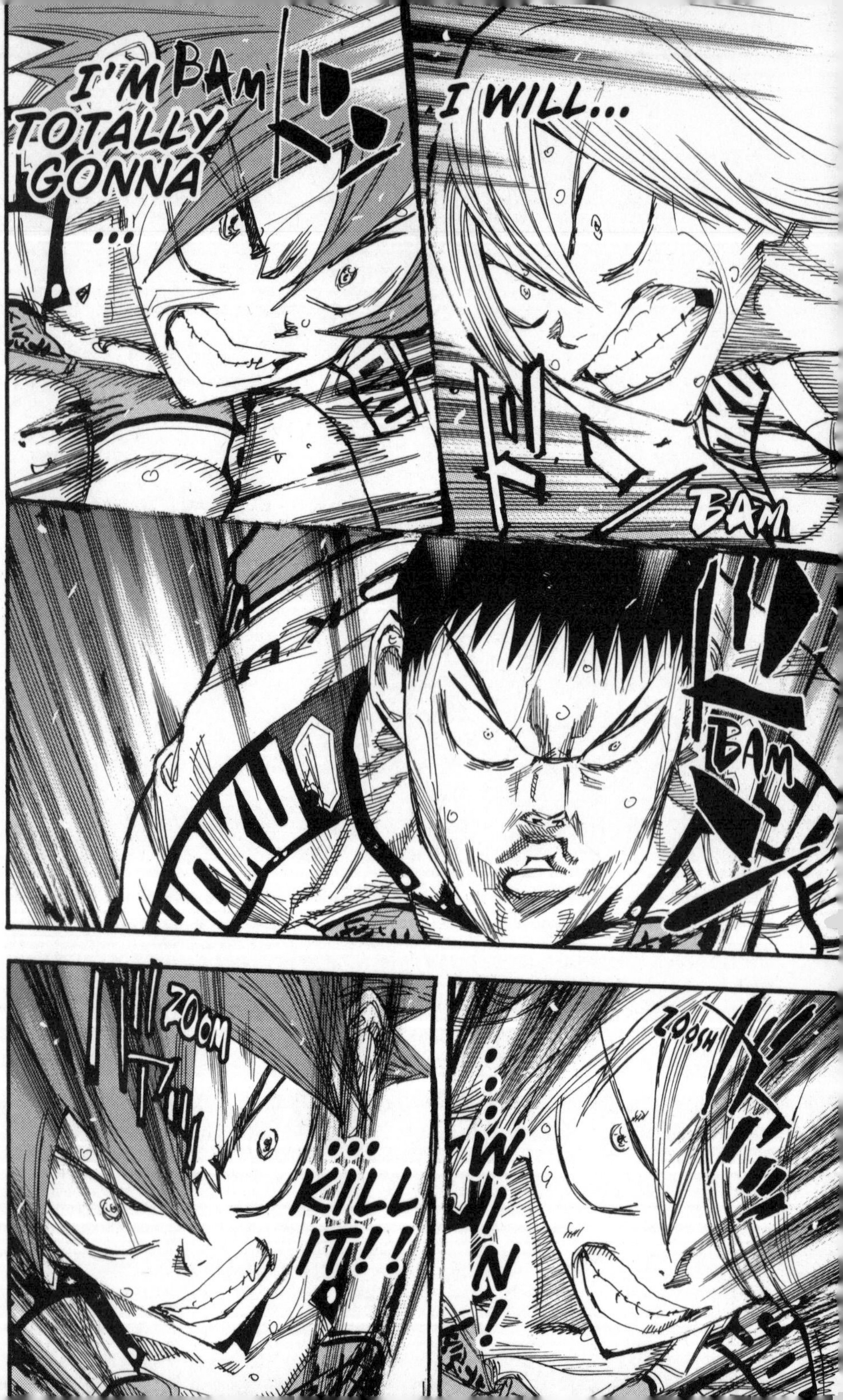
I WILL...
BAM
I'M TOTALLY GONNA
BAM
...
BAM
ZOOSH
...WIN!
ZOOM
...KILL IT!!

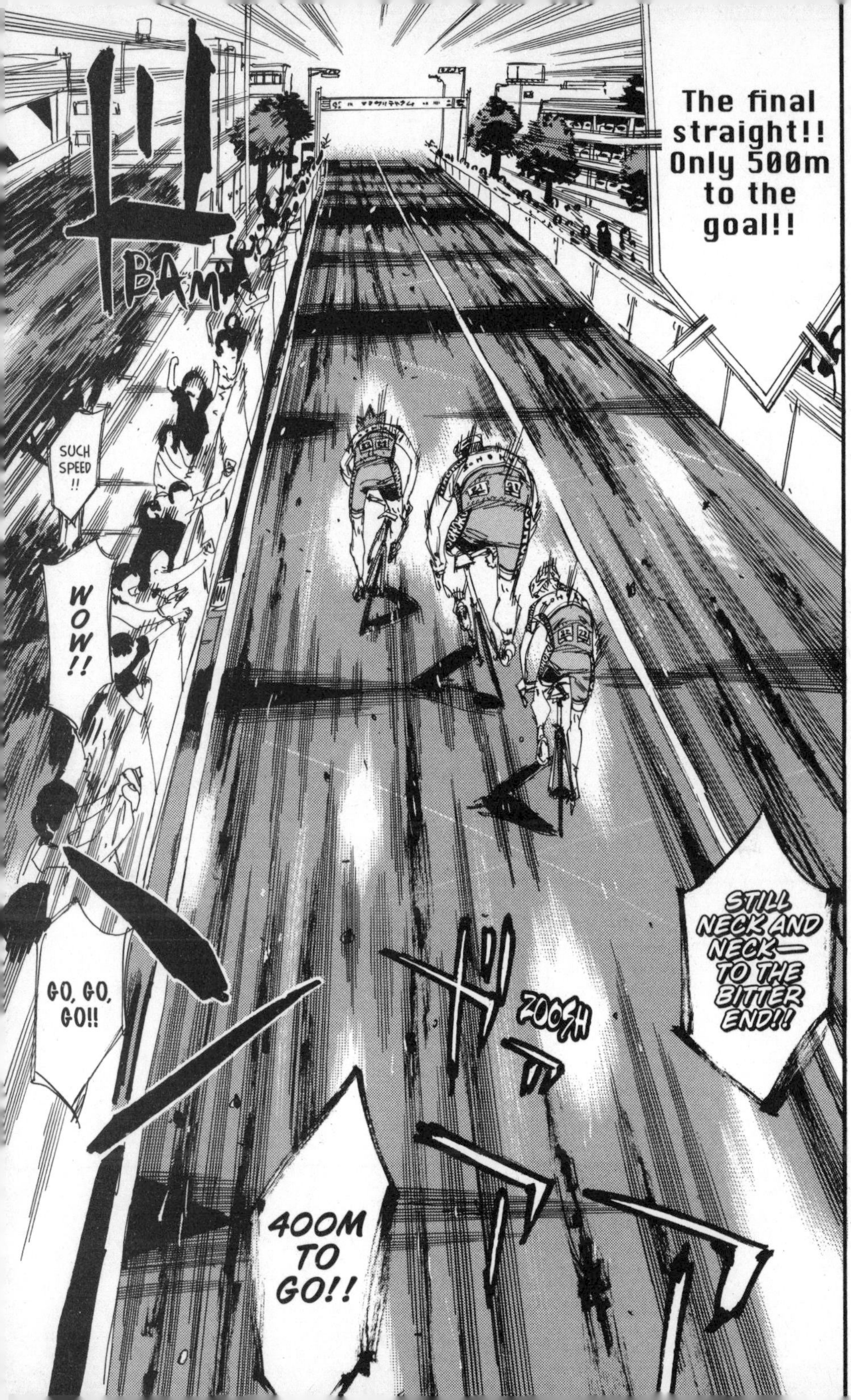
The final straight!! Only 500m to the goal!!
BAM
SUCH SPEED!!
WOW!!
STILL NECK AND NECK—TO THE BITTER END!!
ZOOSH
GO, GO, GO!!
400M TO GO!!

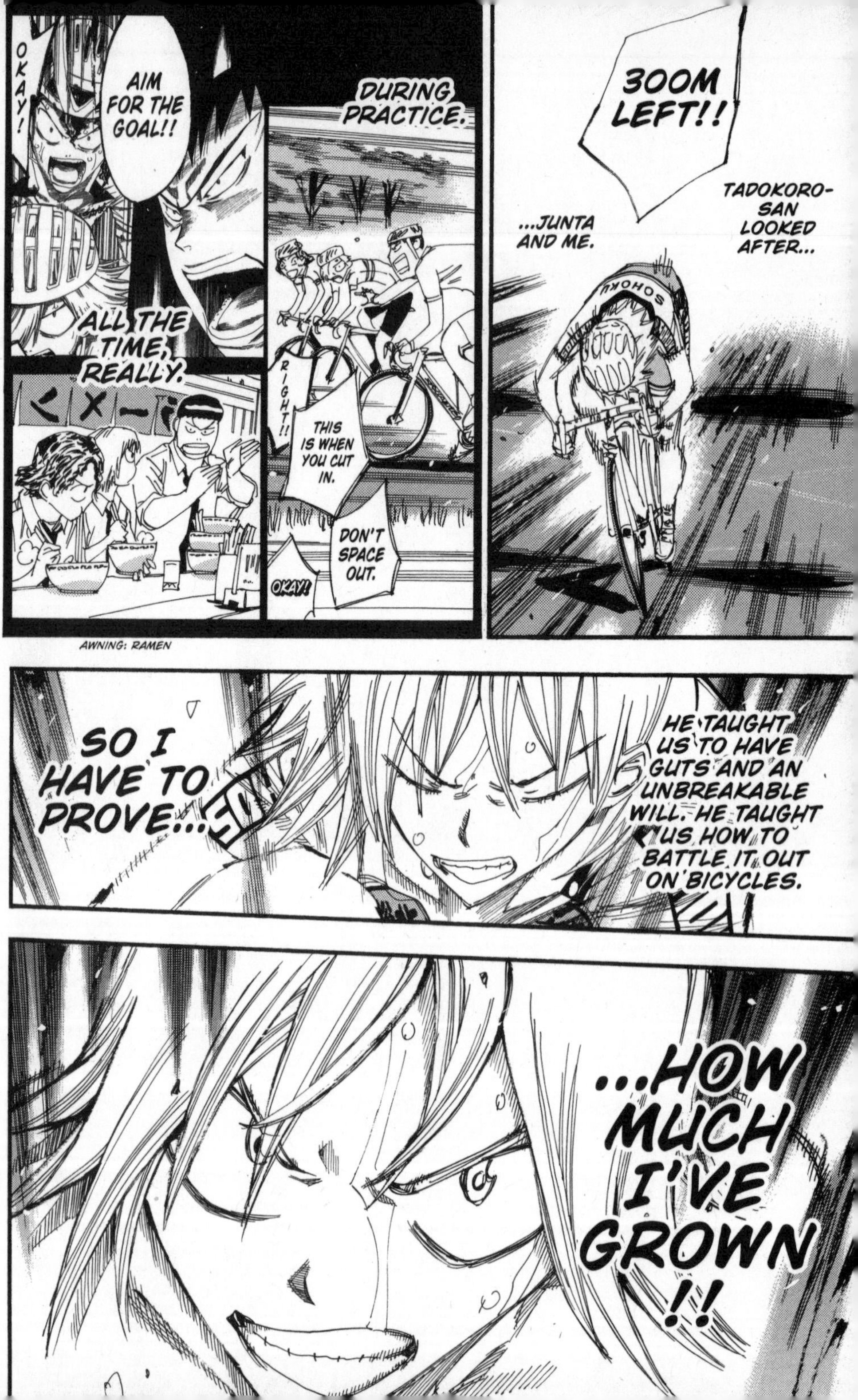
300M LEFT!!
TADOKORO-SAN LOOKED AFTER...
...JUNTA AND ME.
DURING PRACTICE.
THIS IS WHEN YOU CUT IN.
RIGHT!!
DON'T SPACE OUT.
OKAY!
AIM FOR THE GOAL!!
OKAY!
ALL THE TIME, REALLY.
AWNING: RAMEN
HE TAUGHT US TO HAVE GUTS AND AN UNBREAKABLE WILL. HE TAUGHT US HOW TO BATTLE IT OUT ON BICYCLES.
SO I HAVE TO PROVE...
...HOW MUCH I'VE GROWN!!

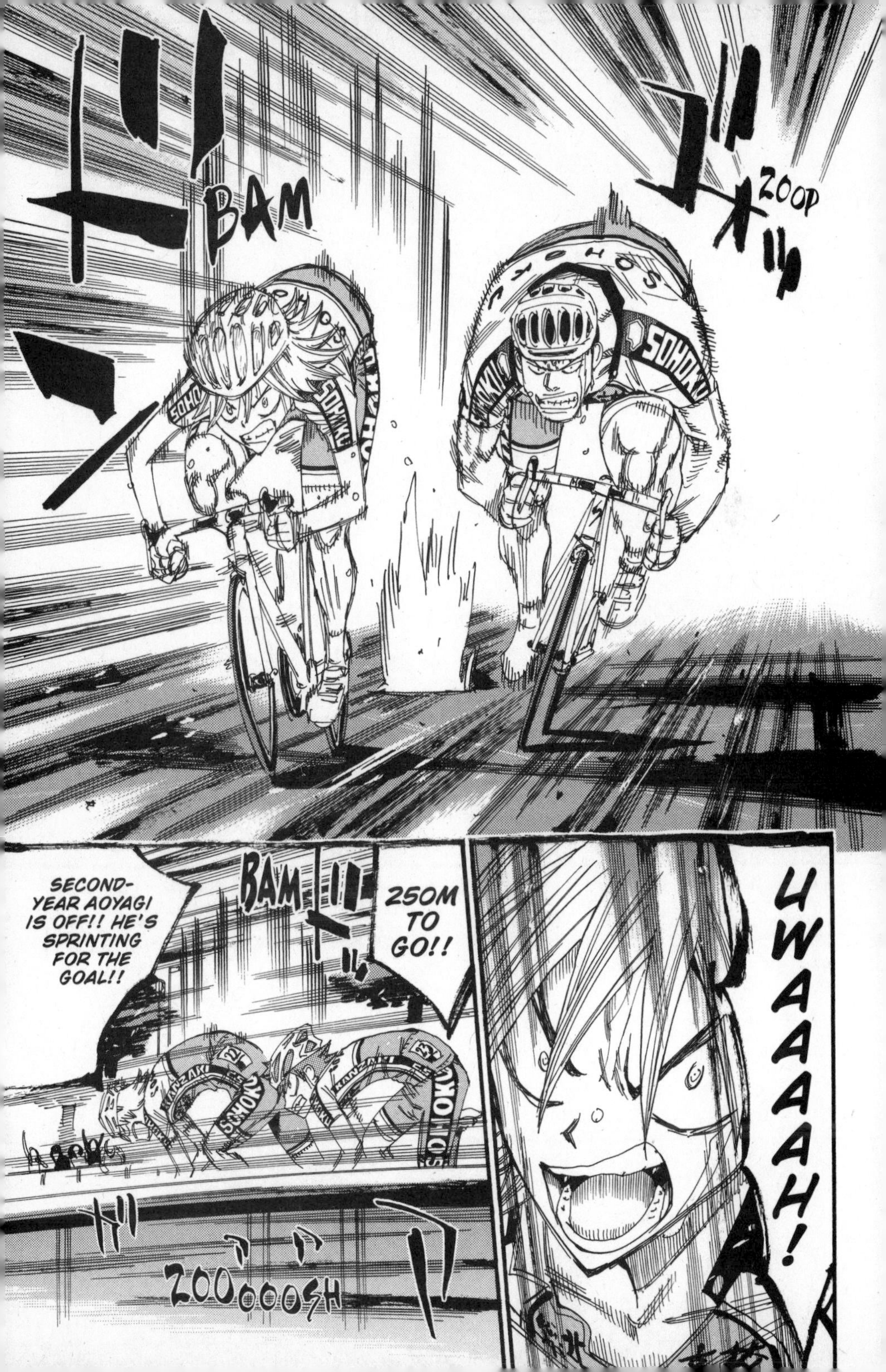
ZOOP
BAM
UWAAAAAAH!
250M TO GO!!
BAM
SECOND-YEAR AOYAGI IS OFF!! HE'S SPRINTING FOR THE GOAL!!
ZOOOOOSH

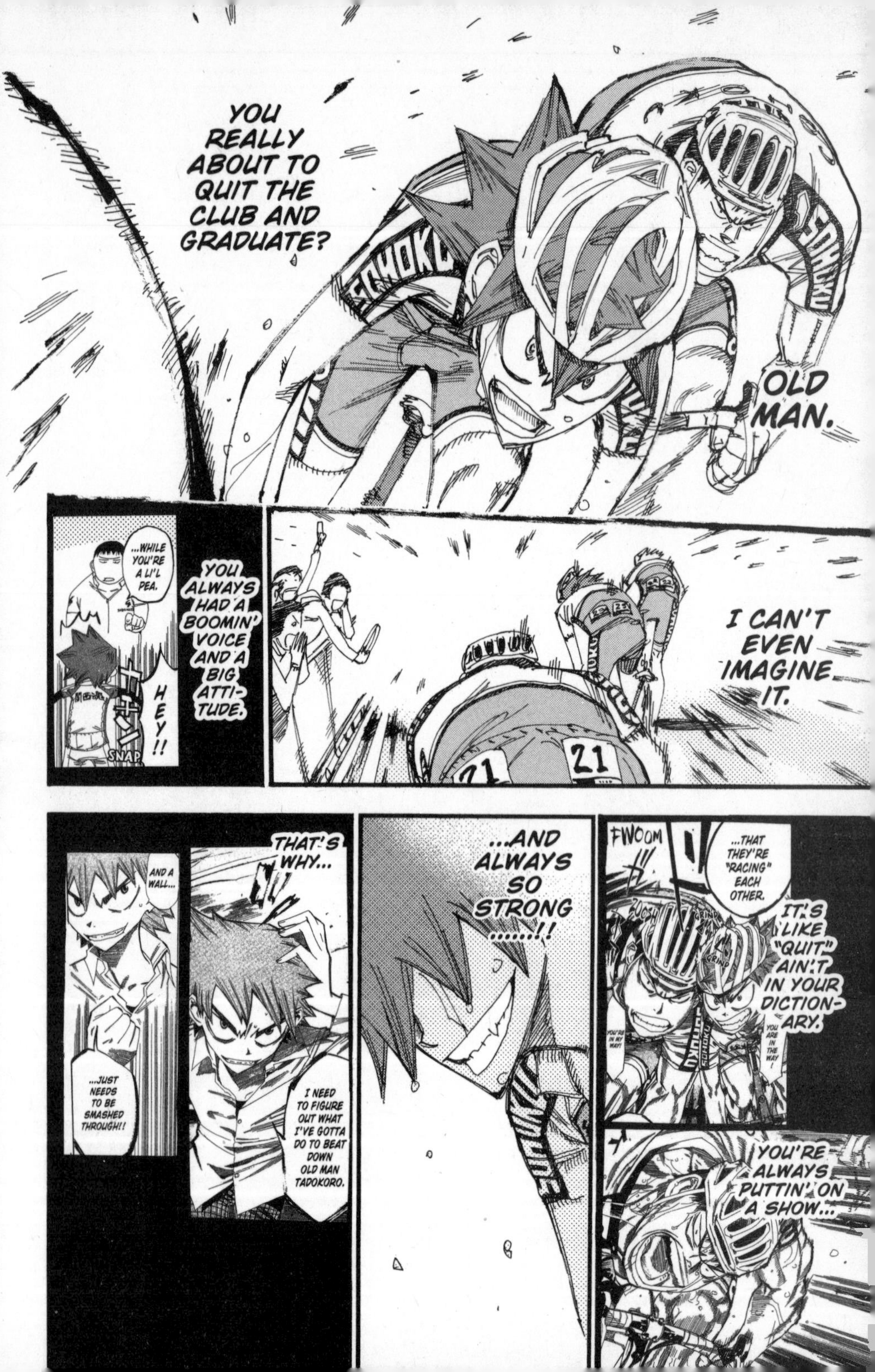

YOU REALLY ABOUT TO QUIT THE CLUB AND GRADUATE?
OLD MAN.
I CAN'T EVEN IMAGINE IT.
YOU ALWAYS HAD A BOOMIN' VOICE AND A BIG ATTITUDE.
...WHILE YOU'RE A LI'L PEA.
HEY!!
SNAP
FWOOM
...THAT THEY'RE "RACING" EACH OTHER.
IT'S LIKE "QUIT" AIN'T IN YOUR DICTIONARY.
ZOOSH
GRIND
YOU'RE IN MY WAY!
YOU ARE IN THE WAY!
YOU'RE ALWAYS PUTTIN' ON A SHOW...
...AND ALWAYS SO STRONG......!!
THAT'S WHY...
I NEED TO FIGURE OUT WHAT I'VE GOTTA DO TO BEAT DOWN OLD MAN TADOKORO.
AND A WALL...
...JUST NEEDS TO BE SMASHED THROUGH!!

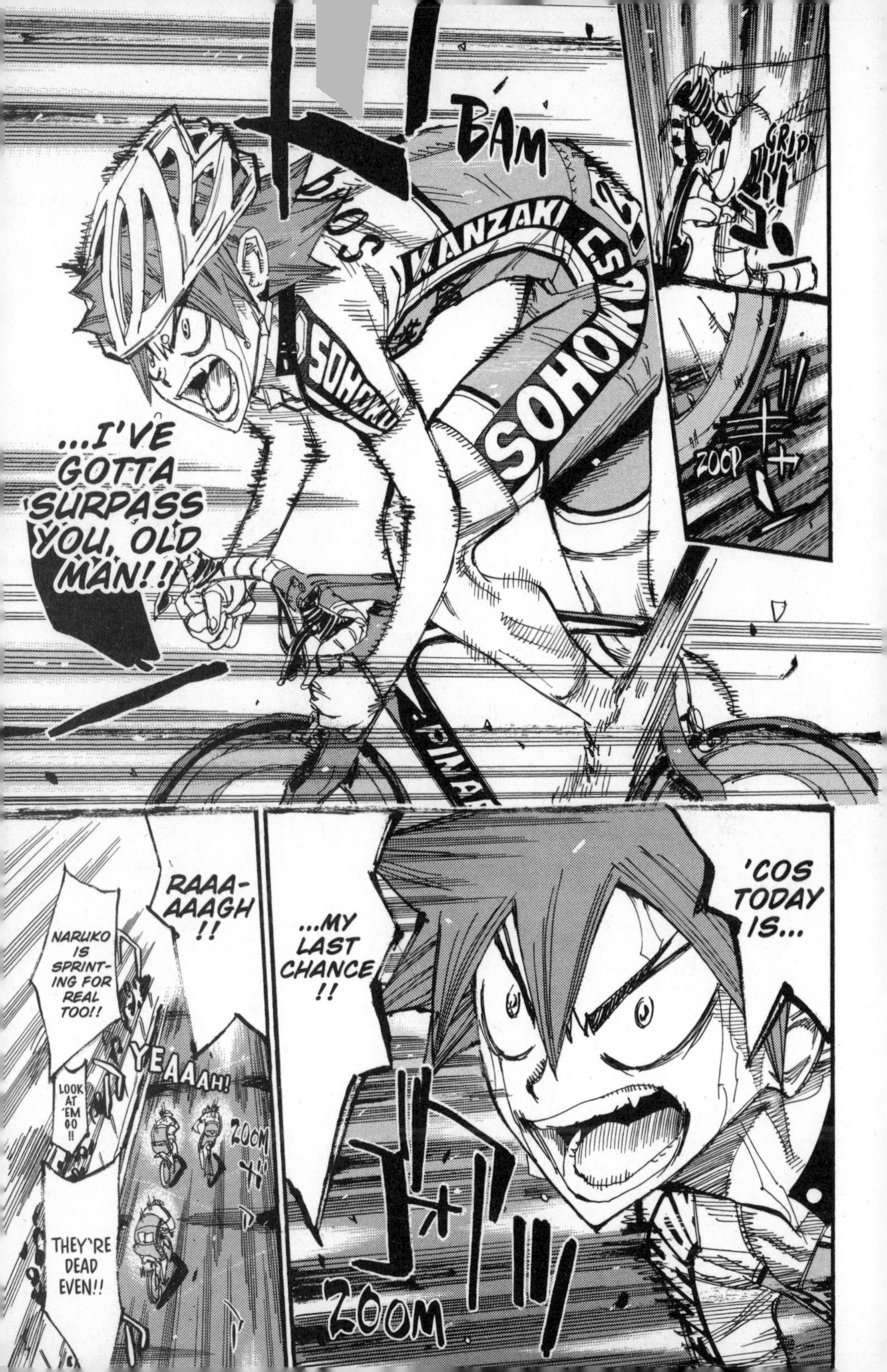
GRIP
ZOOP
BAM
...I'VE GOTTA SURPASS YOU, OLD MAN!!
'COS TODAY IS...
...MY LAST CHANCE!!
ZOOM
RAAA-AAAGH!!
NARUKO IS SPRINT-ING FOR REAL TOO!!
YEAAAAH!
LOOK AT 'EM GO!!
ZOOM
THEY'RE DEAD EVEN!!

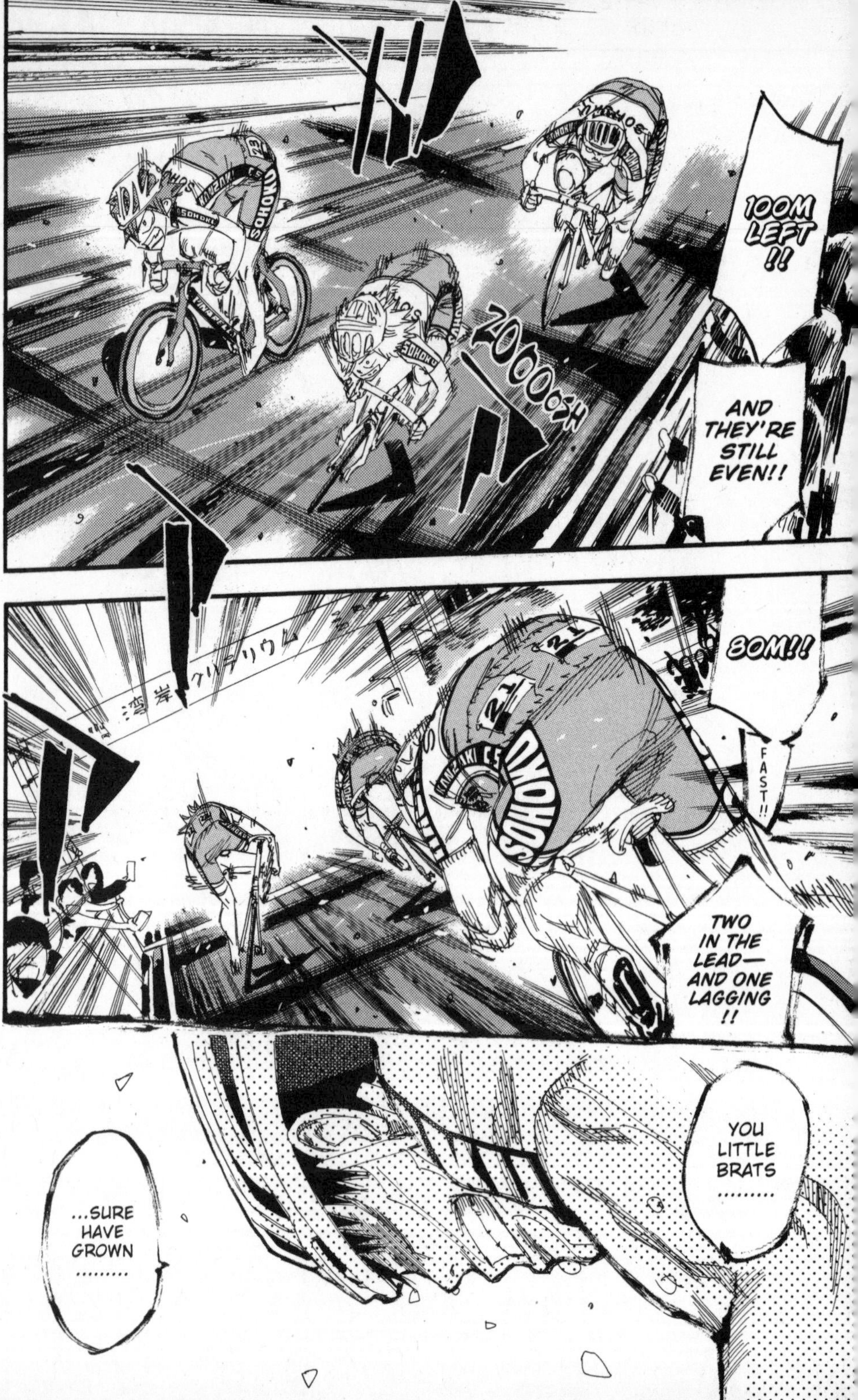
100M LEFT!!
AND THEY'RE STILL EVEN!!
ZOOOOSH
80M!!
FAST!!
TWO IN THE LEAD—AND ONE LAGGING!!
湾岸クリテリウム
YOU LITTLE BRATS.........
...SURE HAVE GROWN.........

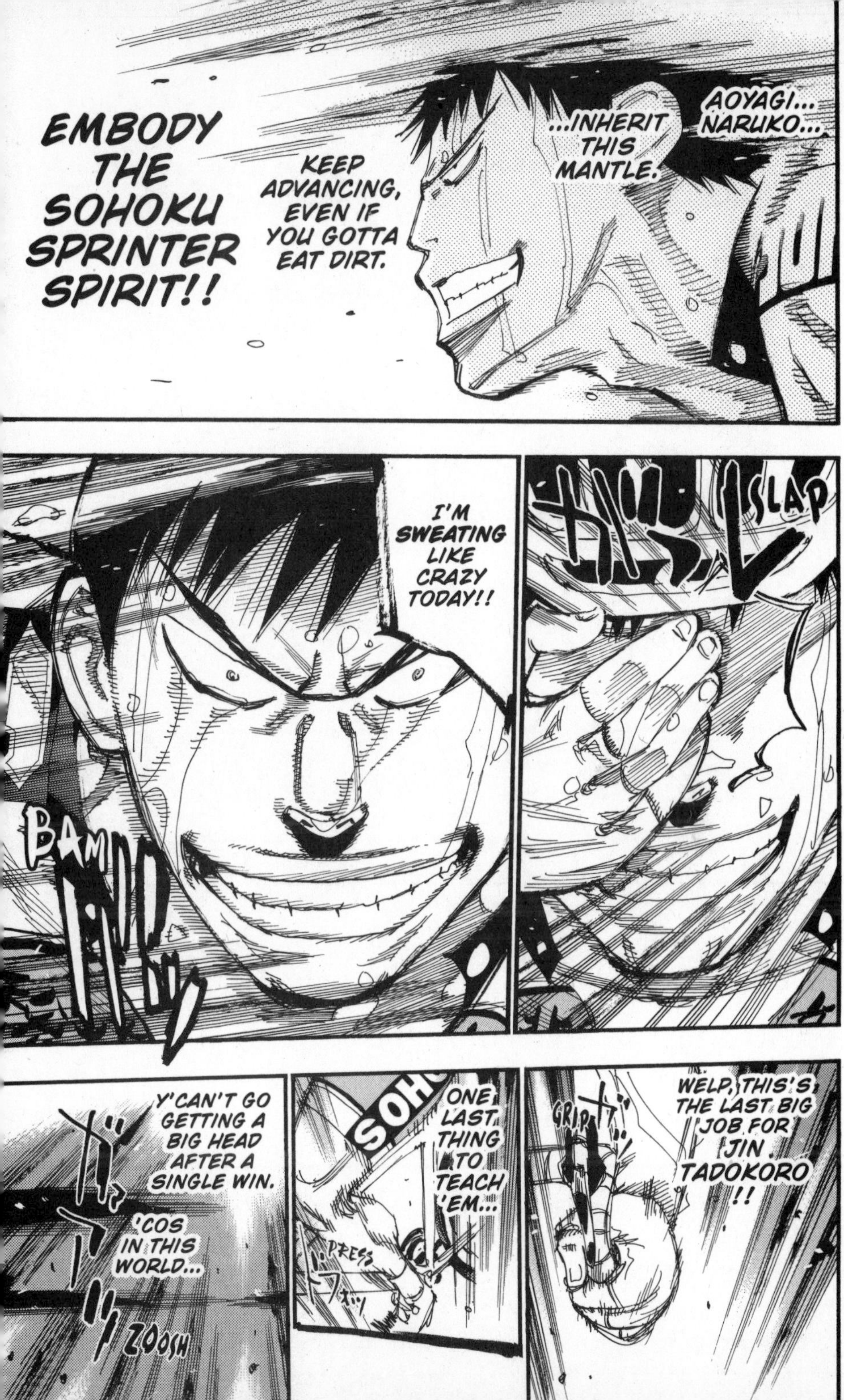
AOYAGI... NARUKO...
...INHERIT THIS MANTLE.
KEEP ADVANCING, EVEN IF YOU GOTTA EAT DIRT.
EMBODY THE SOHOKU SPRINTER SPIRIT!!
SLAP
I'M SWEATING LIKE CRAZY TODAY!!
BAM
GRIP
WELP, THIS'S THE LAST BIG JOB FOR JIN TADOKORO!!
ONE LAST THING TO TEACH 'EM...
PRESS
Y'CAN'T GO GETTING A BIG HEAD AFTER A SINGLE WIN.
'COS IN THIS WORLD...
ZOOSH

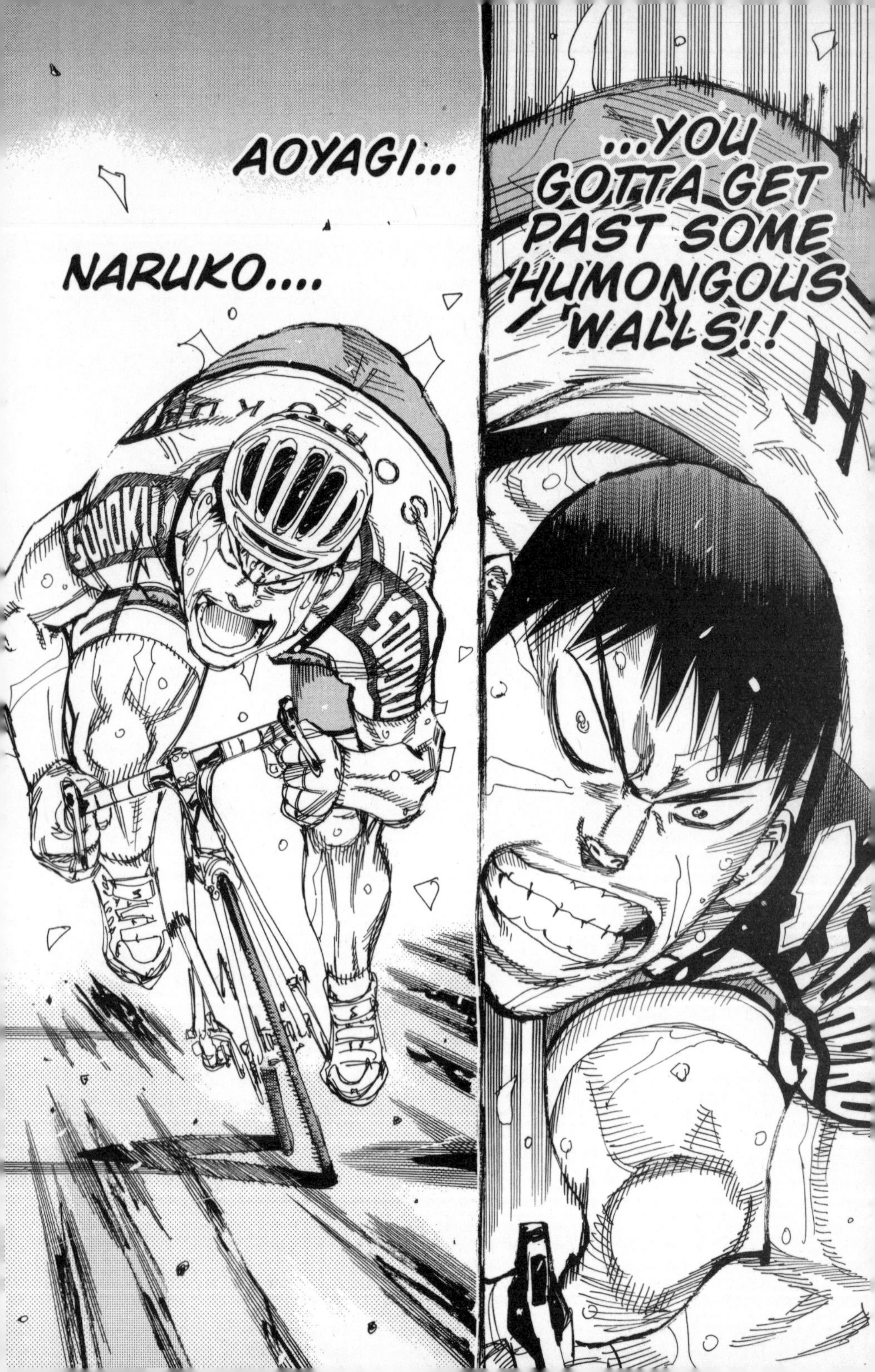
AOYAGI...
NARUKO....
...YOU GOTTA GET PAST SOME HUMONGOUS WALLS!!

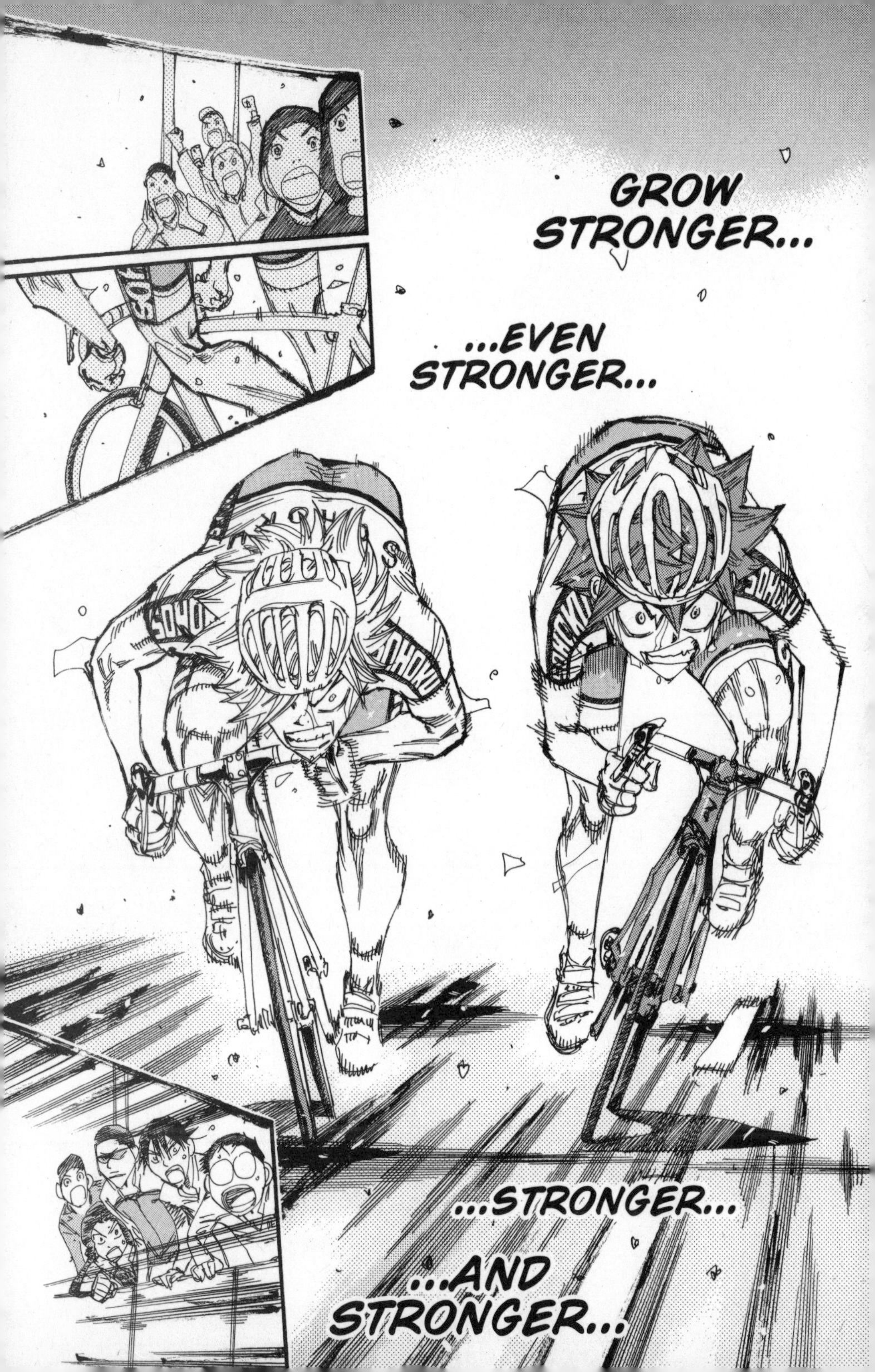
GROW STRONGER...
...EVEN STRONGER...
...STRONGER...
...AND STRONGER...

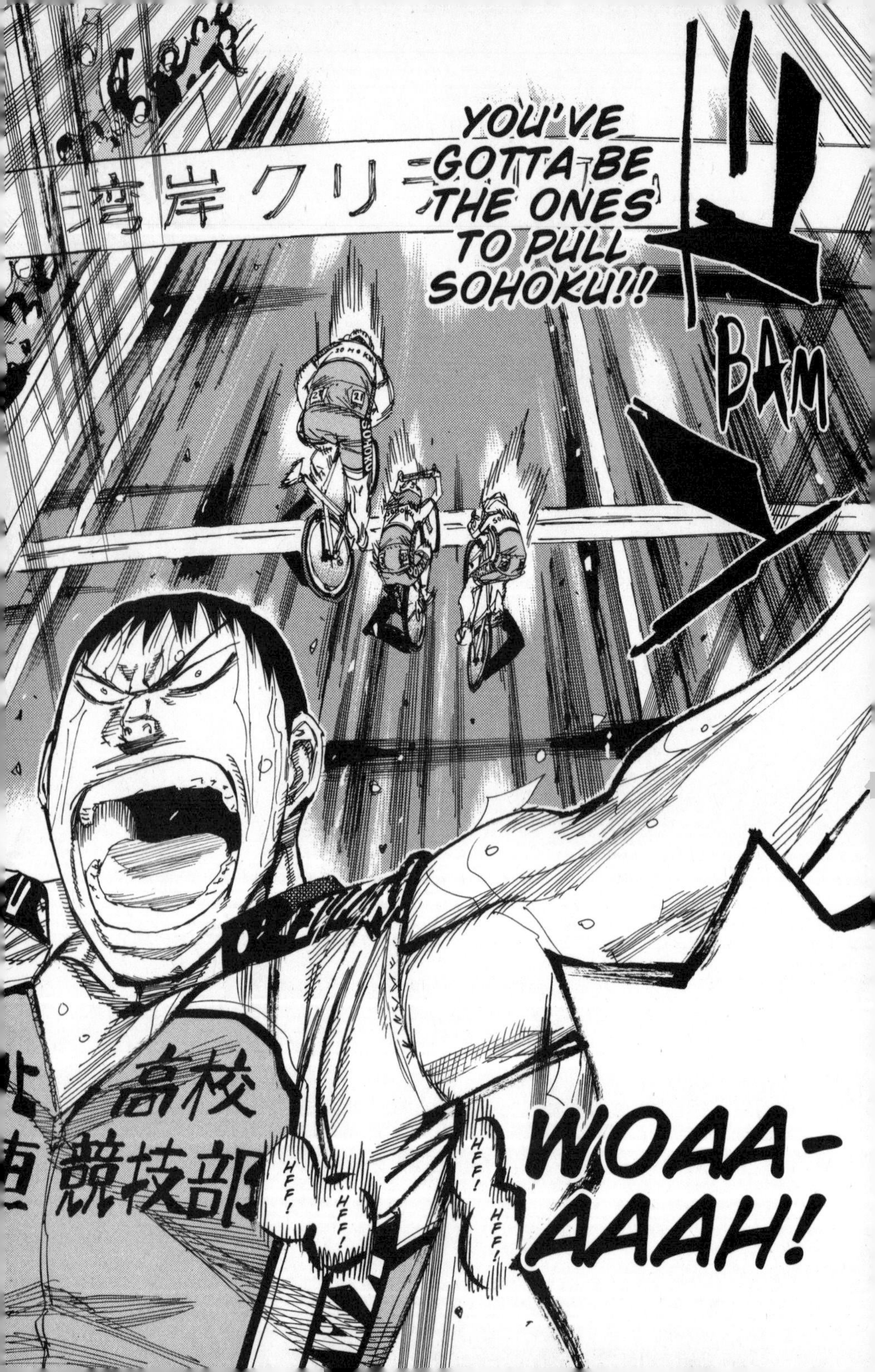
BAM
YOU'VE GOTTA BE THE ONES TO PULL SOHOKU!!
湾岸クリ
WOAA-AAAH!
HFF! HFF!
HFF! HFF!
高校
競技部

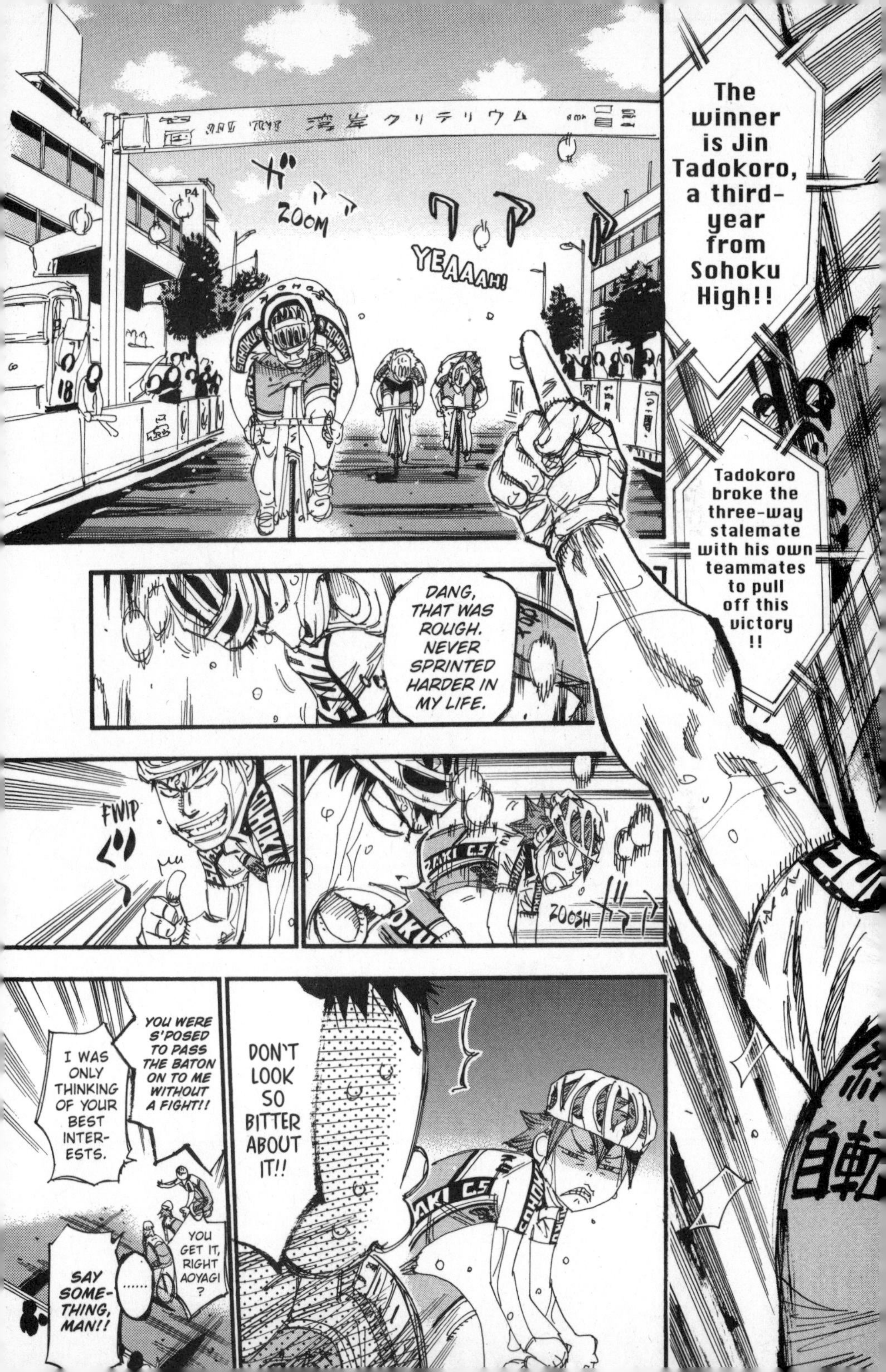
The winner is Jin Tadokoro, a third-year from Sohoku High!!
Tadokoro broke the three-way stalemate with his own teammates to pull off this victory!!
ZOOM
YEAAAH!
DANG, THAT WAS ROUGH. NEVER SPRINTED HARDER IN MY LIFE.
ZOOSH
FWIP
DON'T LOOK SO BITTER ABOUT IT!!
YOU WERE S'POSED TO PASS THE BATON ON TO ME WITHOUT A FIGHT!!
I WAS ONLY THINKING OF YOUR BEST INTERESTS.
YOU GET IT, RIGHT AOYAGI?
......
SAY SOMETHING, MAN!!

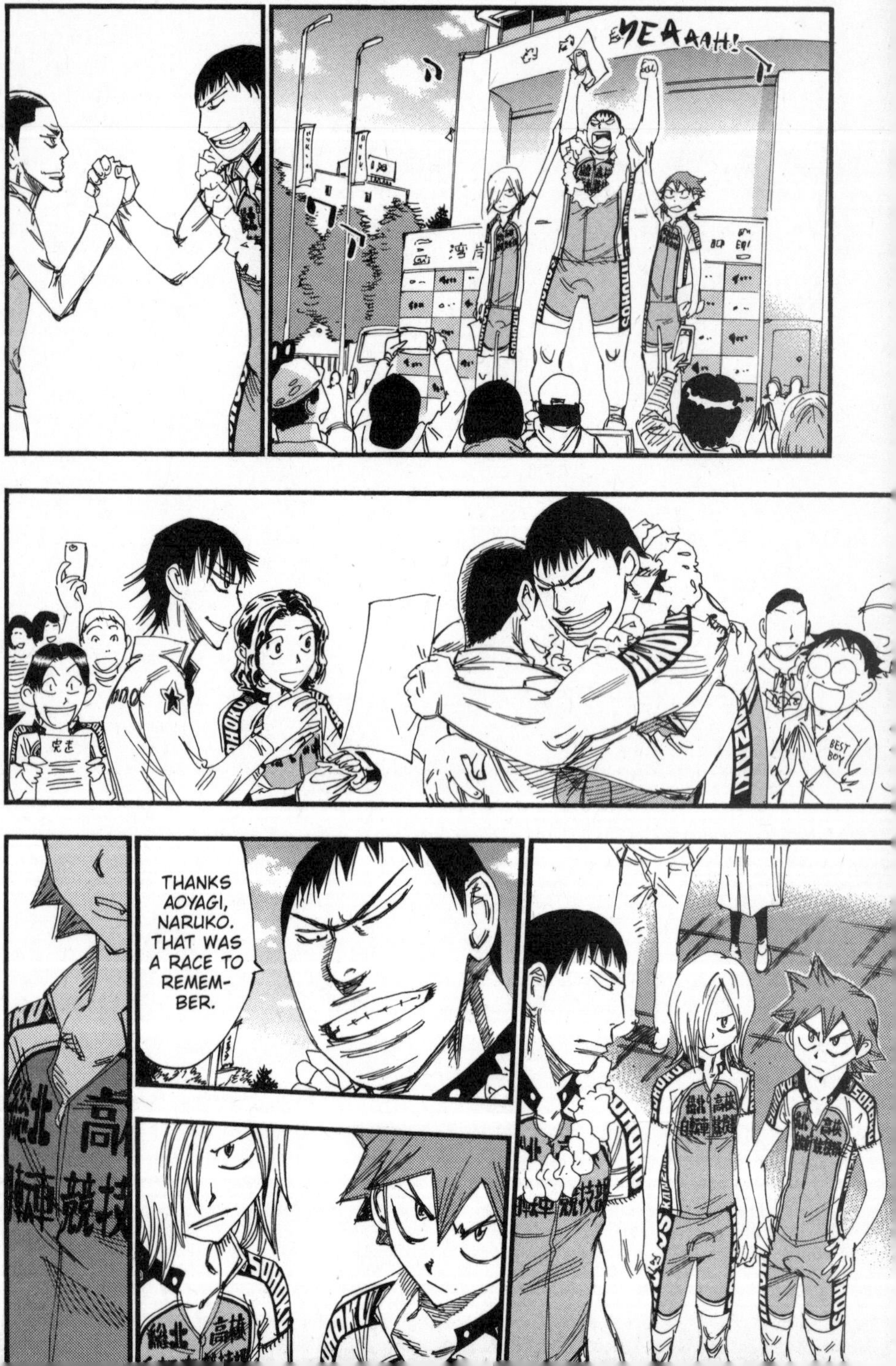
YEAAAH!
BEST BOY
THANKS AOYAGI, NARUKO. THAT WAS A RACE TO REMEMBER.

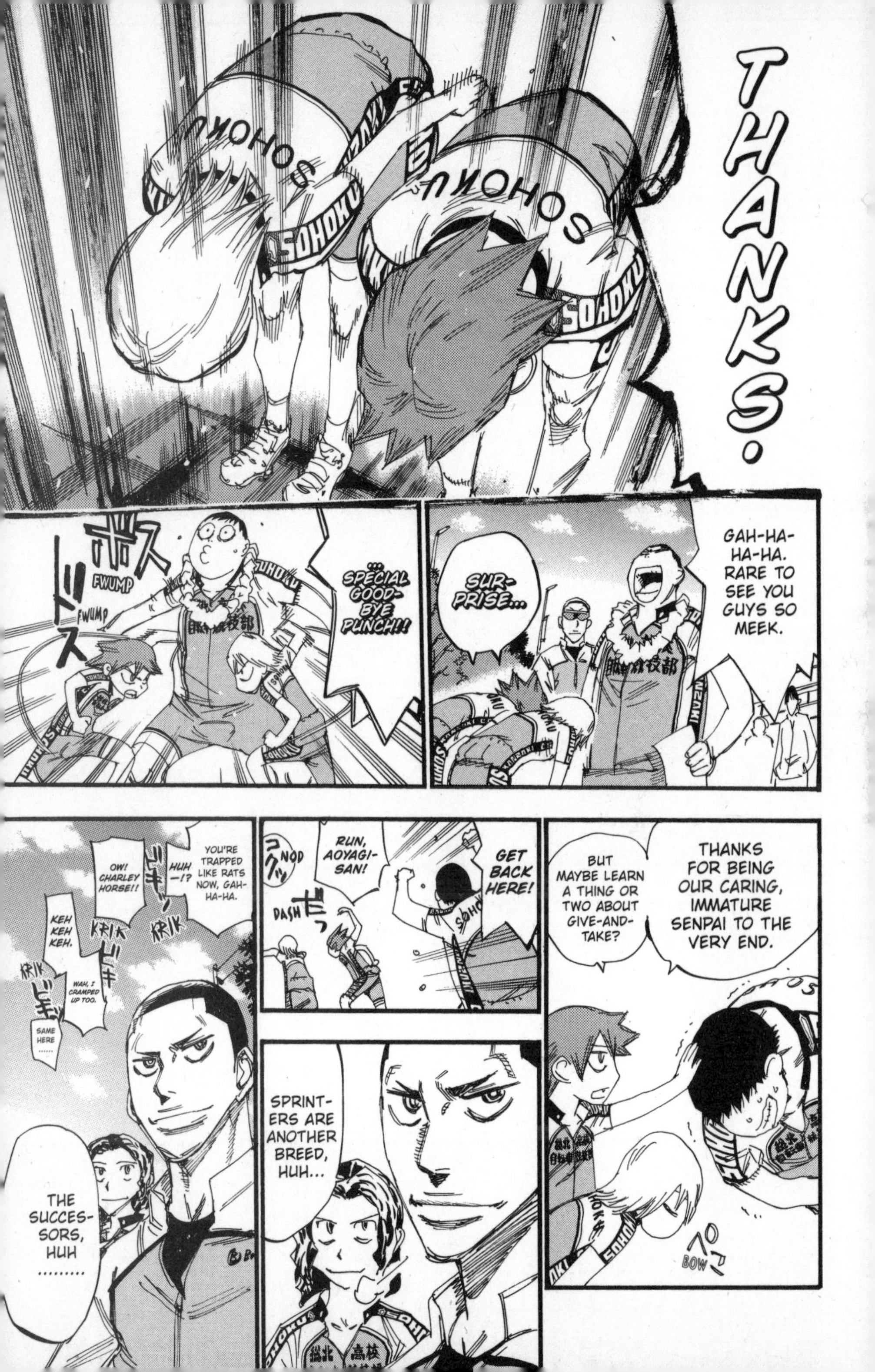
THANKS.
GAH-HA-HA-HA. RARE TO SEE YOU GUYS SO MEEK.
SUR-PRISE...
...SPECIAL GOOD-BYE PUNCH!!
FWUMP
FWUMP
THANKS FOR BEING OUR CARING, IMMATURE SENPAI TO THE VERY END.
BUT MAYBE LEARN A THING OR TWO ABOUT GIVE-AND-TAKE?
BOW
GET BACK HERE!
RUN, AOYAGI-SAN!
NOD
DASH
SPRINT-ERS ARE ANOTHER BREED, HUH...
YOU'RE TRAPPED LIKE RATS NOW, GAH-HA-HA.
HUH-!?
OW! CHARLEY HORSE!!
KRIK
KEH KEH KEH.
KRIK
KRIK
WAH, I CRAMPED UP TOO.
SAME HERE ......
THE SUCCES-SORS, HUH ....

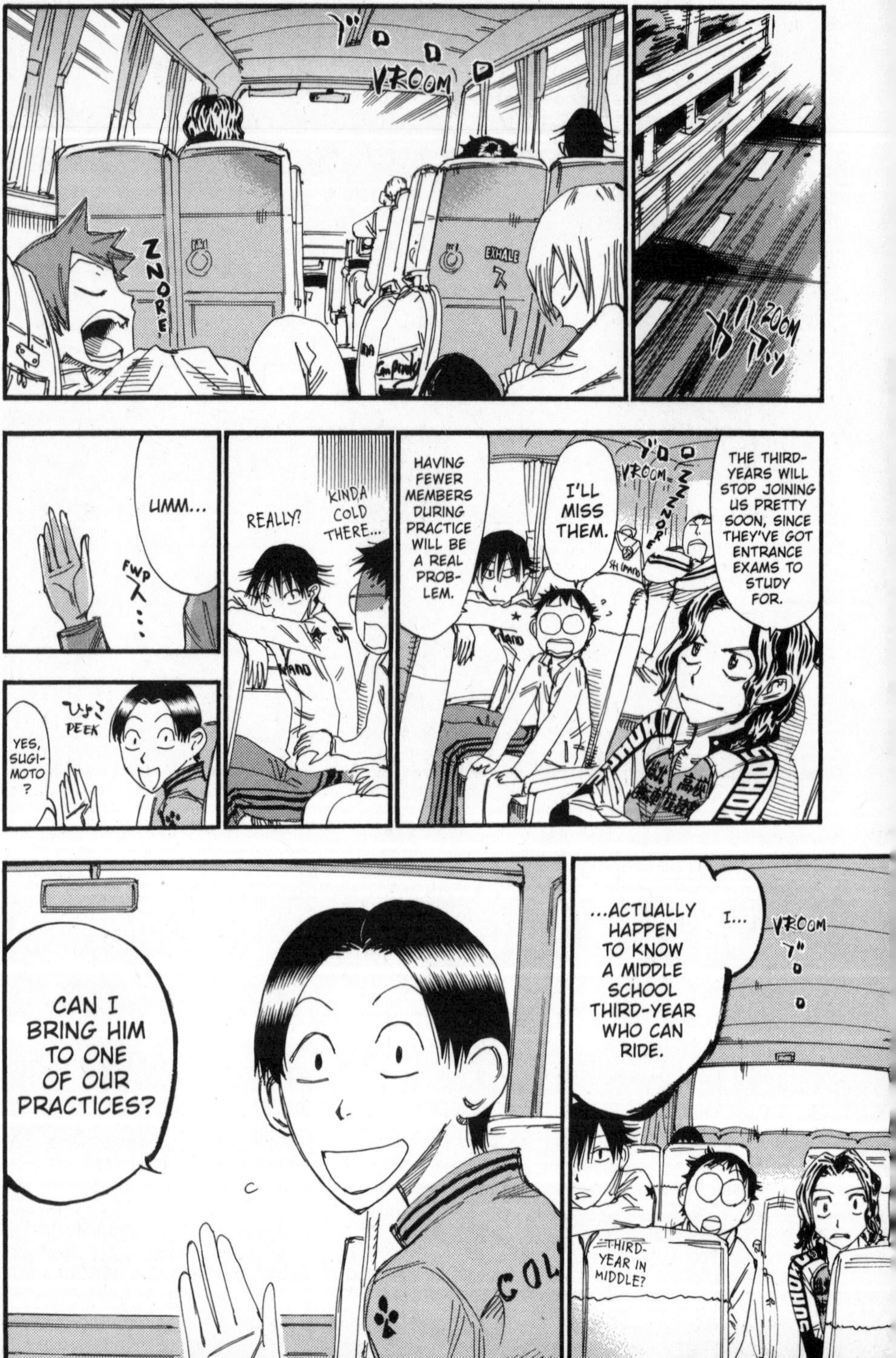
ZOOM
VROOM
EXHALE
ZNORE
THE THIRD-YEARS WILL STOP JOINING US PRETTY SOON, SINCE THEY'VE GOT ENTRANCE EXAMS TO STUDY FOR.
VROOM
ZNORE
I'LL MISS THEM.
HAVING FEWER MEMBERS DURING PRACTICE WILL BE A REAL PROBLEM.
KINDA COLD THERE...
REALLY?
UMM...
FWP
PEEK
YES, SUGIMOTO?
I...
VROOM
...ACTUALLY HAPPEN TO KNOW A MIDDLE SCHOOL THIRD-YEAR WHO CAN RIDE.
THIRD-YEAR IN MIDDLE?
CAN I BRING HIM TO ONE OF OUR PRACTICES?

RIDE.247 SOHOKU: REVAMPED

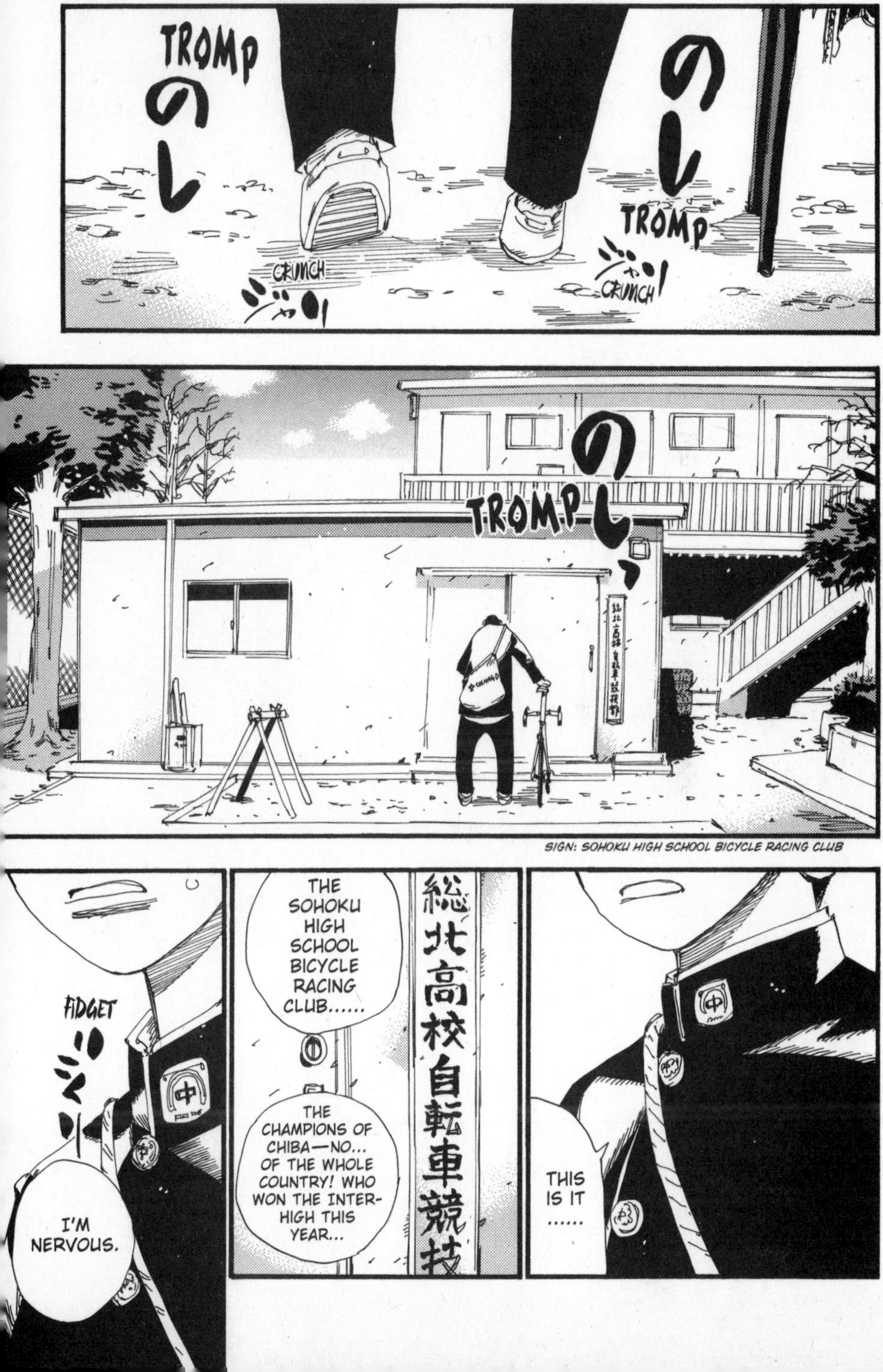
のし
TROMP
ジャリ
CRUNCH
TROMP
のし
CRUNCH
ジャリ
のし
TROMP
SIGN: SOHOKU HIGH SCHOOL BICYCLE RACING CLUB
THIS IS IT......
THE SOHOKU HIGH SCHOOL BICYCLE RACING CLUB......
THE CHAMPIONS OF CHIBA—NO... OF THE WHOLE COUNTRY! WHO WON THE INTER-HIGH THIS YEAR...
総北高校自転車競技
FIDGET
I'M NERVOUS.

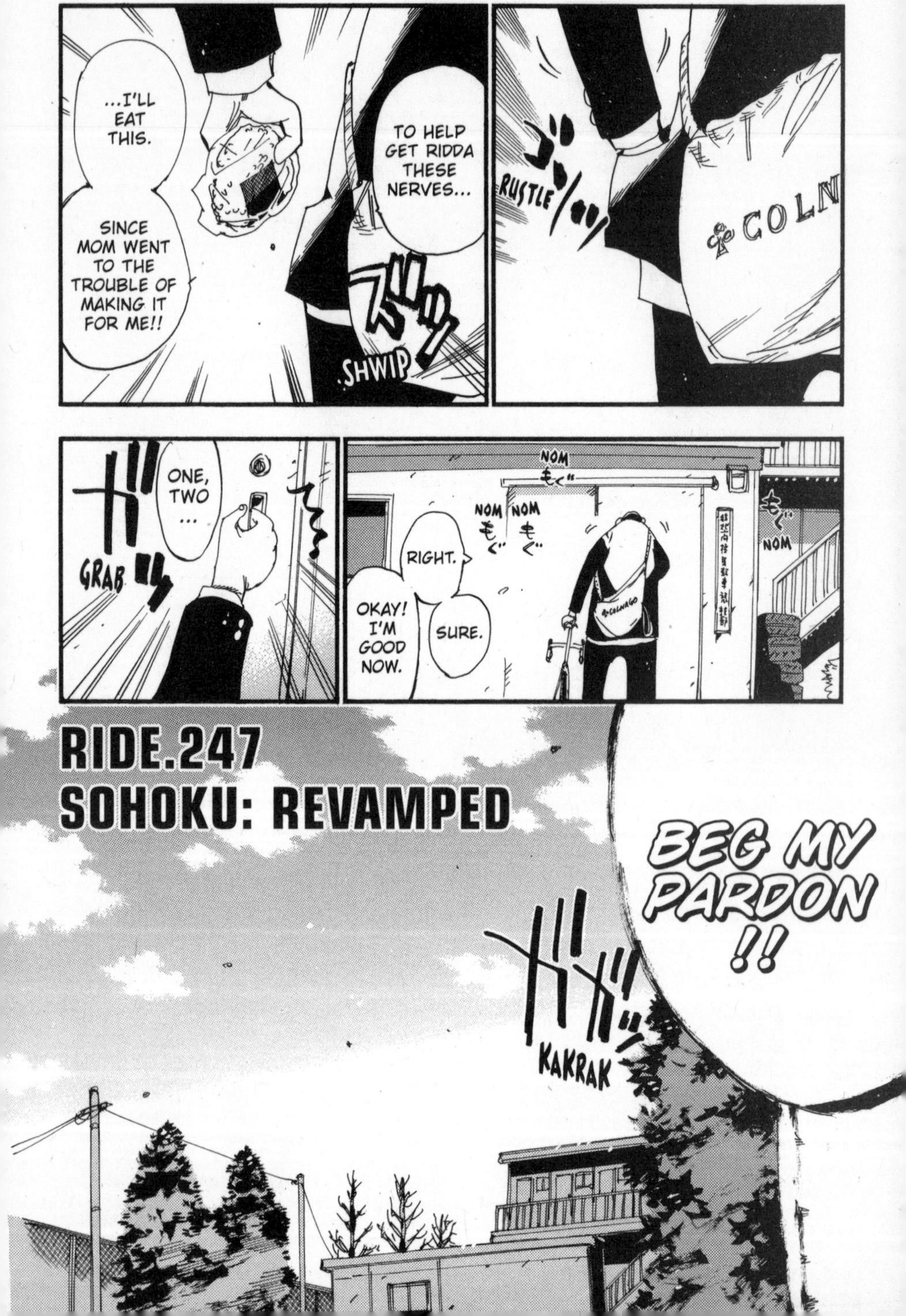
RUSTLE
COLN
TO HELP GET RIDDA THESE NERVES...
...I'LL EAT THIS.
SINCE MOM WENT TO THE TROUBLE OF MAKING IT FOR ME!!
SHWIP
NOM
NOM
NOM
NOM
RIGHT.
SURE.
OKAY! I'M GOOD NOW.
ONE, TWO ...
GRAB
BEG MY PARDON!!
RIDE.247
SOHOKU: REVAMPED
KAKRAK

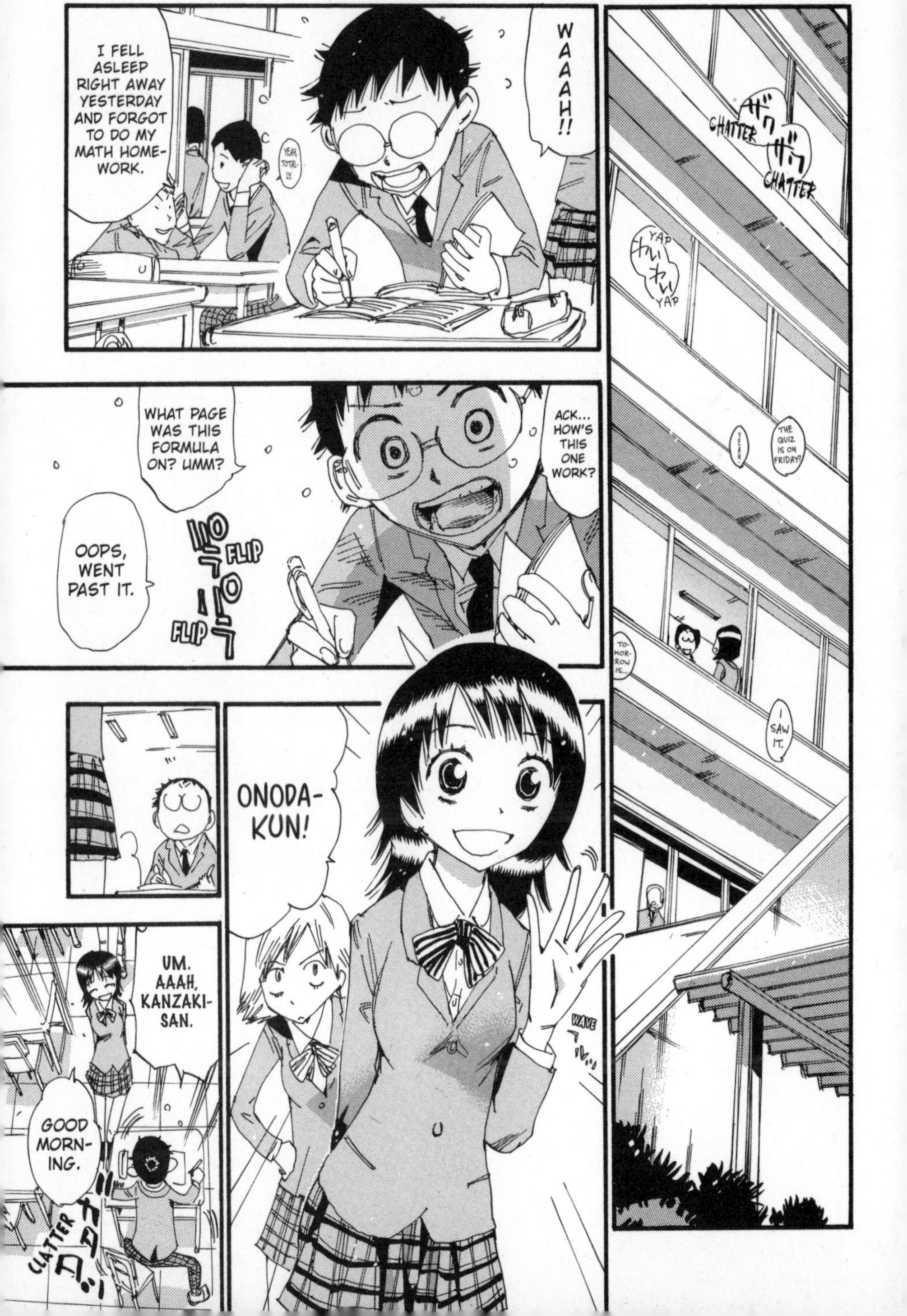
ザワ CHATTER
ザワ CHATTER
YAP わいわい YAP
THE QUIZ IS ON FRIDAY?
YEAH!
TO-MOR-ROW IS...
I SAW IT.
WAAAAH!!
YEAH, TOTALLY.
I FELL ASLEEP RIGHT AWAY YESTERDAY AND FORGOT TO DO MY MATH HOME-WORK.
ACK... HOW'S THIS ONE WORK?
WHAT PAGE WAS THIS FORMULA ON? UMM?
FLIP
FLIP
OOPS, WENT PAST IT.
ONODA-KUN!
WAVE
UM. AAAH, KANZAKI-SAN.
GOOD MORN-ING.
CLATTER

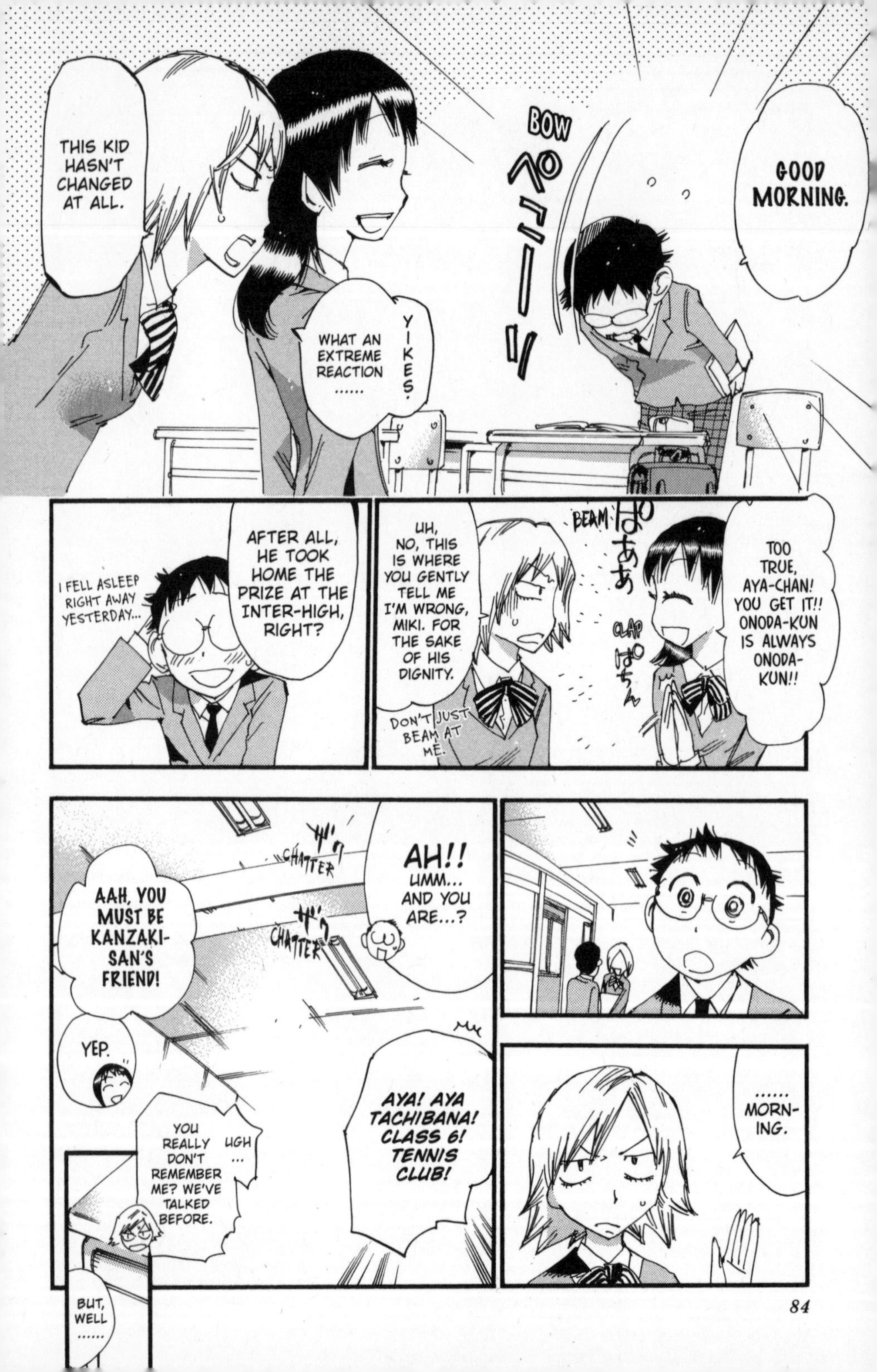
GOOD MORNING.
BOW ペコー
YIKES.
WHAT AN EXTREME REACTION ......
THIS KID HASN'T CHANGED AT ALL.
TOO TRUE, AYA-CHAN! YOU GET IT!! ONODA-KUN IS ALWAYS ONODA-KUN!!
BEAM ぱぁあ
CLAP ぱちん
UH, NO, THIS IS WHERE YOU GENTLY TELL ME I'M WRONG, MIKI. FOR THE SAKE OF HIS DIGNITY.
DON'T JUST BEAM AT ME.
AFTER ALL, HE TOOK HOME THE PRIZE AT THE INTER-HIGH, RIGHT?
I FELL ASLEEP RIGHT AWAY YESTERDAY...
......MORNING.
AH!! UMM... AND YOU ARE...?
CHATTER ザワ
CHATTER ザワ
AAH, YOU MUST BE KANZAKI-SAN'S FRIEND!
YEP.
AYA! AYA TACHIBANA! CLASS 6! TENNIS CLUB!
UGH ...
YOU REALLY DON'T REMEMBER ME? WE'VE TALKED BEFORE.
BUT, WELL ......

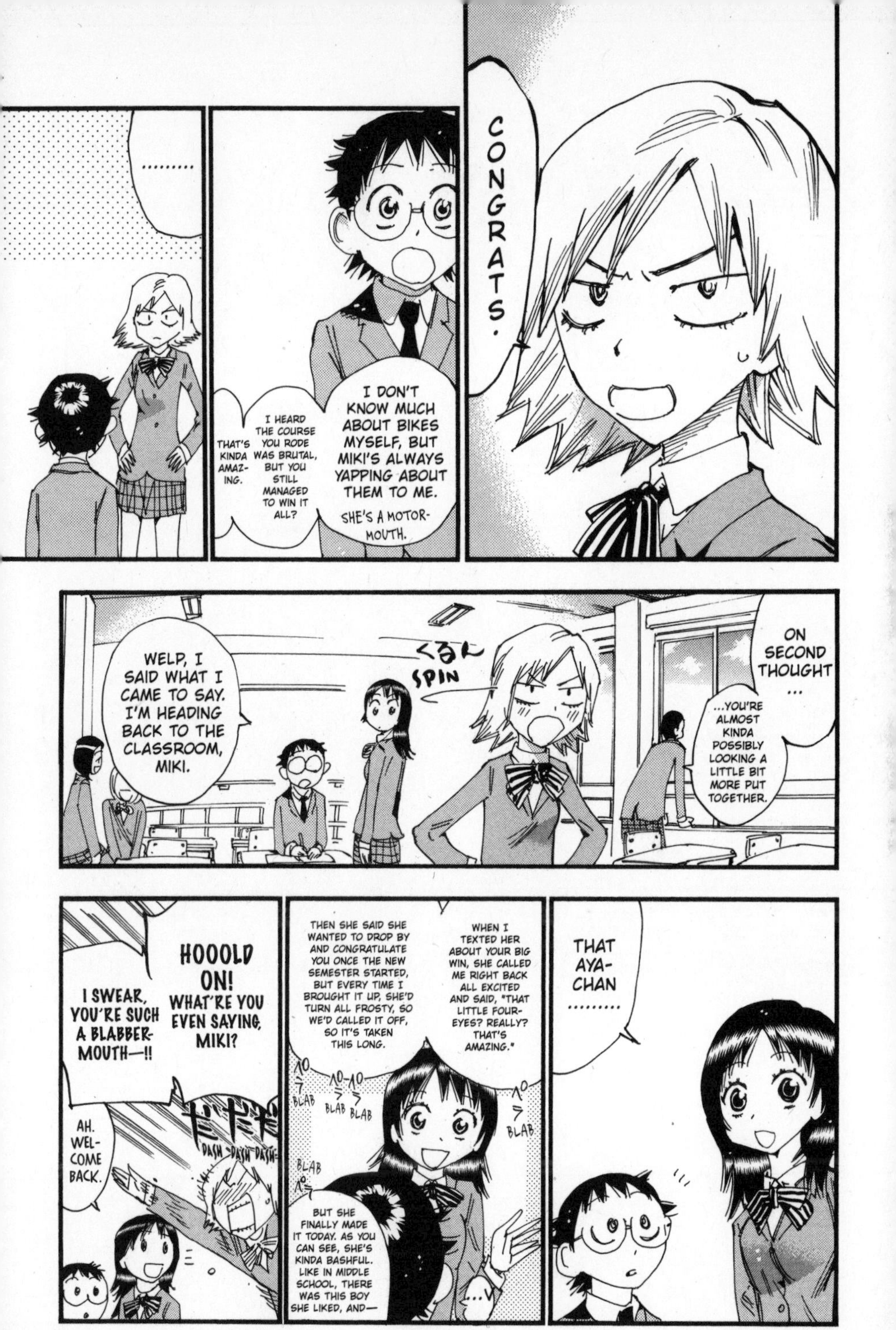
CONGRATS.
I DON'T KNOW MUCH ABOUT BIKES MYSELF, BUT MIKI'S ALWAYS YAPPING ABOUT THEM TO ME.
SHE'S A MOTOR-MOUTH.
I HEARD THE COURSE YOU RODE WAS BRUTAL, BUT YOU STILL MANAGED TO WIN IT ALL?
THAT'S KINDA AMAZ-ING.
....
ON SECOND THOUGHT...
...YOU'RE ALMOST KINDA POSSIBLY LOOKING A LITTLE BIT MORE PUT TOGETHER.
くるん SPIN
WELP, I SAID WHAT I CAME TO SAY. I'M HEADING BACK TO THE CLASSROOM, MIKI.
THAT AYA-CHAN ....
WHEN I TEXTED HER ABOUT YOUR BIG WIN, SHE CALLED ME RIGHT BACK ALL EXCITED AND SAID, "THAT LITTLE FOUR-EYES? REALLY? THAT'S AMAZING."
THEN SHE SAID SHE WANTED TO DROP BY AND CONGRATULATE YOU ONCE THE NEW SEMESTER STARTED, BUT EVERY TIME I BROUGHT IT UP, SHE'D TURN ALL FROSTY, SO WE'D CALLED IT OFF, SO IT'S TAKEN THIS LONG.
BLAB BLAB BLAB BLAB BLAB
BUT SHE FINALLY MADE IT TODAY. AS YOU CAN SEE, SHE'S KINDA BASHFUL. LIKE IN MIDDLE SCHOOL, THERE WAS THIS BOY SHE LIKED, AND—
...
HOOOLD ON! WHAT'RE YOU EVEN SAYING, MIKI?
I SWEAR, YOU'RE SUCH A BLABBER-MOUTH—!!
DASH DASH DASH
AH. WEL-COME BACK.

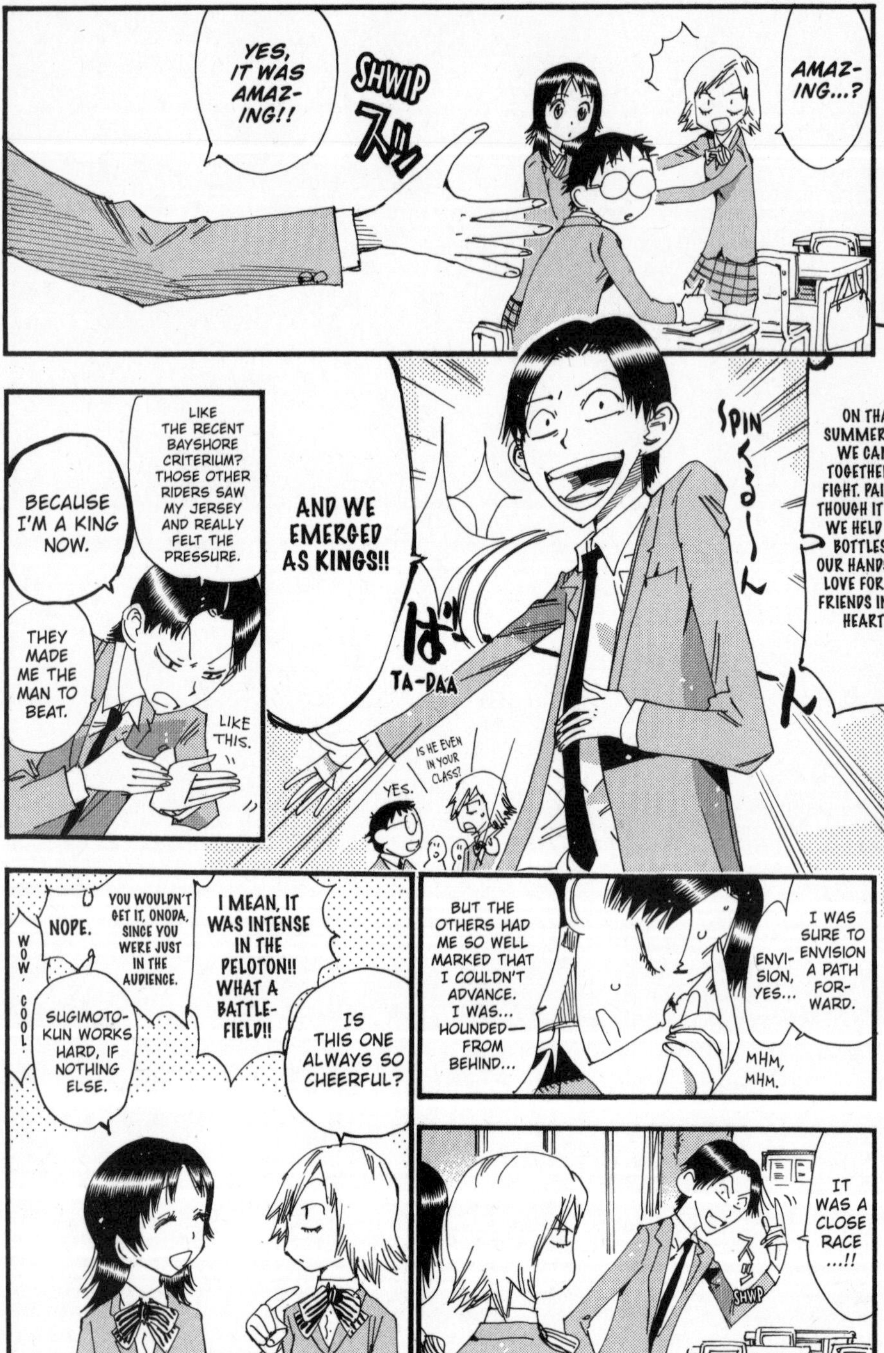
AMAZ-ING...?
SHWIP
スッ
YES, IT WAS AMAZ-ING!!
ON THAT SUMMER DAY, WE CAME TOGETHER TO FIGHT. PAINFUL THOUGH IT WAS, WE HELD OUR BOTTLES IN OUR HANDS AND LOVE FOR OUR FRIENDS IN OUR HEARTS.
SPIN
くるーん
AND WE EMERGED AS KINGS!!
ばっ
TA-DAA
IS HE EVEN IN YOUR CLASS?
YES.
LIKE THE RECENT BAYSHORE CRITERIUM? THOSE OTHER RIDERS SAW MY JERSEY AND REALLY FELT THE PRESSURE.
BECAUSE I'M A KING NOW.
THEY MADE ME THE MAN TO BEAT.
LIKE THIS.
I WAS SURE TO ENVISION A PATH FOR-WARD.
ENVI-SION, YES...
BUT THE OTHERS HAD ME SO WELL MARKED THAT I COULDN'T ADVANCE. I WAS... HOUNDED—FROM BEHIND...
MHM, MHM.
IT WAS A CLOSE RACE ...!!
スッ
SHWP
I MEAN, IT WAS INTENSE IN THE PELOTON!! WHAT A BATTLE-FIELD!!
YOU WOULDN'T GET IT, ONODA, SINCE YOU WERE JUST IN THE AUDIENCE.
NOPE.
WOW. COOL.
IS THIS ONE ALWAYS SO CHEERFUL?
SUGIMOTO-KUN WORKS HARD, IF NOTHING ELSE.

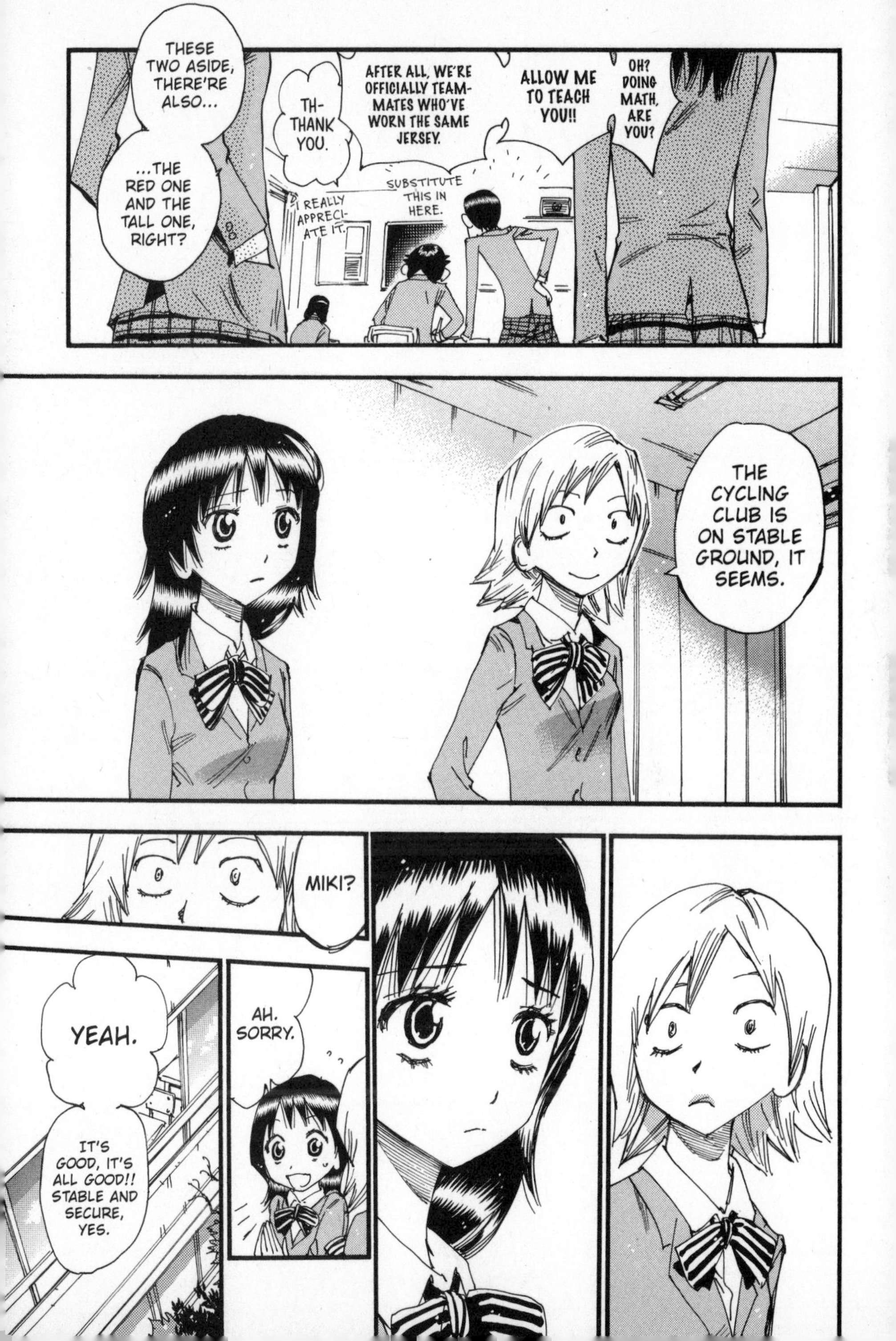
OH? DOING MATH, ARE YOU?
ALLOW ME TO TEACH YOU!!
AFTER ALL, WE'RE OFFICIALLY TEAM-MATES WHO'VE WORN THE SAME JERSEY.
SUBSTITUTE THIS IN HERE.
TH-THANK YOU.
I REALLY APPRECI-ATE IT.
THESE TWO ASIDE, THERE'RE ALSO...
...THE RED ONE AND THE TALL ONE, RIGHT?
THE CYCLING CLUB IS ON STABLE GROUND, IT SEEMS.
MIKI?
AH. SORRY.
YEAH.
IT'S GOOD, IT'S ALL GOOD!! STABLE AND SECURE, YES.

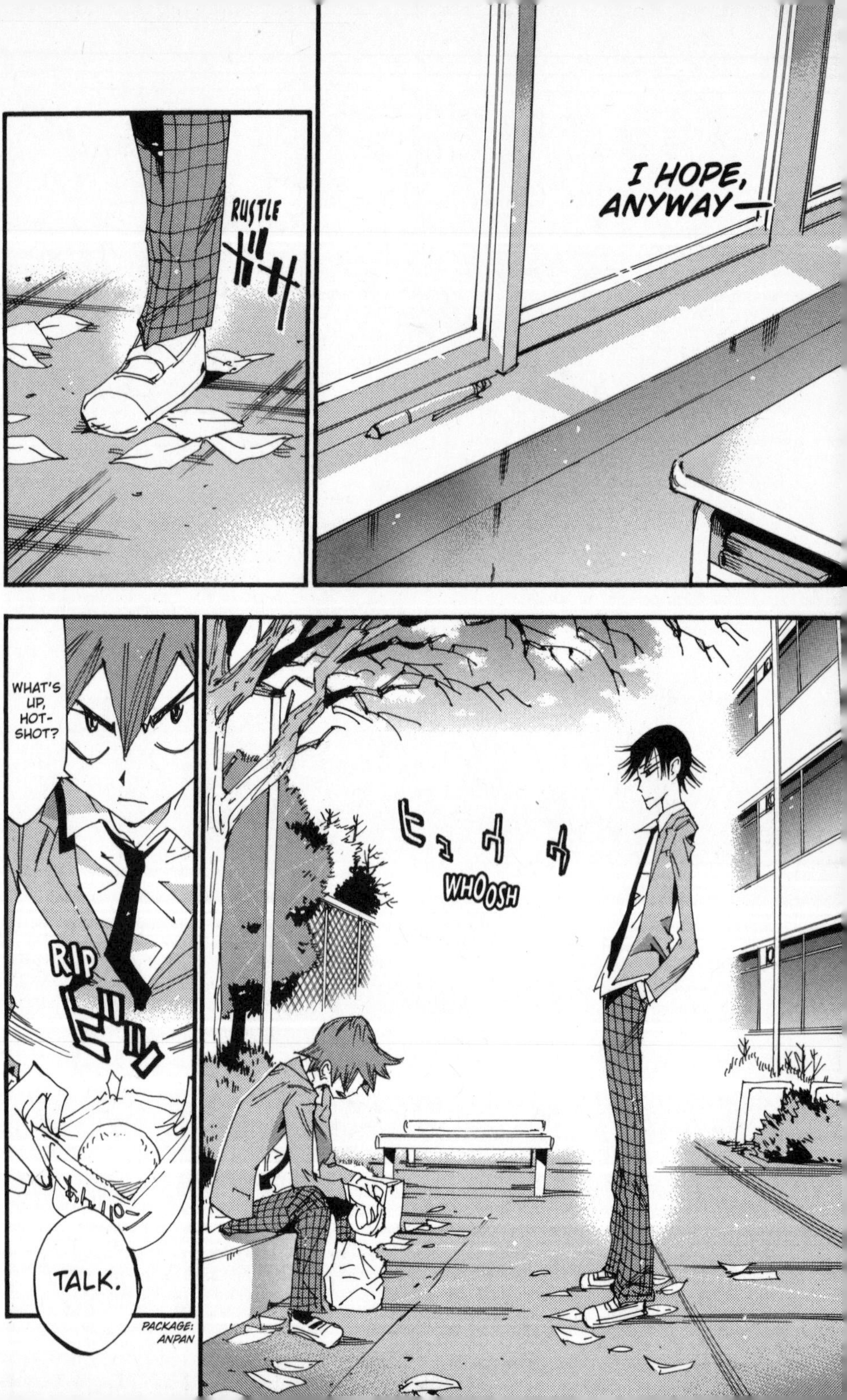
I HOPE, ANYWAY—
RUSTLE
WHOOSH
WHAT'S UP, HOT-SHOT?
RIP
TALK.
PACKAGE: ANPAN

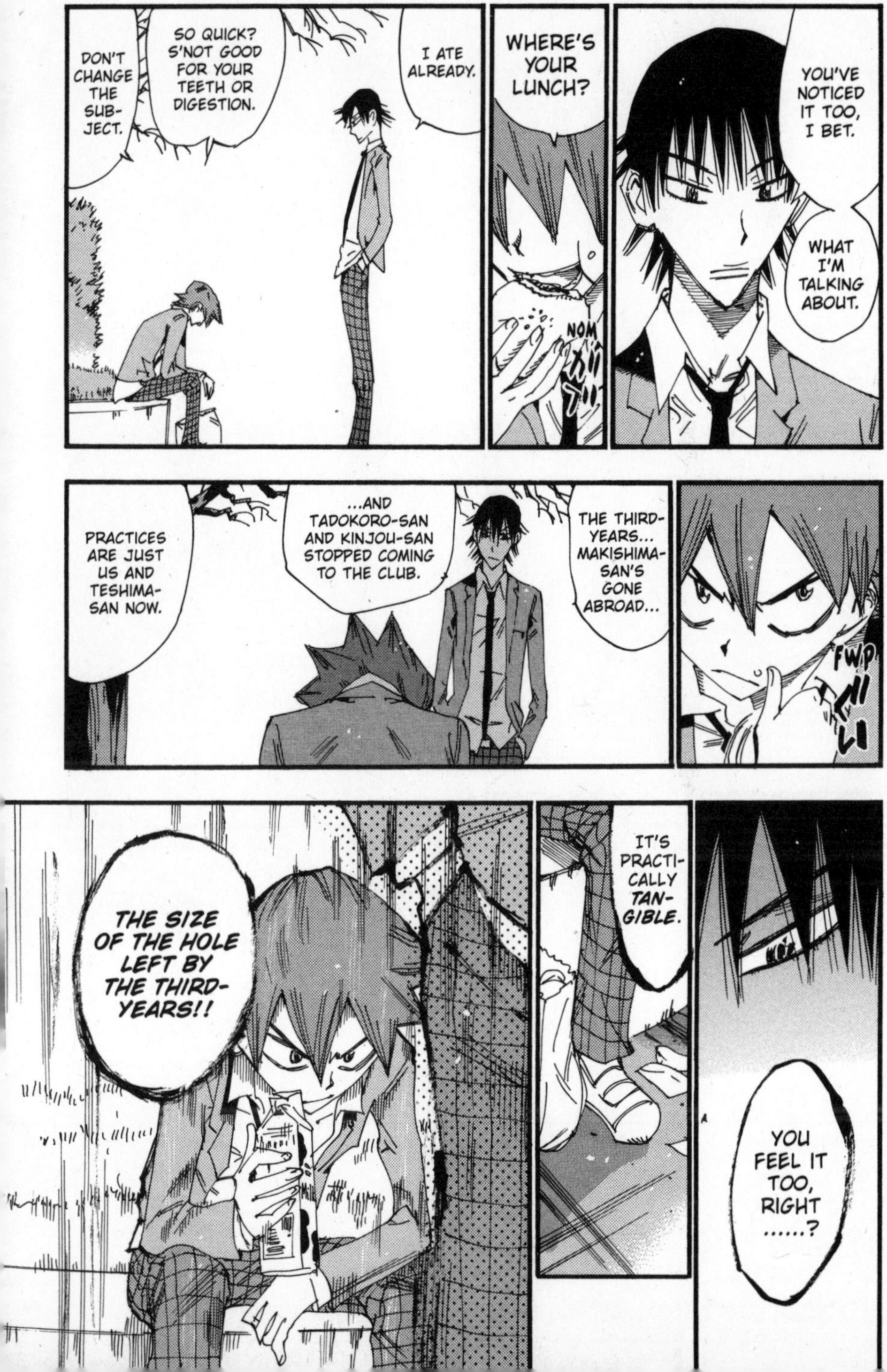
YOU'VE NOTICED IT TOO, I BET.
WHAT I'M TALKING ABOUT.
WHERE'S YOUR LUNCH?
NOM
I ATE ALREADY.
SO QUICK? S'NOT GOOD FOR YOUR TEETH OR DIGESTION.
DON'T CHANGE THE SUB-JECT.
FWP
THE THIRD-YEARS... MAKISHIMA-SAN'S GONE ABROAD...
...AND TADOKORO-SAN AND KINJOU-SAN STOPPED COMING TO THE CLUB.
PRACTICES ARE JUST US AND TESHIMA-SAN NOW.
YOU FEEL IT TOO, RIGHT ......?
IT'S PRACTI-CALLY *TAN-GIBLE*.
THE SIZE OF THE HOLE LEFT BY THE THIRD-YEARS!!

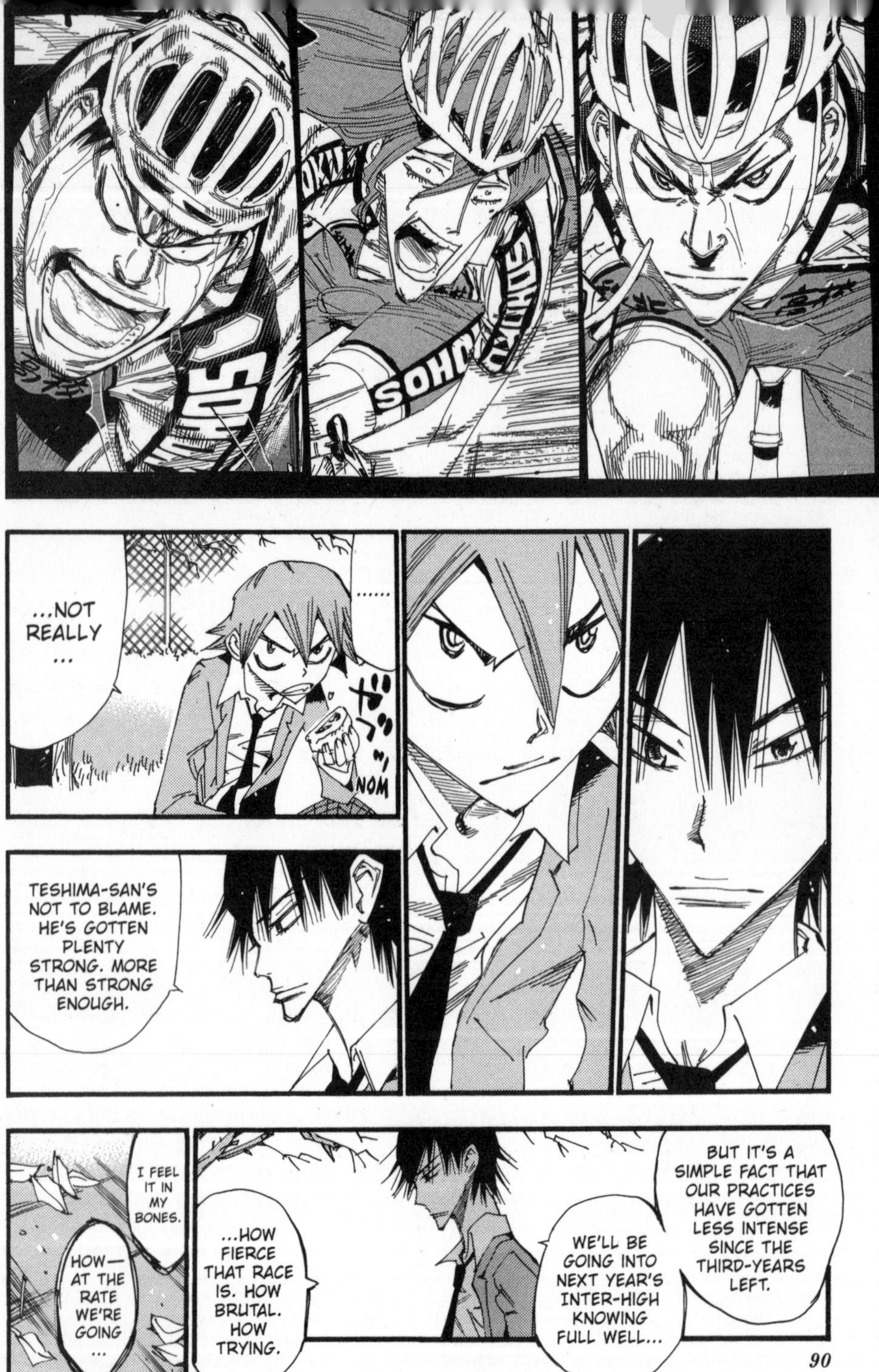
......
...NOT REALLY ...
NOM
TESHIMA-SAN'S NOT TO BLAME. HE'S GOTTEN PLENTY STRONG. MORE THAN STRONG ENOUGH.
BUT IT'S A SIMPLE FACT THAT OUR PRACTICES HAVE GOTTEN LESS INTENSE SINCE THE THIRD-YEARS LEFT.
WE'LL BE GOING INTO NEXT YEAR'S INTER-HIGH KNOWING FULL WELL...
...HOW FIERCE THAT RACE IS. HOW BRUTAL. HOW TRYING.
I FEEL IT IN MY BONES.
HOW— AT THE RATE WE'RE GOING ...

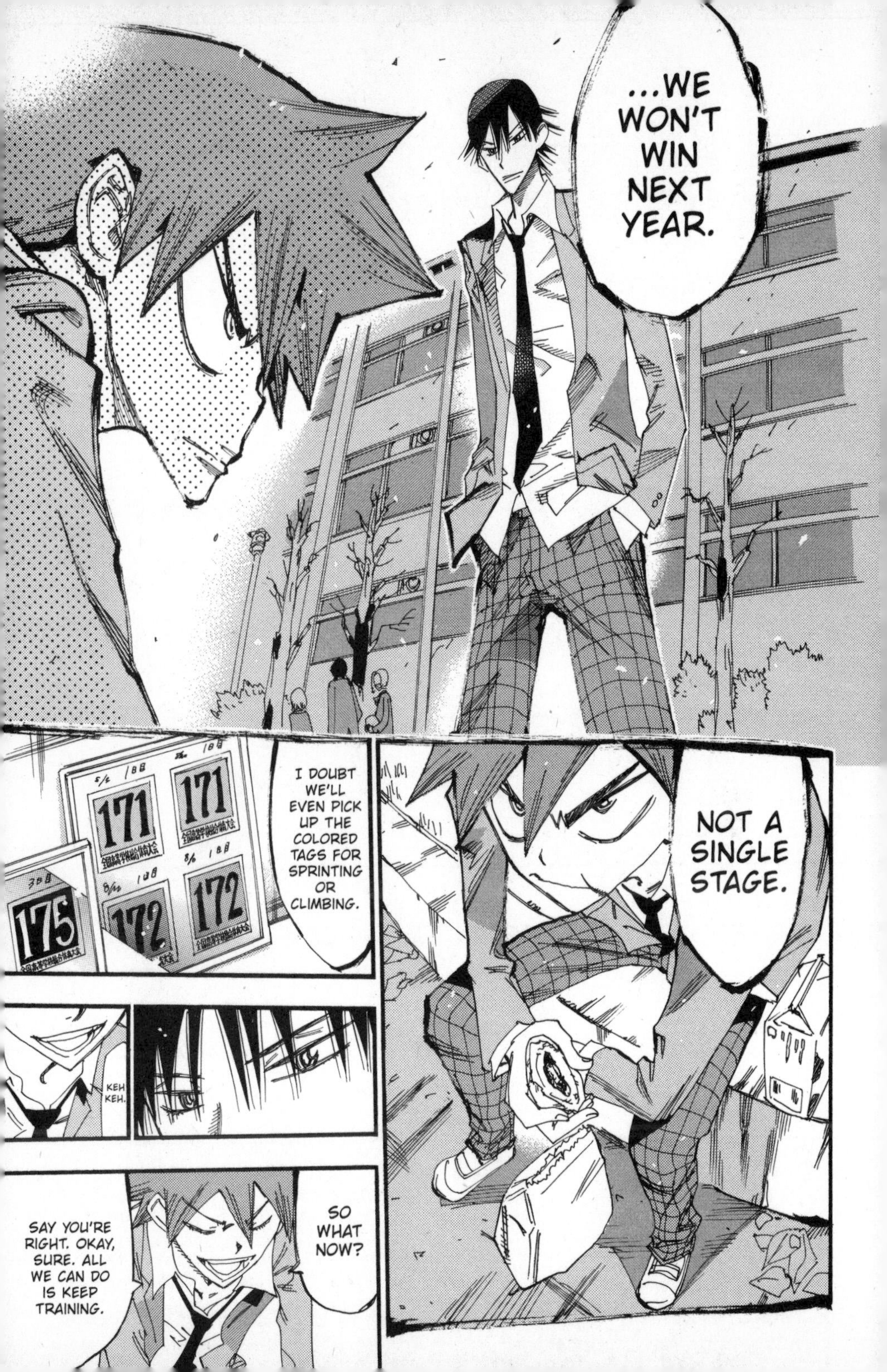
...WE WON'T WIN NEXT YEAR.
NOT A SINGLE STAGE.
I DOUBT WE'LL EVEN PICK UP THE COLORED TAGS FOR SPRINTING OR CLIMBING.
171
171
172
175
KEH KEH.
SO WHAT NOW?
SAY YOU'RE RIGHT. OKAY, SURE. ALL WE CAN DO IS KEEP TRAINING.

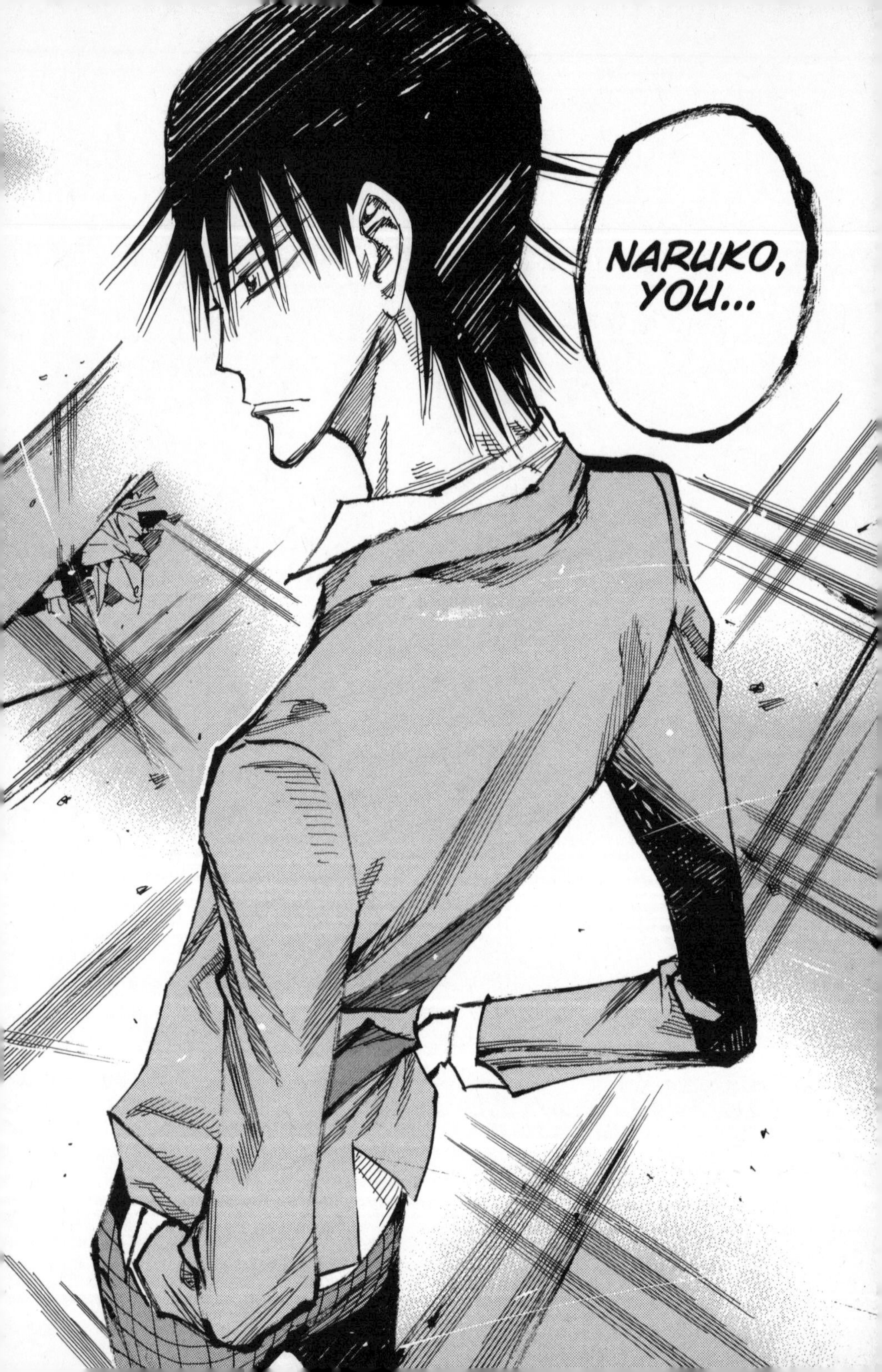
NARUKO, YOU...

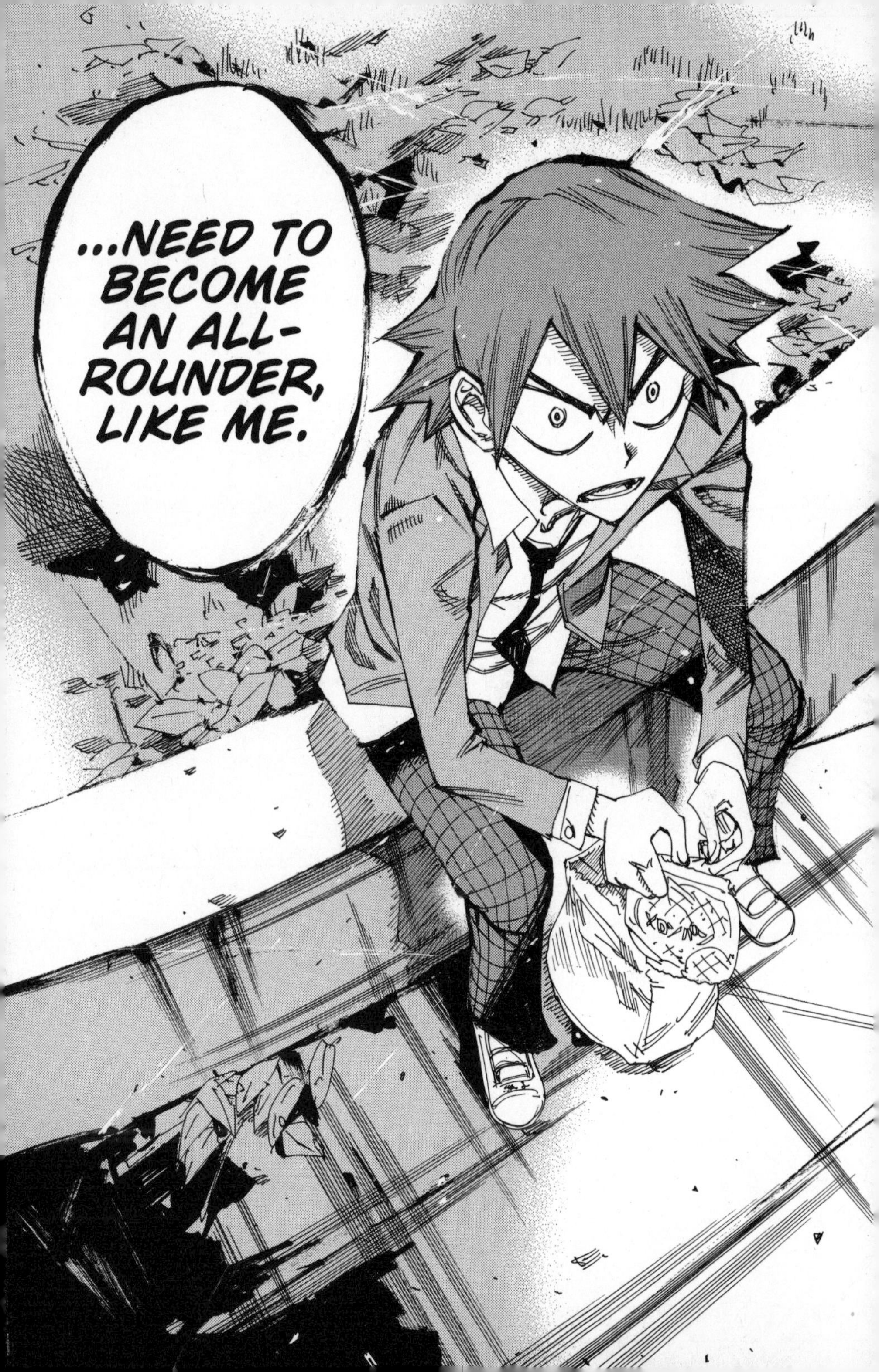
...NEED TO BECOME AN ALL-ROUNDER, LIKE ME.

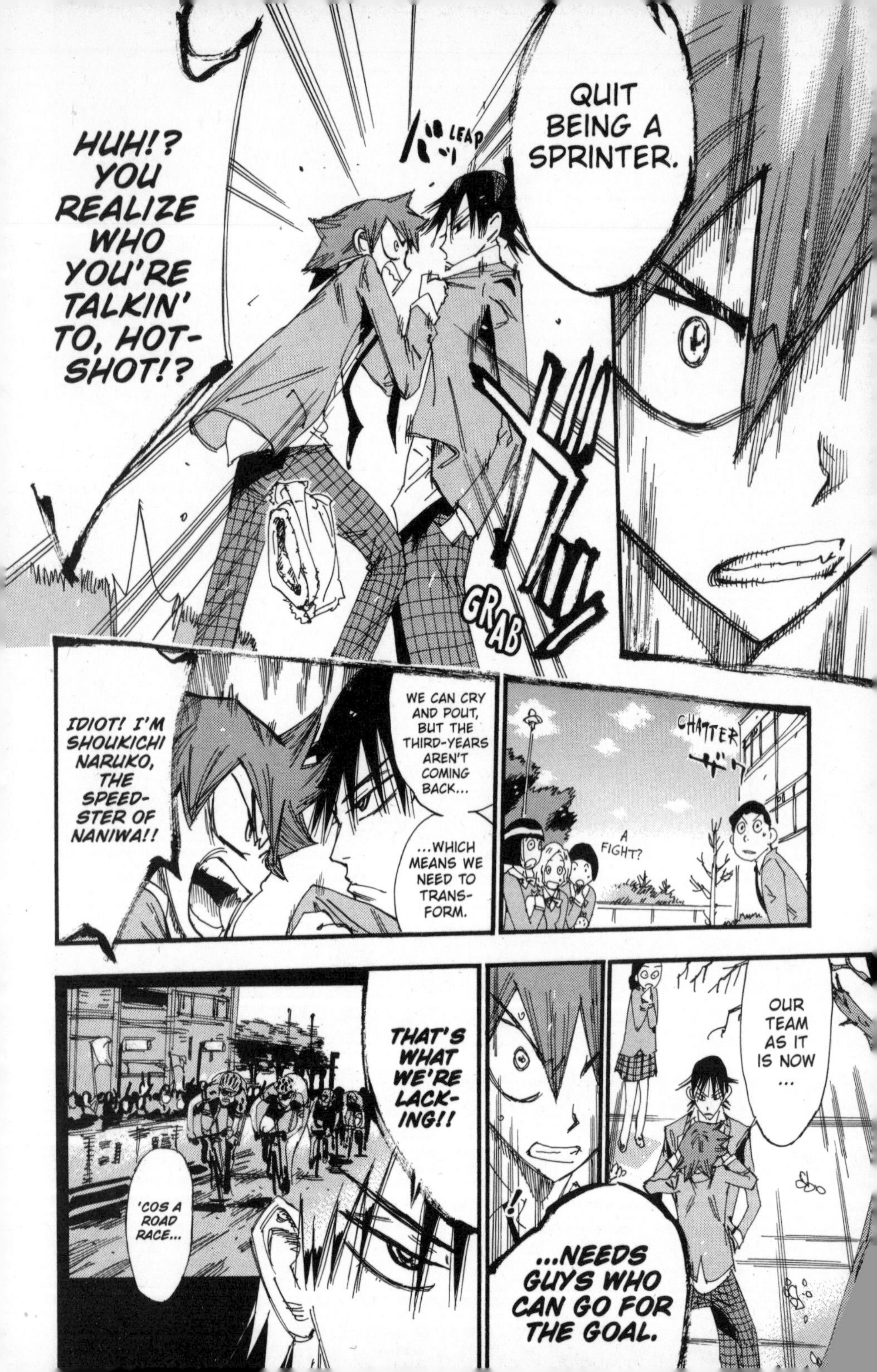
QUIT BEING A SPRINTER.
LEAP
GRAB
HUH!? YOU REALIZE WHO YOU'RE TALKIN' TO, HOT-SHOT!?
CHATTER
A FIGHT?
WE CAN CRY AND POUT, BUT THE THIRD-YEARS AREN'T COMING BACK...
...WHICH MEANS WE NEED TO TRANS-FORM.
IDIOT! I'M SHOUKICHI NARUKO, THE SPEED-STER OF NANIWA!!
OUR TEAM AS IT IS NOW...
!
THAT'S WHAT WE'RE LACK-ING!!
'COS A ROAD RACE...
...NEEDS GUYS WHO CAN GO FOR THE GOAL.

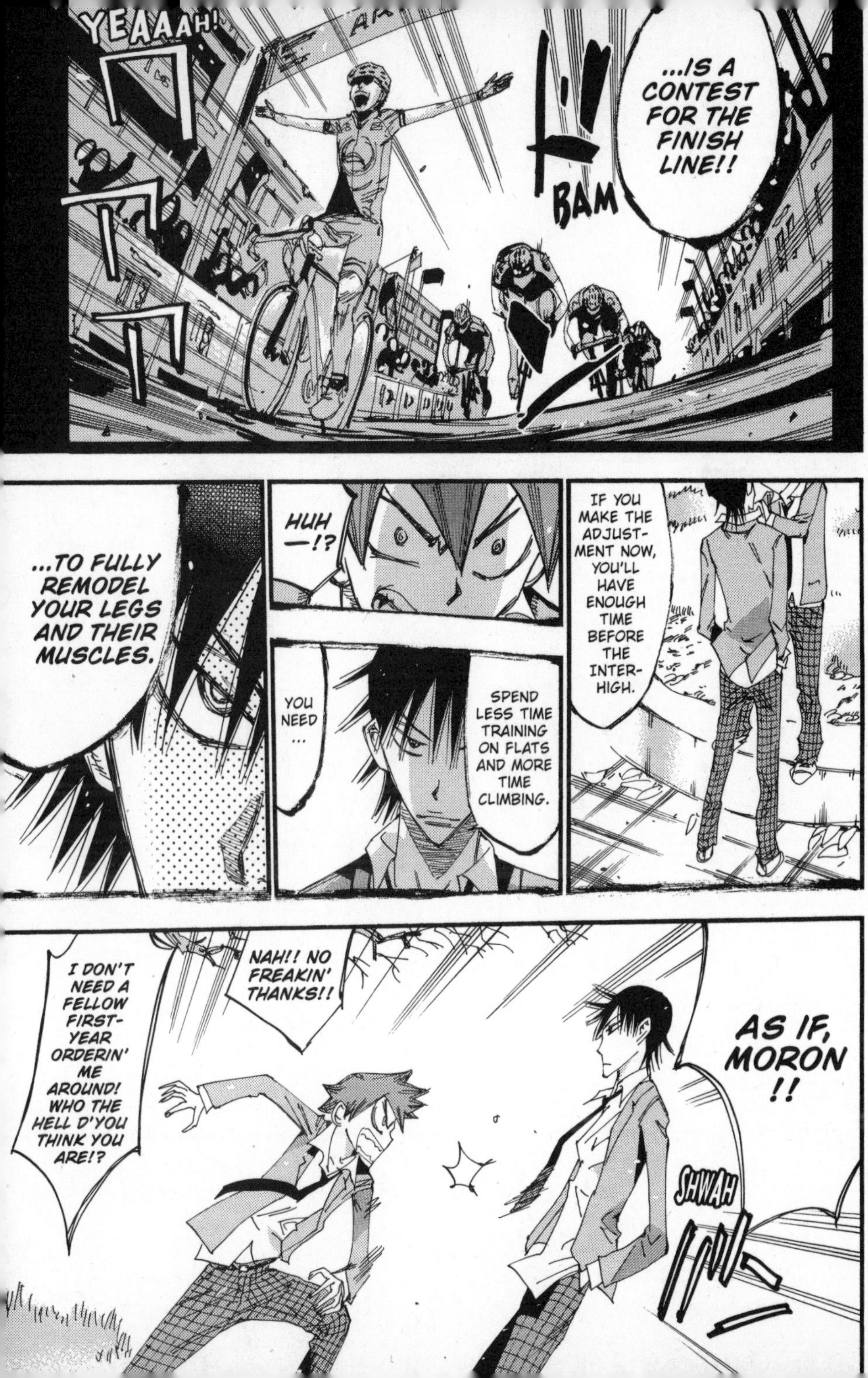
...IS A CONTEST FOR THE FINISH LINE!!
BAM
YEAAAH!
IF YOU MAKE THE ADJUST-MENT NOW, YOU'LL HAVE ENOUGH TIME BEFORE THE INTER-HIGH.
HUH—!?
SPEND LESS TIME TRAINING ON FLATS AND MORE TIME CLIMBING.
YOU NEED...
...TO FULLY REMODEL YOUR LEGS AND THEIR MUSCLES.
AS IF, MORON!!
SHWAH
NAH!! NO FREAKIN' THANKS!!
I DON'T NEED A FELLOW FIRST-YEAR ORDERIN' ME AROUND! WHO THE HELL D'YOU THINK YOU ARE!?

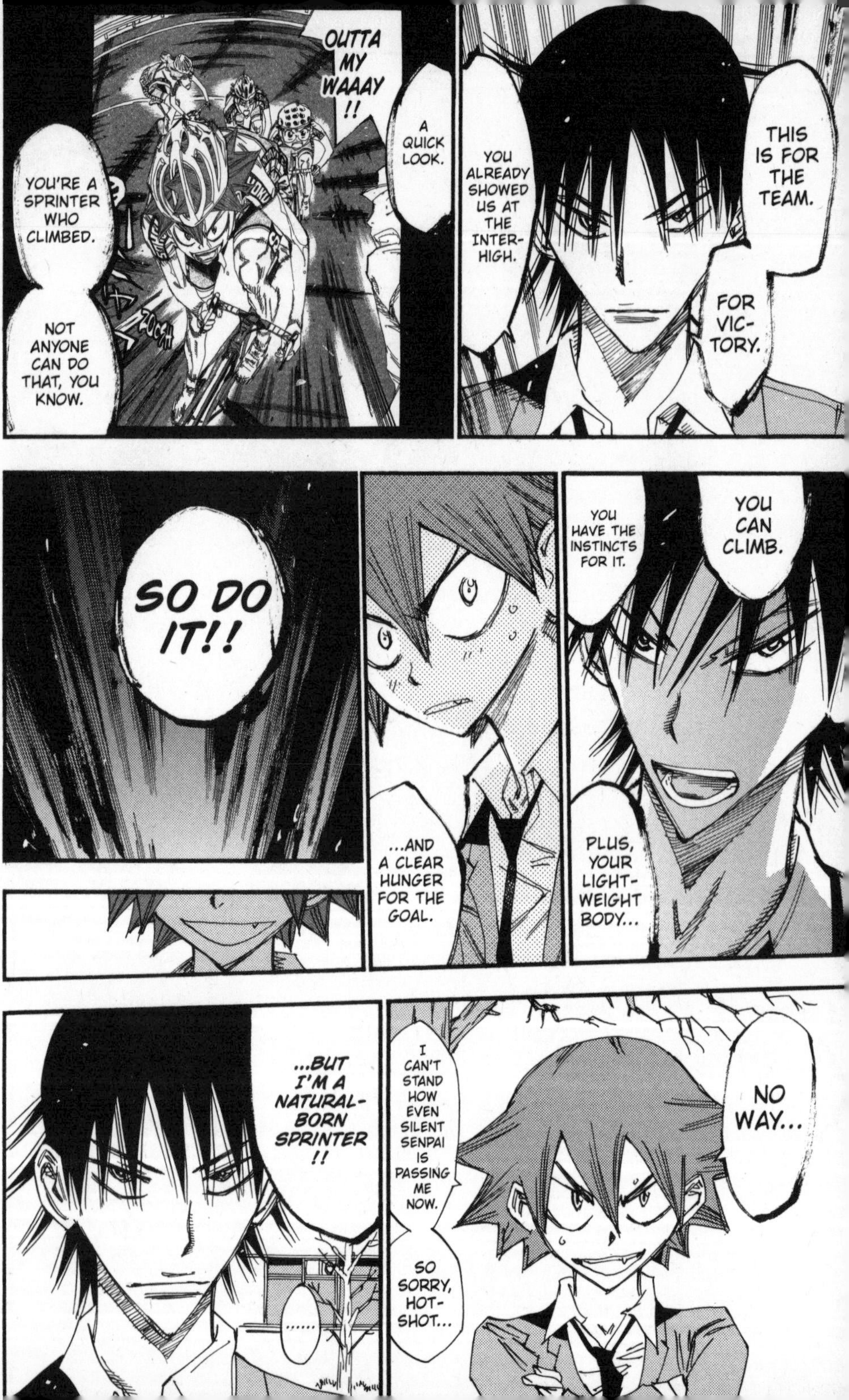
THIS IS FOR THE TEAM.
FOR VICTORY.
YOU ALREADY SHOWED US AT THE INTER-HIGH.
A QUICK LOOK.
OUTTA MY WAAAY!!
YOU'RE A SPRINTER WHO CLIMBED.
NOT ANYONE CAN DO THAT, YOU KNOW.
YOU CAN CLIMB.
YOU HAVE THE INSTINCTS FOR IT.
PLUS, YOUR LIGHT-WEIGHT BODY...
...AND A CLEAR HUNGER FOR THE GOAL.
SO DO IT!!
NO WAY...
I CAN'T STAND HOW EVEN SILENT SENPAI IS PASSING ME NOW.
SO SORRY, HOT-SHOT...
...BUT I'M A NATURAL-BORN SPRINTER!!
......

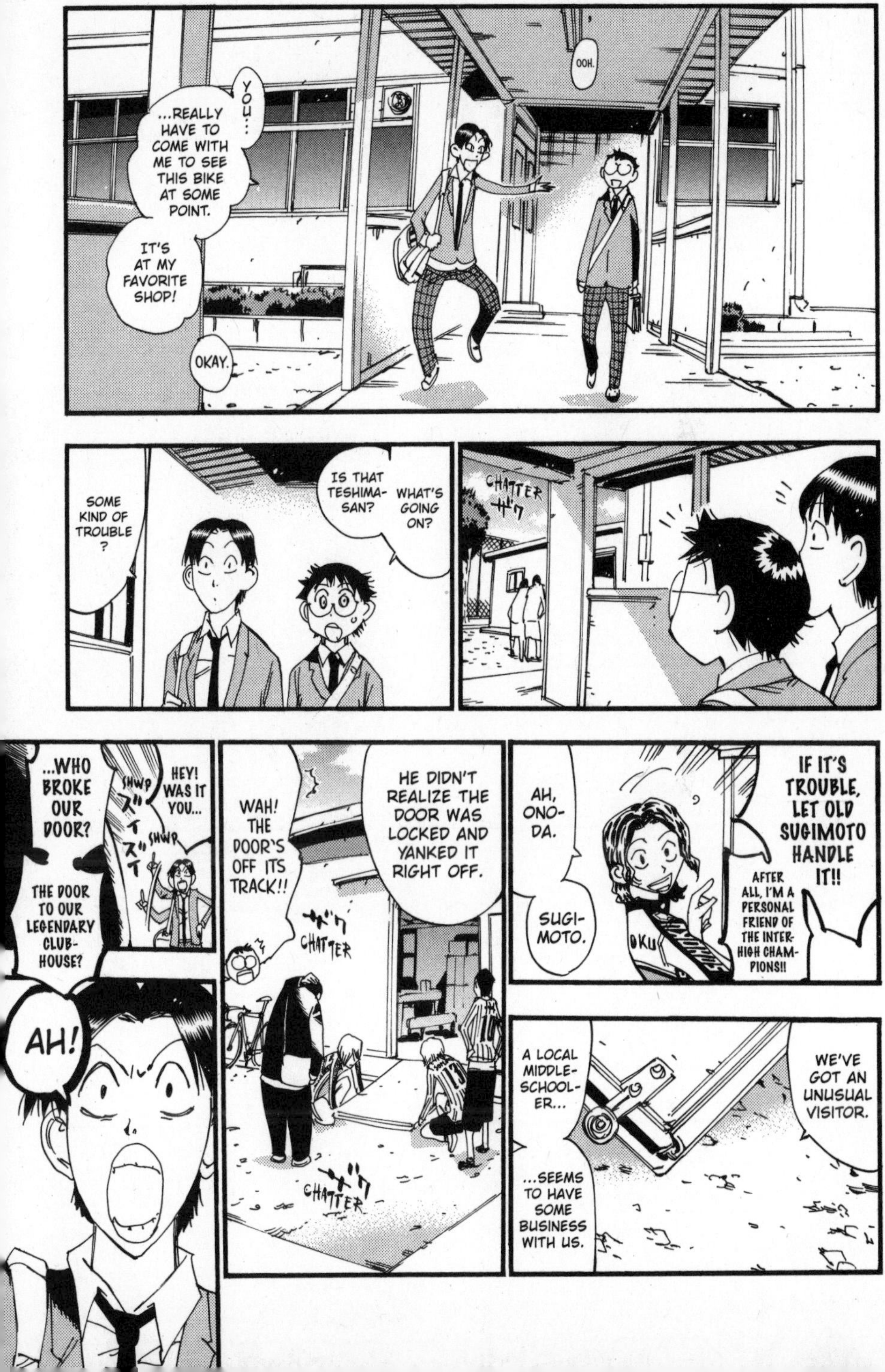
OOH.
YOU...
...REALLY HAVE TO COME WITH ME TO SEE THIS BIKE AT SOME POINT.
IT'S AT MY FAVORITE SHOP!
OKAY.
CHATTER
WHAT'S GOING ON?
IS THAT TESHIMA-SAN?
SOME KIND OF TROUBLE?
IF IT'S TROUBLE, LET OLD SUGIMOTO HANDLE IT!!
AFTER ALL, I'M A PERSONAL FRIEND OF THE INTER-HIGH CHAMPIONS!!
AH, ONODA.
SUGI-MOTO.
WE'VE GOT AN UNUSUAL VISITOR.
A LOCAL MIDDLE-SCHOOLER...
...SEEMS TO HAVE SOME BUSINESS WITH US.
HE DIDN'T REALIZE THE DOOR WAS LOCKED AND YANKED IT RIGHT OFF.
WAH! THE DOOR'S OFF ITS TRACK!!
CHATTER
CHATTER
HEY! WAS IT YOU...
SHWP
SHWP
...WHO BROKE OUR DOOR?
THE DOOR TO OUR LEGENDARY CLUB-HOUSE?
AH!

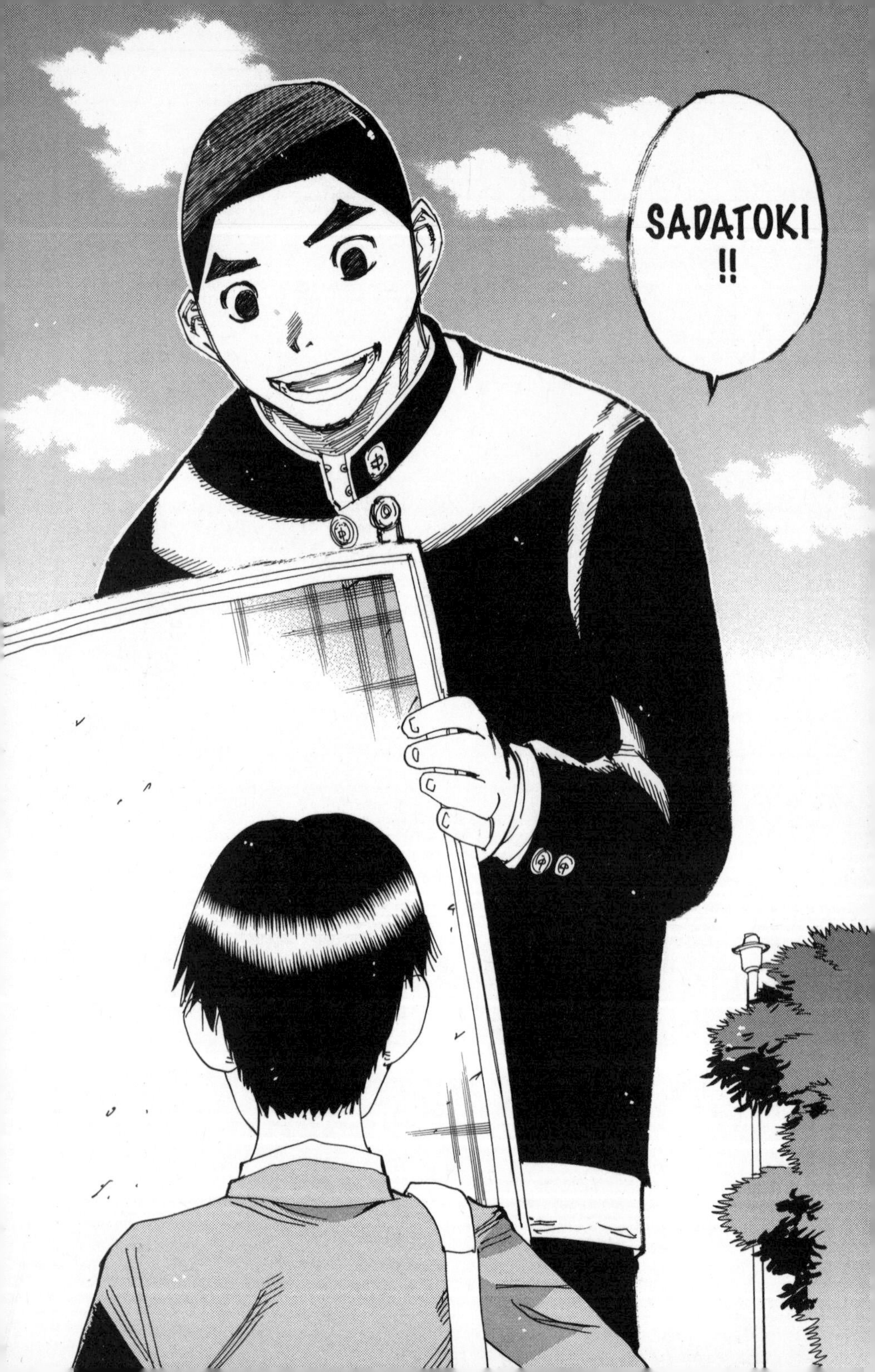
SADATOKI !!

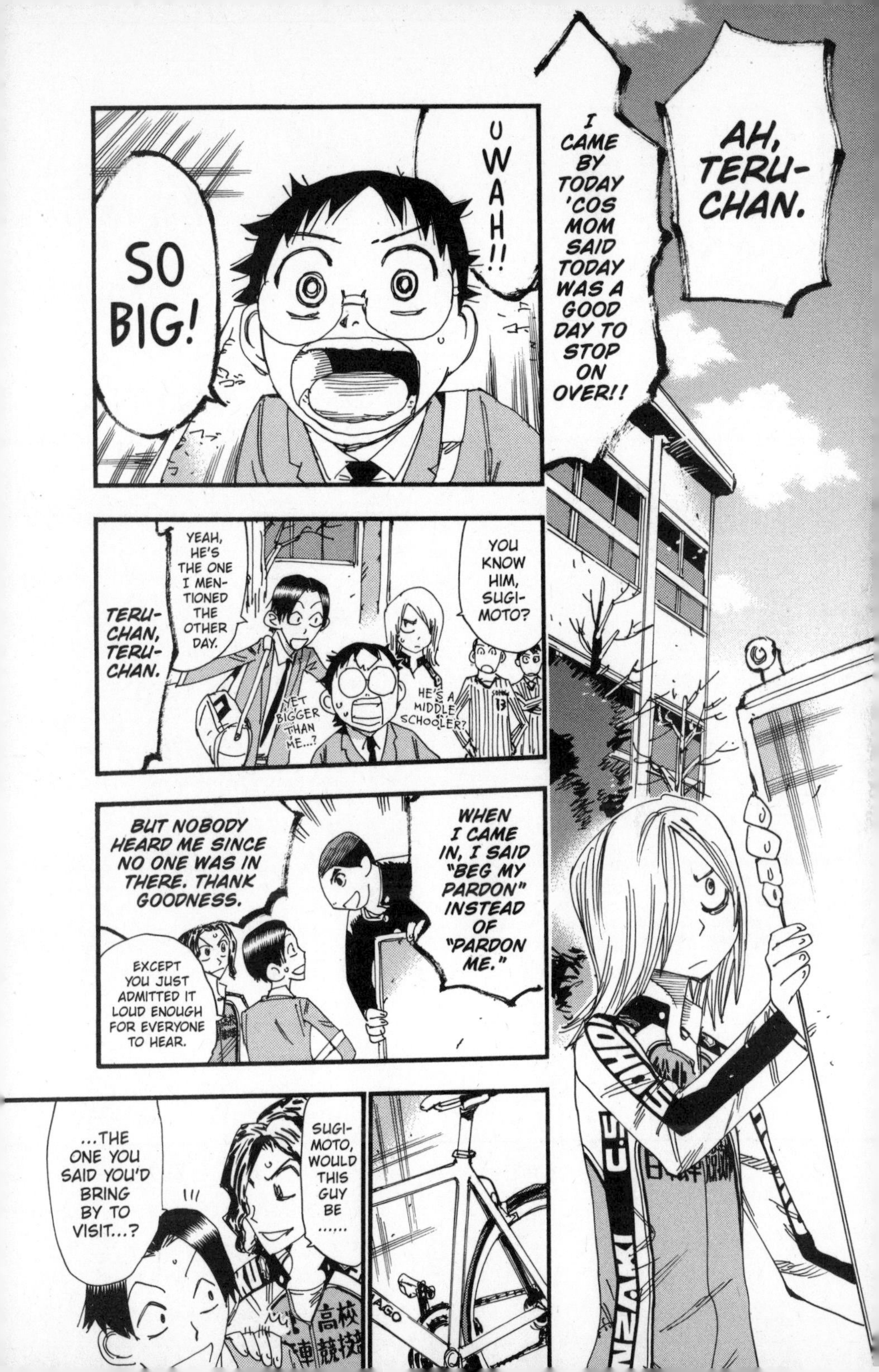
AH, TERU-CHAN.
I CAME BY TODAY 'COS MOM SAID TODAY WAS A GOOD DAY TO STOP ON OVER!!
UWAH!!
SO BIG!
YOU KNOW HIM, SUGIMOTO?
HE'S A MIDDLE SCHOOLER?
YEAH, HE'S THE ONE I MENTIONED THE OTHER DAY.
YET BIGGER THAN ME...?
TERU-CHAN, TERU-CHAN.
WHEN I CAME IN, I SAID "BEG MY PARDON" INSTEAD OF "PARDON ME."
BUT NOBODY HEARD ME SINCE NO ONE WAS IN THERE. THANK GOODNESS.
EXCEPT YOU JUST ADMITTED IT LOUD ENOUGH FOR EVERYONE TO HEAR.
SUGIMOTO, WOULD THIS GUY BE ......
...THE ONE YOU SAID YOU'D BRING BY TO VISIT...?

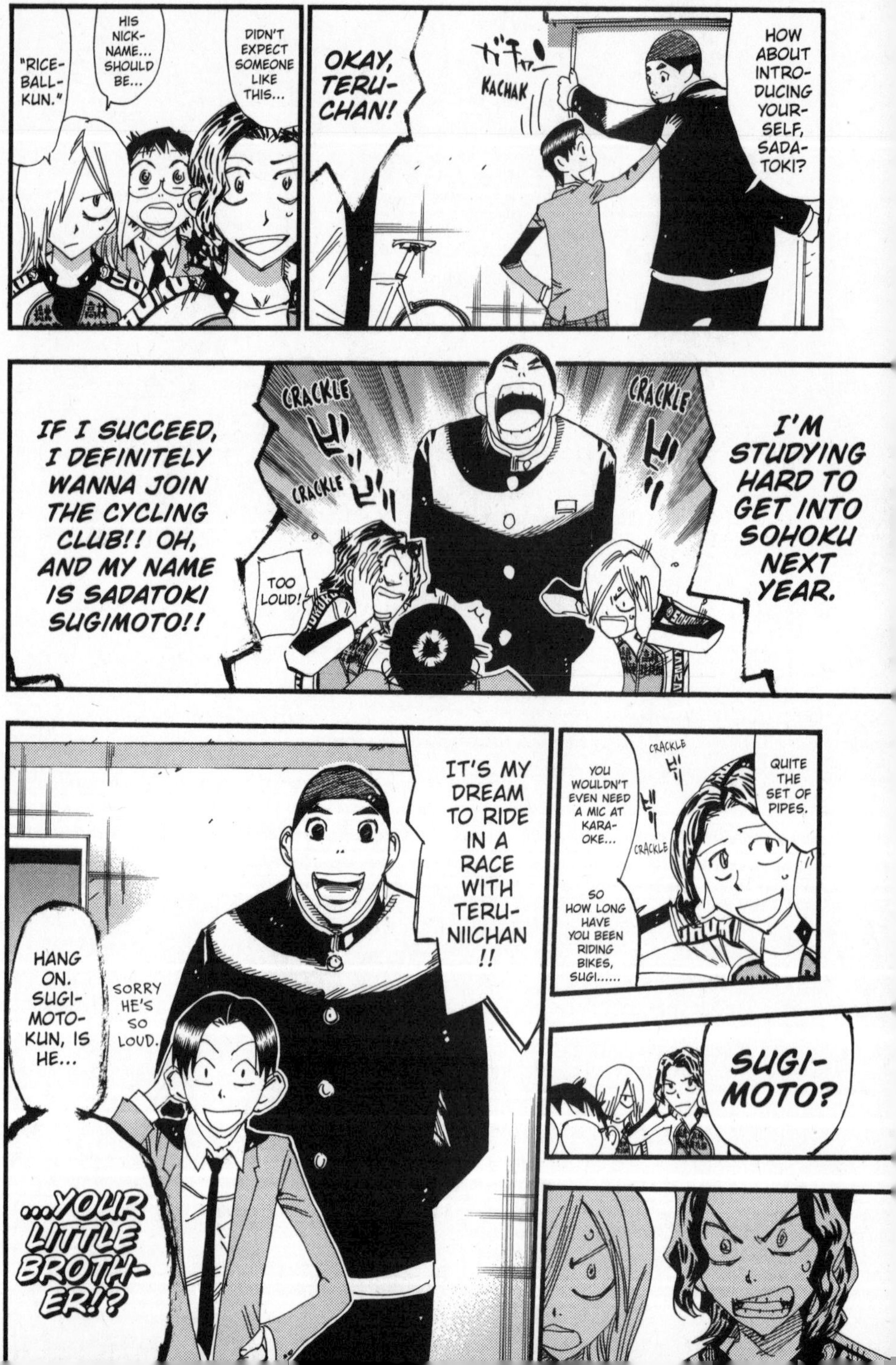
HOW ABOUT INTRO-DUCING YOUR-SELF, SADA-TOKI?
KACHAK
OKAY, TERU-CHAN!
DIDN'T EXPECT SOMEONE LIKE THIS...
HIS NICK-NAME... SHOULD BE...
"RICE-BALL-KUN."
I'M STUDYING HARD TO GET INTO SOHOKU NEXT YEAR.
CRACKLE
CRACKLE
CRACKLE
IF I SUCCEED, I DEFINITELY WANNA JOIN THE CYCLING CLUB!! OH, AND MY NAME IS SADATOKI SUGIMOTO!!
TOO LOUD!
QUITE THE SET OF PIPES.
CRACKLE
YOU WOULDN'T EVEN NEED A MIC AT KARA-OKE...
CRACKLE
SO HOW LONG HAVE YOU BEEN RIDING BIKES, SUGI......
SUGI-MOTO?
IT'S MY DREAM TO RIDE IN A RACE WITH TERU-NIICHAN !!
SORRY HE'S SO LOUD.
HANG ON. SUGI-MOTO-KUN, IS HE...
...YOUR LITTLE BROTH-ER!?

RIDE.248 SUGIMOTO'S LITTLE BROTHER

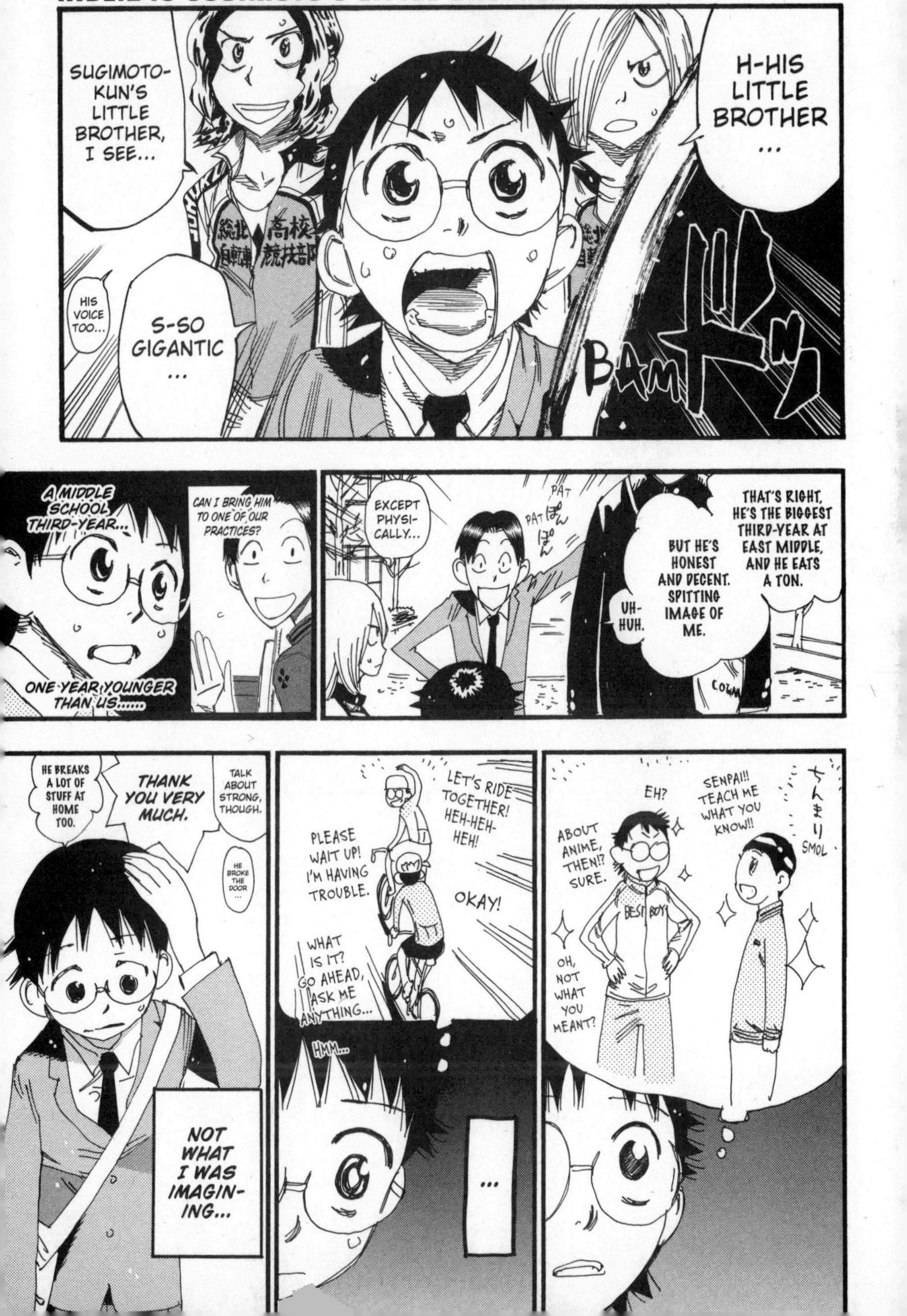
H-HIS LITTLE BROTHER ...
SUGIMOTO-KUN'S LITTLE BROTHER, I SEE...
BAM
S-SO GIGANTIC ...
HIS VOICE TOO...
THAT'S RIGHT, HE'S THE BIGGEST THIRD-YEAR AT EAST MIDDLE, AND HE EATS A TON.
BUT HE'S HONEST AND DECENT. SPITTING IMAGE OF ME.
UH-HUH.
PAT PAT
EXCEPT PHYSICALLY...
CAN I BRING HIM TO ONE OF OUR PRACTICES?
A MIDDLE SCHOOL THIRD-YEAR...
ONE YEAR YOUNGER THAN US......
SENPAI!! TEACH ME WHAT YOU KNOW!!
SMOL
EH?
ABOUT ANIME, THEN!? SURE.
OH, NOT WHAT YOU MEANT?
LET'S RIDE TOGETHER! HEH-HEH-HEH!
PLEASE WAIT UP! I'M HAVING TROUBLE.
OKAY!
WHAT IS IT? GO AHEAD, ASK ME ANYTHING...
HMM...
...
TALK ABOUT STRONG, THOUGH.
THANK YOU VERY MUCH.
HE BREAKS A LOT OF STUFF AT HOME TOO.
HE BROKE THE DOOR ...
NOT WHAT I WAS IMAGINING...

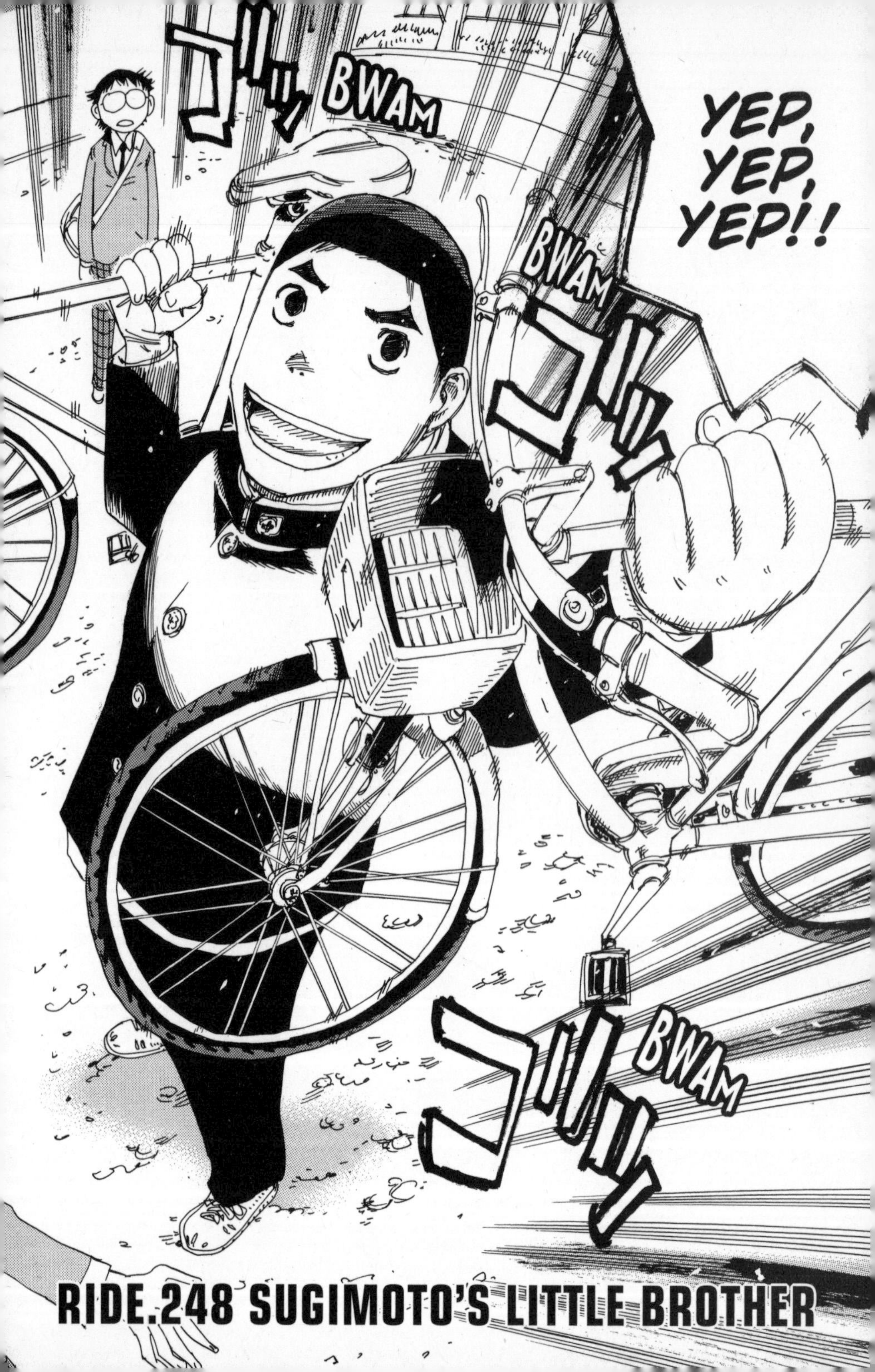
YEP, YEP, YEP!!
BWAM
BWAM
BWAM

RIDE.248 SUGIMOTO'S LITTLE BROTHER

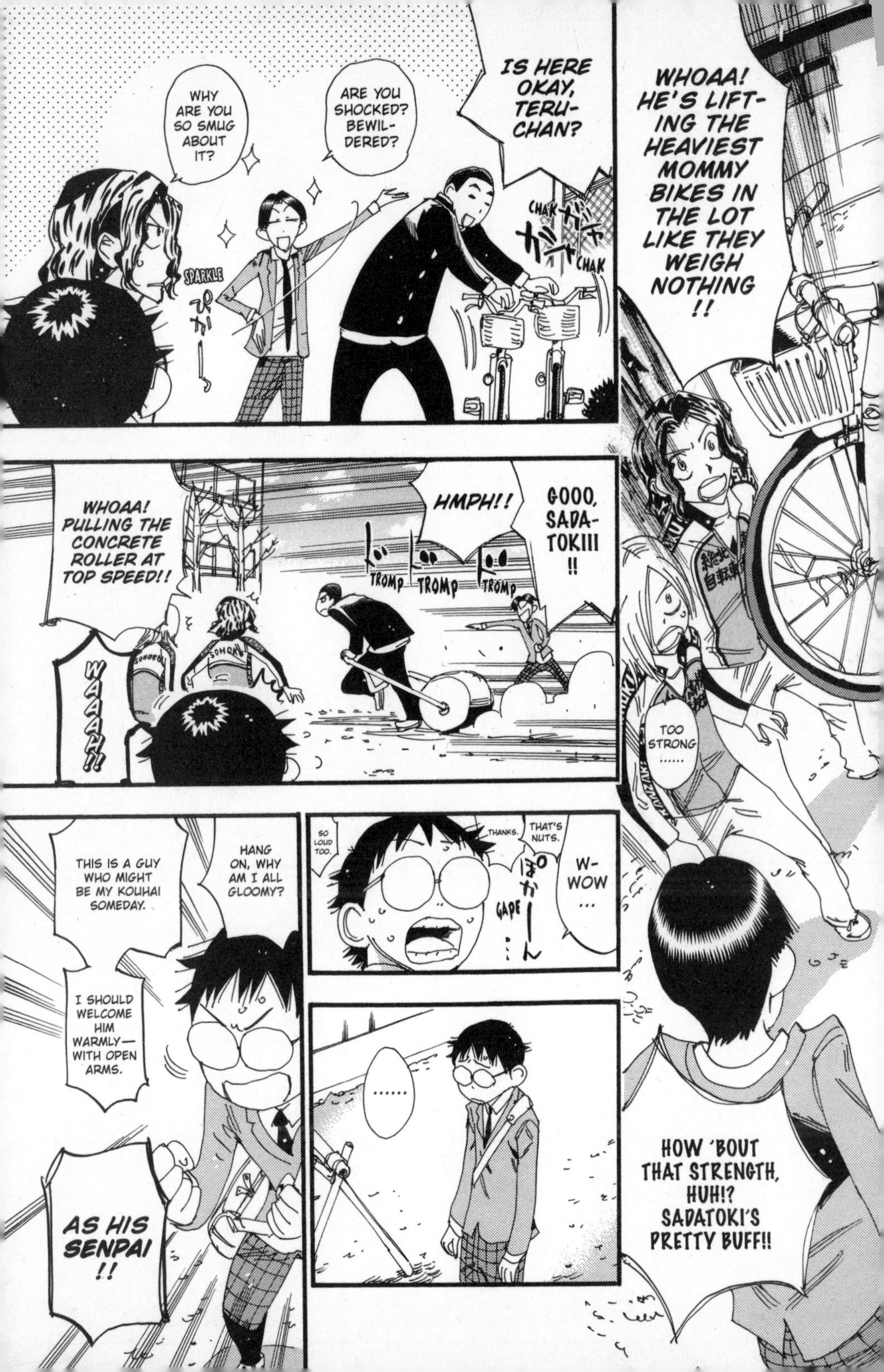
WHOAA! HE'S LIFTING THE HEAVIEST MOMMY BIKES IN THE LOT LIKE THEY WEIGH NOTHING!!
TOO STRONG......
HOW 'BOUT THAT STRENGTH, HUH!? SADATOKI'S PRETTY BUFF!!
IS HERE OKAY, TERU-CHAN?
CHAK
CHAK
ARE YOU SHOCKED? BEWILDERED?
WHY ARE YOU SO SMUG ABOUT IT?
SPARKLE
GOOO, SADATOKIII!!
HMPH!!
TROMP
TROMP
TROMP
WHOAA! PULLING THE CONCRETE ROLLER AT TOP SPEED!!
WAAAAH!!
W-WOW...
THAT'S NUTS.
THANKS.
SO LOUD TOO.
GAPE
......
HANG ON, WHY AM I ALL GLOOMY?
THIS IS A GUY WHO MIGHT BE MY KOUHAI SOMEDAY.
I SHOULD WELCOME HIM WARMLY—WITH OPEN ARMS.
AS HIS SENPAI!!

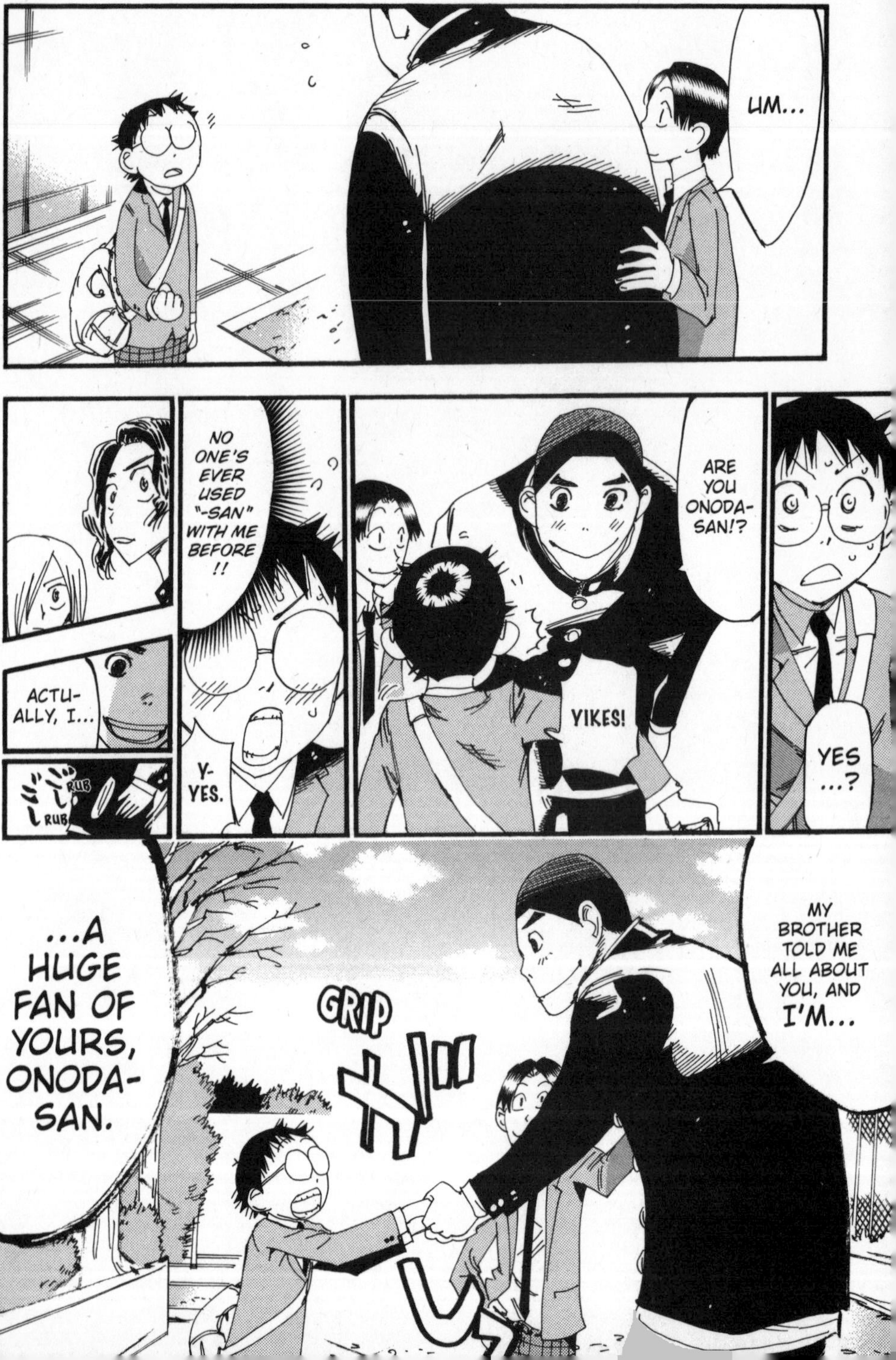
UM...
YES ...?
ARE YOU ONODA-SAN!?
YIKES!
NO ONE'S EVER USED "-SAN" WITH ME BEFORE !!
Y- YES.
ACTU-ALLY, I...
RUB
RUB
MY BROTHER TOLD ME ALL ABOUT YOU, AND I'M...
GRIP
...A HUGE FAN OF YOURS, ONODA-SAN.

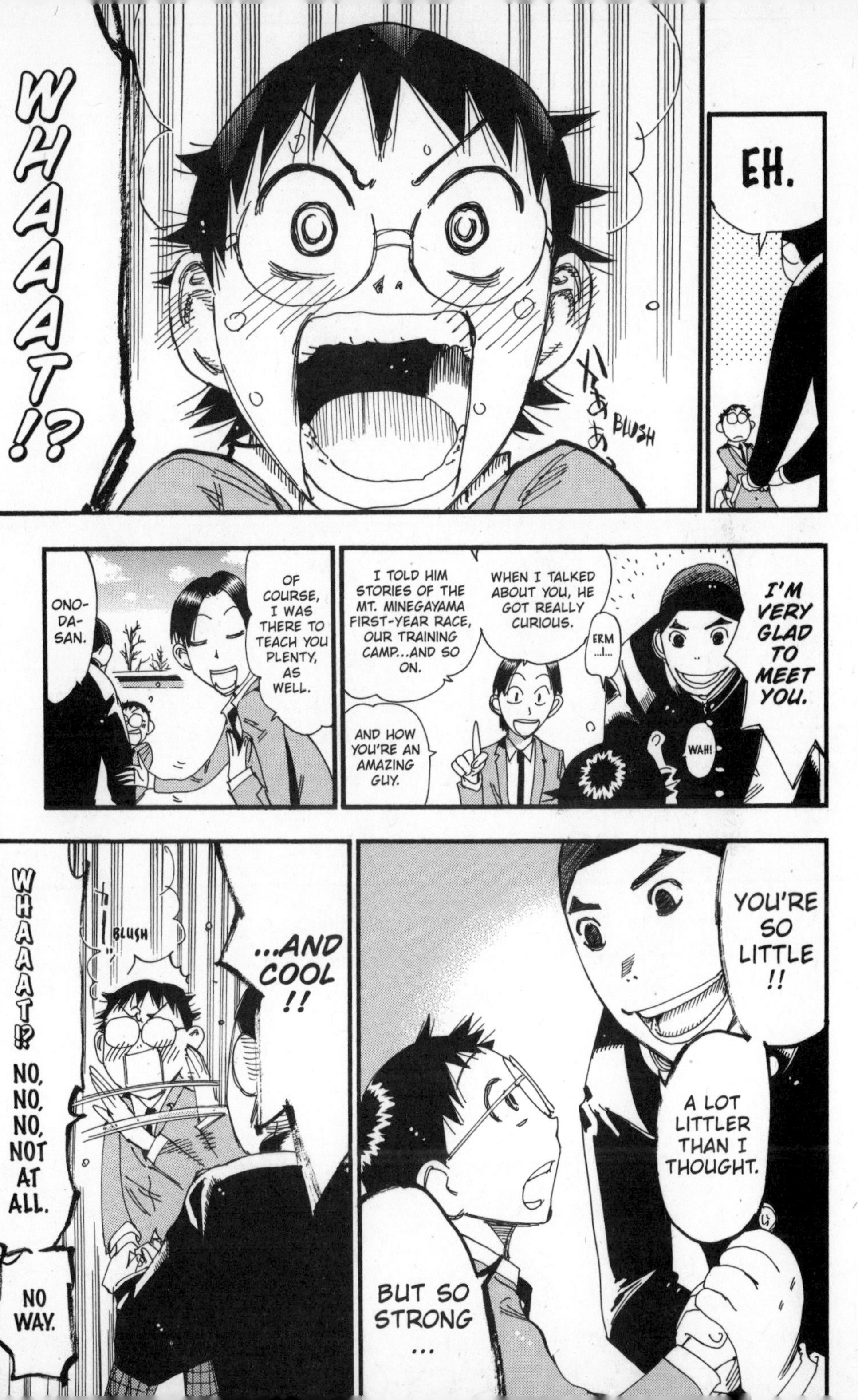
EH.
WHAAAAT!?
BLUSH
I'M VERY GLAD TO MEET YOU.
ERM ...I...
WAH!
WHEN I TALKED ABOUT YOU, HE GOT REALLY CURIOUS.
I TOLD HIM STORIES OF THE MT. MINEGAYAMA FIRST-YEAR RACE, OUR TRAINING CAMP...AND SO ON.
AND HOW YOU'RE AN AMAZING GUY.
OF COURSE, I WAS THERE TO TEACH YOU PLENTY, AS WELL.
ONO-DA-SAN.
YOU'RE SO LITTLE!!
A LOT LITTLER THAN I THOUGHT.
BUT SO STRONG...
...AND COOL!!
WHAAAAT!?
BLUSH
NO, NO, NO, NOT AT ALL.
NO WAY.

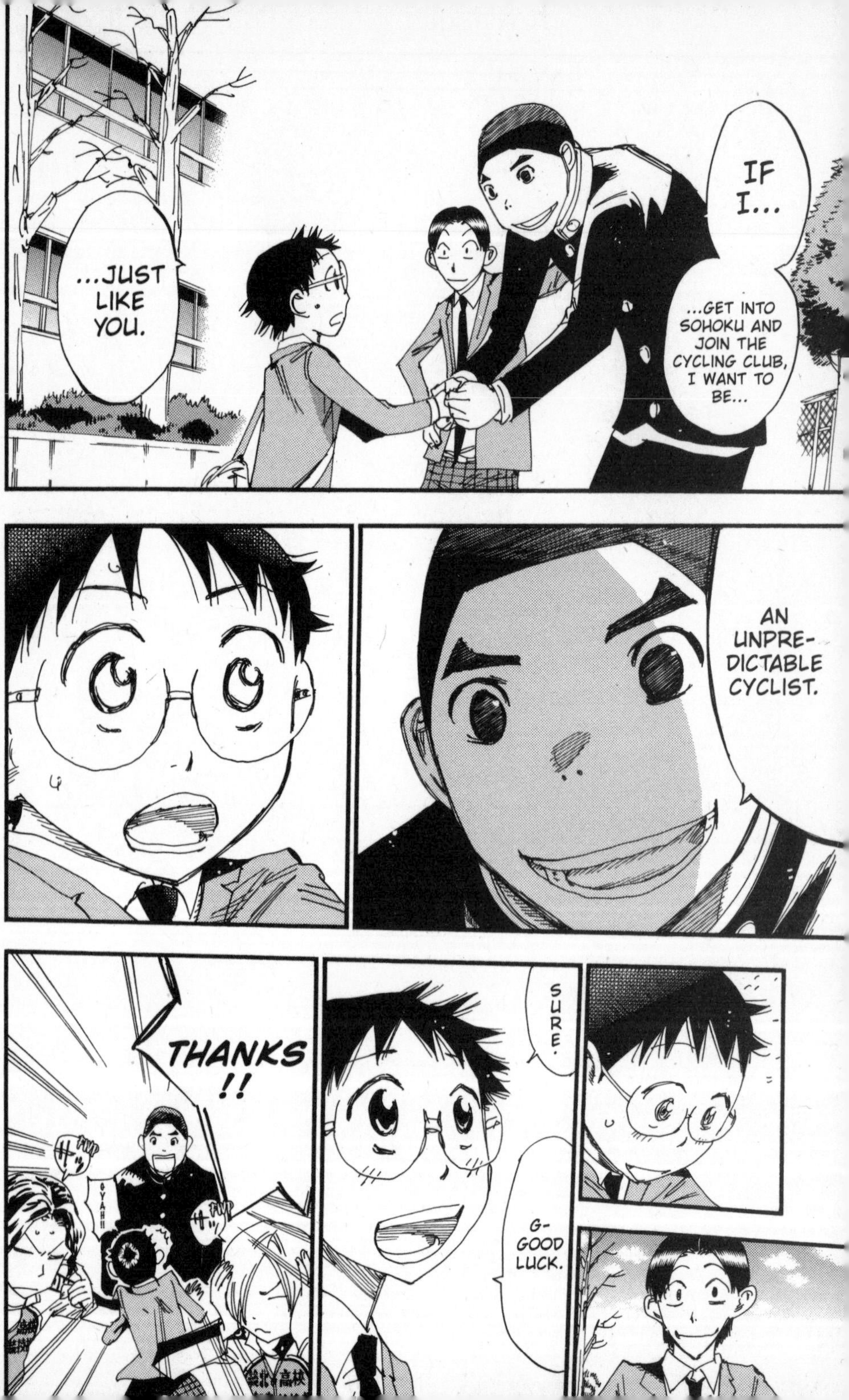
IF I...
...GET INTO SOHOKU AND JOIN THE CYCLING CLUB, I WANT TO BE...
...JUST LIKE YOU.
AN UNPRE-DICTABLE CYCLIST.
SURE.
G-GOOD LUCK.
THANKS!!

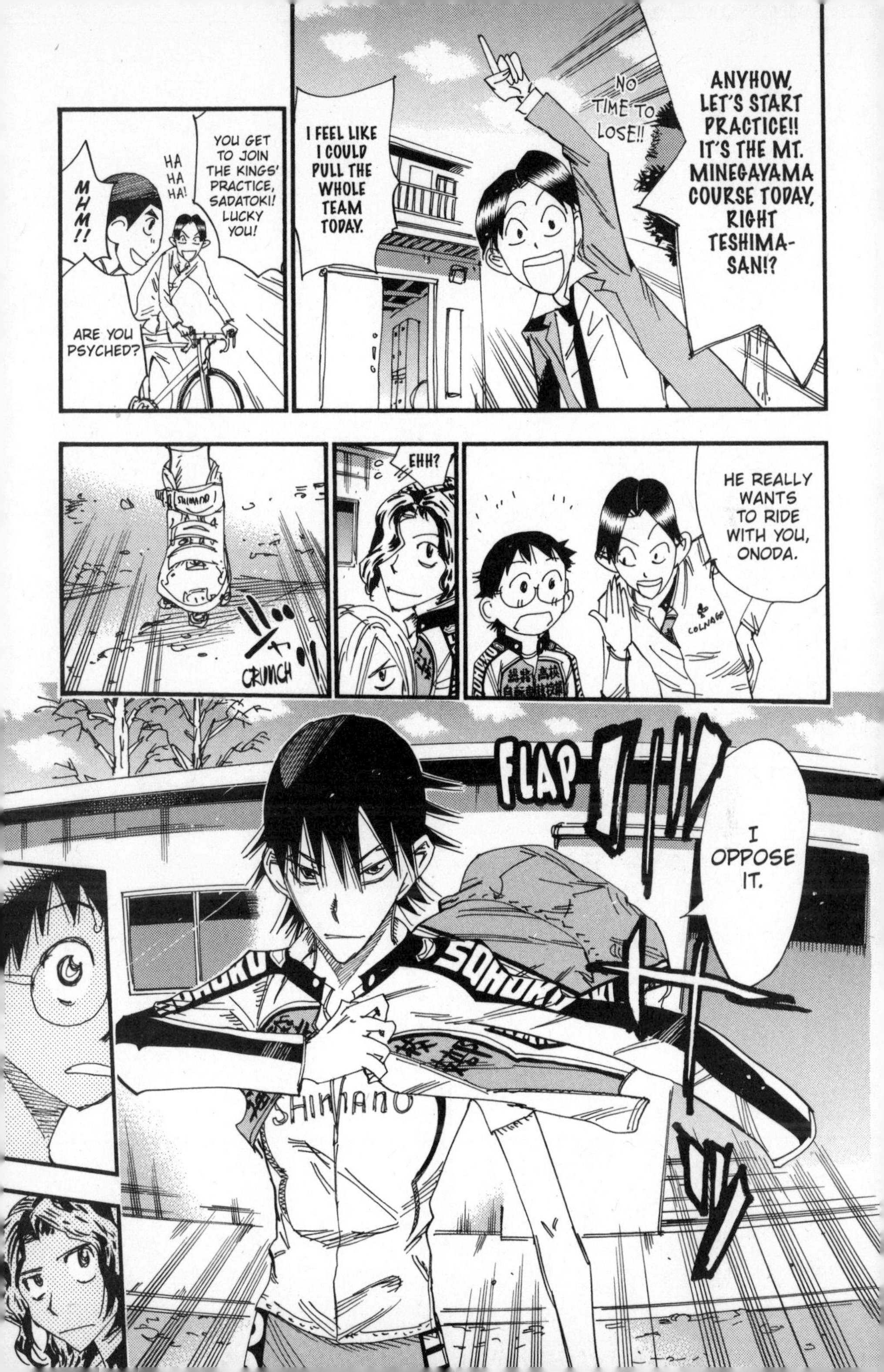
ANYHOW, LET'S START PRACTICE!! IT'S THE MT. MINEGAYAMA COURSE TODAY, RIGHT TESHIMA-SAN!?
NO TIME TO LOSE!!
I FEEL LIKE I COULD PULL THE WHOLE TEAM TODAY.
YOU GET TO JOIN THE KINGS' PRACTICE, SADATOKI! LUCKY YOU!
HA HA HA!
MHM!!
ARE YOU PSYCHED?
HE REALLY WANTS TO RIDE WITH YOU, ONODA.
COLNAGO
EHH?
SHIMANO
CRUNCH
FLAP
I OPPOSE IT.
SOHOKU
SOHOKU
SHIMANO

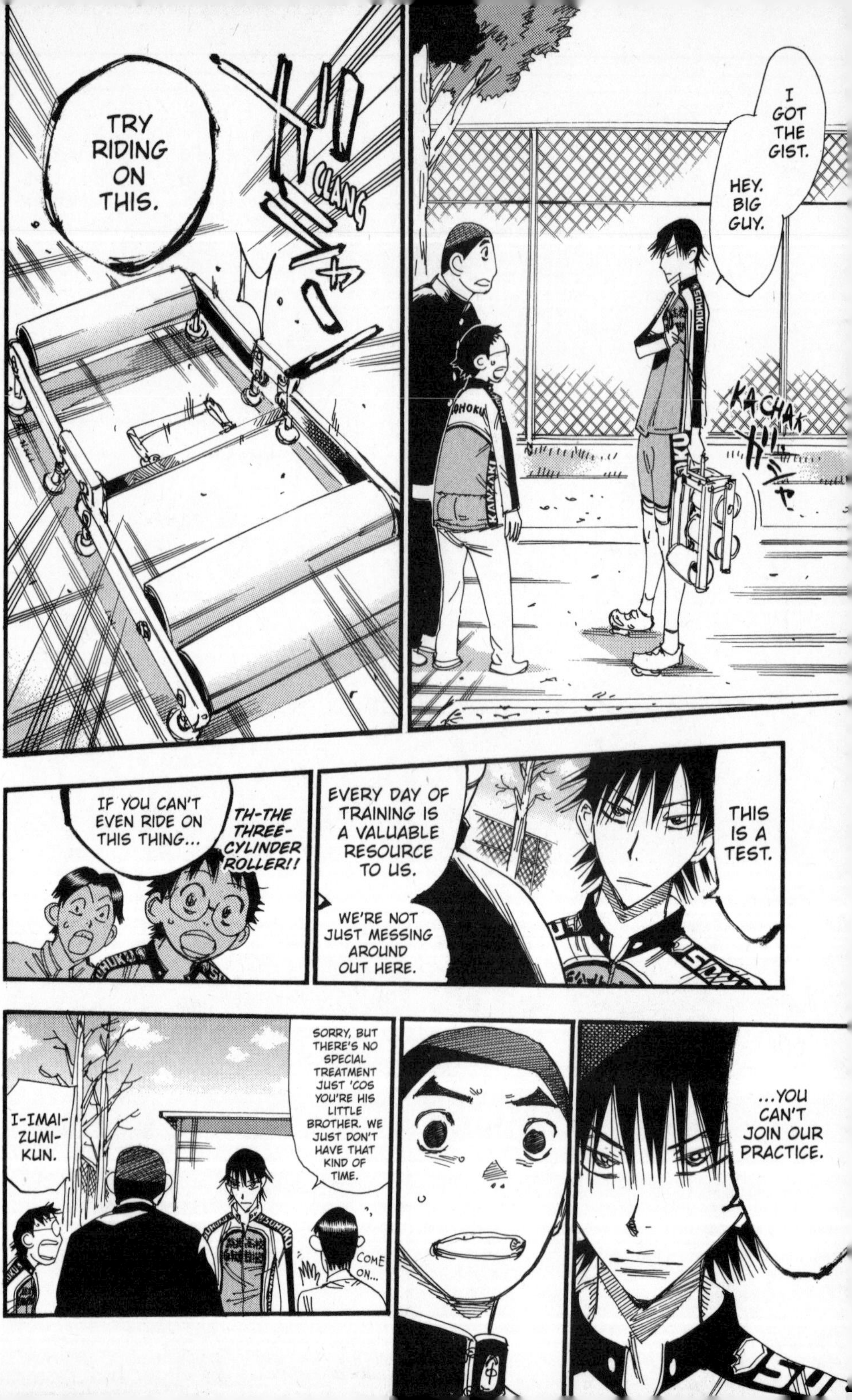
I GOT THE GIST.
HEY. BIG GUY.
KACHA
CLANG
TRY RIDING ON THIS.
THIS IS A TEST.
EVERY DAY OF TRAINING IS A VALUABLE RESOURCE TO US.
WE'RE NOT JUST MESSING AROUND OUT HERE.
IF YOU CAN'T EVEN RIDE ON THIS THING...
TH-THE THREE-CYLINDER ROLLER!!
...YOU CAN'T JOIN OUR PRACTICE.
SORRY, BUT THERE'S NO SPECIAL TREATMENT JUST 'COS YOU'RE HIS LITTLE BROTHER. WE JUST DON'T HAVE THAT KIND OF TIME.
I-IMAI-ZUMI-KUN.
COME ON...

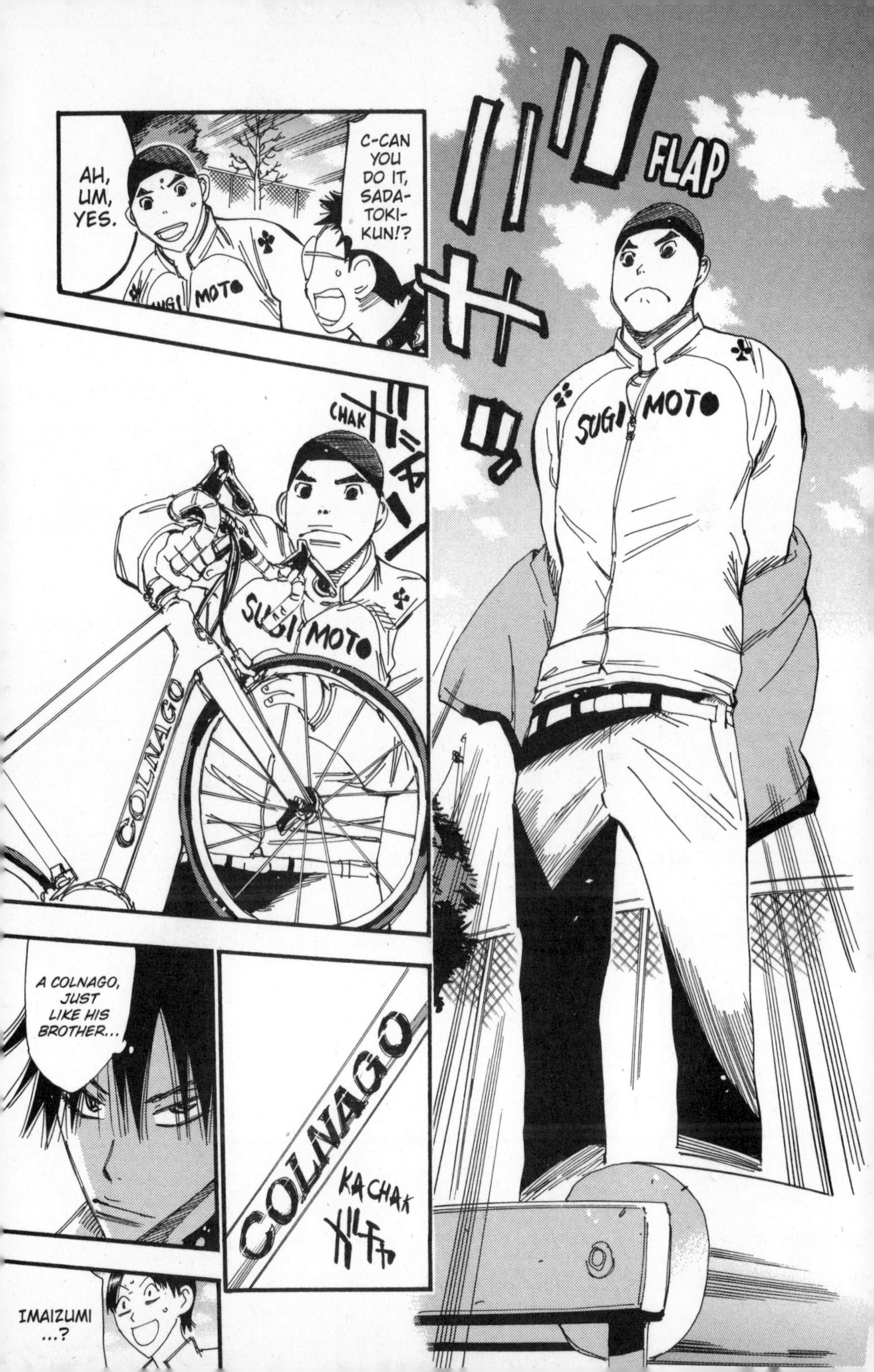
FLAP
SUGI MOTO
C-CAN YOU DO IT, SADA-TOKI-KUN!?
AH, UM, YES.
CHAK
COLNAGO
COLNAGO
KACHAK
A COLNAGO, JUST LIKE HIS BROTHER...
IMAIZUMI ...?

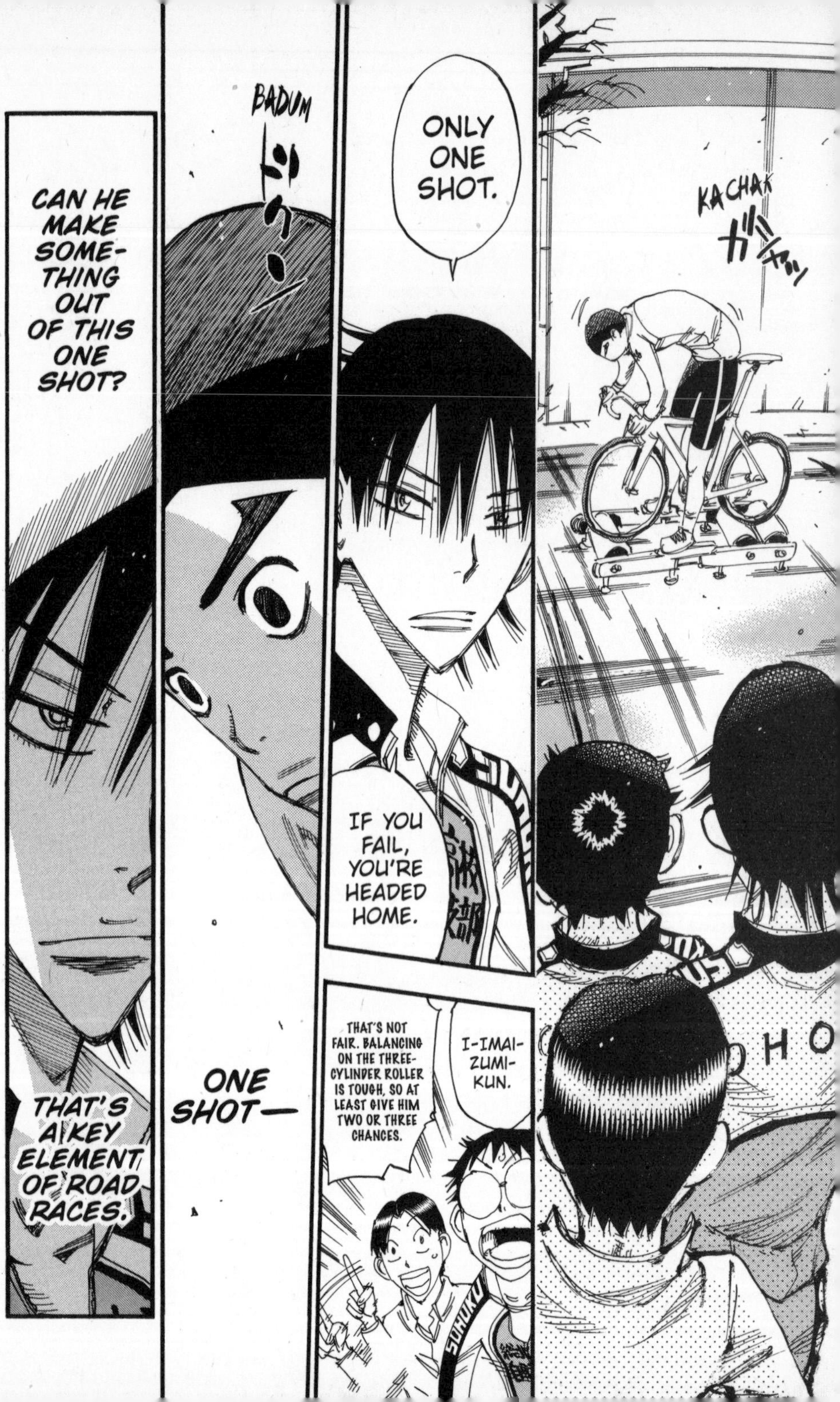
KACHAK
ONLY ONE SHOT.
IF YOU FAIL, YOU'RE HEADED HOME.
I-IMAIZUMI-KUN.
THAT'S NOT FAIR. BALANCING ON THE THREE-CYLINDER ROLLER IS TOUGH, SO AT LEAST GIVE HIM TWO OR THREE CHANCES.
BADUM
ONE SHOT—
CAN HE MAKE SOMETHING OUT OF THIS ONE SHOT?
THAT'S A KEY ELEMENT OF ROAD RACES.

BADUM

ONE SHOT.

HE EVEN SANG THE LOVE☆HIME ENDING THEME.

BUT SADA-TOKI'S NEVER TRIED THIS BEFORE.

BADUM

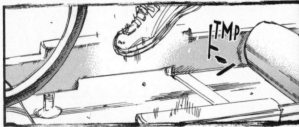

TMP

TMP

INHALE

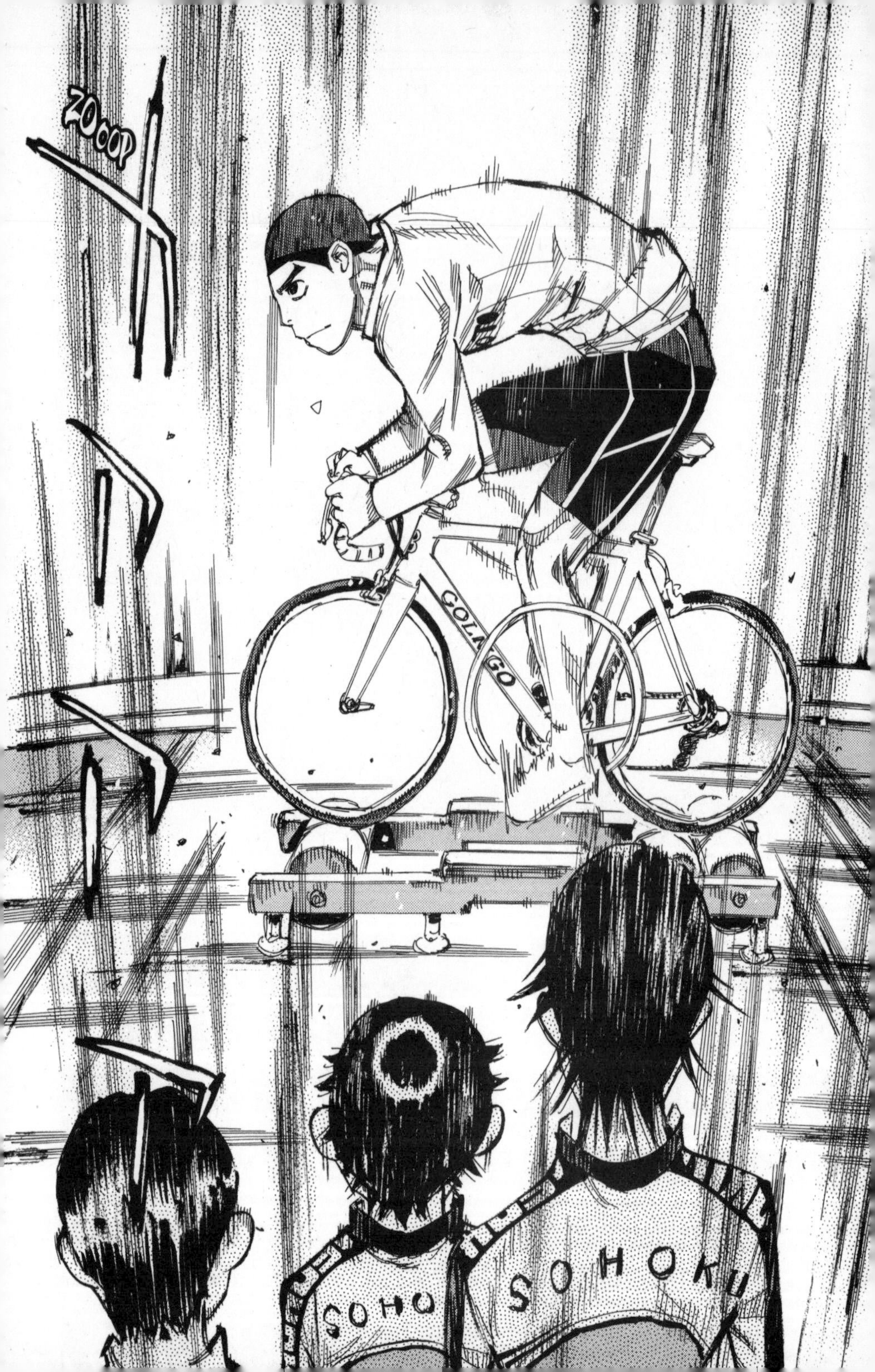
ZOOOP
SOHOKU
SOHO

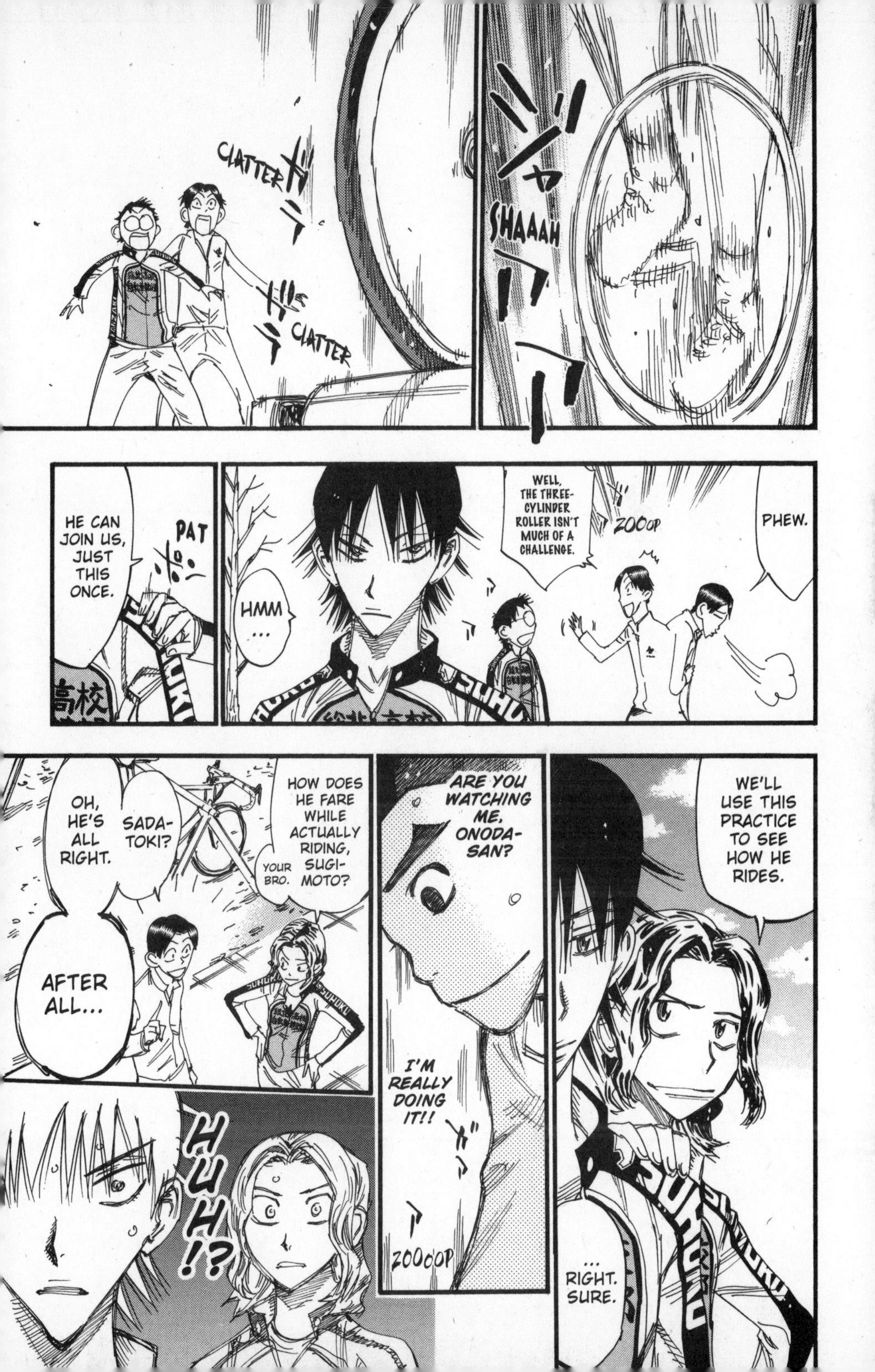
SHAAAH
CLATTER
CLATTER
PHEW.
ZOOOP
WELL, THE THREE-CYLINDER ROLLER ISN'T MUCH OF A CHALLENGE.
HMM...
HE CAN JOIN US, JUST THIS ONCE.
PAT
WE'LL USE THIS PRACTICE TO SEE HOW HE RIDES.
...RIGHT. SURE.
ARE YOU WATCHING ME, ONODA-SAN?
I'M REALLY DOING IT!!
ZOOOOOP
HOW DOES HE FARE WHILE ACTUALLY RIDING, SUGI-MOTO?
YOUR BRO.
SADA-TOKI?
OH, HE'S ALL RIGHT.
AFTER ALL...
HUH!?

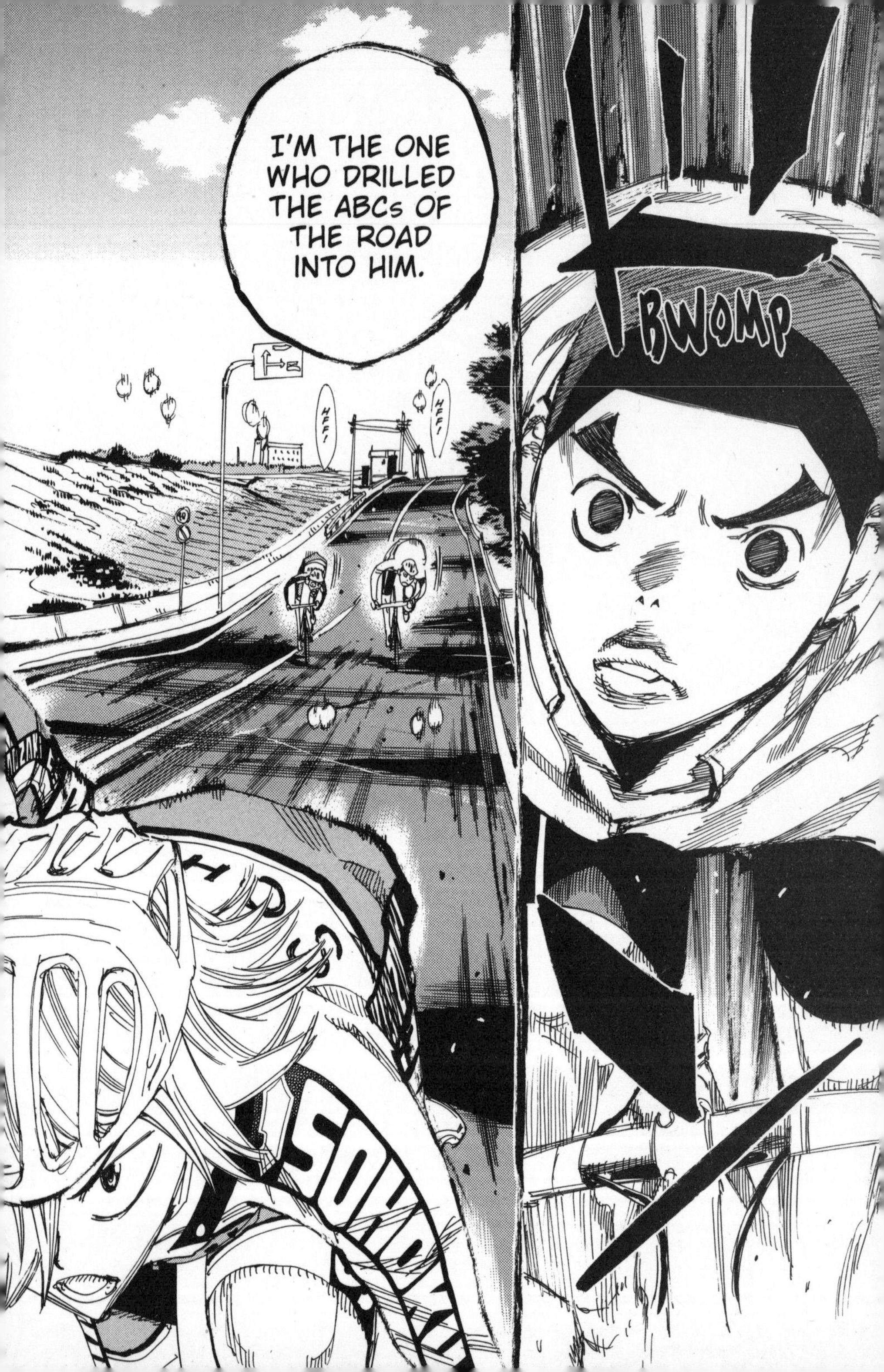
BWOMP
I'M THE ONE WHO DRILLED THE ABCs OF THE ROAD INTO HIM.
HFF!
HFF!

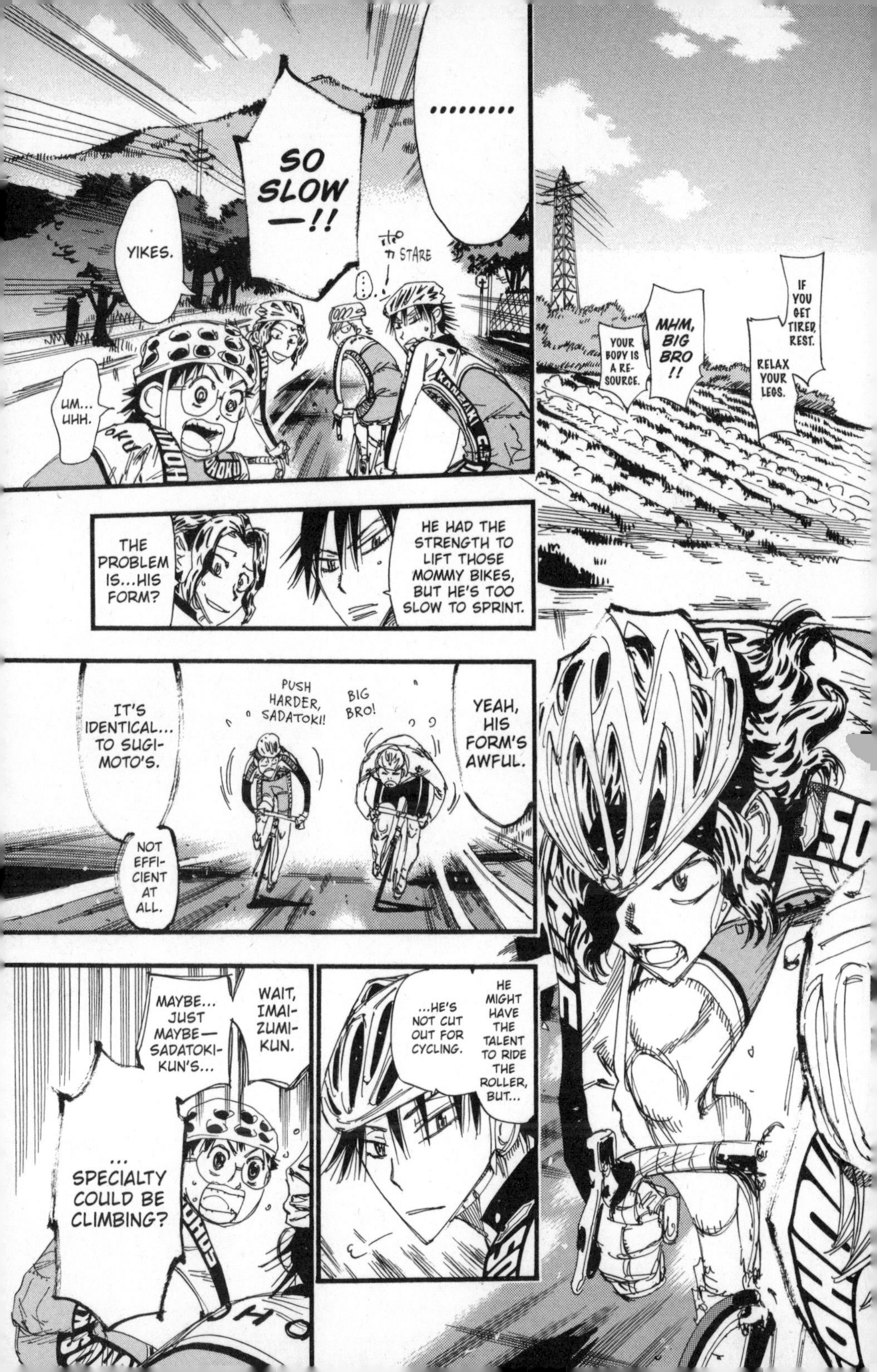
IF YOU GET TIRED, REST.
RELAX YOUR LEGS.
MHM, BIG BRO!!
YOUR BODY IS A RESOURCE.
....
SO SLOW—!!
STARE
...!
YIKES.
UM... UHH.
HE HAD THE STRENGTH TO LIFT THOSE MOMMY BIKES, BUT HE'S TOO SLOW TO SPRINT.
THE PROBLEM IS...HIS FORM?
YEAH, HIS FORM'S AWFUL.
BIG BRO!
PUSH HARDER, SADATOKI!
IT'S IDENTICAL... TO SUGIMOTO'S.
NOT EFFICIENT AT ALL.
HE MIGHT HAVE THE TALENT TO RIDE THE ROLLER, BUT...
...HE'S NOT CUT OUT FOR CYCLING.
WAIT, IMAIZUMI-KUN.
MAYBE... JUST MAYBE— SADATOKI-KUN'S...
...SPECIALTY COULD BE CLIMBING?

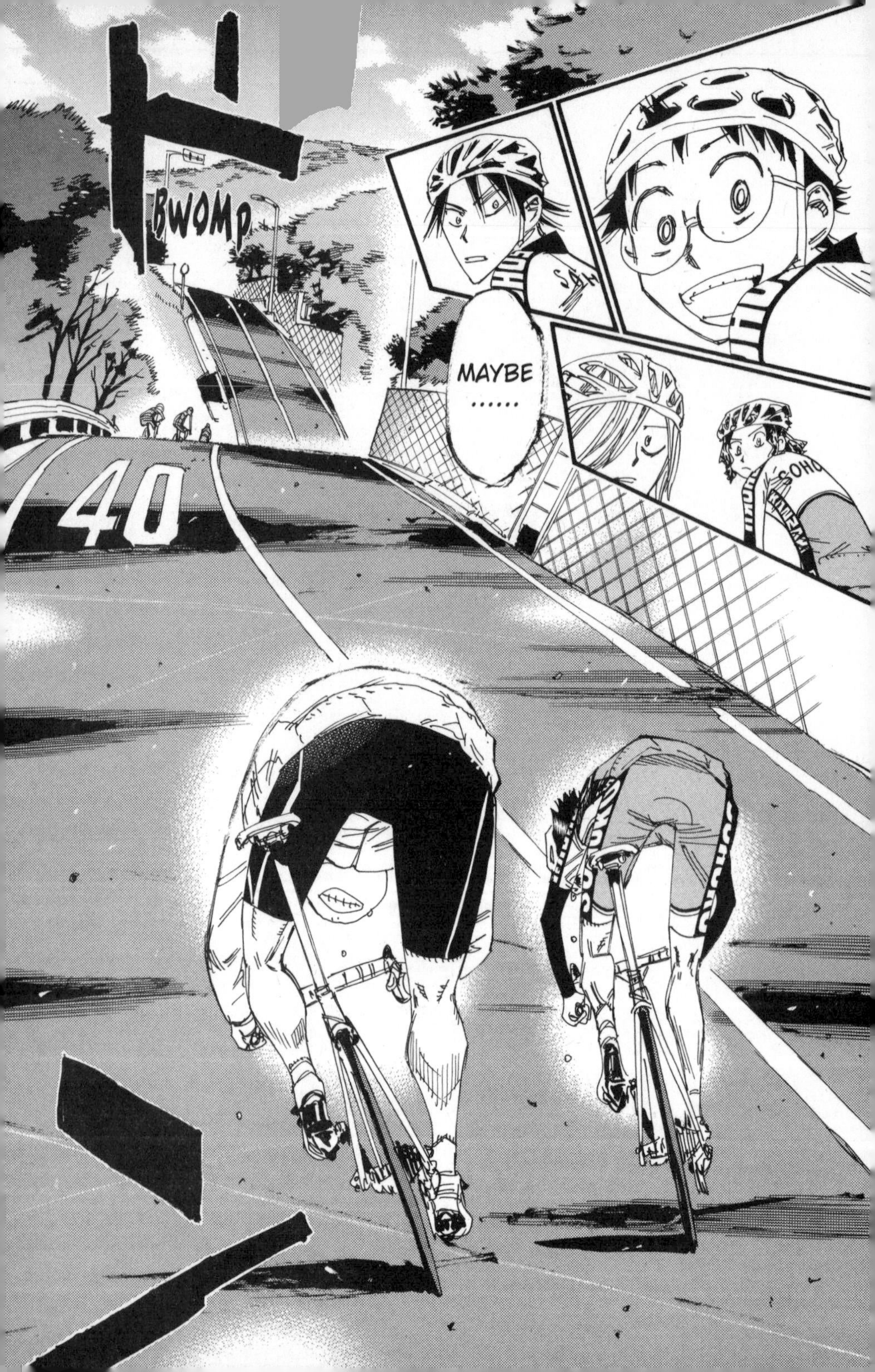
BWOMP
MAYBE ......

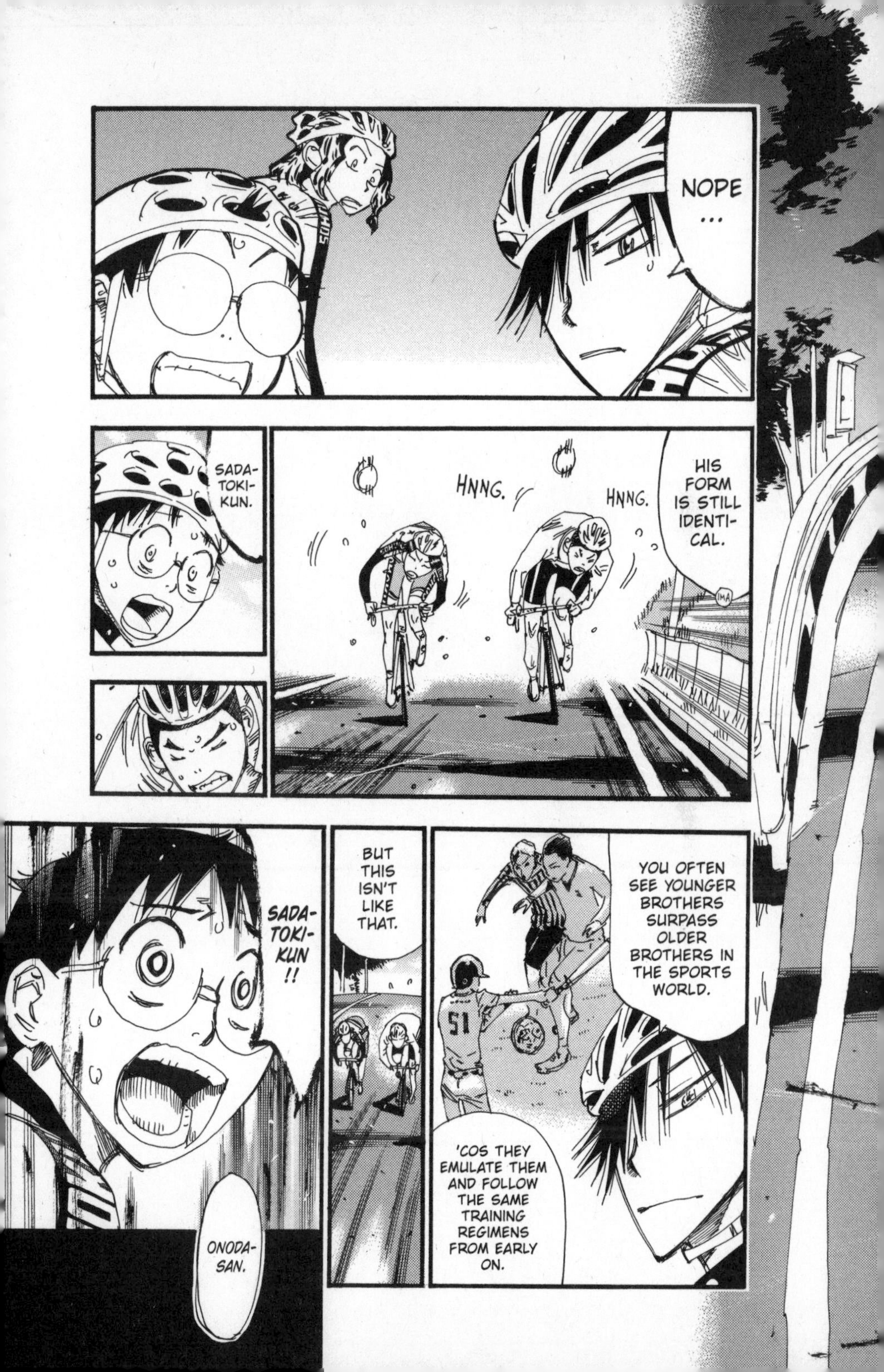
NOPE ...
HIS FORM IS STILL IDENTI-CAL.
HNNG.
HNNG.
SADA-TOKI-KUN.
YOU OFTEN SEE YOUNGER BROTHERS SURPASS OLDER BROTHERS IN THE SPORTS WORLD.
'COS THEY EMULATE THEM AND FOLLOW THE SAME TRAINING REGIMENS FROM EARLY ON.
BUT THIS ISN'T LIKE THAT.
SADA-TOKI-KUN !!
ONODA-SAN.

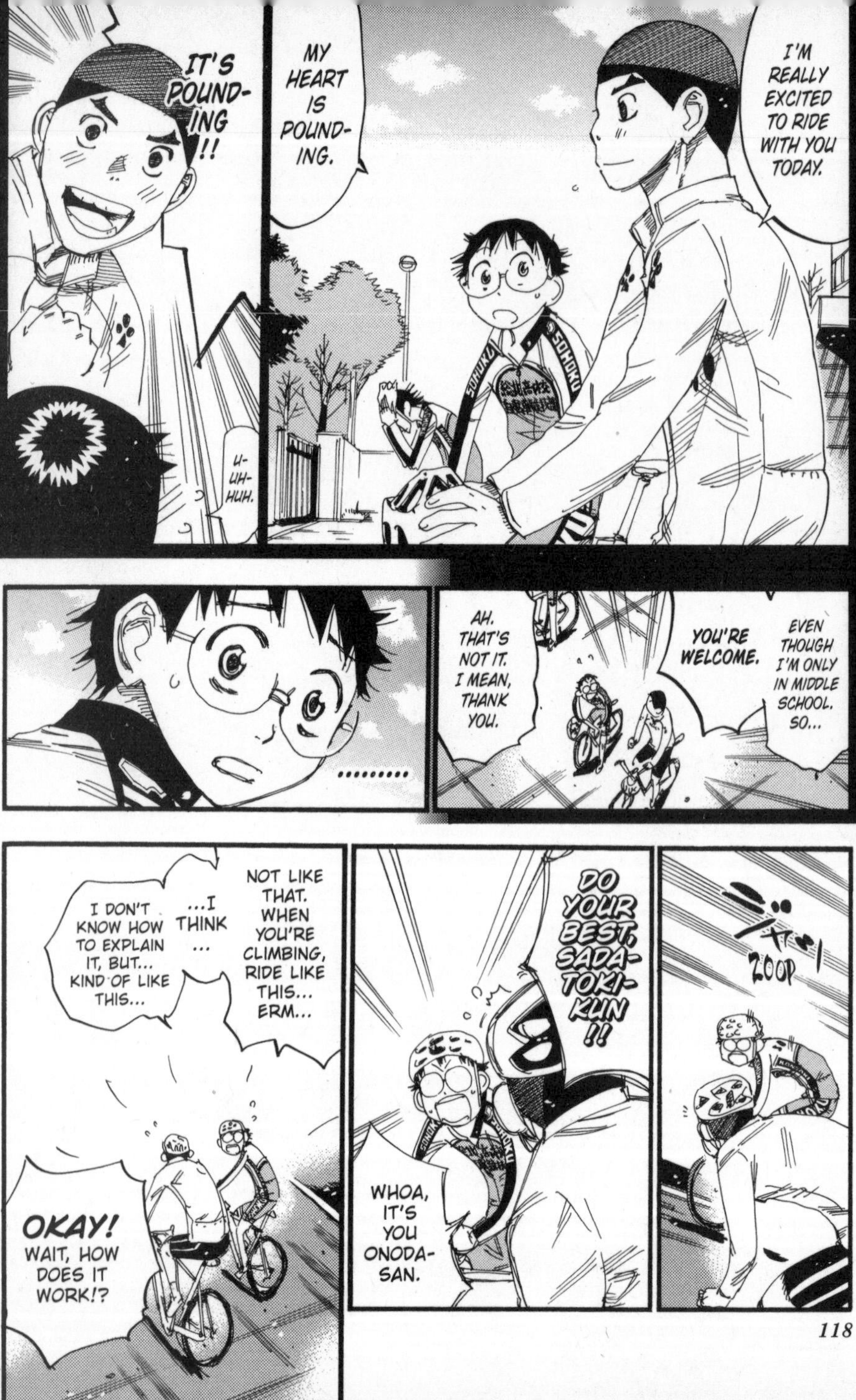
I'M REALLY EXCITED TO RIDE WITH YOU TODAY.
MY HEART IS POUNDING.
IT'S POUNDING!!
U-UH-HUH.
EVEN THOUGH I'M ONLY IN MIDDLE SCHOOL, SO...
YOU'RE WELCOME.
AH. THAT'S NOT IT. I MEAN, THANK YOU.
....
ZOOP
DO YOUR BEST, SADATOKI-KUN!!
WHOA, IT'S YOU ONODA-SAN.
NOT LIKE THAT. WHEN YOU'RE CLIMBING, RIDE LIKE THIS... ERM...
...I THINK...
I DON'T KNOW HOW TO EXPLAIN IT, BUT... KIND OF LIKE THIS...
OKAY! WAIT, HOW DOES IT WORK!?

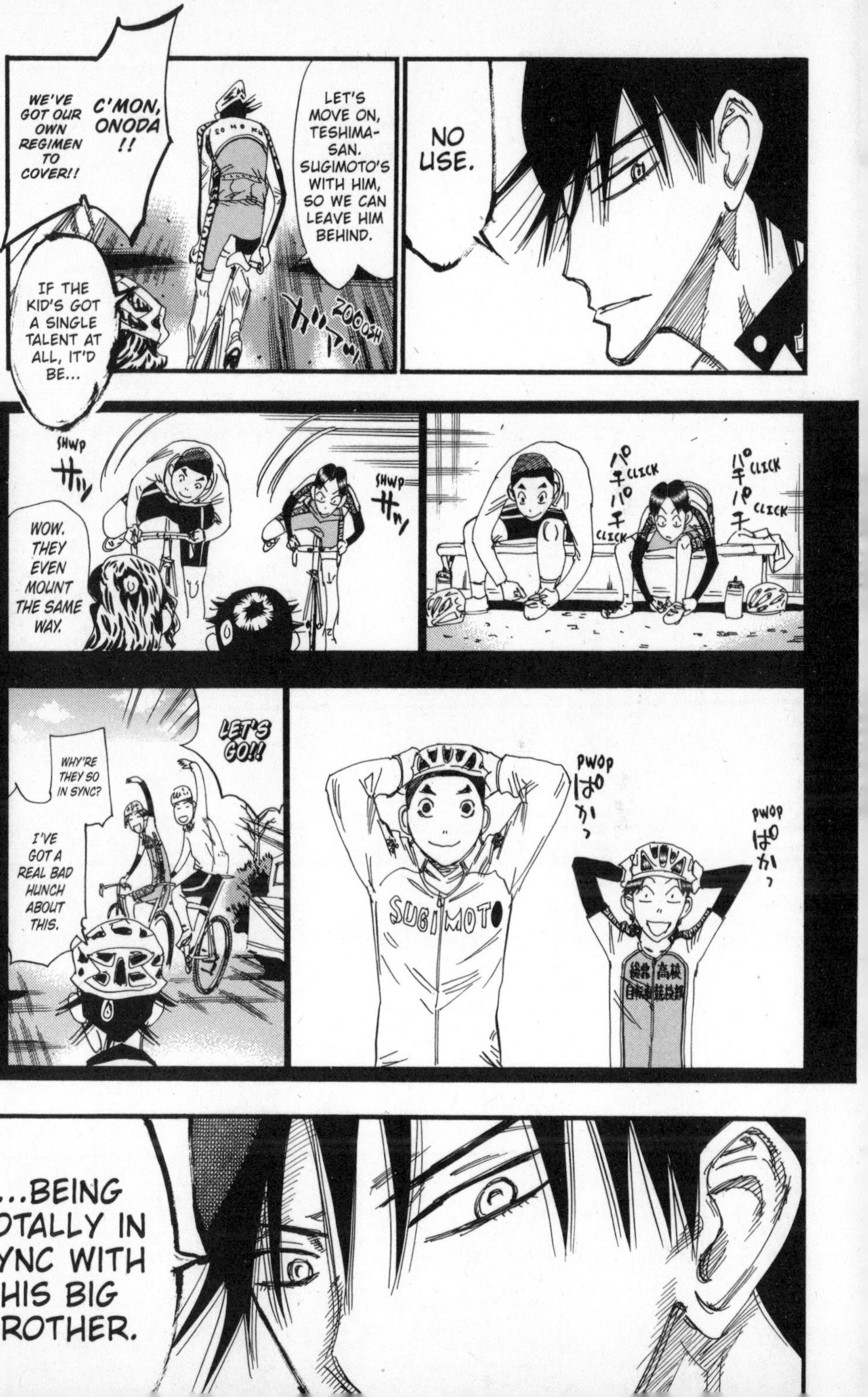
NO USE.
LET'S MOVE ON, TESHIMA-SAN. SUGIMOTO'S WITH HIM, SO WE CAN LEAVE HIM BEHIND.
C'MON, ONODA!!
WE'VE GOT OUR OWN REGIMEN TO COVER!!
ZOOOSH
IF THE KID'S GOT A SINGLE TALENT AT ALL, IT'D BE...
CLICK
CLICK
CLICK
SHWP
SHWP
WOW. THEY EVEN MOUNT THE SAME WAY.
PWOP
PWOP
LET'S GO!!
WHY'RE THEY SO IN SYNC?
I'VE GOT A REAL BAD HUNCH ABOUT THIS.
...BEING TOTALLY IN SYNC WITH HIS BIG BROTHER.

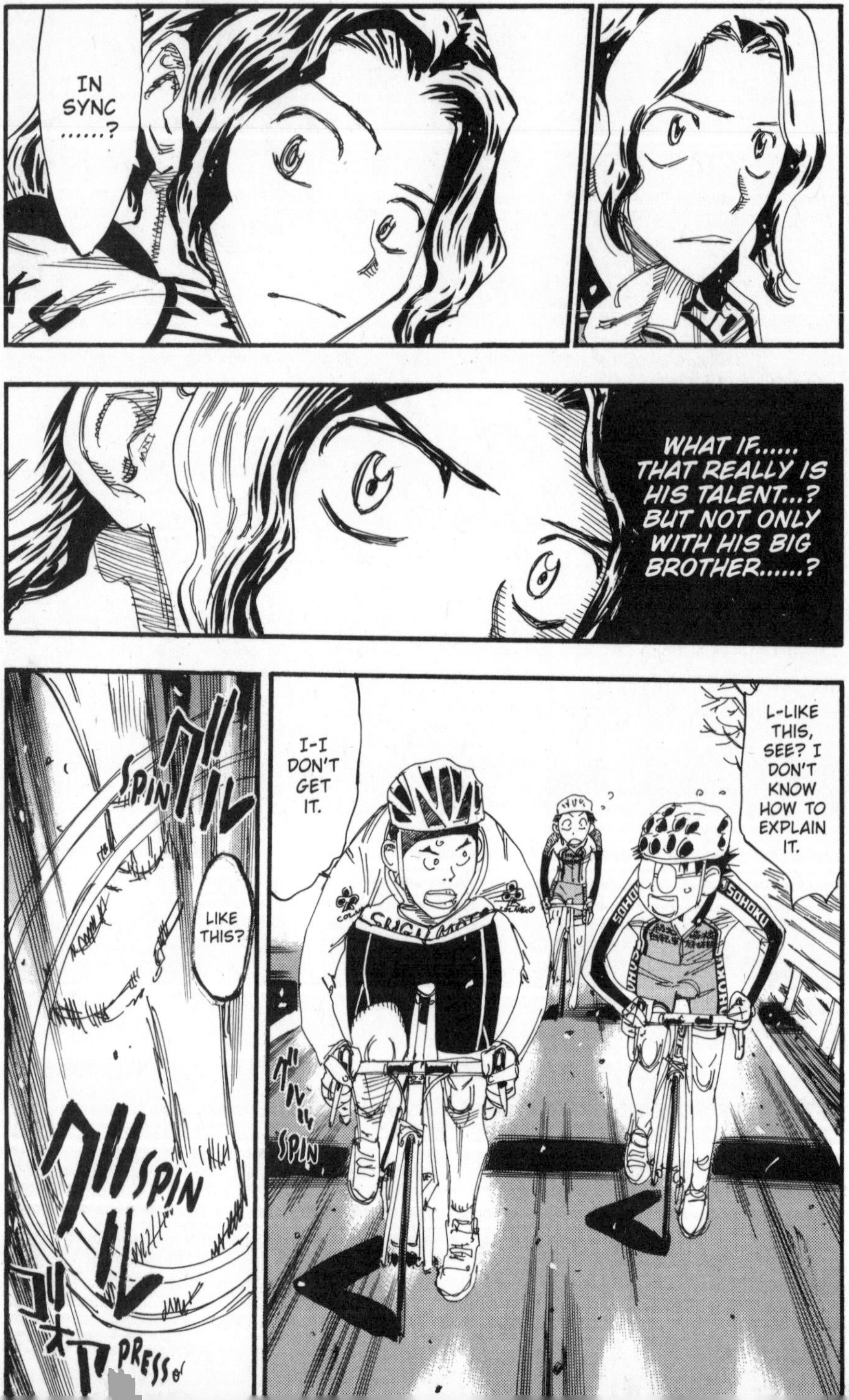
IN SYNC ......?
WHAT IF...... THAT REALLY IS HIS TALENT...? BUT NOT ONLY WITH HIS BIG BROTHER......?
L-LIKE THIS, SEE? I DON'T KNOW HOW TO EXPLAIN IT.
I-I DON'T GET IT.
SPIN
SPIN
LIKE THIS?
SPIN
PRESS

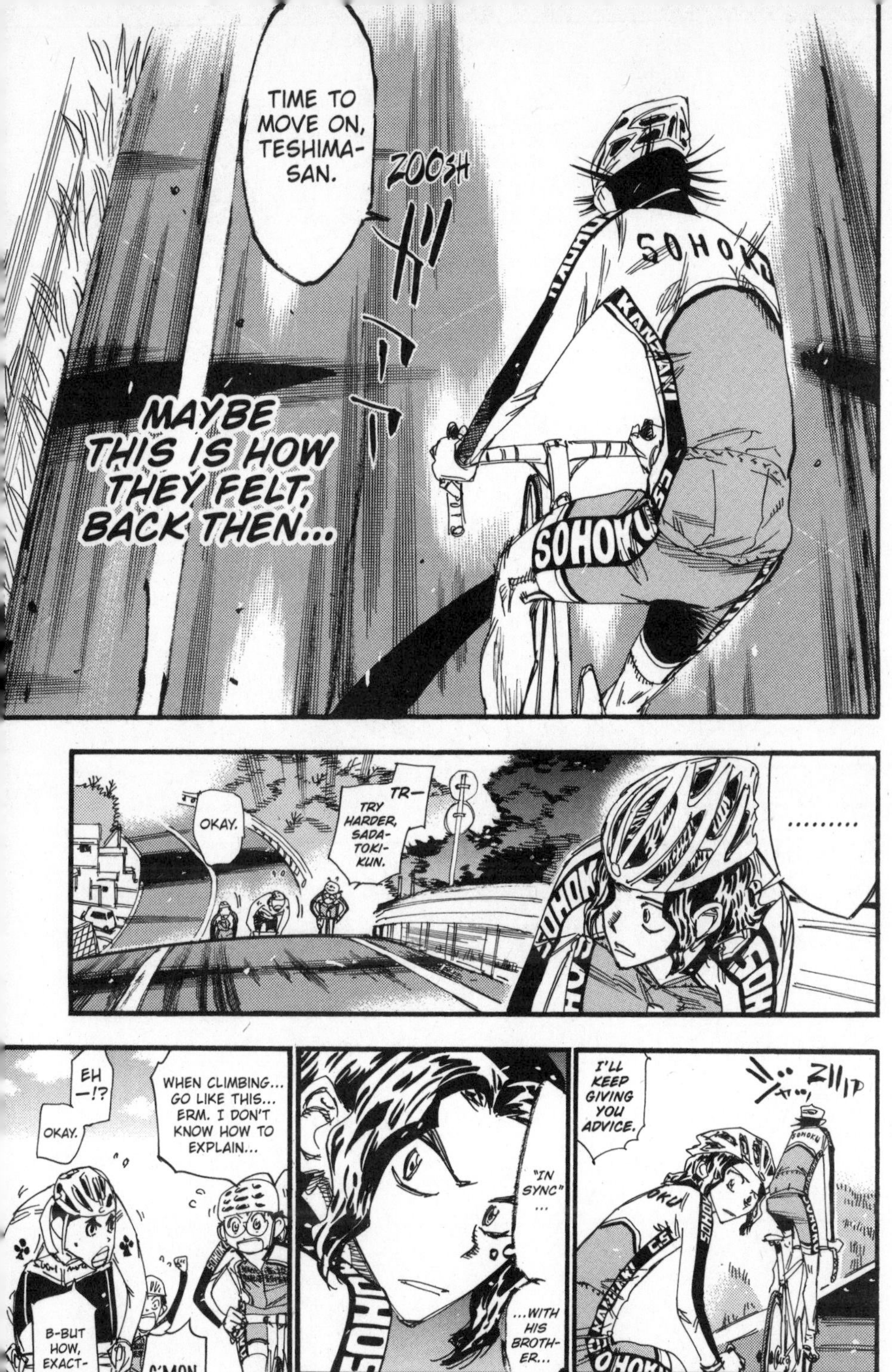
TIME TO MOVE ON, TESHIMA-SAN.
ZOOSH
MAYBE THIS IS HOW THEY FELT, BACK THEN...
....
TR— TRY HARDER, SADA-TOKI-KUN.
OKAY.
ZIIIP
I'LL KEEP GIVING YOU ADVICE.
"IN SYNC"...
...WITH HIS BROTHER...
WHEN CLIMBING... GO LIKE THIS... ERM. I DON'T KNOW HOW TO EXPLAIN...
EH —!?
OKAY.
C'MON, SADA-TOKI!!
B-BUT HOW, EXACT-LY?

RIDE.249 THREE MINUTES

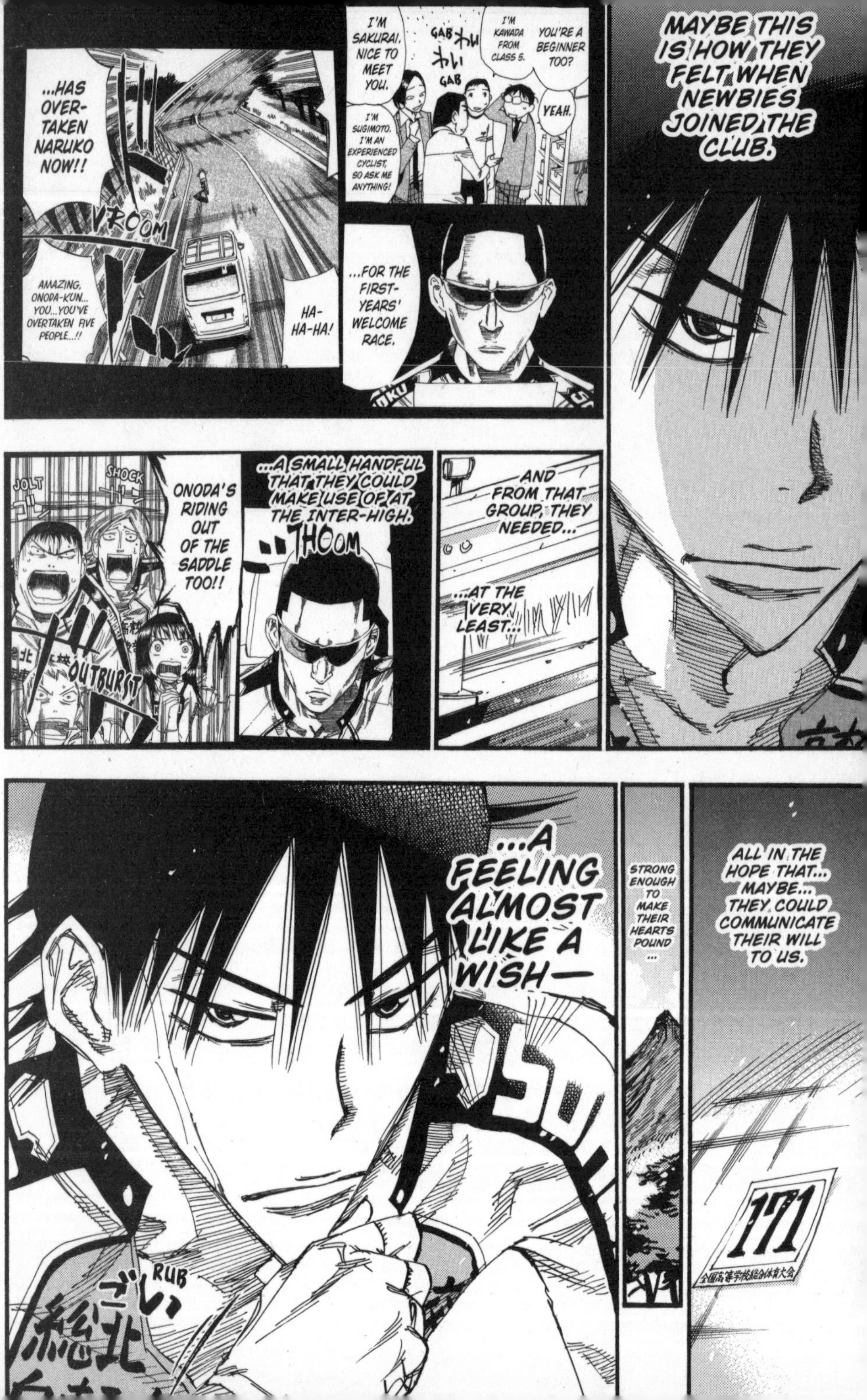

MAYBE THIS IS HOW THEY FELT WHEN NEWBIES JOINED THE CLUB.
YOU'RE A BEGINNER TOO?
I'M KAWADA FROM CLASS 5.
YEAH.
GAB GAB
I'M SAKURAI. NICE TO MEET YOU.
I'M SUGIMOTO. I'M AN EXPERIENCED CYCLIST, SO ASK ME ANYTHING!
...FOR THE FIRST-YEARS' WELCOME RACE.
...HAS OVER-TAKEN NARUKO NOW!!
VROOM
HA-HA-HA!
AMAZING, ONODA-KUN... YOU...YOU'VE OVERTAKEN FIVE PEOPLE...!!
AND FROM THAT GROUP, THEY NEEDED...
...AT THE VERY LEAST...
...A SMALL HANDFUL THAT THEY COULD MAKE USE OF AT THE INTER-HIGH.
THOOM
ONODA'S RIDING OUT OF THE SADDLE TOO!!
SHOCK
JOLT
OUTBURST
ALL IN THE HOPE THAT... MAYBE... THEY COULD COMMUNICATE THEIR WILL TO US.
STRONG ENOUGH TO MAKE THEIR HEARTS POUND...
...A FEELING ALMOST LIKE A WISH—
RUB
171

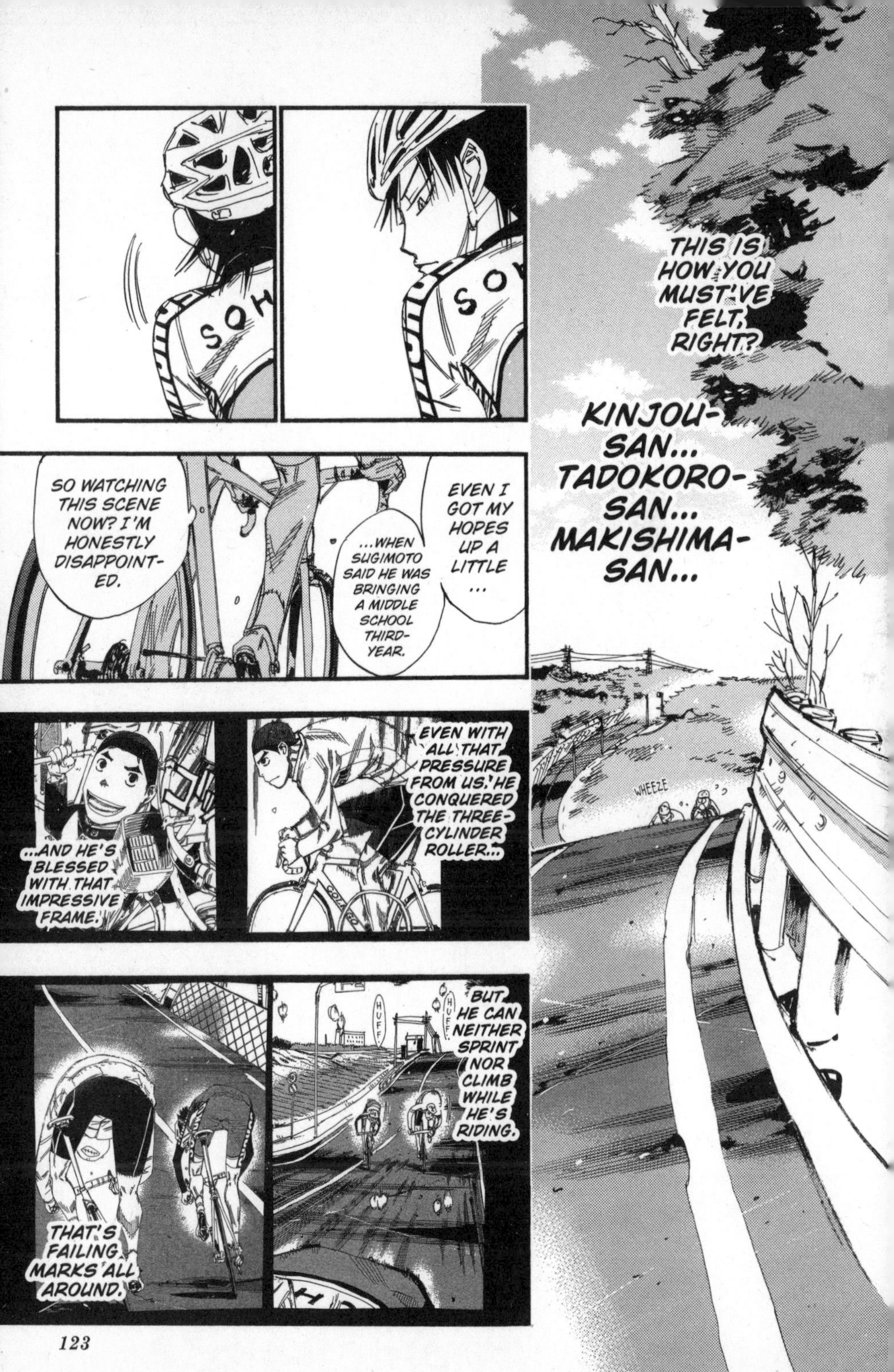
THIS IS HOW YOU MUST'VE FELT, RIGHT?
KINJOU-SAN... TADOKORO-SAN... MAKISHIMA-SAN...
WHEEZE
EVEN I GOT MY HOPES UP A LITTLE ...
...WHEN SUGIMOTO SAID HE WAS BRINGING A MIDDLE SCHOOL THIRD-YEAR.
SO WATCHING THIS SCENE NOW? I'M HONESTLY DISAPPOINT-ED.
EVEN WITH ALL THAT PRESSURE FROM US, HE CONQUERED THE THREE-CYLINDER ROLLER...
...AND HE'S BLESSED WITH THAT IMPRESSIVE FRAME.
HUFF
HUFF
BUT HE CAN NEITHER SPRINT NOR CLIMB WHILE HE'S RIDING.
THAT'S FAILING MARKS ALL AROUND.

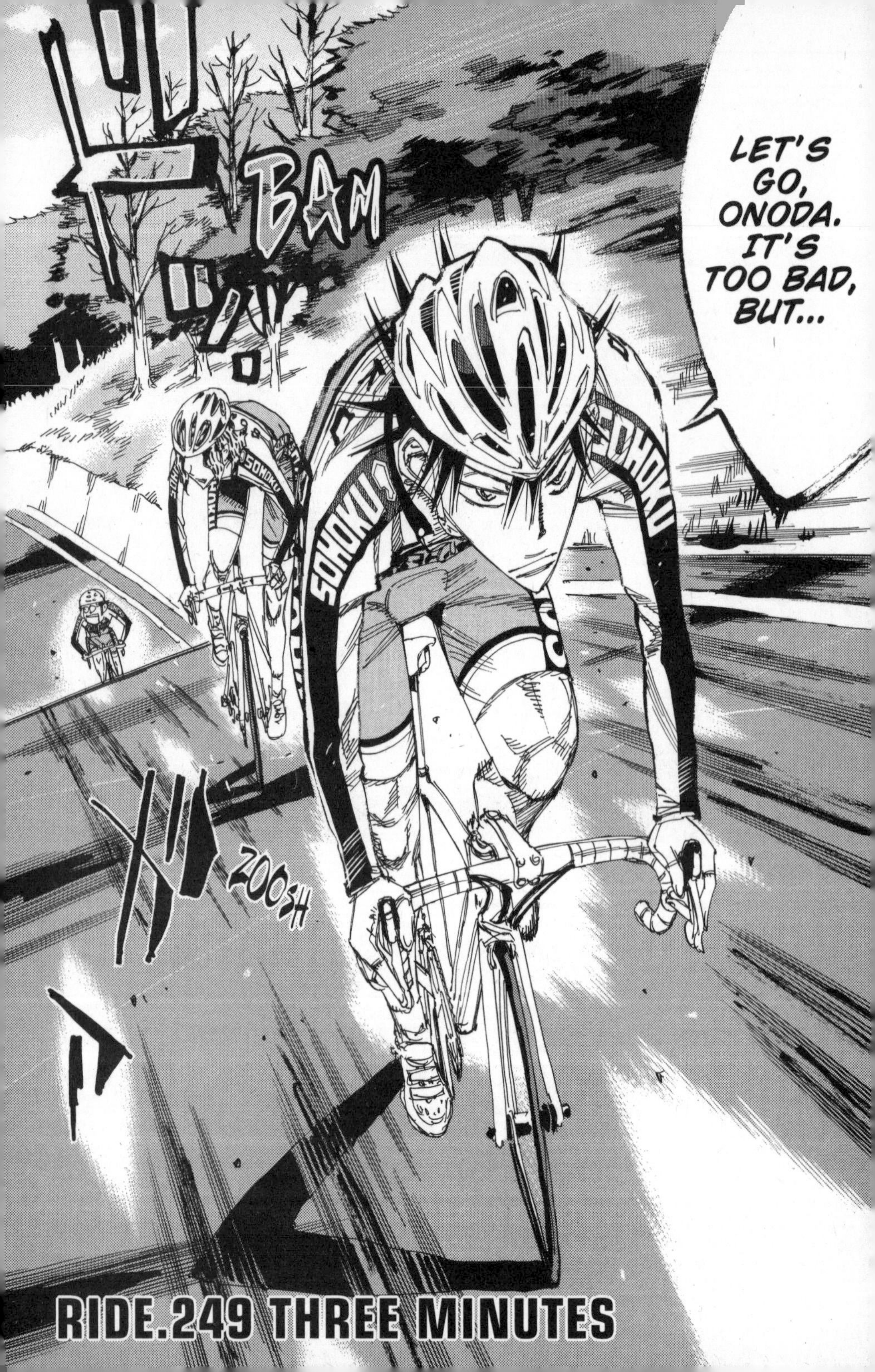
BAM
LET'S GO, ONODA. IT'S TOO BAD, BUT...
ZOOSH

RIDE.249 THREE MINUTES

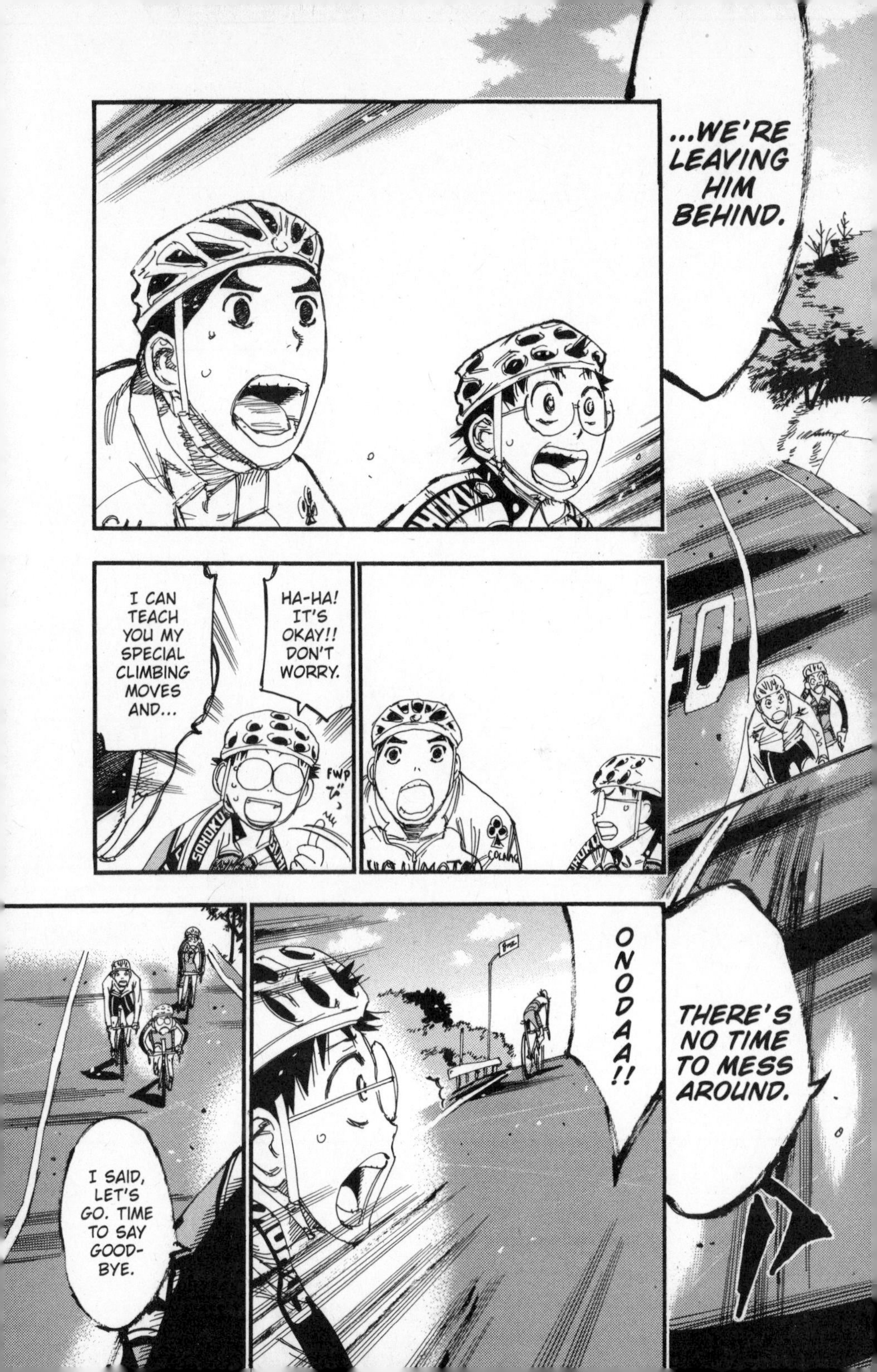

...WE'RE LEAVING HIM BEHIND.
HA-HA! IT'S OKAY!! DON'T WORRY.
I CAN TEACH YOU MY SPECIAL CLIMBING MOVES AND...
FWP
THERE'S NO TIME TO MESS AROUND.
ONODAA!!
I SAID, LET'S GO. TIME TO SAY GOOD-BYE.

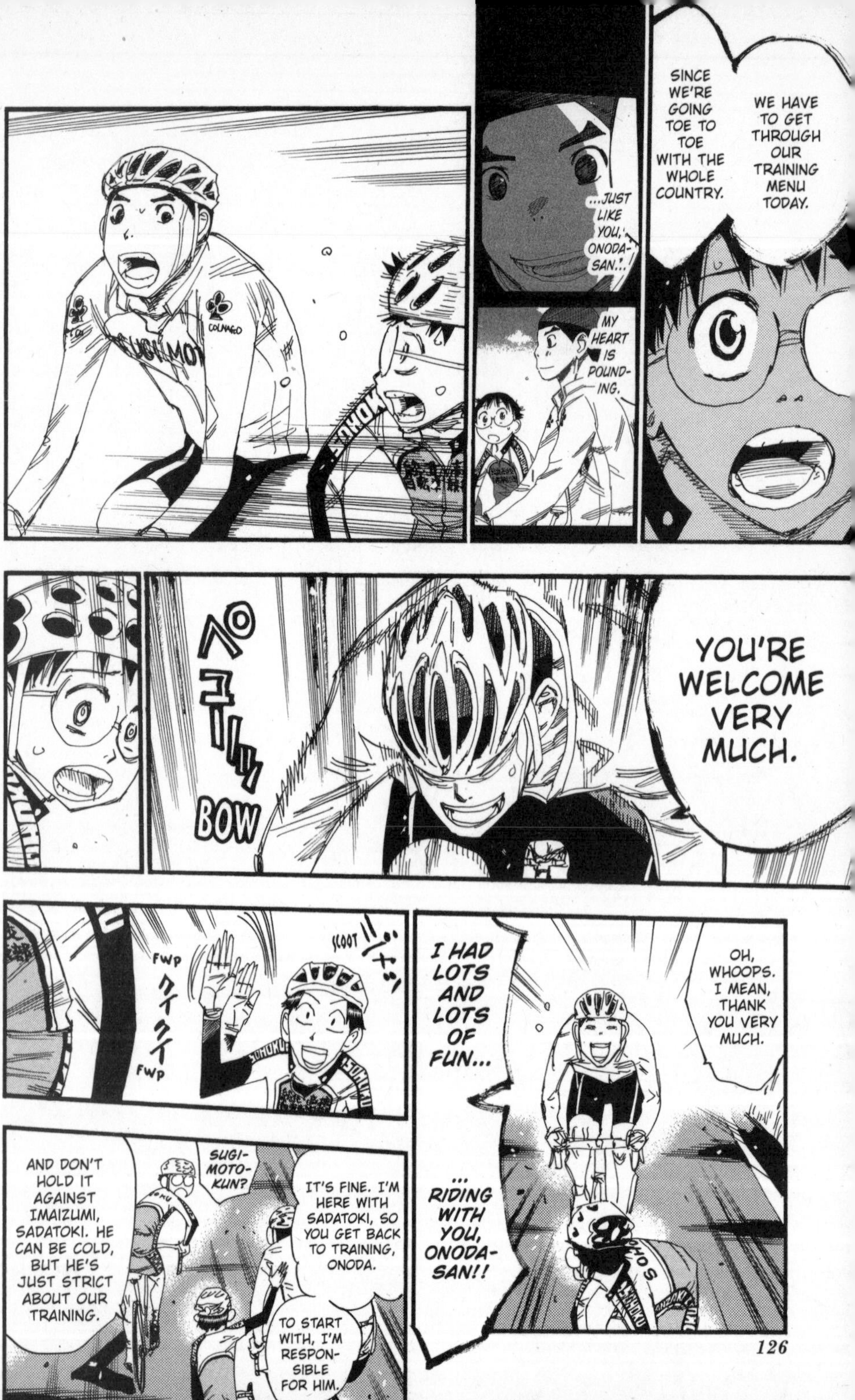
WE HAVE TO GET THROUGH OUR TRAINING MENU TODAY.
SINCE WE'RE GOING TOE TO TOE WITH THE WHOLE COUNTRY.
...JUST LIKE YOU, ONODA-SAN...
MY HEART IS POUNDING.
YOU'RE WELCOME VERY MUCH.
ペコーッ
BOW
OH, WHOOPS. I MEAN, THANK YOU VERY MUCH.
I HAD LOTS AND LOTS OF FUN...
...RIDING WITH YOU, ONODA-SAN!!
SCOOT
ジャッ
FWP
クイクイ
FWP
SUGIMOTO-KUN?
IT'S FINE. I'M HERE WITH SADATOKI, SO YOU GET BACK TO TRAINING, ONODA.
TO START WITH, I'M RESPONSIBLE FOR HIM.
AND DON'T HOLD IT AGAINST IMAIZUMI, SADATOKI. HE CAN BE COLD, BUT HE'S JUST STRICT ABOUT OUR TRAINING.

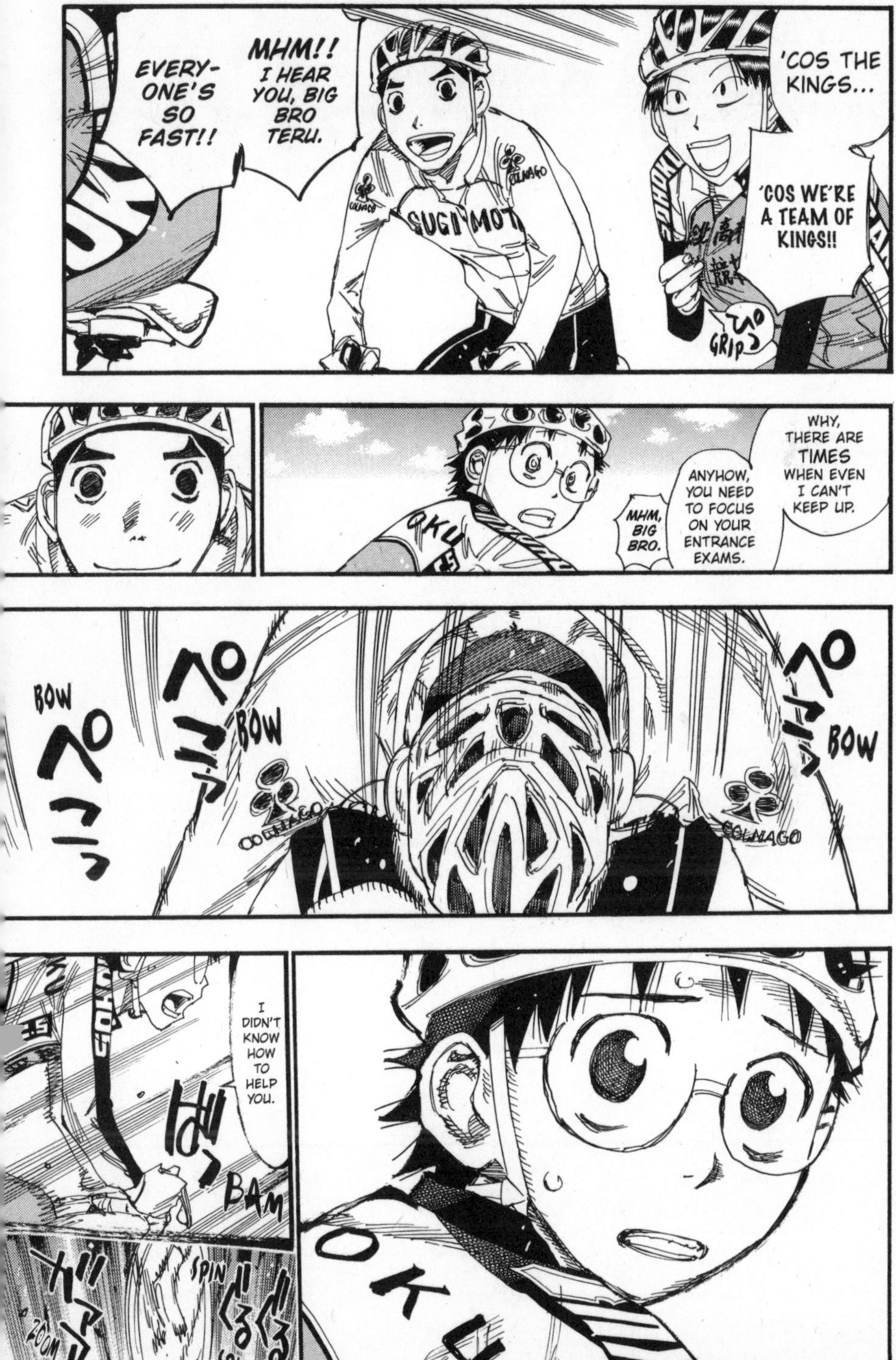
'COS THE KINGS...
'COS WE'RE A TEAM OF KINGS!!
GRIP
MHM!! I HEAR YOU, BIG BRO TERU.
EVERY-ONE'S SO FAST!!
WHY, THERE ARE TIMES WHEN EVEN I CAN'T KEEP UP.
ANYHOW, YOU NEED TO FOCUS ON YOUR ENTRANCE EXAMS.
MHM, BIG BRO.
BOW
BOW
BOW
I DIDN'T KNOW HOW TO HELP YOU.
BAM
SPIN
SPIN
ZOOM

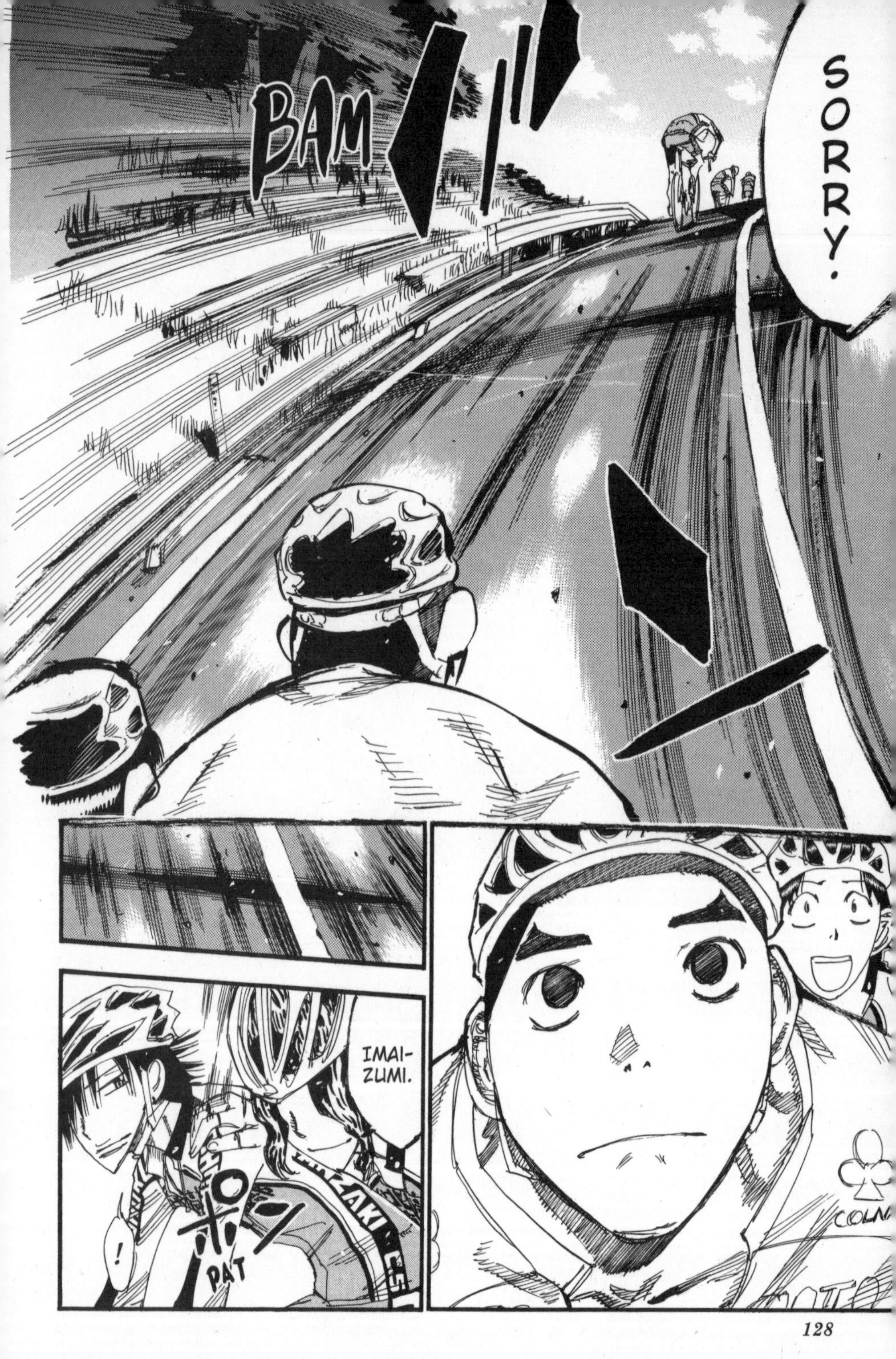
SORRY.
BAM
IMAI-ZUMI.
PAT
!

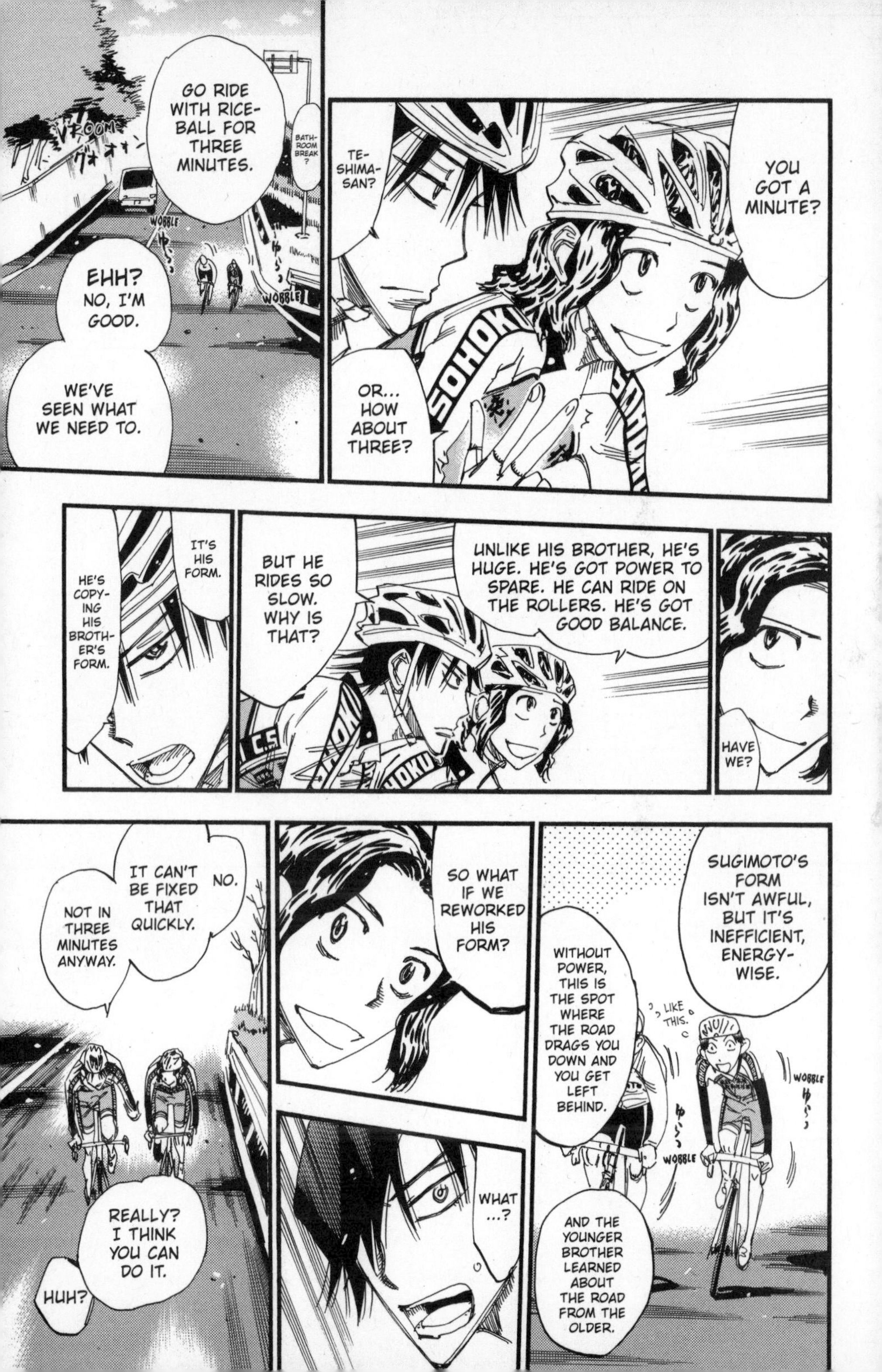
YOU GOT A MINUTE?
TE-SHIMA-SAN?
OR... HOW ABOUT THREE?
GO RIDE WITH RICE-BALL FOR THREE MINUTES.
BATH-ROOM BREAK?
VROOM
グオオン
WOBBLE
WOBBLE
EHH? NO, I'M GOOD.
WE'VE SEEN WHAT WE NEED TO.
HAVE WE?
UNLIKE HIS BROTHER, HE'S HUGE. HE'S GOT POWER TO SPARE. HE CAN RIDE ON THE ROLLERS. HE'S GOT GOOD BALANCE.
BUT HE RIDES SO SLOW. WHY IS THAT?
IT'S HIS FORM.
HE'S COPYING HIS BROTHER'S FORM.
SUGIMOTO'S FORM ISN'T AWFUL, BUT IT'S INEFFICIENT, ENERGY-WISE.
LIKE THIS.
WOBBLE
WOBBLE
WITHOUT POWER, THIS IS THE SPOT WHERE THE ROAD DRAGS YOU DOWN AND YOU GET LEFT BEHIND.
AND THE YOUNGER BROTHER LEARNED ABOUT THE ROAD FROM THE OLDER.
SO WHAT IF WE REWORKED HIS FORM?
WHAT ...?
NO.
IT CAN'T BE FIXED THAT QUICKLY.
NOT IN THREE MINUTES ANYWAY.
REALLY? I THINK YOU CAN DO IT.
HUH?

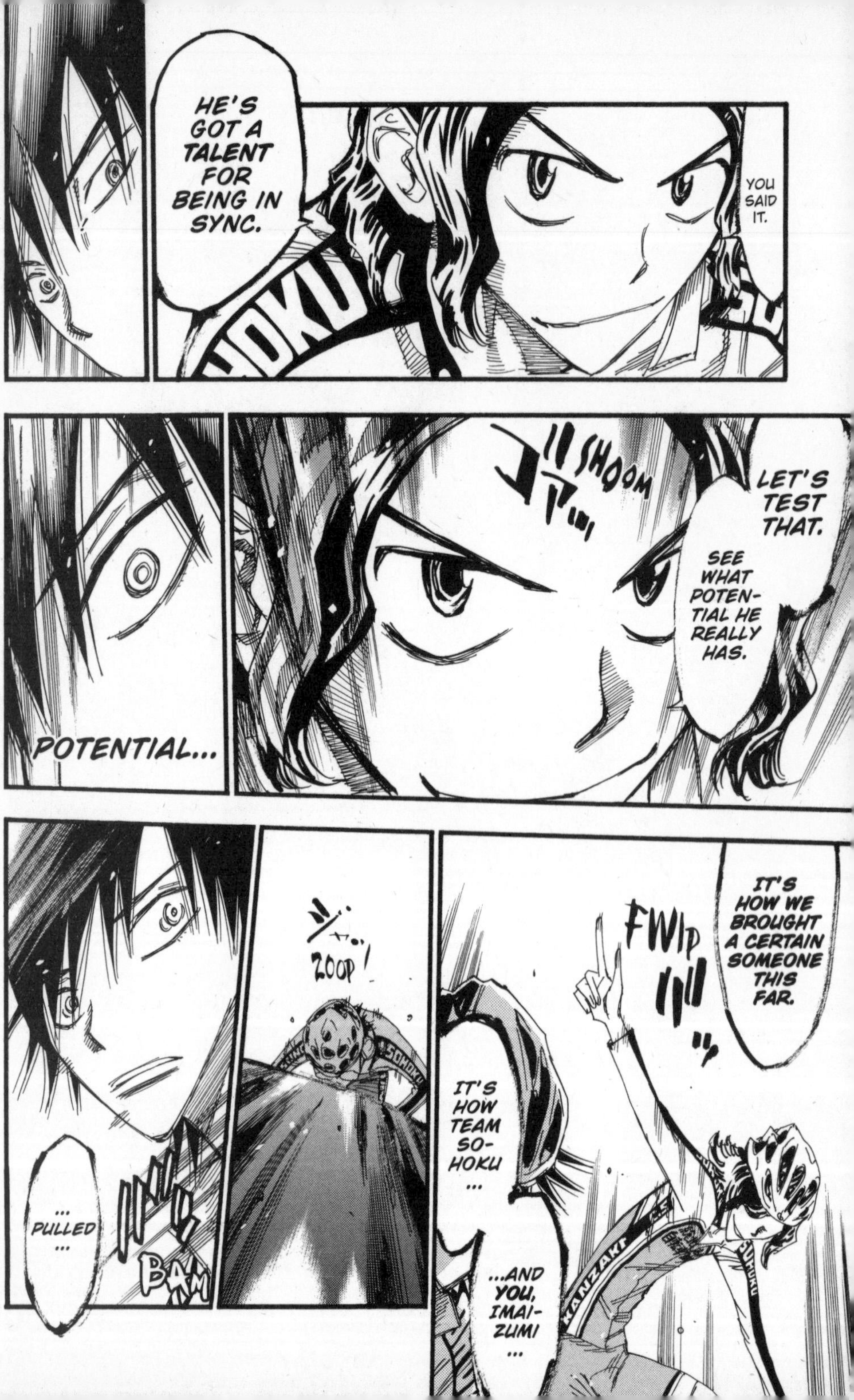
HE'S GOT A TALENT FOR BEING IN SYNC.
YOU SAID IT.
SHOOM
LET'S TEST THAT.
SEE WHAT POTENTIAL HE REALLY HAS.
POTENTIAL...
IT'S HOW WE BROUGHT A CERTAIN SOMEONE THIS FAR.
FWIP
IT'S HOW TEAM SO-HOKU...
...AND YOU, IMAIZUMI...
ZOOP
...PULLED...
BAM

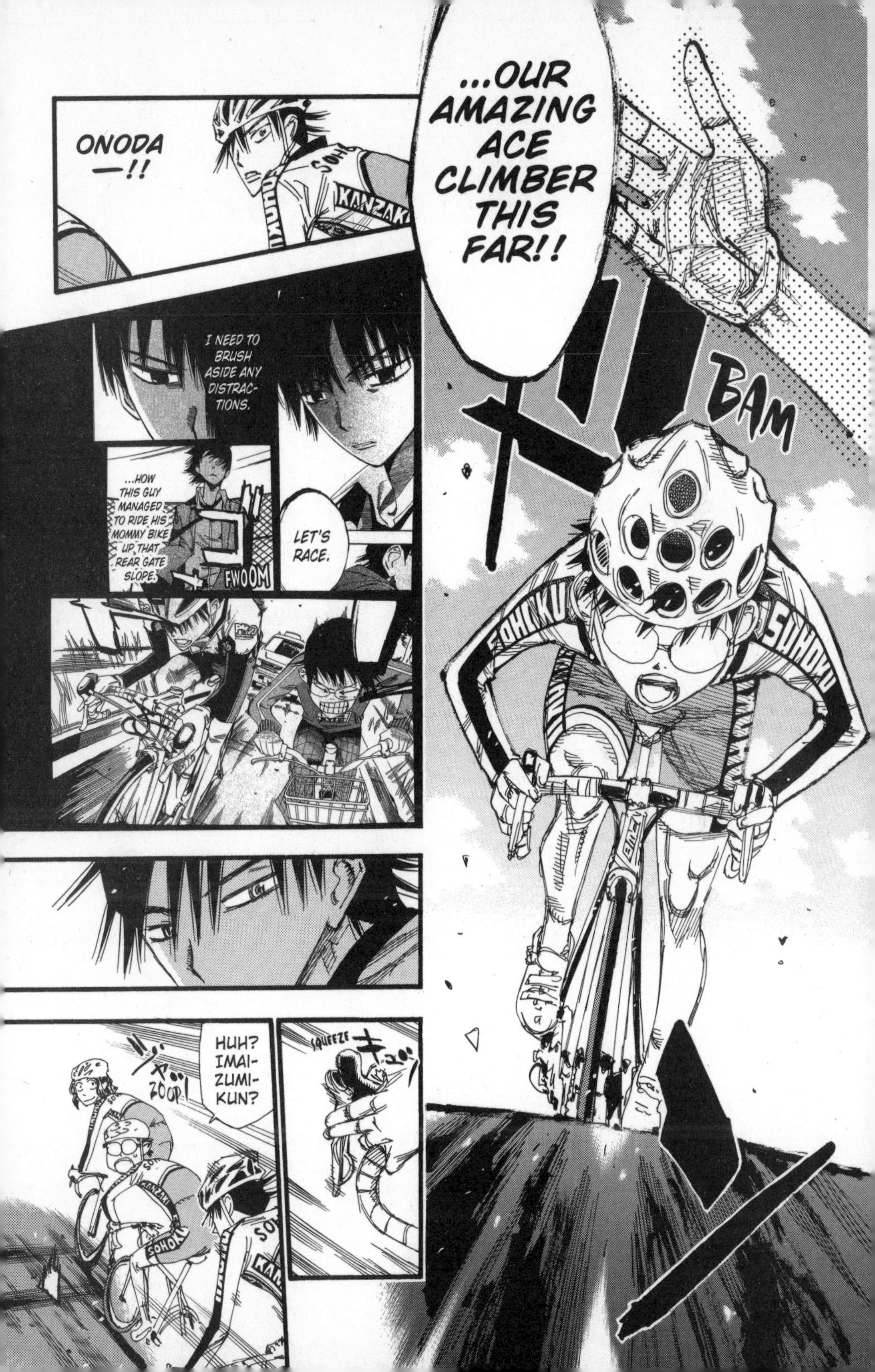
...OUR AMAZING ACE CLIMBER THIS FAR!!
BAM
ONODA—!!
LET'S RACE.
I NEED TO BRUSH ASIDE ANY DISTRACTIONS.
...HOW THIS GUY MANAGED TO RIDE HIS MOMMY BIKE UP THAT REAR GATE SLOPE.
FWOOM
SQUEEZE
HUH? IMAI-ZUMI-KUN?
ZOOP!

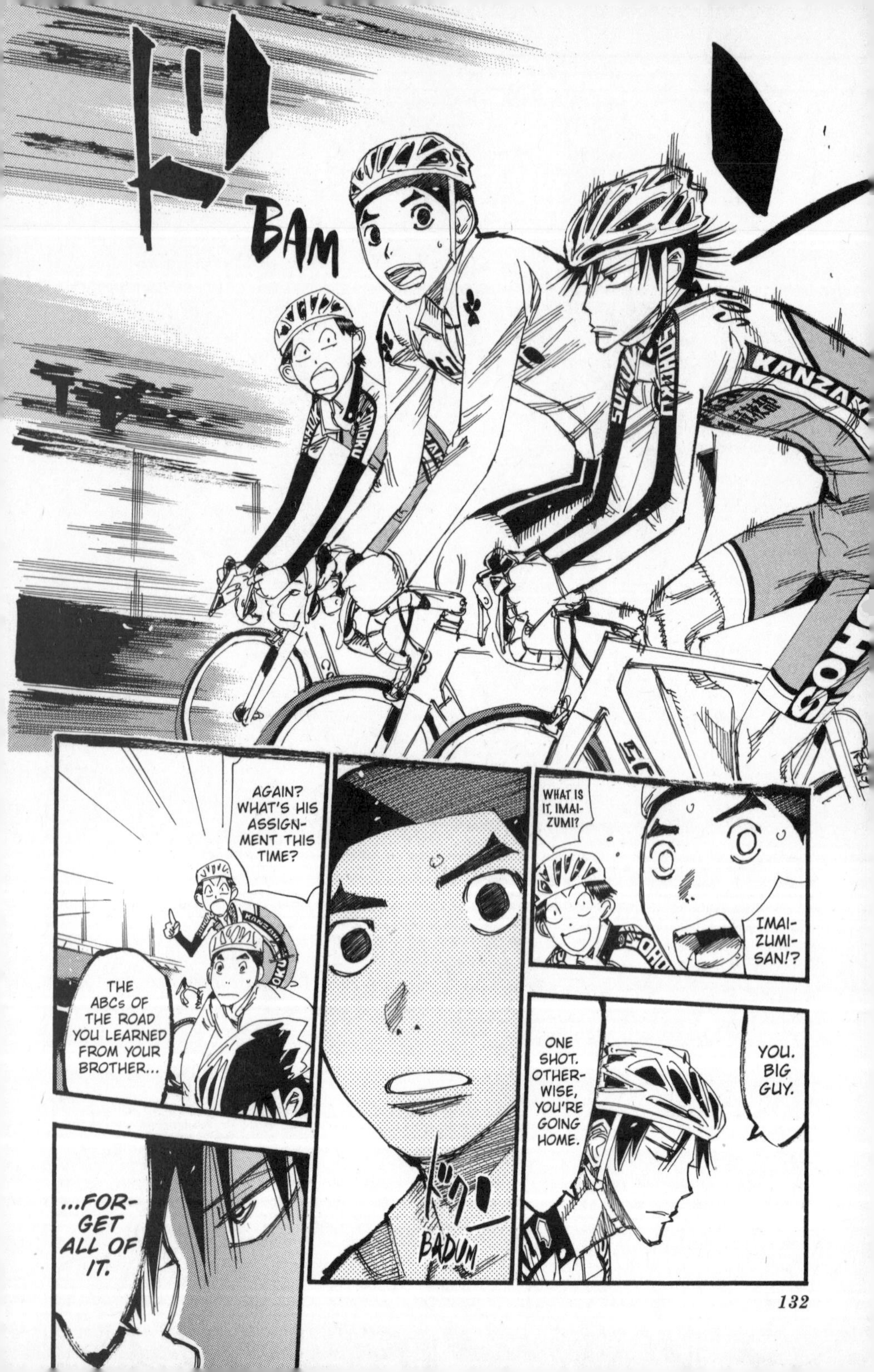
BAM
IMAI-ZUMI-SAN!?
WHAT IS IT, IMAI-ZUMI?
YOU. BIG GUY.
ONE SHOT. OTHER-WISE, YOU'RE GOING HOME.
BADUM
AGAIN? WHAT'S HIS ASSIGN-MENT THIS TIME?
THE ABCs OF THE ROAD YOU LEARNED FROM YOUR BROTHER...
...FOR-GET ALL OF IT.

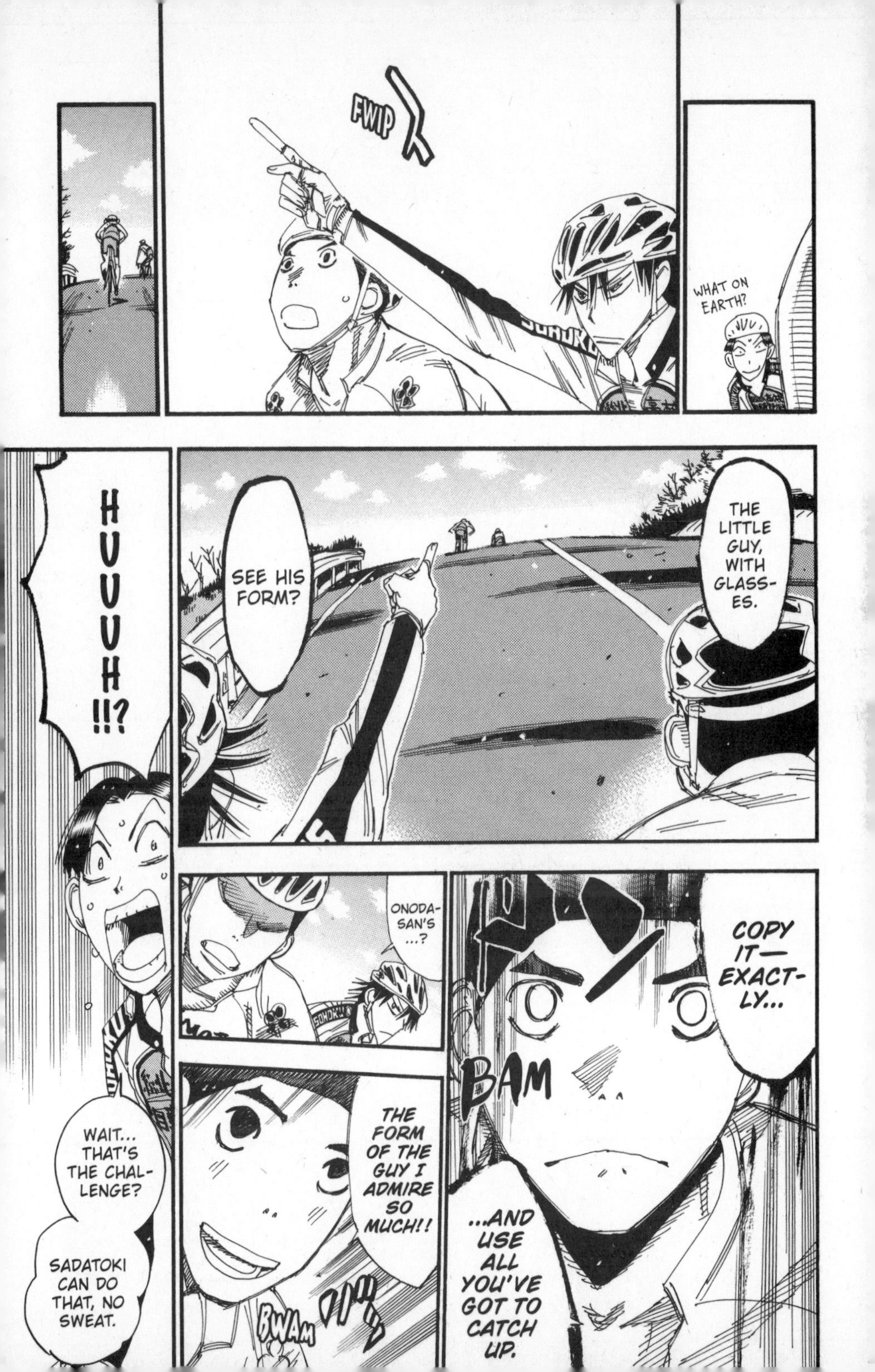
WHAT ON EARTH?
FWIP
THE LITTLE GUY, WITH GLASSES.
SEE HIS FORM?
HUUUUH!!?
COPY IT—EXACTLY...
BAM
...AND USE ALL YOU'VE GOT TO CATCH UP.
ONODA-SAN'S ...?
THE FORM OF THE GUY I ADMIRE SO MUCH!!
BWAM
WAIT... THAT'S THE CHALLENGE?
SADATOKI CAN DO THAT, NO SWEAT.

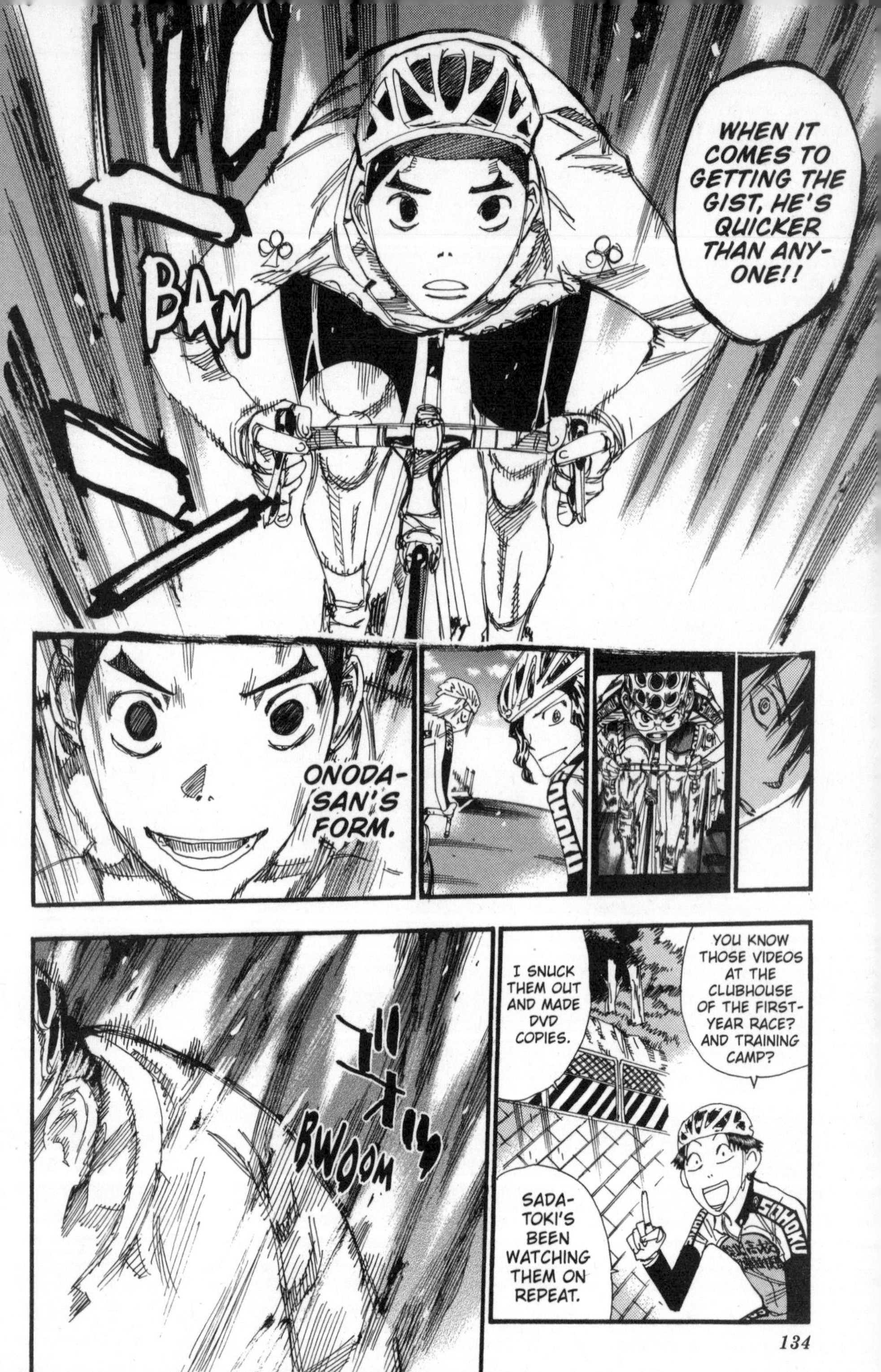
WHEN IT COMES TO GETTING THE GIST, HE'S QUICKER THAN ANY-ONE!!
BAM
ONODA-SAN'S FORM.
YOU KNOW THOSE VIDEOS AT THE CLUBHOUSE OF THE FIRST-YEAR RACE? AND TRAINING CAMP?
I SNUCK THEM OUT AND MADE DVD COPIES.
SADA-TOKI'S BEEN WATCHING THEM ON REPEAT.
BWOOM

SHOOM

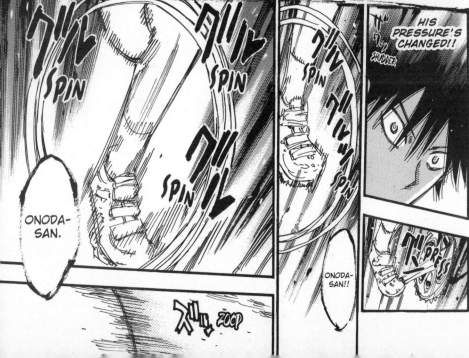

SPIN

SPIN

SPIN

SPIN

SPIN

ONODA-SAN.

ONODA-SAN!!

SHUDDER

HIS PRESSURE'S CHANGED!!

PRESS

ZOOP

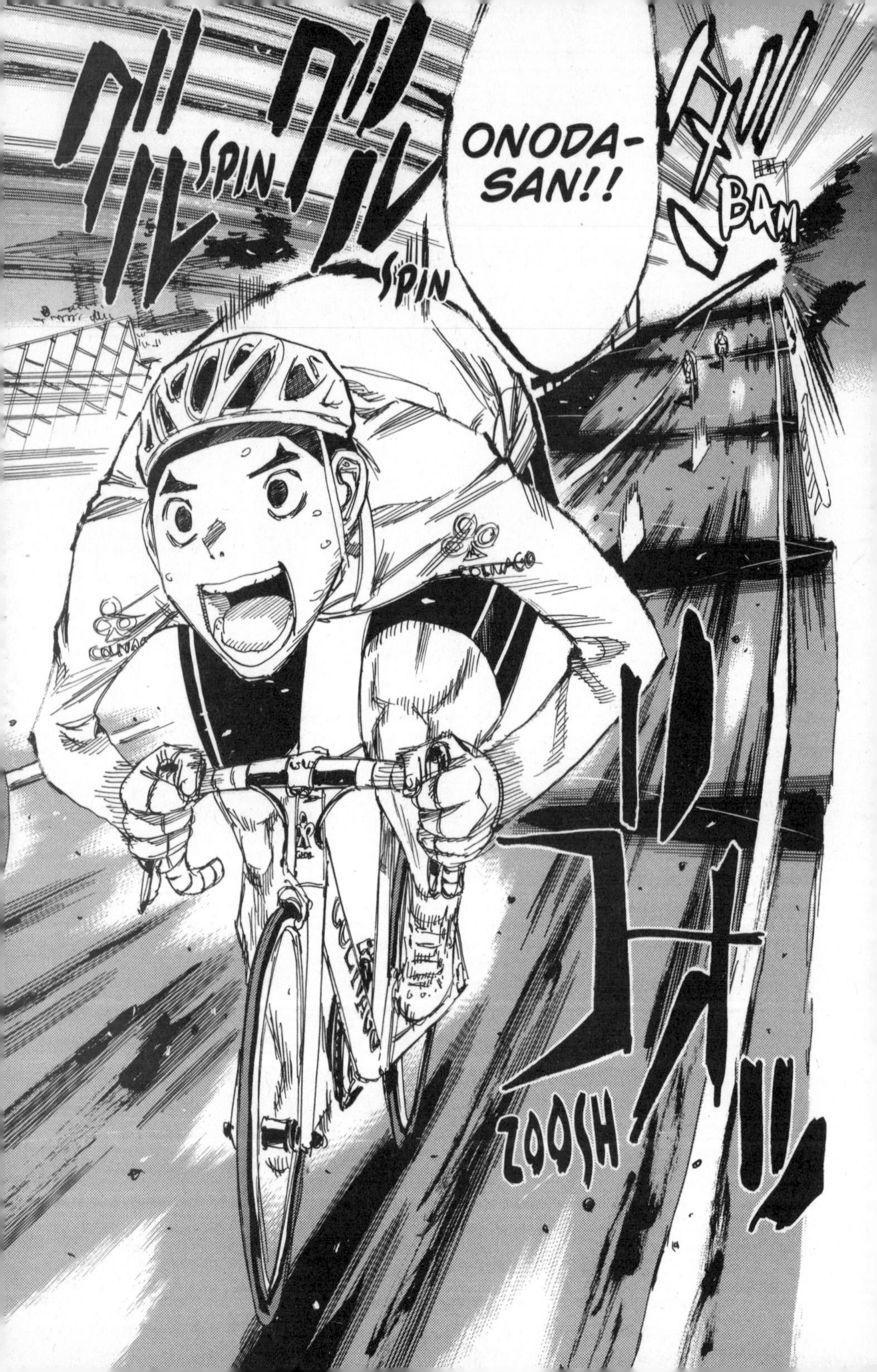
BAM
ONODA-SAN!!
SPIN
SPIN
ZOOSH

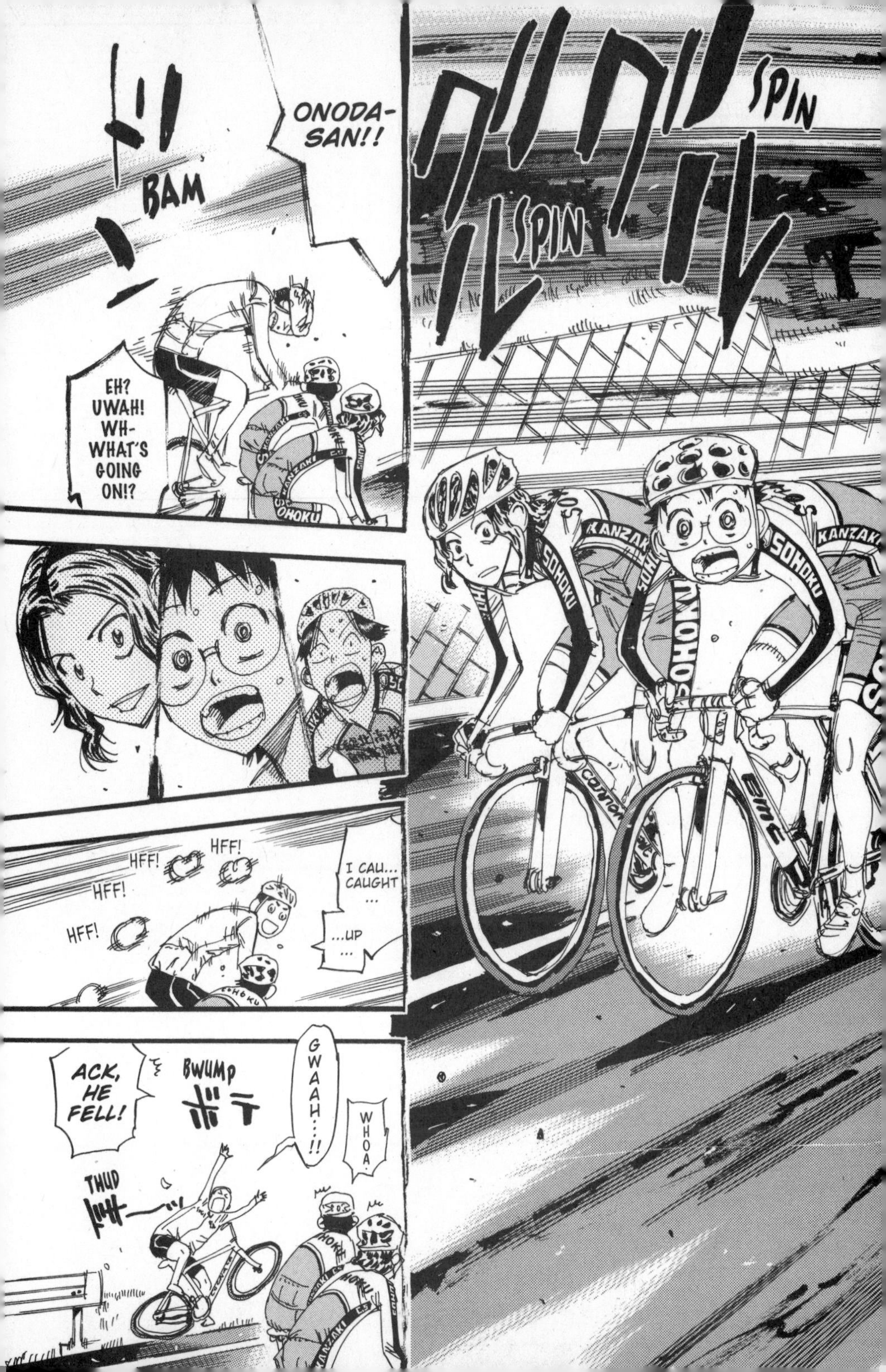
SPIN
SPIN
ONODA-SAN!!
BAM
EH? UWAH! WH-WHAT'S GOING ON!?
I CAU... CAUGHT ...
...UP ...
HFF!
HFF!
HFF!
HFF!
GWAAAH...!!
WHOA.
BWUMP
ACK, HE FELL!
THUD

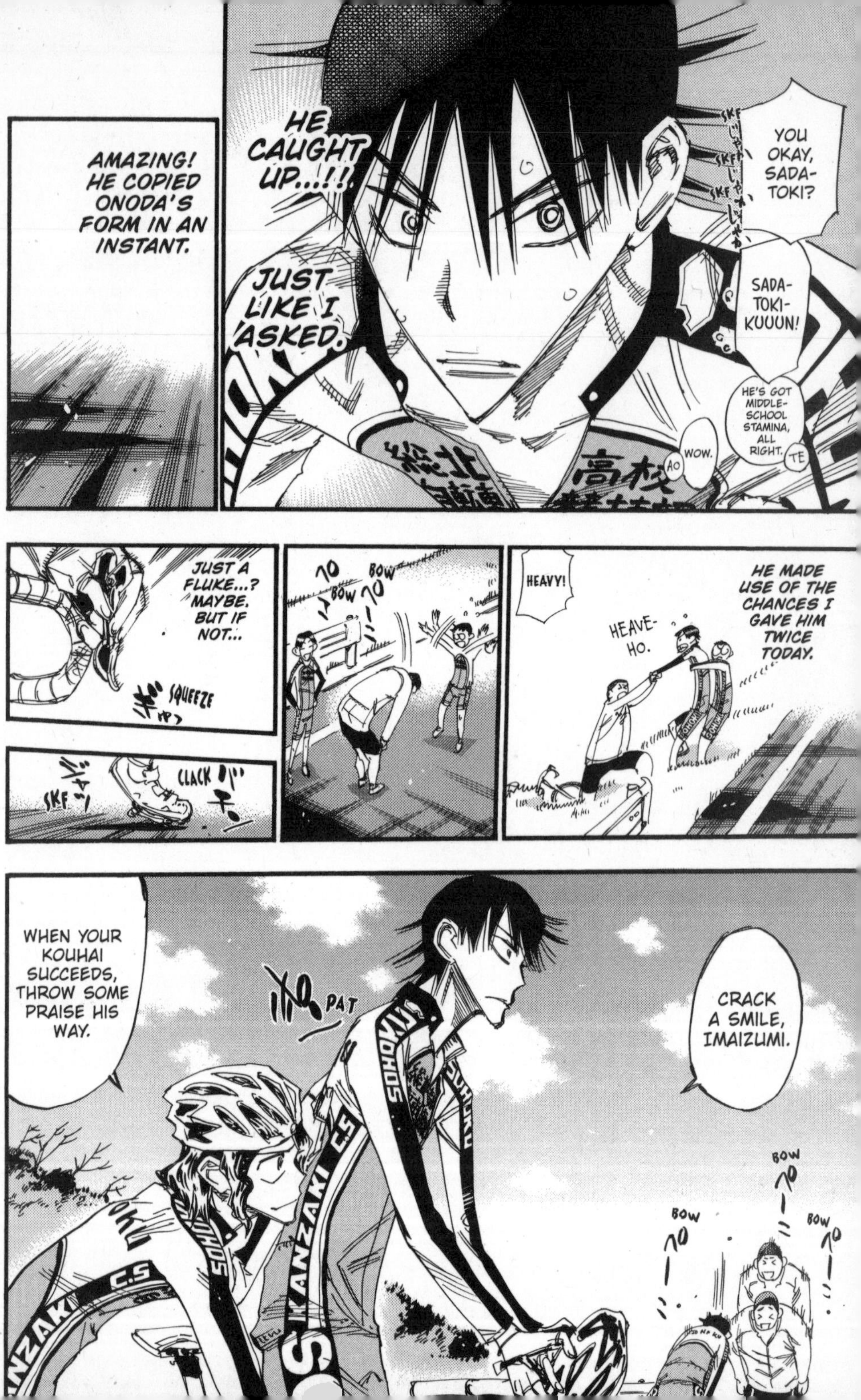
SKF
SKF
SKF
YOU OKAY, SADA-TOKI?
SADA-TOKI-KUUUN!
HE'S GOT MIDDLE-SCHOOL STAMINA, ALL RIGHT.
TE
WOW.
AO
HE CAUGHT UP...!!
JUST LIKE I ASKED.
AMAZING! HE COPIED ONODA'S FORM IN AN INSTANT.
HE MADE USE OF THE CHANCES I GAVE HIM TWICE TODAY.
HEAVY!
HEAVE-HO.
BOW
BOW
JUST A FLUKE...? MAYBE. BUT IF NOT...
SQUEEZE
CLACK
SKF
CRACK A SMILE, IMAIZUMI.
WHEN YOUR KOUHAI SUCCEEDS, THROW SOME PRAISE HIS WAY.
PAT
BOW
BOW
BOW

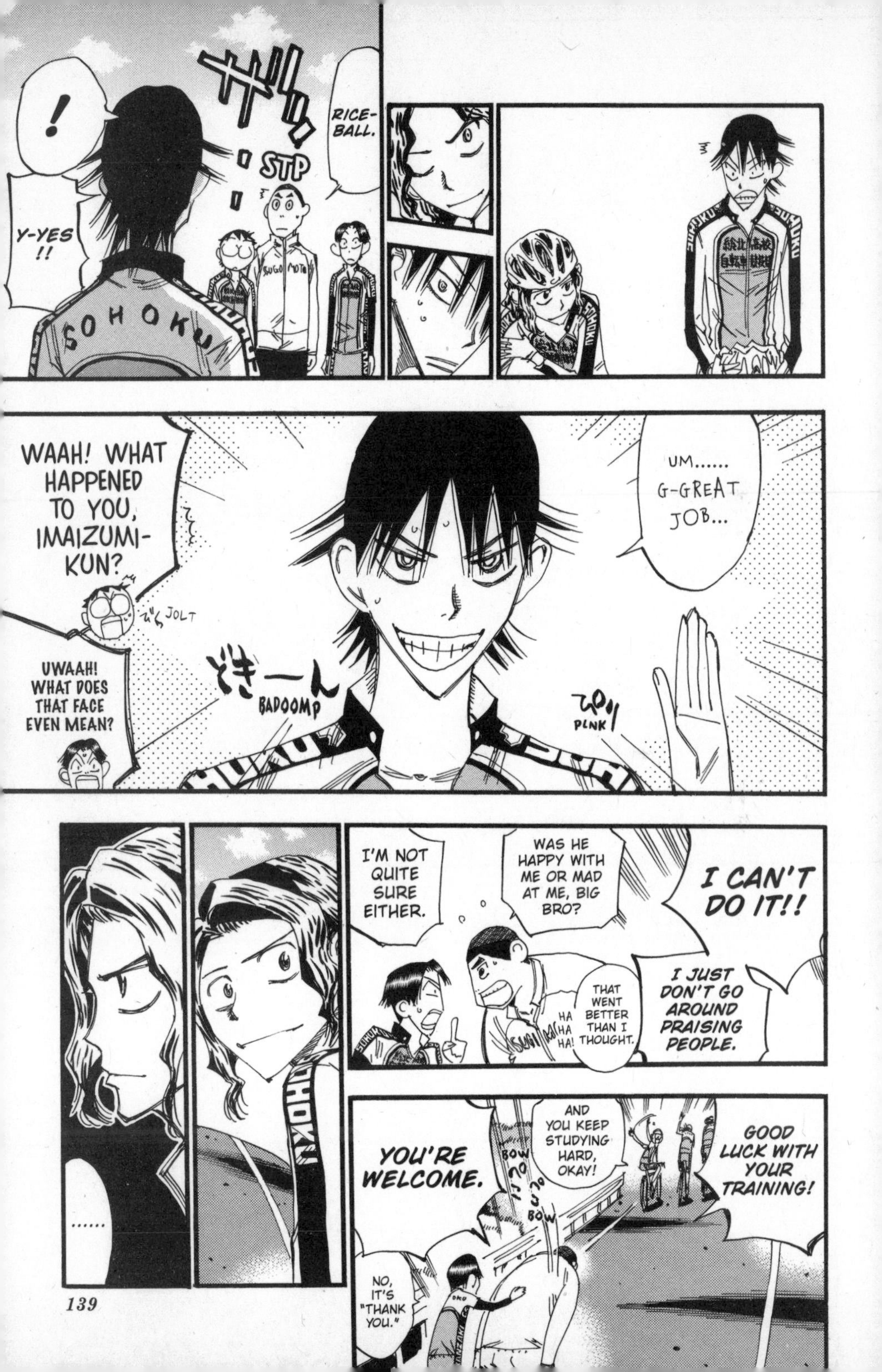
RICE-BALL.
STP
!
Y-YES !!
UM...... G-GREAT JOB...
PLNK
どきーん
BADOOMP
WAAH! WHAT HAPPENED TO YOU, IMAIZUMI-KUN?
JOLT
UWAAH! WHAT DOES THAT FACE EVEN MEAN?
I CAN'T DO IT!!
I JUST DON'T GO AROUND PRAISING PEOPLE.
WAS HE HAPPY WITH ME OR MAD AT ME, BIG BRO?
THAT WENT BETTER THAN I THOUGHT.
HA HA HA!
I'M NOT QUITE SURE EITHER.
GOOD LUCK WITH YOUR TRAINING!
AND YOU KEEP STUDYING HARD, OKAY!
BOW
BOW
YOU'RE WELCOME.
NO, IT'S "THANK YOU."
......

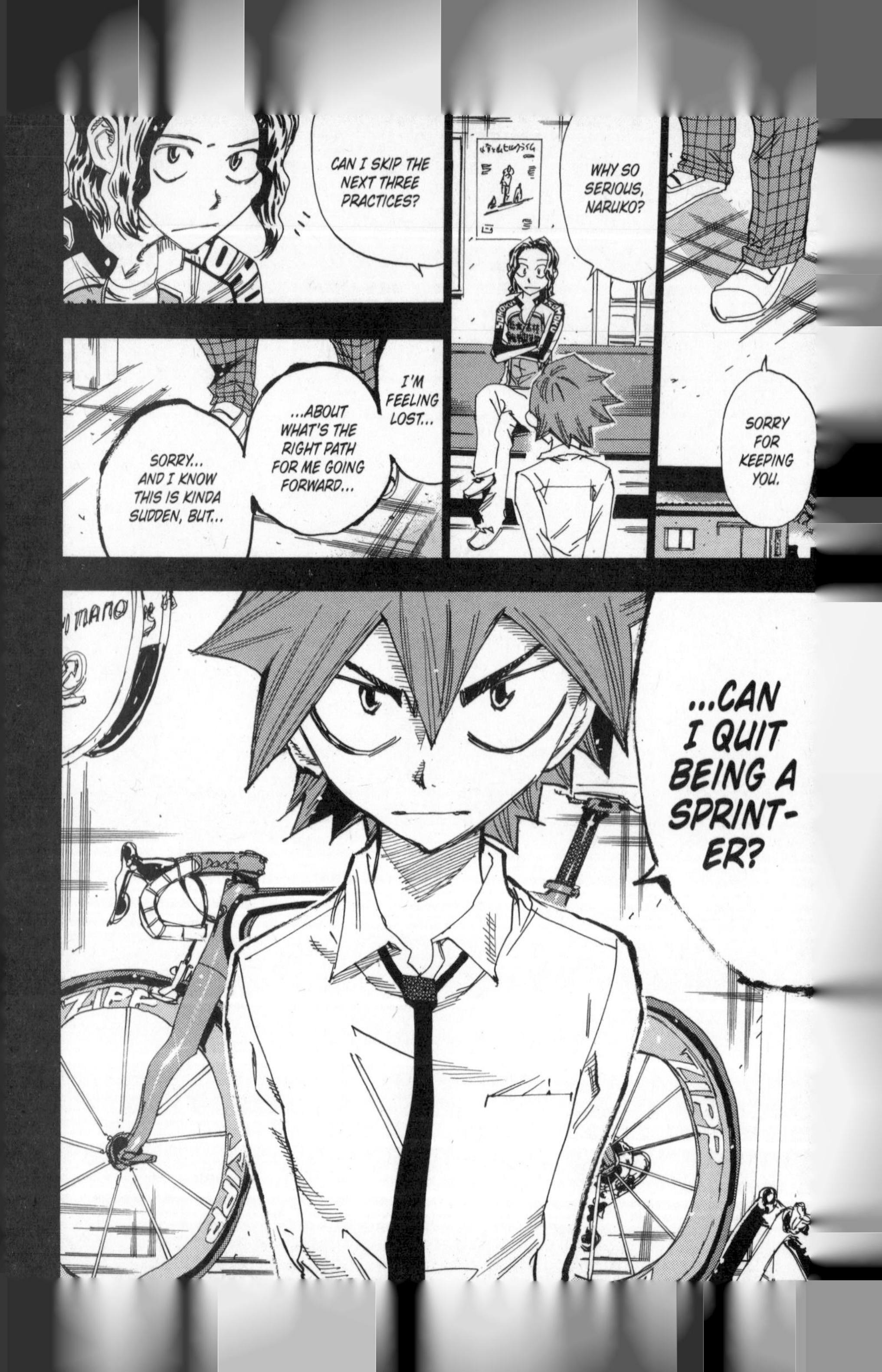
SORRY FOR KEEPING YOU.
WHY SO SERIOUS, NARUKO?
CAN I SKIP THE NEXT THREE PRACTICES?
I'M FEELING LOST...
...ABOUT WHAT'S THE RIGHT PATH FOR ME GOING FORWARD...
SORRY... AND I KNOW THIS IS KINDA SUDDEN, BUT...
...CAN I QUIT BEING A SPRINT-ER?

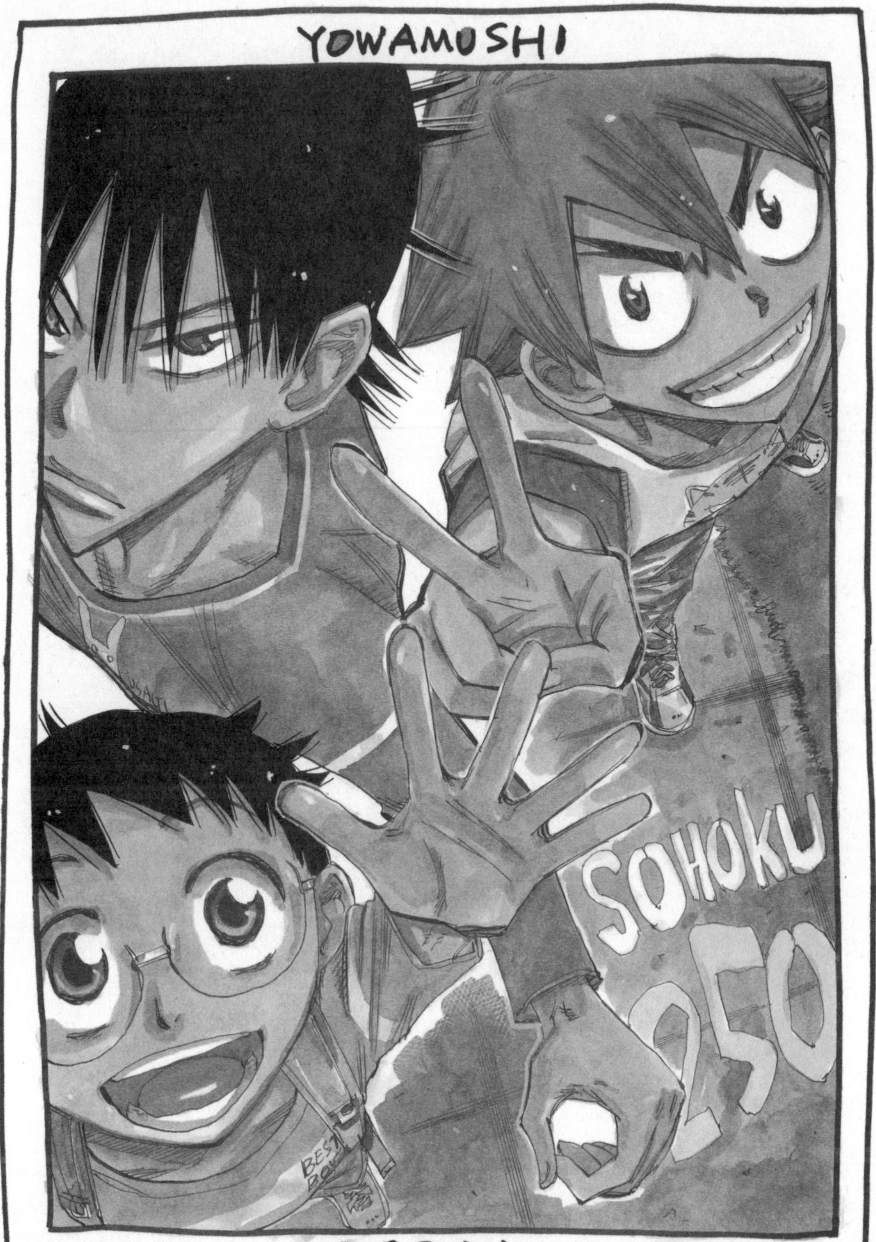
YOWAMOSHI
SOHOKU
250
PEDAL

RIDE.250 OSAKA

SADATOKI

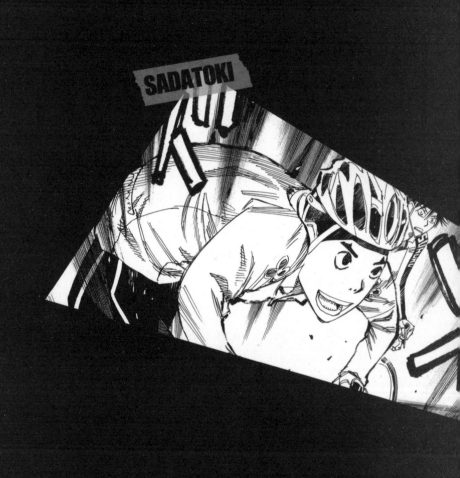

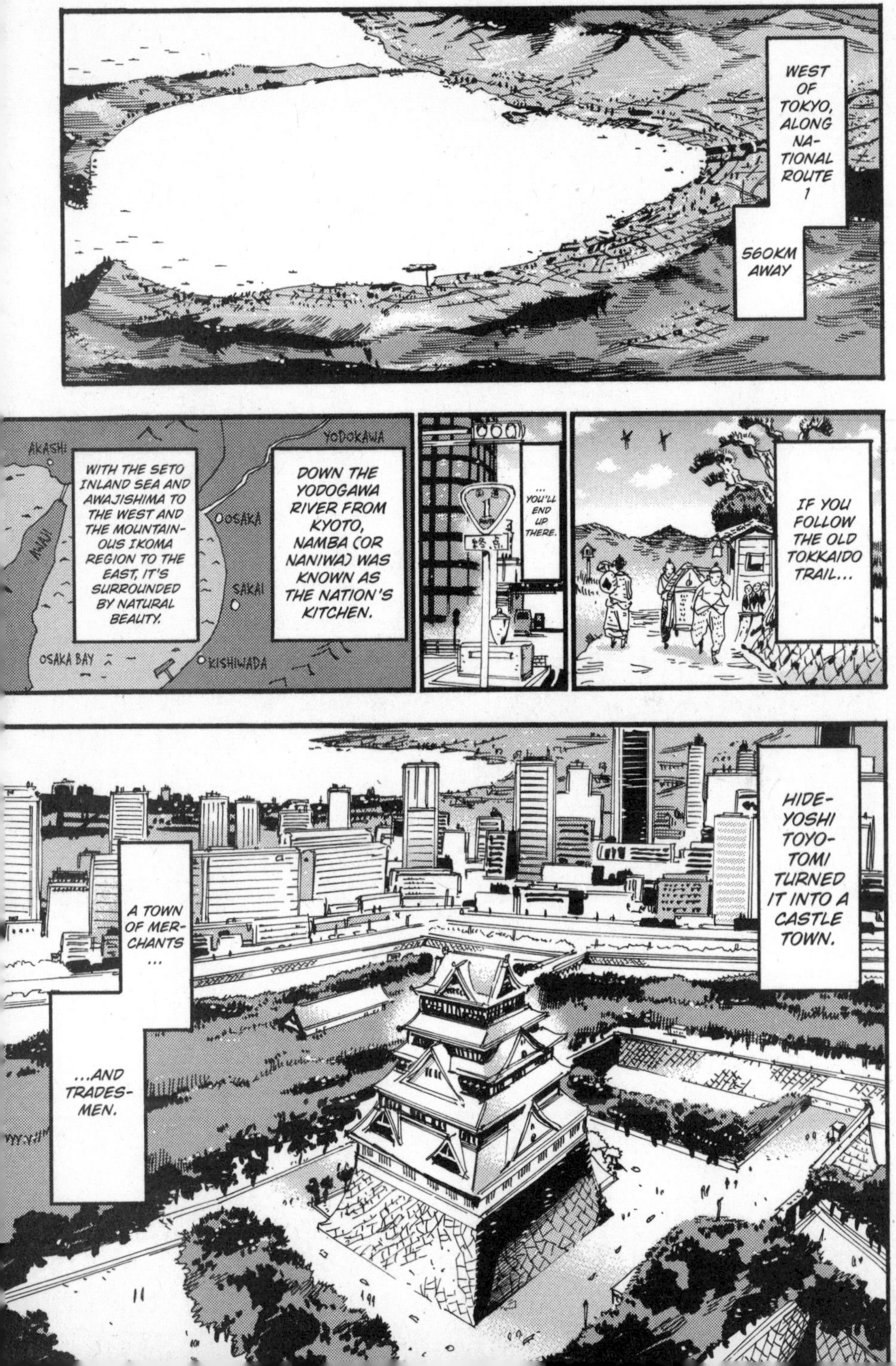
WEST OF TOKYO, ALONG NATIONAL ROUTE 1
560KM AWAY
IF YOU FOLLOW THE OLD TOKKAIDO TRAIL...
...YOU'LL END UP THERE.
YODOKAWA
DOWN THE YODOGAWA RIVER FROM KYOTO, NAMBA (OR NANIWA) WAS KNOWN AS THE NATION'S KITCHEN.
AKASHI
WITH THE SETO INLAND SEA AND AWAJISHIMA TO THE WEST AND THE MOUNTAINOUS IKOMA REGION TO THE EAST, IT'S SURROUNDED BY NATURAL BEAUTY.
OOSAKA
AWAJI
SAKAI
OSAKA BAY
KISHIWADA
HIDEYOSHI TOYOTOMI TURNED IT INTO A CASTLE TOWN.
A TOWN OF MERCHANTS...
...AND TRADESMEN.

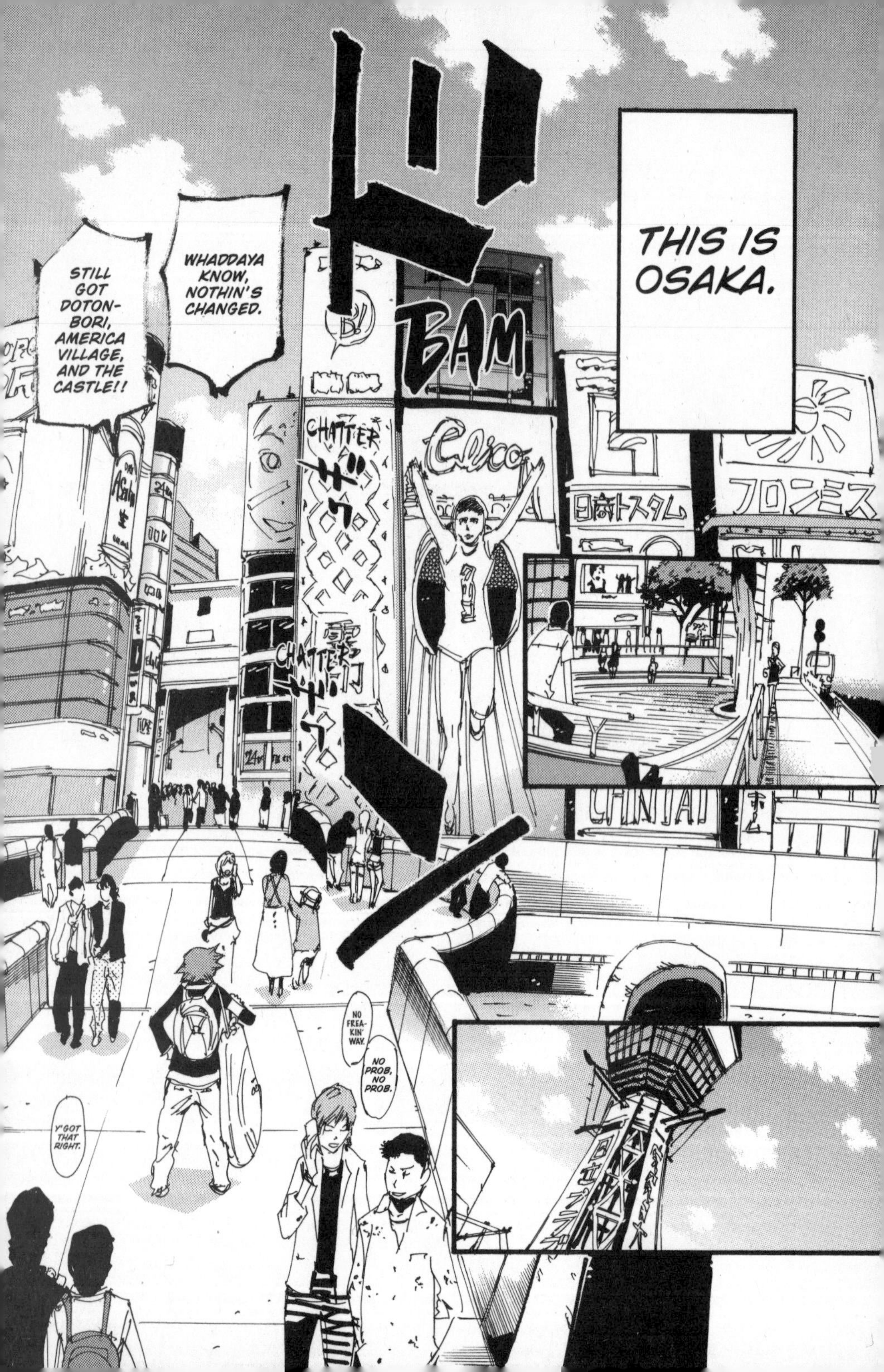
THIS IS OSAKA.
WHADDAYA KNOW, NOTHIN'S CHANGED.
STILL GOT DOTON-BORI, AMERICA VILLAGE, AND THE CASTLE!!
BAM
CHATTER
CHATTER
NO FREA-KIN' WAY.
NO PROB, NO PROB.
Y'GOT THAT RIGHT.

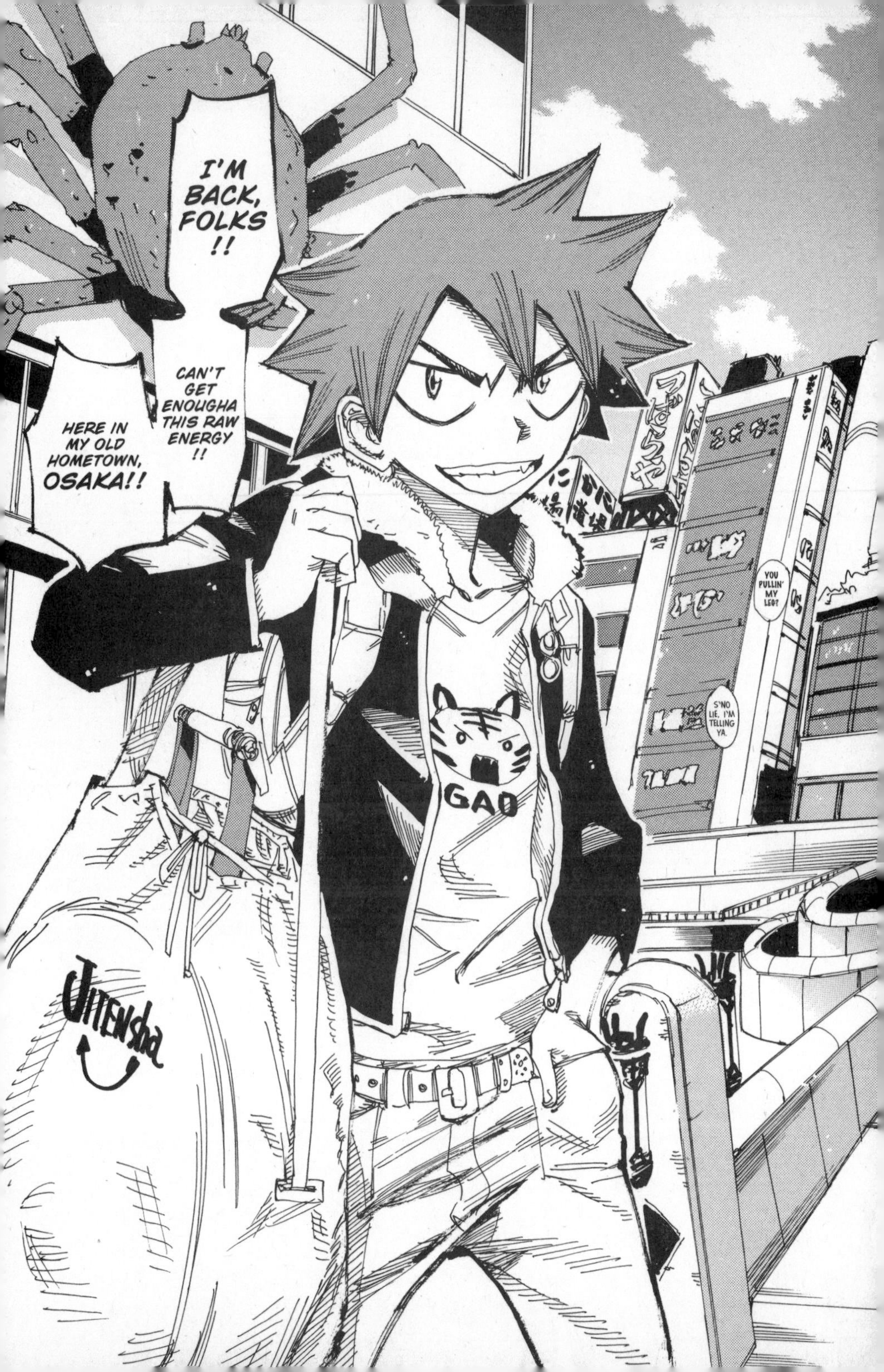
I'M BACK, FOLKS!!
CAN'T GET ENOUGHA THIS RAW ENERGY!!
HERE IN MY OLD HOMETOWN, OSAKA!!
YOU PULLIN' MY LEG?
S'NO LIE, I'M TELLING YA.
GAO
JITENsha

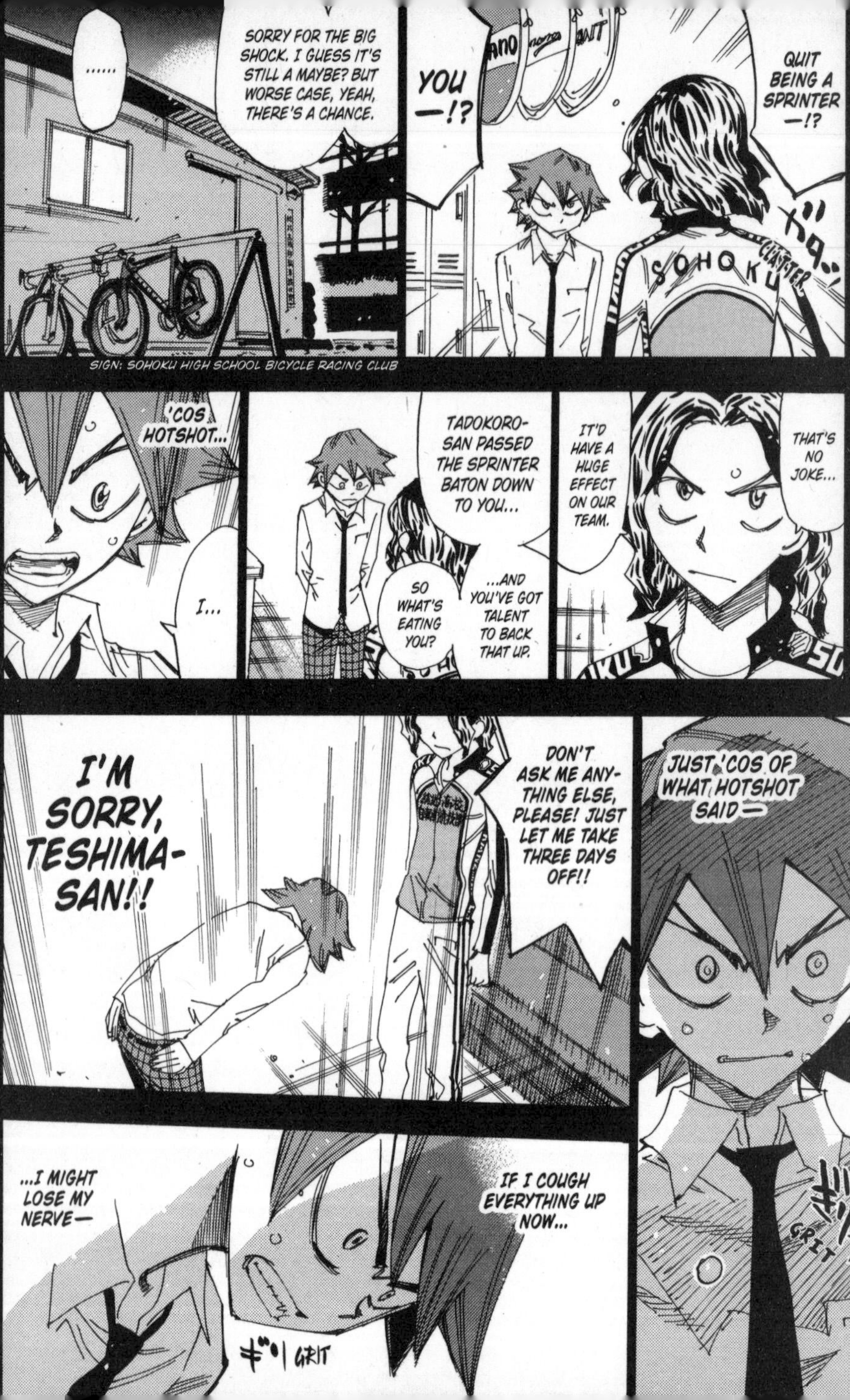
QUIT BEING A SPRINTER—!?
CLATTER
YOU—!?
SORRY FOR THE BIG SHOCK. I GUESS IT'S STILL A MAYBE? BUT WORSE CASE, YEAH, THERE'S A CHANCE.
......
SIGN: SOHOKU HIGH SCHOOL BICYCLE RACING CLUB
THAT'S NO JOKE...
IT'D HAVE A HUGE EFFECT ON OUR TEAM.
TADOKORO-SAN PASSED THE SPRINTER BATON DOWN TO YOU...
...AND YOU'VE GOT TALENT TO BACK THAT UP.
SO WHAT'S EATING YOU?
'COS HOTSHOT...
I...
JUST 'COS OF WHAT HOTSHOT SAID—
GRIT
DON'T ASK ME ANYTHING ELSE, PLEASE! JUST LET ME TAKE THREE DAYS OFF!!
I'M SORRY, TESHIMA-SAN!!
IF I COUGH EVERYTHING UP NOW...
...I MIGHT LOSE MY NERVE—
GRIT

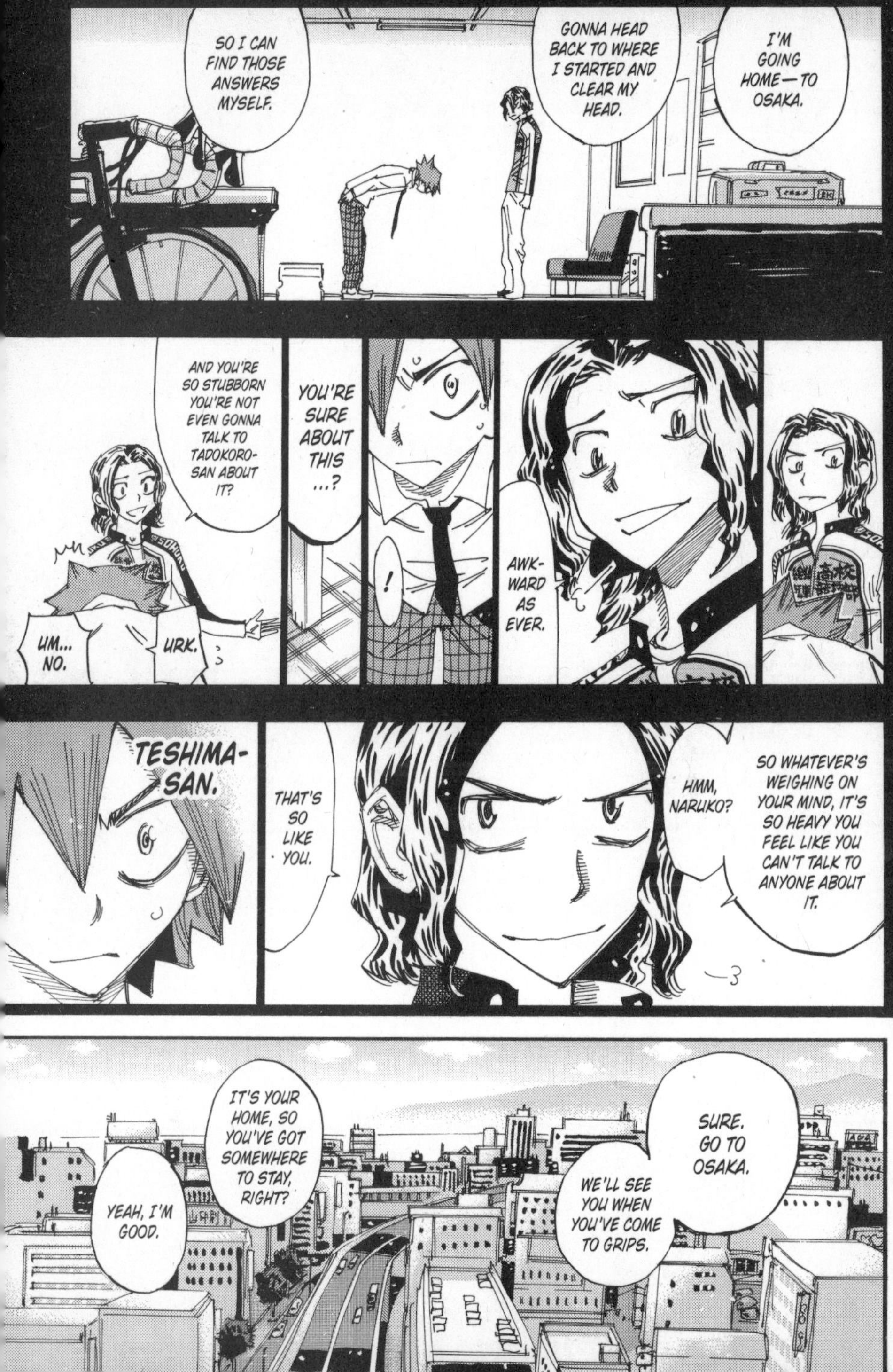
I'M GOING HOME—TO OSAKA.
GONNA HEAD BACK TO WHERE I STARTED AND CLEAR MY HEAD.
SO I CAN FIND THOSE ANSWERS MYSELF.
AWK-WARD AS EVER.
YOU'RE SURE ABOUT THIS ...?
!
AND YOU'RE SO STUBBORN YOU'RE NOT EVEN GONNA TALK TO TADOKORO-SAN ABOUT IT?
URK.
UM... NO.
SO WHATEVER'S WEIGHING ON YOUR MIND, IT'S SO HEAVY YOU FEEL LIKE YOU CAN'T TALK TO ANYONE ABOUT IT.
HMM, NARUKO?
THAT'S SO LIKE YOU.
TESHIMA-SAN.
SURE. GO TO OSAKA.
WE'LL SEE YOU WHEN YOU'VE COME TO GRIPS.
IT'S YOUR HOME, SO YOU'VE GOT SOMEWHERE TO STAY, RIGHT?
YEAH, I'M GOOD.

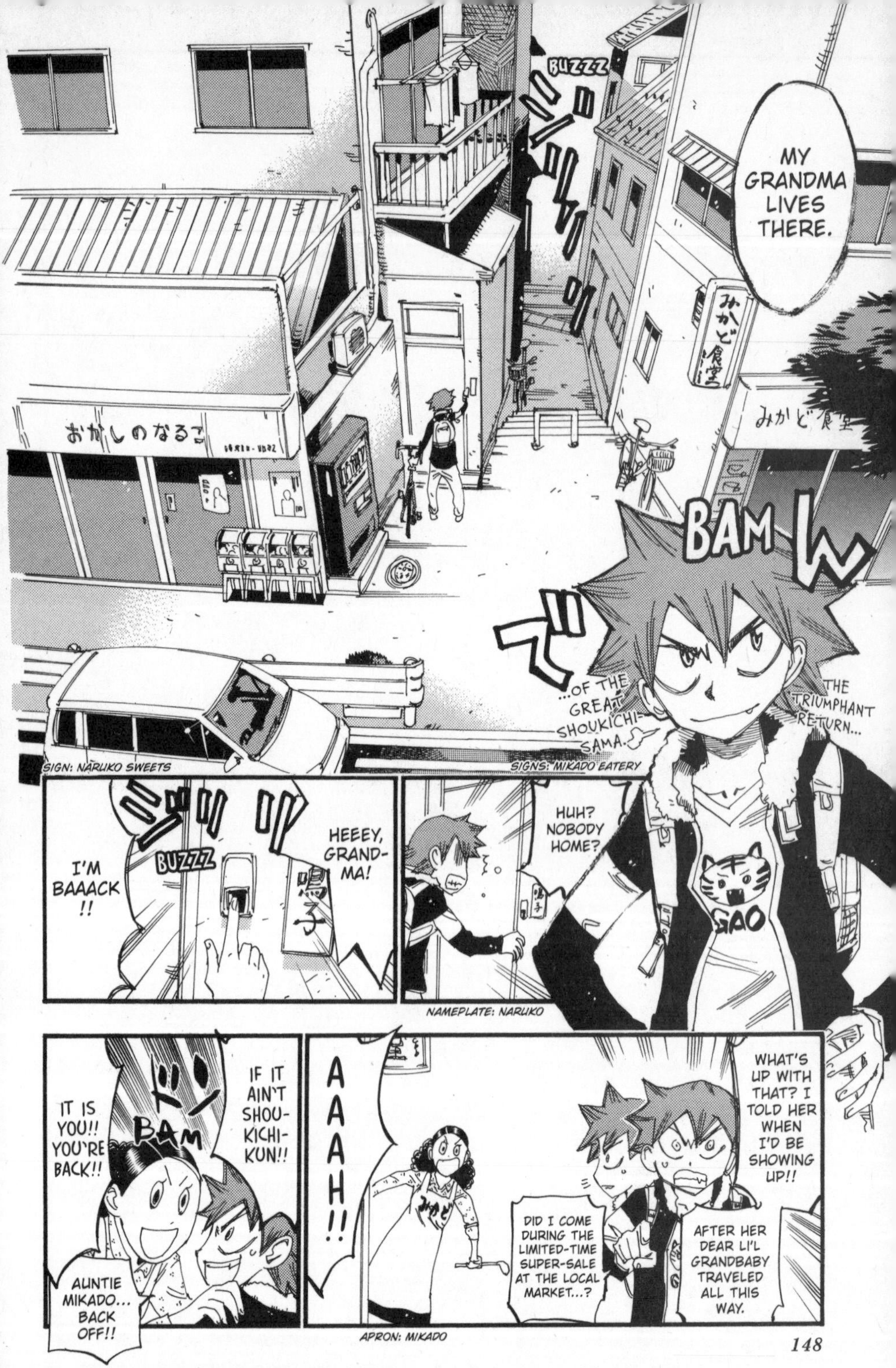
BUZZZ
MY GRANDMA LIVES THERE.
おかしのなるこ
みかど食堂
BAM
THE TRIUMPHANT RE-TURN...
...OF THE GREAT SHOUKICHI-SAMA.
SIGN: NARUKO SWEETS
SIGNS: MIKADO EATERY
HUH? NOBODY HOME?
NAMEPLATE: NARUKO
HEEEY, GRANDMA!
BUZZZ
I'M BAAACK!!
WHAT'S UP WITH THAT? I TOLD HER WHEN I'D BE SHOWING UP!!
AFTER HER DEAR LI'L GRANDBABY TRAVELED ALL THIS WAY.
DID I COME DURING THE LIMITED-TIME SUPER-SALE AT THE LOCAL MARKET...?
AAAAH!!
APRON: MIKADO
IF IT AIN'T SHOU-KICHI-KUN!!
BAM
IT IS YOU!! YOU'RE BACK!!
AUNTIE MIKADO... BACK OFF!!

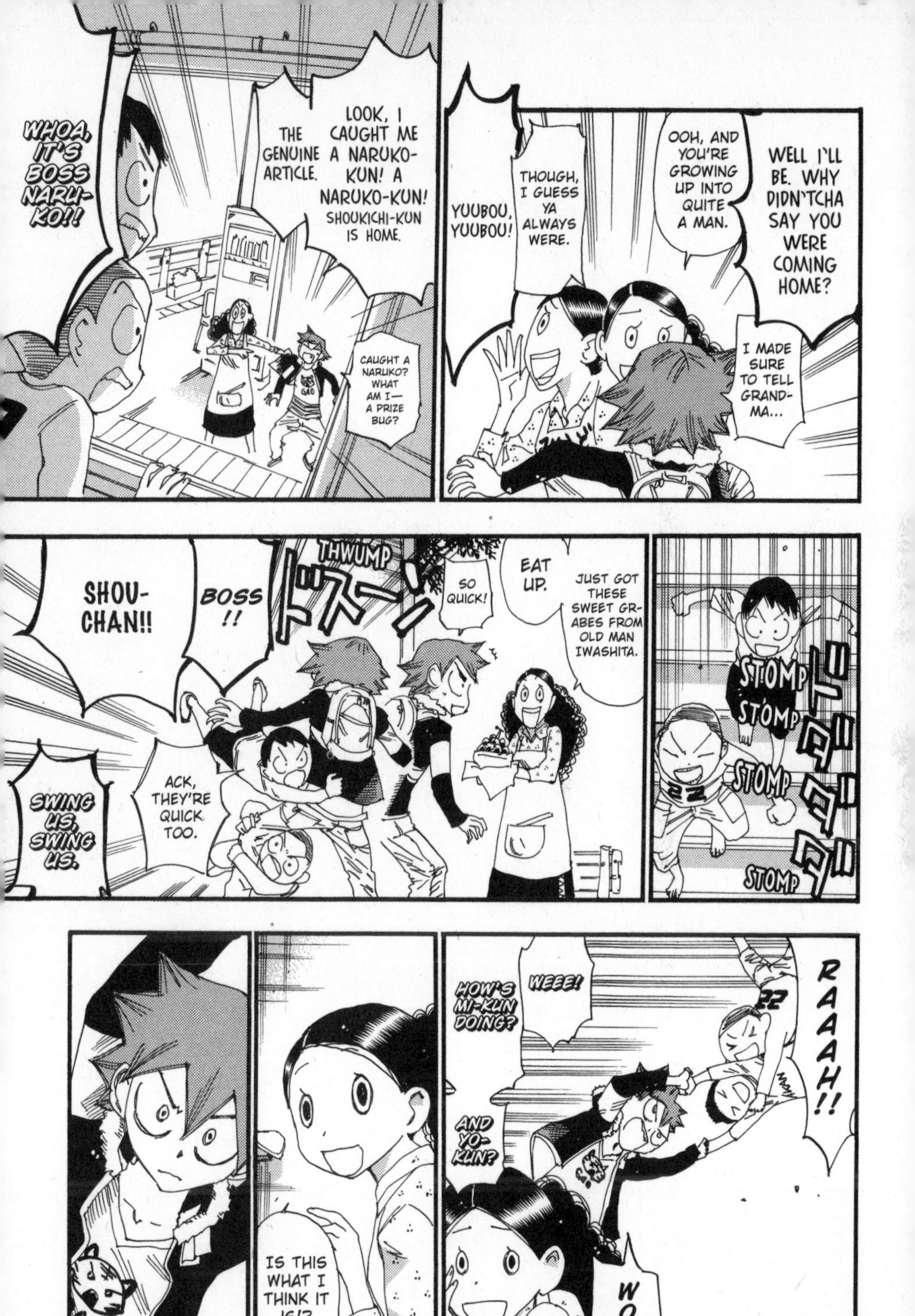
WELL I'LL BE. WHY DIDN'TCHA SAY YOU WERE COMING HOME?
OOH, AND YOU'RE GROWING UP INTO QUITE A MAN.
THOUGH, I GUESS YA ALWAYS WERE.
YUUBOU, YUUBOU!
I MADE SURE TO TELL GRAND-MA...
LOOK, I CAUGHT ME A NARUKO-KUN! A NARUKO-KUN! SHOUKICHI-KUN IS HOME.
THE GENUINE ARTICLE.
WHOA, IT'S BOSS NARU-KO!!
CAUGHT A NARUKO? WHAT AM I— A PRIZE BUG?
STOMP
STOMP
STOMP
STOMP
JUST GOT THESE SWEET GR-ABES FROM OLD MAN IWASHITA.
EAT UP.
SO QUICK!
THWUMP
BOSS !!
SHOU-CHAN!!
ACK, THEY'RE QUICK TOO.
SWING US, SWING US.
RAAAAH!!
WEEE!
HOW'S MI-KUN DOING?
AND YO-KUN?
WOOO!!
WOW.
IS THIS WHAT I THINK IT IS!?

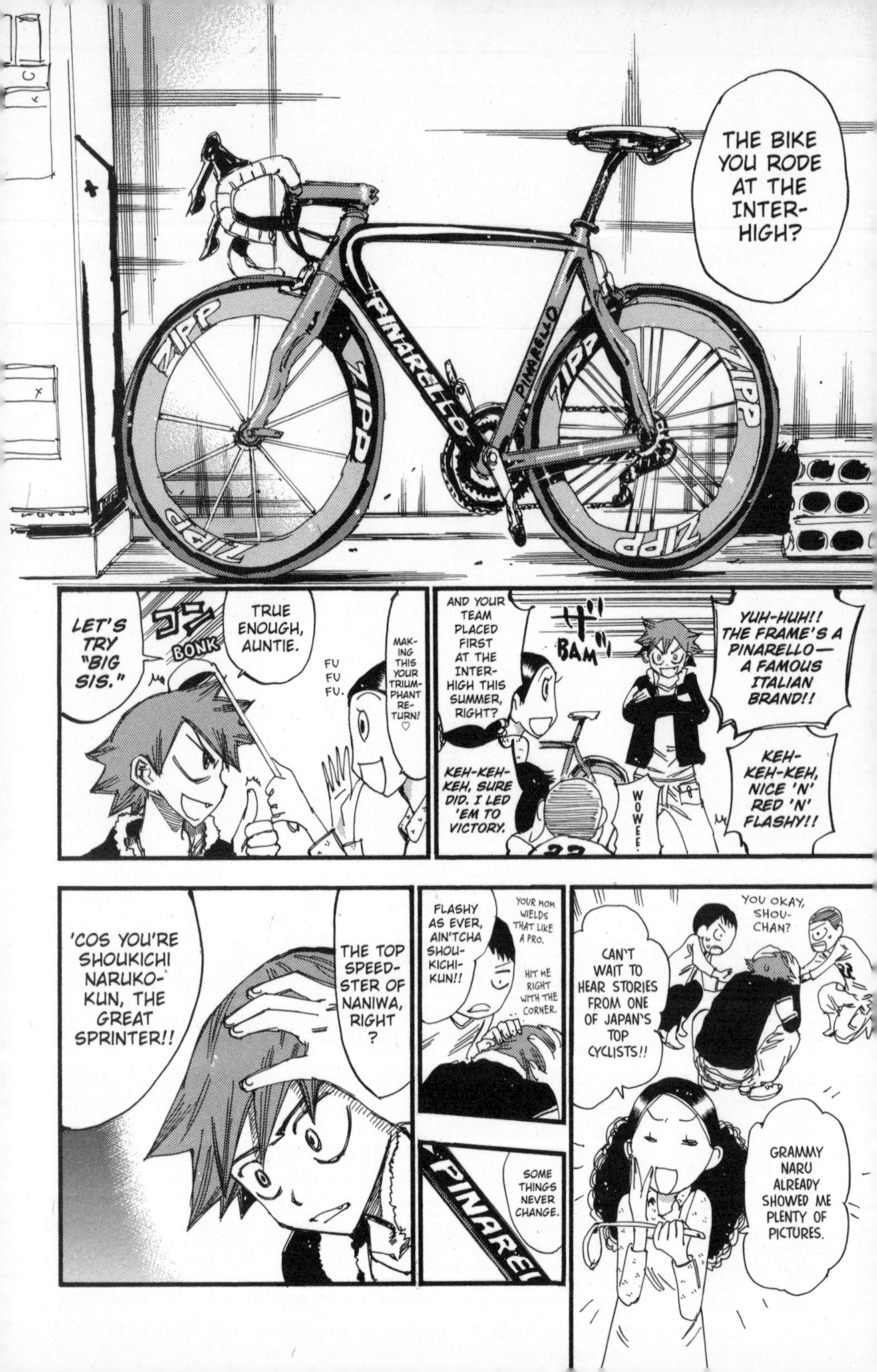
THE BIKE YOU RODE AT THE INTER-HIGH?
YUH-HUH!! THE FRAME'S A PINARELLO— A FAMOUS ITALIAN BRAND!!
BAM
AND YOUR TEAM PLACED FIRST AT THE INTER-HIGH THIS SUMMER, RIGHT?
KEH-KEH-KEH, NICE 'N' RED 'N' FLASHY!!
WOWEE.
KEH-KEH-KEH, SURE DID. I LED 'EM TO VICTORY.
MAKING THIS YOUR TRIUMPHANT RETURN! ♡
FU FU FU.
TRUE ENOUGH, AUNTIE.
BONK
LET'S TRY "BIG SIS."
YOU OKAY, SHOU-CHAN?
CAN'T WAIT TO HEAR STORIES FROM ONE OF JAPAN'S TOP CYCLISTS!!
GRAMMY NARU ALREADY SHOWED ME PLENTY OF PICTURES.
YOUR MOM WIELDS THAT LIKE A PRO.
HIT ME RIGHT WITH THE CORNER.
FLASHY AS EVER, AIN'TCHA SHOUKICHI-KUN!!
SOME THINGS NEVER CHANGE.
THE TOP SPEEDSTER OF NANIWA, RIGHT?
'COS YOU'RE SHOUKICHI NARUKO-KUN, THE GREAT SPRINTER!!

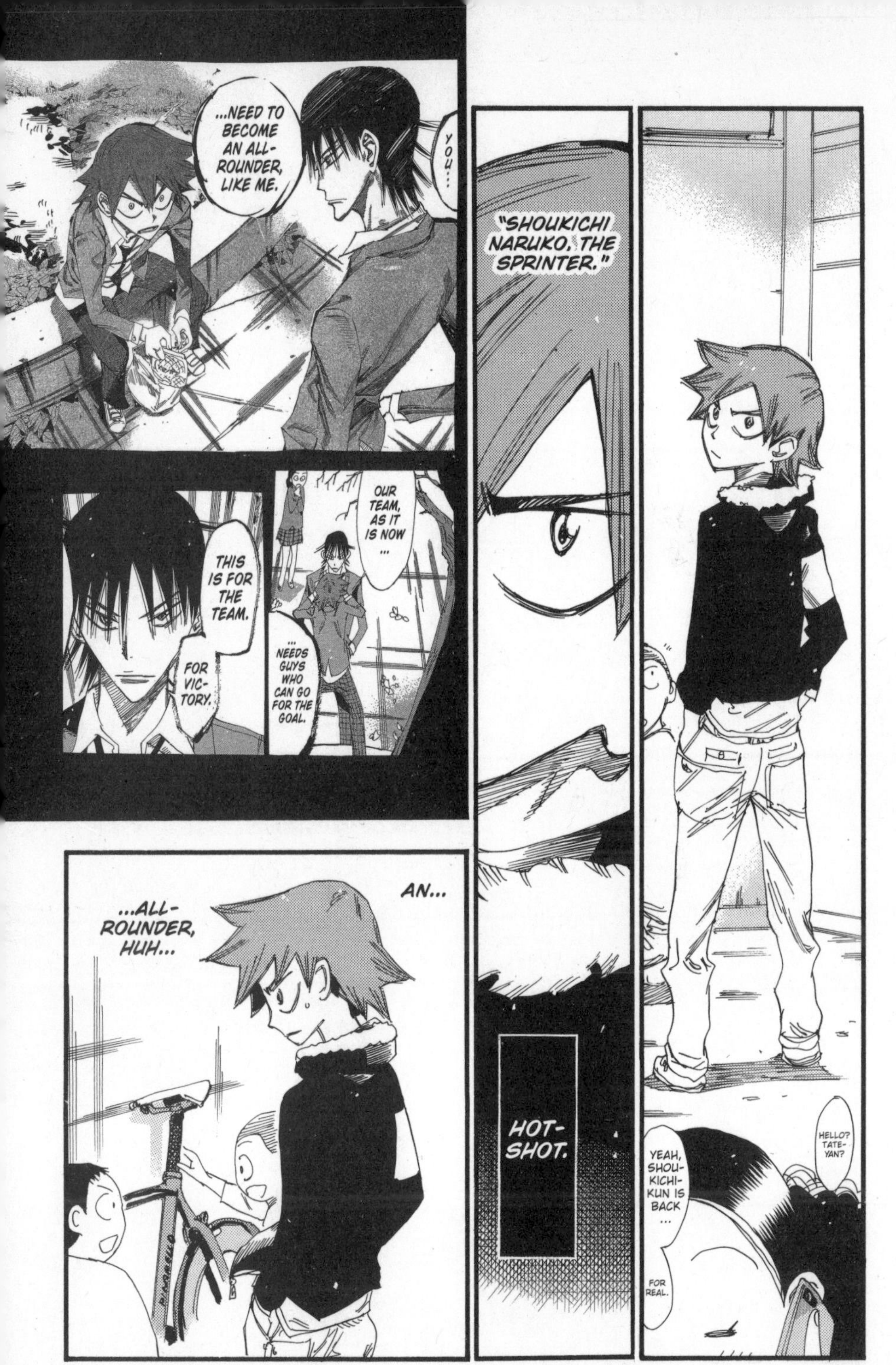
HELLO? TATE-YAN?
YEAH, SHOUKICHI-KUN IS BACK...
FOR REAL.
"SHOUKICHI NARUKO, THE SPRINTER."
HOT-SHOT.
YOU...
...NEED TO BECOME AN ALL-ROUNDER, LIKE ME.
OUR TEAM, AS IT IS NOW...
...NEEDS GUYS WHO CAN GO FOR THE GOAL.
THIS IS FOR THE TEAM.
FOR VICTORY.
AN...
...ALL-ROUNDER, HUH...

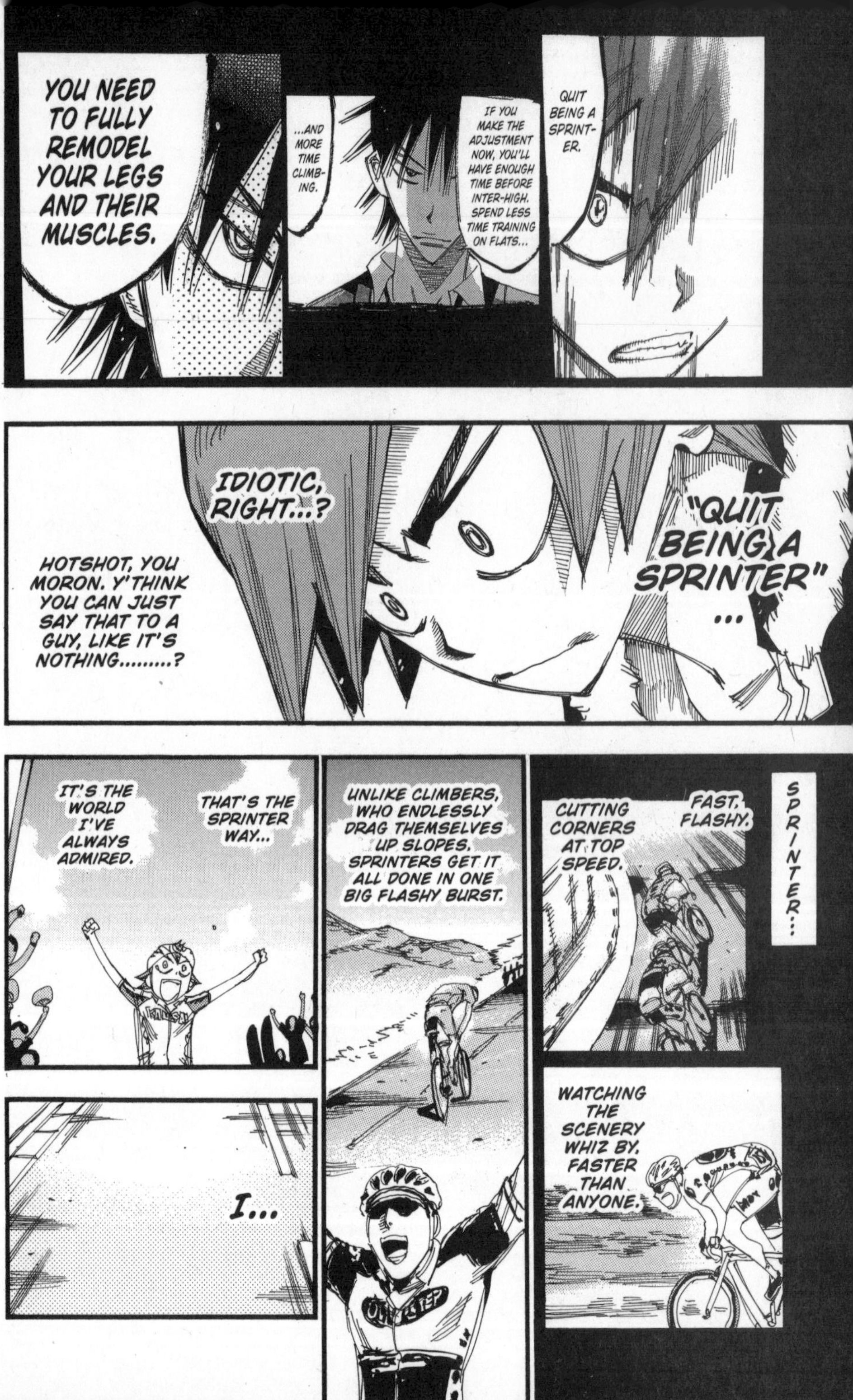
QUIT BEING A SPRINTER.
IF YOU MAKE THE ADJUSTMENT NOW, YOU'LL HAVE ENOUGH TIME BEFORE INTER-HIGH. SPEND LESS TIME TRAINING ON FLATS...
...AND MORE TIME CLIMBING.
YOU NEED TO FULLY REMODEL YOUR LEGS AND THEIR MUSCLES.
"QUIT BEING A SPRINTER"...
IDIOTIC, RIGHT...?
HOTSHOT, YOU MORON. Y'THINK YOU CAN JUST SAY THAT TO A GUY, LIKE IT'S NOTHING.........?
SPRINTER...
FAST. FLASHY.
CUTTING CORNERS AT TOP SPEED.
WATCHING THE SCENERY WHIZ BY. FASTER THAN ANYONE.
UNLIKE CLIMBERS, WHO ENDLESSLY DRAG THEMSELVES UP SLOPES, SPRINTERS GET IT ALL DONE IN ONE BIG FLASHY BURST.
THAT'S THE SPRINTER WAY...
IT'S THE WORLD I'VE ALWAYS ADMIRED.
I...

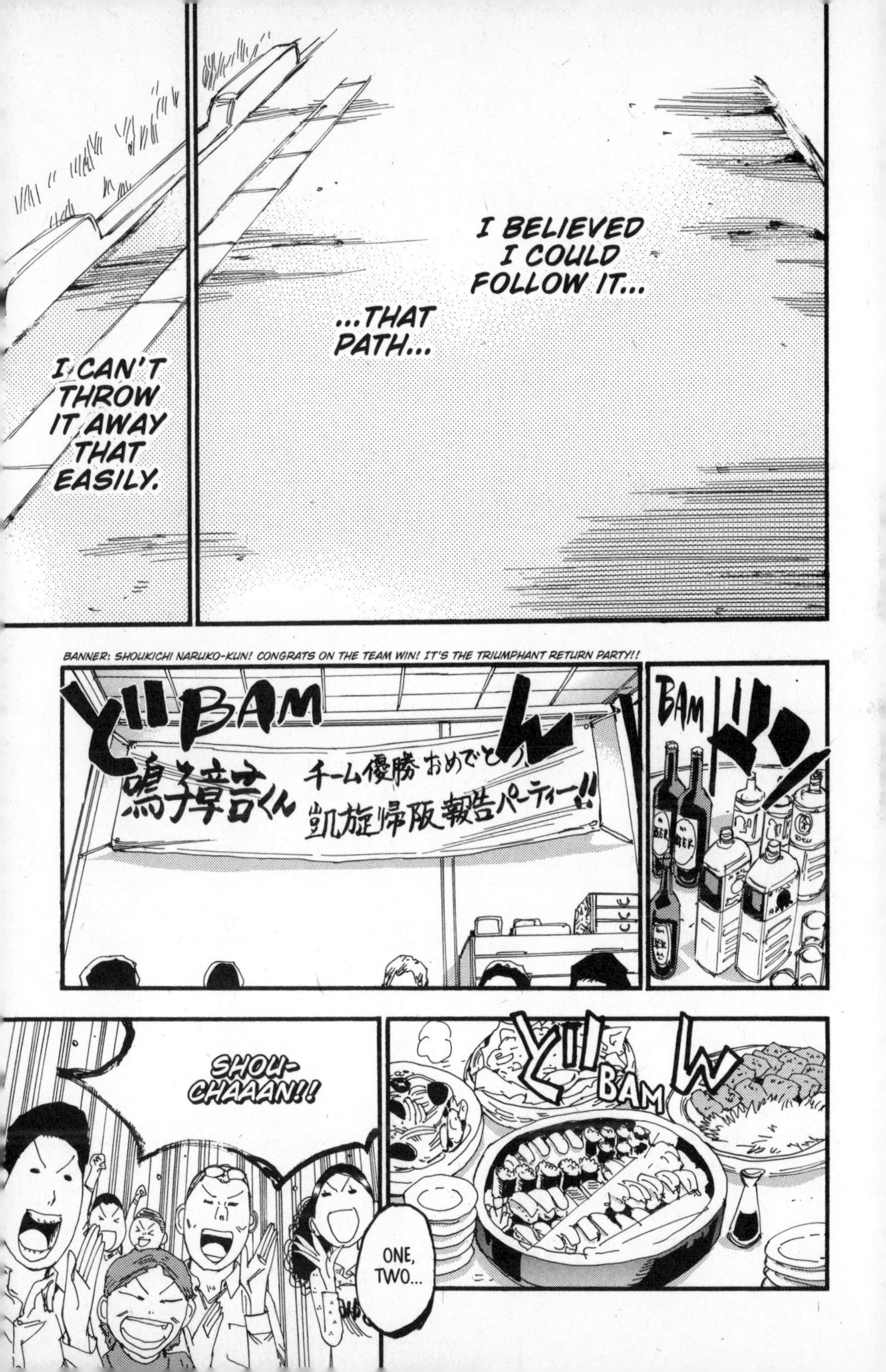
I BELIEVED I COULD FOLLOW IT...
...THAT PATH...
I CAN'T THROW IT AWAY THAT EASILY.
BANNER: SHOUKICHI NARUKO-KUN! CONGRATS ON THE TEAM WIN! IT'S THE TRIUMPHANT RETURN PARTY!!
BAM
BAM
鳴子章吉くん
チーム優勝おめでとう
凱旋帰阪報告パーティー!!
BAM
SHOU-CHAAAN!!
ONE, TWO...

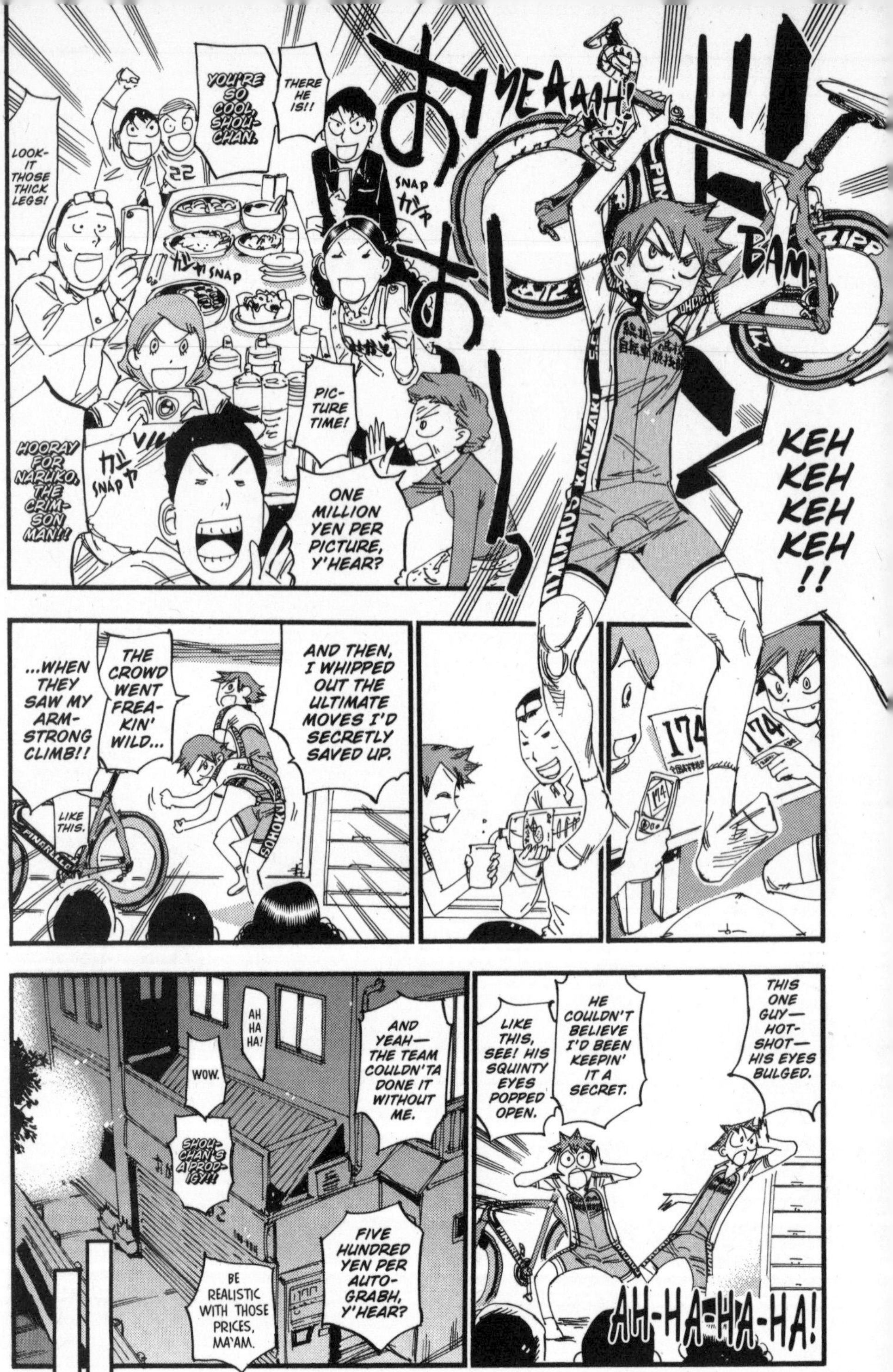
KEH KEH KEH KEH!!
BAM
YEAAAAH!
SNAP
THERE HE IS!!
YOU'RE SO COOL, SHOU-CHAN.
LOOK-IT THOSE THICK LEGS!
SNAP
PIC-TURE TIME!
ONE MILLION YEN PER PICTURE, Y'HEAR?
SNAP
HOORAY FOR NARUKO, THE CRIM-SON MAN!!
AND THEN, I WHIPPED OUT THE ULTIMATE MOVES I'D SECRETLY SAVED UP.
THE CROWD WENT FREA-KIN' WILD...
...WHEN THEY SAW MY ARM-STRONG CLIMB!!
LIKE THIS.
THIS ONE GUY—HOT-SHOT—HIS EYES BULGED.
HE COULDN'T BELIEVE I'D BEEN KEEPIN' IT A SECRET.
LIKE THIS, SEE! HIS SQUINTY EYES POPPED OPEN.
AH-HA-HA-HA!
AND YEAH—THE TEAM COULDN'TA DONE IT WITHOUT ME.
AH HA HA!
WOW.
SHOU-CHAN'S A PRODIGY!!
FIVE HUNDRED YEN PER AUTO-GRABH, Y'HEAR?
BE REALISTIC WITH THOSE PRICES, MA'AM.

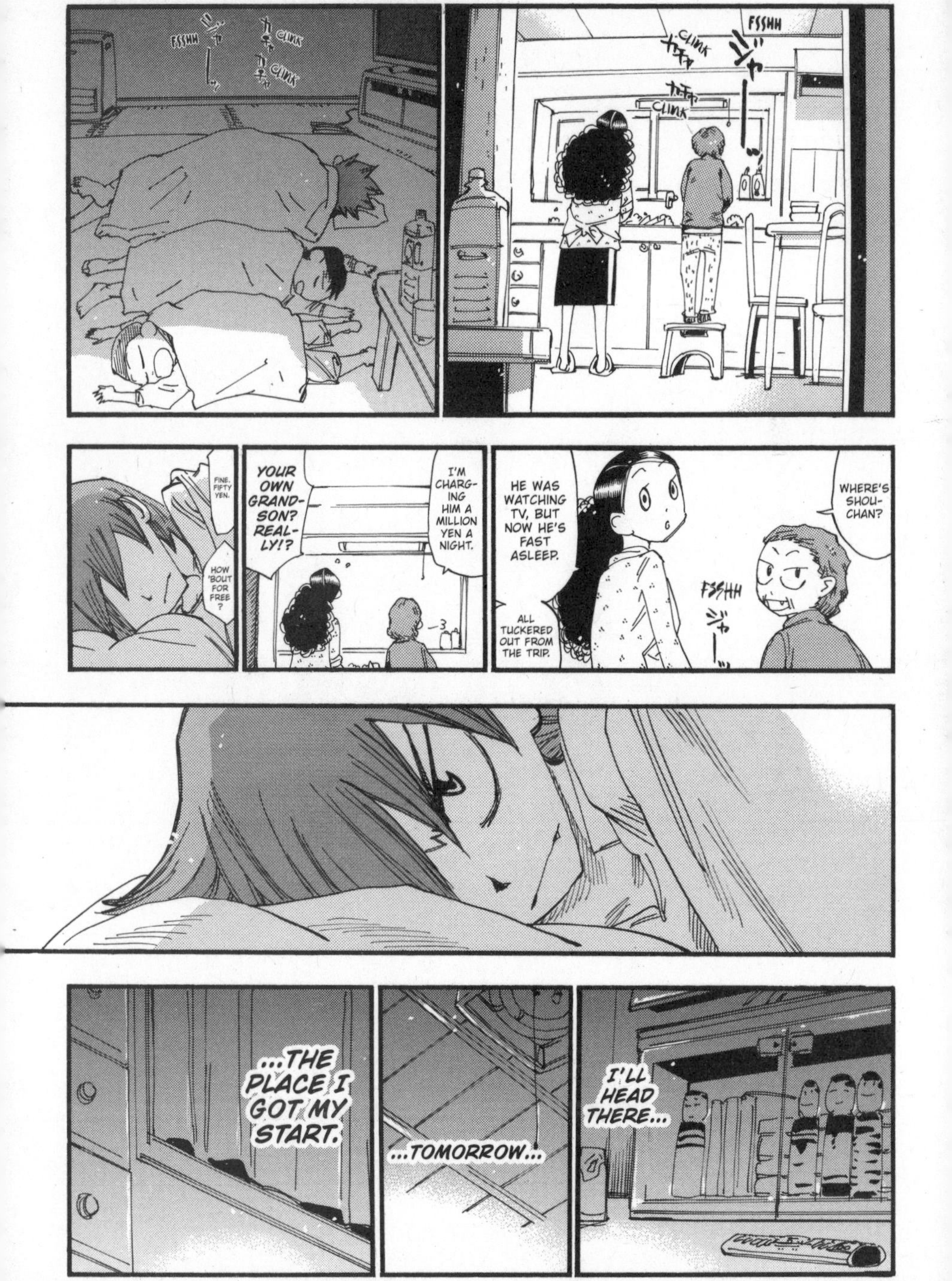
FSSHH
CLINK
CLINK
FSSHH
CLINK
CLINK
WHERE'S SHOU-CHAN?
FSSHH
HE WAS WATCHING TV, BUT NOW HE'S FAST ASLEEP.
ALL TUCKERED OUT FROM THE TRIP.
I'M CHARGING HIM A MILLION YEN A NIGHT.
YOUR OWN GRANDSON? REALLY!?
FINE. FIFTY YEN.
HOW 'BOUT FOR FREE?
I'LL HEAD THERE...
...TOMORROW...
...THE PLACE I GOT MY START.

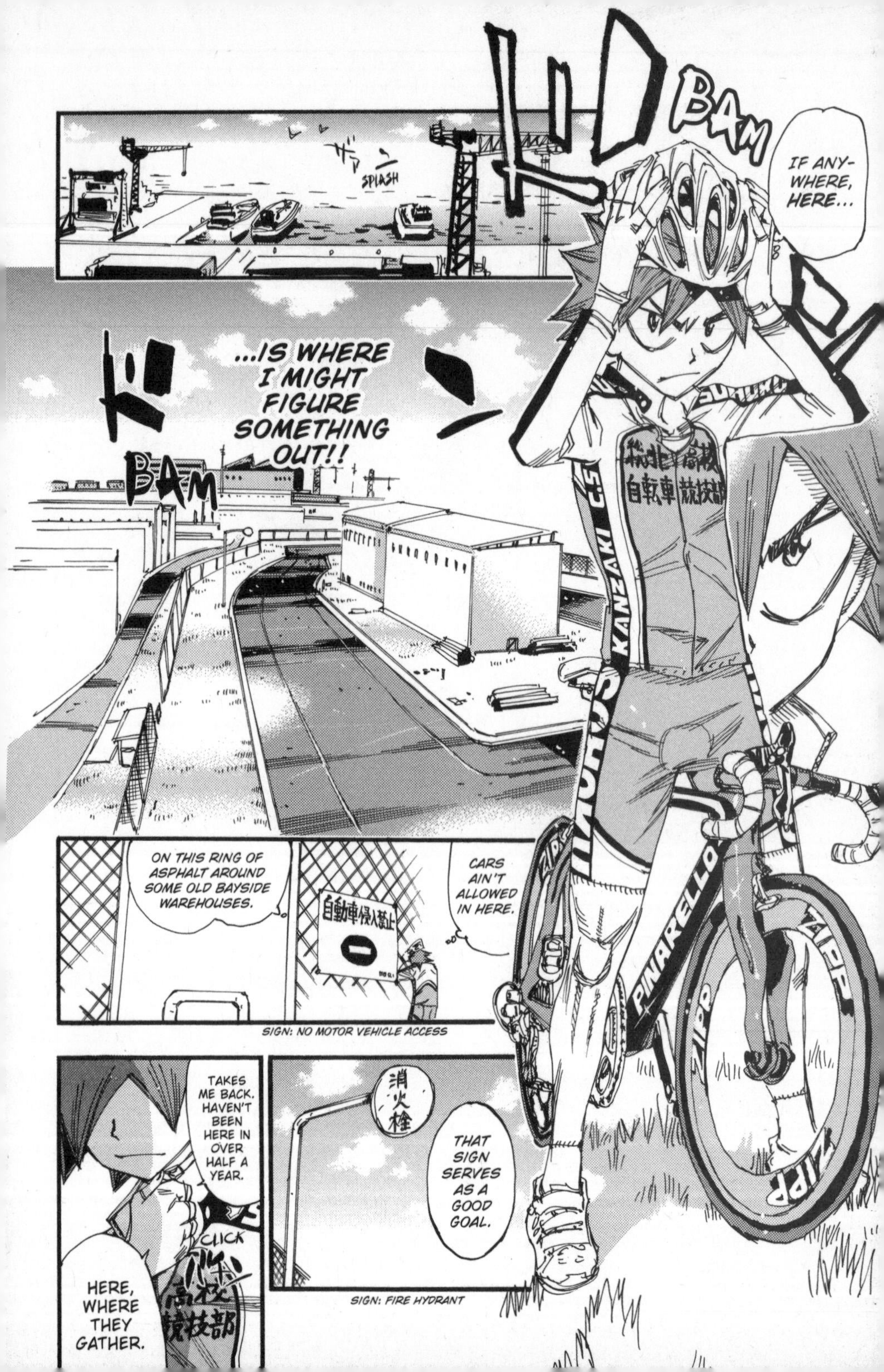
BAM
IF ANY-WHERE, HERE...
SPLASH
...IS WHERE I MIGHT FIGURE SOMETHING OUT!!
BAM
ON THIS RING OF ASPHALT AROUND SOME OLD BAYSIDE WAREHOUSES.
CARS AIN'T ALLOWED IN HERE.
自動車侵入禁止
SIGN: NO MOTOR VEHICLE ACCESS
消火栓
THAT SIGN SERVES AS A GOOD GOAL.
SIGN: FIRE HYDRANT
TAKES ME BACK. HAVEN'T BEEN HERE IN OVER HALF A YEAR.
CLICK
HERE, WHERE THEY GATHER.

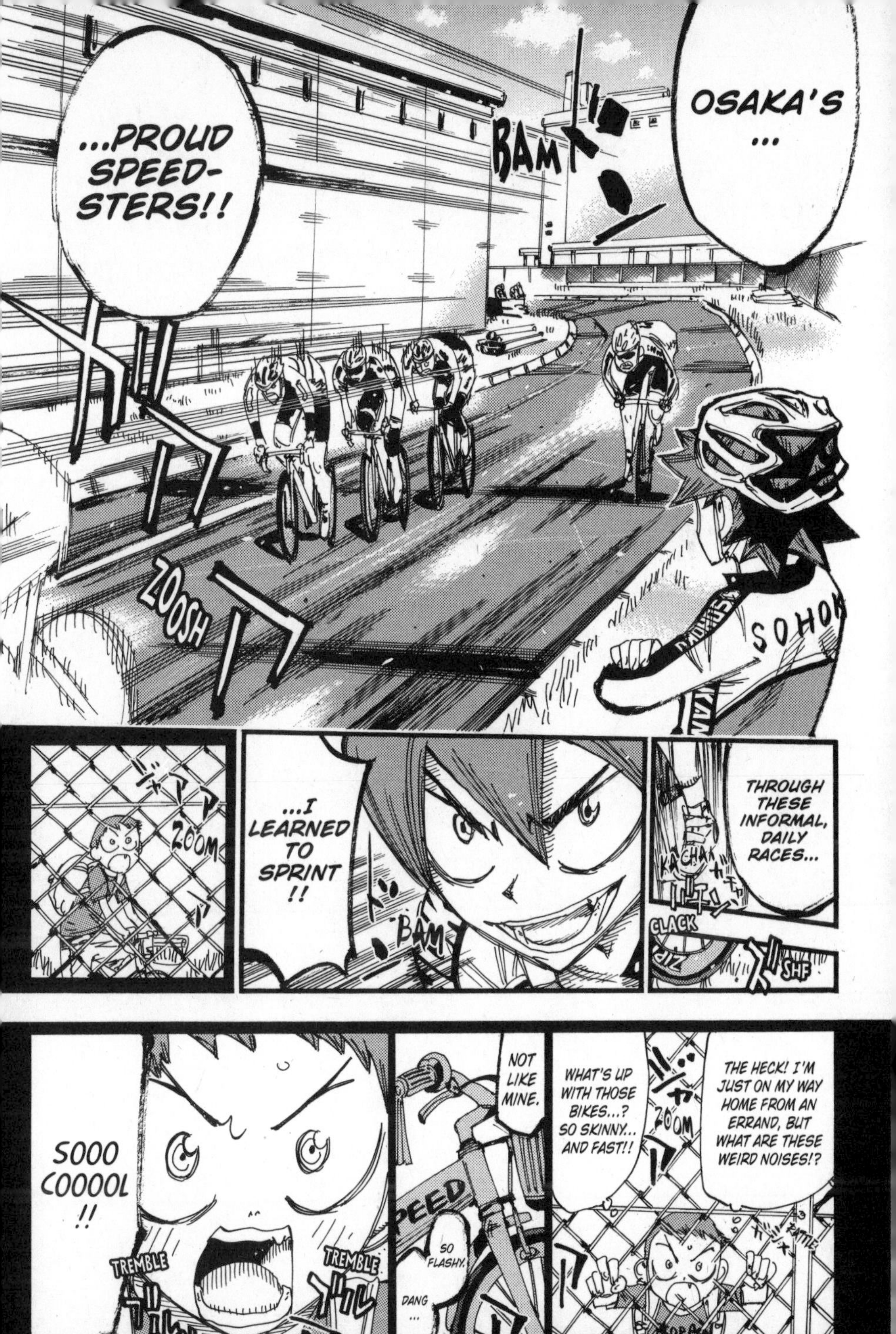
OSAKA'S ...
BAM
...PROUD SPEEDSTERS!!
ZOOSH
THROUGH THESE INFORMAL, DAILY RACES...
KACHAK
CLACK
ZIP
SHF
...I LEARNED TO SPRINT!!
BAM
ZOOM
THE HECK! I'M JUST ON MY WAY HOME FROM AN ERRAND, BUT WHAT ARE THESE WEIRD NOISES!?
WHAT'S UP WITH THOSE BIKES...? SO SKINNY... AND FAST!!
ZOOM
RATTLE
NOT LIKE MINE.
SO FLASHY.
DANG...
SOOO COOOOL!!
TREMBLE
TREMBLE

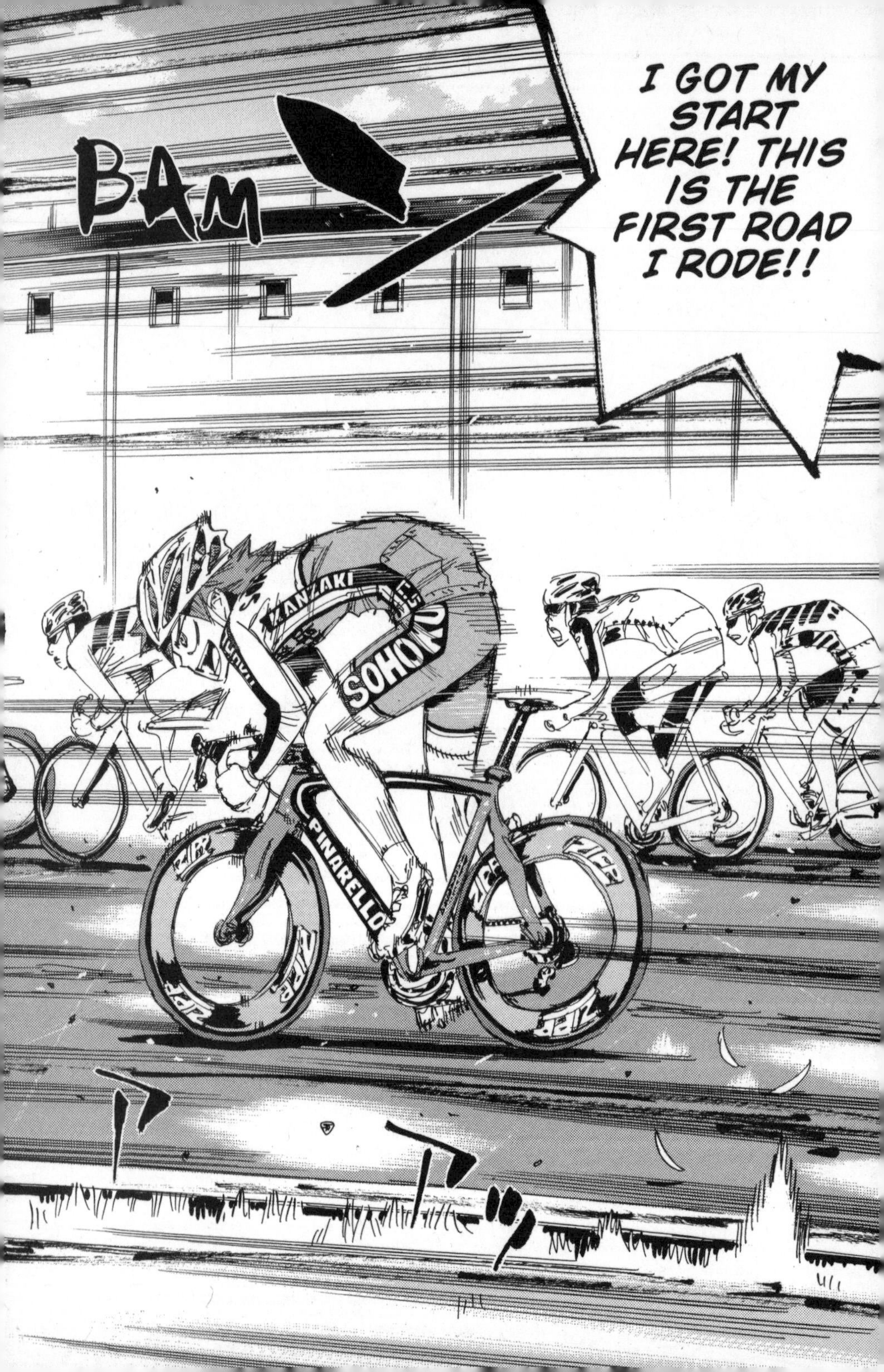
I GOT MY START HERE! THIS IS THE FIRST ROAD I RODE!!
BAM

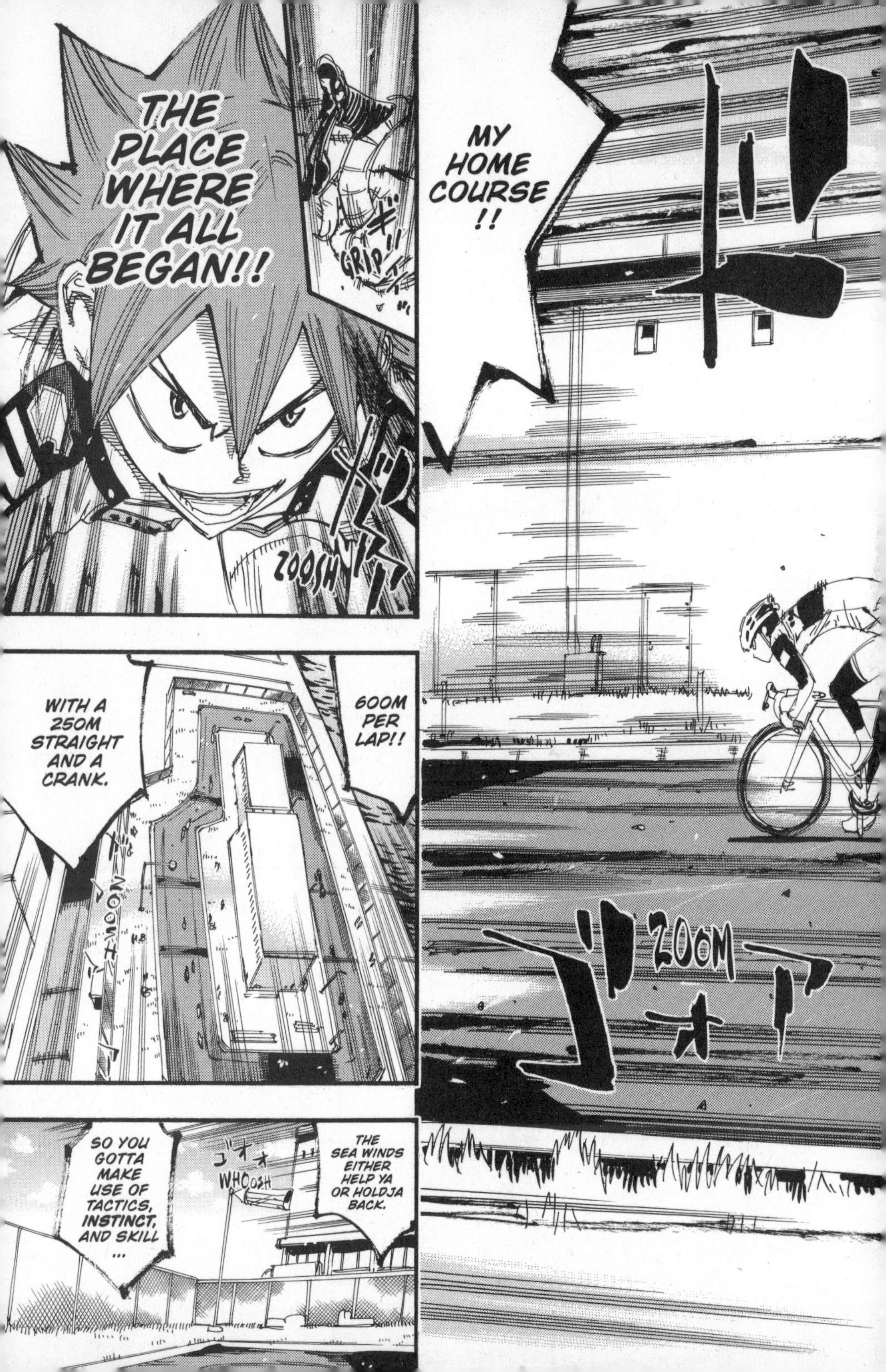
MY HOME COURSE!!
ZOOM
THE PLACE WHERE IT ALL BEGAN!!
GRIP
ZOOSH
600M PER LAP!!
WITH A 250M STRAIGHT AND A CRANK.
ZOOSH
THE SEA WINDS EITHER HELP YA OR HOLDJA BACK.
SO YOU GOTTA MAKE USE OF TACTICS, INSTINCT, AND SKILL...
WHOOSH

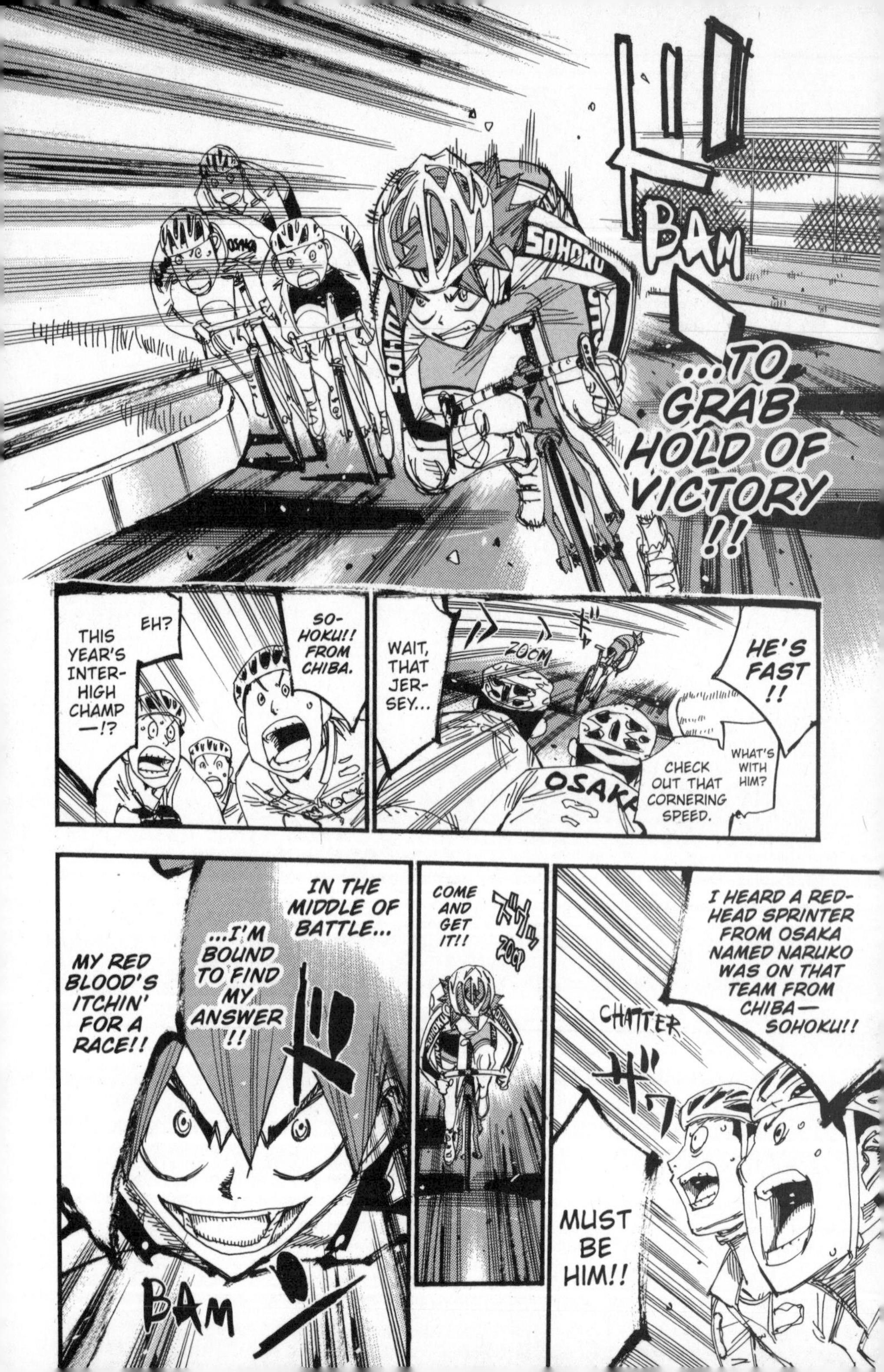
BAM
...TO GRAB HOLD OF VICTORY!!
HE'S FAST!!
WHAT'S WITH HIM?
CHECK OUT THAT CORNERING SPEED.
WAIT, THAT JERSEY...
ZOOM
SO-HOKU!! FROM CHIBA.
EH?
THIS YEAR'S INTER-HIGH CHAMP—!?
I HEARD A RED-HEAD SPRINTER FROM OSAKA NAMED NARUKO WAS ON THAT TEAM FROM CHIBA—SOHOKU!!
CHATTER
MUST BE HIM!!
COME AND GET IT!!
ZOOM
IN THE MIDDLE OF BATTLE...
...I'M BOUND TO FIND MY ANSWER!!
MY RED BLOOD'S ITCHIN' FOR A RACE!!
BAM

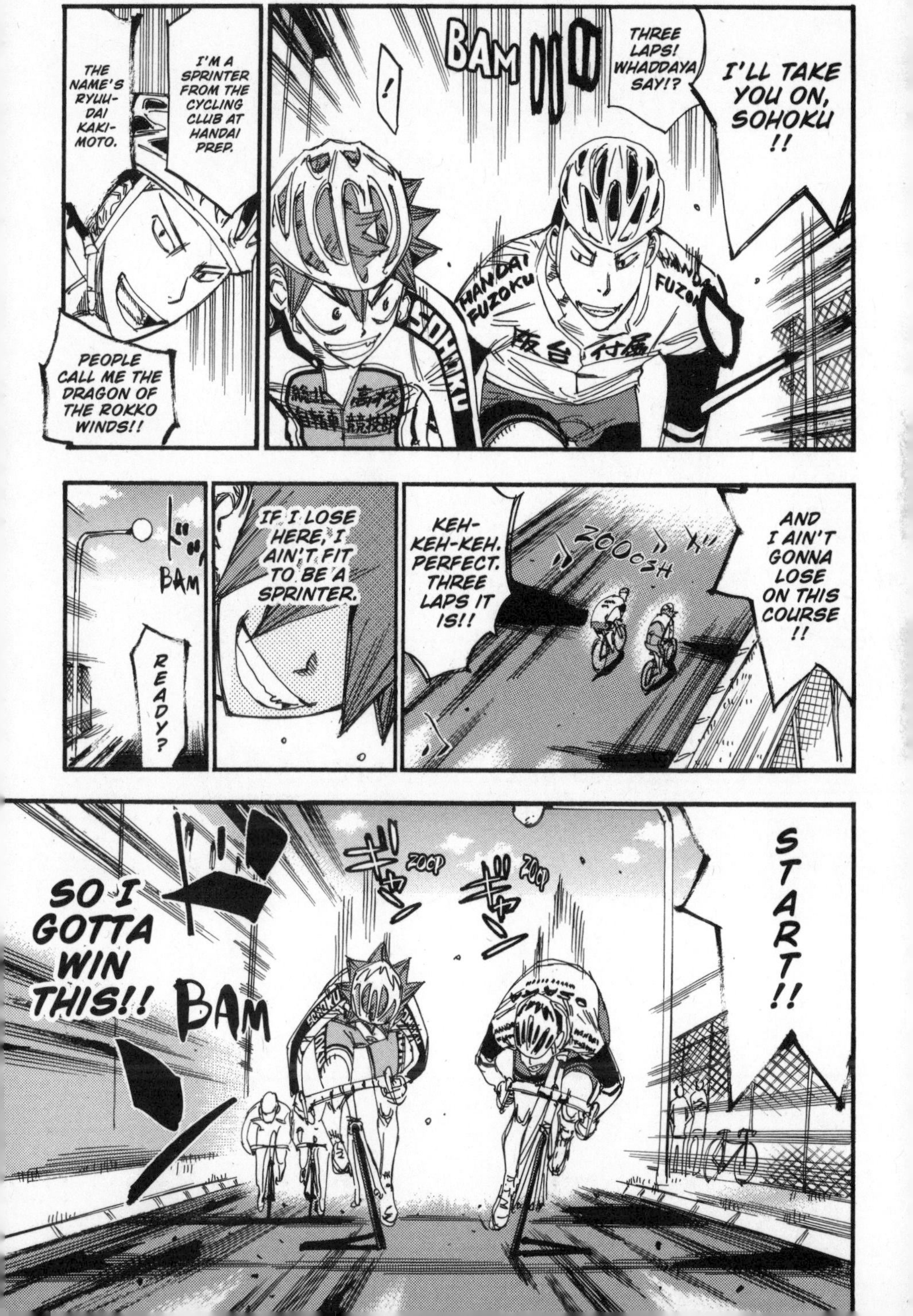
I'LL TAKE YOU ON, SOHOKU!!
THREE LAPS! WHADDAYA SAY!?
BAM
!
I'M A SPRINTER FROM THE CYCLING CLUB AT HANDAI PREP.
THE NAME'S RYUU-DAI KAKI-MOTO.
PEOPLE CALL ME THE DRAGON OF THE ROKKO WINDS!!
AND I AIN'T GONNA LOSE ON THIS COURSE!!
ZOOOSH
KEH-KEH-KEH. PERFECT. THREE LAPS IT IS!!
IF I LOSE HERE, I AIN'T FIT TO BE A SPRINTER.
BAM
READY?
START!!
SO I GOTTA WIN THIS!!
BAM

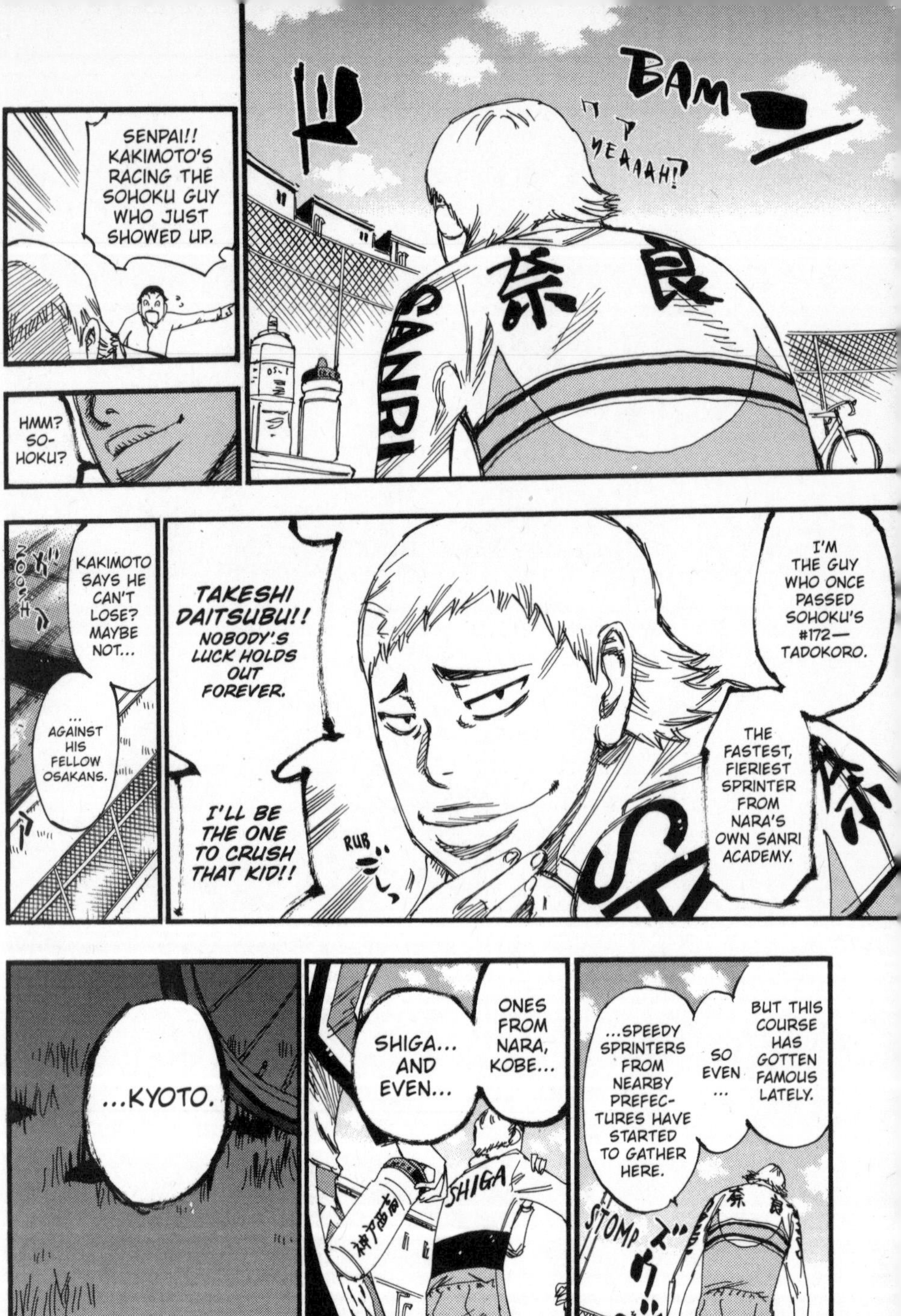
BAM
YEAAAH!?
SENPAI!! KAKIMOTO'S RACING THE SOHOKU GUY WHO JUST SHOWED UP.
HMM? SO-HOKU?
I'M THE GUY WHO ONCE PASSED SOHOKU'S #172—TADOKORO.
THE FASTEST, FIERIEST SPRINTER FROM NARA'S OWN SANRI ACADEMY.
TAKESHI DAITSUBU!! NOBODY'S LUCK HOLDS OUT FOREVER.
I'LL BE THE ONE TO CRUSH THAT KID!!
RUB
KAKIMOTO SAYS HE CAN'T LOSE? MAYBE NOT...
...AGAINST HIS FELLOW OSAKANS.
WOOSH
BUT THIS COURSE HAS GOTTEN FAMOUS LATELY.
SO EVEN...
...SPEEDY SPRINTERS FROM NEARBY PREFEC-TURES HAVE STARTED TO GATHER HERE.
STOMP
ONES FROM NARA, KOBE...
SHIGA... AND EVEN...
SHIGA
...KYOTO.
BOTTLE: KOBE WEST HIGH

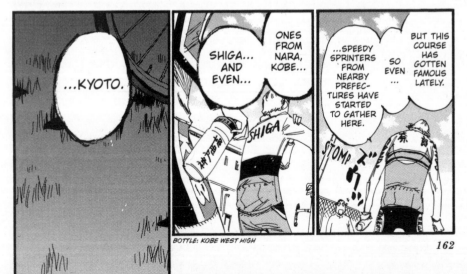

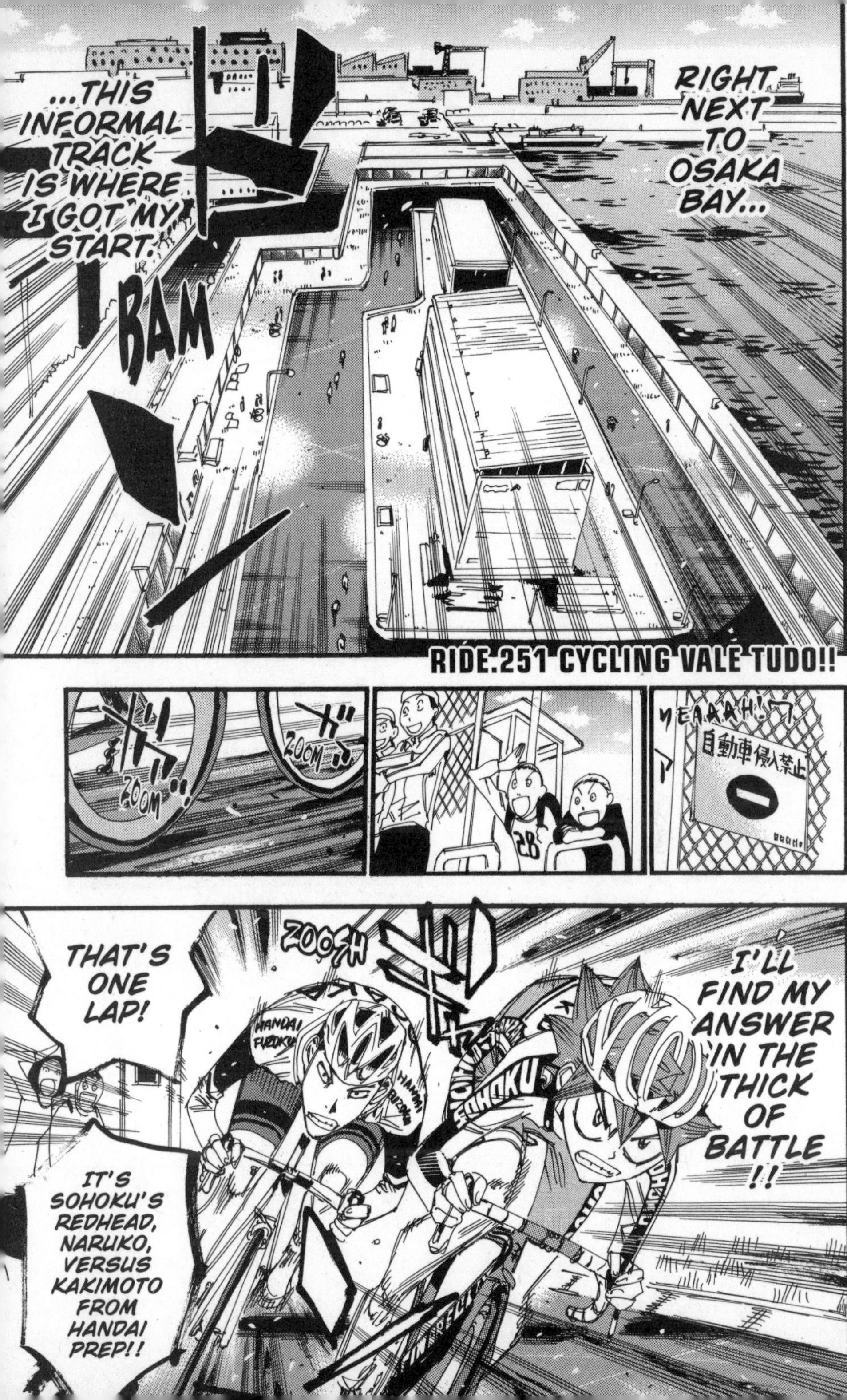
RIGHT NEXT TO OSAKA BAY...
...THIS INFORMAL TRACK IS WHERE I GOT MY START.
BAM
RIDE.251 CYCLING VALE TUDO!!
YEAAAAH!
自動車侵入禁止
ZOOM
ZOOM
I'LL FIND MY ANSWER IN THE THICK OF BATTLE!!
ZOOSH
THAT'S ONE LAP!
IT'S SOHOKU'S REDHEAD, NARUKO, VERSUS KAKIMOTO FROM HANDAI PREP!!
HANDAI FUZOKU
SOHOKU

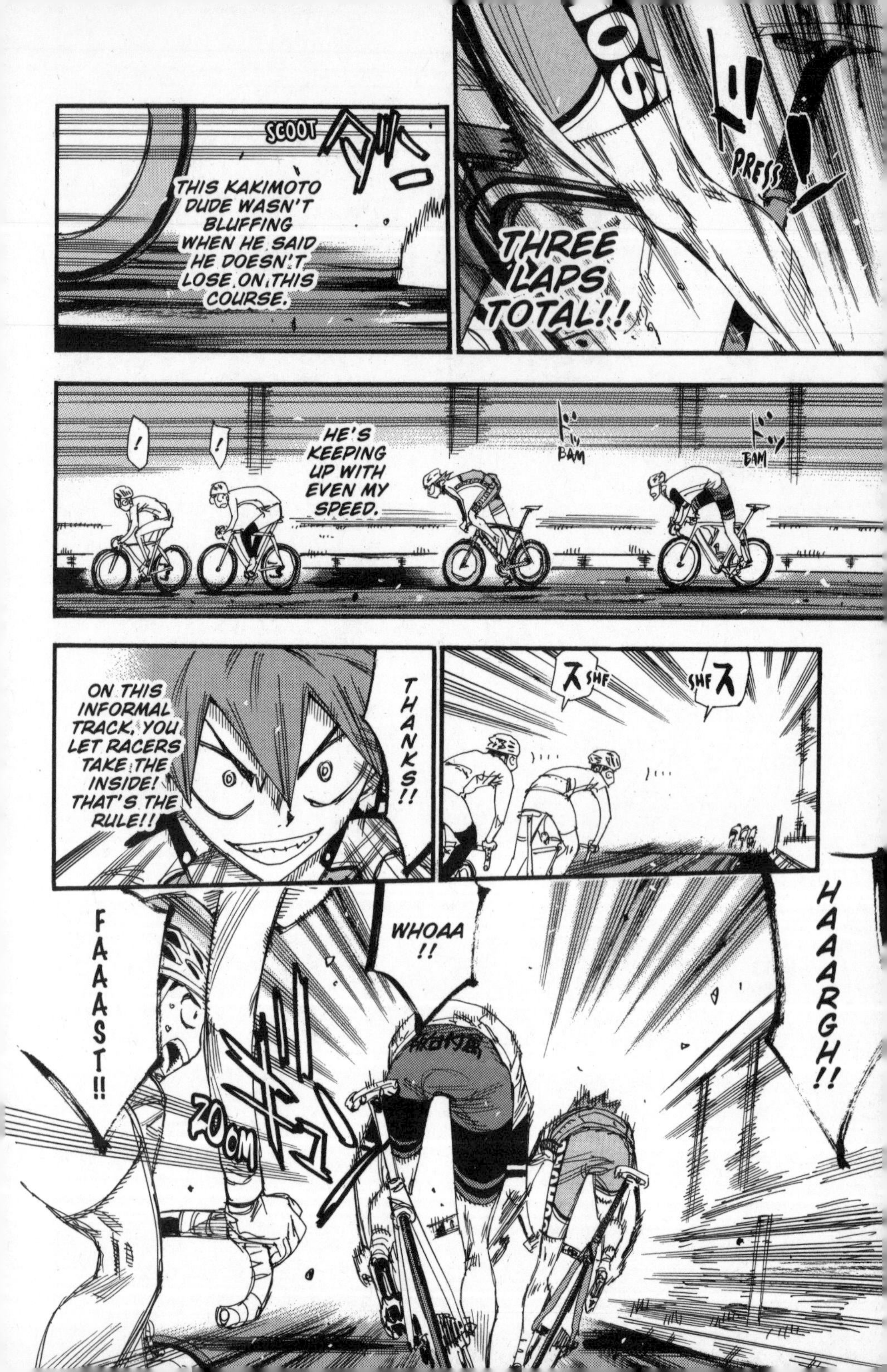
PRESS
THREE LAPS TOTAL!!
SCOOT
THIS KAKIMOTO DUDE WASN'T BLUFFING WHEN HE SAID HE DOESN'T LOSE ON THIS COURSE.
BAM
BAM
HE'S KEEPING UP WITH EVEN MY SPEED.
!
!
SHF
SHF
THANKS!!
ON THIS INFORMAL TRACK, YOU LET RACERS TAKE THE INSIDE! THAT'S THE RULE!!
HAAAARGH!!
WHOAA!!
ZOOM
FAAAST!!

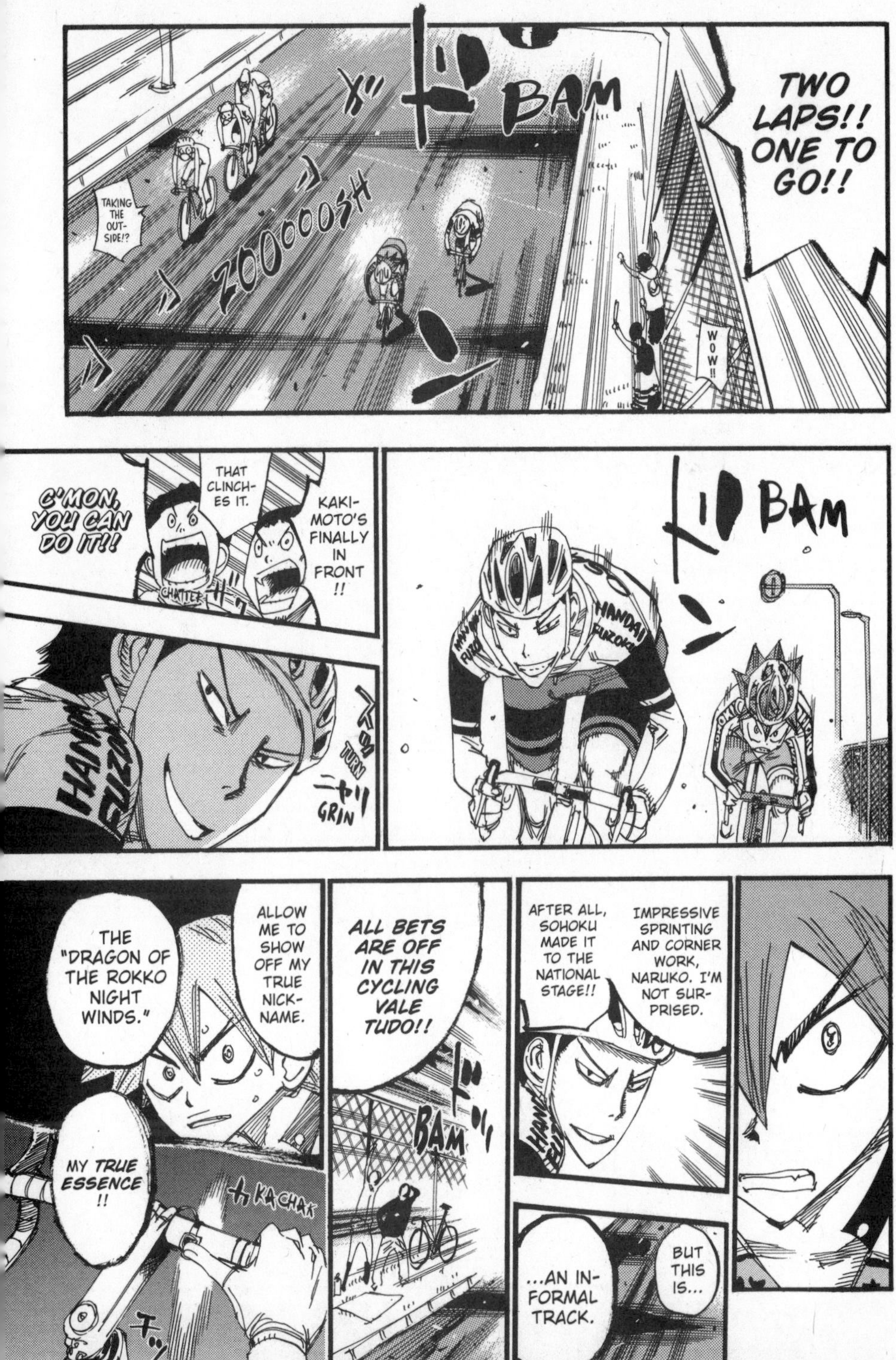

TWO LAPS!! ONE TO GO!!
BAM
WOW!!
ZOOOOOSH
TAKING THE OUT-SIDE!?
BAM
KAKI-MOTO'S FINALLY IN FRONT!!
THAT CLINCH-ES IT.
C'MON, YOU CAN DO IT!!
CHATTER
TURN
GRIN
IMPRESSIVE SPRINTING AND CORNER WORK, NARUKO. I'M NOT SUR-PRISED.
AFTER ALL, SOHOKU MADE IT TO THE NATIONAL STAGE!!
BUT THIS IS...
...AN IN-FORMAL TRACK.
ALL BETS ARE OFF IN THIS CYCLING VALE TUDO!!
BAM
ALLOW ME TO SHOW OFF MY TRUE NICK-NAME.
THE "DRAGON OF THE ROKKO NIGHT WINDS."
MY TRUE ESSENCE!!
KA CHAK

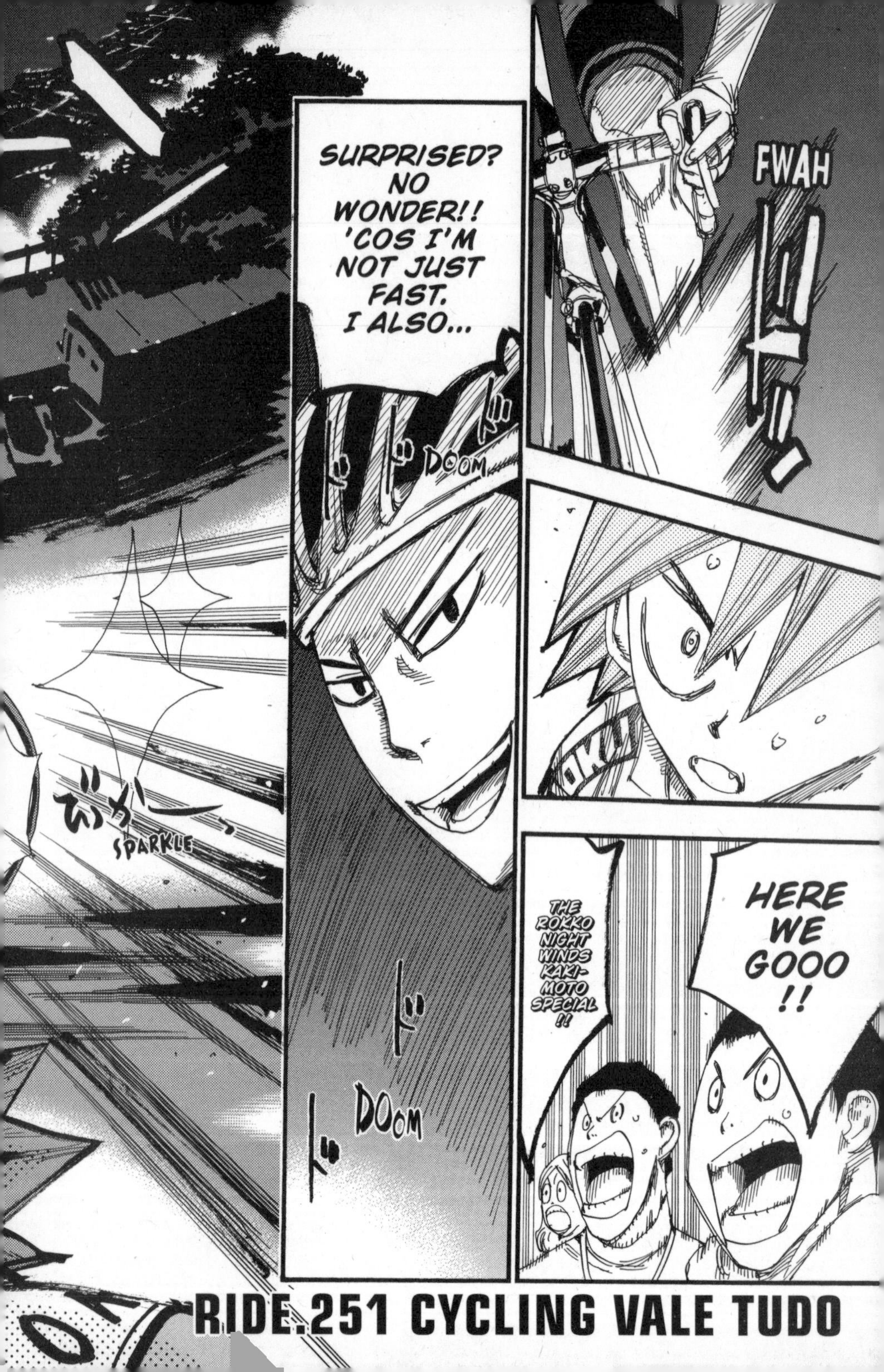
FWAH
HERE WE GOOO!!
THE ROKKO NIGHT WINDS KAKI-MOTO SPECIAL!!
SURPRISED? NO WONDER!! 'COS I'M NOT JUST FAST. I ALSO...
DOOM
DOOM
SPARKLE

RIDE.251 CYCLING VALE TUDO

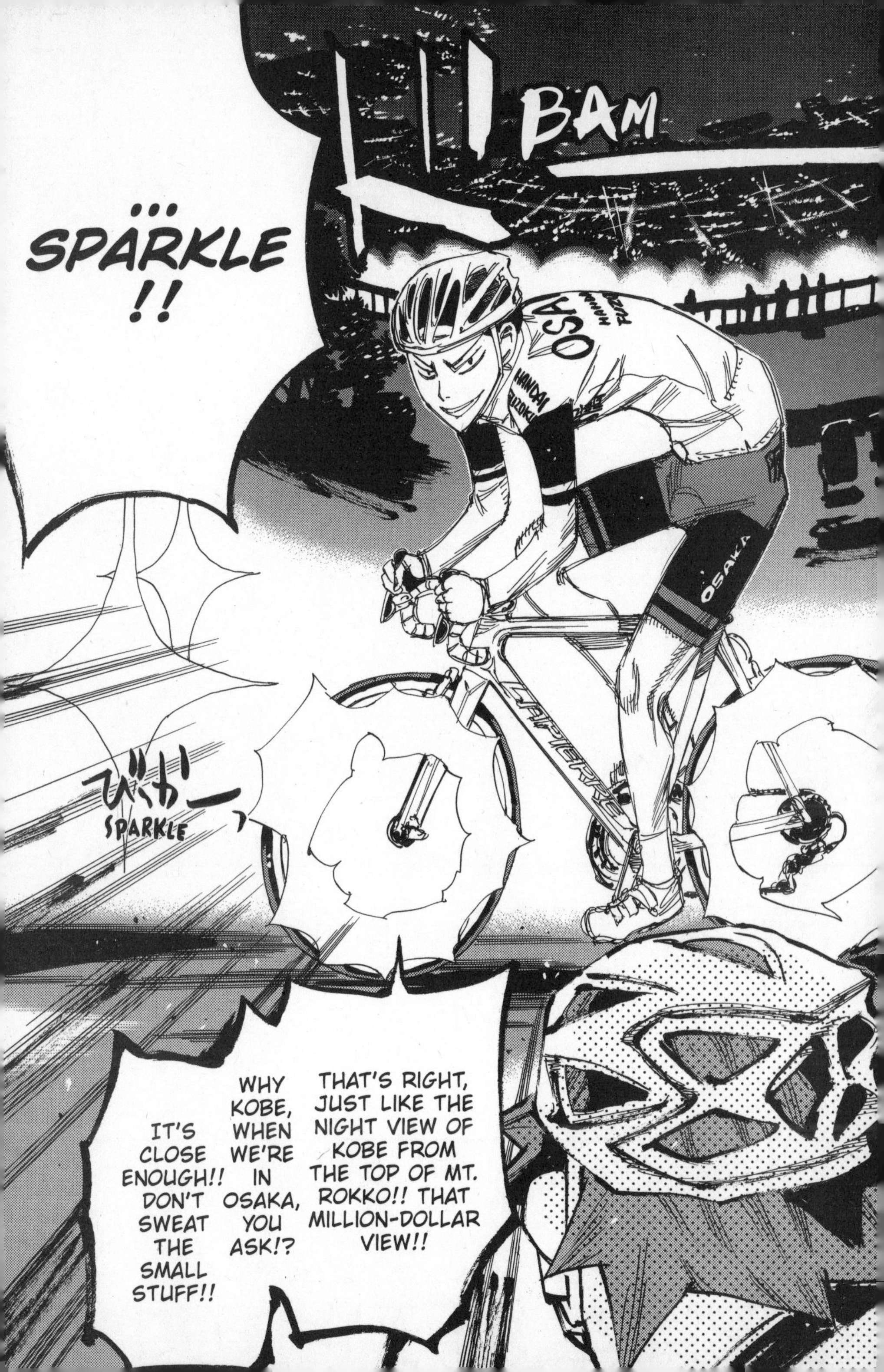
BAM
...SPÄRKLE!!
ぴかー
SPARKLE
THAT'S RIGHT, JUST LIKE THE NIGHT VIEW OF KOBE FROM THE TOP OF MT. ROKKO!! THAT MILLION-DOLLAR VIEW!!
WHY KOBE, WHEN WE'RE IN OSAKA, YOU ASK!?
IT'S CLOSE ENOUGH!! DON'T SWEAT THE SMALL STUFF!!
OSAKA
HANDAI
OSAKA

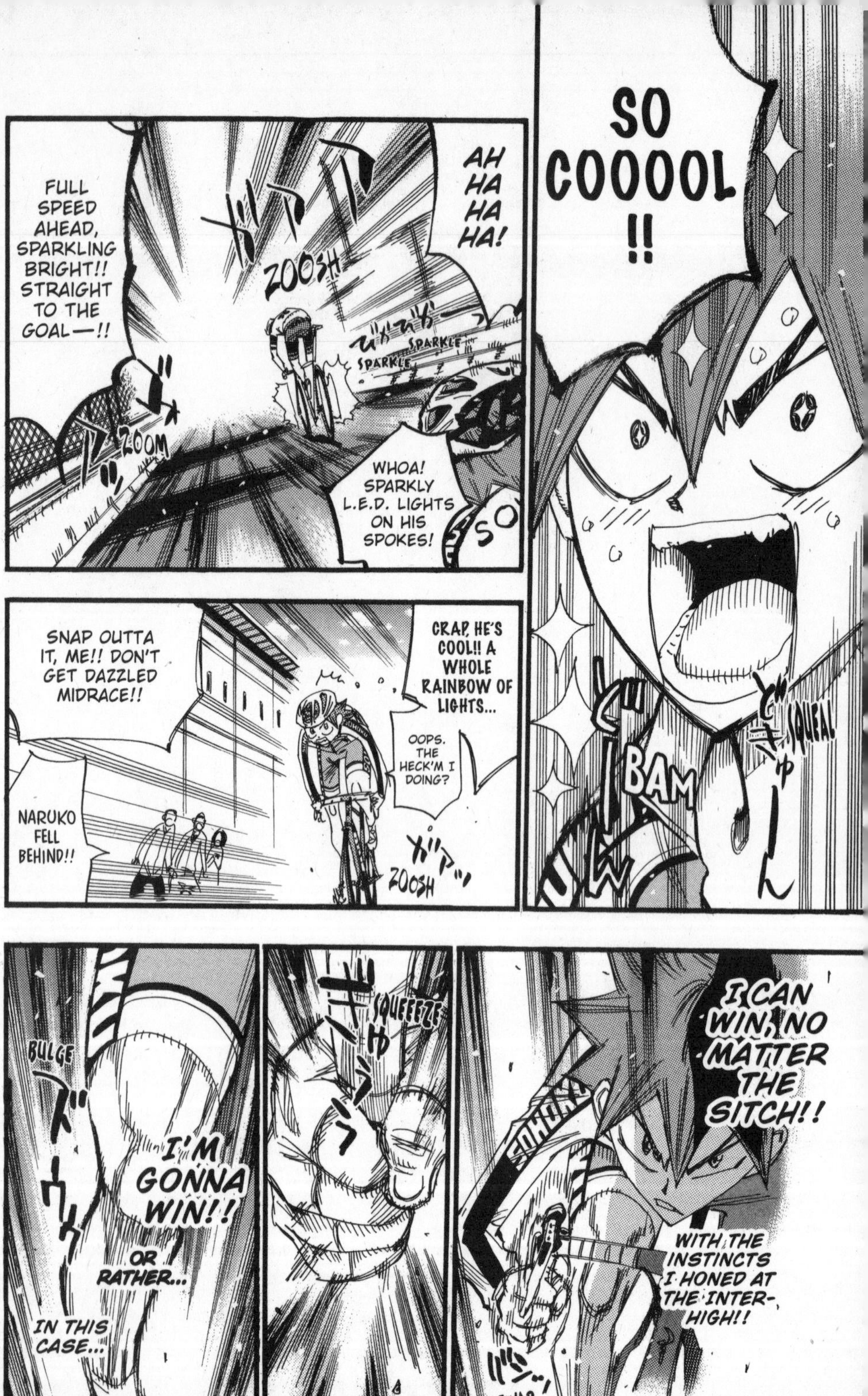
FULL SPEED AHEAD, SPARKLING BRIGHT!! STRAIGHT TO THE GOAL—!!
AH HA HA HA!
ZOOSH
SPARKLE SPARKLE
ZOOM
WHOA! SPARKLY L.E.D. LIGHTS ON HIS SPOKES!
SO
SO COOOOL !!
BAM
SQUEAL
CRAP, HE'S COOL!! A WHOLE RAINBOW OF LIGHTS...
OOPS. THE HECK'M I DOING?
SNAP OUTTA IT, ME!! DON'T GET DAZZLED MIDRACE!!
NARUKO FELL BEHIND!!
ZOOSH
I CAN WIN, NO MATTER THE SITCH!!
WITH THE INSTINCTS I HONED AT THE INTER-HIGH!!
FWAP
SQUEEEZE
BULGE
I'M GONNA WIN!!
OR RATHER...
IN THIS CASE...

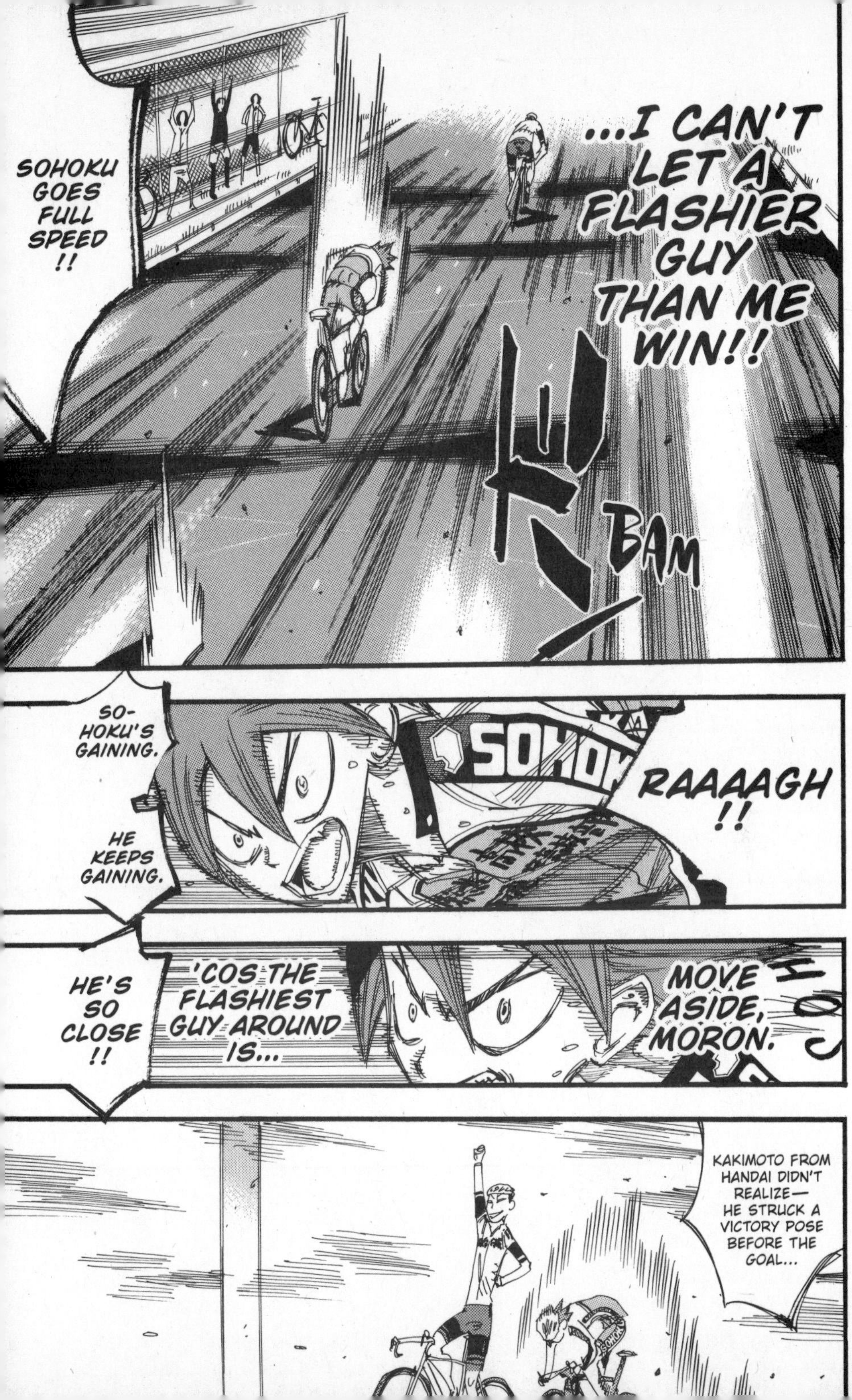
...I CAN'T LET A FLASHIER GUY THAN ME WIN!!
SOHOKU GOES FULL SPEED!!
BAM
RAAAAGH!!
SO-HOKU'S GAINING.
HE KEEPS GAINING.
MOVE ASIDE, MORON.
'COS THE FLASHIEST GUY AROUND IS...
HE'S SO CLOSE!!
KAKIMOTO FROM HANDAI DIDN'T REALIZE—HE STRUCK A VICTORY POSE BEFORE THE GOAL...

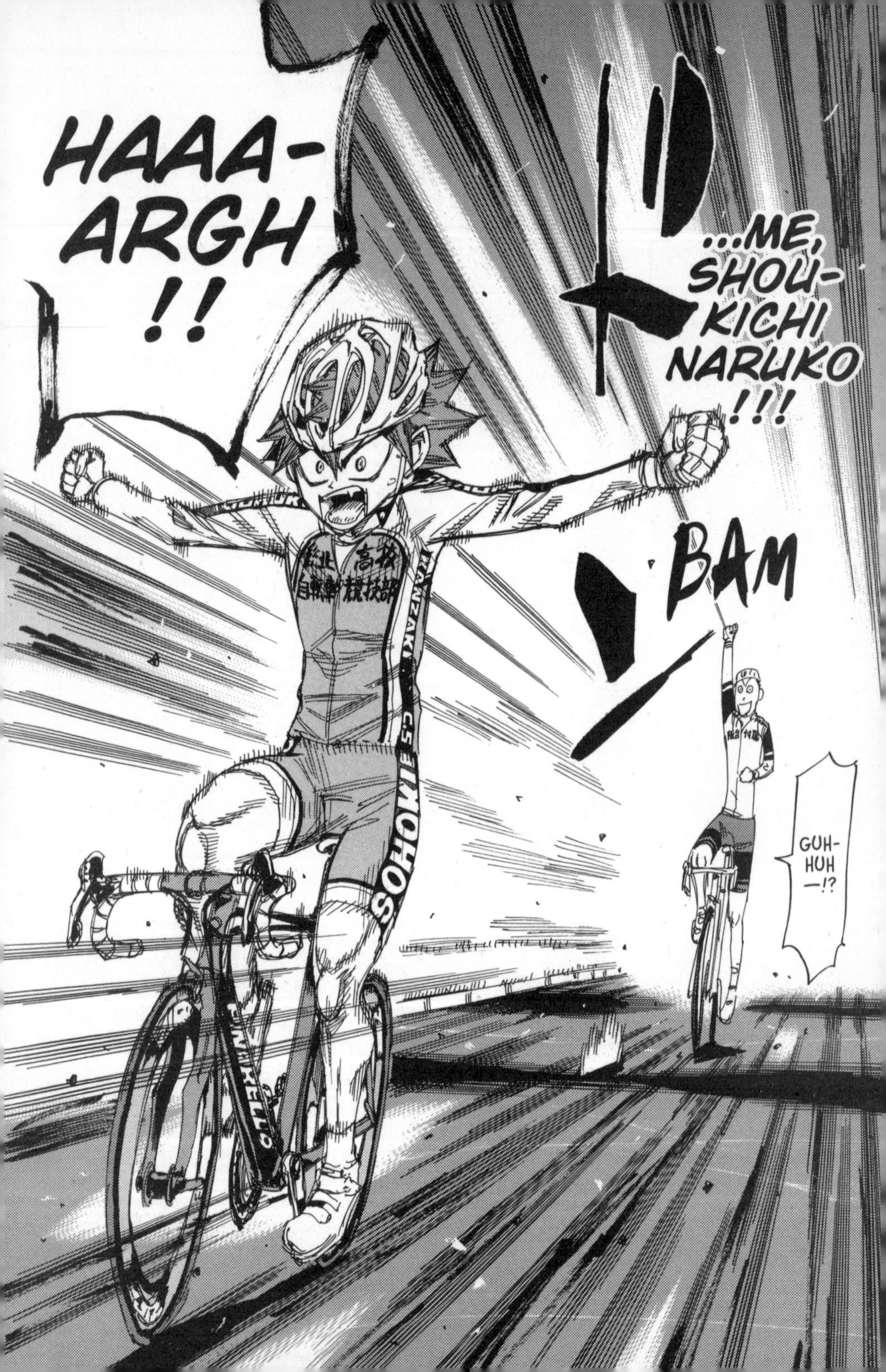
...ME, SHOU-KICHI NARUKO!!!
HAAA-ARGH!!
BAM
GUH-HUH—!?

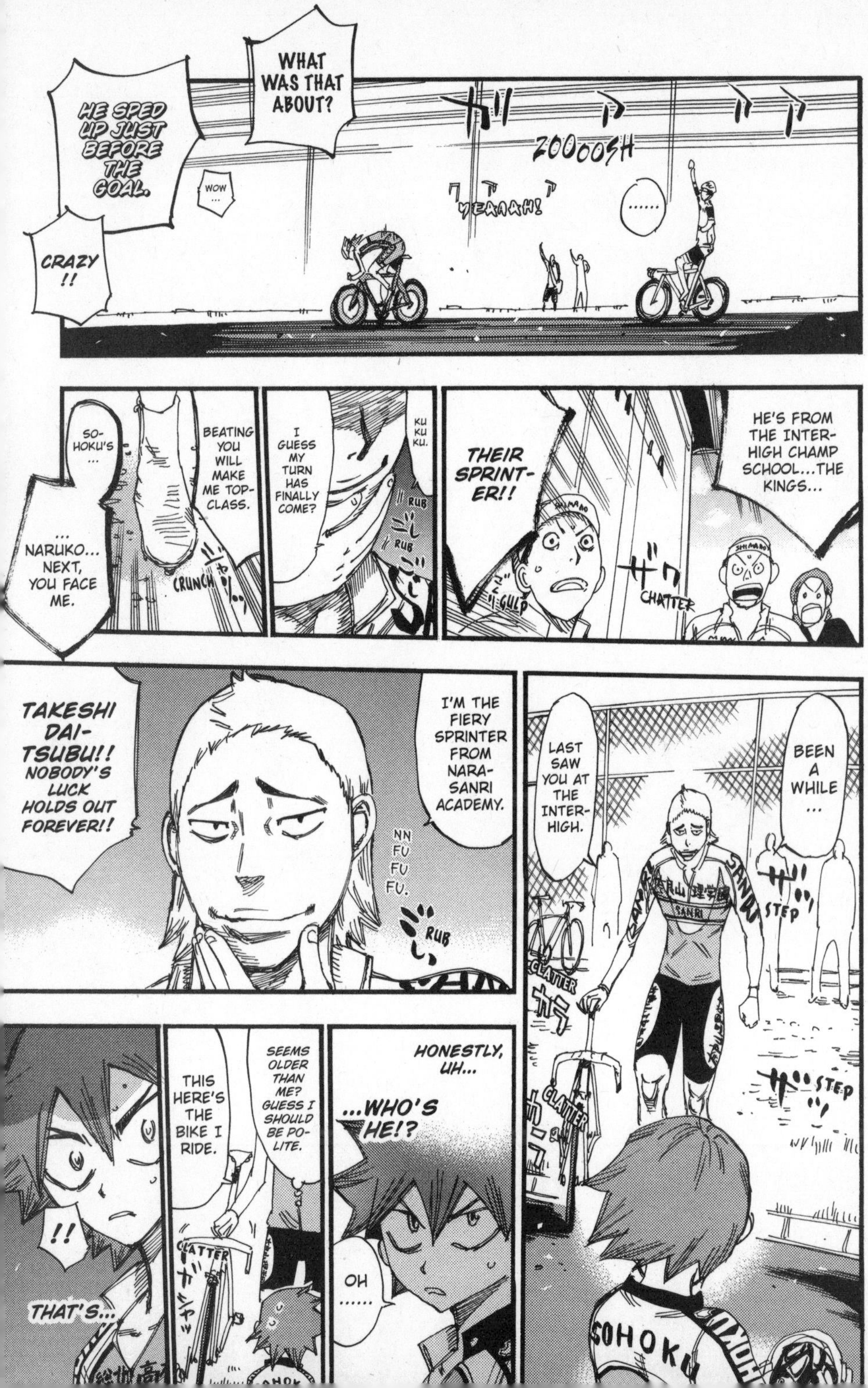
ZOOOOSH
WHAT WAS THAT ABOUT?
HE SPED UP JUST BEFORE THE GOAL.
......
YEAAAH!
WOW ...
CRAZY !!
HE'S FROM THE INTER-HIGH CHAMP SCHOOL...THE KINGS...
CHATTER
THEIR SPRINTER!!
GULP
KU KU KU.
I GUESS MY TURN HAS FINALLY COME?
RUB
RUB
BEATING YOU WILL MAKE ME TOP-CLASS.
SO-HOKU'S ...
CRUNCH
... NARUKO... NEXT, YOU FACE ME.
BEEN A WHILE ...
LAST SAW YOU AT THE INTER-HIGH.
STEP
CLATTER
STEP
CLATTER
I'M THE FIERY SPRINTER FROM NARA-SANRI ACADEMY.
TAKESHI DAI-TSUBU!! NOBODY'S LUCK HOLDS OUT FOREVER!!
NN FU FU FU.
RUB
HONESTLY, UH...
...WHO'S HE!?
OH ......
SEEMS OLDER THAN ME? GUESS I SHOULD BE PO-LITE.
THIS HERE'S THE BIKE I RIDE.
CLATTER
!!
THAT'S...

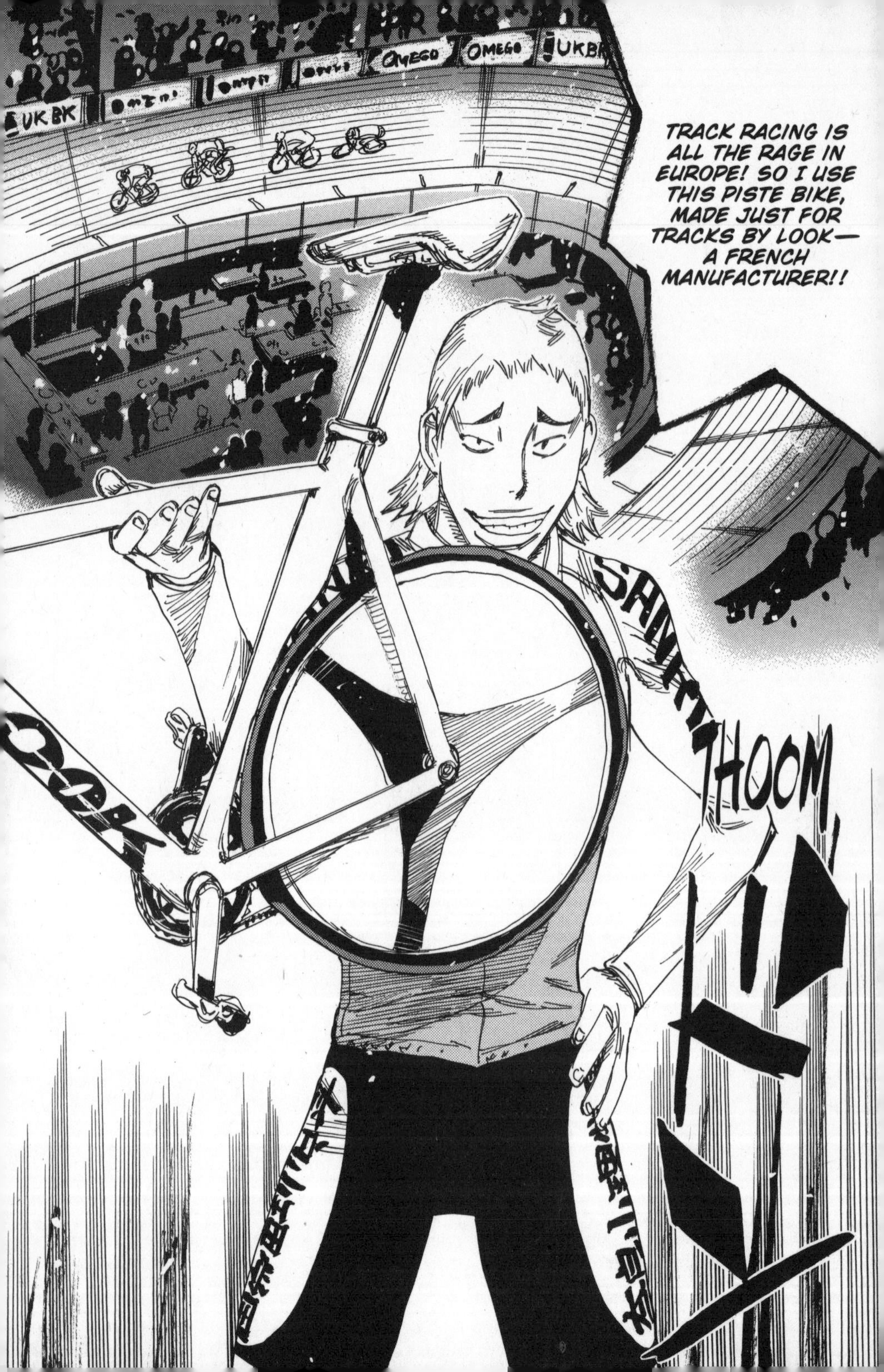
TRACK RACING IS ALL THE RAGE IN EUROPE! SO I USE THIS PISTE BIKE, MADE JUST FOR TRACKS BY LOOK— A FRENCH MANUFACTURER!!
THOOM

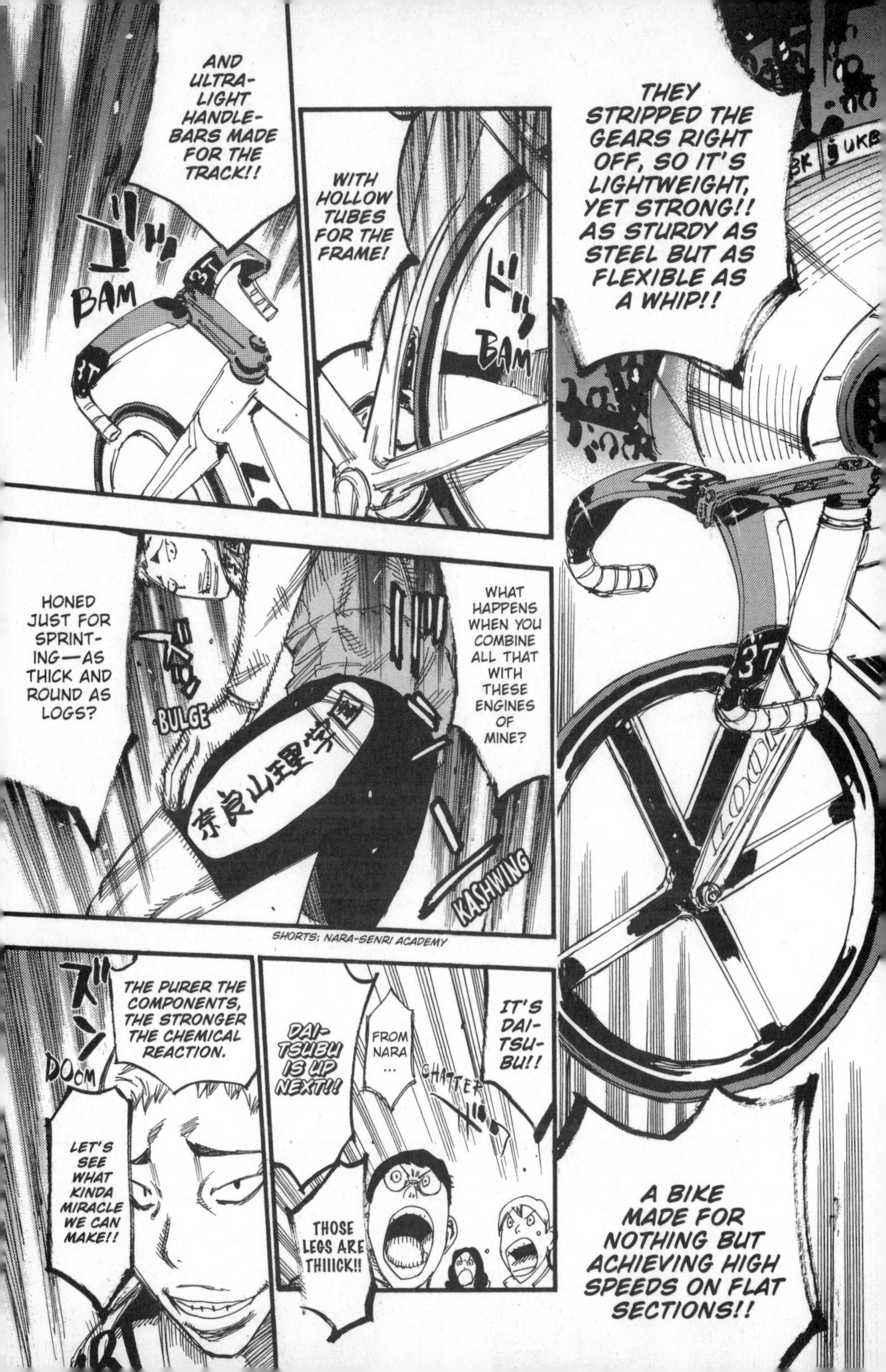
THEY STRIPPED THE GEARS RIGHT OFF, SO IT'S LIGHTWEIGHT, YET STRONG!! AS STURDY AS STEEL BUT AS FLEXIBLE AS A WHIP!!
A BIKE MADE FOR NOTHING BUT ACHIEVING HIGH SPEEDS ON FLAT SECTIONS!!
WITH HOLLOW TUBES FOR THE FRAME!
BAM
AND ULTRA-LIGHT HANDLE-BARS MADE FOR THE TRACK!!
BAM
WHAT HAPPENS WHEN YOU COMBINE ALL THAT WITH THESE ENGINES OF MINE?
HONED JUST FOR SPRINT-ING—AS THICK AND ROUND AS LOGS?
BULGE
KASHWING
SHORTS: NARA-SENRI ACADEMY
IT'S DAI-TSU-BU!!
FROM NARA ...
DAI-TSUBU IS UP NEXT!!
CHATTER
THOSE LEGS ARE THIIICK!!
THE PURER THE COMPONENTS, THE STRONGER THE CHEMICAL REACTION.
DOOM
LET'S SEE WHAT KINDA MIRACLE WE CAN MAKE!!

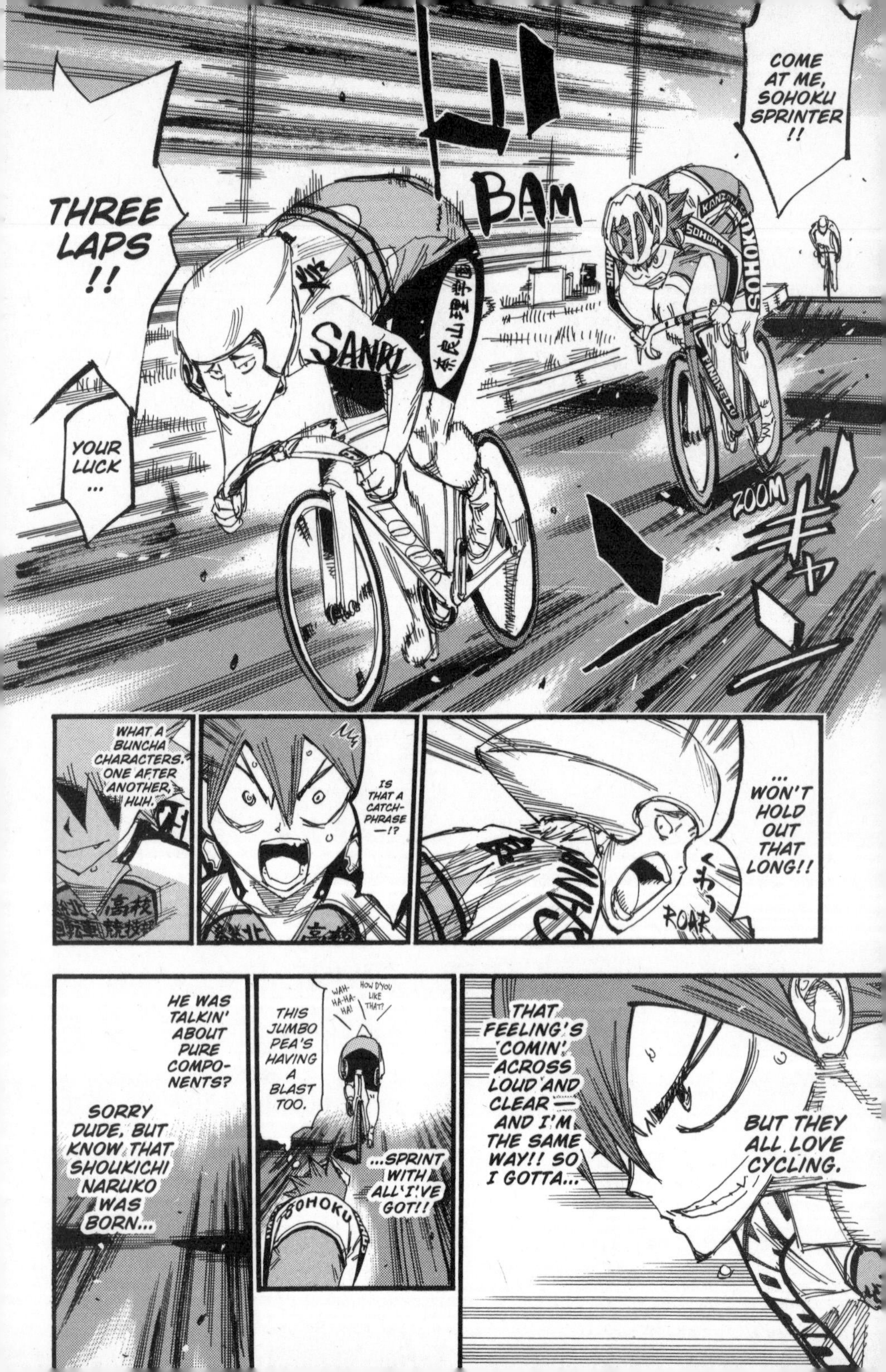
COME AT ME, SOHOKU SPRINTER !!
BAM
THREE LAPS !!
YOUR LUCK ...
ZOOM
... WON'T HOLD OUT THAT LONG!!
ROAR
IS THAT A CATCH-PHRASE —!?
WHAT A BUNCHA CHARACTERS. ONE AFTER ANOTHER, HUH.
BUT THEY ALL LOVE CYCLING.
THAT FEELING'S COMIN' ACROSS LOUD AND CLEAR — AND I'M THE SAME WAY!! SO I GOTTA...
WAH-HA-HA-HA!
HOW D'YOU LIKE THAT?!
THIS JUMBO PEA'S HAVING A BLAST TOO.
...SPRINT WITH ALL I'VE GOT!!
HE WAS TALKIN' ABOUT PURE COMPO-NENTS?
SORRY DUDE, BUT KNOW THAT SHOUKICHI NARUKO WAS BORN...

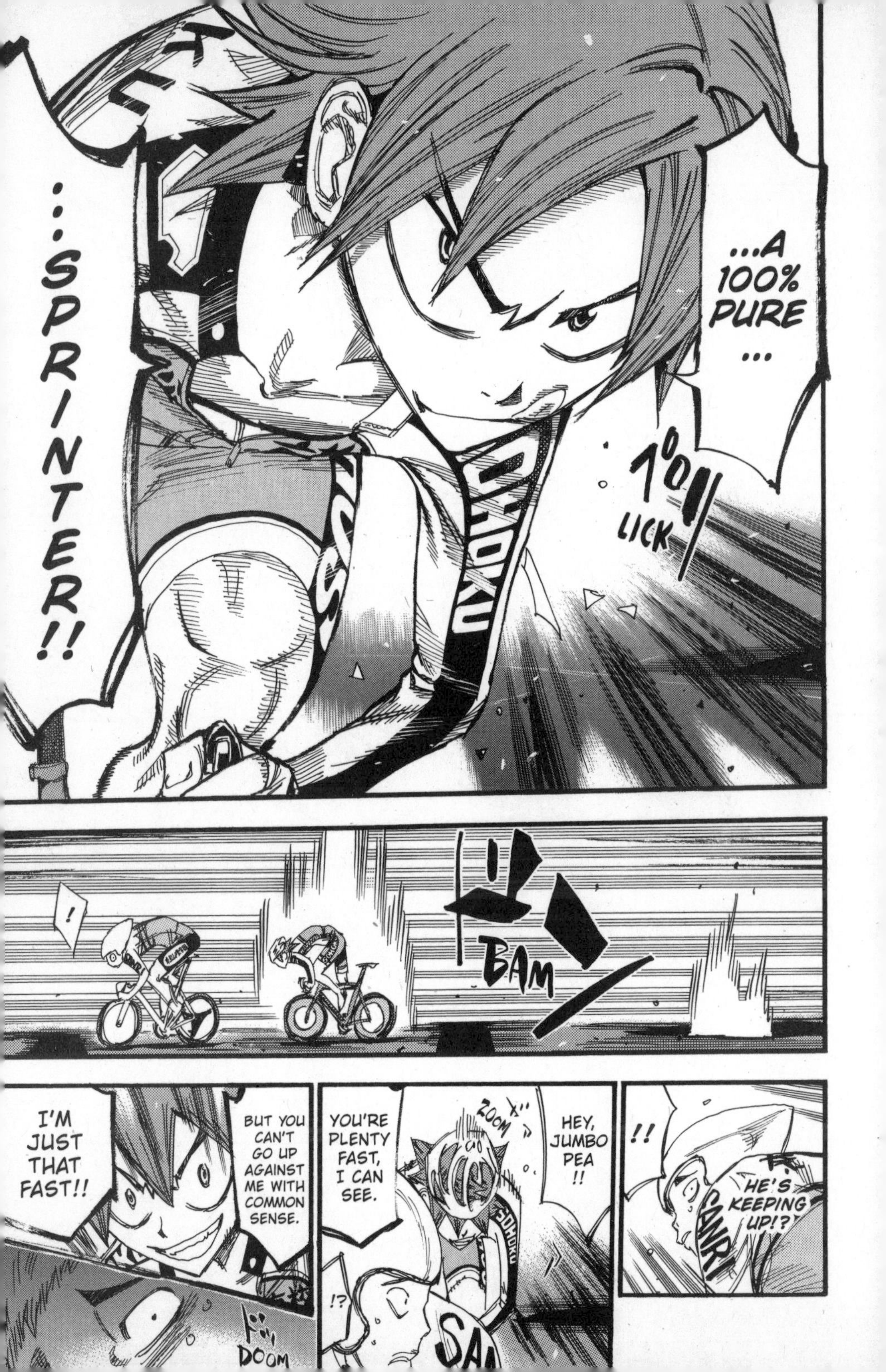
...A 100% PURE ...
LICK
...SPRINTER!!
BAM
!
!!
HE'S KEEPING UP!?
HEY, JUMBO PEA!!
ZOOM
YOU'RE PLENTY FAST, I CAN SEE.
!?
BUT YOU CAN'T GO UP AGAINST ME WITH COMMON SENSE.
I'M JUST THAT FAST!!
DOOM

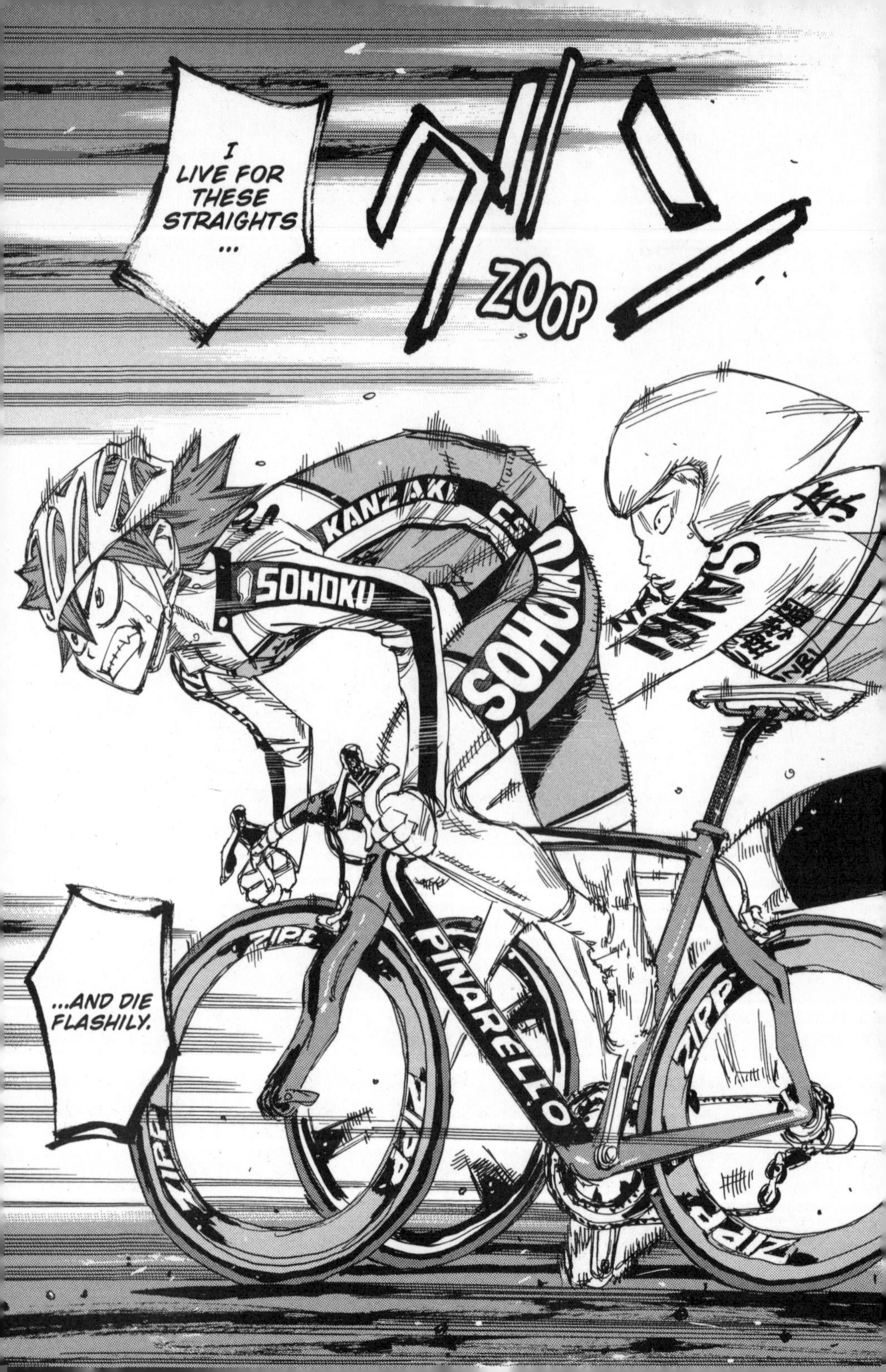
ZOOP
I LIVE FOR THESE STRAIGHTS...
...AND DIE FLASHILY.

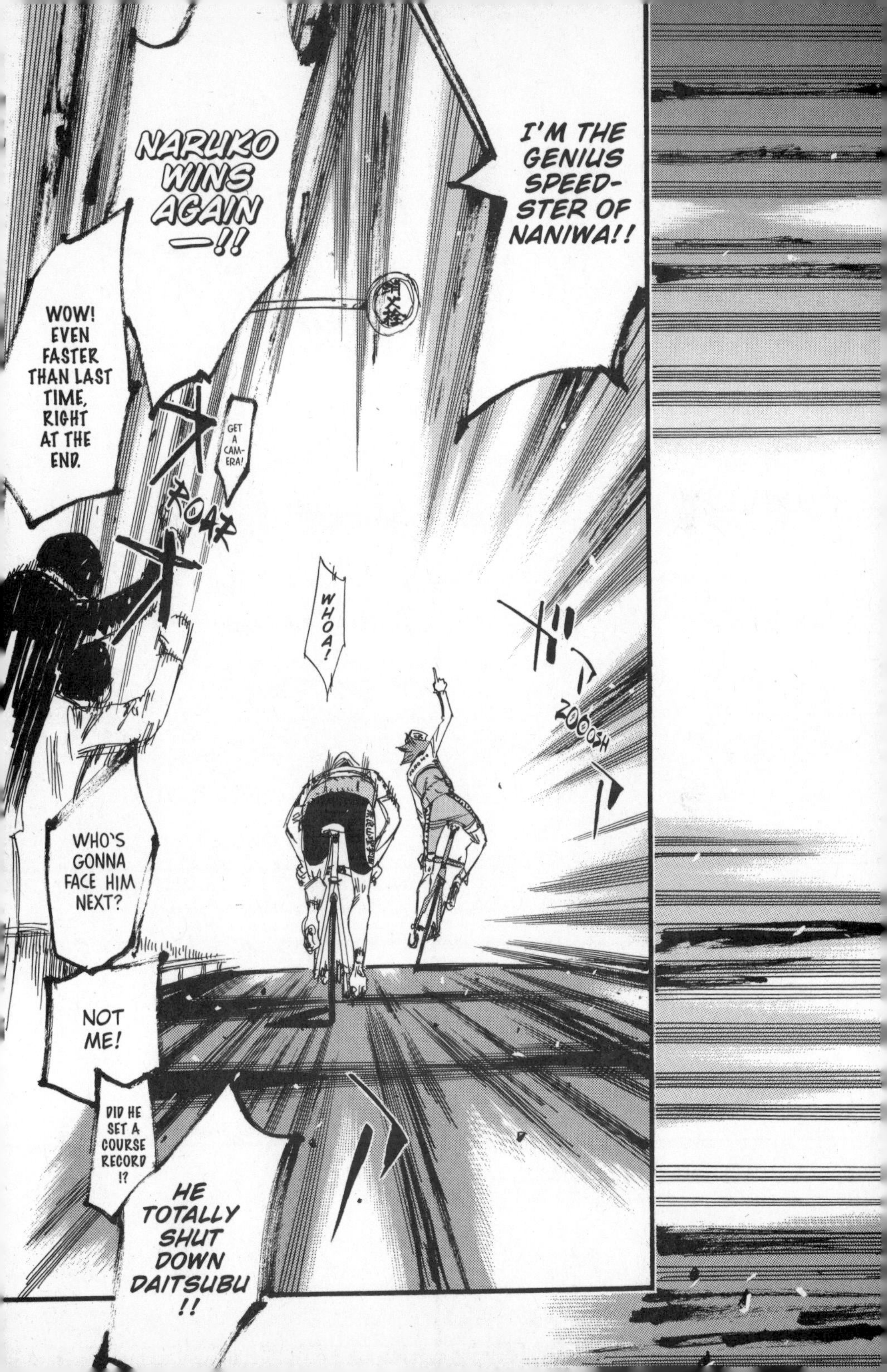

I'M THE GENIUS SPEED-STER OF NANIWA!!
NARUKO WINS AGAIN—!!
WOW! EVEN FASTER THAN LAST TIME, RIGHT AT THE END.
GET A CAM-ERA!
ROAR
WHOA!
ZOOOSH
WHO'S GONNA FACE HIM NEXT?
NOT ME!
DID HE SET A COURSE RECORD!?
HE TOTALLY SHUT DOWN DAITSUBU!!

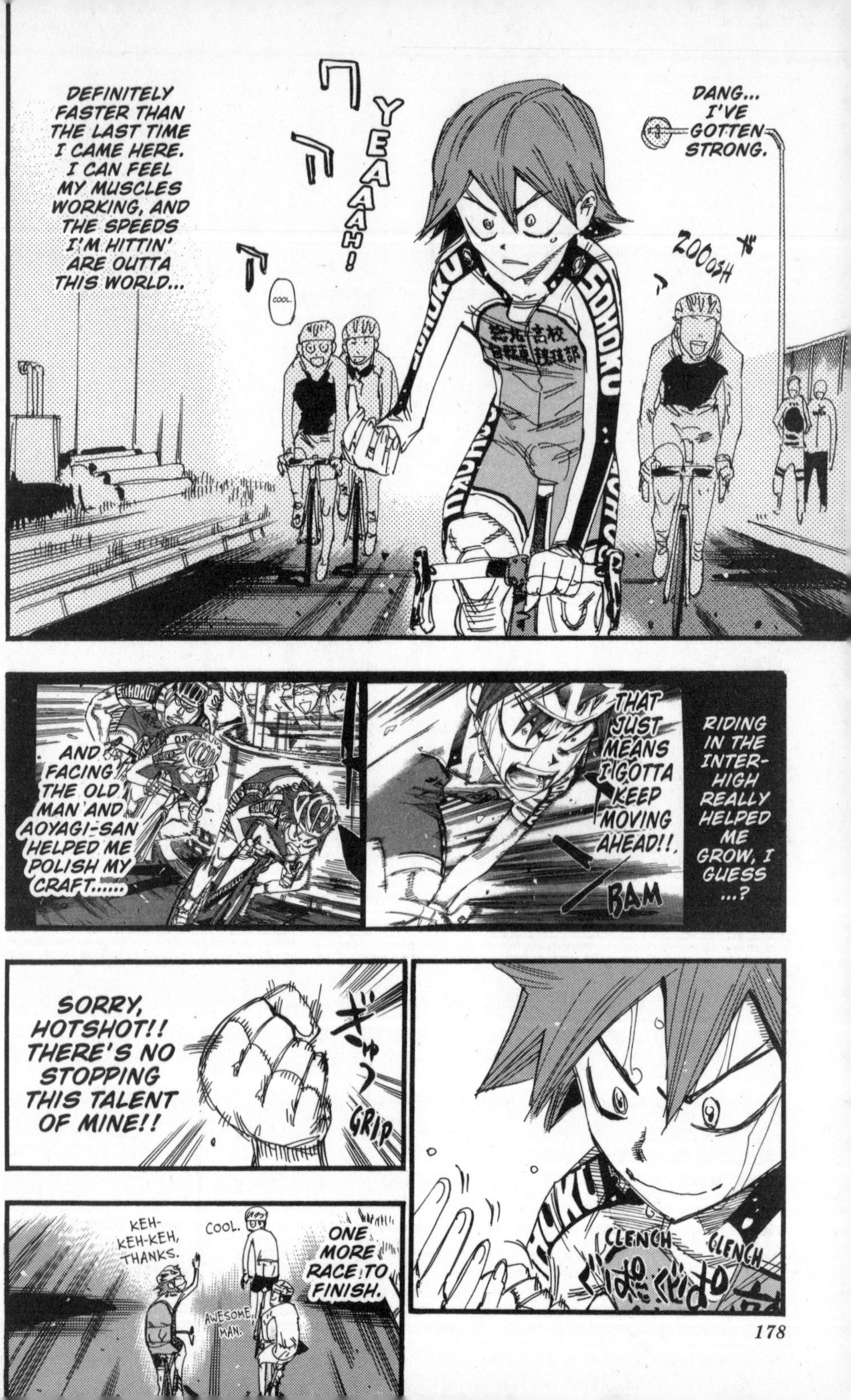

DANG... I'VE GOTTEN STRONG.
ZOOOSH
YEAAAAH!
COOL.
DEFINITELY FASTER THAN THE LAST TIME I CAME HERE. I CAN FEEL MY MUSCLES WORKING, AND THE SPEEDS I'M HITTIN' ARE OUTTA THIS WORLD...
RIDING IN THE INTER-HIGH REALLY HELPED ME GROW, I GUESS ...?
THAT JUST MEANS I GOTTA KEEP MOVING AHEAD!!
BAM
AND FACING THE OLD MAN AND AOYAGI-SAN HELPED ME POLISH MY CRAFT......
CLENCH
CLENCH
SORRY, HOTSHOT!! THERE'S NO STOPPING THIS TALENT OF MINE!!
GRIP
ONE MORE RACE TO FINISH.
COOL.
KEH-KEH-KEH, THANKS.
AWESOME, MAN.

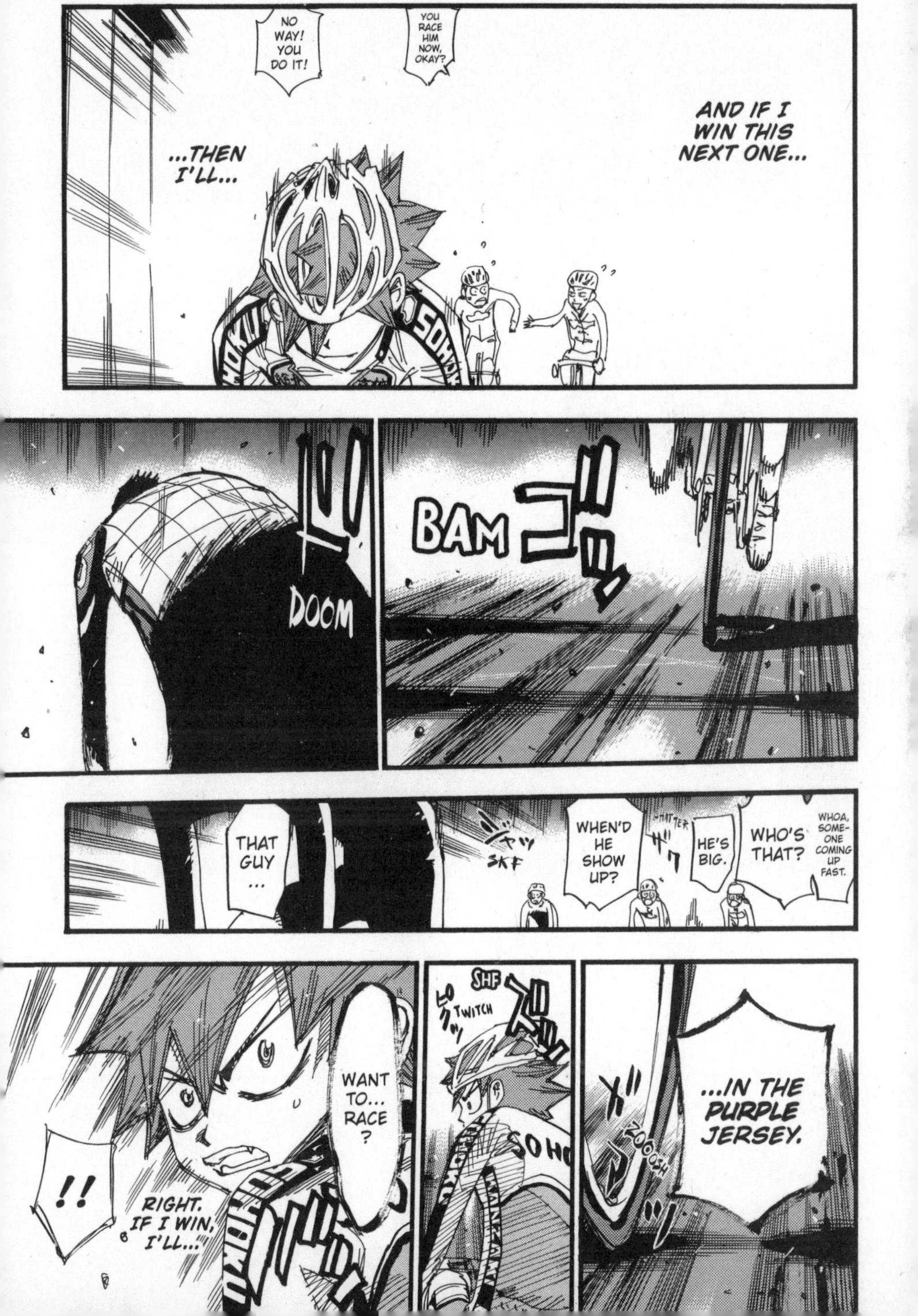
AND IF I WIN THIS NEXT ONE...
YOU RACE HIM NOW, OKAY?
NO WAY! YOU DO IT!
...THEN I'LL...
BAM
DOOM
WHOA, SOME-ONE COMING UP FAST.
WHO'S THAT?
HE'S BIG.
CHATTER
WHEN'D HE SHOW UP?
SKF
THAT GUY ...
...IN THE PURPLE JERSEY.
ZOOOSH
SHF
TWITCH
WANT TO... RACE?
!!
RIGHT. IF I WIN, I'LL...

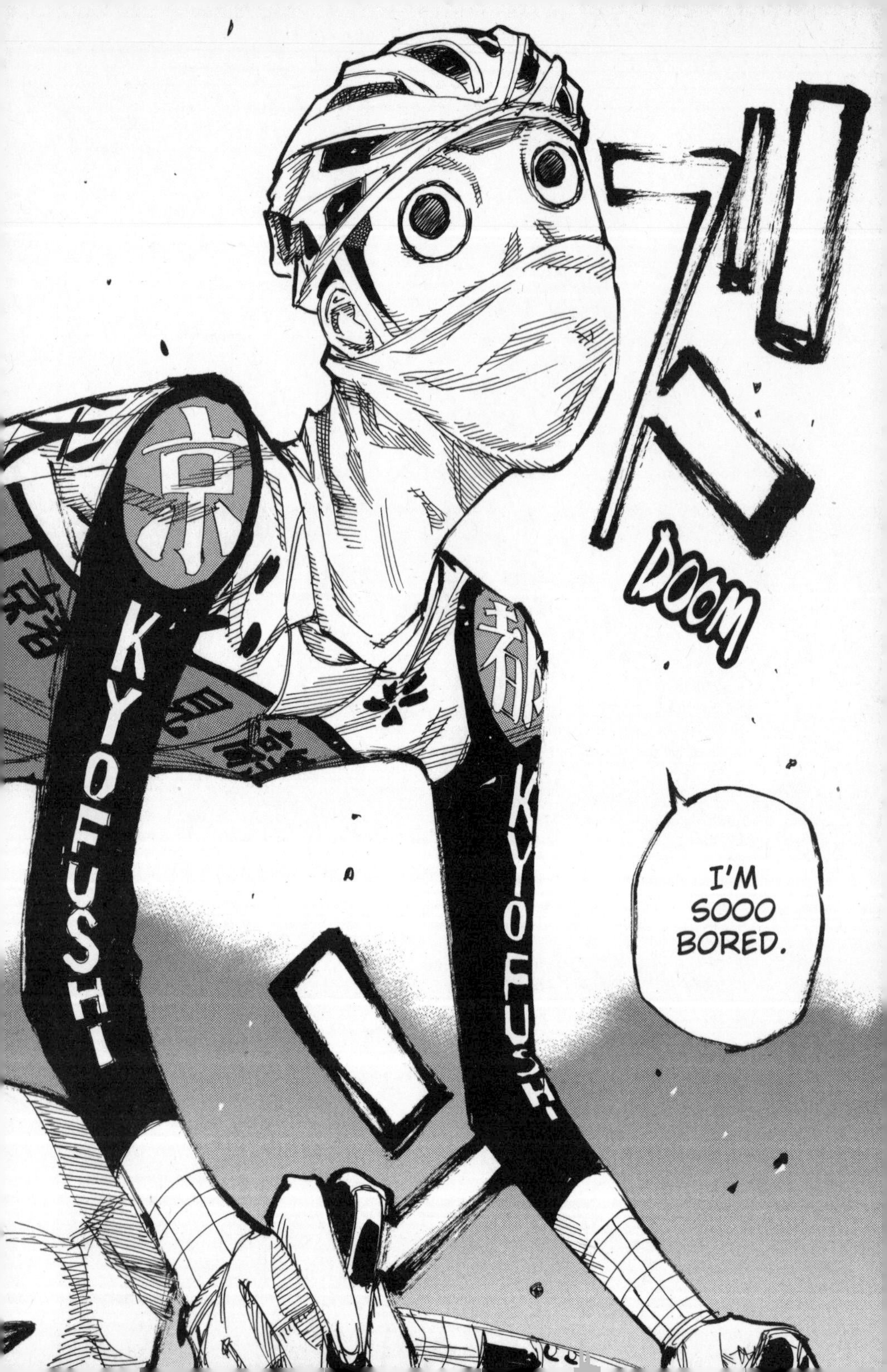
DOOM
I'M SOOO BORED.
KYOFUSHI
KYOFUSHI

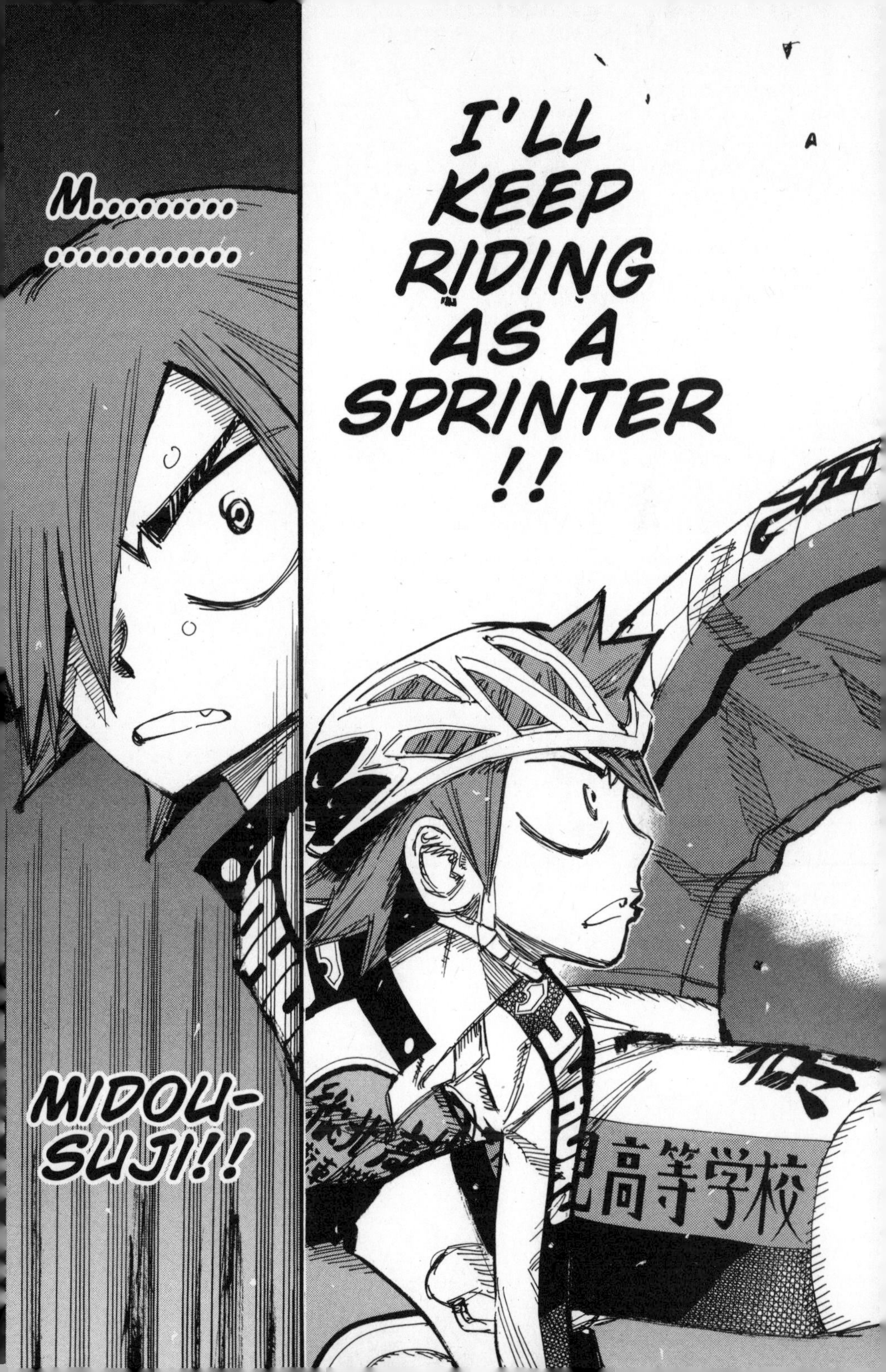
I'LL KEEP RIDING AS A SPRINTER !!
高等学校
M...........
....
MIDOU-SUJI!!

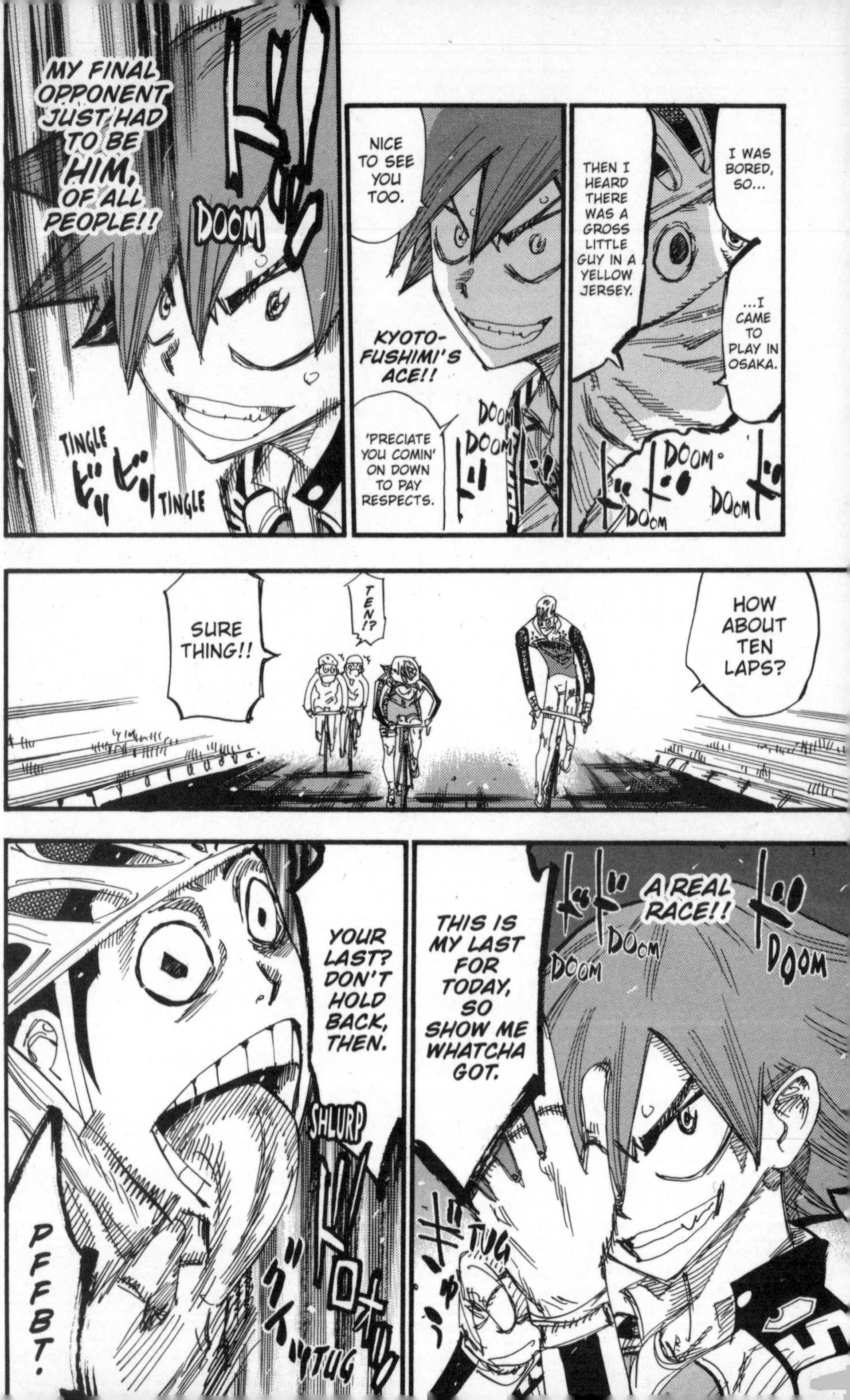
I WAS BORED, SO...
THEN I HEARD THERE WAS A GROSS LITTLE GUY IN A YELLOW JERSEY.
...I CAME TO PLAY IN OSAKA.
DOOM
DOOM
DOOM
NICE TO SEE YOU TOO.
KYOTO-FUSHIMI'S ACE!!
'PRECIATE YOU COMIN' ON DOWN TO PAY RESPECTS.
DOOM
DOOM
MY FINAL OPPONENT JUST HAD TO BE HIM, OF ALL PEOPLE!!
DOOM
TINGLE
TINGLE
HOW ABOUT TEN LAPS?
TEN!?
SURE THING!!
A REAL RACE!!
THIS IS MY LAST FOR TODAY, SO SHOW ME WHATCHA GOT.
DOOM
DOOM
DOOM
TUG
YOUR LAST? DON'T HOLD BACK, THEN.
SHLURP
TUG
PFFBT.

RIDE.252 NARUKO VS. MIDOUSUJI

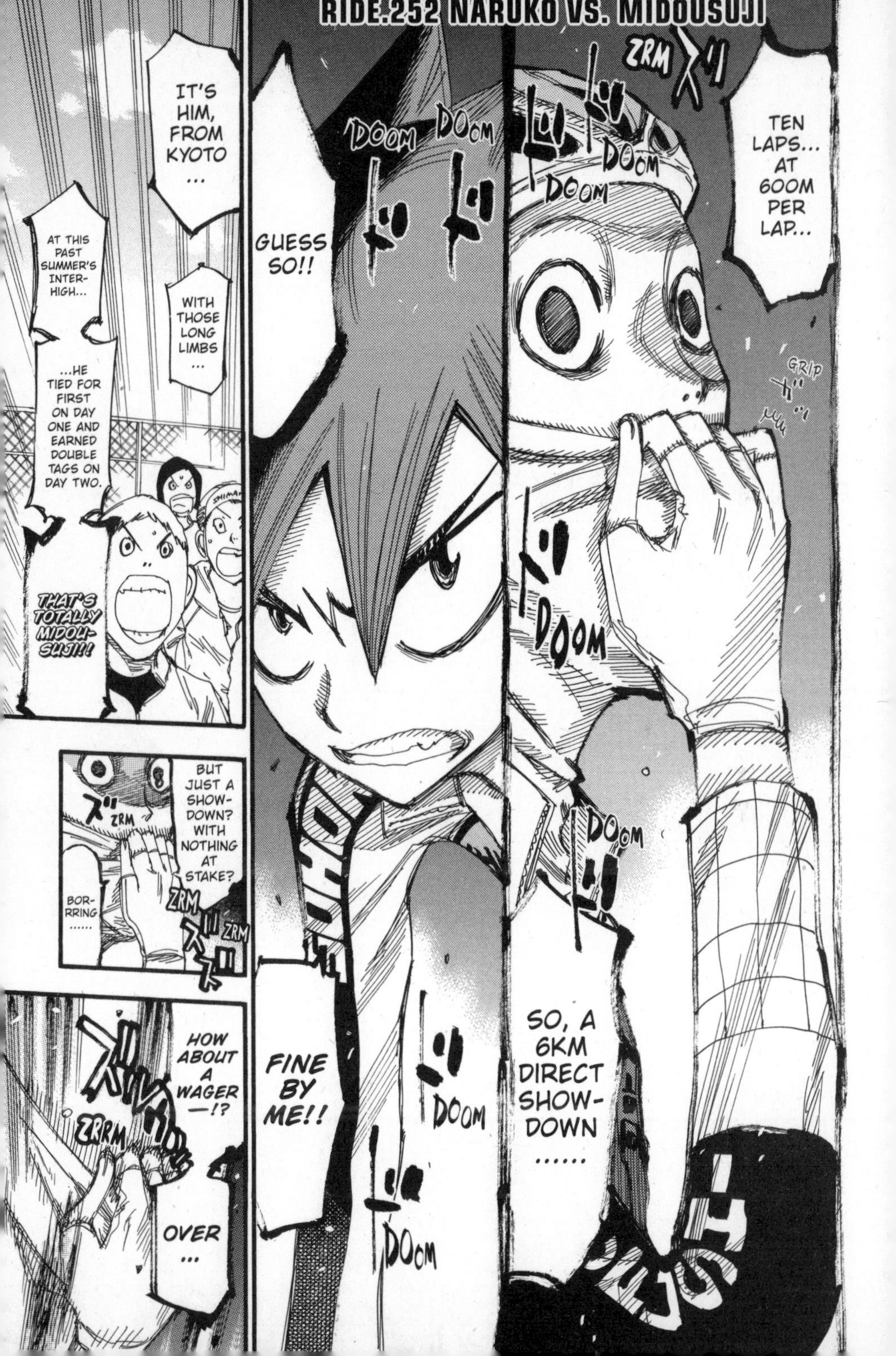
ZRM
TEN LAPS... AT 600M PER LAP...
DOOM
DOOM
GRIP
DOOM
DOOM
SO, A 6KM DIRECT SHOW-DOWN......
DOOM DOOM
GUESS SO!!
FINE BY ME!!
DOOM
DOOM
IT'S HIM, FROM KYOTO...
WITH THOSE LONG LIMBS...
AT THIS PAST SUMMER'S INTER-HIGH...
...HE TIED FOR FIRST ON DAY ONE AND EARNED DOUBLE TAGS ON DAY TWO.
THAT'S TOTALLY MIDOU-SUJI!!
ZRM
BUT JUST A SHOW-DOWN? WITH NOTHING AT STAKE?
BOR-RRING......
ZRM
ZRM
HOW ABOUT A WAGER—!?
ZRRM
OVER...

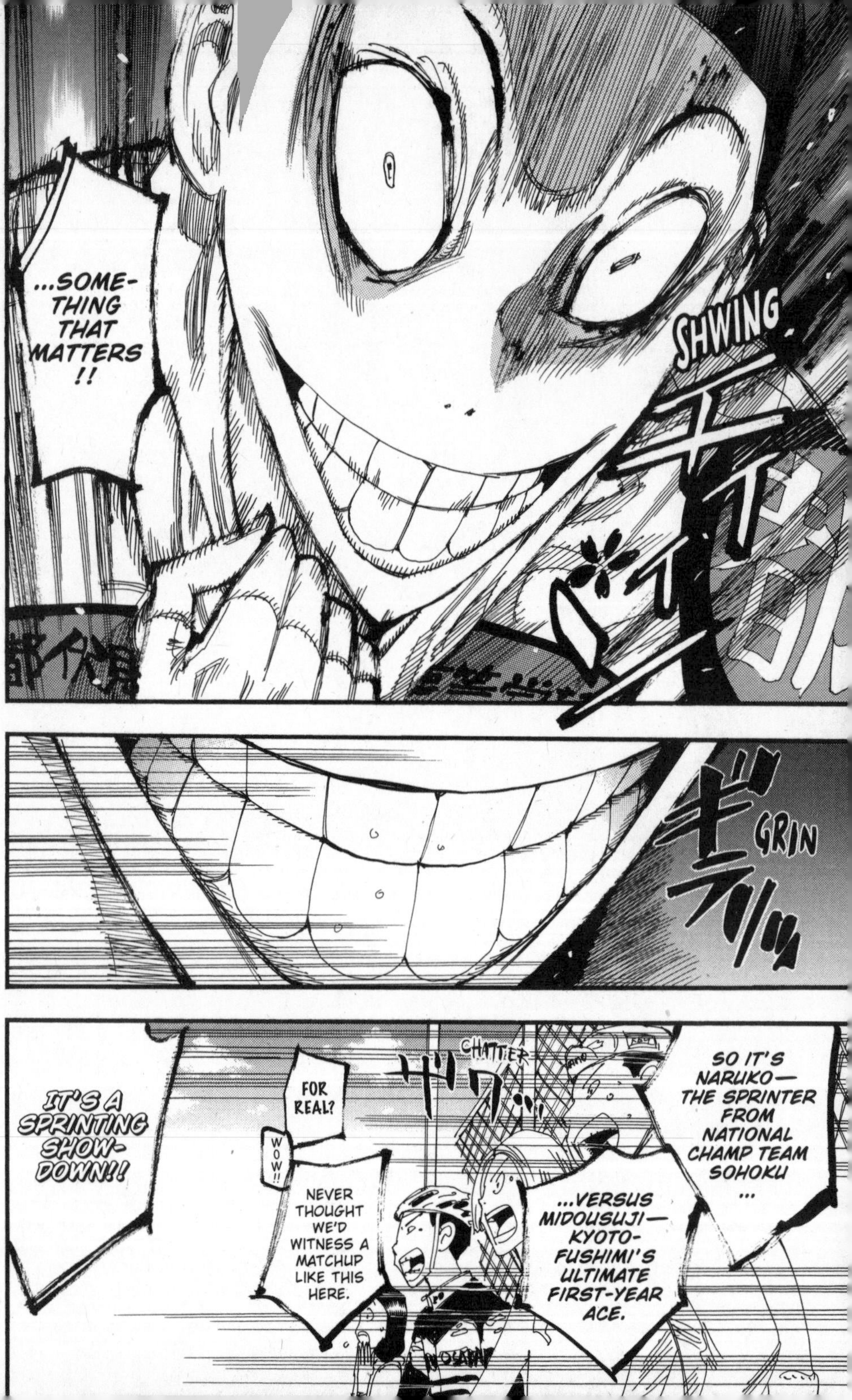
...SOME-THING THAT MATTERS!!
SHWING
GRIN
SO IT'S NARUKO—THE SPRINTER FROM NATIONAL CHAMP TEAM SOHOKU...
...VERSUS MIDOUSUJI—KYOTO-FUSHIMI'S ULTIMATE FIRST-YEAR ACE.
CHATTER
FOR REAL?
WOW!!
NEVER THOUGHT WE'D WITNESS A MATCHUP LIKE THIS HERE.
IT'S A SPRINTING SHOW-DOWN!!

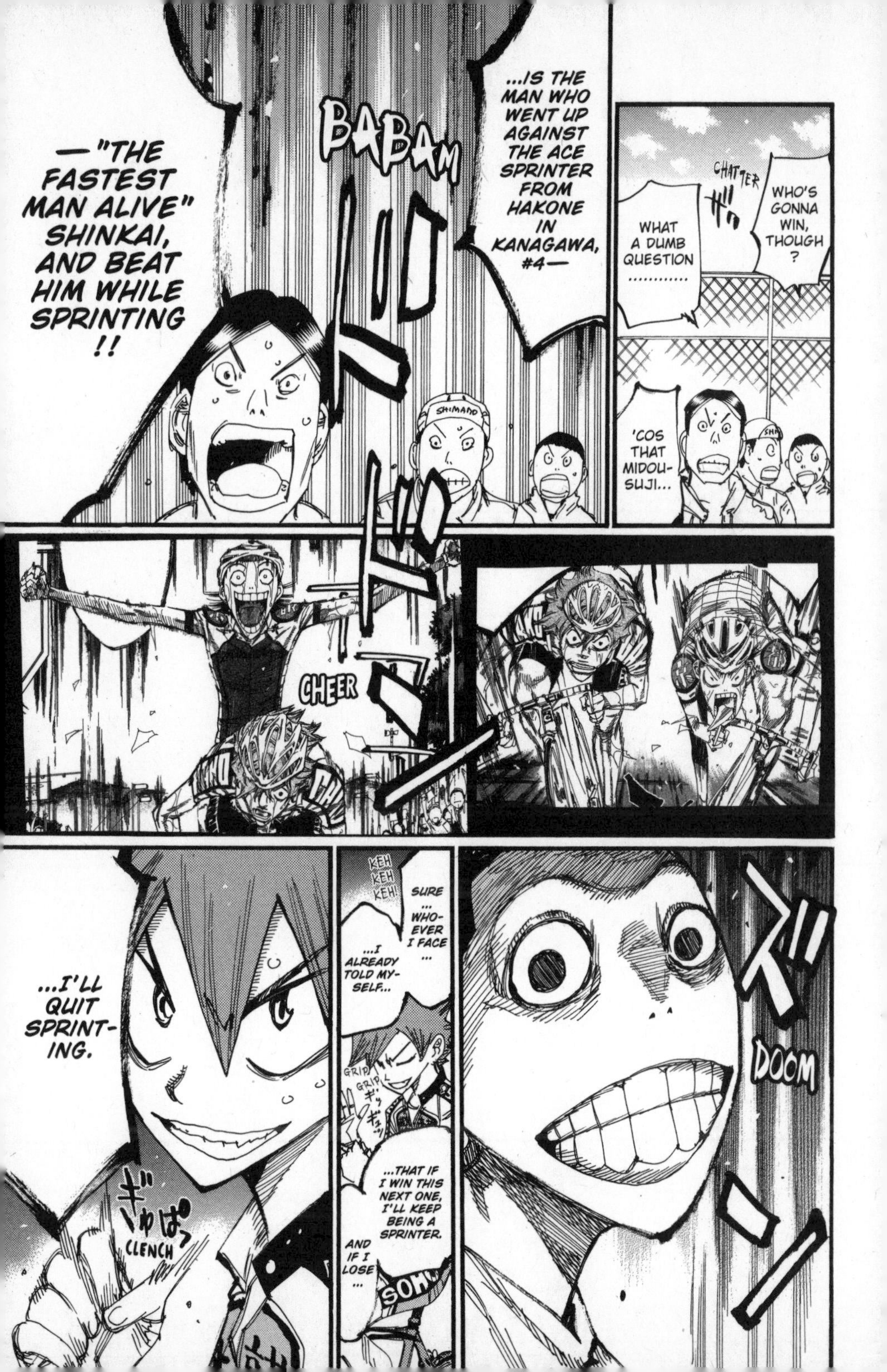
CHATTER
WHO'S GONNA WIN, THOUGH?
WHAT A DUMB QUESTION............
'COS THAT MIDOU-SUJI...
...IS THE MAN WHO WENT UP AGAINST THE ACE SPRINTER FROM HAKONE IN KANAGAWA, #4—
BABAM
—"THE FASTEST MAN ALIVE" SHINKAI, AND BEAT HIM WHILE SPRINTING!!
CHEER
DOOM
KEH KEH KEH!
SURE... WHO-EVER I FACE...
...I ALREADY TOLD MY-SELF...
GRIP GRIP
...THAT IF I WIN THIS NEXT ONE, I'LL KEEP BEING A SPRINTER.
AND IF I LOSE...
...I'LL QUIT SPRINT-ING.
CLENCH

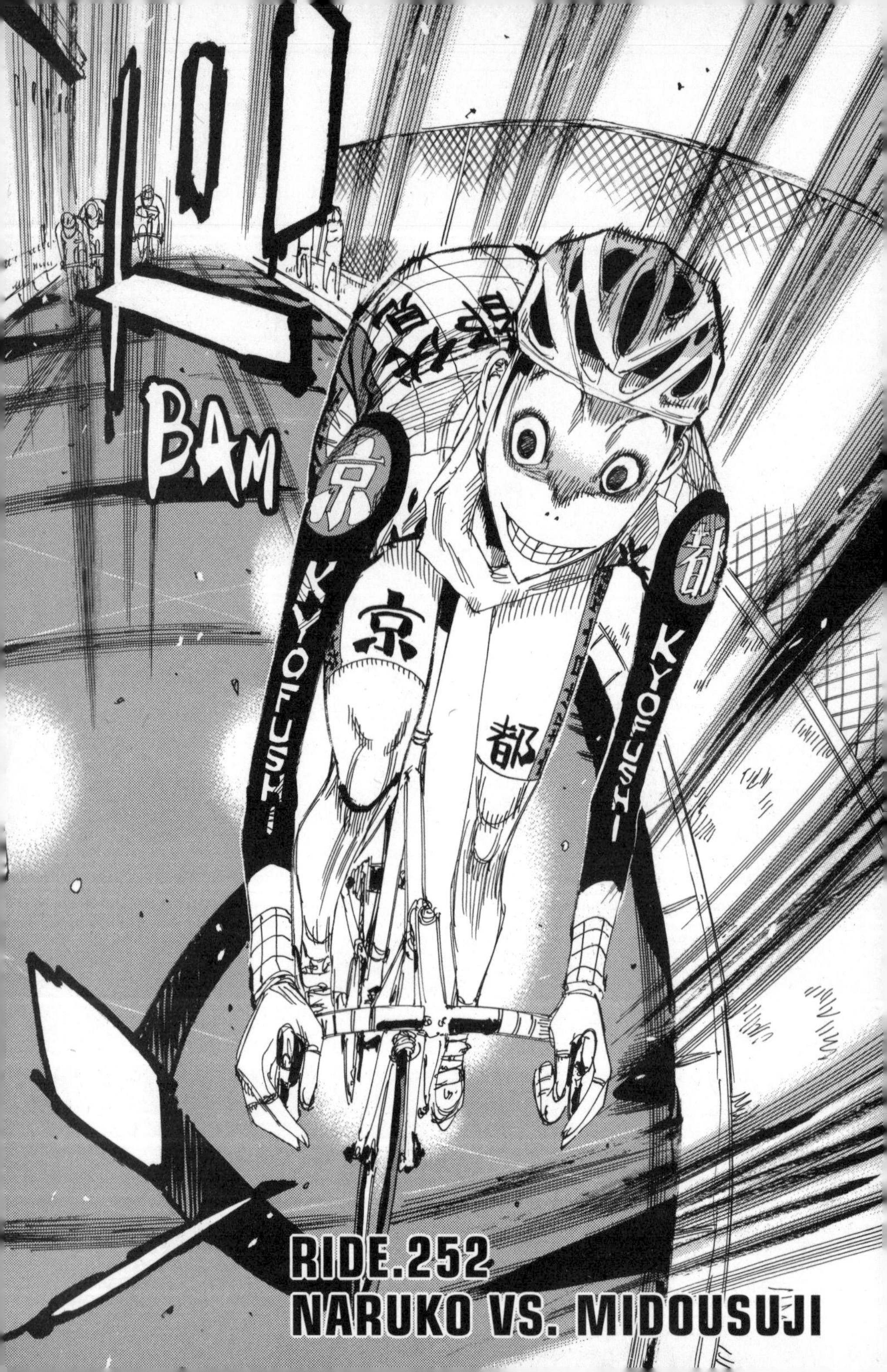
BAM
KYOFUSHI
KYOFUSHI

RIDE.252
NARUKO VS. MIDOUSUJI

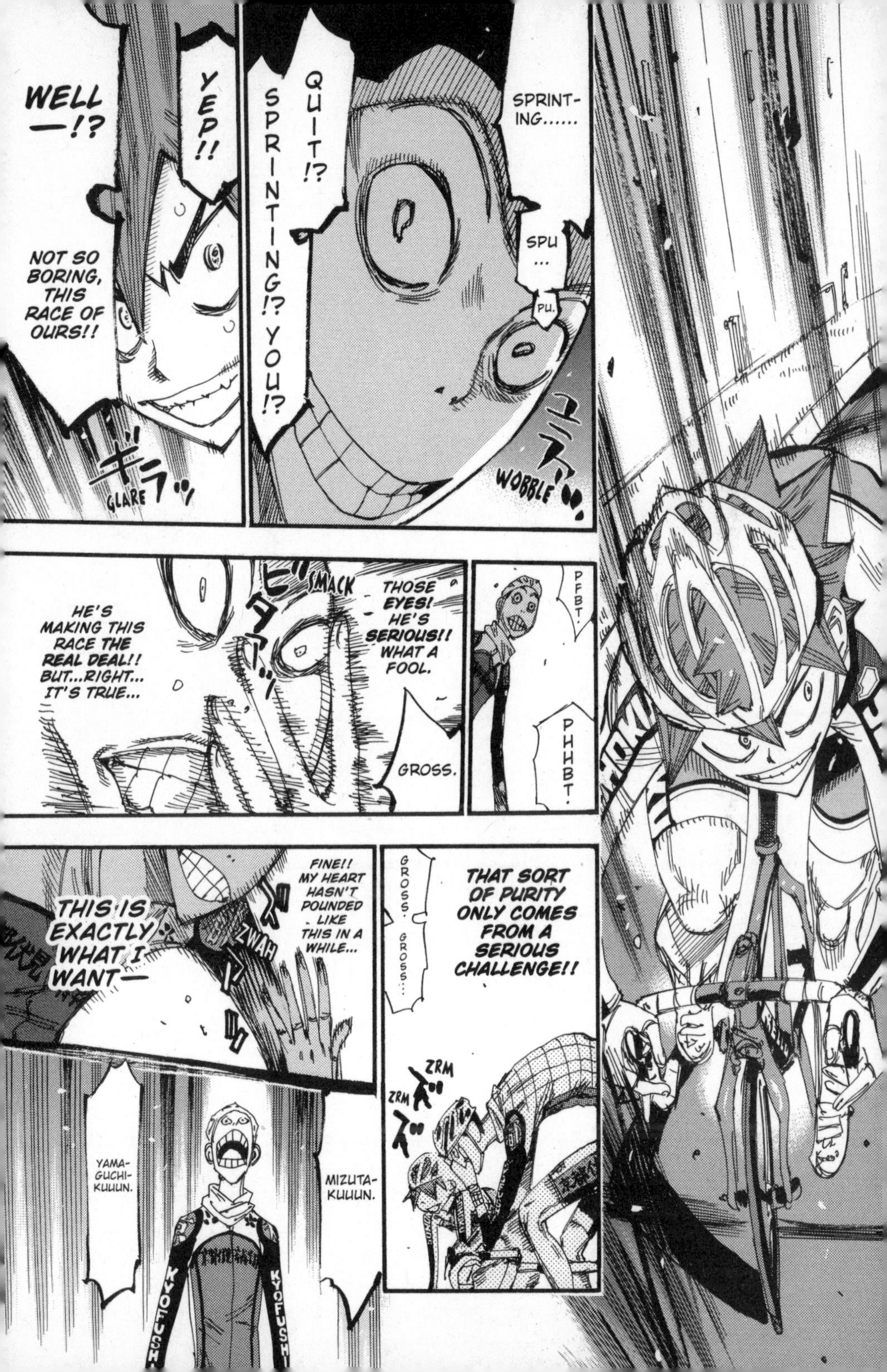
SPRINT-ING......
SPU...
PU.
QUIT!? SPRINTING!? YOU!?
WOBBLE
YEP!!
WELL—!?
NOT SO BORING, THIS RACE OF OURS!!
GLARE
PFBT.
PHHBT.
SMACK
THOSE EYES! HE'S SERIOUS!! WHAT A FOOL.
GROSS.
HE'S MAKING THIS RACE THE REAL DEAL!! BUT...RIGHT... IT'S TRUE...
THAT SORT OF PURITY ONLY COMES FROM A SERIOUS CHALLENGE!!
GROSS. GROSS. GROSS...
ZRM
ZRM
FINE!! MY HEART HASN'T POUNDED LIKE THIS IN A WHILE...
ZWAH
THIS IS EXACTLY WHAT I WANT—
MIZUTA-KUUUN.
YAMA-GUCHI-KUUUN.
KYOFUSHI
KYOFUSHI

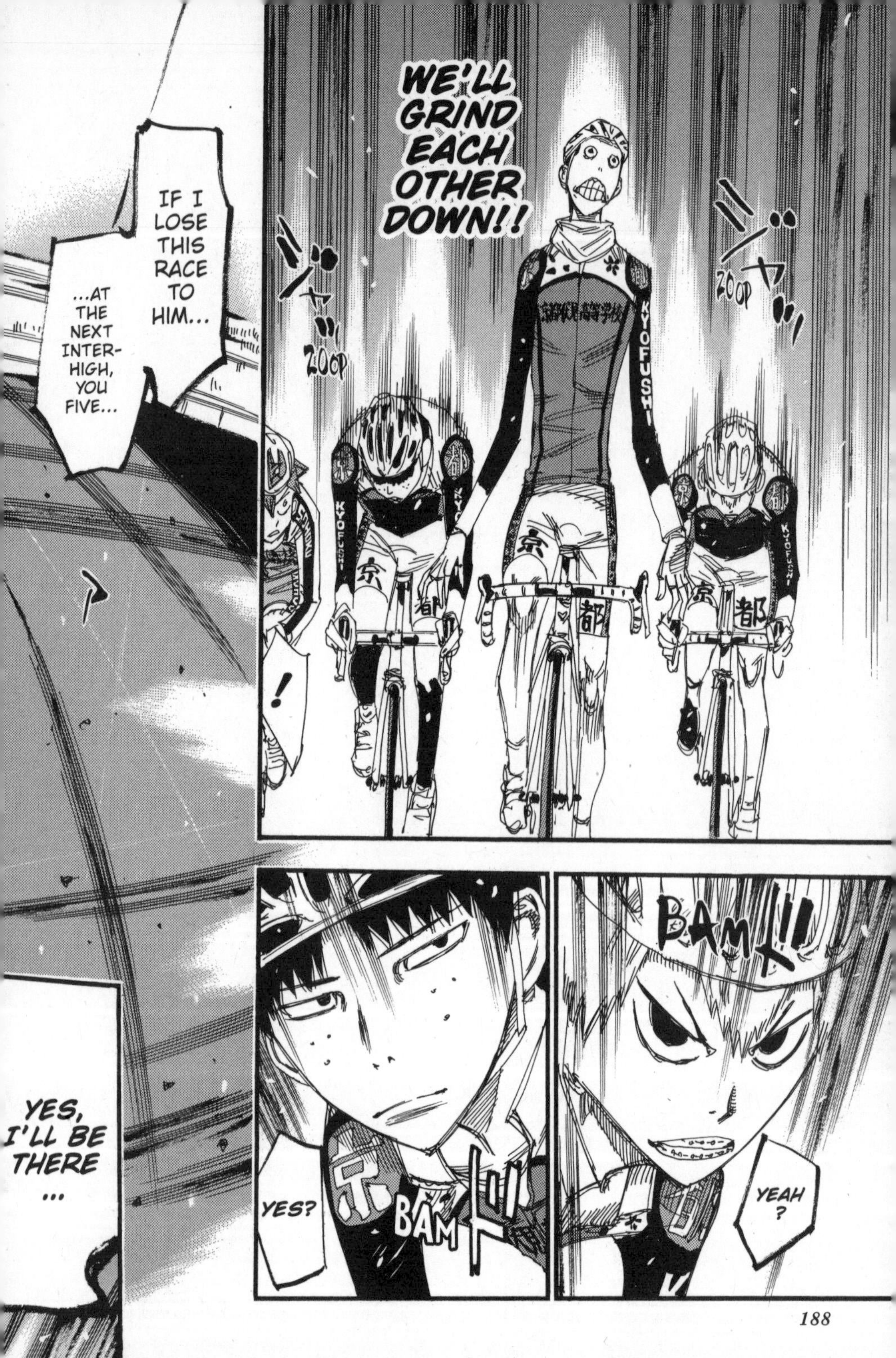
WE'LL GRIND EACH OTHER DOWN!!
ZOOP
ZOOP
!
BAM!!
YEAH?
YES?
BAM!!
IF I LOSE THIS RACE TO HIM...
...AT THE NEXT INTER-HIGH, YOU FIVE...
YES, I'LL BE THERE...

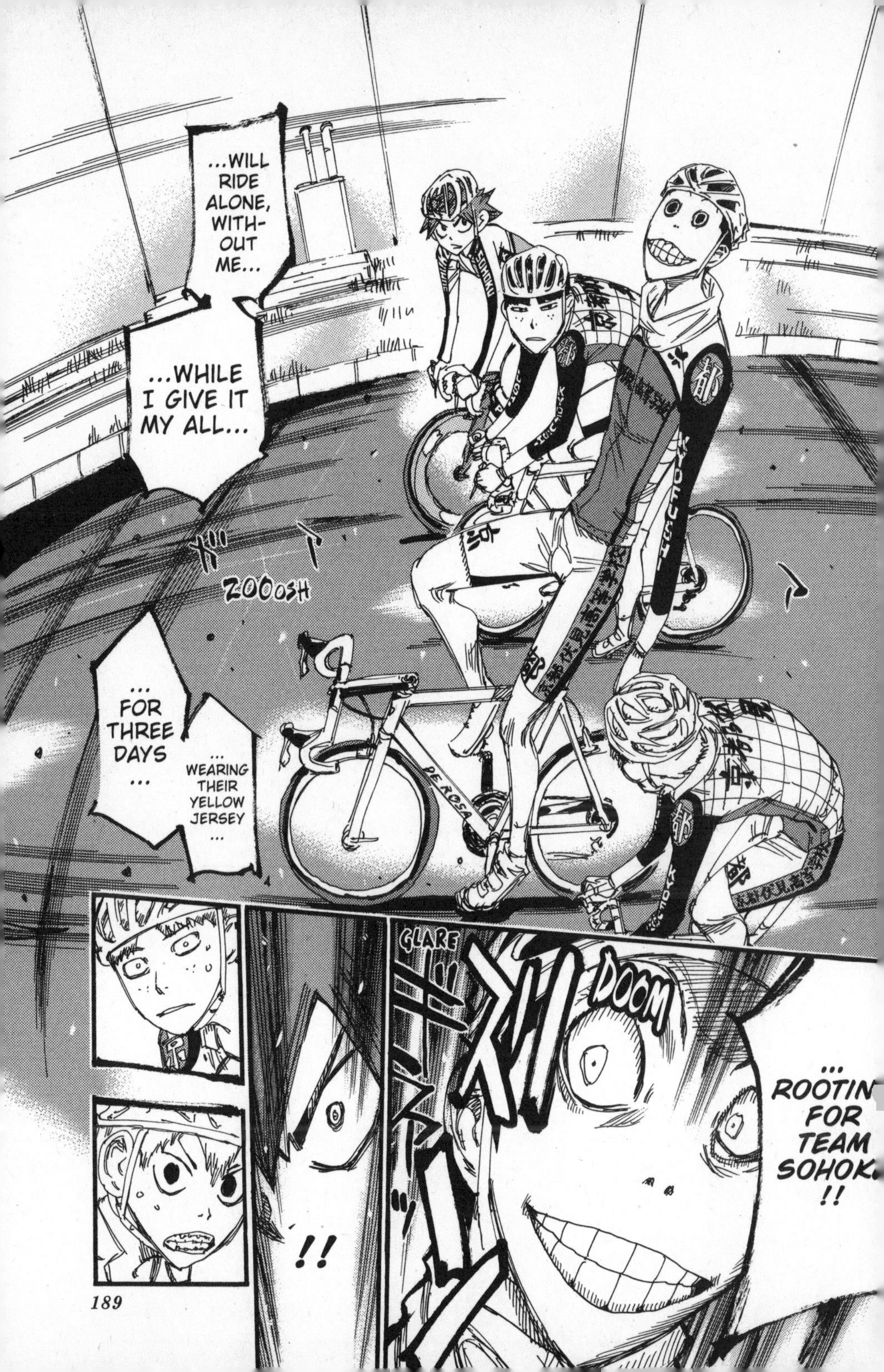
...WILL RIDE ALONE, WITH-OUT ME...
...WHILE I GIVE IT MY ALL...
ZOOOSH
...FOR THREE DAYS...
...WEARING THEIR YELLOW JERSEY...
GLARE
DOOM
...ROOTIN FOR TEAM SOHOK !!
!!

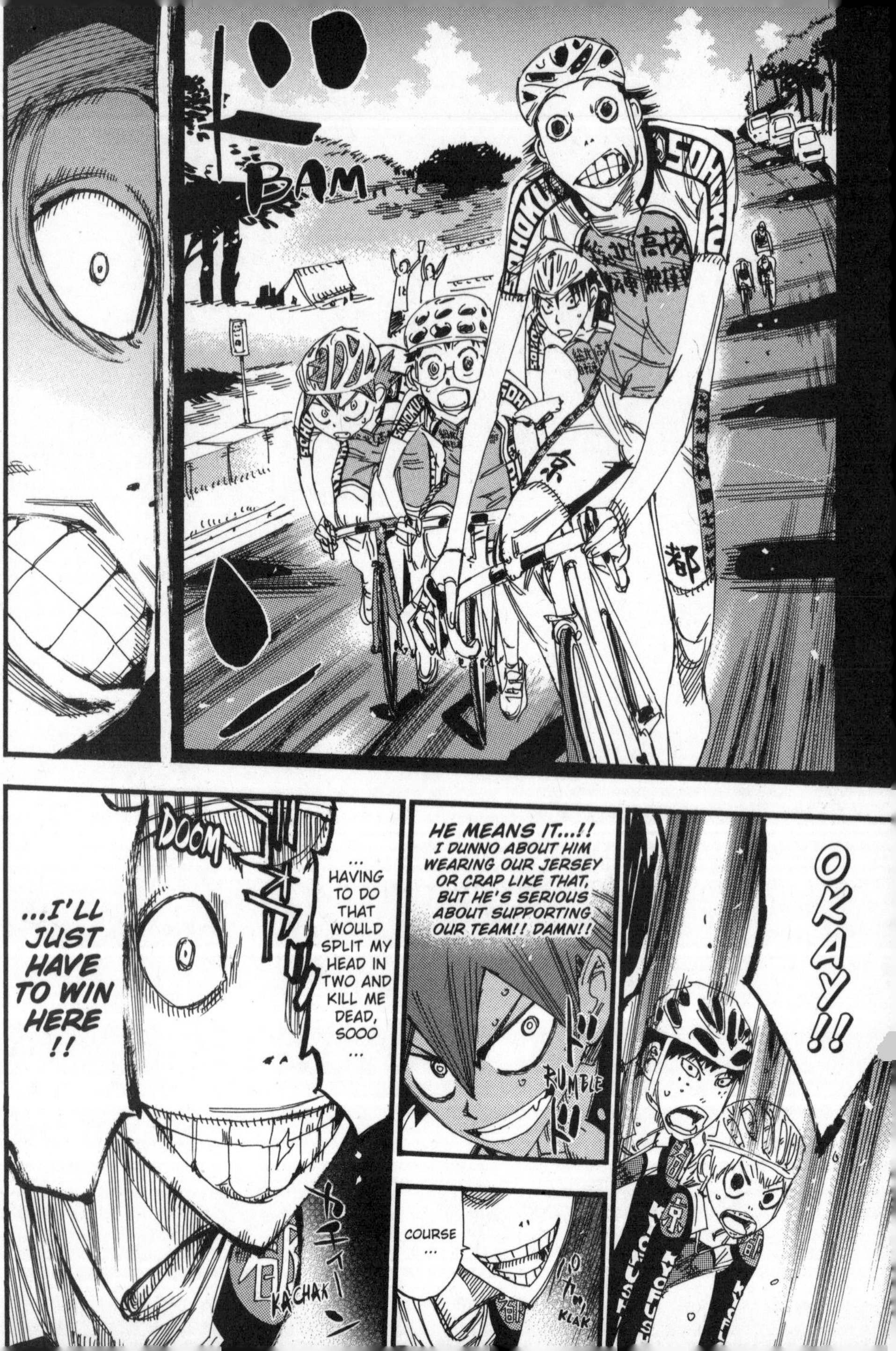
BAM
OKAY!!
HE MEANS IT...!! I DUNNO ABOUT HIM WEARING OUR JERSEY OR CRAP LIKE THAT, BUT HE'S SERIOUS ABOUT SUPPORTING OUR TEAM!! DAMN!!
RUMBLE
COURSE ...
KLAK
DOOM
... HAVING TO DO THAT WOULD SPLIT MY HEAD IN TWO AND KILL ME DEAD, SOOO ...
...I'LL JUST HAVE TO WIN HERE !!
KACHAK

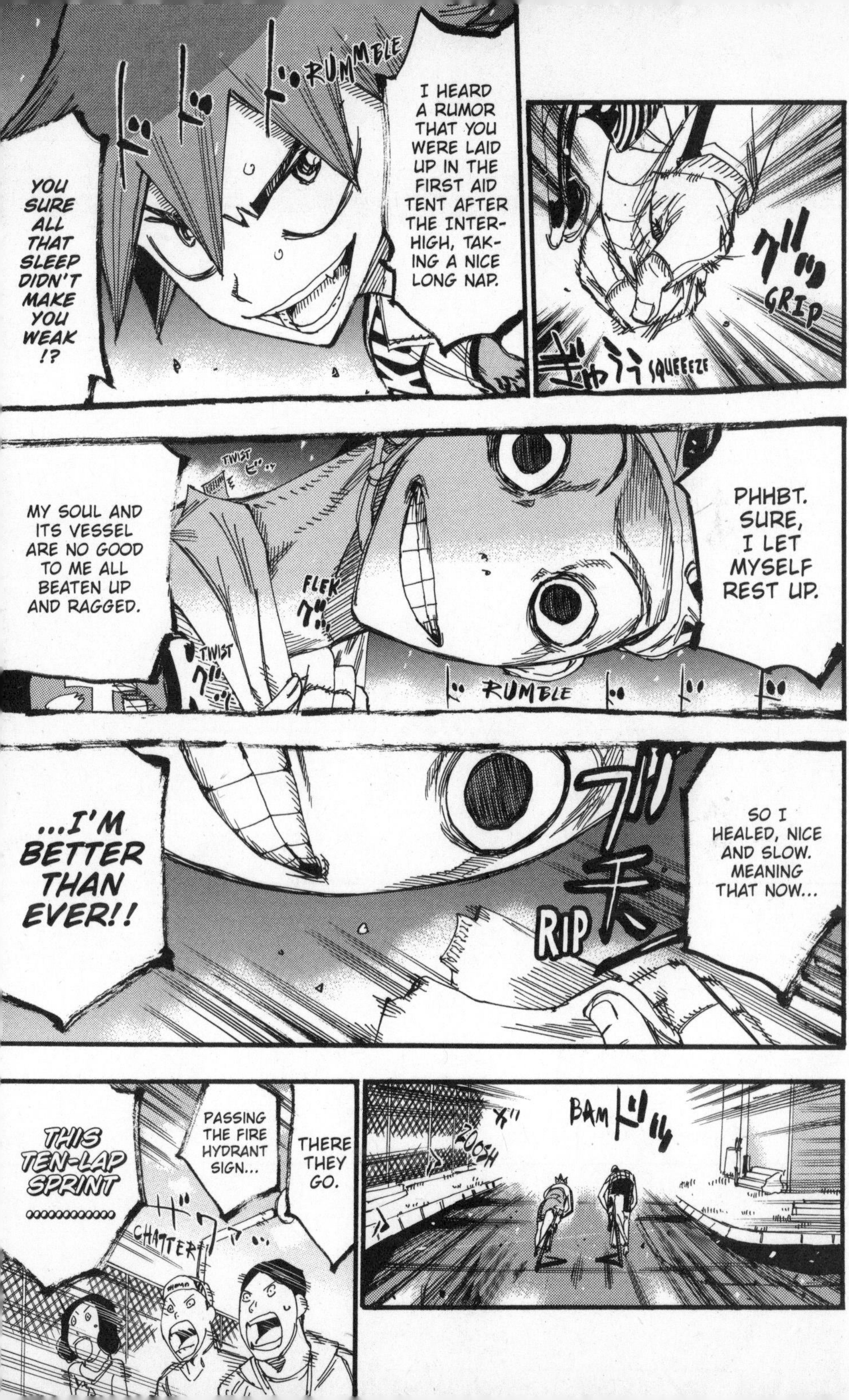
GRIP
SQUEEEZE
RUMMBLE
I HEARD A RUMOR THAT YOU WERE LAID UP IN THE FIRST AID TENT AFTER THE INTER-HIGH, TAKING A NICE LONG NAP.
YOU SURE ALL THAT SLEEP DIDN'T MAKE YOU WEAK !?
PHHBT. SURE, I LET MYSELF REST UP.
TWIST
MY SOUL AND ITS VESSEL ARE NO GOOD TO ME ALL BEATEN UP AND RAGGED.
FLEK
TWIST
RUMBLE
SO I HEALED, NICE AND SLOW. MEANING THAT NOW...
RIP
...I'M BETTER THAN EVER!!
BAM
ZOOSH
THERE THEY GO.
PASSING THE FIRE HYDRANT SIGN...
THIS TEN-LAP SPRINT..........
CHATTER

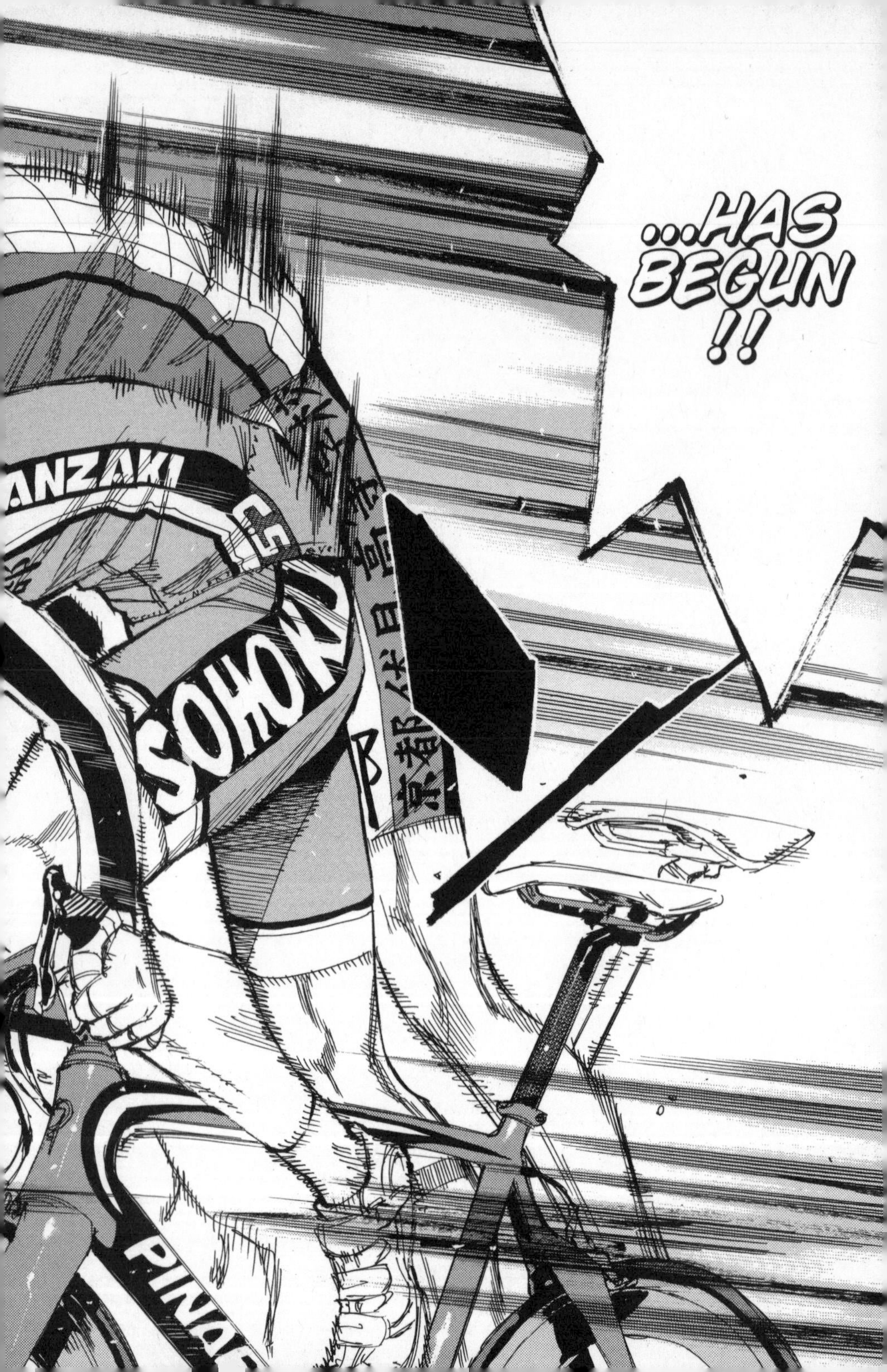
...HAS BEGUN!!

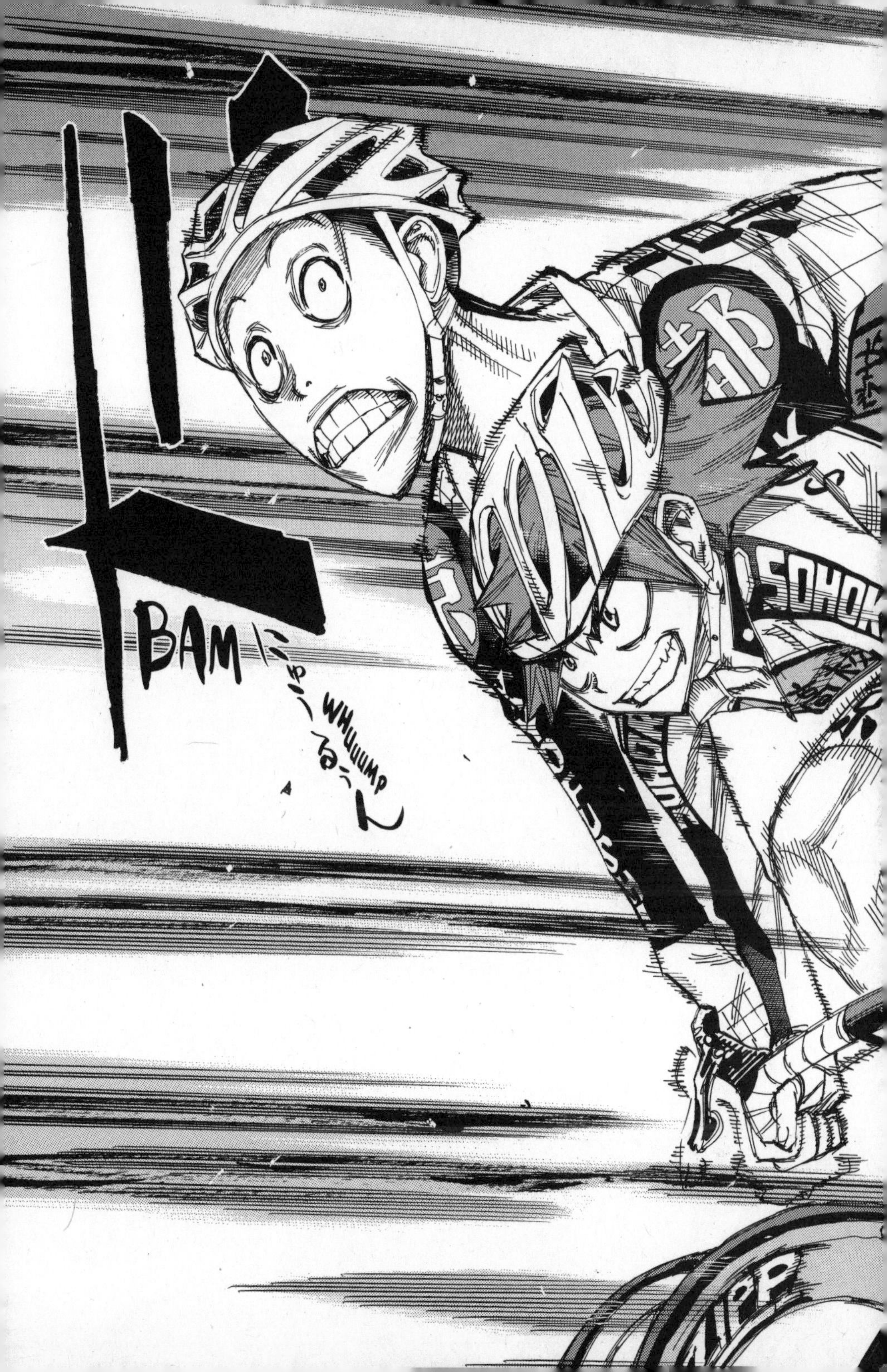
にゅ～る～ん
WHUUUMP
BAM

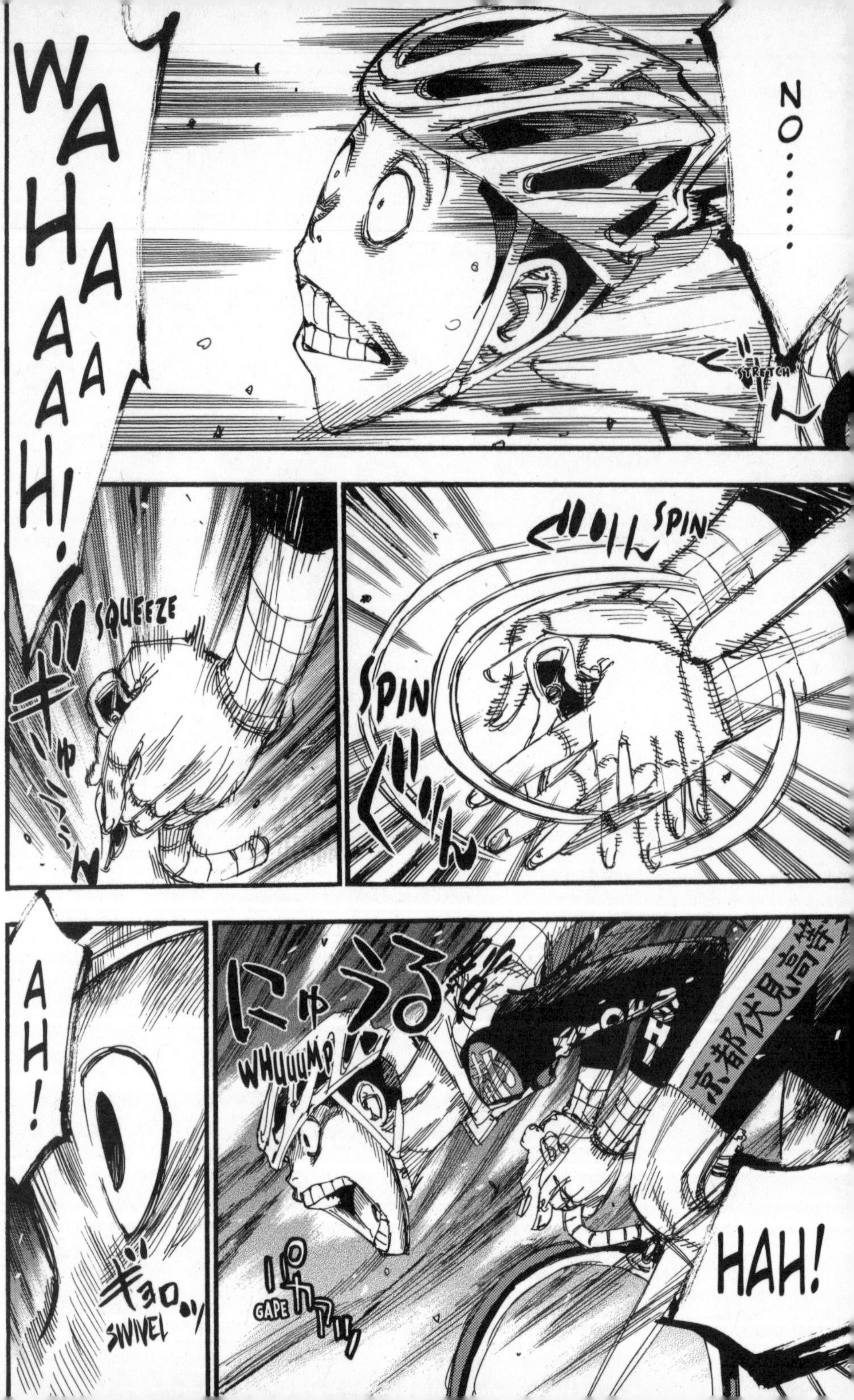
NO......
STRETCH
WAHAAAAAH!
SPIN
SPIN
SQUEEZE
京都伏見高校
HAH!
にゅうる
WHUUUMP
GAPE
AH!
SWIVEL

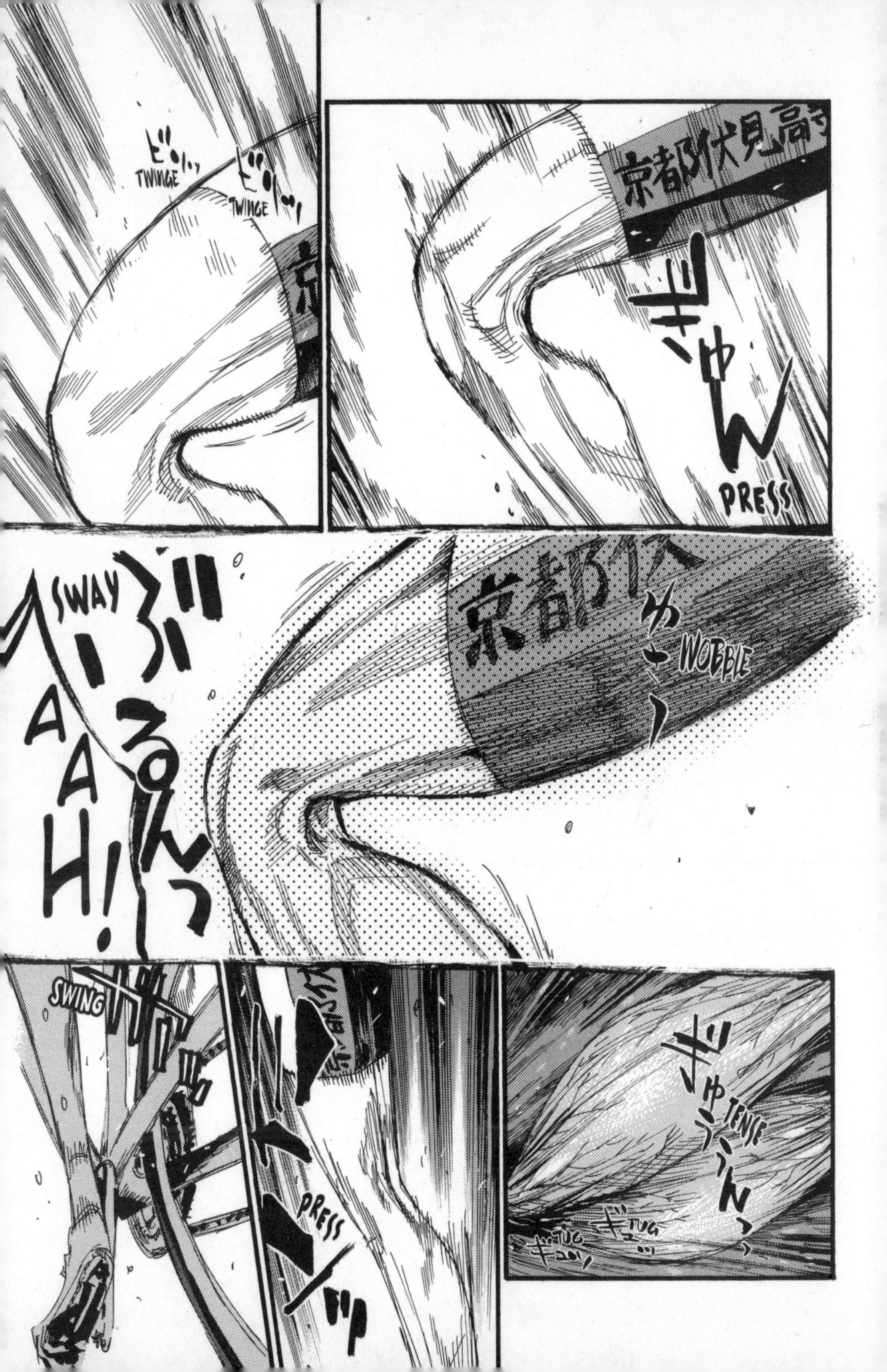
ぎゅん
PRESS
TWINGE
TWINGE
WOBBLE
SWAY
AAAH!
TENSE
TUG
TUG
PRESS
SWING

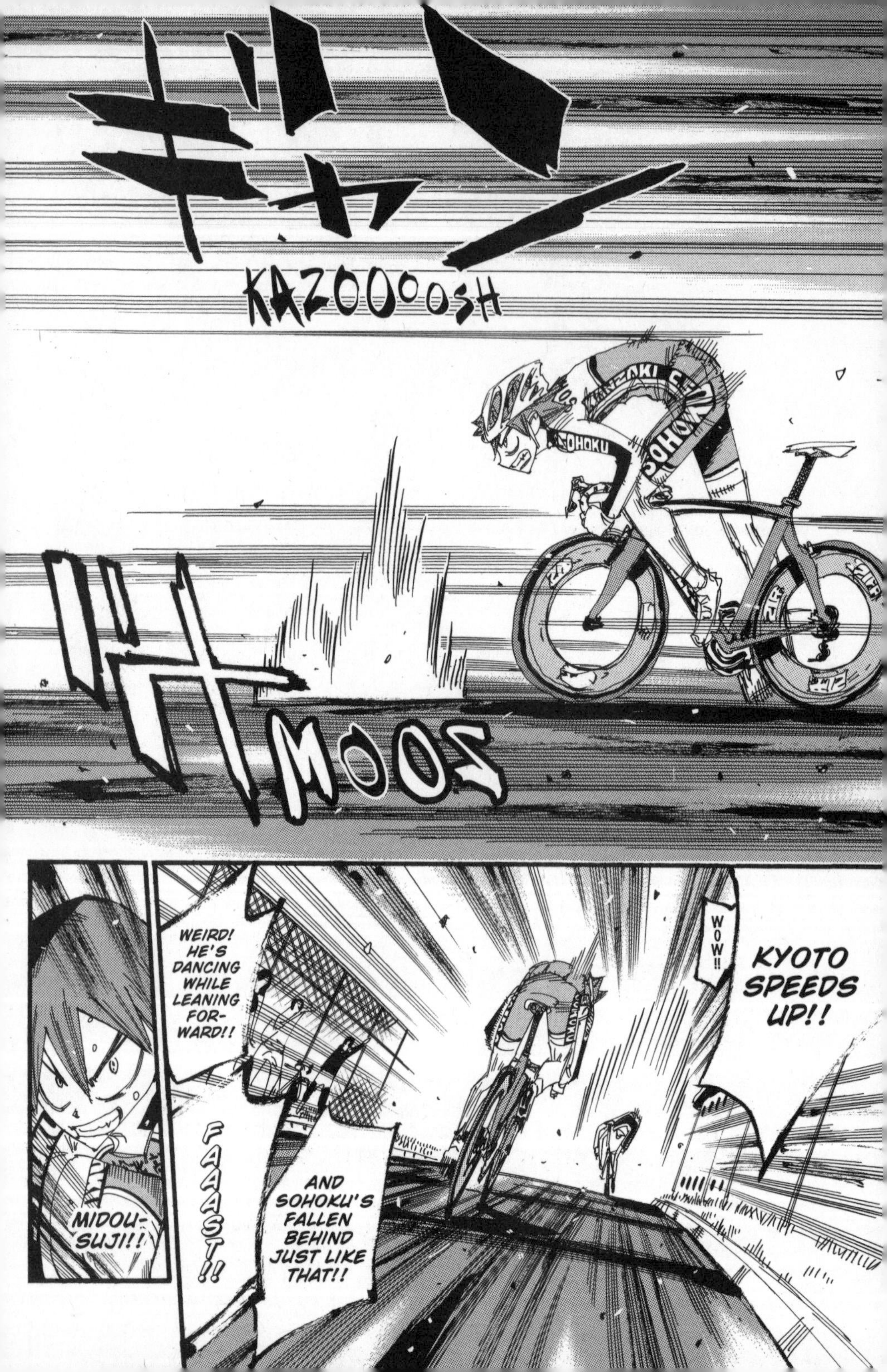
KAZOOOOSH
ZOOM
KYOTO SPEEDS UP!!
WOW!!
WEIRD! HE'S DANCING WHILE LEANING FOR-WARD!!
AND SOHOKU'S FALLEN BEHIND JUST LIKE THAT!!
FAAAAST!!
MIDOU-SUJI!!

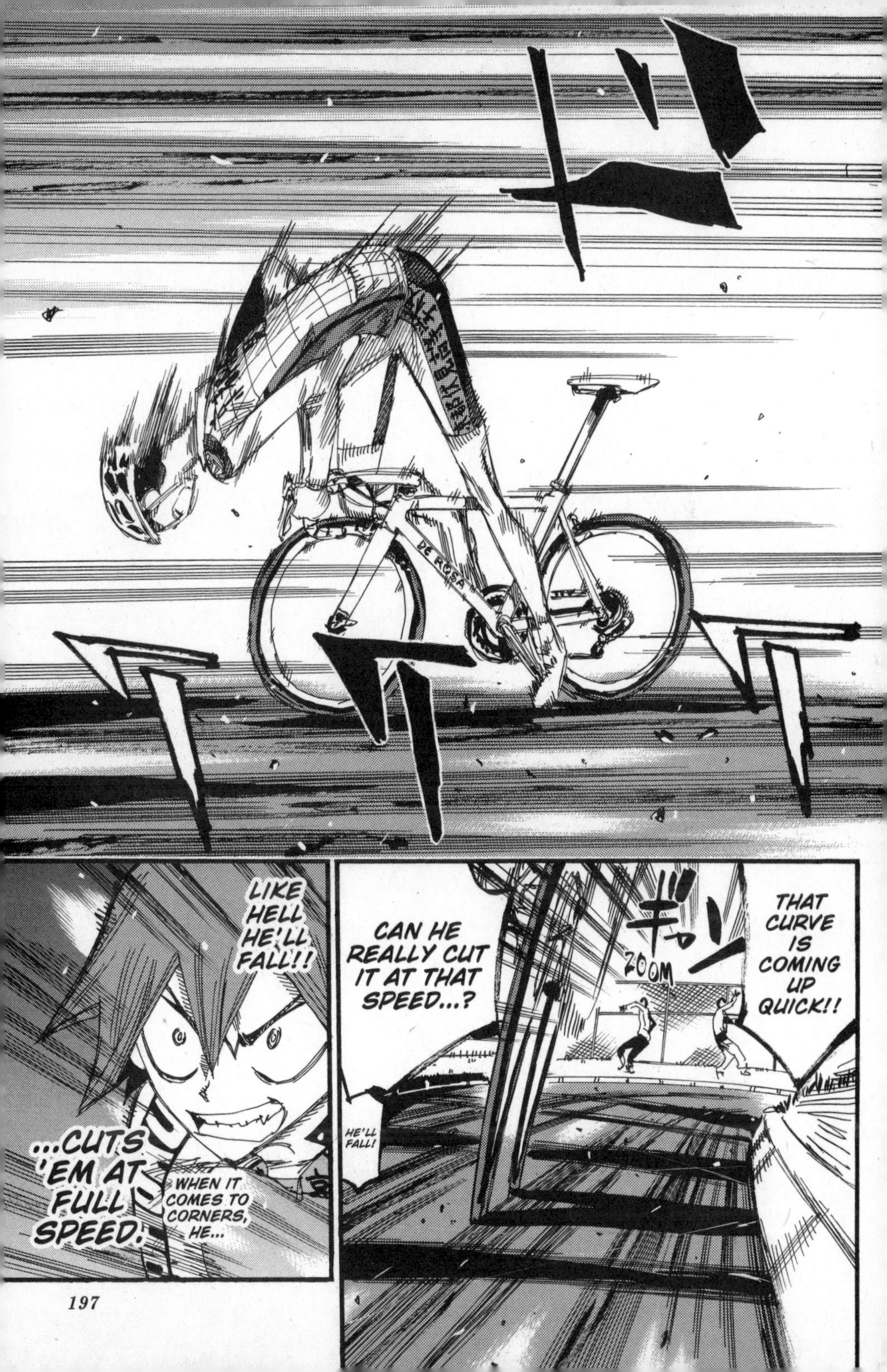
THAT CURVE IS COMING UP QUICK!!
ZOOM
CAN HE REALLY CUT IT AT THAT SPEED...?
HE'LL FALL!
LIKE HELL HE'LL FALL!!
WHEN IT COMES TO CORNERS, HE...
...CUTS 'EM AT FULL SPEED.

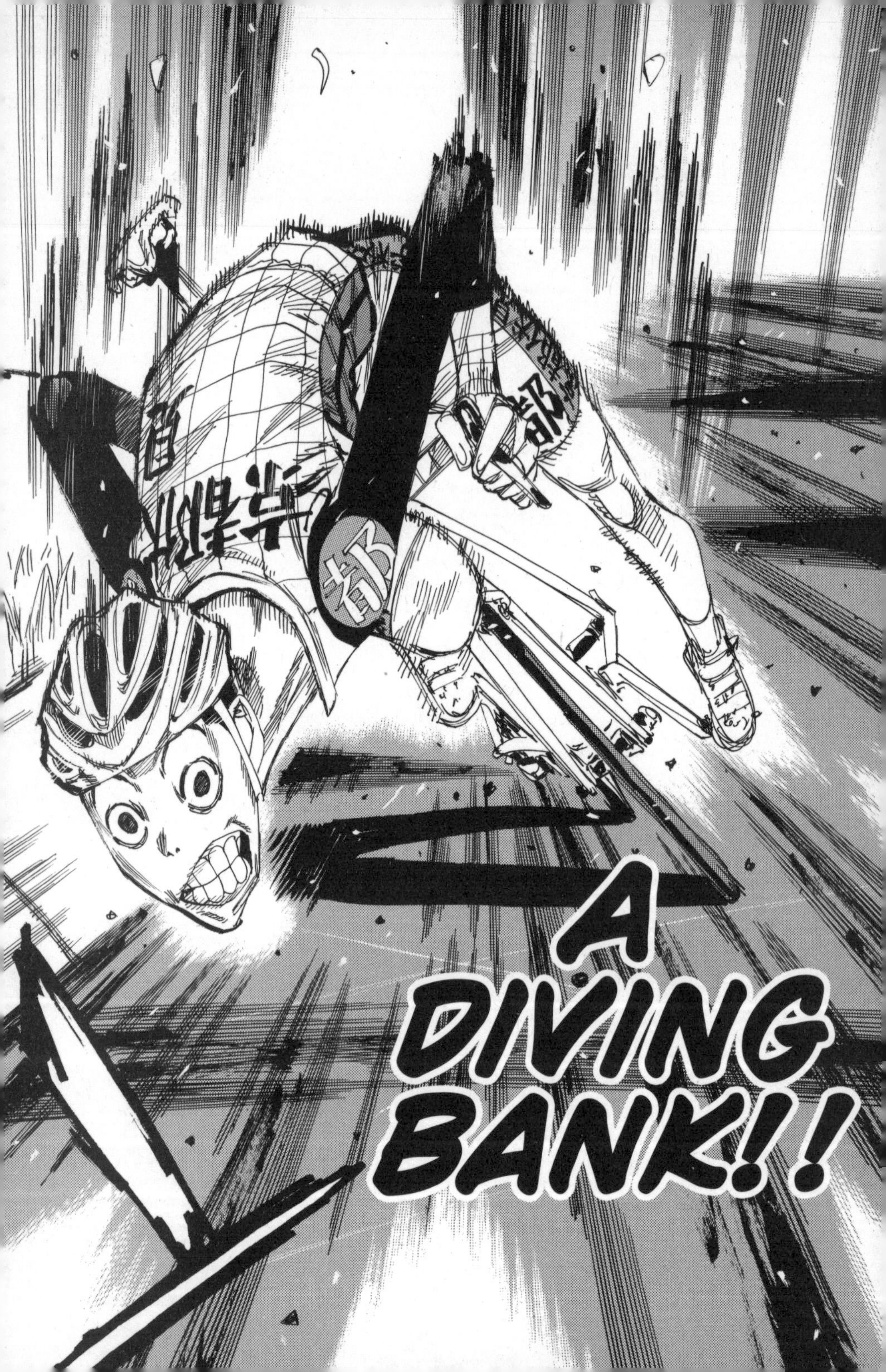
A DIVING BANK!!

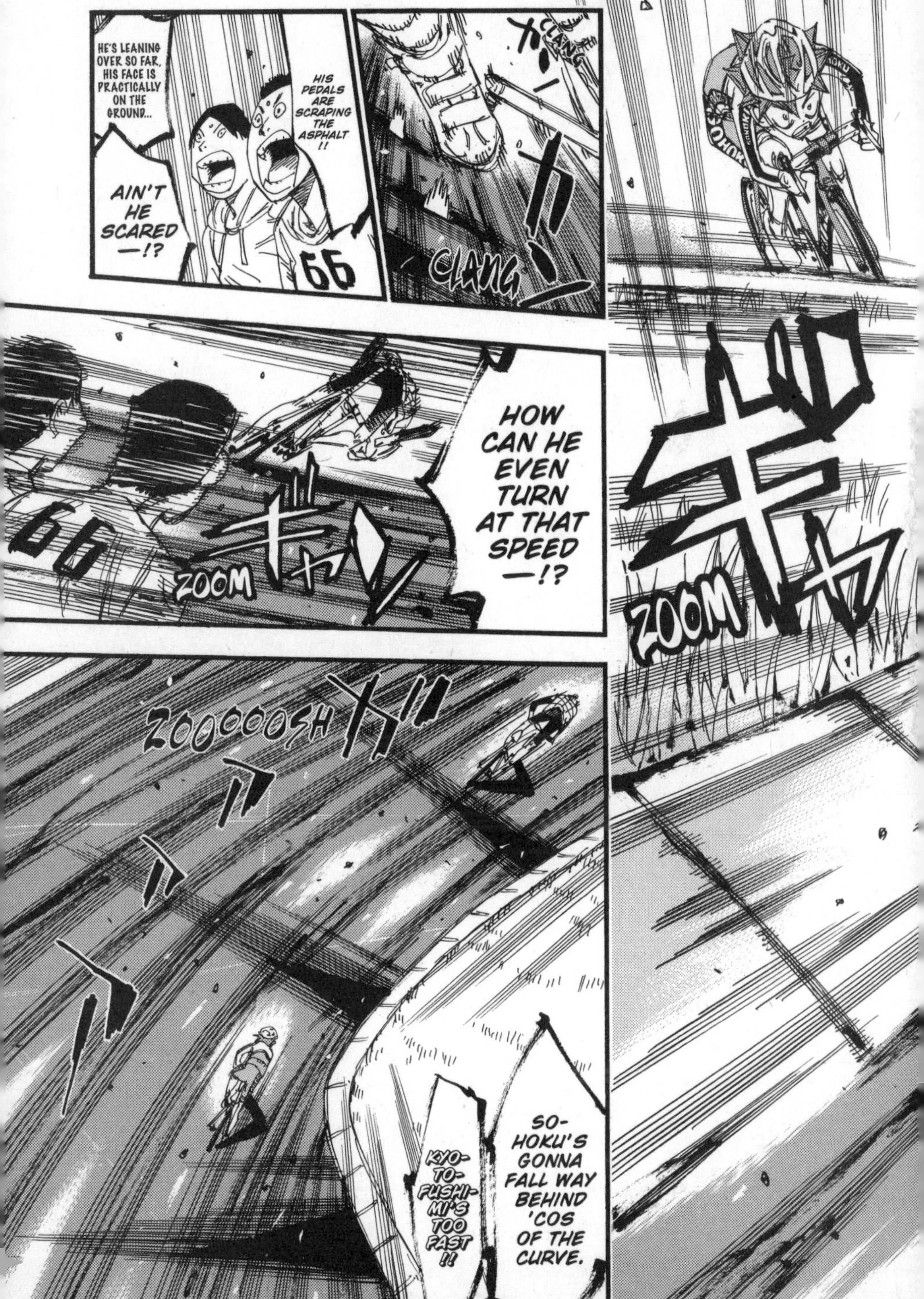
ZOOM
CLANG
CLANG
HIS PEDALS ARE SCRAPING THE ASPHALT!!
HE'S LEANING OVER SO FAR, HIS FACE IS PRACTICALLY ON THE GROUND...
AIN'T HE SCARED—!?
HOW CAN HE EVEN TURN AT THAT SPEED—!?
ZOOM
ZOOOOOSH
SO-HOKU'S GONNA FALL WAY BEHIND 'COS OF THE CURVE.
KYOTO-FUSHIMI'S TOO FAST!!

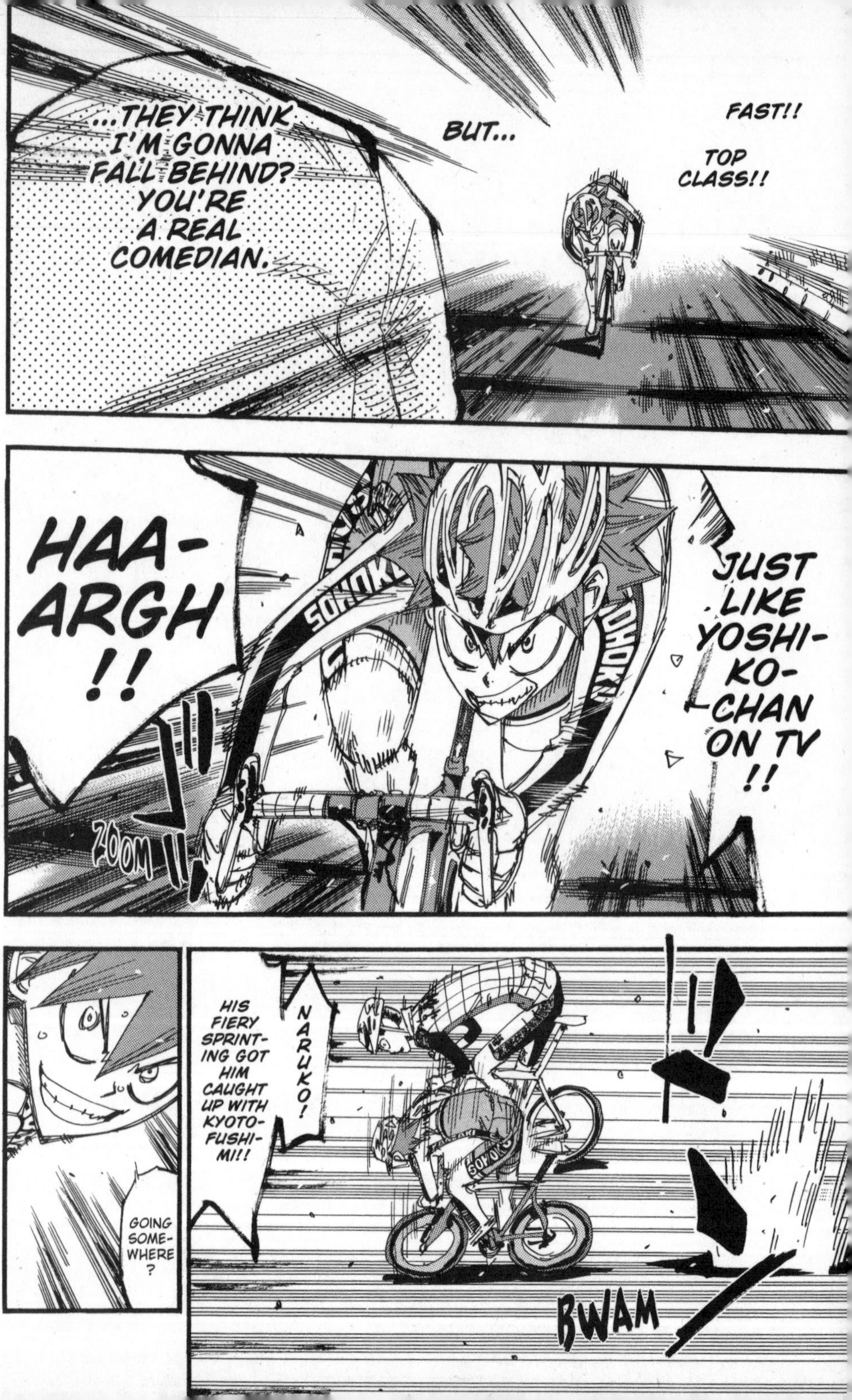
FAST!!
TOP CLASS!!
BUT...
...THEY THINK I'M GONNA FALL BEHIND? YOU'RE A REAL COMEDIAN.
JUST LIKE YOSHI-KO-CHAN ON TV!!
HAA-ARGH!!
ZOOM
NARUKO!
HIS FIERY SPRINT-ING GOT HIM CAUGHT UP WITH KYOTO-FUSHI-MI!!
BWAM
GOING SOME-WHERE?

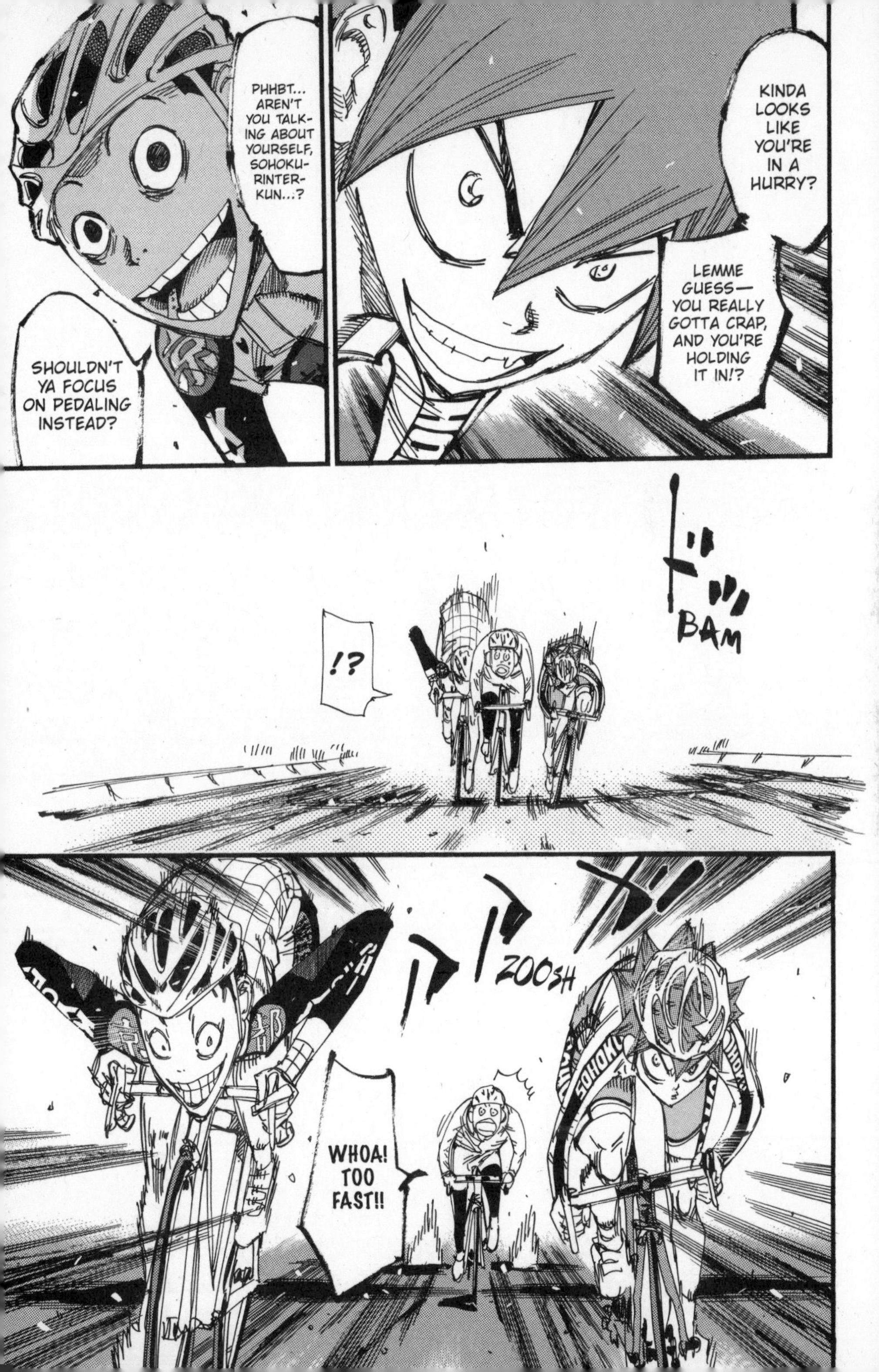
KINDA LOOKS LIKE YOU'RE IN A HURRY?
LEMME GUESS—YOU REALLY GOTTA CRAP, AND YOU'RE HOLDING IT IN!?
PHHBT... AREN'T YOU TALKING ABOUT YOURSELF, SOHOKU-RINTER-KUN...?
SHOULDN'T YA FOCUS ON PEDALING INSTEAD?
BAM
!?
ZOOSH
WHOA! TOO FAST!!

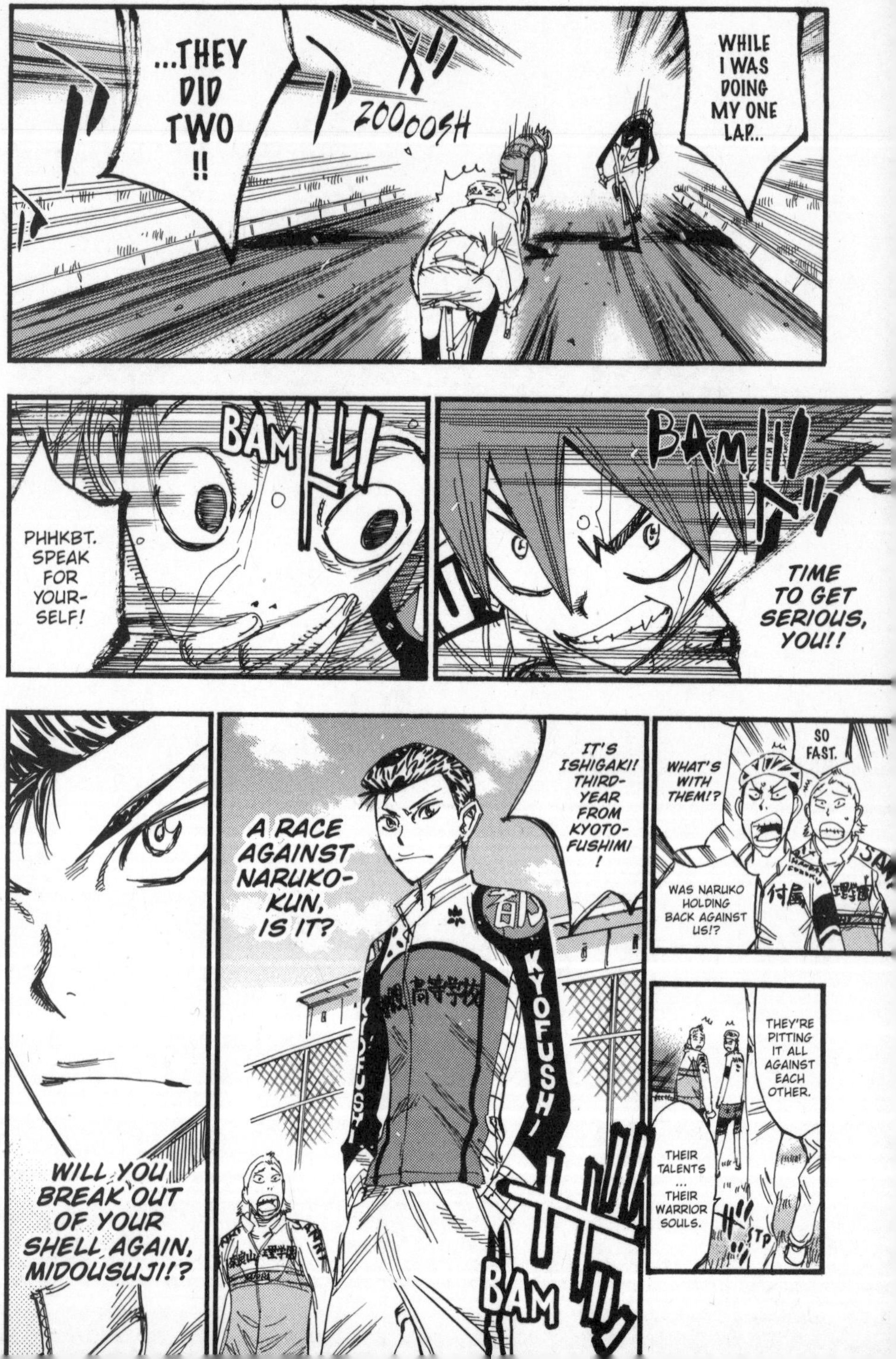
WHILE I WAS DOING MY ONE LAP...
ZOOoOSH
...THEY DID TWO !!
BAM
TIME TO GET SERIOUS, YOU!!
BAM
PHHKBT. SPEAK FOR YOUR-SELF!
SO FAST.
WHAT'S WITH THEM!?
WAS NARUKO HOLDING BACK AGAINST US!?
THEY'RE PITTING IT ALL AGAINST EACH OTHER.
THEIR TALENTS ... THEIR WARRIOR SOULS.
STP
IT'S ISHIGAKI! THIRD-YEAR FROM KYOTO-FUSHIMI!
A RACE AGAINST NARUKO-KUN, IS IT?
BAM
WILL YOU BREAK OUT OF YOUR SHELL AGAIN, MIDOUSUJI!?

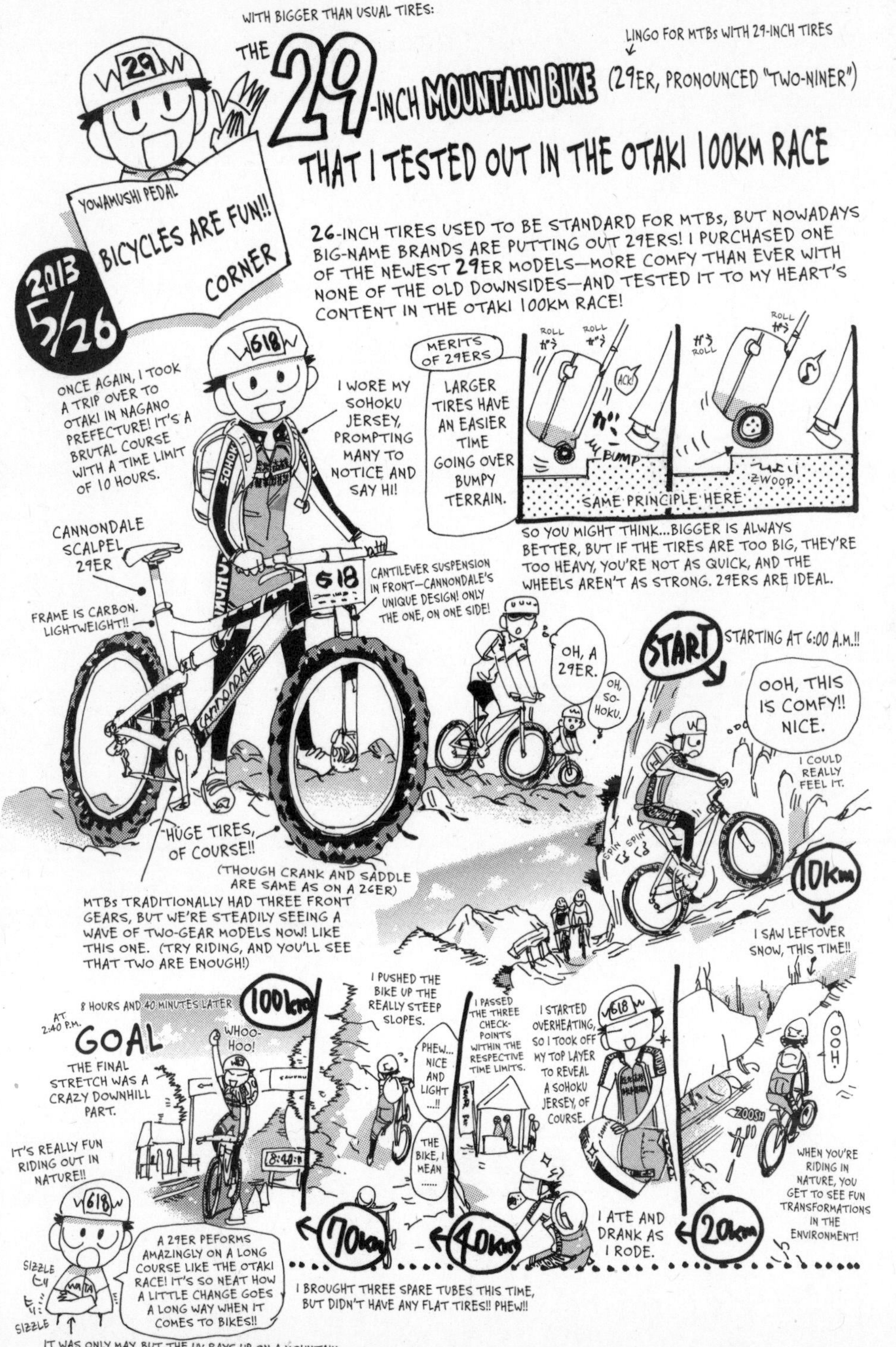

WITH BIGGER THAN USUAL TIRES:
LINGO FOR MTBs WITH 29-INCH TIRES
THE 29-INCH MOUNTAIN BIKE (29ER, PRONOUNCED "TWO-NINER")
THAT I TESTED OUT IN THE OTAKI 100KM RACE
29
YOWAMUSHI PEDAL
BICYCLES ARE FUN!!
CORNER
2013 5/26
26-INCH TIRES USED TO BE STANDARD FOR MTBs, BUT NOWADAYS BIG-NAME BRANDS ARE PUTTING OUT 29ERS! I PURCHASED ONE OF THE NEWEST 29ER MODELS—MORE COMFY THAN EVER WITH NONE OF THE OLD DOWNSIDES—AND TESTED IT TO MY HEART'S CONTENT IN THE OTAKI 100KM RACE!
MERITS OF 29ERS
LARGER TIRES HAVE AN EASIER TIME GOING OVER BUMPY TERRAIN.
ROLL
ROLL
ROLL
ACK!
BUMP
ROLL
ZWOOP
SAME PRINCIPLE HERE
SO YOU MIGHT THINK...BIGGER IS ALWAYS BETTER, BUT IF THE TIRES ARE TOO BIG, THEY'RE TOO HEAVY, YOU'RE NOT AS QUICK, AND THE WHEELS AREN'T AS STRONG. 29ERS ARE IDEAL.
618
ONCE AGAIN, I TOOK A TRIP OVER TO OTAKI IN NAGANO PREFECTURE! IT'S A BRUTAL COURSE WITH A TIME LIMIT OF 10 HOURS.
I WORE MY SOHOKU JERSEY, PROMPTING MANY TO NOTICE AND SAY HI!
CANNONDALE SCALPEL 29ER
FRAME IS CARBON. LIGHTWEIGHT!!
CANTILEVER SUSPENSION IN FRONT—CANNONDALE'S UNIQUE DESIGN! ONLY THE ONE, ON ONE SIDE!
618
HUGE TIRES, OF COURSE!!
(THOUGH CRANK AND SADDLE ARE SAME AS ON A 26ER)
MTBs TRADITIONALLY HAD THREE FRONT GEARS, BUT WE'RE STEADILY SEEING A WAVE OF TWO-GEAR MODELS NOW! LIKE THIS ONE. (TRY RIDING, AND YOU'LL SEE THAT TWO ARE ENOUGH!)
OH, A 29ER.
OH, SO-HOKU.
START
STARTING AT 6:00 A.M.!!
OOH, THIS IS COMFY!! NICE.
I COULD REALLY FEEL IT.
SPIN SPIN
10km
I SAW LEFTOVER SNOW, THIS TIME!!
OOH.
ZOOSH
WHEN YOU'RE RIDING IN NATURE, YOU GET TO SEE FUN TRANSFORMATIONS IN THE ENVIRONMENT!
20km
618
I STARTED OVERHEATING, SO I TOOK OFF MY TOP LAYER TO REVEAL A SOHOKU JERSEY, OF COURSE.
I ATE AND DRANK AS I RODE.
I PASSED THE THREE CHECK-POINTS WITHIN THE RESPECTIVE TIME LIMITS.
40km
I PUSHED THE BIKE UP THE REALLY STEEP SLOPES.
PHEW... NICE AND LIGHT...!!
THE BIKE, I MEAN......
70km
100km
8 HOURS AND 40 MINUTES LATER
AT 2:40 P.M.
GOAL
WHOO-HOO!
THE FINAL STRETCH WAS A CRAZY DOWNHILL PART.
8:40
IT'S REALLY FUN RIDING OUT IN NATURE!!
618
A 29ER PEFORMS AMAZINGLY ON A LONG COURSE LIKE THE OTAKI RACE! IT'S SO NEAT HOW A LITTLE CHANGE GOES A LONG WAY WHEN IT COMES TO BIKES!!
SIZZLE
SIZZLE
IT WAS ONLY MAY, BUT THE UV RAYS UP ON A MOUNTAIN ARE NO JOKE, SO MY ARMS GOT SUNBURNED.
I BROUGHT THREE SPARE TUBES THIS TIME, BUT DIDN'T HAVE ANY FLAT TIRES!! PHEW!!

YOWAMUSHI PEDAL

RIDE.253: WHITTLING AWAY

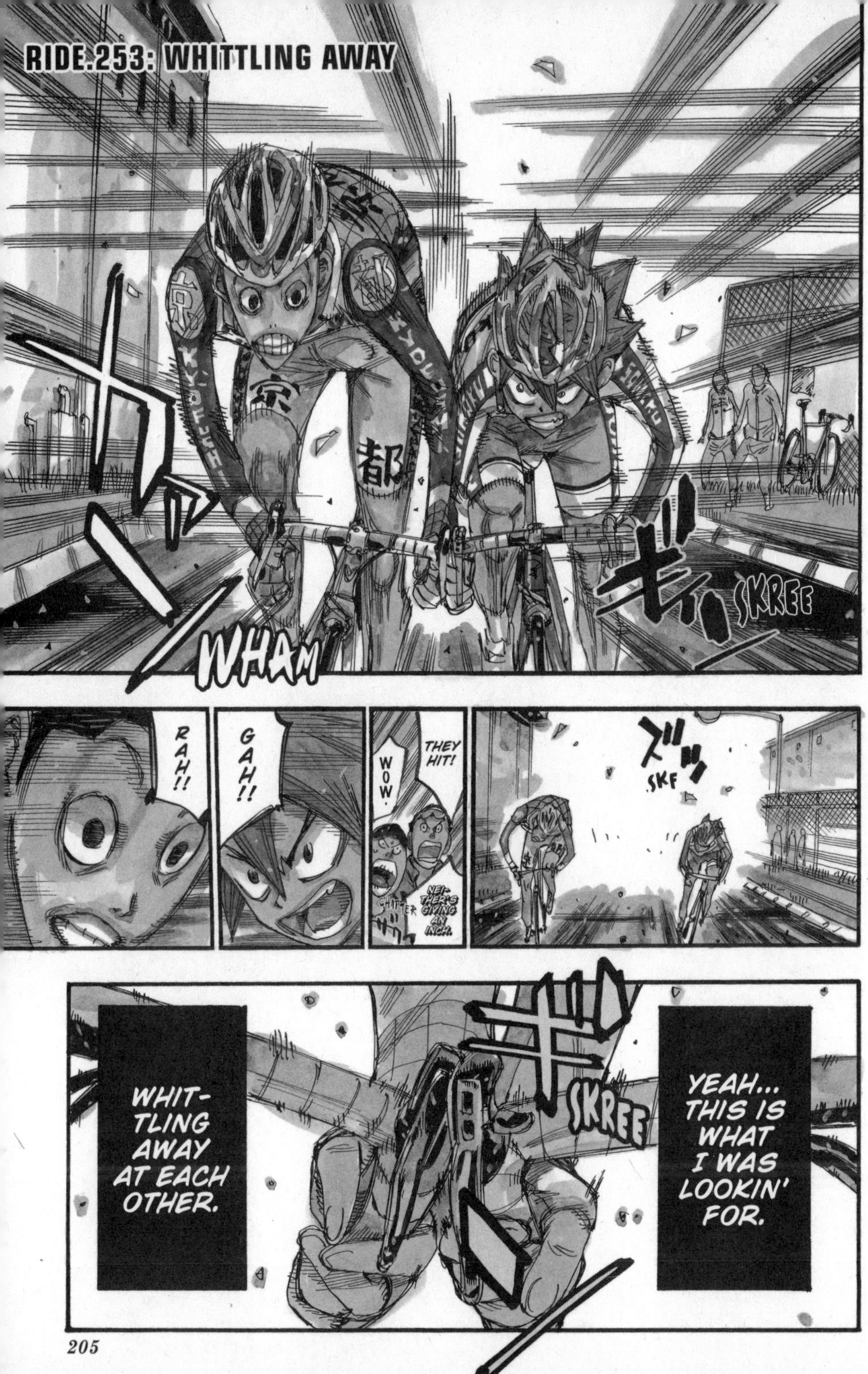
SKREE
WHAM
SKF
THEY HIT!
WOW.
NEITHER'S GIVING AN INCH.
CHATTER
GAH!!
RAH!!
YEAH... THIS IS WHAT I WAS LOOKIN' FOR.
SKREE
WHIT-TLING AWAY AT EACH OTHER.

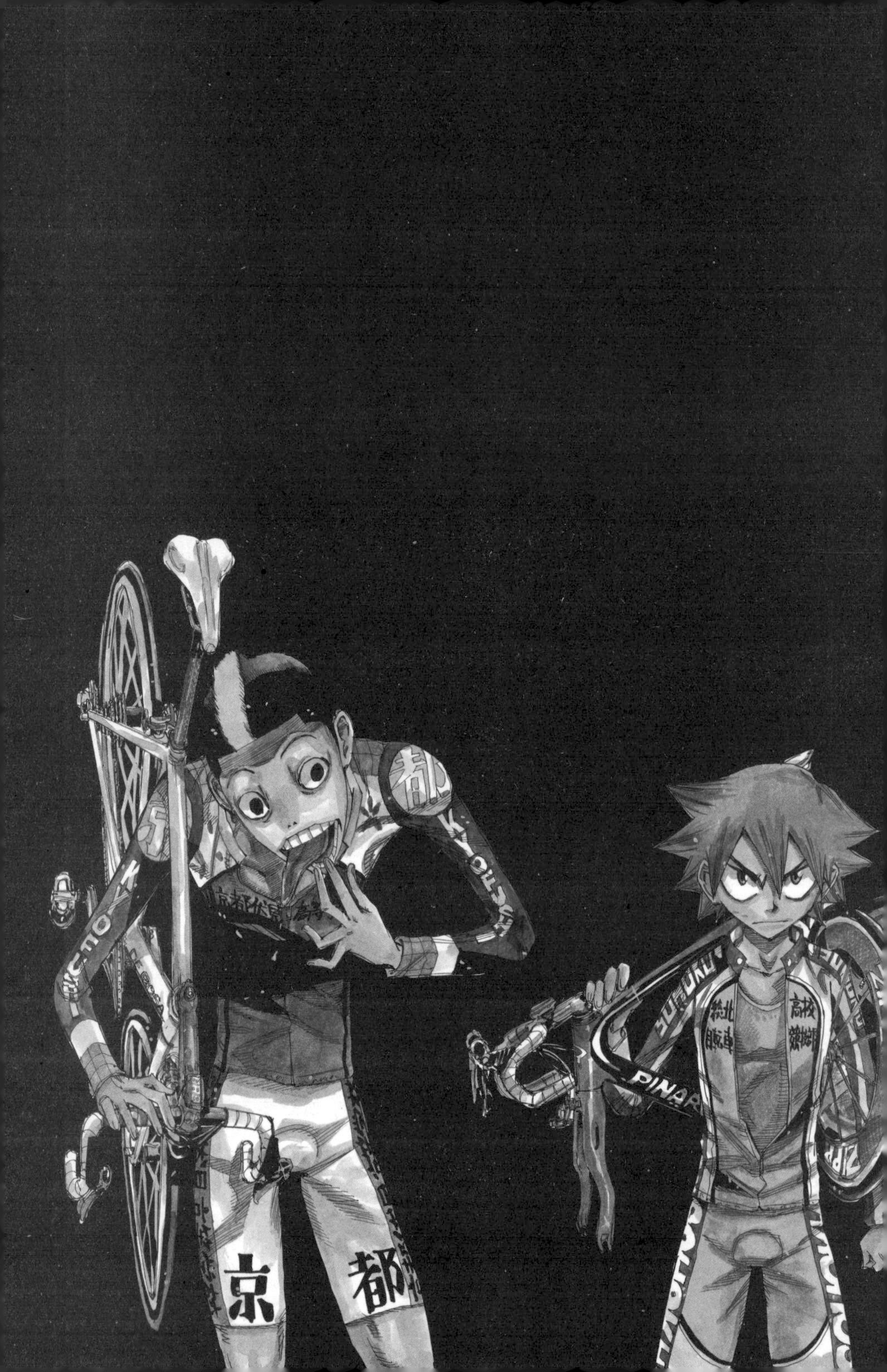
京都
PINAR

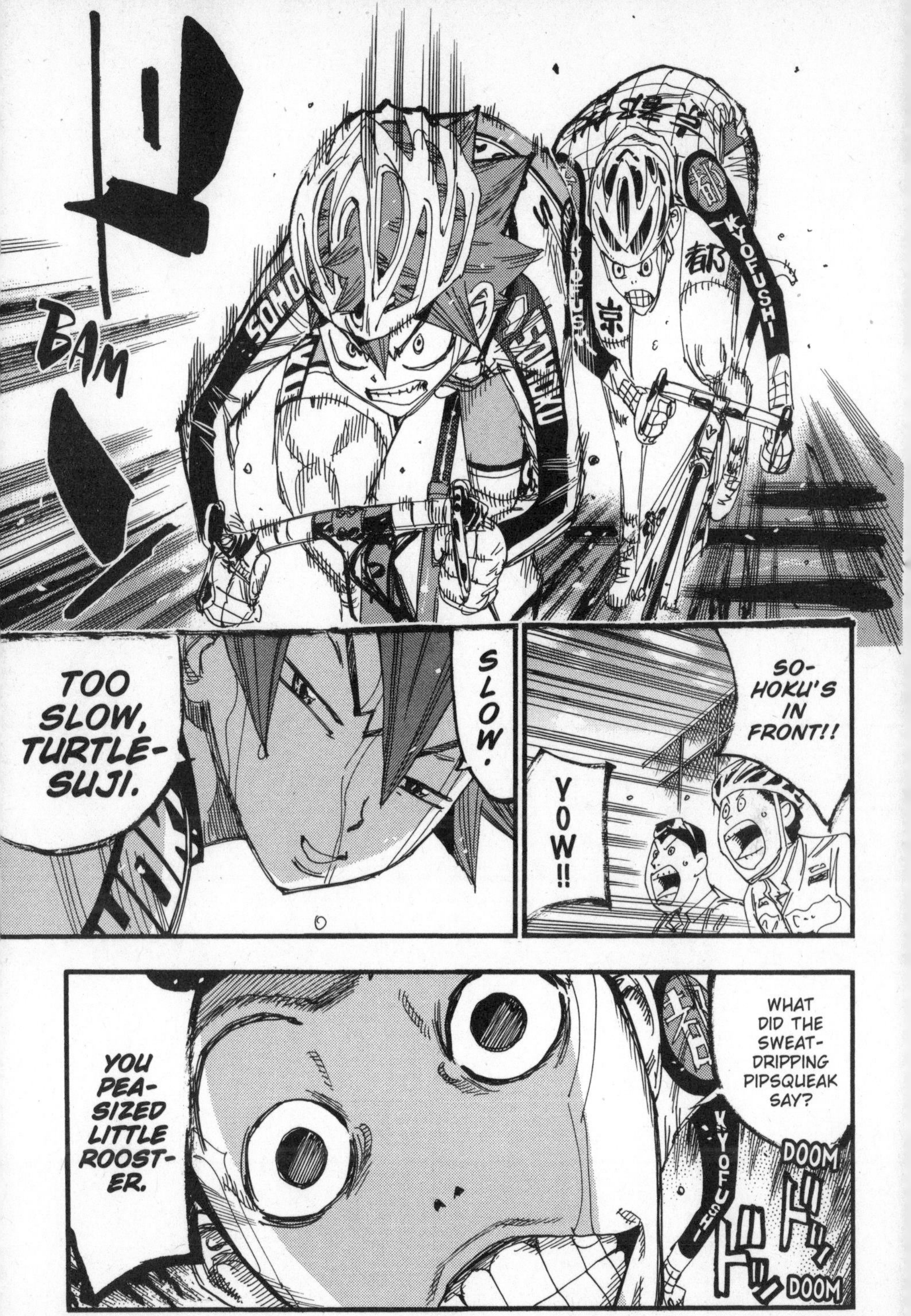
BAM
SO-HOKU'S IN FRONT!!
YOW!!
SLOW.
TOO SLOW, TURTLE-SUJI.
WHAT DID THE SWEAT-DRIPPING PIPSQUEAK SAY?
DOOM
DOOM
YOU PEA-SIZED LITTLE ROOSTER.

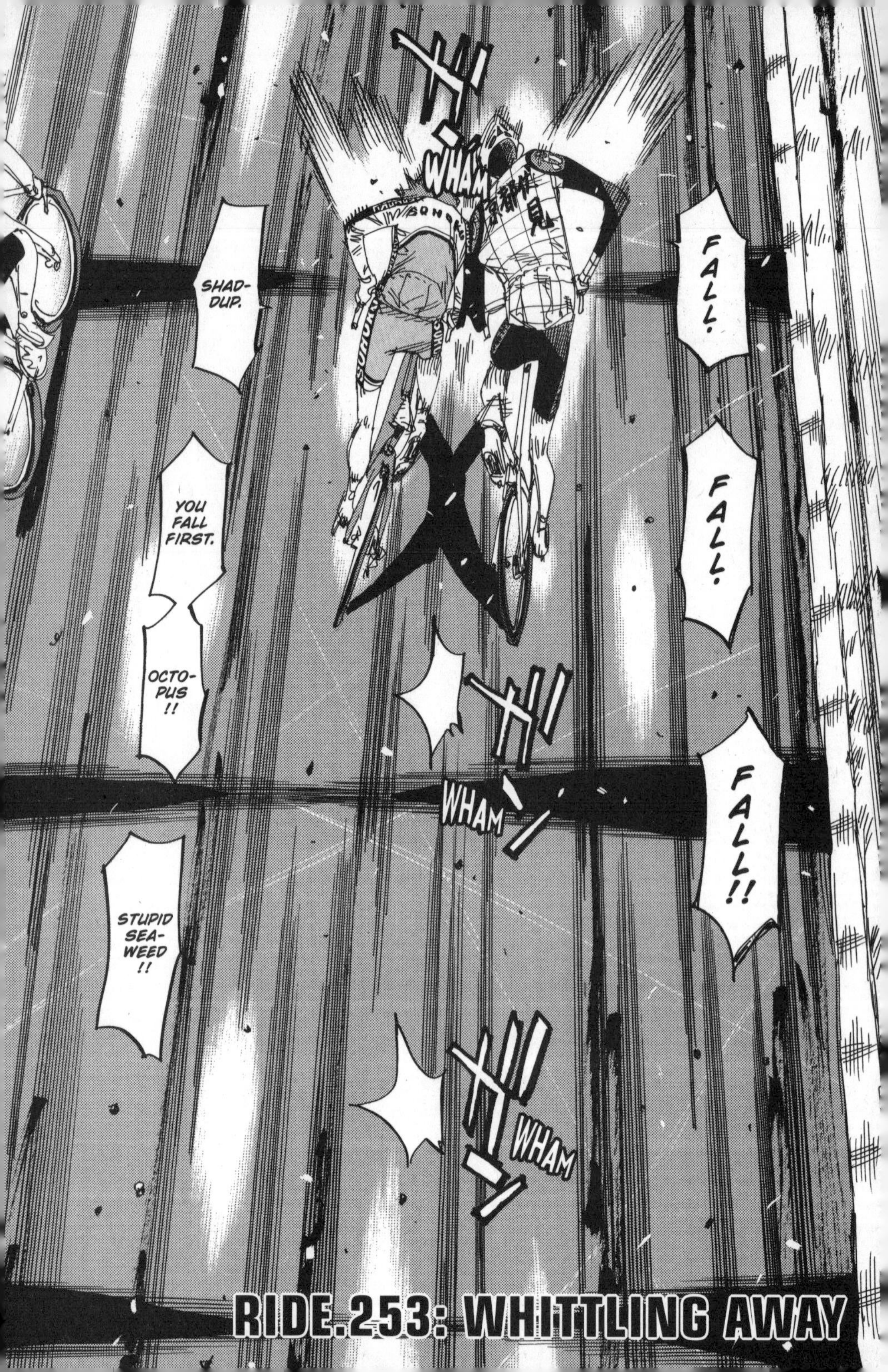
WHAM
FALL.
SHAD-DUP.
FALL.
YOU FALL FIRST.
OCTO-PUS!!
WHAM
FALL!!
STUPID SEA-WEED!!
WHAM

RIDE.253: WHITTLING AWAY

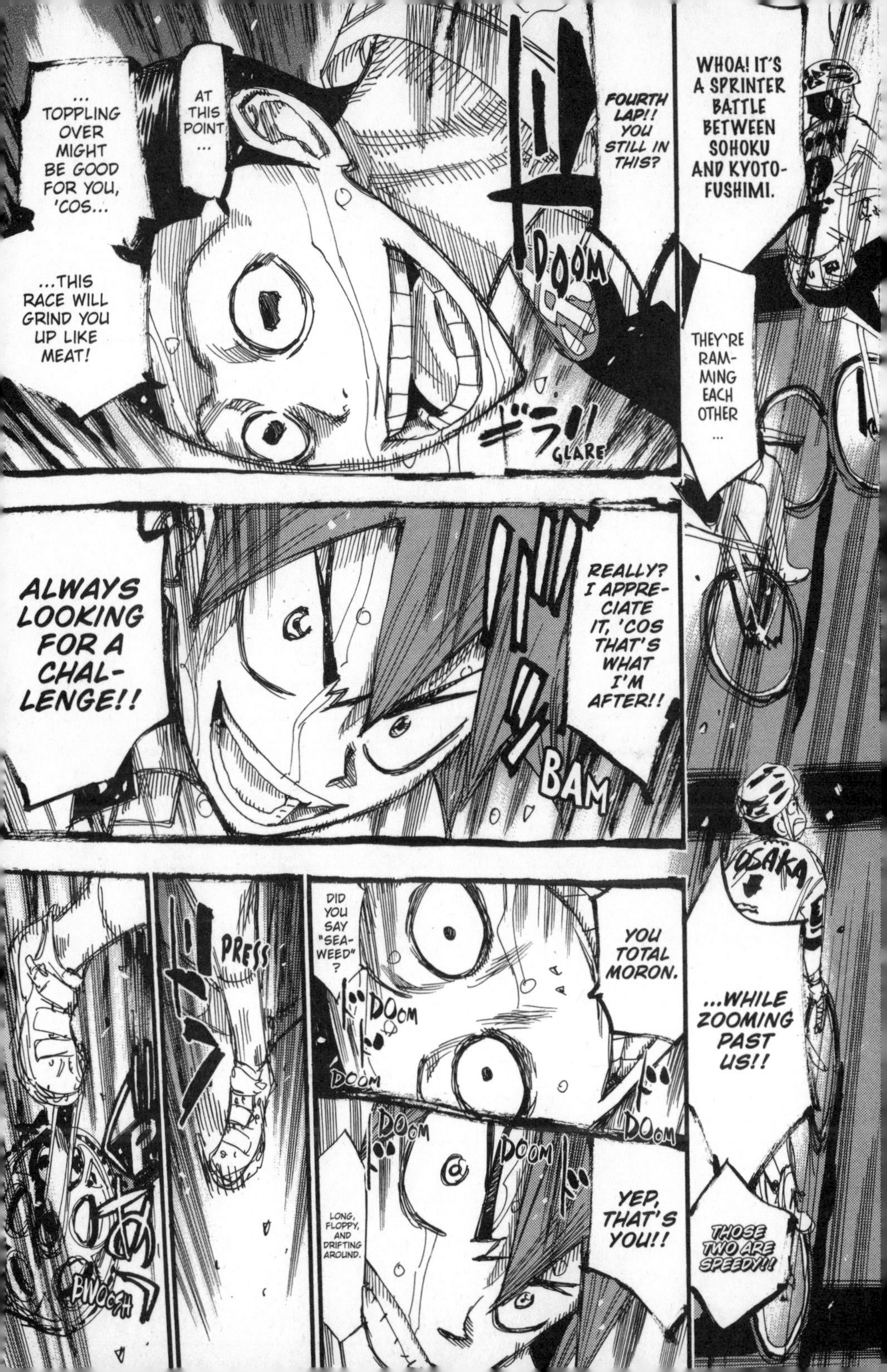
WHOA! IT'S A SPRINTER BATTLE BETWEEN SOHOKU AND KYOTO-FUSHIMI.
THEY'RE RAM-MING EACH OTHER...
...WHILE ZOOMING PAST US!!
THOSE TWO ARE SPEEDY!!
FOURTH LAP!! YOU STILL IN THIS?
DOOM
AT THIS POINT...
...TOPPLING OVER MIGHT BE GOOD FOR YOU, 'COS...
...THIS RACE WILL GRIND YOU UP LIKE MEAT!
ギラ
GLARE
REALLY? I APPRE-CIATE IT, 'COS THAT'S WHAT I'M AFTER!!
BAM
ALWAYS LOOKING FOR A CHAL-LENGE!!
OSAKA
YOU TOTAL MORON.
DID YOU SAY "SEA-WEED"?
DOOM
DOOM
DOOM
YEP, THAT'S YOU!!
DOOM
DOOM
LONG, FLOPPY, AND DRIFTING AROUND.
PRESS
BWOOSH

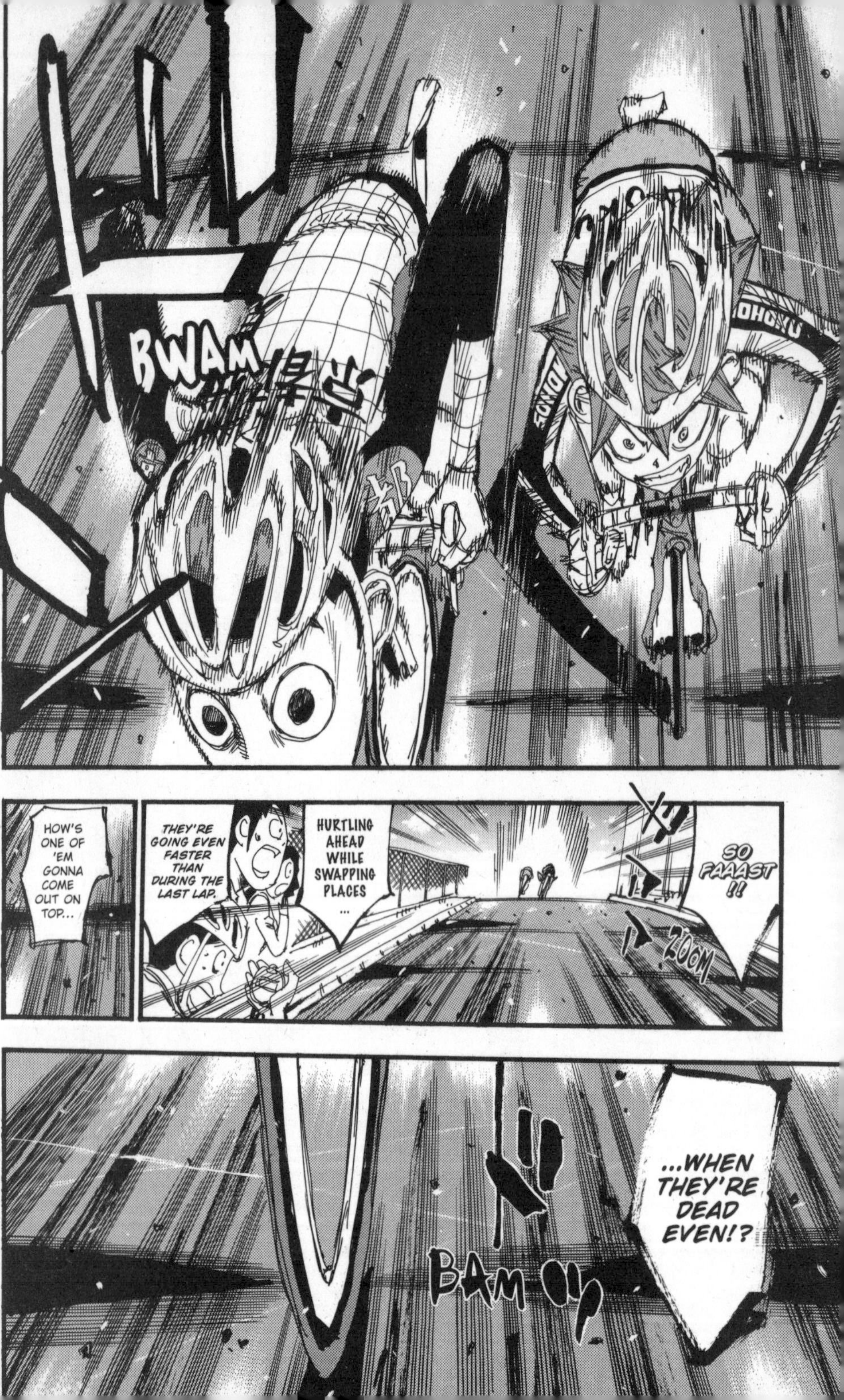
BWAM
SO FAAAST!!
ZOOM
HURTLING AHEAD WHILE SWAPPING PLACES...
THEY'RE GOING EVEN FASTER THAN DURING THE LAST LAP.
HOW'S ONE OF 'EM GONNA COME OUT ON TOP...
...WHEN THEY'RE DEAD EVEN!?
BAM

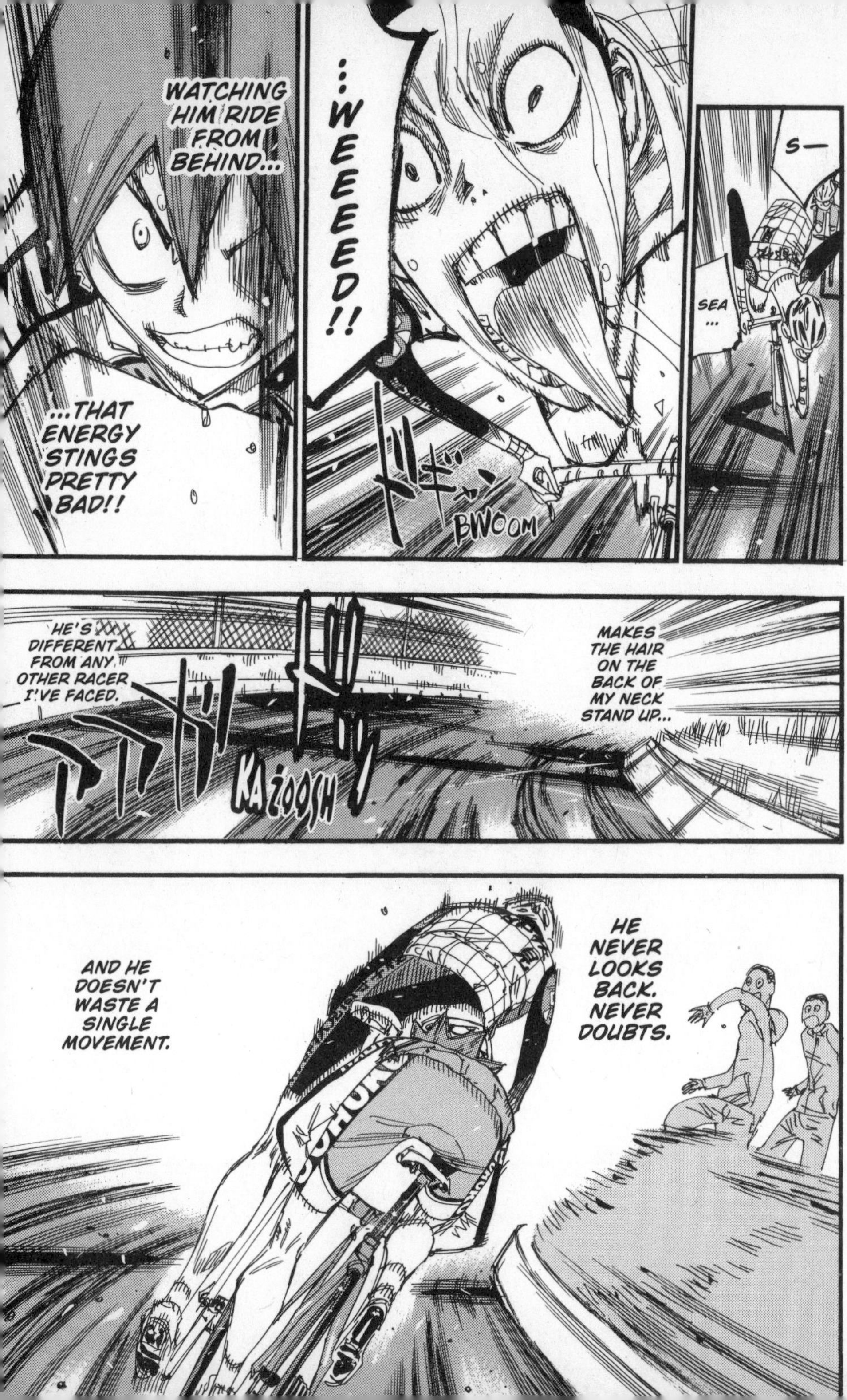
S—
SEA...
...WEEEEEED!!
BWOOM
WATCHING HIM RIDE FROM BEHIND...
...THAT ENERGY STINGS PRETTY BAD!!
MAKES THE HAIR ON THE BACK OF MY NECK STAND UP...
KAZOOSH
HE'S DIFFERENT FROM ANY OTHER RACER I'VE FACED.
HE NEVER LOOKS BACK. NEVER DOUBTS.
AND HE DOESN'T WASTE A SINGLE MOVEMENT.

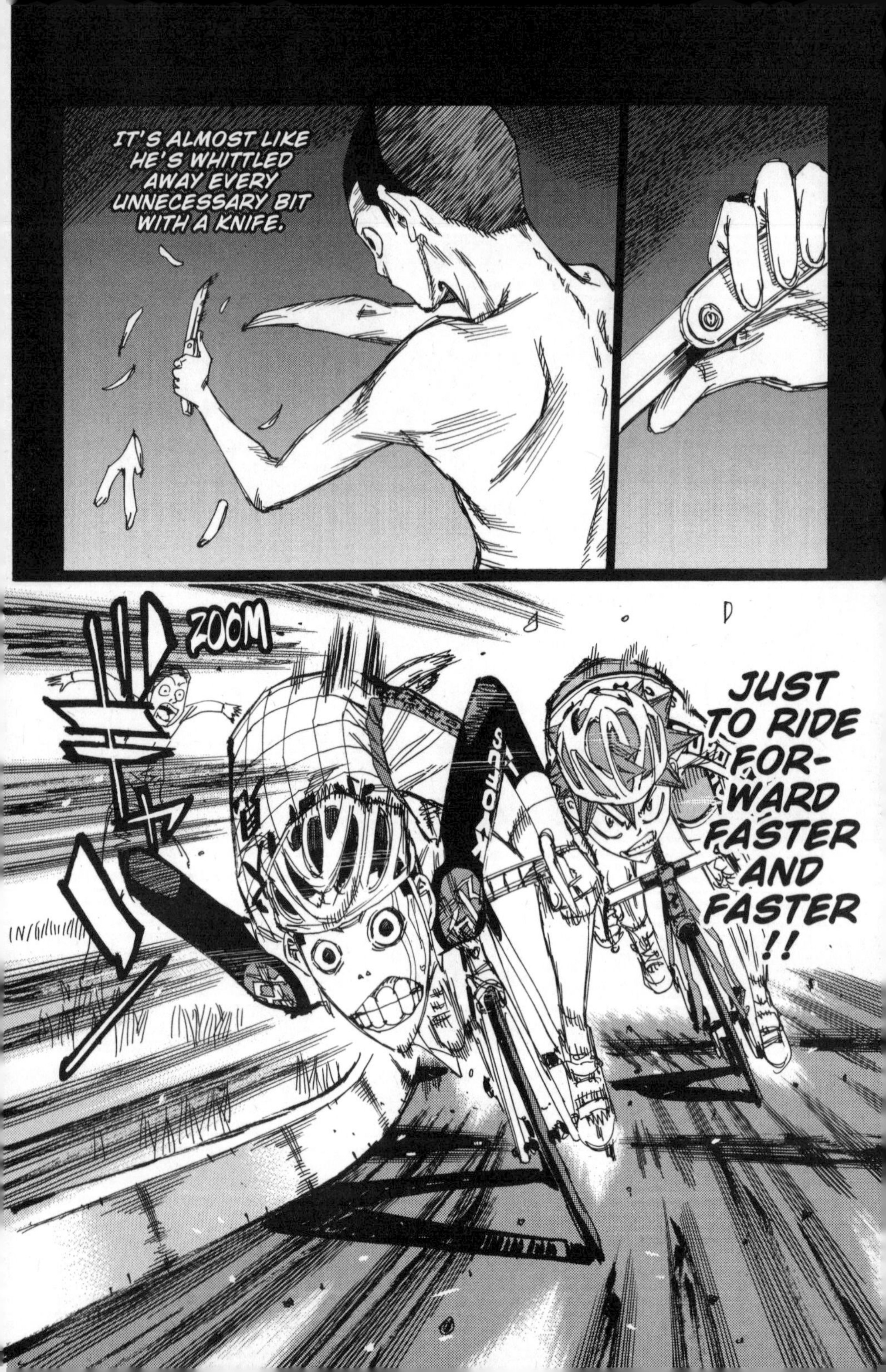
IT'S ALMOST LIKE HE'S WHITTLED AWAY EVERY UNNECESSARY BIT WITH A KNIFE.
JUST TO RIDE FOR-WARD FASTER AND FASTER!!
ZOOM

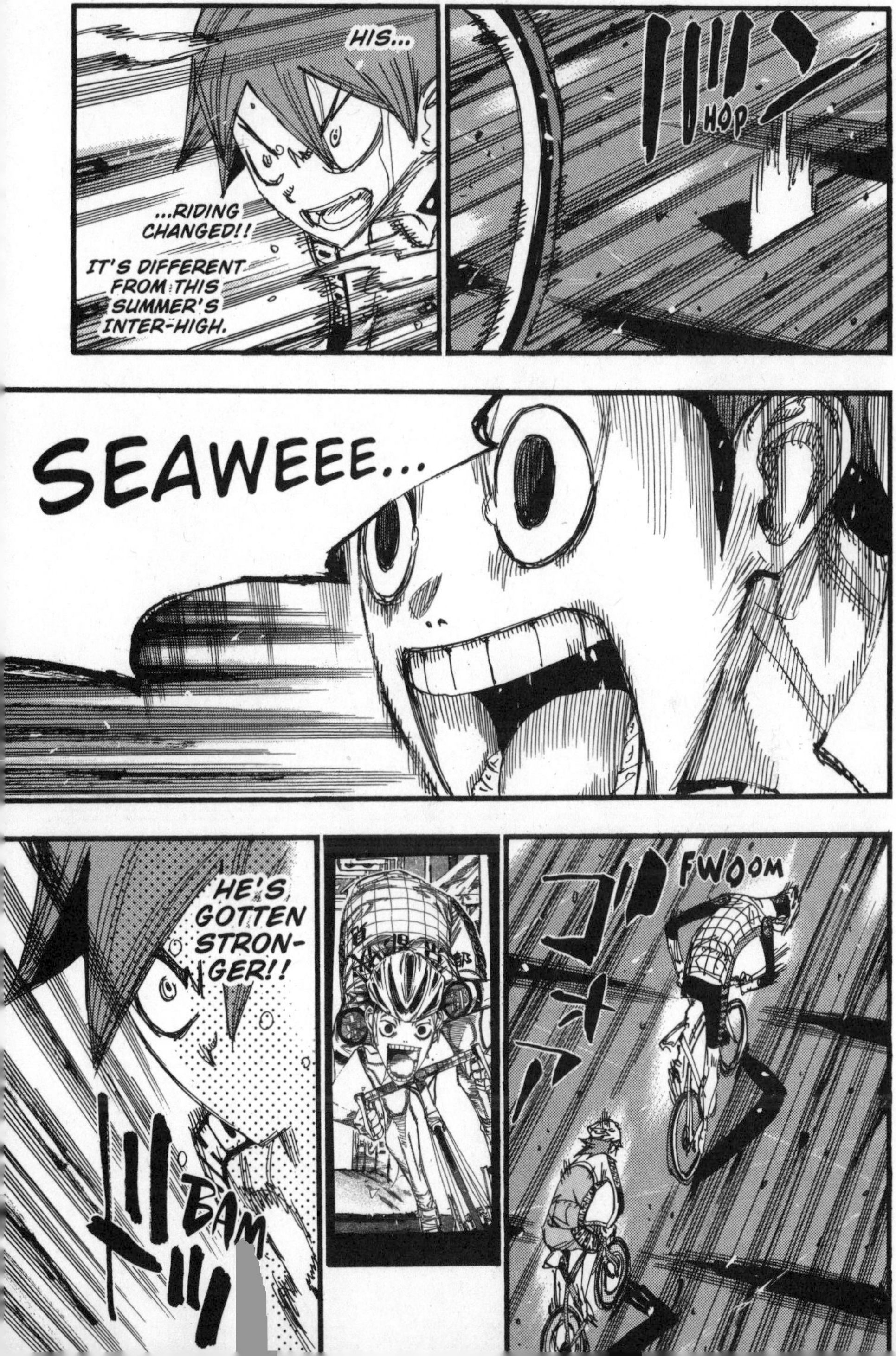
HOP
HIS...
...RIDING CHANGED!!
IT'S DIFFERENT FROM THIS SUMMER'S INTER-HIGH.
SEAWEEE...
FWOOM
HE'S GOTTEN STRON-GER!!
BAM

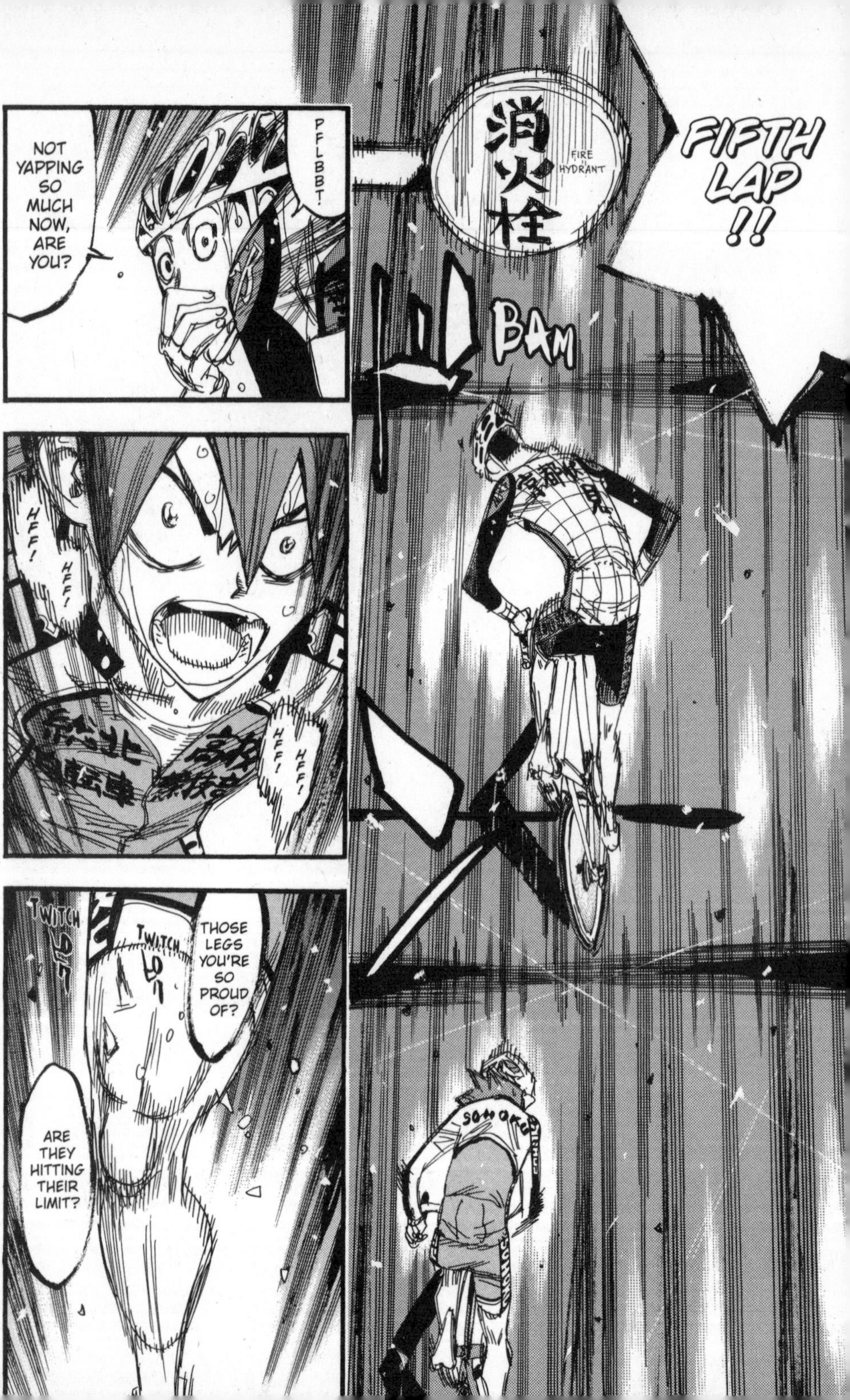
FIFTH LAP!!
消火栓
FIRE HYDRANT
BAM
PFLBBT!
NOT YAPPING SO MUCH NOW, ARE YOU?
HFF! HFF!
HFF! HFF!
TWITCH
TWITCH
THOSE LEGS YOU'RE SO PROUD OF?
ARE THEY HITTING THEIR LIMIT?

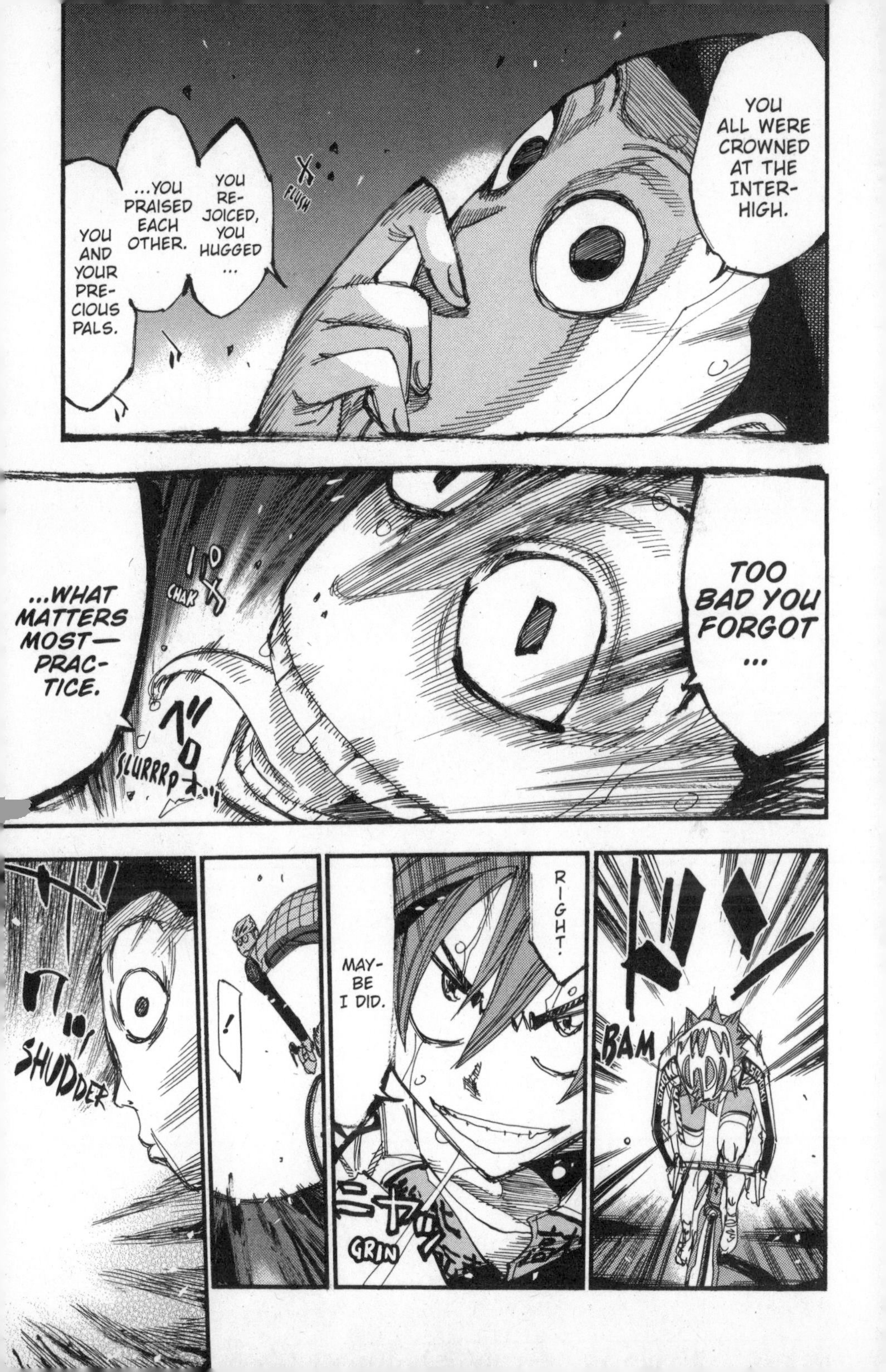
YOU ALL WERE CROWNED AT THE INTER-HIGH.
YOU RE-JOICED, YOU HUGGED...
FLUSH
...YOU PRAISED EACH OTHER.
YOU AND YOUR PRE-CIOUS PALS.
TOO BAD YOU FORGOT...
CHAK
...WHAT MATTERS MOST— PRAC-TICE.
SLURRRP
BAM
RIGHT.
MAY-BE I DID.
GRIN
!
SHUDDER

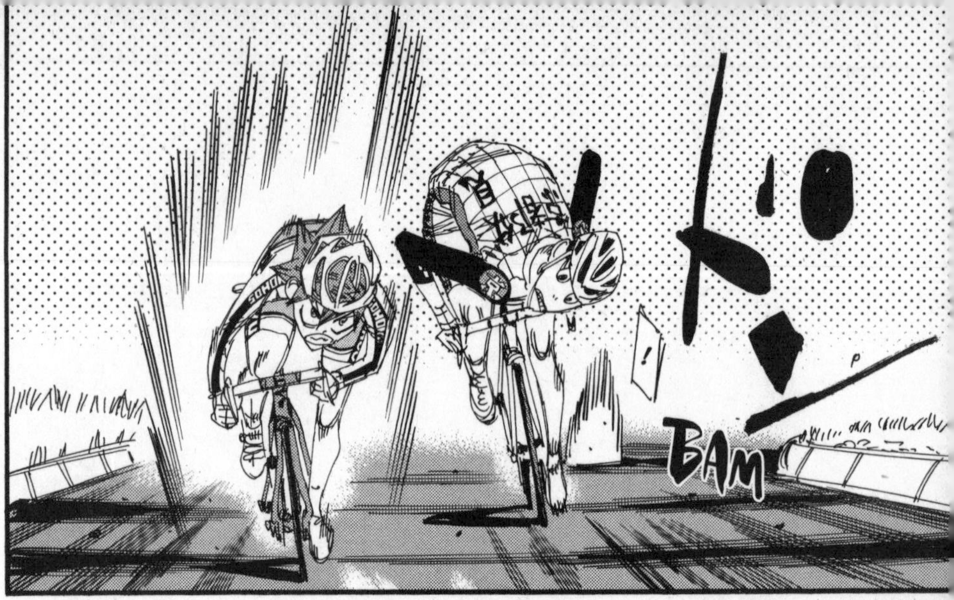
BAM

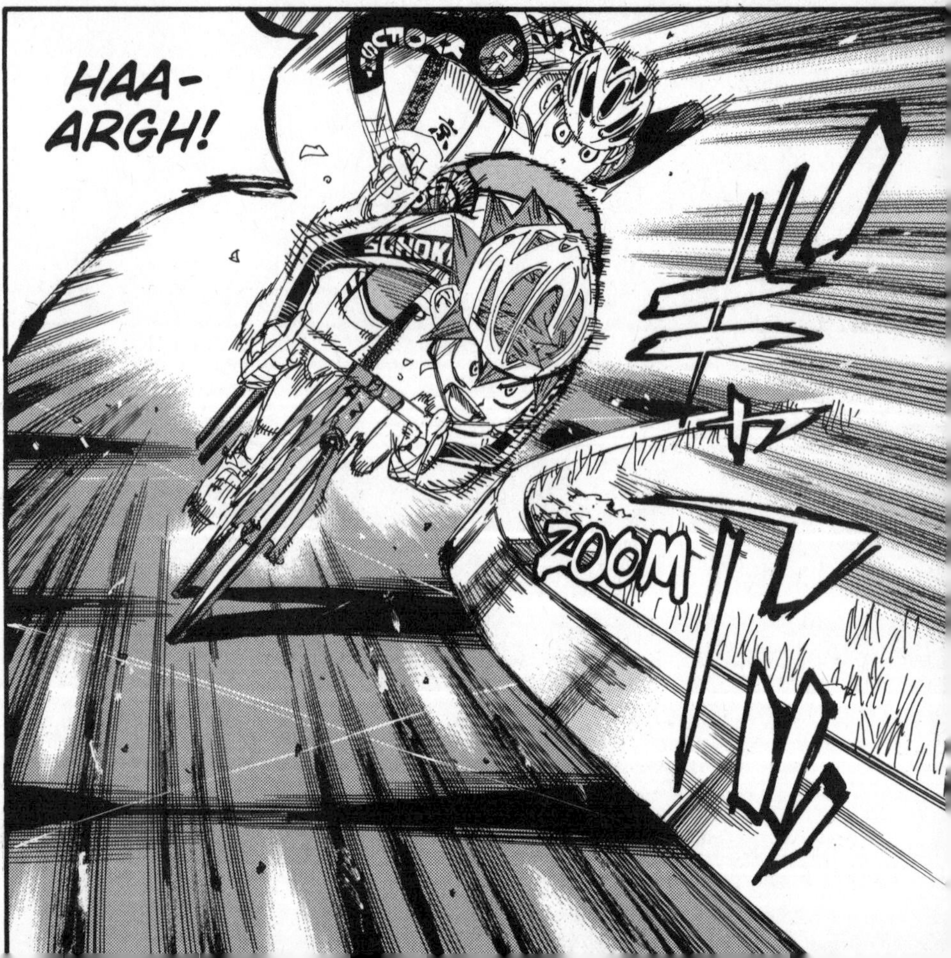
HAA-
ARGH!
ZOOM

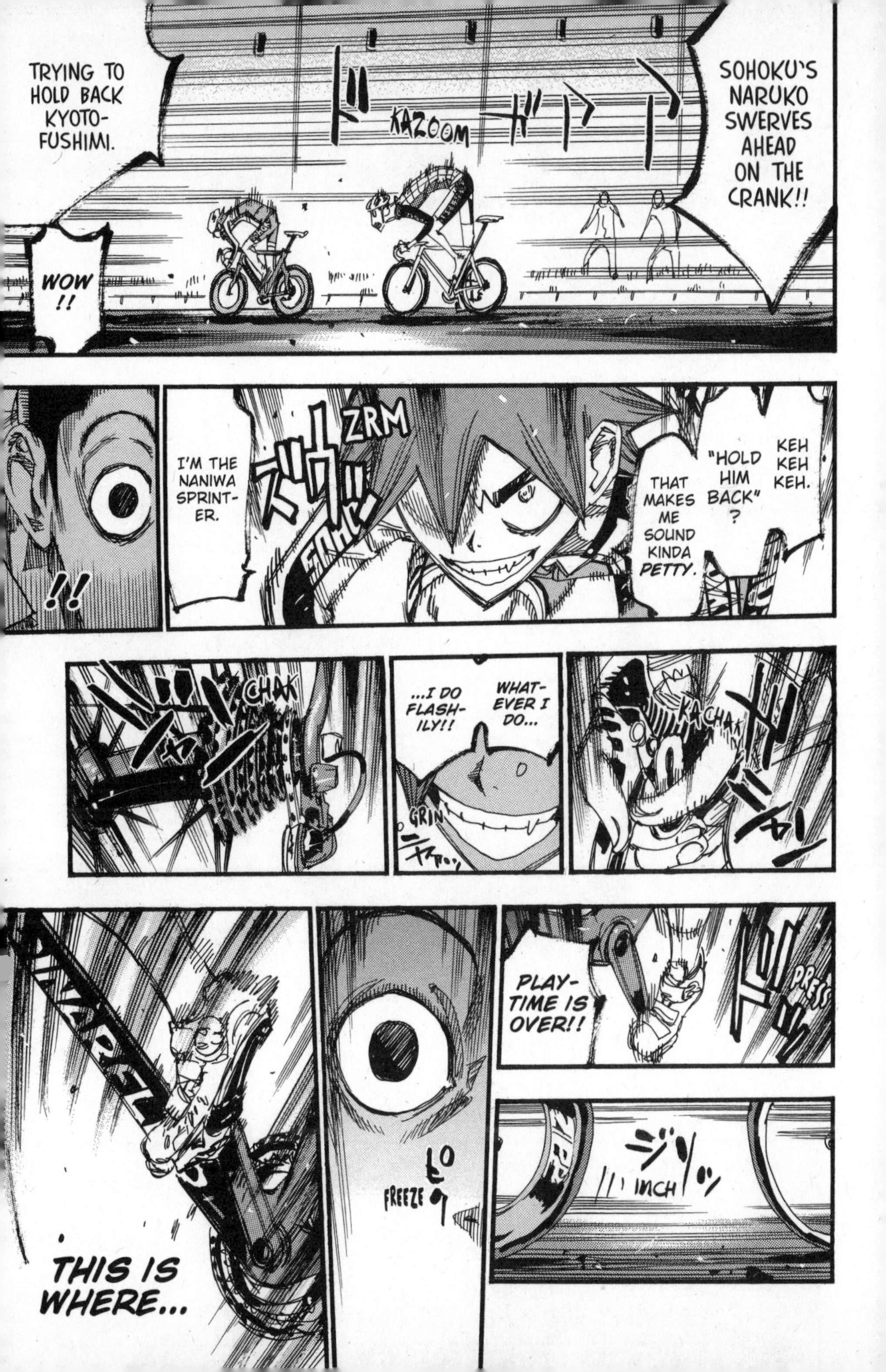
SOHOKU'S NARUKO SWERVES AHEAD ON THE CRANK!!
KAZOOM
TRYING TO HOLD BACK KYOTO-FUSHIMI.
WOW!!
KEH KEH KEH.
"HOLD HIM BACK"?
THAT MAKES ME SOUND KINDA PETTY.
ZRM
I'M THE NANIWA SPRINT-ER.
!!
KACHAK
WHAT-EVER I DO...
...I DO FLASH-ILY!!
GRIN
CHAK
PRESS
PLAY-TIME IS OVER!!
INCH
FREEZE
THIS IS WHERE...

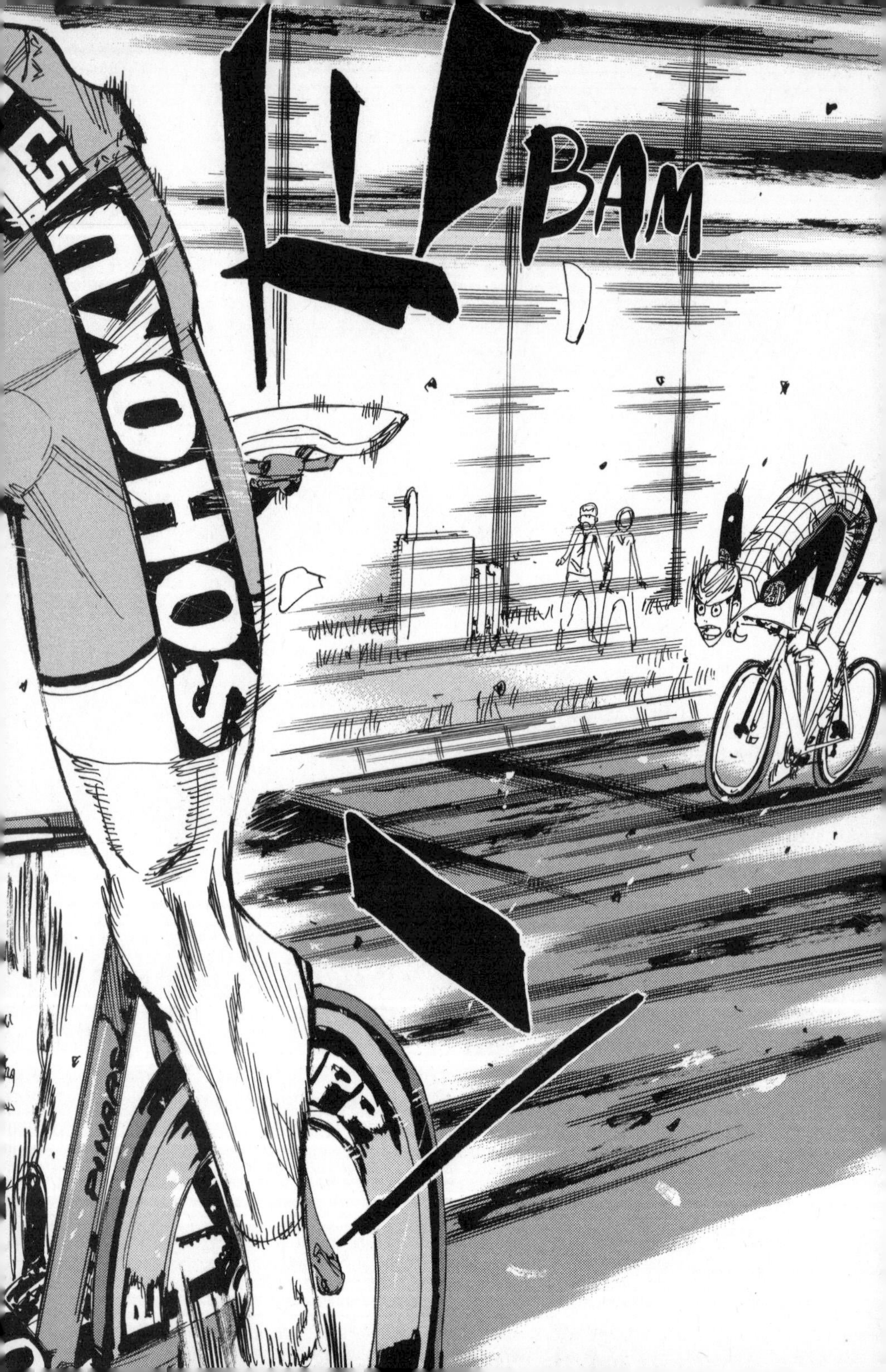
BAM
SOHOKU

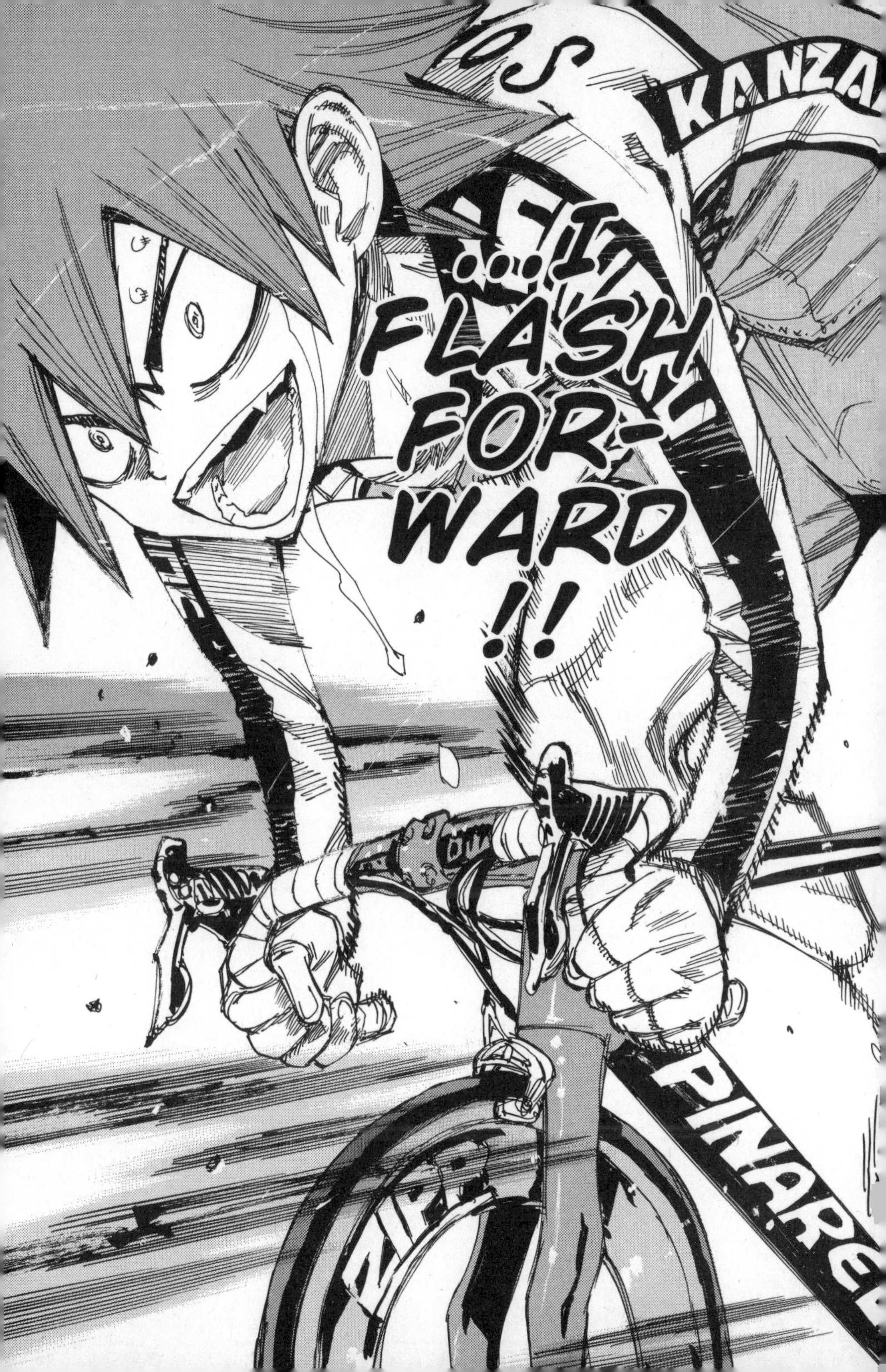

...I FLASH FOR-WARD!!

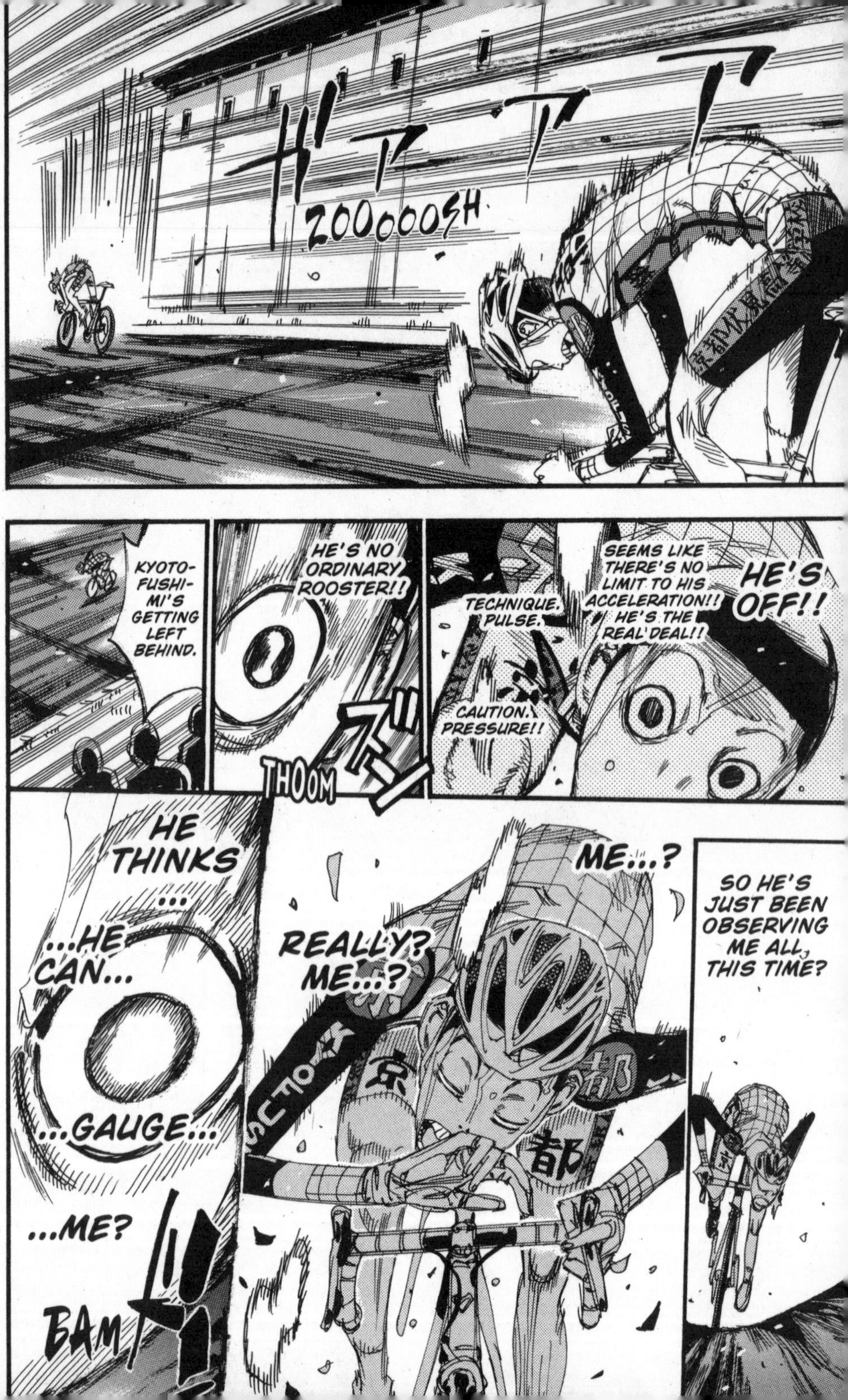
ZOOOOOSH
HE'S OFF!!
SEEMS LIKE THERE'S NO LIMIT TO HIS ACCELERATION!! HE'S THE REAL DEAL!!
TECHNIQUE. PULSE.
CAUTION. PRESSURE!!
HE'S NO ORDINARY ROOSTER!!
THOOM
KYOTO-FUSHIMI'S GETTING LEFT BEHIND.
SO HE'S JUST BEEN OBSERVING ME ALL THIS TIME?
ME...?
REALLY? ME...?
HE THINKS...
...HE CAN...
...GAUGE...
...ME?
BAM

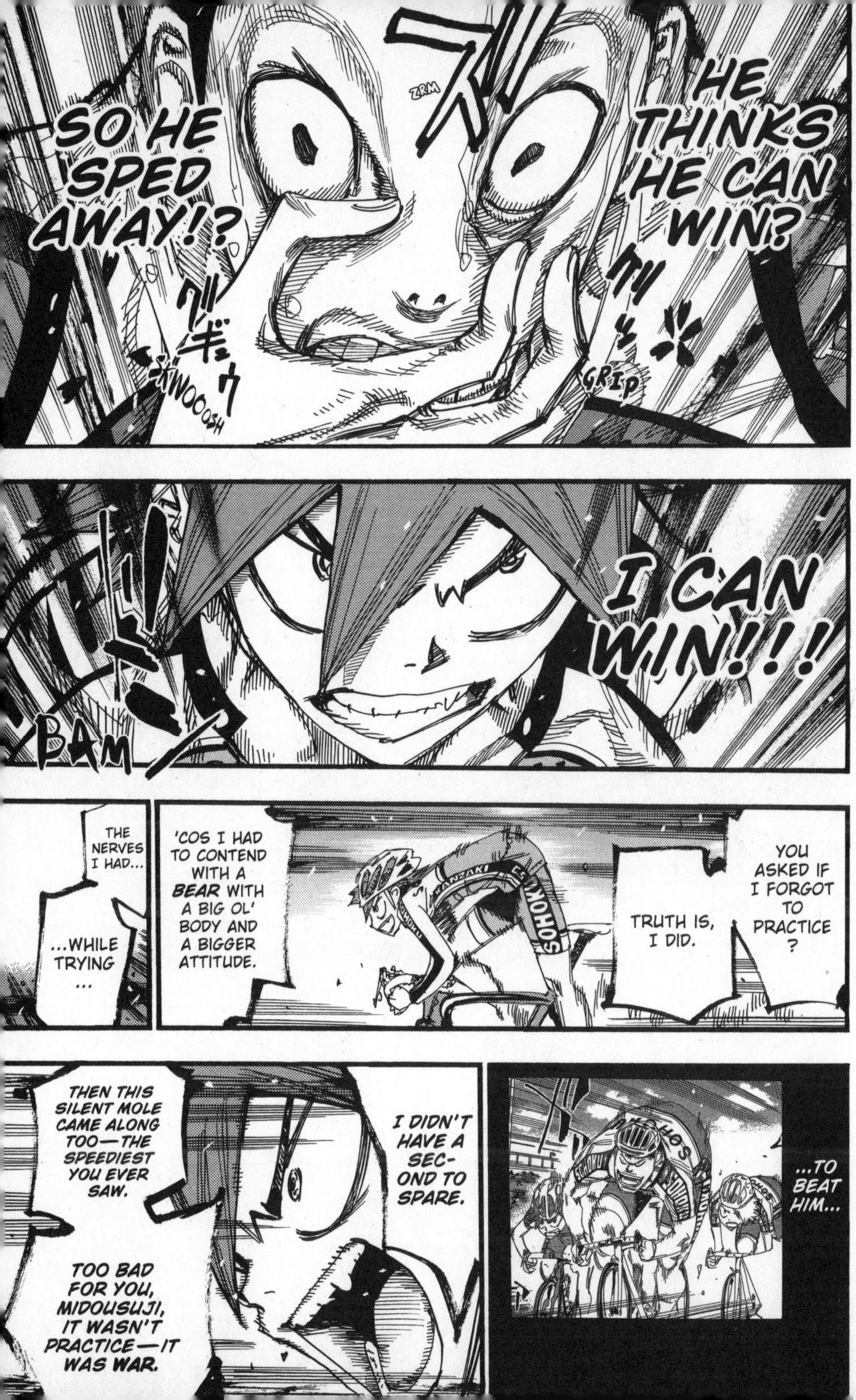

HE THINKS HE CAN WIN?
ZRM
SO HE SPED AWAY!?
GRIP
WOOOSH
I CAN WIN!!!
BAM
YOU ASKED IF I FORGOT TO PRACTICE?
TRUTH IS, I DID.
'COS I HAD TO CONTEND WITH A BEAR WITH A BIG OL' BODY AND A BIGGER ATTITUDE.
THE NERVES I HAD...
...WHILE TRYING...
...TO BEAT HIM...
I DIDN'T HAVE A SEC-OND TO SPARE.
THEN THIS SILENT MOLE CAME ALONG TOO—THE SPEEDIEST YOU EVER SAW.
TOO BAD FOR YOU, MIDOUSUJI, IT WASN'T PRACTICE—IT WAS WAR.

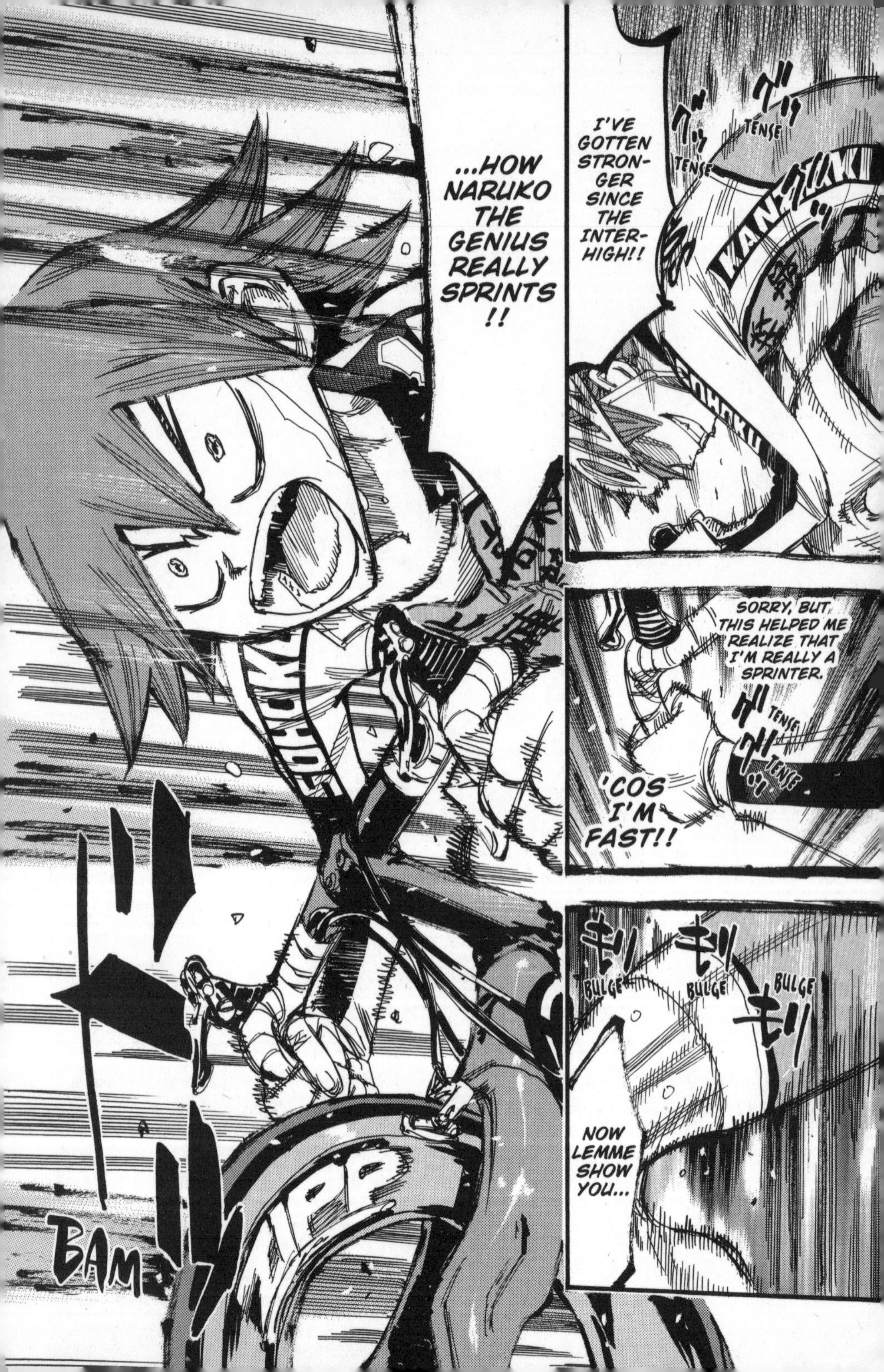

TENSE
TENSE
I'VE GOTTEN STRONGER SINCE THE INTER-HIGH!!
SORRY, BUT THIS HELPED ME REALIZE THAT I'M REALLY A SPRINTER.
TENSE
TENSE
'COS I'M FAST!!
BULGE
BULGE
BULGE
NOW LEMME SHOW YOU...
...HOW NARUKO THE GENIUS REALLY SPRINTS!!
BAM

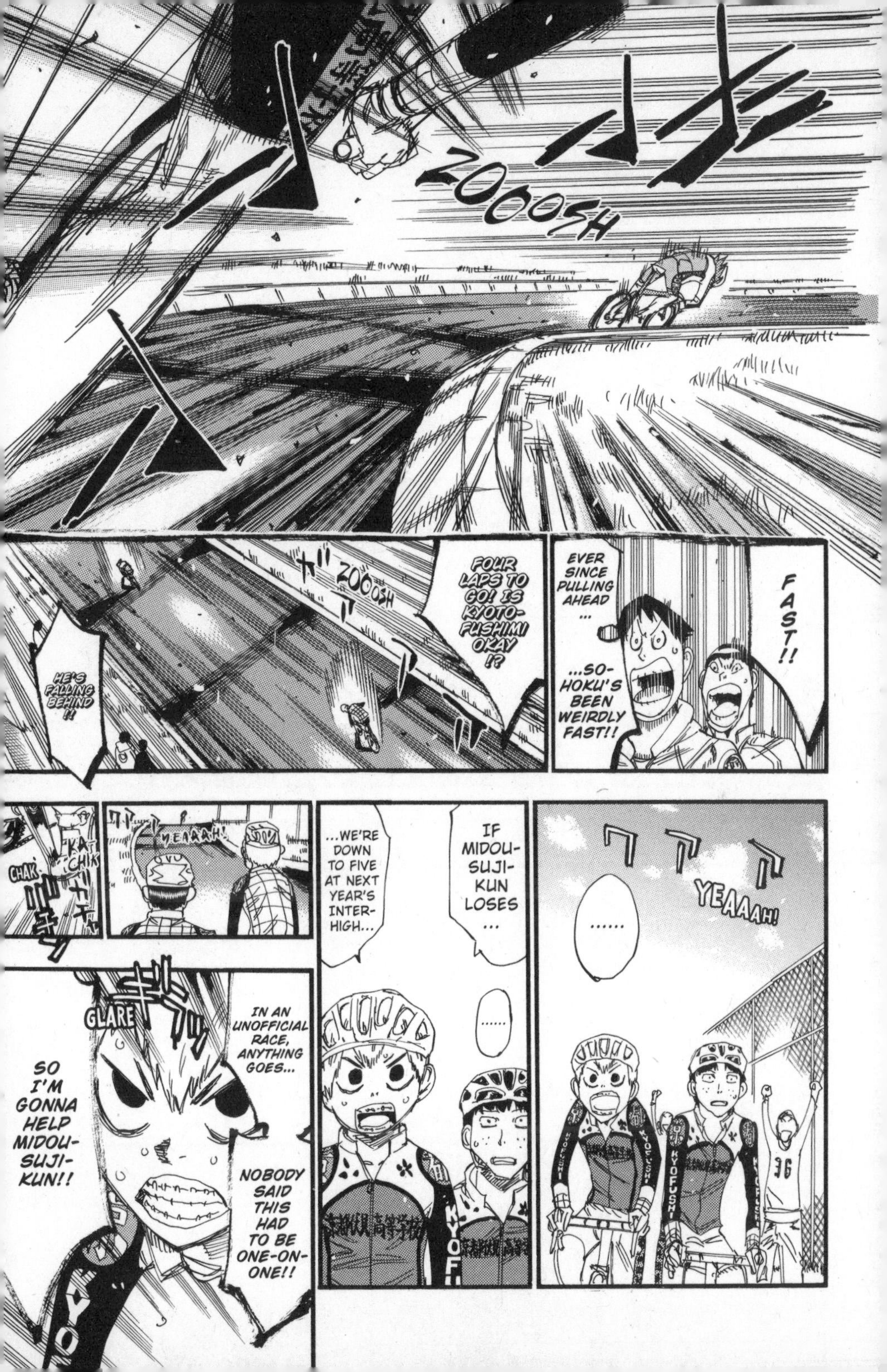
ZOOOSH
FAST!!
EVER SINCE PULLING AHEAD ...
...SO-HOKU'S BEEN WEIRDLY FAST!!
FOUR LAPS TO GO! IS KYOTO-FUSHIMI OKAY !?
ZOOOSH
HE'S FALLING BEHIND !!
YEAAAH!
......
IF MIDOU-SUJI-KUN LOSES ...
...WE'RE DOWN TO FIVE AT NEXT YEAR'S INTER-HIGH...
......
YEAAAH!
KA CHIK
CHAK
IN AN UNOFFICIAL RACE, ANYTHING GOES...
NOBODY SAID THIS HAD TO BE ONE-ON-ONE!!
GLARE
SO I'M GONNA HELP MIDOU-SUJI-KUN!!

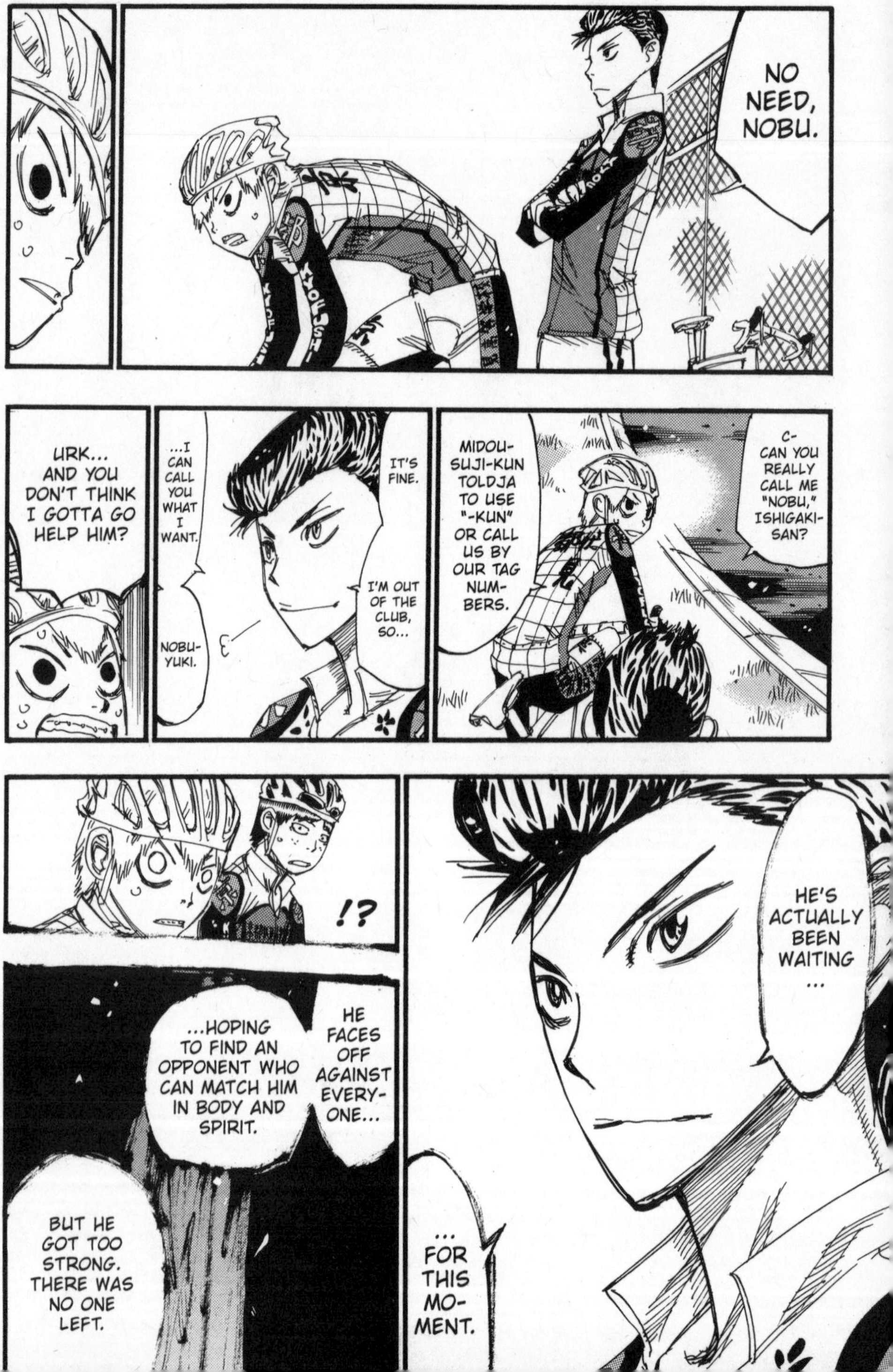
NO NEED, NOBU.
C-CAN YOU REALLY CALL ME "NOBU," ISHIGAKI-SAN?
MIDOU-SUJI-KUN TOLDJA TO USE "-KUN" OR CALL US BY OUR TAG NUM-BERS.
IT'S FINE.
I'M OUT OF THE CLUB, SO...
...I CAN CALL YOU WHAT I WANT.
NOBU-YUKI.
URK... AND YOU DON'T THINK I GOTTA GO HELP HIM?
HE'S ACTUALLY BEEN WAITING ...
... FOR THIS MO-MENT.
!?
HE FACES OFF AGAINST EVERY-ONE...
...HOPING TO FIND AN OPPONENT WHO CAN MATCH HIM IN BODY AND SPIRIT.
BUT HE GOT TOO STRONG. THERE WAS NO ONE LEFT.

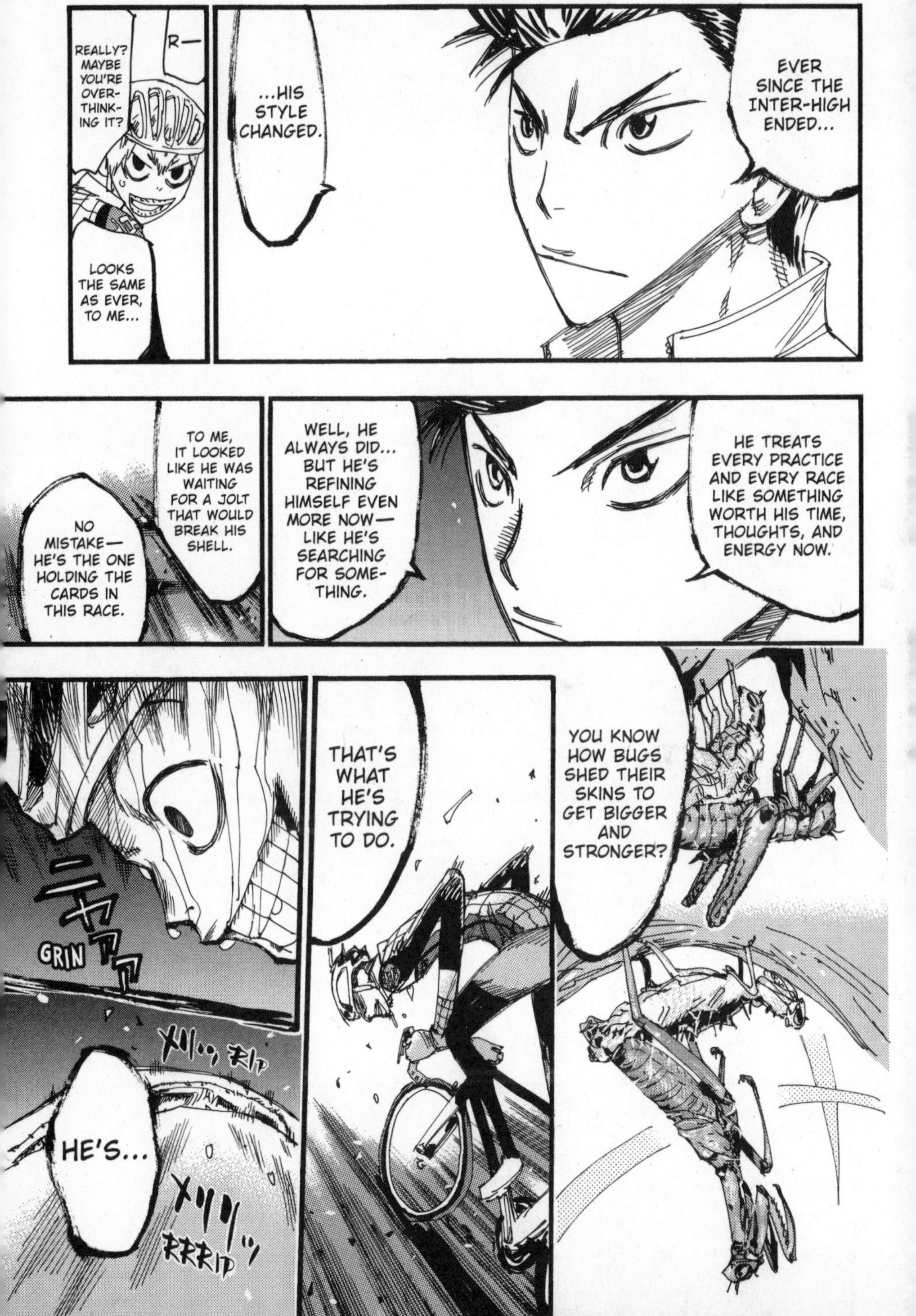
EVER SINCE THE INTER-HIGH ENDED...
...HIS STYLE CHANGED.
R—
REALLY? MAYBE YOU'RE OVER-THINKING IT?
LOOKS THE SAME AS EVER, TO ME...
HE TREATS EVERY PRACTICE AND EVERY RACE LIKE SOMETHING WORTH HIS TIME, THOUGHTS, AND ENERGY NOW.
WELL, HE ALWAYS DID... BUT HE'S REFINING HIMSELF EVEN MORE NOW—LIKE HE'S SEARCHING FOR SOME-THING.
TO ME, IT LOOKED LIKE HE WAS WAITING FOR A JOLT THAT WOULD BREAK HIS SHELL.
NO MISTAKE—HE'S THE ONE HOLDING THE CARDS IN THIS RACE.
YOU KNOW HOW BUGS SHED THEIR SKINS TO GET BIGGER AND STRONGER?
THAT'S WHAT HE'S TRYING TO DO.
ニヤァァ GRIN
メリッ RIP
HE'S...
メリリッ RRRIP

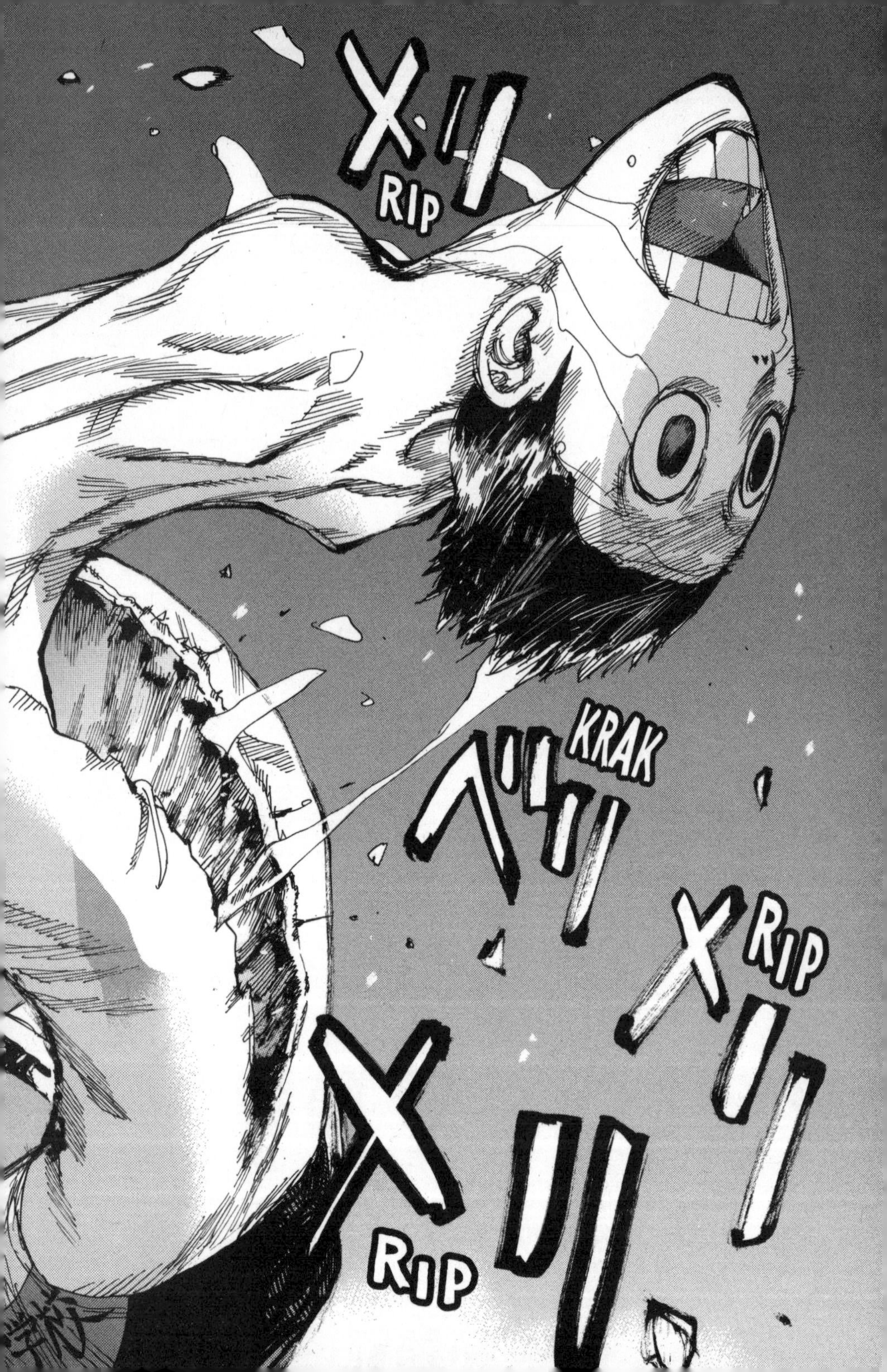

RIP
KRAK
RIP
RIP

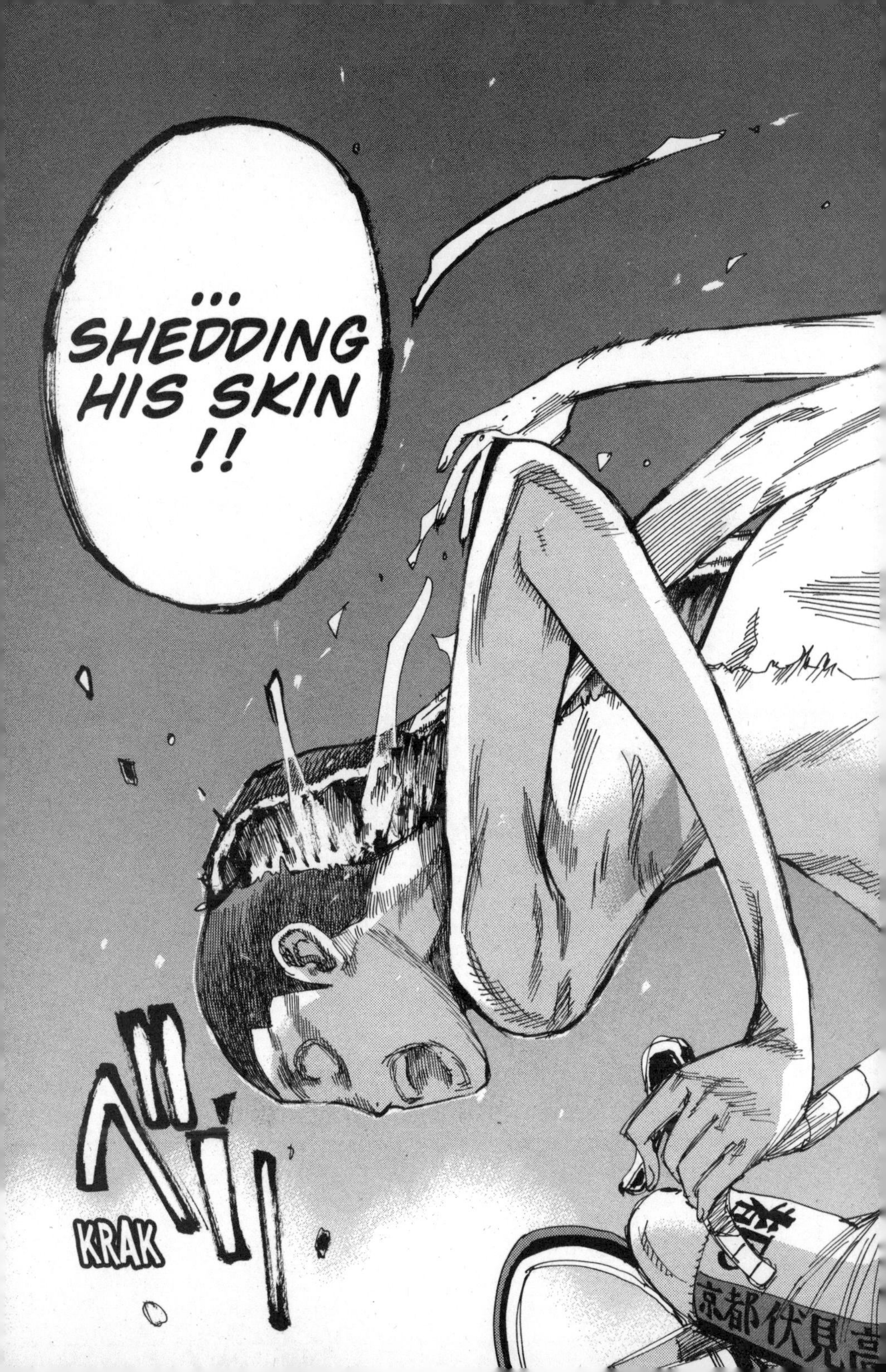
...SHEDDING HIS SKIN !!
KRAK
京都伏見

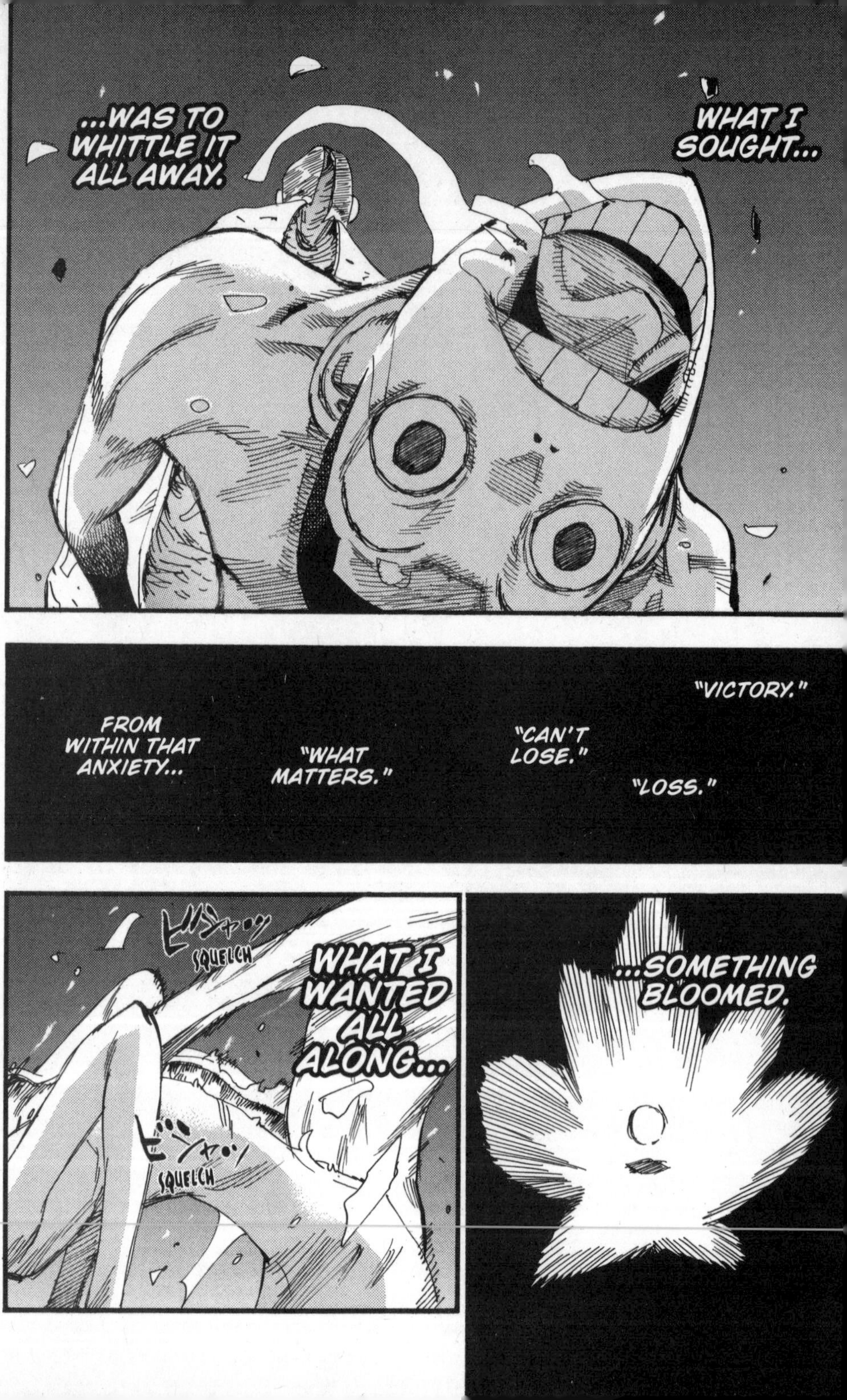
WHAT I SOUGHT...
...WAS TO WHITTLE IT ALL AWAY.
"VICTORY."
"LOSS."
"CAN'T LOSE."
"WHAT MATTERS."
FROM WITHIN THAT ANXIETY...
...SOMETHING BLOOMED.
SQUELCH
WHAT I WANTED ALL ALONG...
SQUELCH

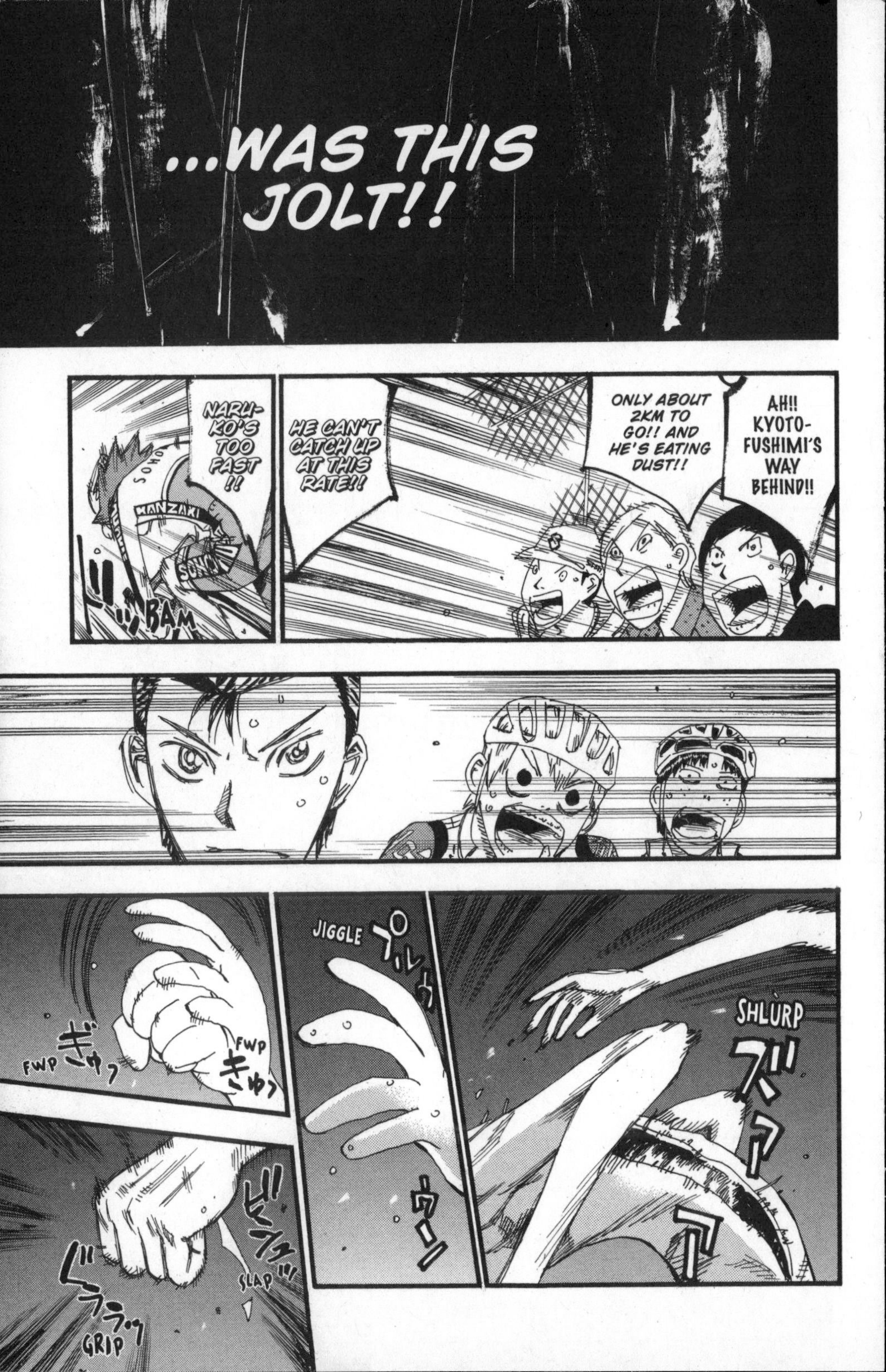
...WAS THIS JOLT!!
AH!! KYOTO-FUSHIMI'S WAY BEHIND!!
ONLY ABOUT 2KM TO GO!! AND HE'S EATING DUST!!
HE CAN'T CATCH UP AT THIS RATE!!
NARU-KO'S TOO FAST!!
BAM
SHLURP
JIGGLE
FWP
FWP
SLAP
GRIP

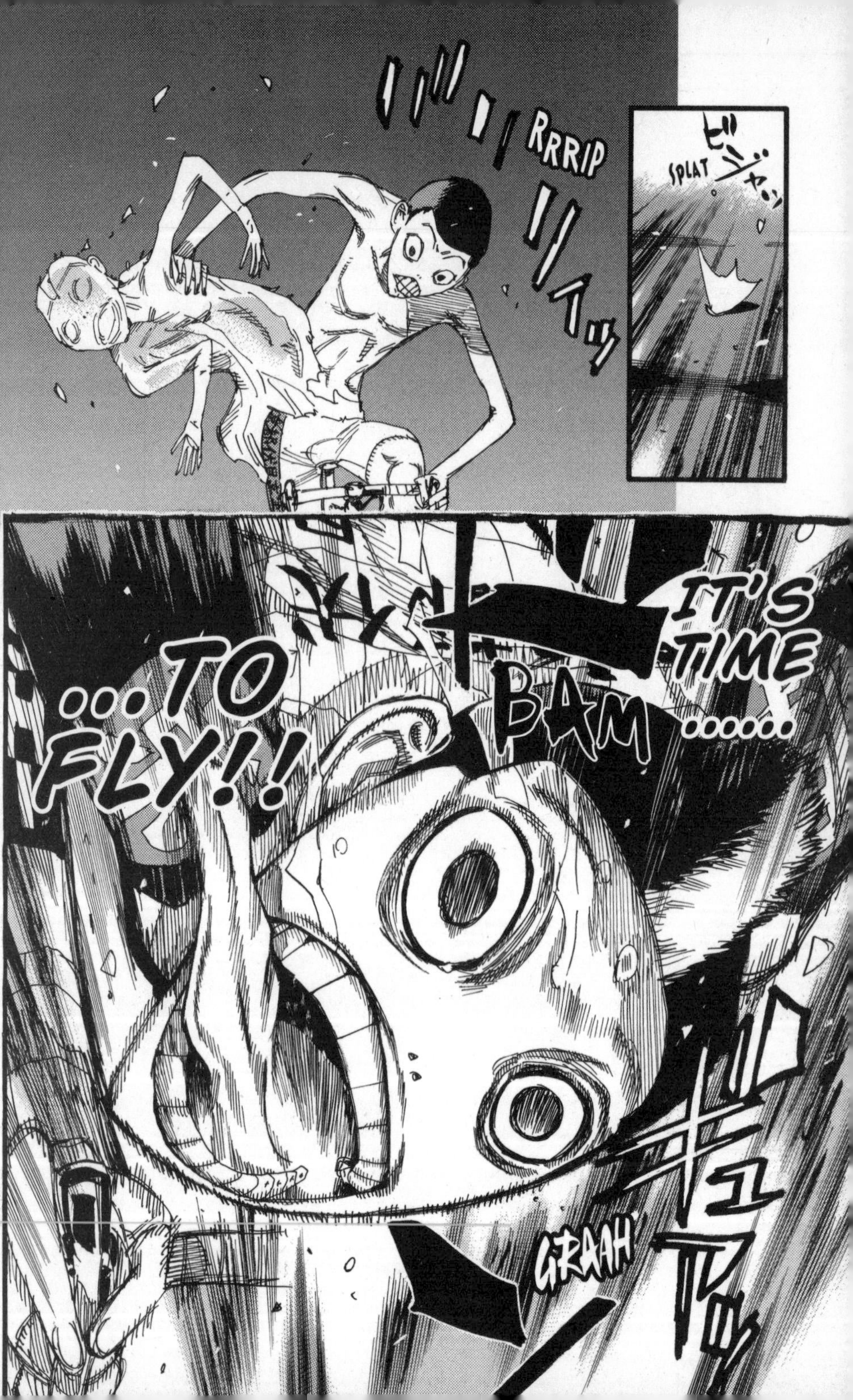
SPLAT
RRRIP
IT'S TIME ......
BAM
...TO FLY!!
GRAAH

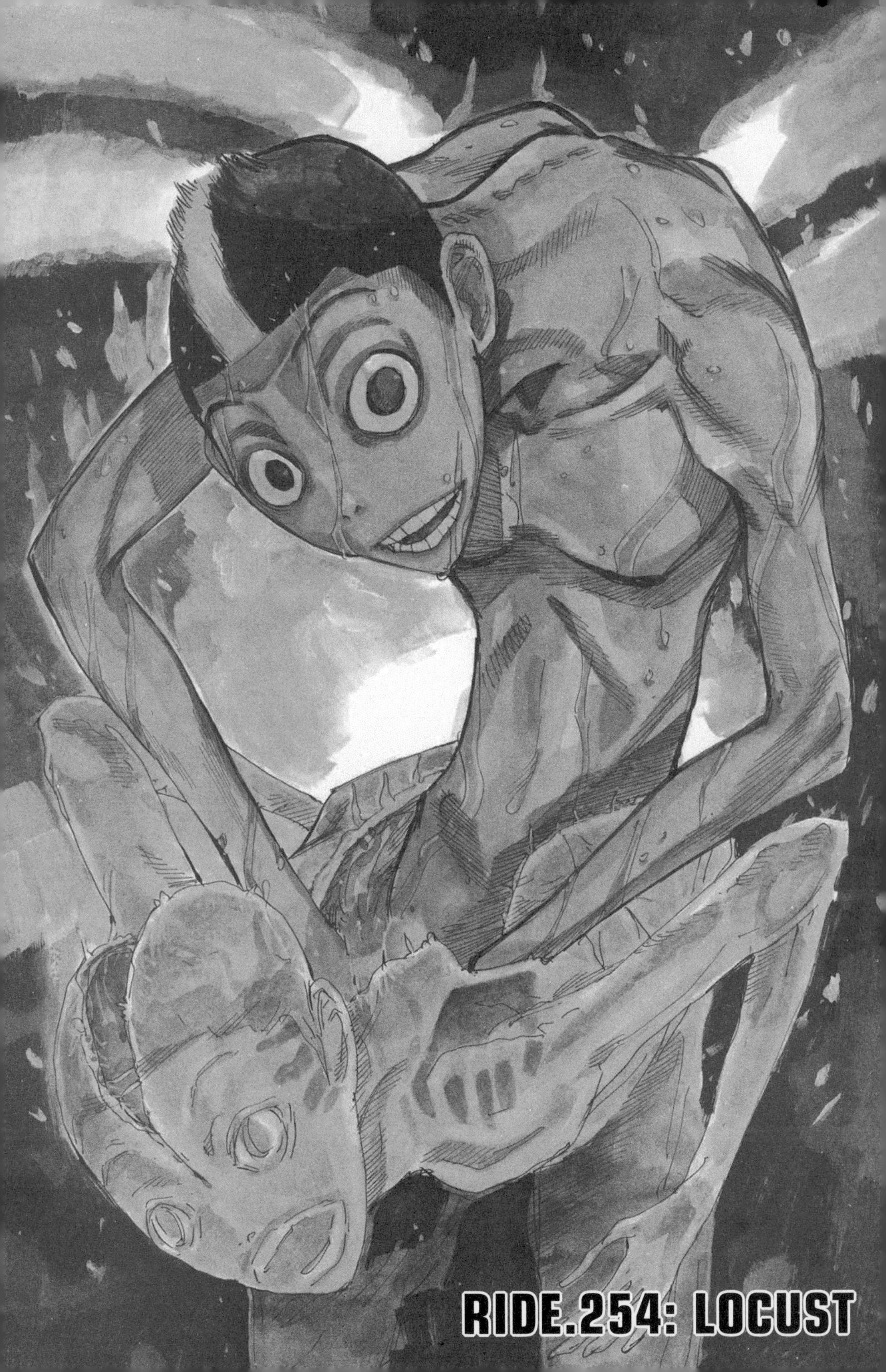
RIDE.254: LOCUST

WAKING

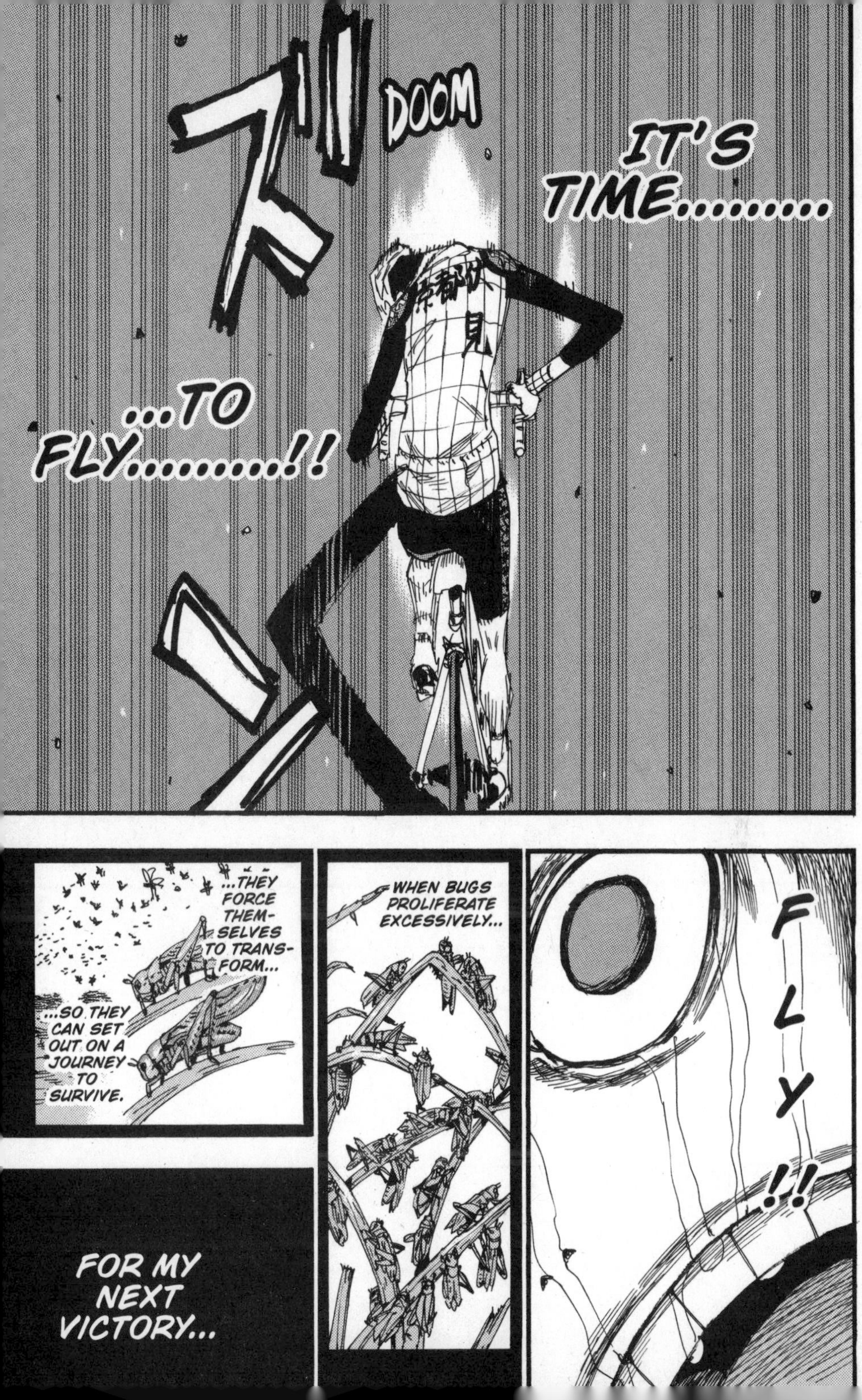
IT'S TIME.........
DOOM
...TO FLY..........!!
FLY!!
WHEN BUGS PROLIFERATE EXCESSIVELY...
...THEY FORCE THEMSELVES TO TRANSFORM...
...SO THEY CAN SET OUT ON A JOURNEY TO SURVIVE.
FOR MY NEXT VICTORY...

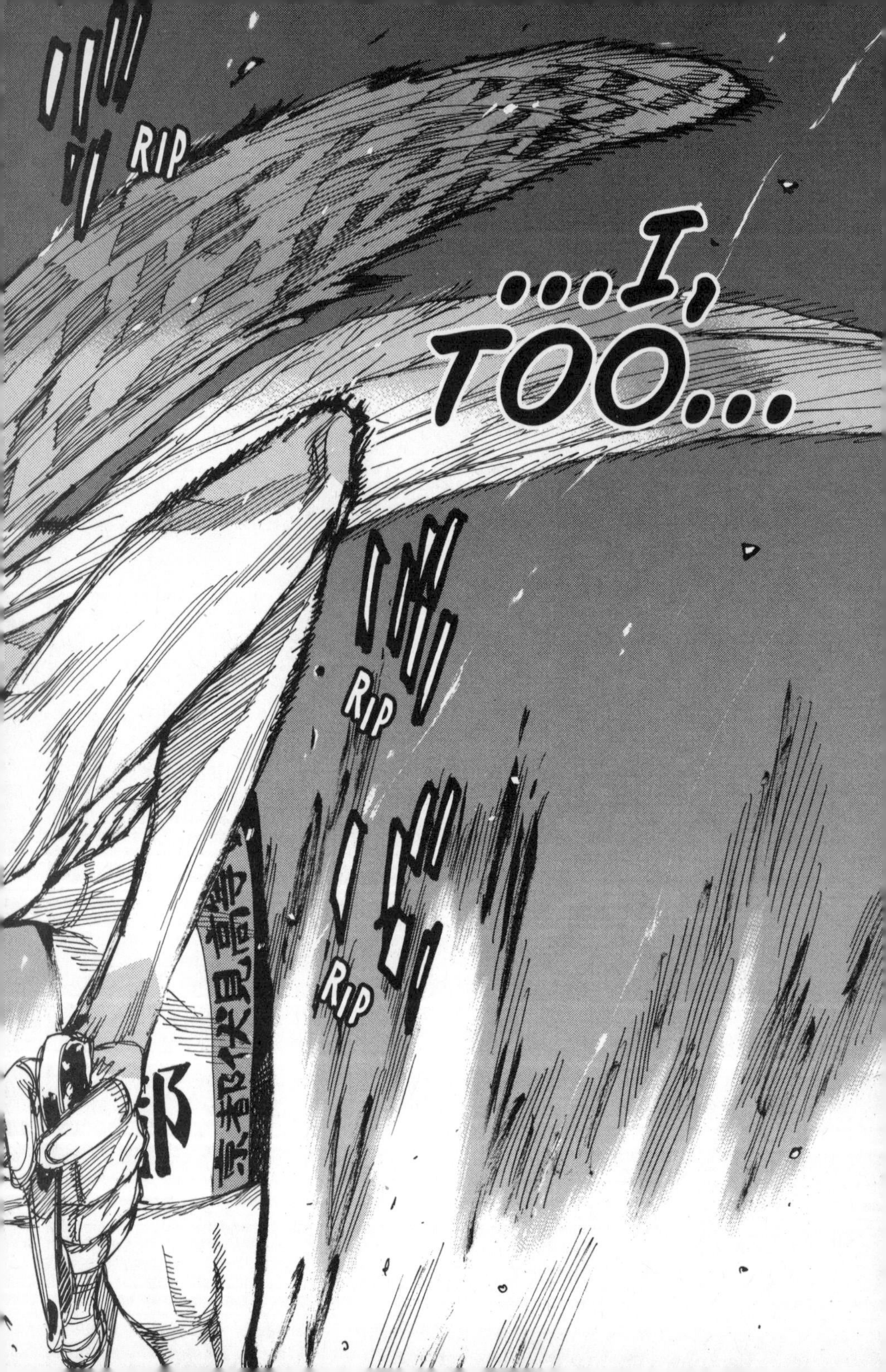
RIP
...I, TOO...
RIP
RIP

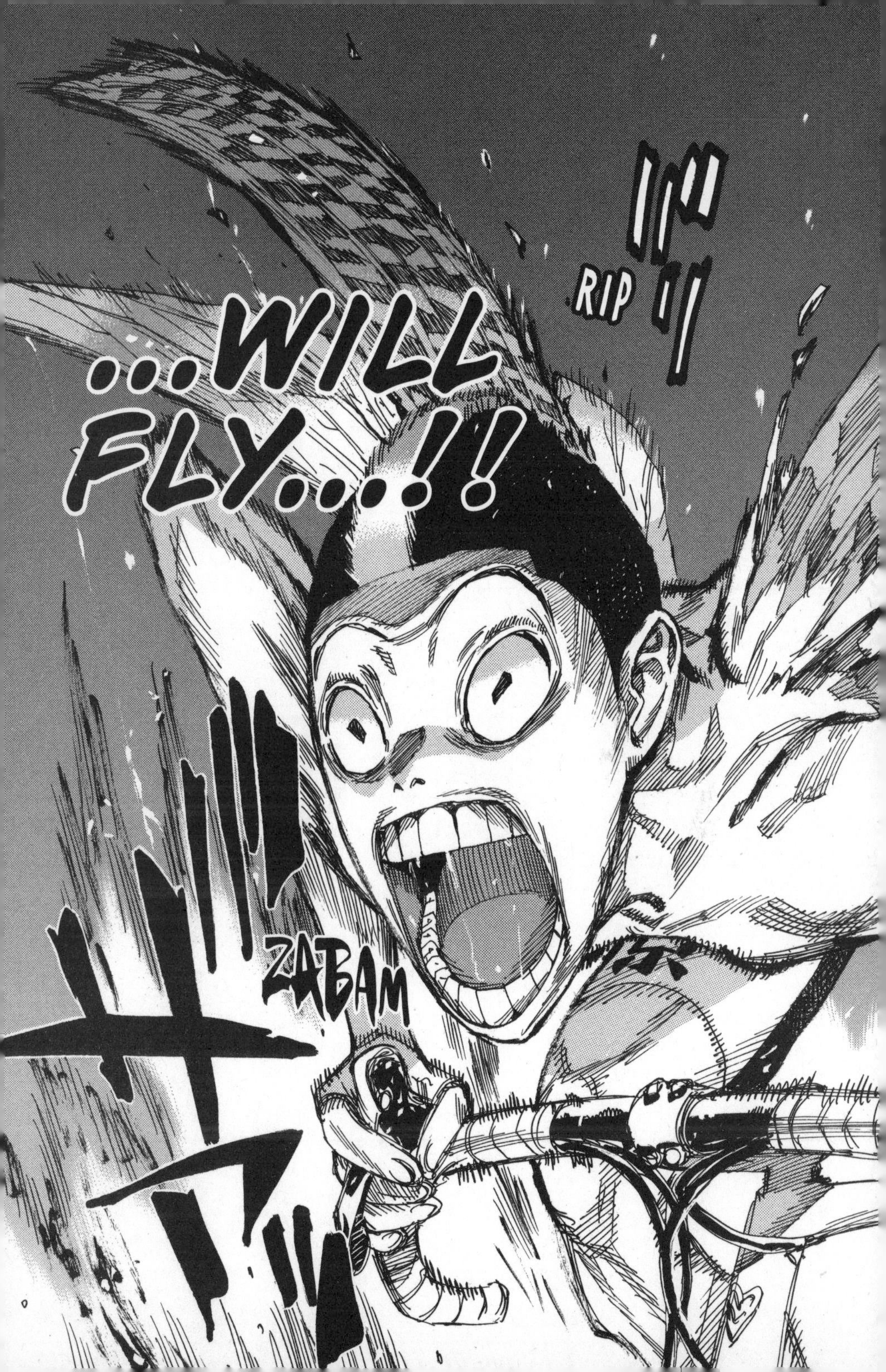
RIP
...WILL FLY...!!
ZABAM

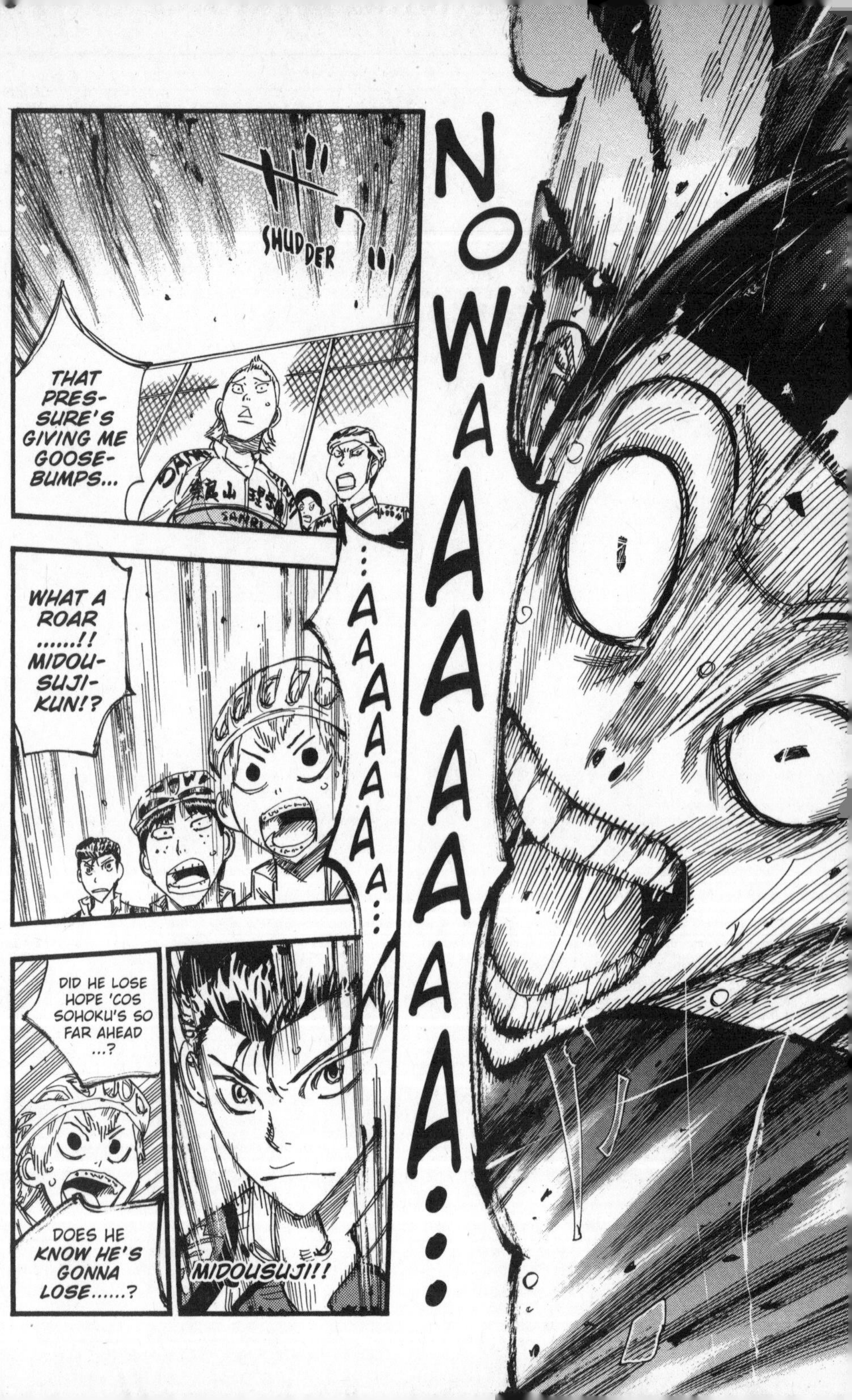
NOWAAAAAAAAA...
ザッ
SHUDDER
THAT PRES-SURE'S GIVING ME GOOSE-BUMPS...
...AAAAAAAAA...
WHAT A ROAR ......!! MIDOU-SUJI-KUN!?
MIDOUSUJI!!
DID HE LOSE HOPE 'COS SOHOKU'S SO FAR AHEAD ...?
DOES HE KNOW HE'S GONNA LOSE......?

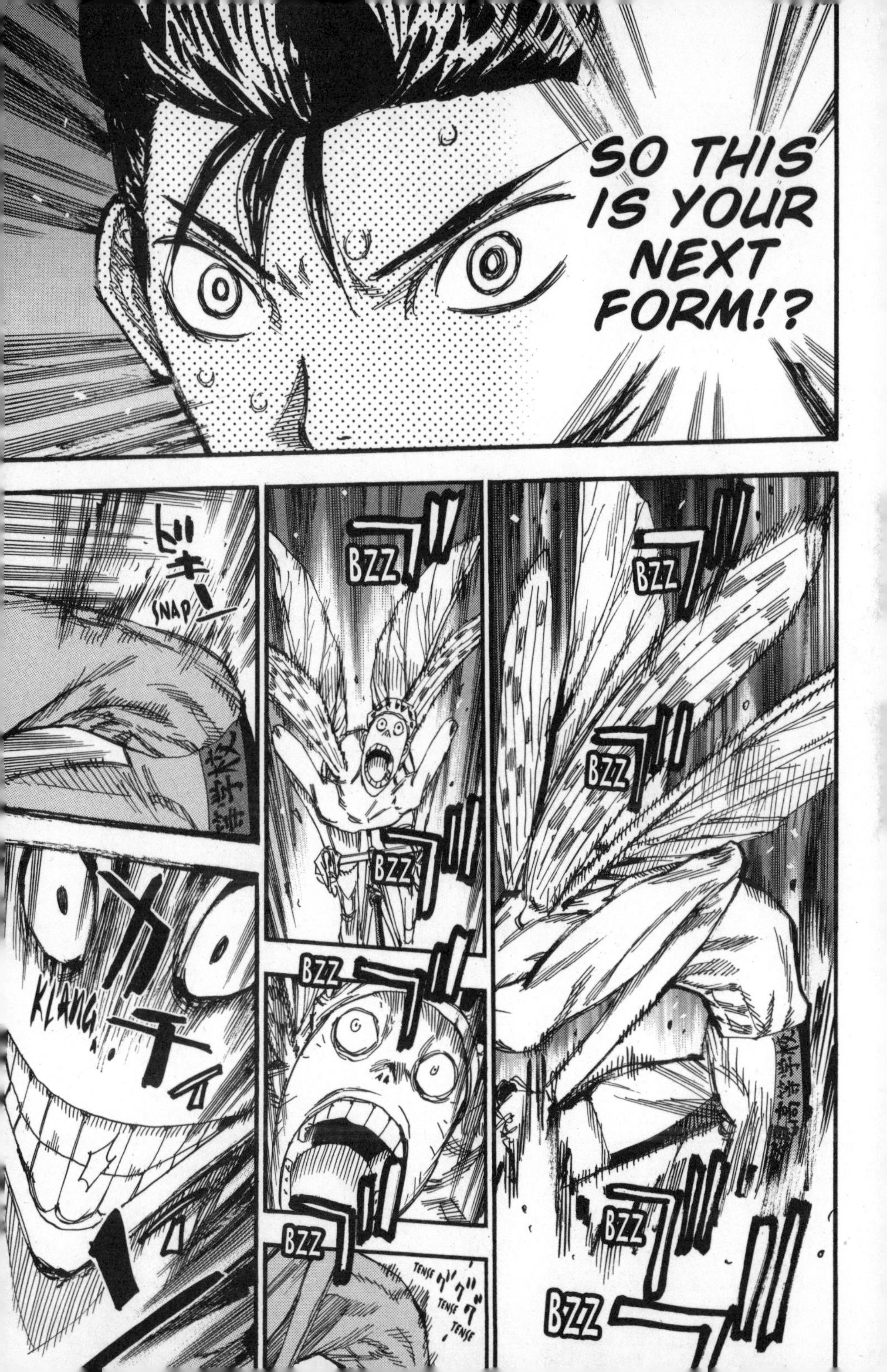
SO THIS IS YOUR NEXT FORM!?
BZZ
BZZ
BZZ
BZZ
BZZ
BZZ
BZZ
BZZ
TENSE
TENSE
TENSE
SNAP
KLANG

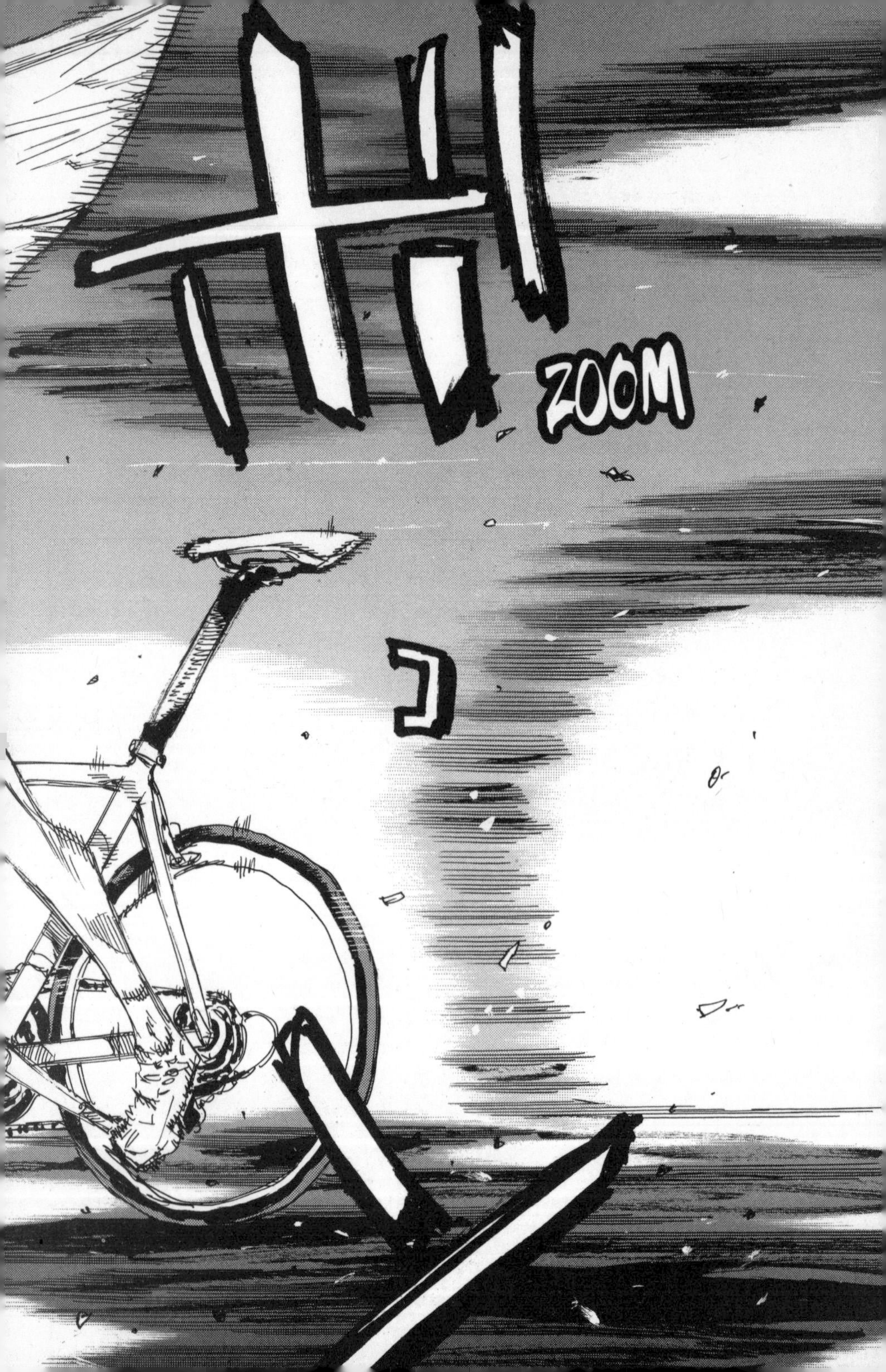
ZOOM

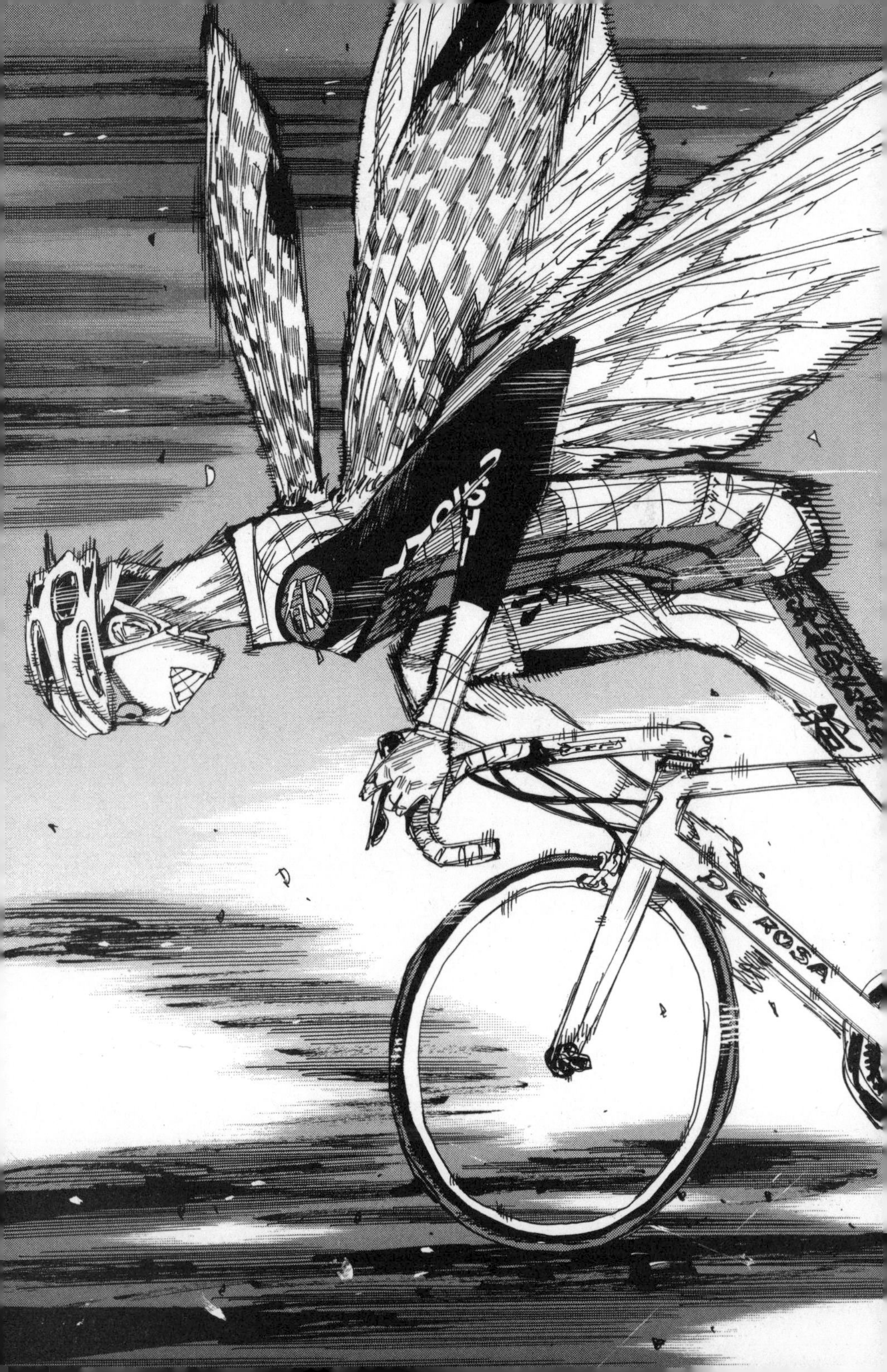
DE ROSA

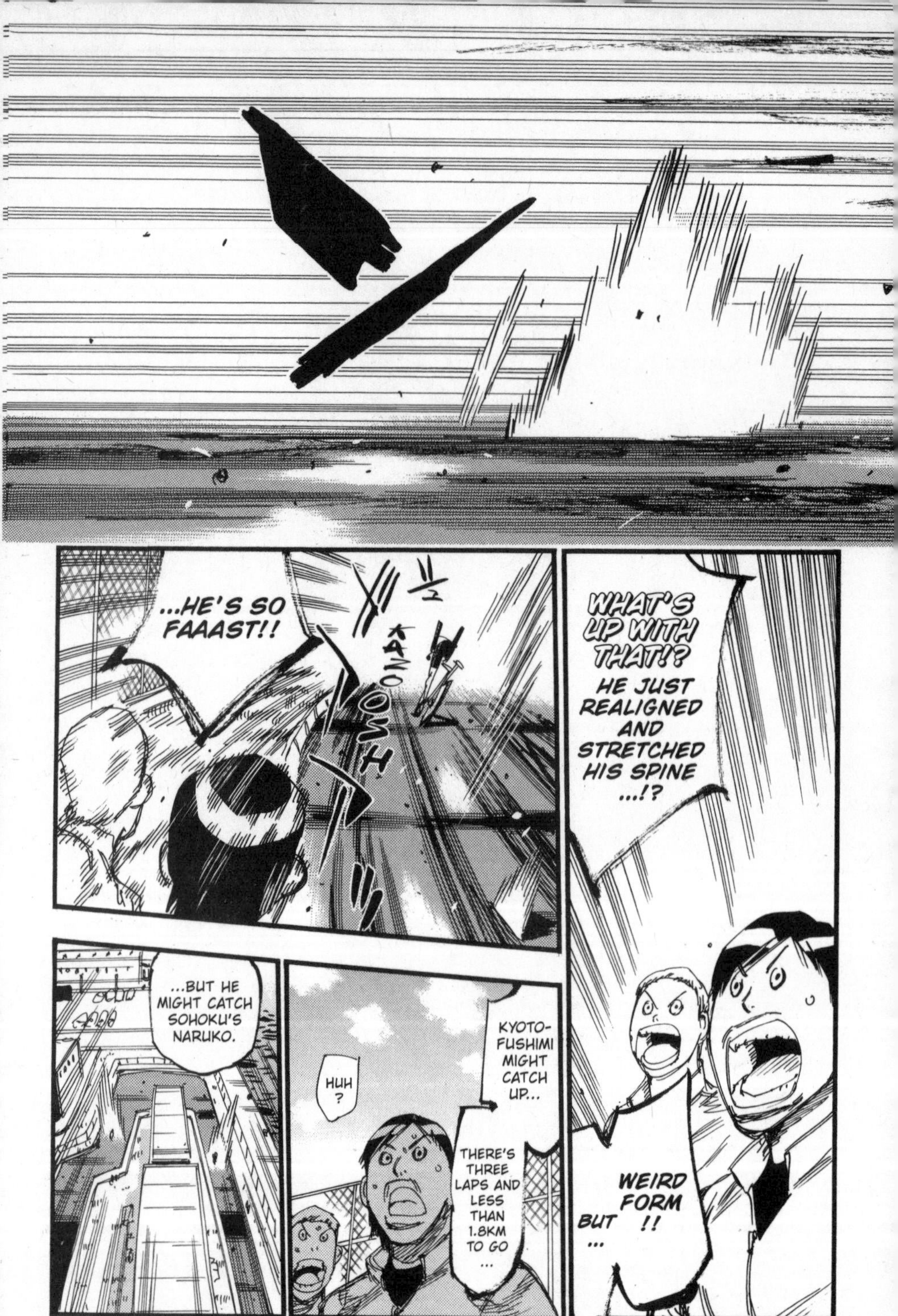
WHAT'S UP WITH THAT!?
HE JUST REALIGNED AND STRETCHED HIS SPINE ...!?
WEIRD FORM!!
BUT...
...HE'S SO FAAAST!!
KAZOOSH
KYOTO-FUSHIMI MIGHT CATCH UP...
HUH?
THERE'S THREE LAPS AND LESS THAN 1.8KM TO GO...
...BUT HE MIGHT CATCH SOHOKU'S NARUKO.

BWAM

ZOOOSH!!

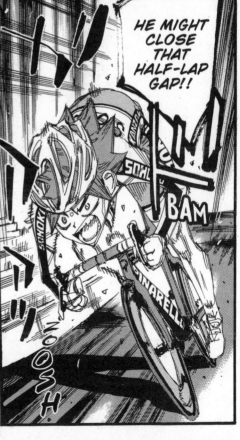

HE MIGHT CLOSE THAT HALF-LAP GAP!!

BAM

ZOOOSH!!

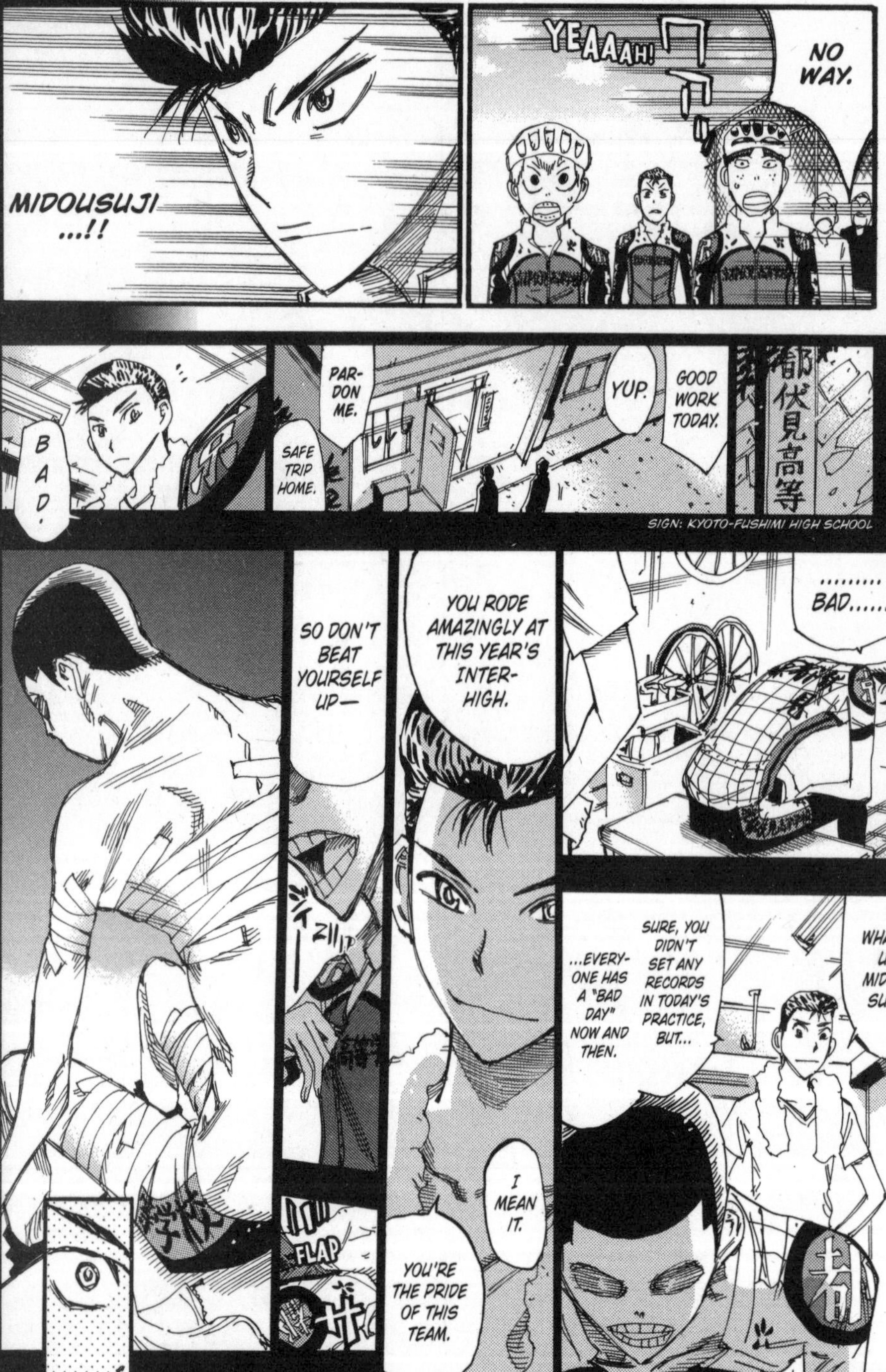
YEAAAAH!
NO WAY.
MIDOUSUJI ...!!
GOOD WORK TODAY.
YUP.
PARDON ME.
SAFE TRIP HOME.
B A D.
SIGN: KYOTO-FUSHIMI HIGH SCHOOL
.... BAD......
WHAT'S UP, MIDOUSUJI?
SURE, YOU DIDN'T SET ANY RECORDS IN TODAY'S PRACTICE, BUT...
...EVERYONE HAS A "BAD DAY" NOW AND THEN.
YOU RODE AMAZINGLY AT THIS YEAR'S INTER-HIGH.
SO DON'T BEAT YOURSELF UP—
ZIIIP
I MEAN IT.
YOU'RE THE PRIDE OF THIS TEAM.
FLAP

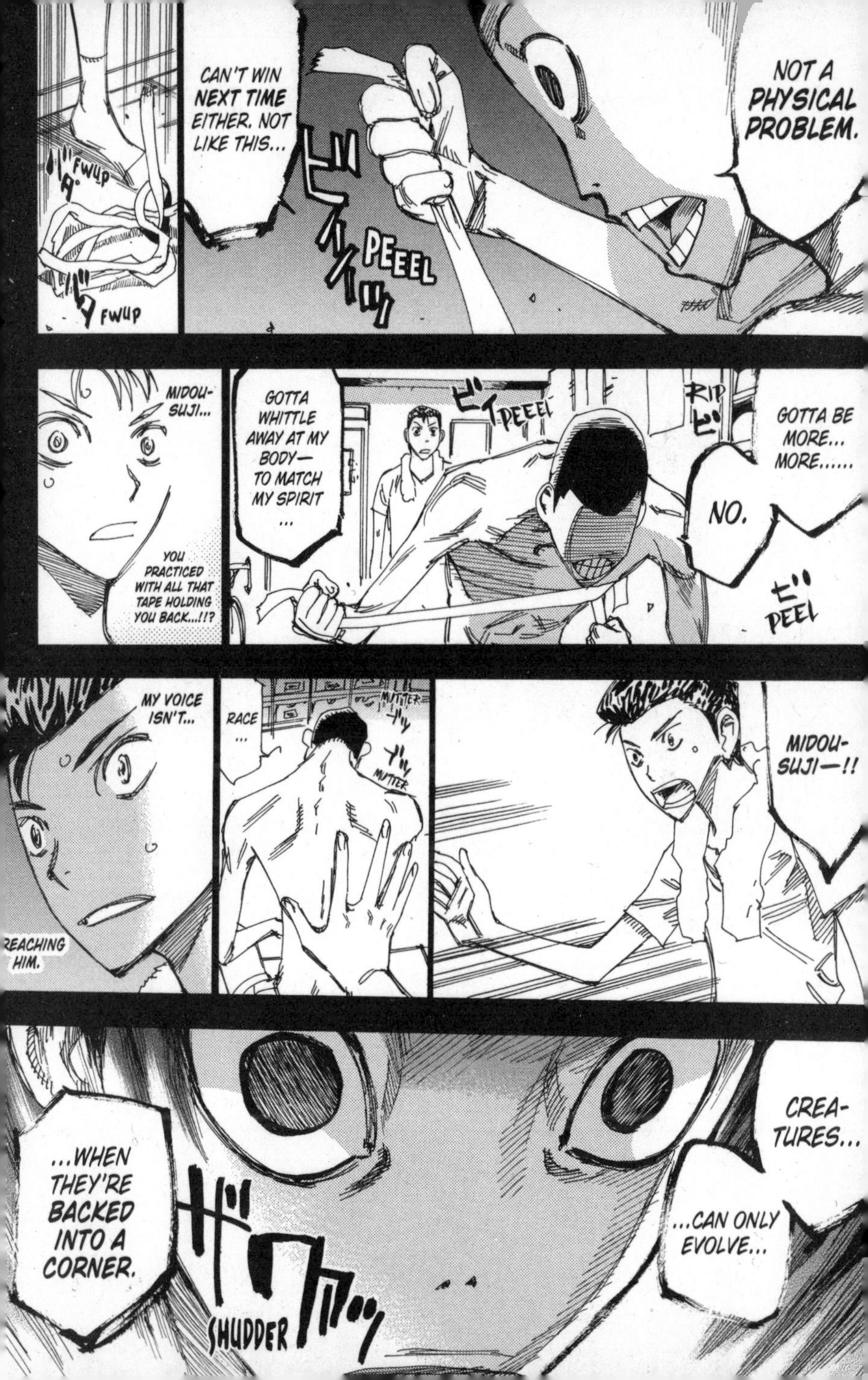
NOT A PHYSICAL PROBLEM.
CAN'T WIN NEXT TIME EITHER. NOT LIKE THIS...
PEEEL
FWUP
FWUP
GOTTA BE MORE... MORE......
NO.
RIP
PEEL
GOTTA WHITTLE AWAY AT MY BODY— TO MATCH MY SPIRIT ...
PEEEL
MIDOU-SUJI...
YOU PRACTICED WITH ALL THAT TAPE HOLDING YOU BACK...!?
MIDOU-SUJI—!!
MUTTER
MUTTER
RACE ...
MY VOICE ISN'T...
REACHING HIM.
CREA-TURES...
...CAN ONLY EVOLVE...
...WHEN THEY'RE BACKED INTO A CORNER.
SHUDDER

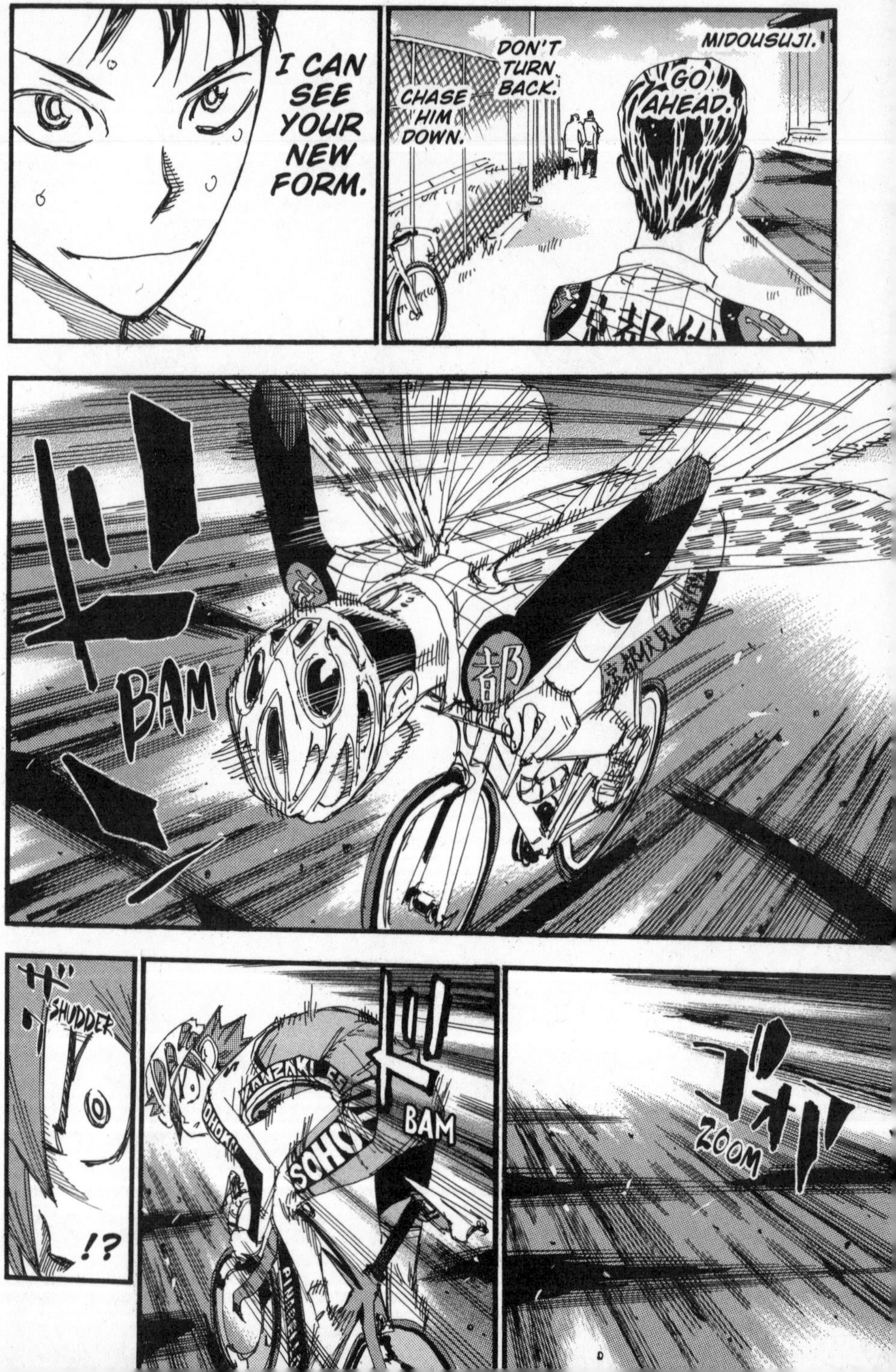
MIDOUSUJI.
GO AHEAD.
DON'T TURN BACK.
CHASE HIM DOWN.
I CAN SEE YOUR NEW FORM.
BAM
ZOOM
BAM
SHUDDER
!?

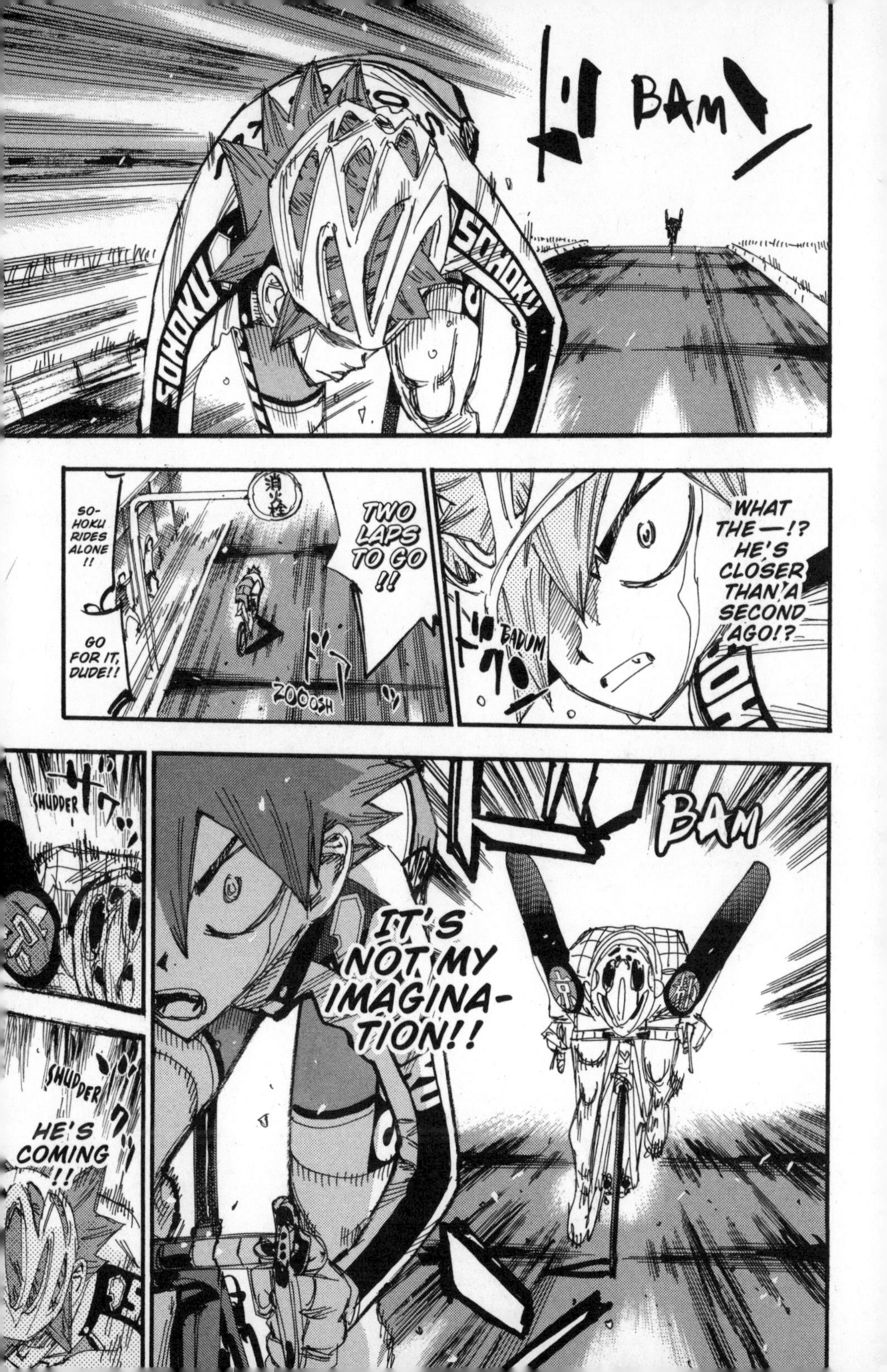
BAM
WHAT THE—!? HE'S CLOSER THAN A SECOND AGO!?
BADUM
消火栓
TWO LAPS TO GO!!
SO-HOKU RIDES ALONE!!
GO FOR IT, DUDE!!
ZOOOSH
BAM
IT'S NOT MY IMAGINATION!!
SHUDDER
SHUDDER
HE'S COMING!!

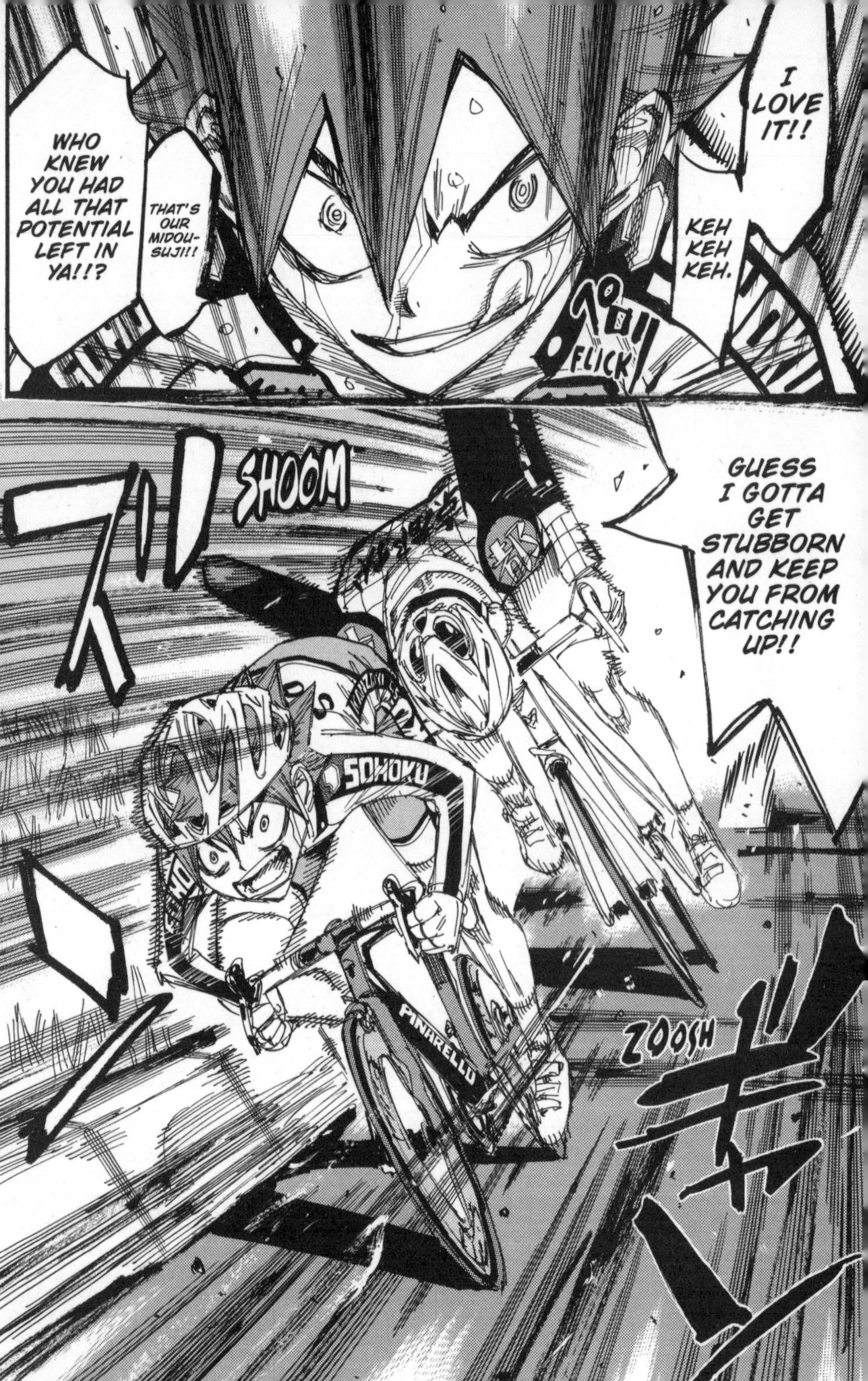
I LOVE IT!!
KEH KEH KEH.
FLICK
THAT'S OUR MIDOU-SUJI!!
WHO KNEW YOU HAD ALL THAT POTENTIAL LEFT IN YA!!?
GUESS I GOTTA GET STUBBORN AND KEEP YOU FROM CATCHING UP!!
SHOOM
SOHOKU
PINARELLO
ZOOSH

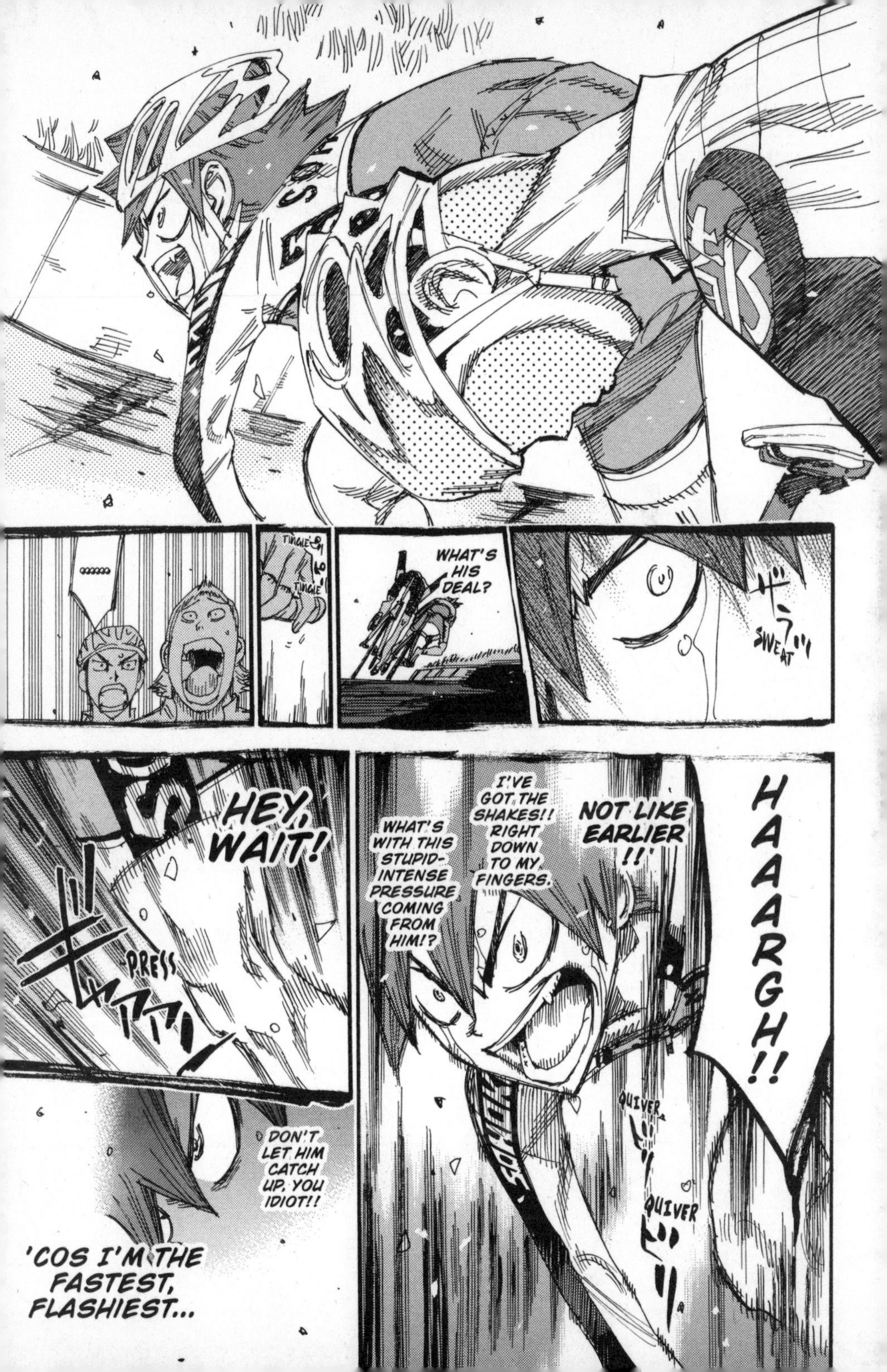
SWEAT
WHAT'S HIS DEAL?
TINGLE
TINGLE
......
HAAAARGH!!
NOT LIKE EARLIER!!
I'VE GOT THE SHAKES!! RIGHT DOWN TO MY FINGERS.
WHAT'S WITH THIS STUPID-INTENSE PRESSURE COMING FROM HIM!?
QUIVER
QUIVER
HEY, WAIT!
PRESS
DON'T LET HIM CATCH UP, YOU IDIOT!!
'COS I'M THE FASTEST, FLASHIEST...

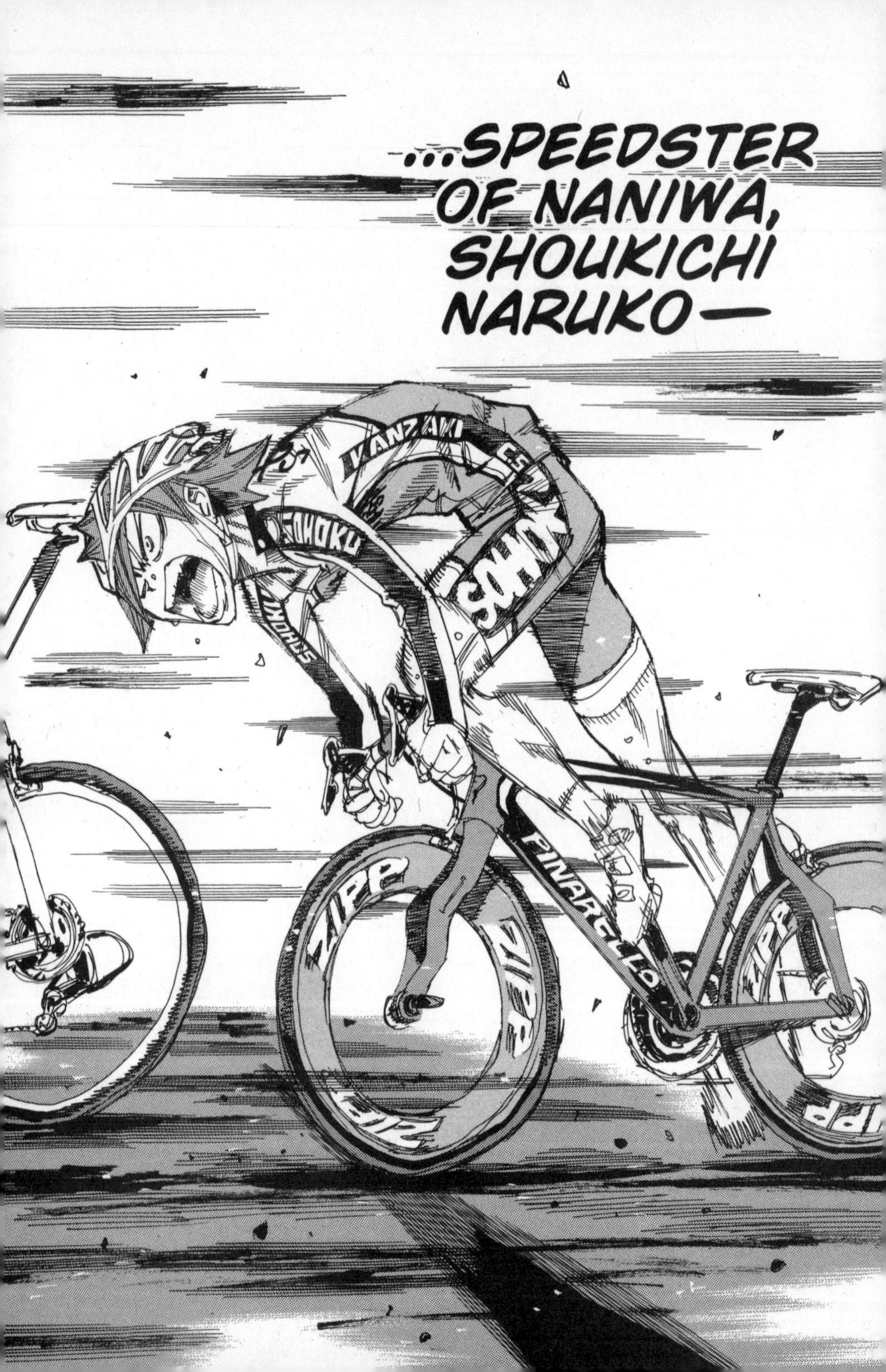
...SPEEDSTER OF NANIWA, SHOUKICHI NARUKO—

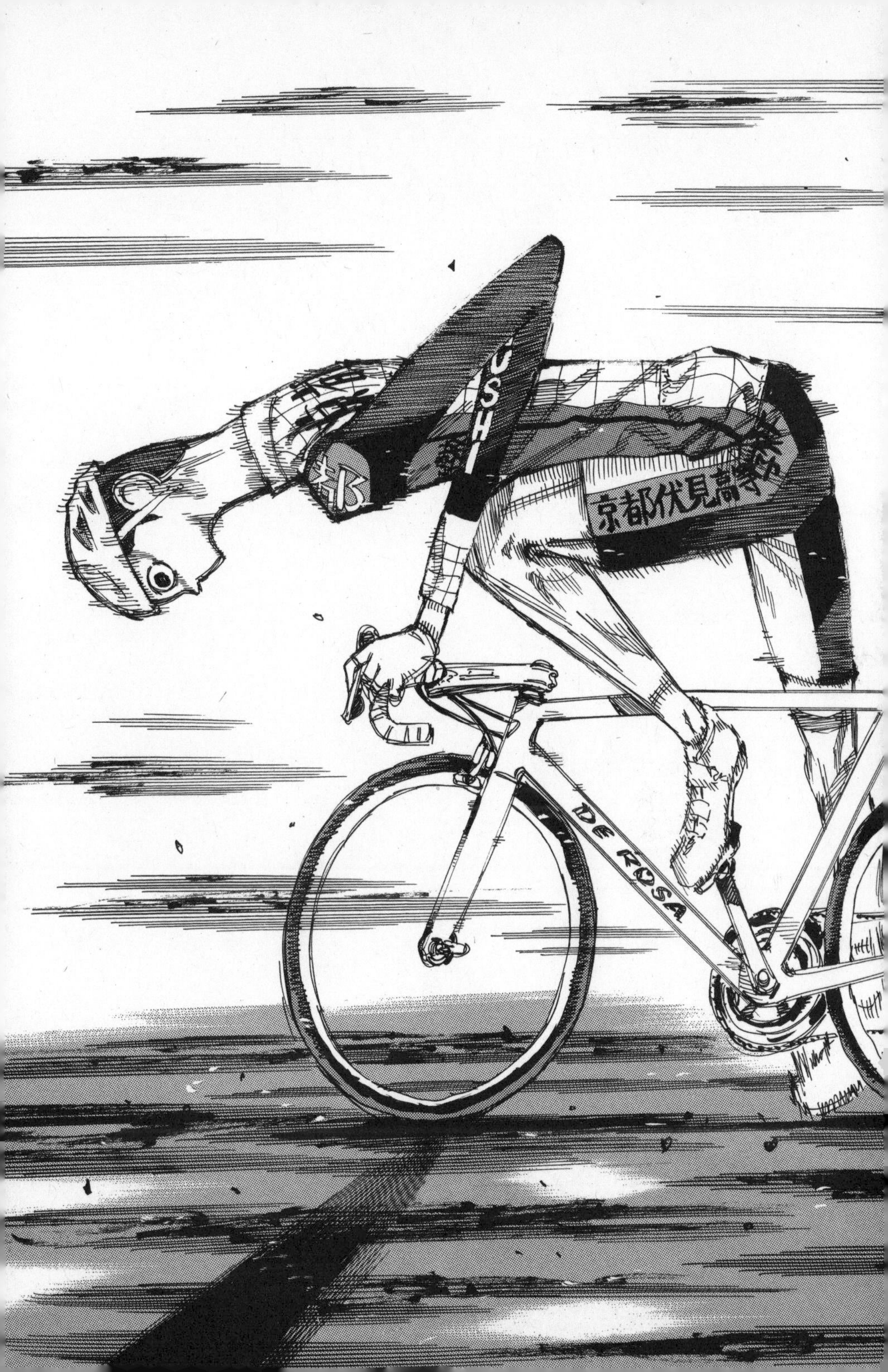
京都伏見高等
DE ROSA

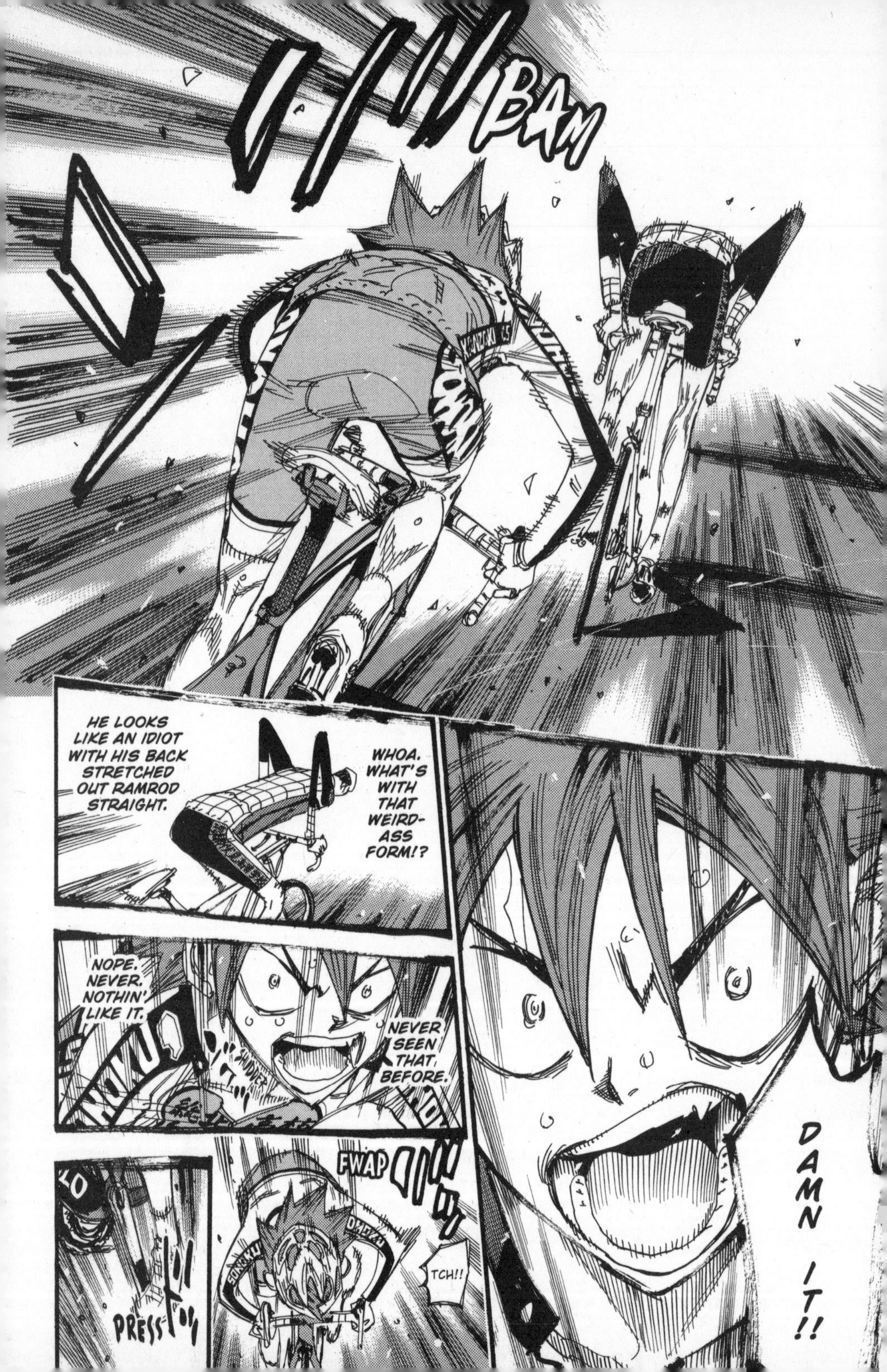
BAM
DAMN IT!!
WHOA. WHAT'S WITH THAT WEIRD-ASS FORM!?
HE LOOKS LIKE AN IDIOT WITH HIS BACK STRETCHED OUT RAMROD STRAIGHT.
NOPE. NEVER. NOTHIN' LIKE IT.
SHUDDER
NEVER SEEN THAT BEFORE.
FWAP
TCH!!
PRESS

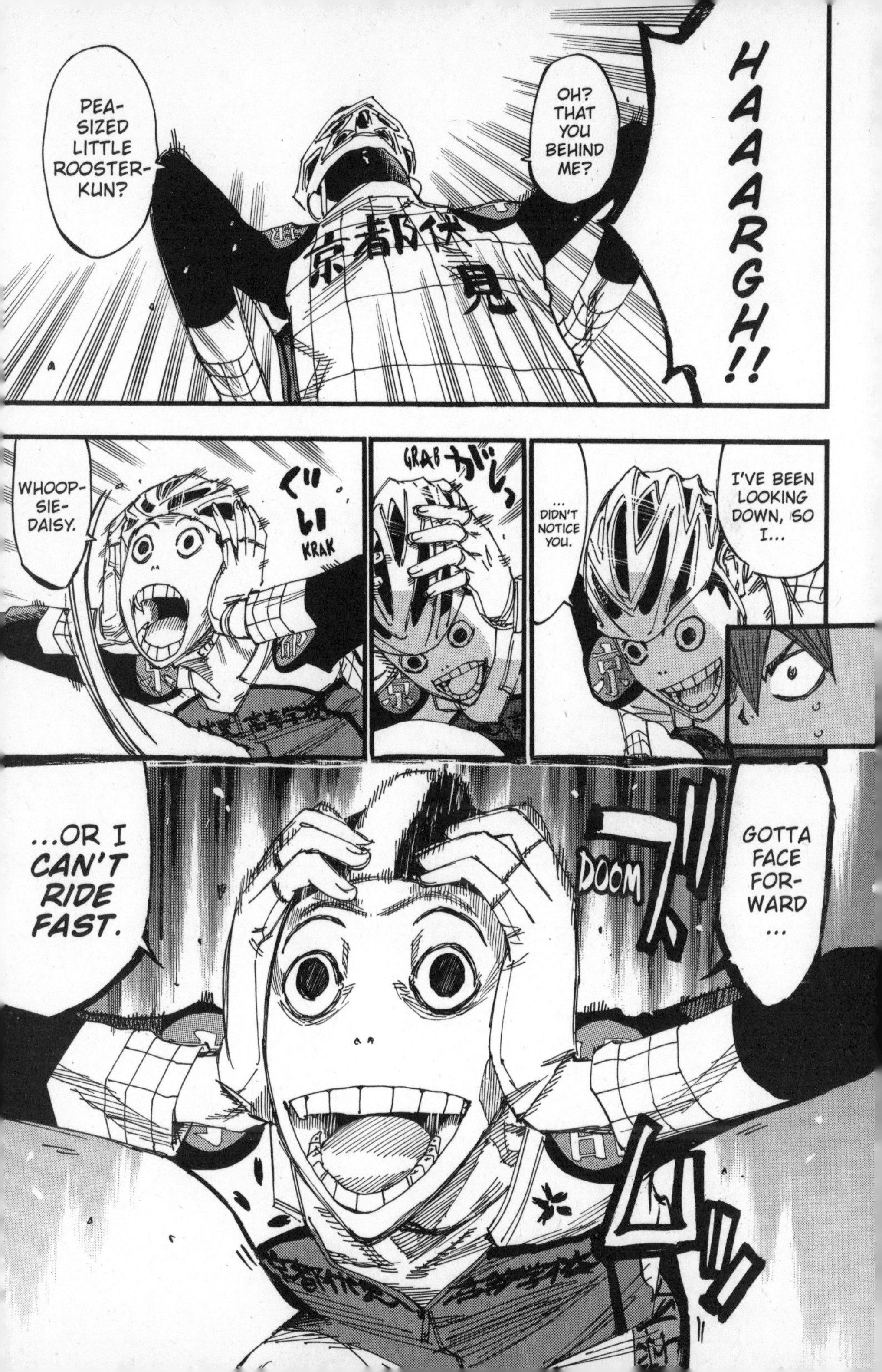
HAAAARGH!!
OH? THAT YOU BEHIND ME?
京都伏見
PEA-SIZED LITTLE ROOSTER-KUN?
I'VE BEEN LOOKING DOWN, SO I...
...DIDN'T NOTICE YOU.
がしっ
GRAB
ぐい
KRAK
WHOOPSIE-DAISY.
GOTTA FACE FORWARD...
DOOM
...OR I CAN'T RIDE FAST.

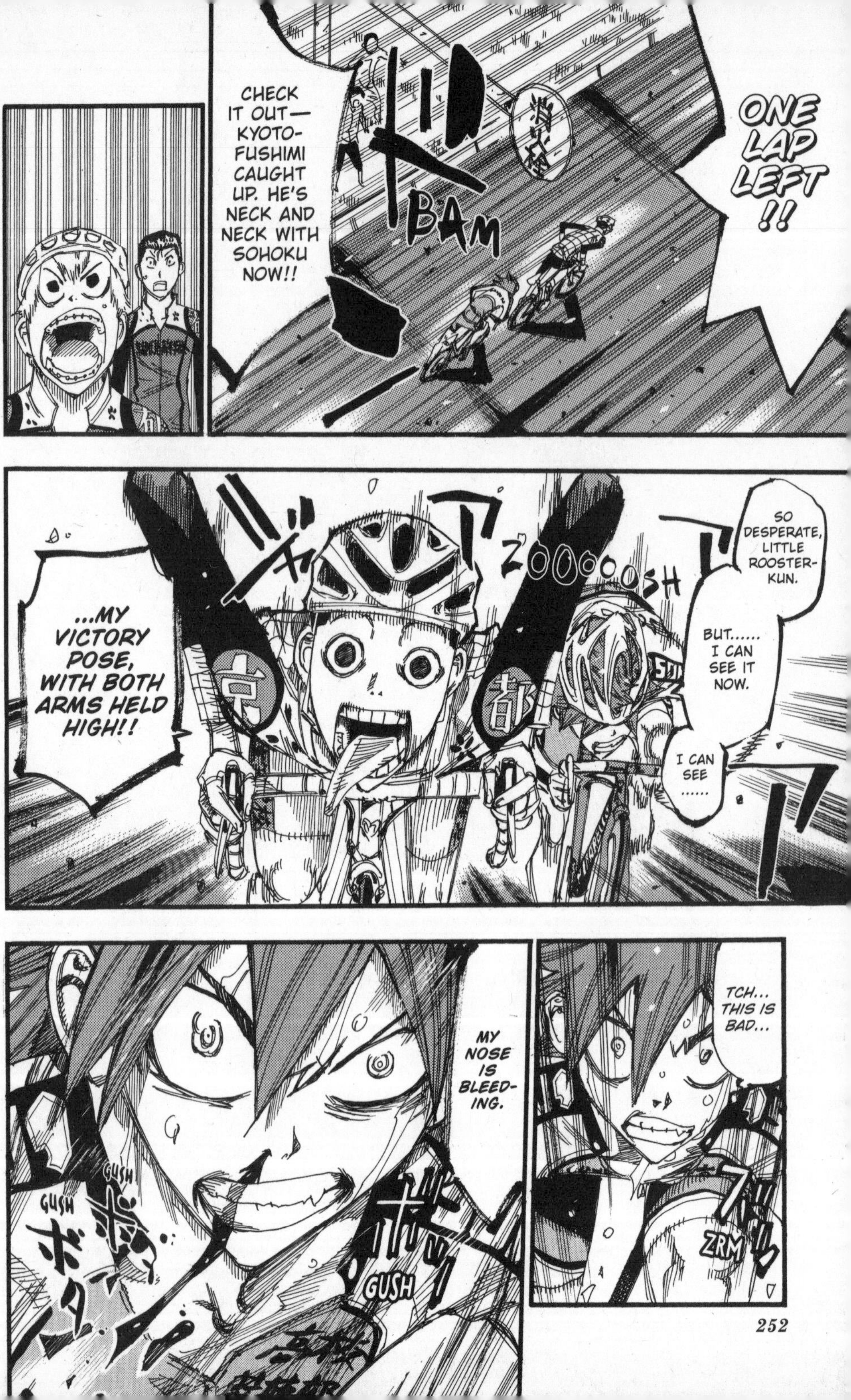
ONE LAP LEFT!!
BAM
CHECK IT OUT—KYOTO-FUSHIMI CAUGHT UP. HE'S NECK AND NECK WITH SOHOKU NOW!!
SO DESPERATE, LITTLE ROOSTER-KUN.
ZOOOOOOSH
BUT...... I CAN SEE IT NOW.
I CAN SEE ......
...MY VICTORY POSE, WITH BOTH ARMS HELD HIGH!!
TCH... THIS IS BAD...
ZRM
MY NOSE IS BLEED-ING.
GUSH
GUSH
GUSH

RIDE.255: THE MAN FROM OSAKA

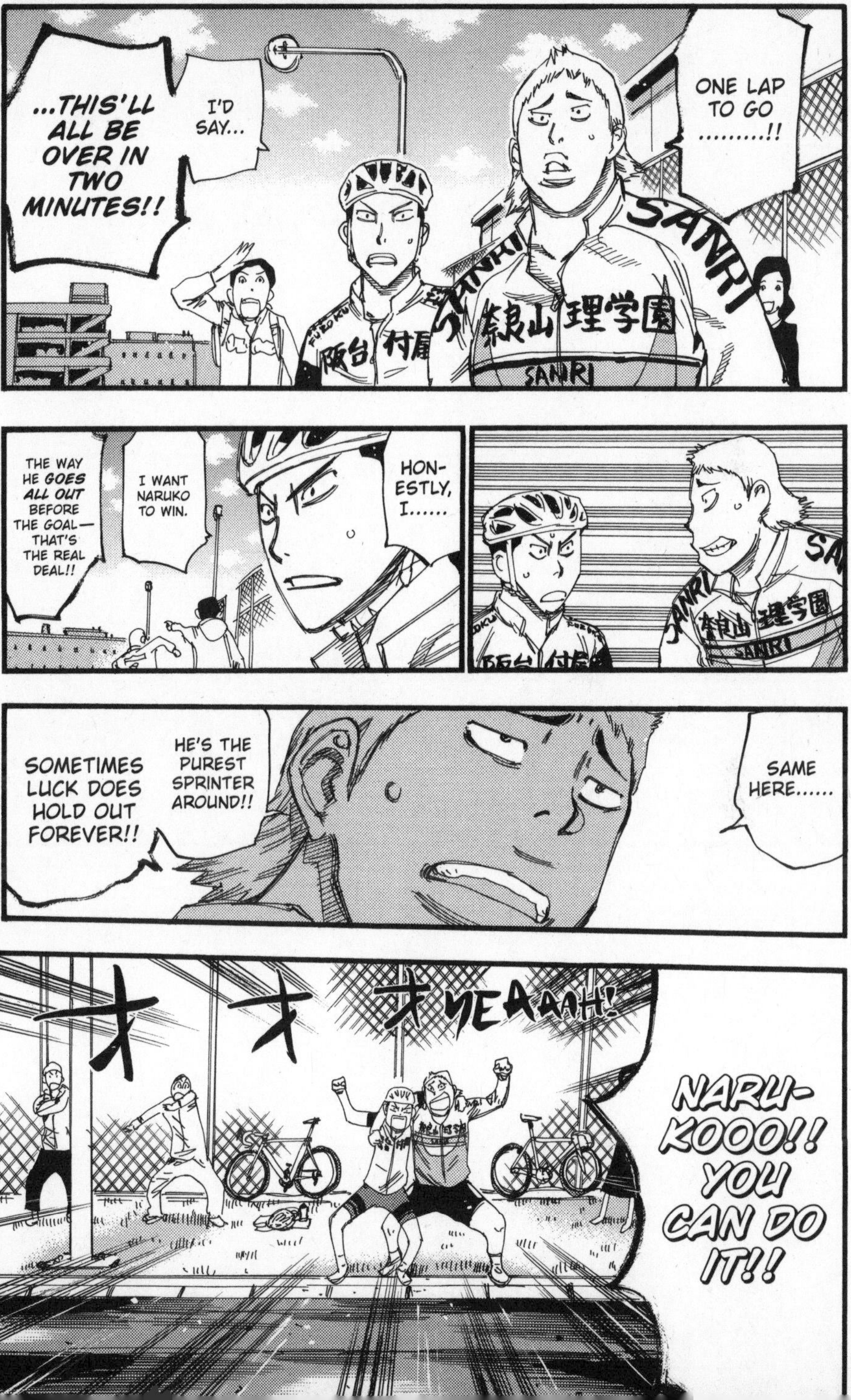
ONE LAP TO GO ....!!
I'D SAY...
...THIS'LL ALL BE OVER IN TWO MINUTES!!
SANRI
HON-ESTLY, I......
I WANT NARUKO TO WIN.
THE WAY HE GOES ALL OUT BEFORE THE GOAL—THAT'S THE REAL DEAL!!
SAME HERE......
HE'S THE PUREST SPRINTER AROUND!!
SOMETIMES LUCK DOES HOLD OUT FOREVER!!
NARU-KOOO!! YOU CAN DO IT!!
オオオYEAAAH!

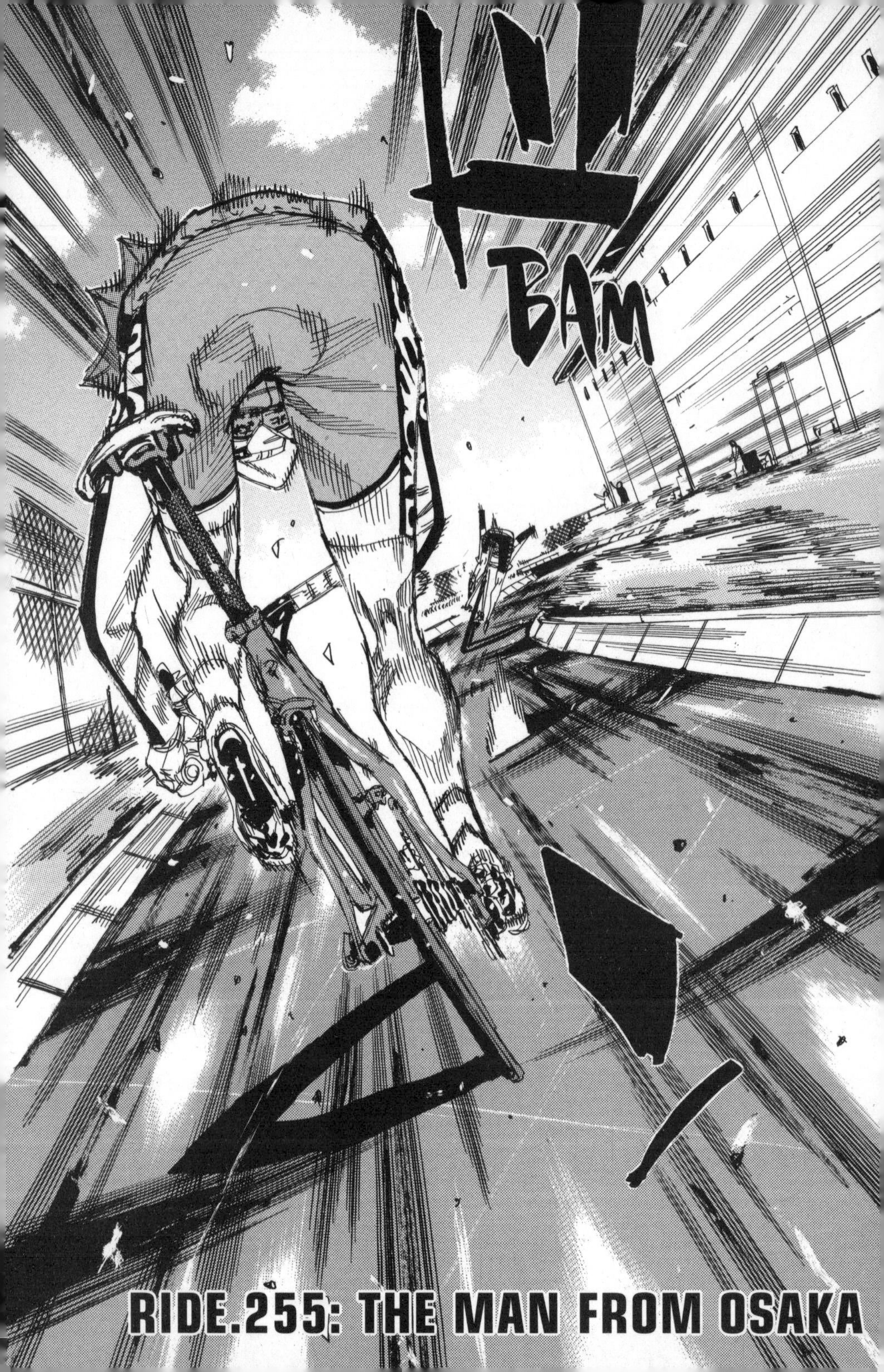
BAM
RIDE.255: THE MAN FROM OSAKA

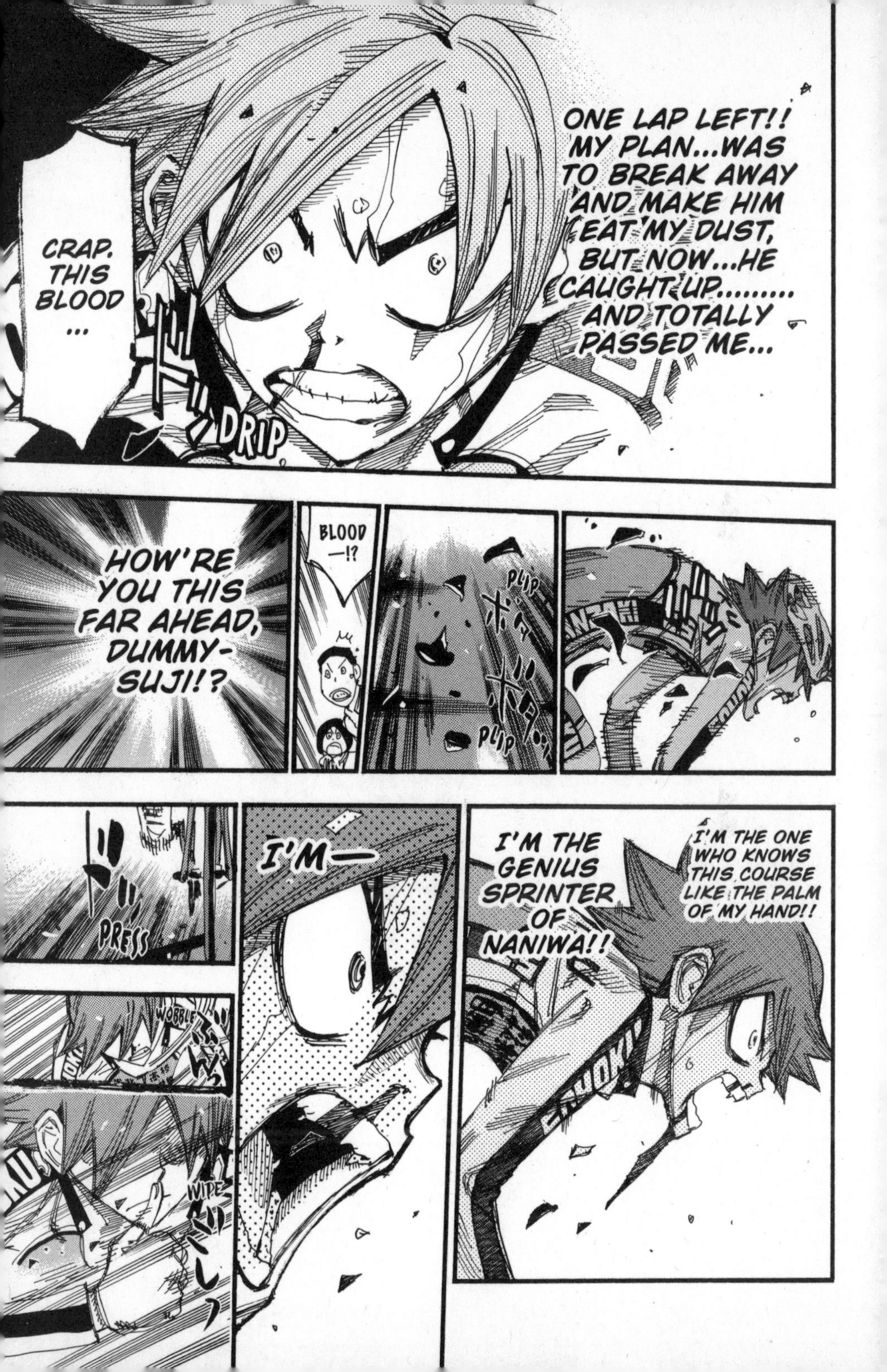

ONE LAP LEFT!! MY PLAN...WAS TO BREAK AWAY AND MAKE HIM EAT MY DUST, BUT NOW...HE CAUGHT UP......... AND TOTALLY PASSED ME...
CRAP. THIS BLOOD ...
DRIP
PLIP
PLIP
BLOOD —!?
HOW'RE YOU THIS FAR AHEAD, DUMMY-SUJI!?
I'M THE ONE WHO KNOWS THIS COURSE LIKE THE PALM OF MY HAND!!
I'M THE GENIUS SPRINTER OF NANIWA!!
I'M—
PRESS
WOBBLE
WIPE

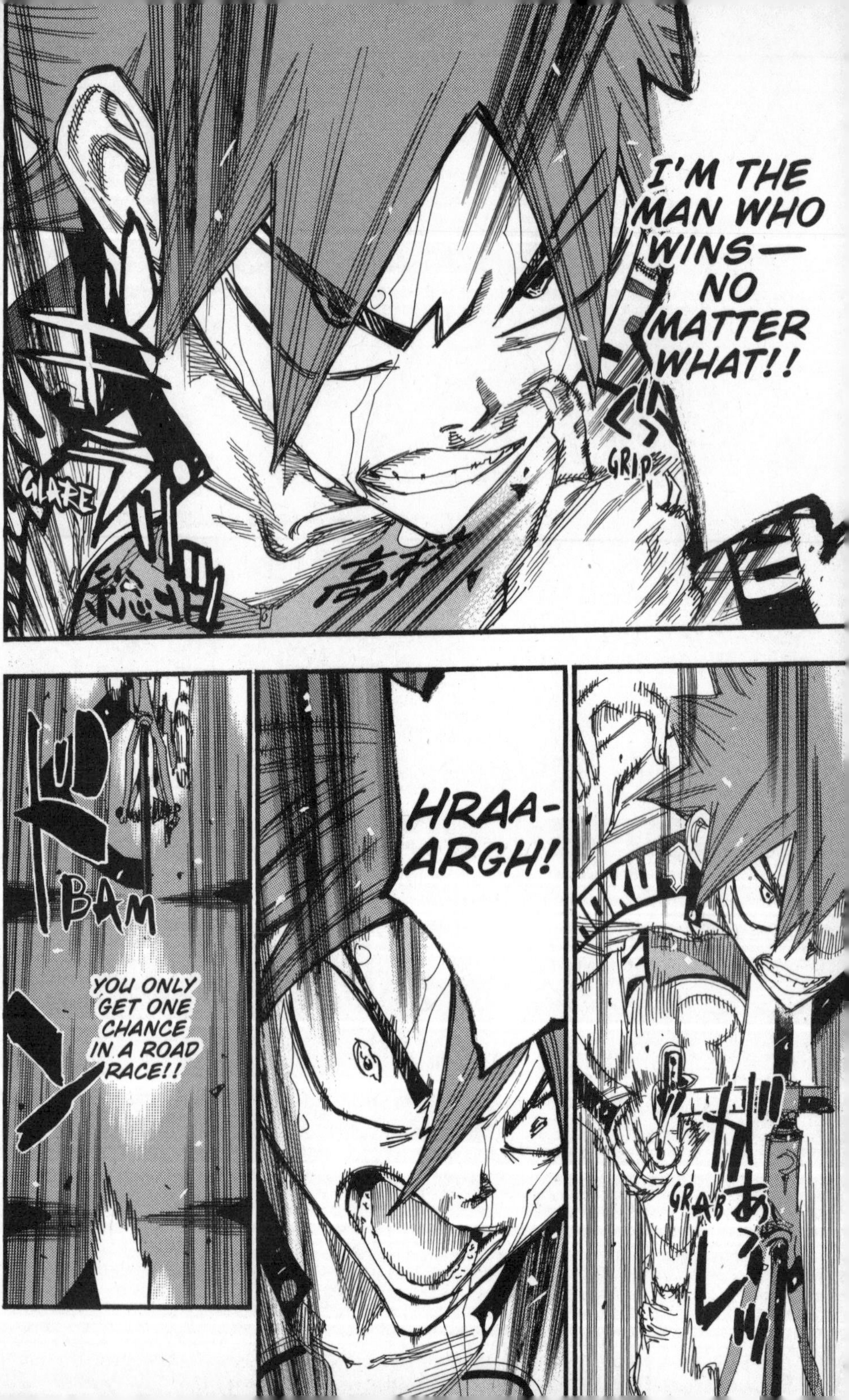
I'M THE MAN WHO WINS— NO MATTER WHAT!!
GRIP
GLARE
GRAB
HRAA-ARGH!
BAM
YOU ONLY GET ONE CHANCE IN A ROAD RACE!!

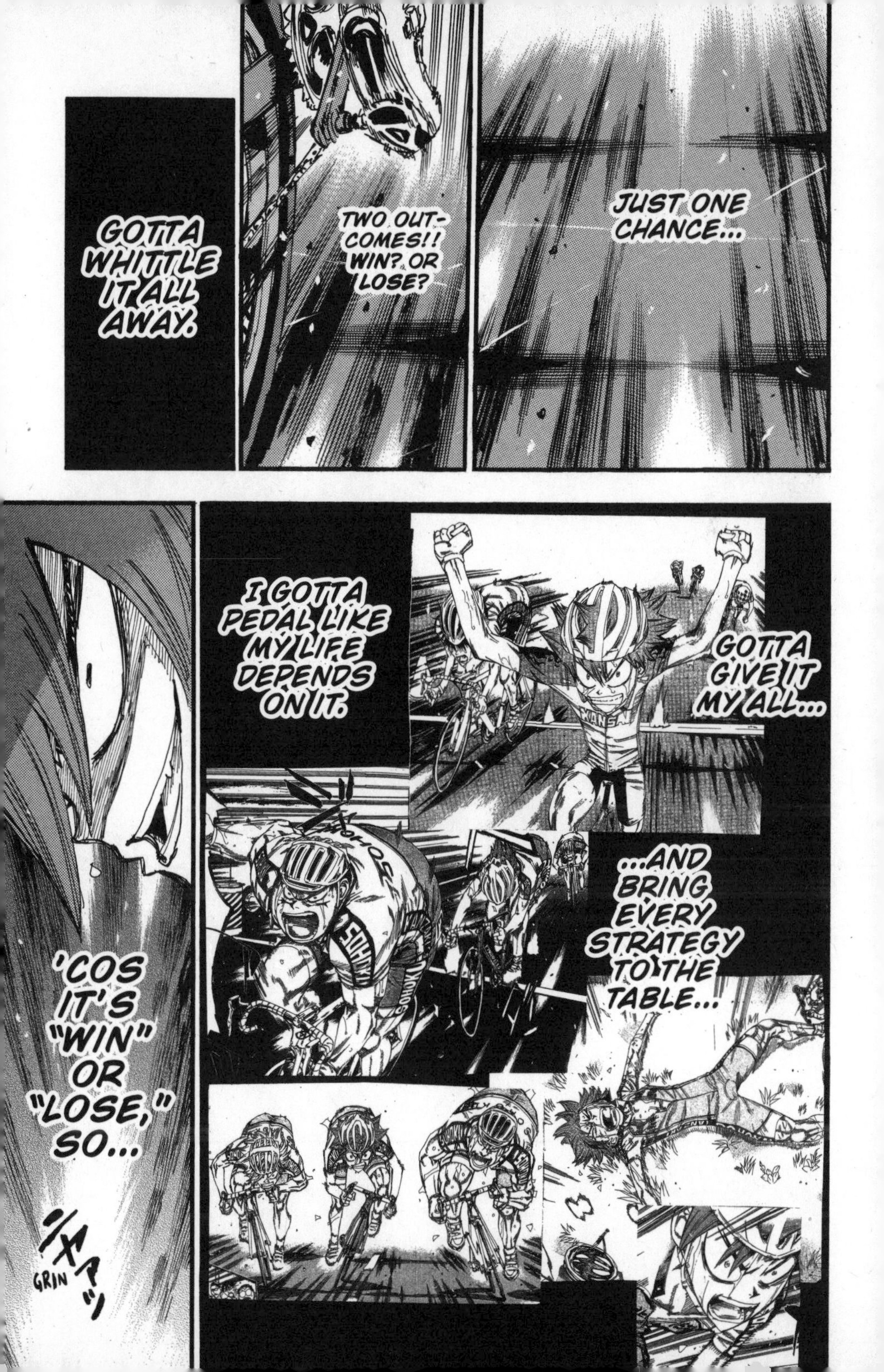

JUST ONE CHANCE...
TWO OUT-COMES!! WIN? OR LOSE?
GOTTA WHITTLE IT ALL AWAY.
I GOTTA PEDAL LIKE MY LIFE DEPENDS ON IT.
GOTTA GIVE IT MY ALL...
...AND BRING EVERY STRATEGY TO THE TABLE...
'COS IT'S "WIN" OR "LOSE," SO...
ニヤッ
GRIN

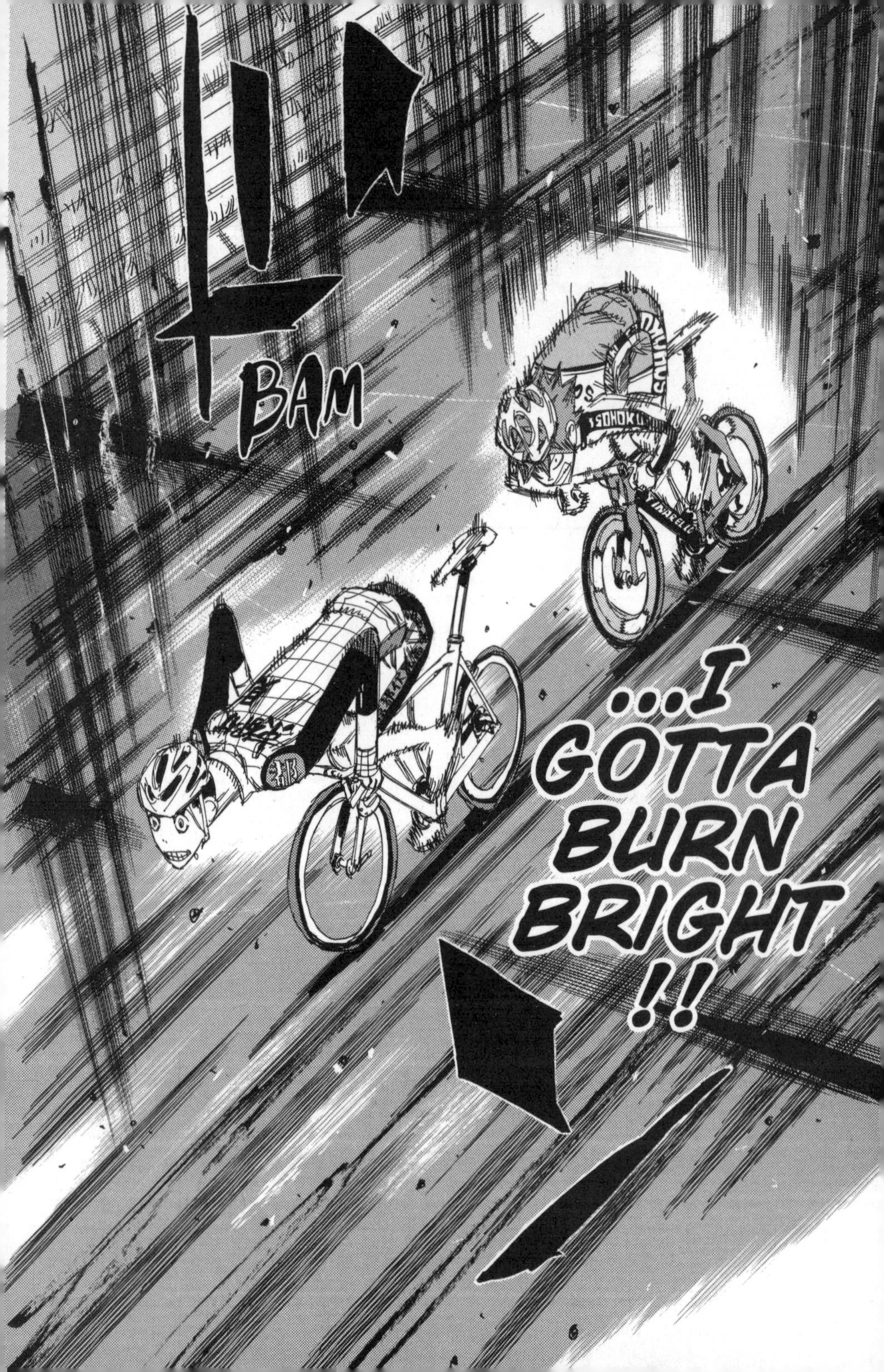
BAM
...I GOTTA BURN BRIGHT!!

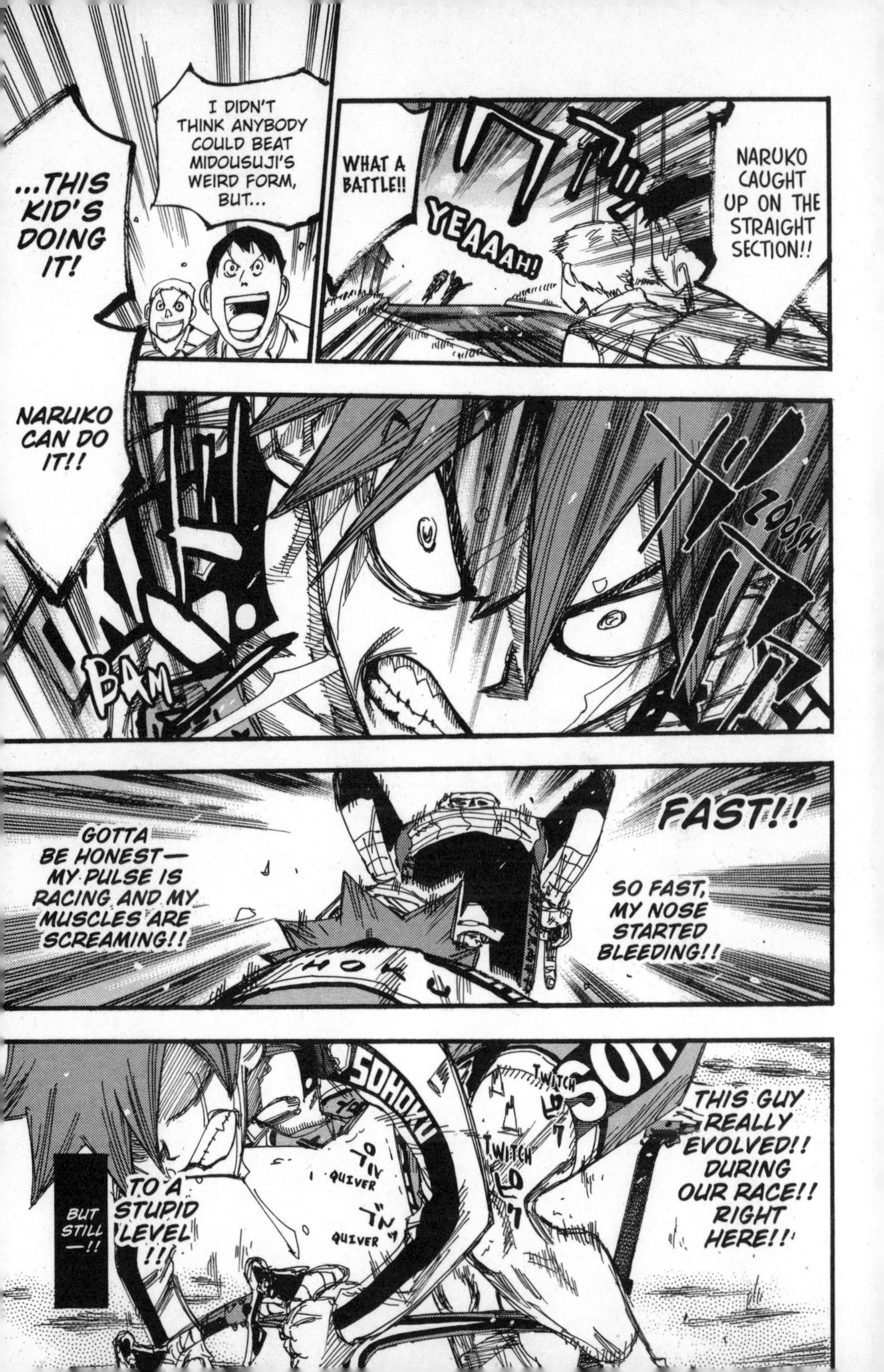
NARUKO CAUGHT UP ON THE STRAIGHT SECTION!!
YEAAAAH!
WHAT A BATTLE!!
I DIDN'T THINK ANYBODY COULD BEAT MIDOUSUJI'S WEIRD FORM, BUT...
...THIS KID'S DOING IT!
ZOOSH
BAM
NARUKO CAN DO IT!!
FAST!!
SO FAST, MY NOSE STARTED BLEEDING!!
GOTTA BE HONEST—MY PULSE IS RACING AND MY MUSCLES ARE SCREAMING!!
THIS GUY REALLY EVOLVED!! DURING OUR RACE!! RIGHT HERE!!
TWITCH
TWITCH
SOHOKU
QUIVER
QUIVER
TO A STUPID LEVEL!!
BUT STILL—!!

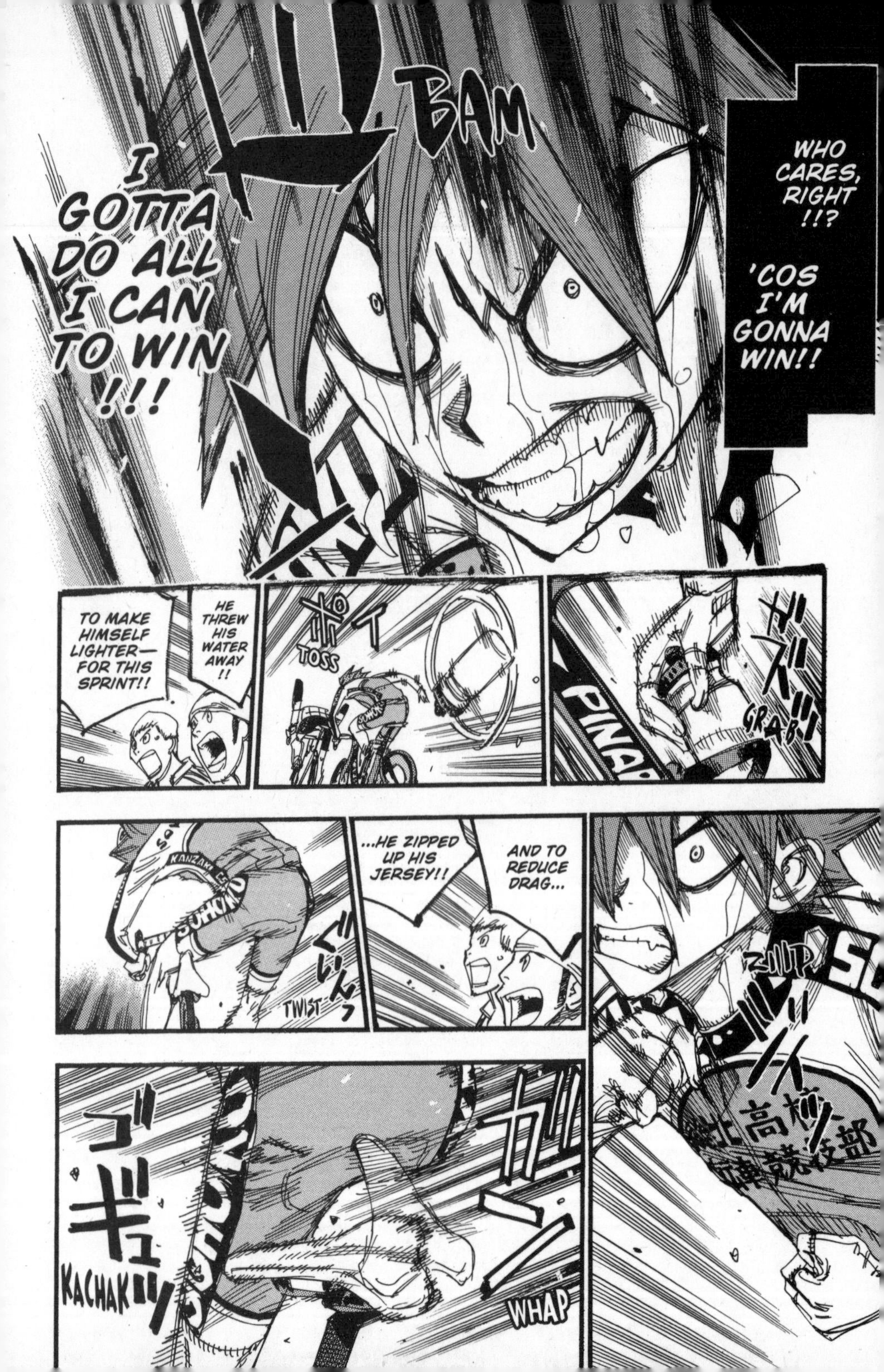
WHO CARES, RIGHT!!?
'COS I'M GONNA WIN!!
BAM
I GOTTA DO ALL I CAN TO WIN!!!
GRAB!!
PINA
TOSS
HE THREW HIS WATER AWAY!!
TO MAKE HIMSELF LIGHTER—FOR THIS SPRINT!!
ZIIIP
AND TO REDUCE DRAG...
...HE ZIPPED UP HIS JERSEY!!
TWIST
KANZAKI
KACHAK
WHAP

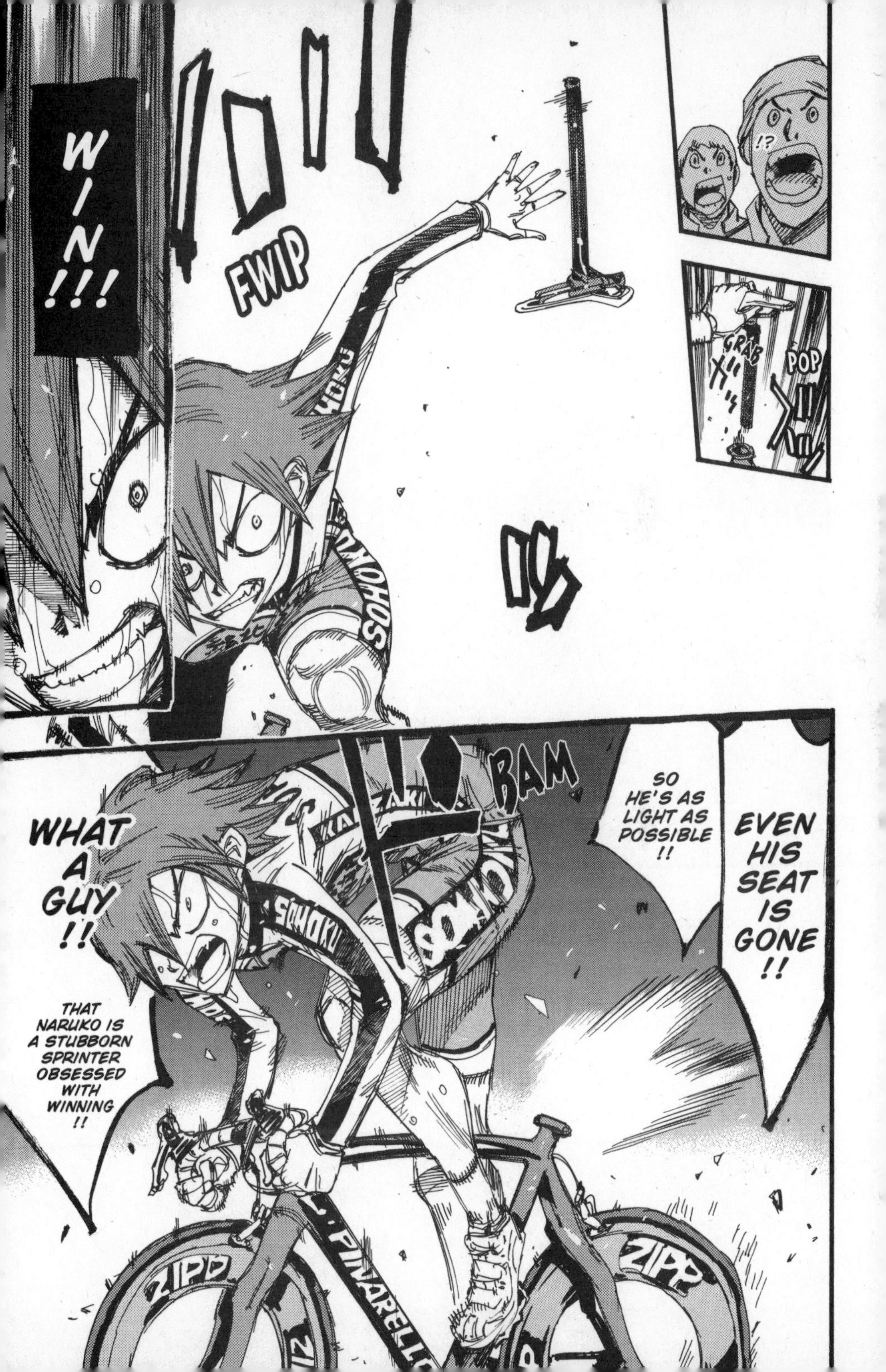

!?
GRAB
POP
WIN!!!
FWIP
BAM
EVEN HIS SEAT IS GONE!!
SO HE'S AS LIGHT AS POSSIBLE!!
WHAT A GUY!!
THAT NARUKO IS A STUBBORN SPRINTER OBSESSED WITH WINNING!!

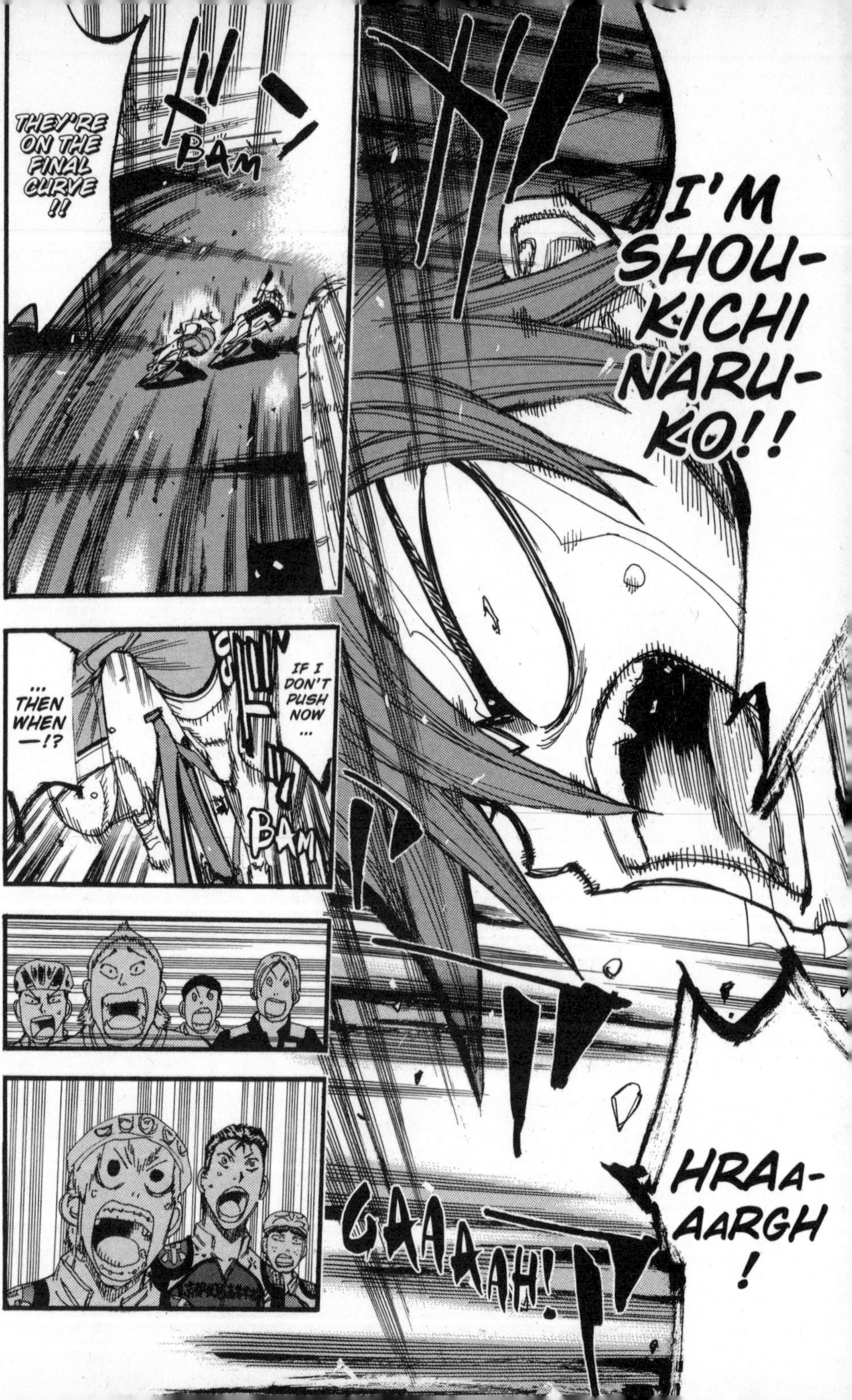
I'M SHOUKICHI NARUKO!!
HRAA-AARGH!
GAAAAAH!
THEY'RE ON THE FINAL CURVE!!
BAM
IF I DON'T PUSH NOW...
...THEN WHEN—!?
BAM

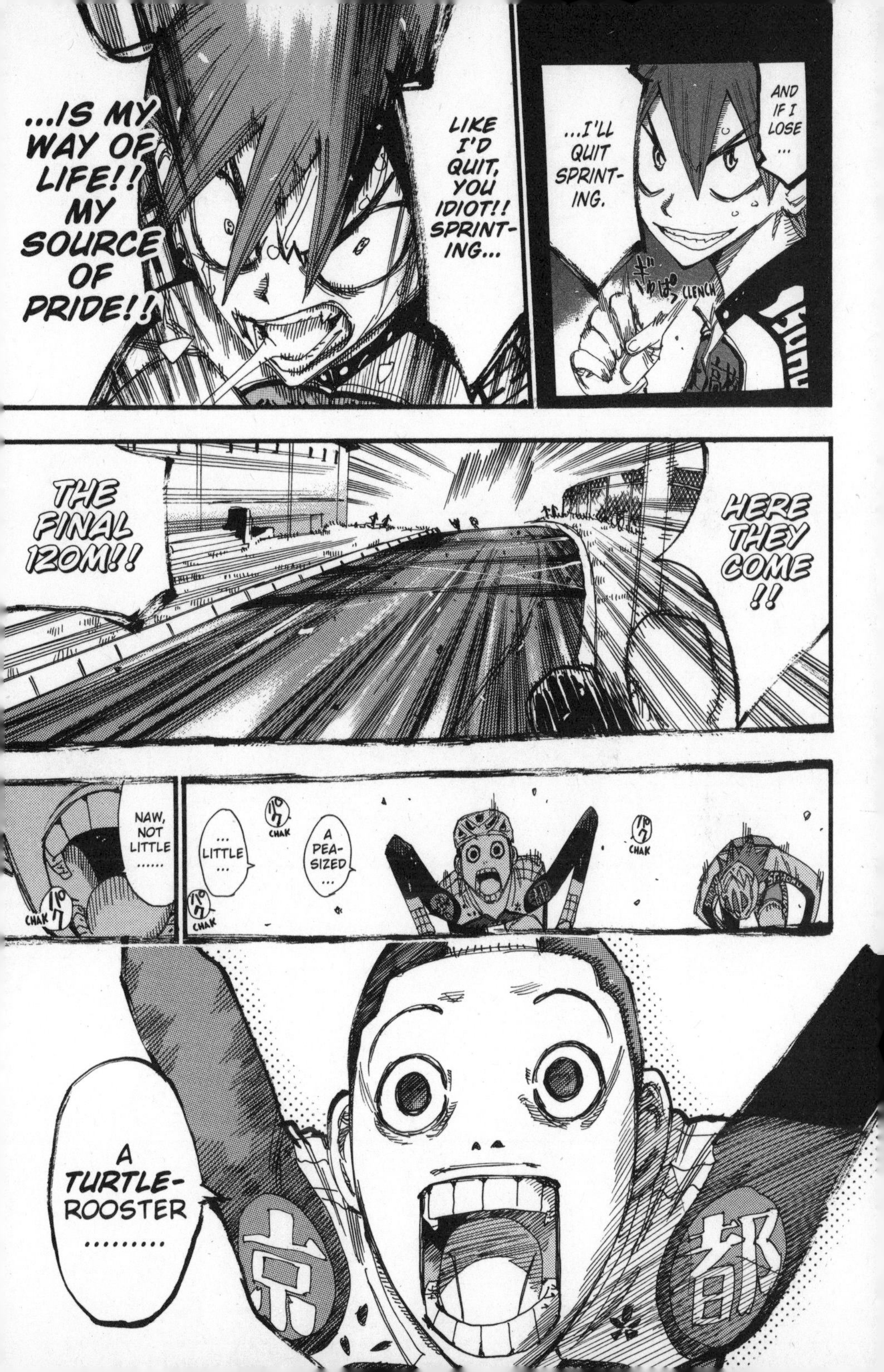

AND IF I LOSE ...
...I'LL QUIT SPRINT-ING.
CLENCH
LIKE I'D QUIT, YOU IDIOT!! SPRINT-ING...
...IS MY WAY OF LIFE!! MY SOURCE OF PRIDE!!
HERE THEY COME!!
THE FINAL 120M!!
CHAK
A PEA-SIZED ...
... LITTLE ...
CHAK
CHAK
NAW, NOT LITTLE ......
CHAK
A TURTLE-ROOSTER ....

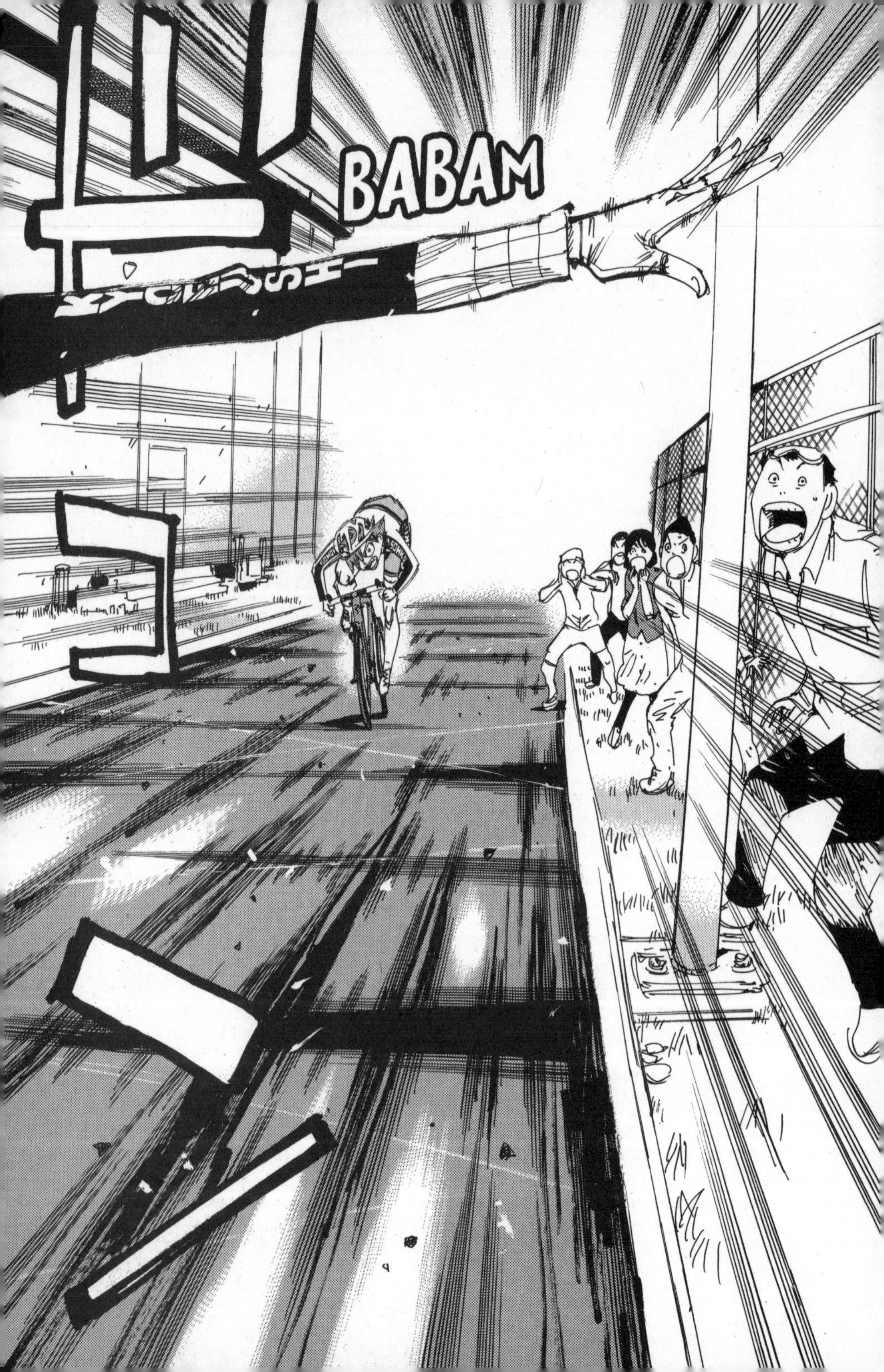
BABAM

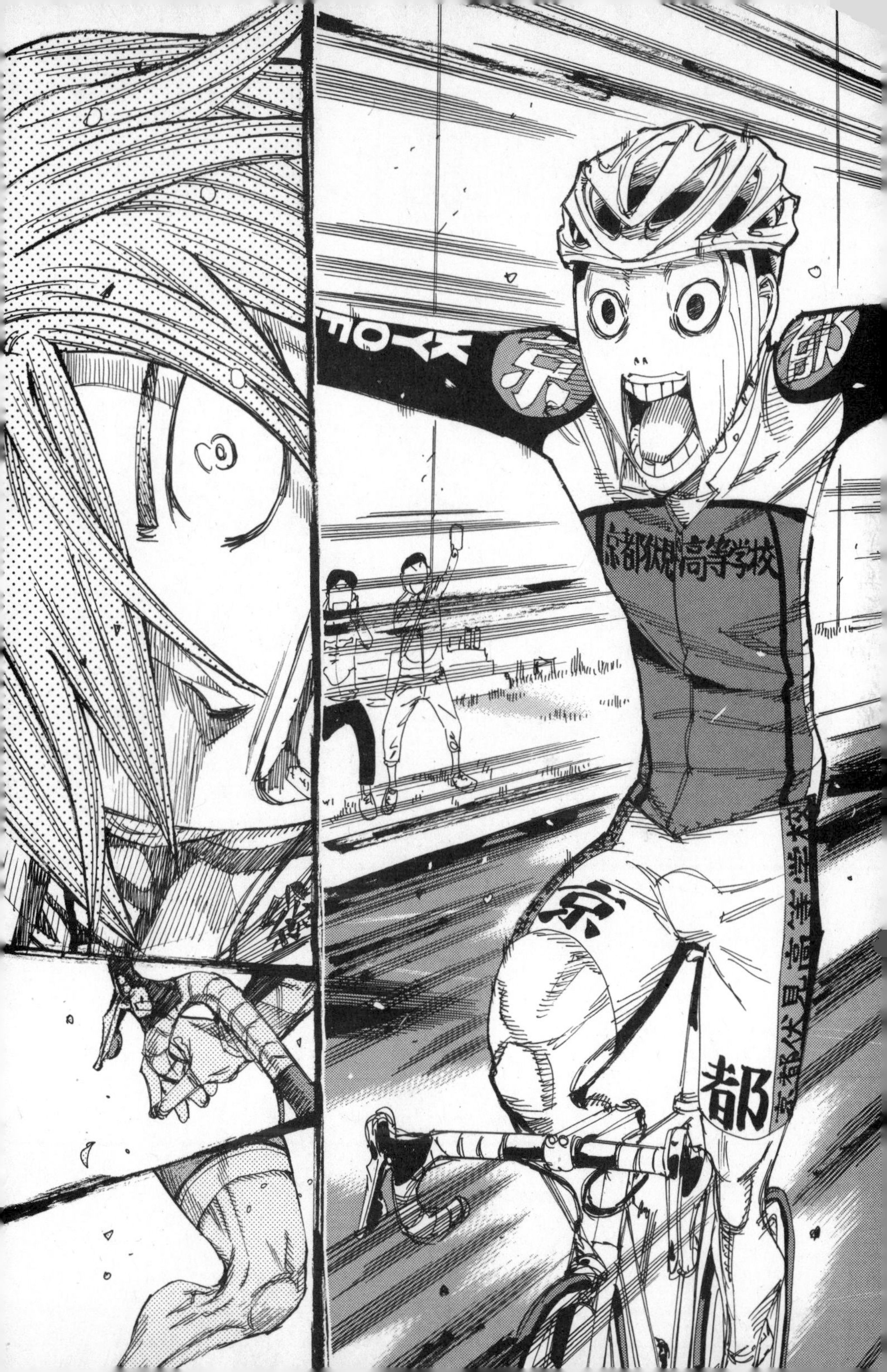
京都伏見高等学校

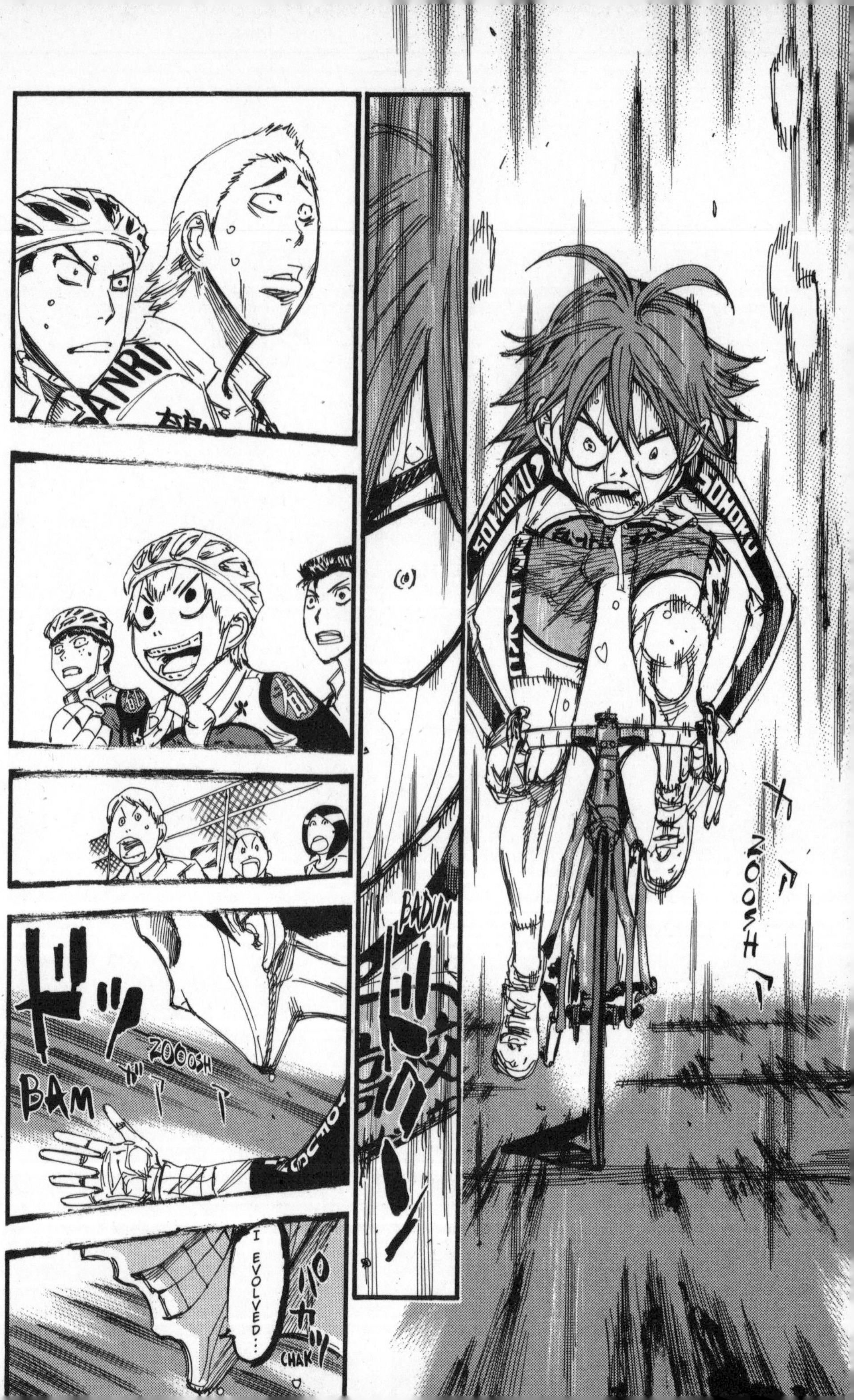
WHOOSH
BADUM
ZOOOSH
BAM
I EVOLVED...
CHAK

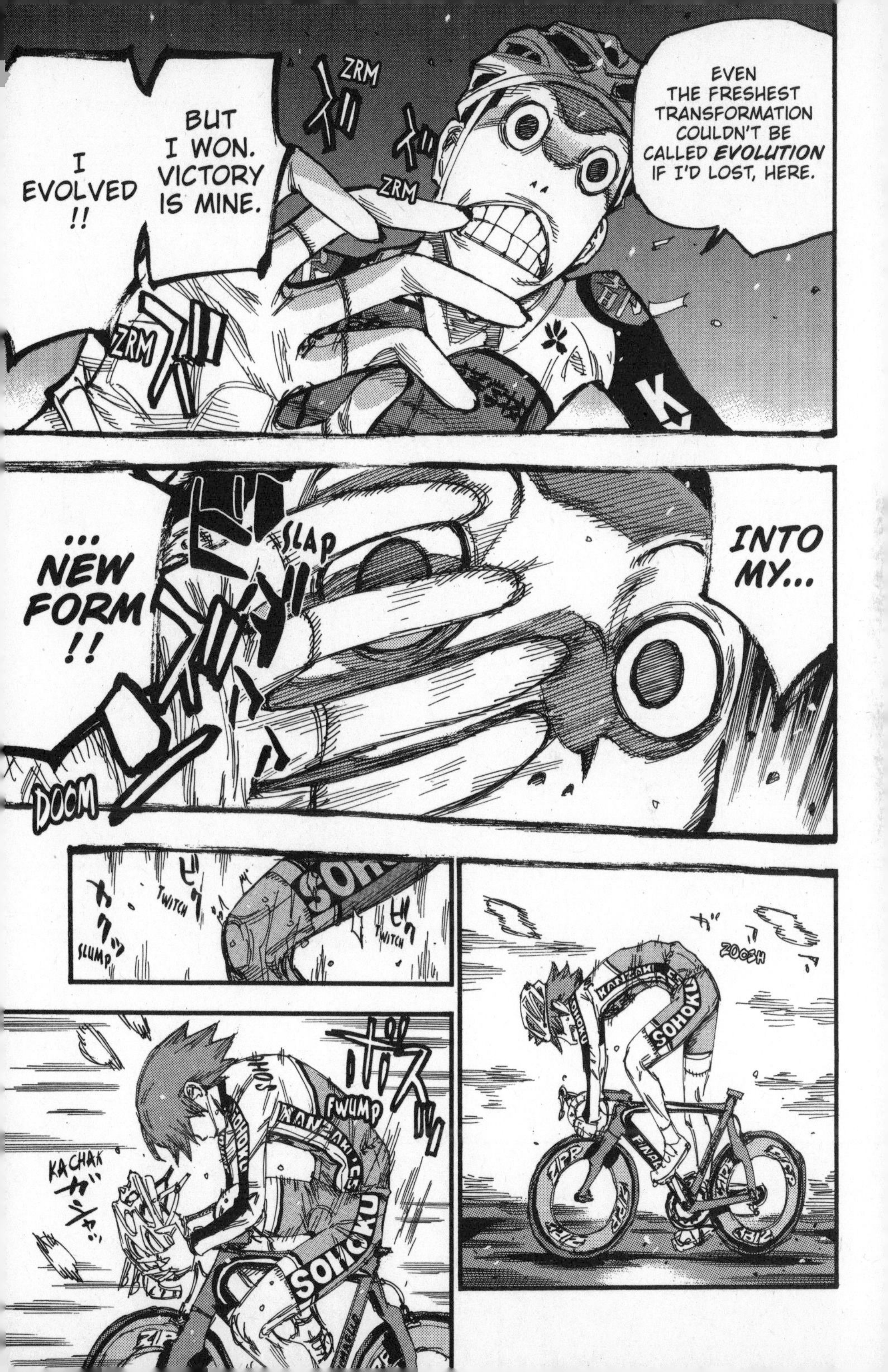
EVEN THE FRESHEST TRANSFORMATION COULDN'T BE CALLED *EVOLUTION* IF I'D LOST, HERE.
ZRM
ZRM
BUT I WON. VICTORY IS MINE.
I EVOLVED!!
ZRM
INTO MY...
SLAP
...NEW FORM!!
DOOM
ZOOSH
TWITCH
TWITCH
SLUMP
FWUMP
KACHAK

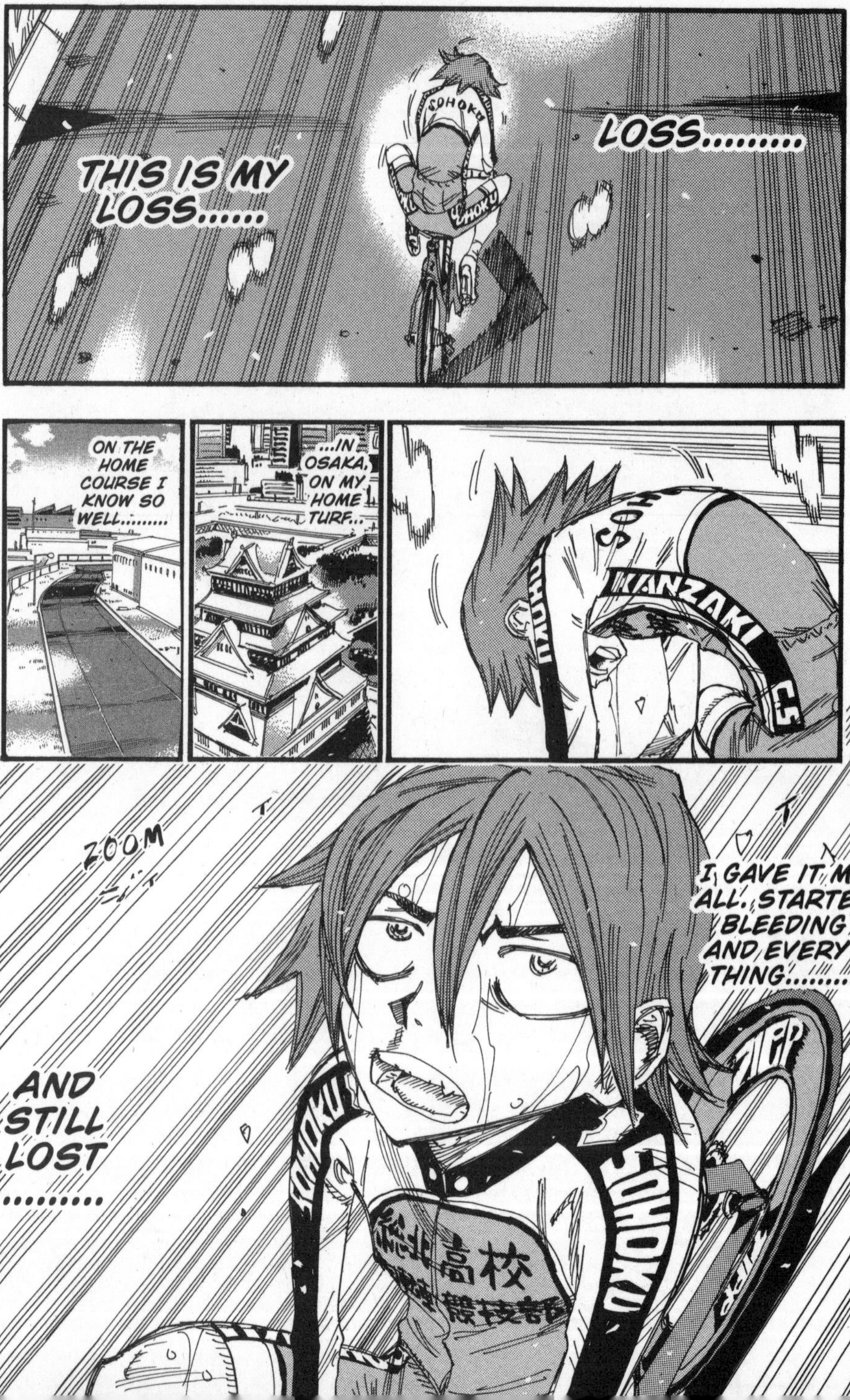
LOSS.........
THIS IS MY LOSS......
...IN OSAKA, ON MY HOME TURF...
ON THE HOME COURSE I KNOW SO WELL........
KANZAKI
I GAVE IT MY ALL, STARTED BLEEDING AND EVERYTHING.........
ZOOM
AND STILL LOST ....
SOHOKU
総北高校

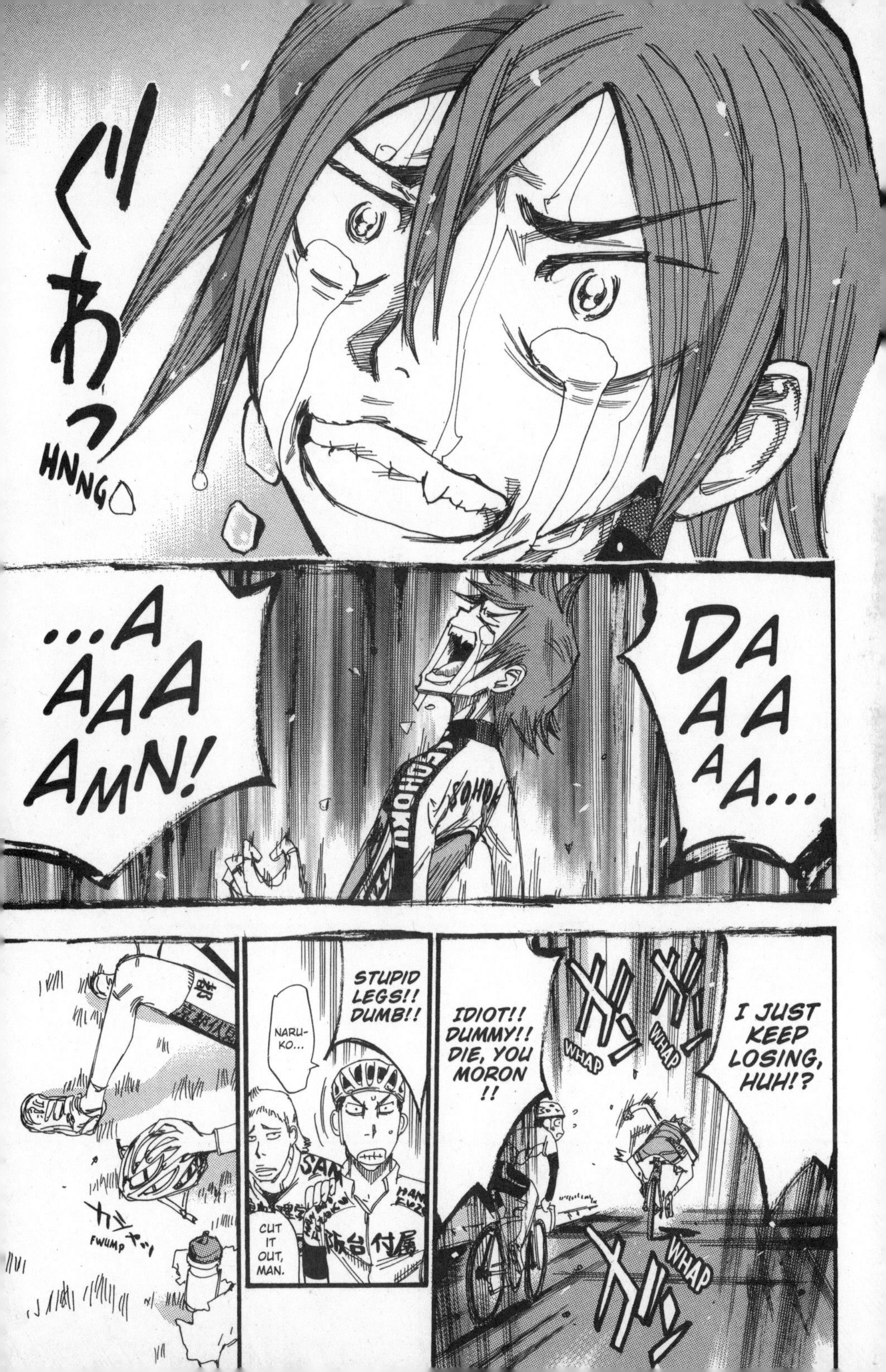
くわっ
HNNG
DAAAAA...
...AAAAAMN!
I JUST KEEP LOSING, HUH!?
WHAP
WHAP
IDIOT!! DUMMY!! DIE, YOU MORON!!
WHAP
STUPID LEGS!! DUMB!!
NARUKO...
CUT IT OUT, MAN.
FWUMP

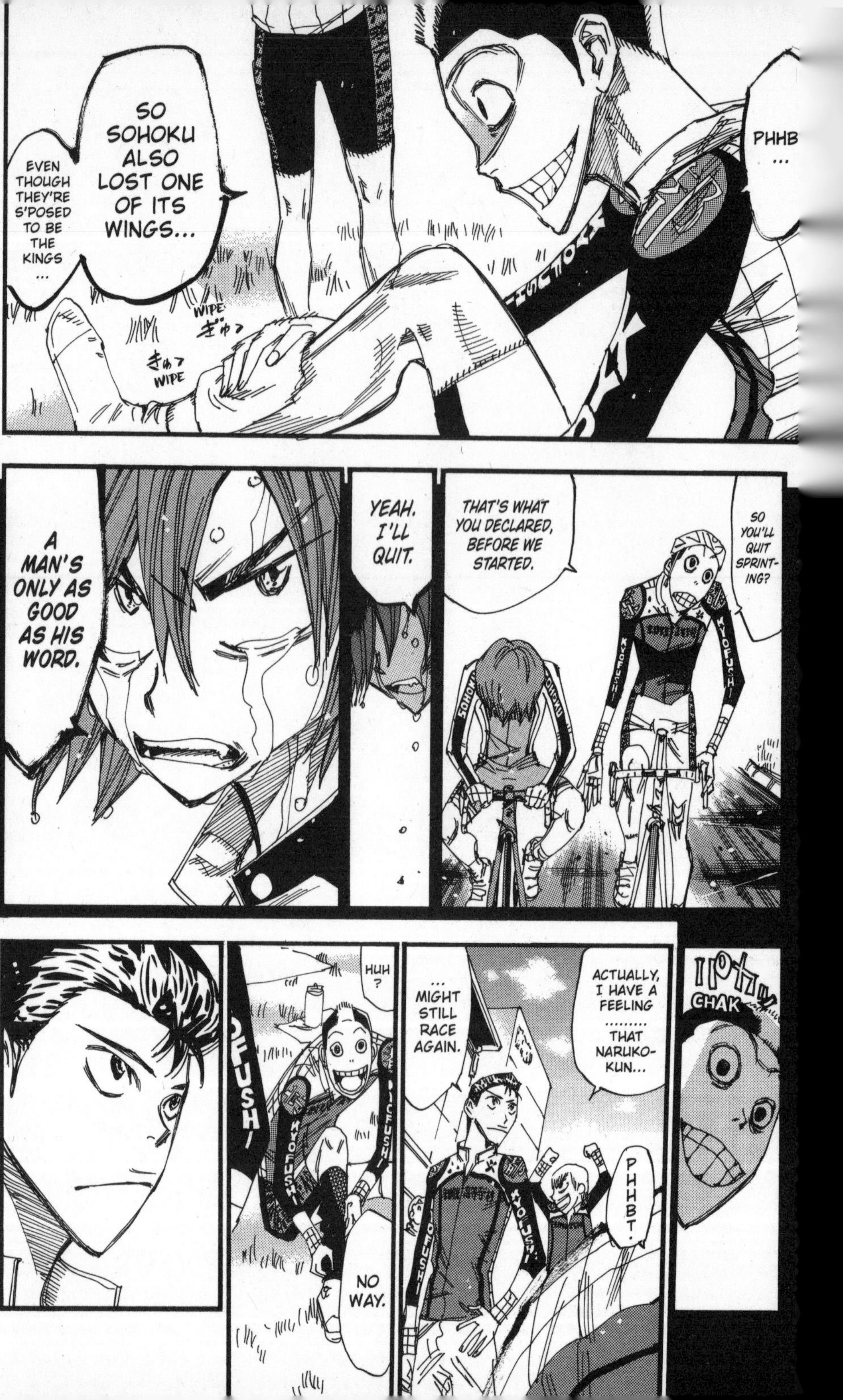
PHHB ...
SO SOHOKU ALSO LOST ONE OF ITS WINGS...
EVEN THOUGH THEY'RE S'POSED TO BE THE KINGS ...
WIPE
WIPE
SO YOU'LL QUIT SPRINT-ING?
THAT'S WHAT YOU DECLARED, BEFORE WE STARTED.
YEAH. I'LL QUIT.
A MAN'S ONLY AS GOOD AS HIS WORD.
CHAK
PHHBT.
ACTUALLY, I HAVE A FEELING .... THAT NARUKO-KUN...
... MIGHT STILL RACE AGAIN.
HUH?
NO WAY.
...

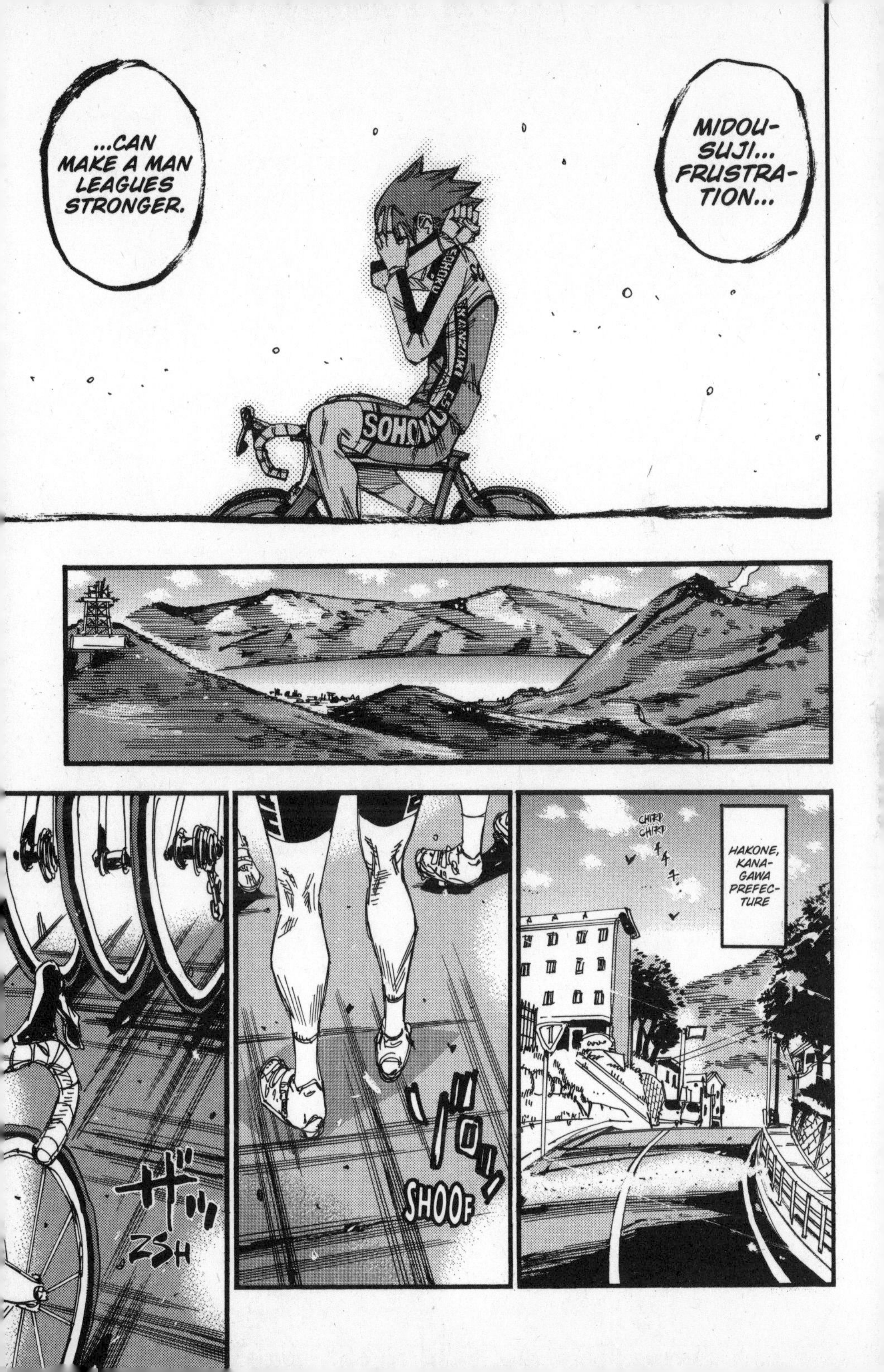
MIDOU-SUJI... FRUSTRATION...
...CAN MAKE A MAN LEAGUES STRONGER.
CHIRP CHIRP
HAKONE, KANAGAWA PREFECTURE
SHOOF
ザッ
ZSH

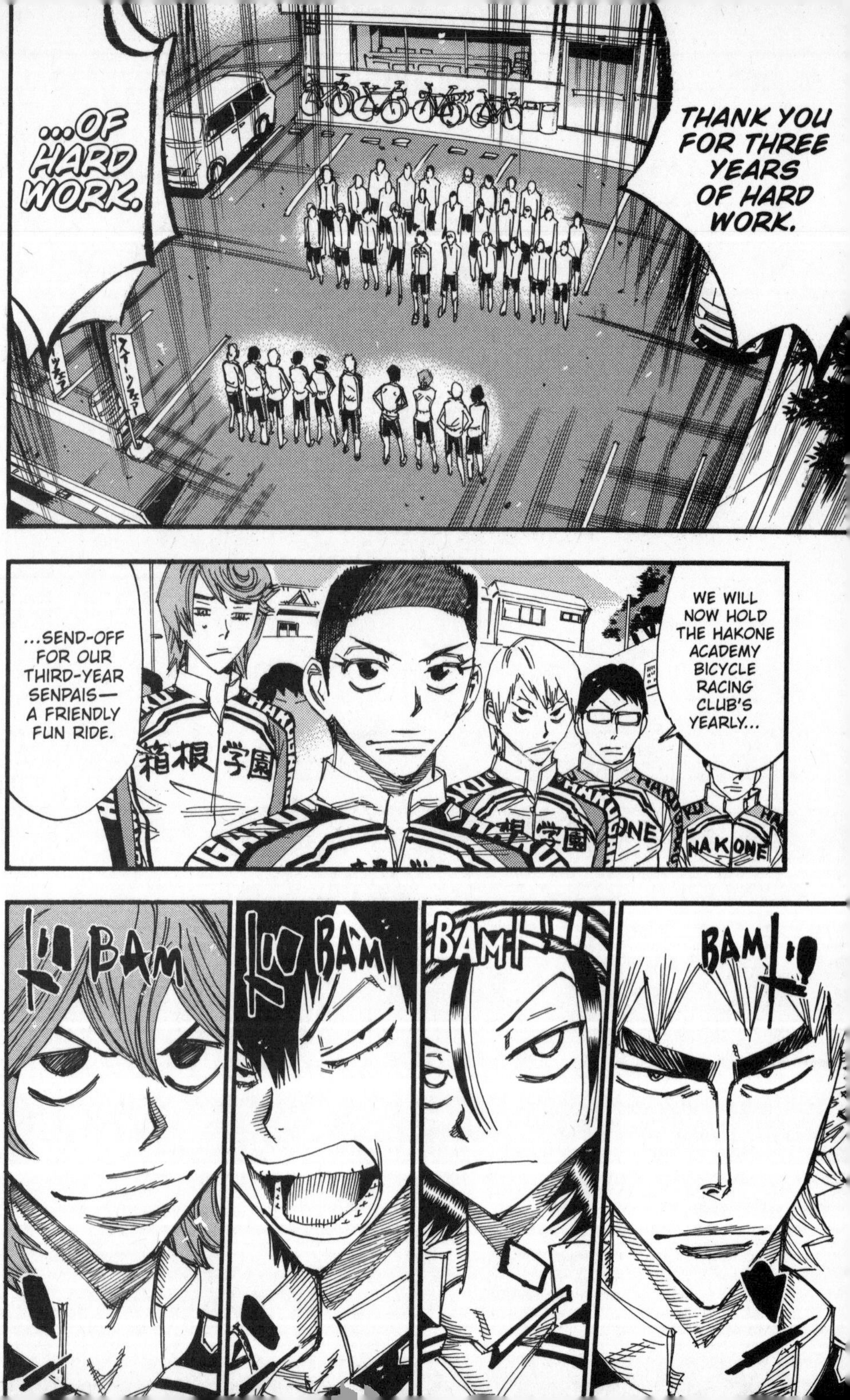
THANK YOU FOR THREE YEARS OF HARD WORK.
...OF HARD WORK.
WE WILL NOW HOLD THE HAKONE ACADEMY BICYCLE RACING CLUB'S YEARLY...
...SEND-OFF FOR OUR THIRD-YEAR SENPAIS—A FRIENDLY FUN RIDE.
箱根学園
NAKONE
BAM
BAM
BAM
BAM

RIDE.256: HAKONE'S FINAL FUN RIDE

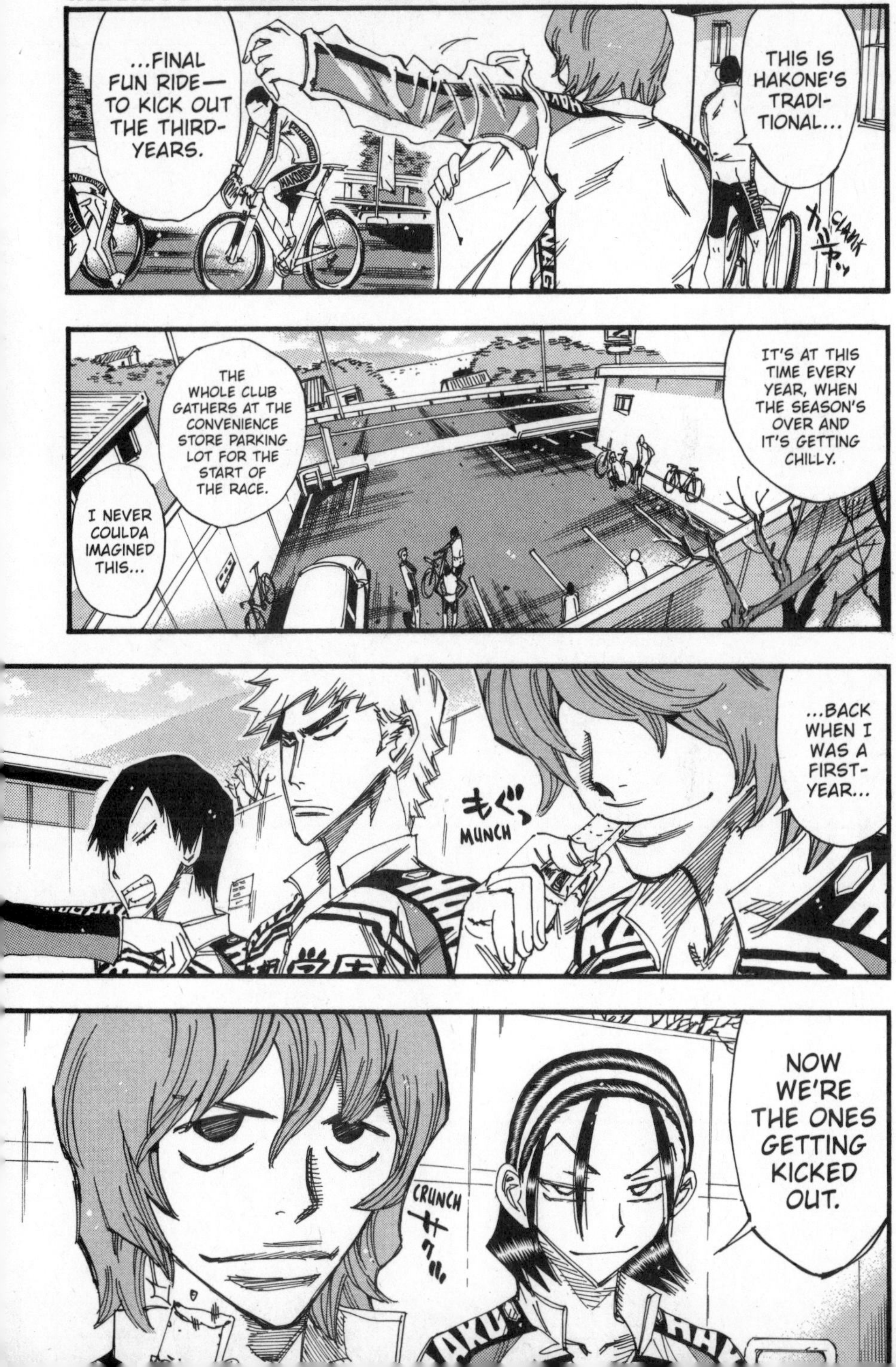

THIS IS HAKONE'S TRADITIONAL...
CLANK
...FINAL FUN RIDE—TO KICK OUT THE THIRD-YEARS.
IT'S AT THIS TIME EVERY YEAR, WHEN THE SEASON'S OVER AND IT'S GETTING CHILLY.
THE WHOLE CLUB GATHERS AT THE CONVENIENCE STORE PARKING LOT FOR THE START OF THE RACE.
I NEVER COULDA IMAGINED THIS...
...BACK WHEN I WAS A FIRST-YEAR...
MUNCH
NOW WE'RE THE ONES GETTING KICKED OUT.
CRUNCH

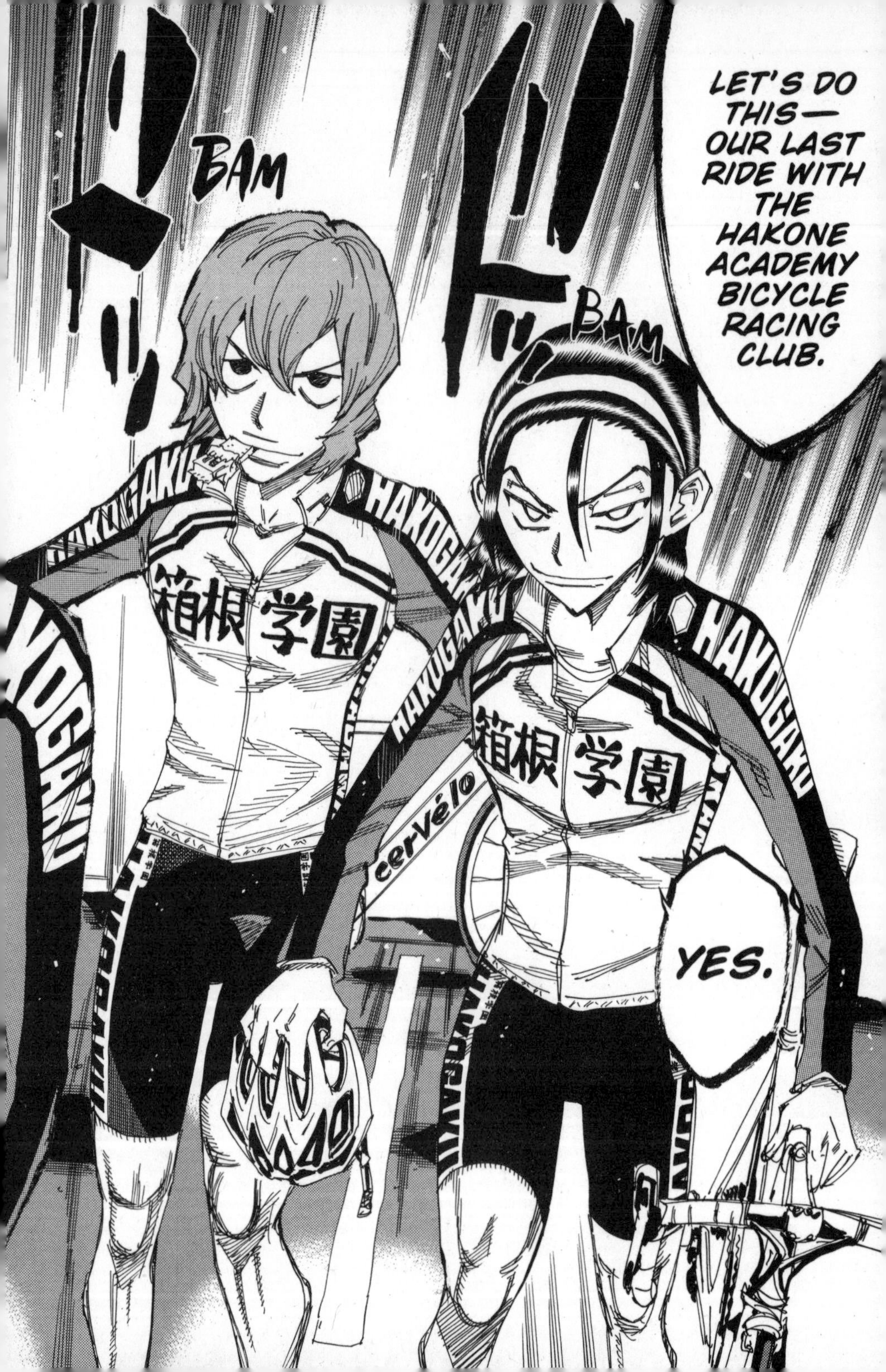
LET'S DO THIS— OUR LAST RIDE WITH THE HAKONE ACADEMY BICYCLE RACING CLUB.
BAM
BAM
HAKOGAKU
箱根学園
cervélo
箱根学園
YES.

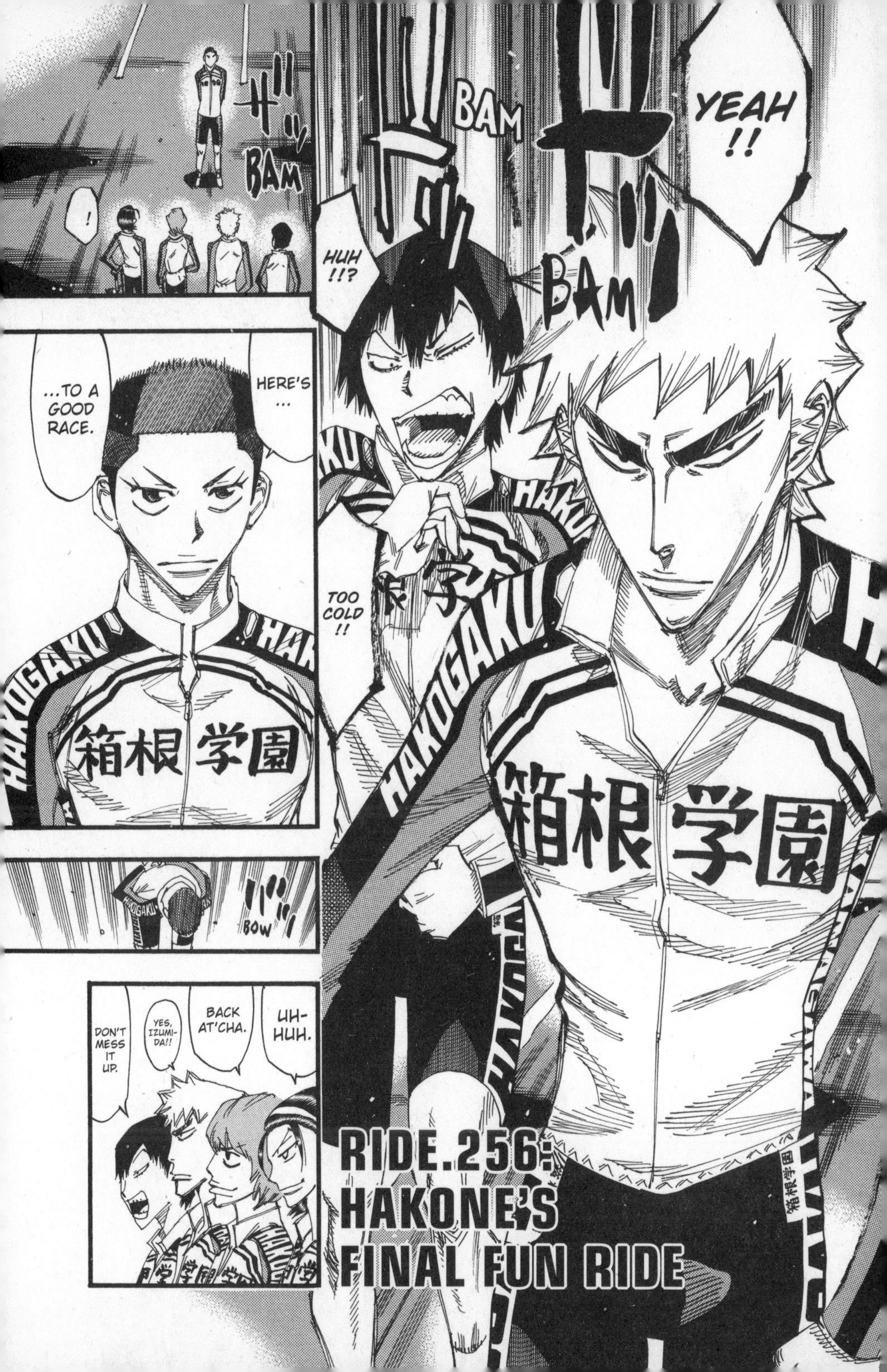
YEAH!!
BAM
BAM
HUH!!?
TOO COLD!!
RIDE.256: HAKONE'S FINAL FUN RIDE
BAM
!
HERE'S...
...TO A GOOD RACE.
BOW
UH-HUH.
BACK AT'CHA.
YES, IZUMIDA!!
DON'T MESS IT UP.

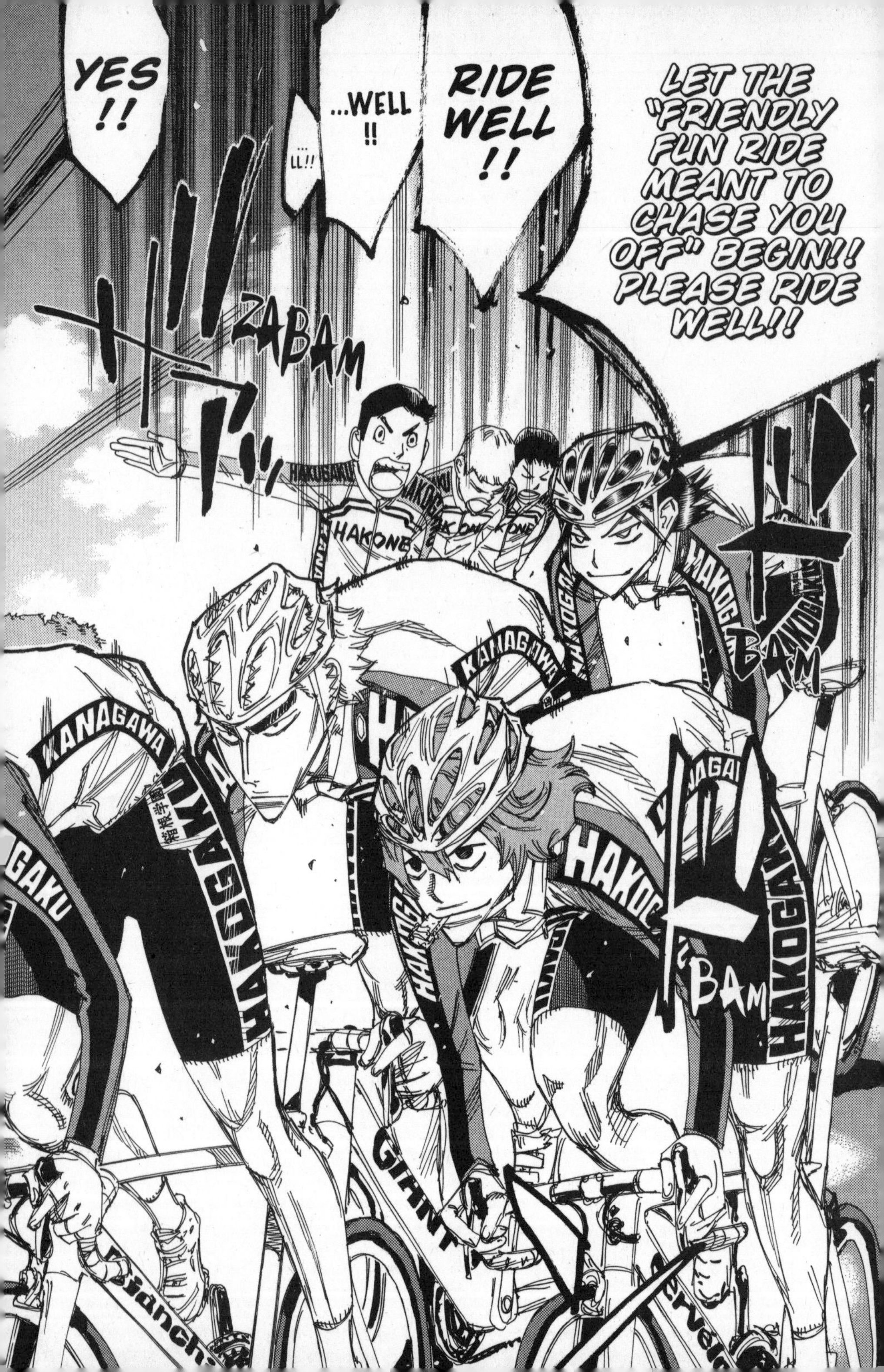
LET THE "FRIENDLY FUN RIDE MEANT TO CHASE YOU OFF" BEGIN!! PLEASE RIDE WELL!!
RIDE WELL!!
...WELL!!
...LL!!
YES!!
ZABAM
BAM
BAM

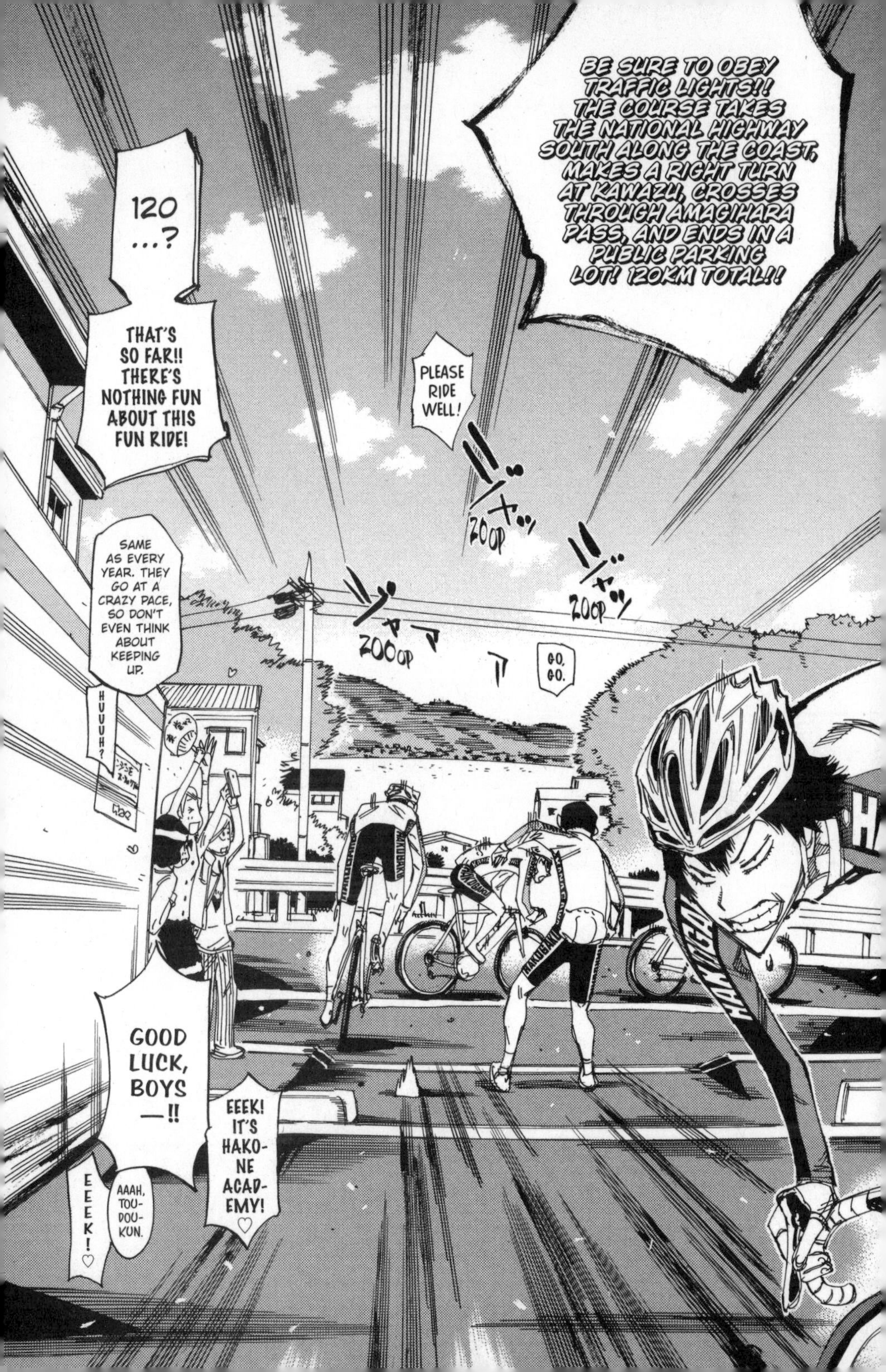
BE SURE TO OBEY TRAFFIC LIGHTS!! THE COURSE TAKES THE NATIONAL HIGHWAY SOUTH ALONG THE COAST, MAKES A RIGHT TURN AT KAWAZU, CROSSES THROUGH AMAGIHARA PASS, AND ENDS IN A PUBLIC PARKING LOT! 120KM TOTAL!!
120 ...?
THAT'S SO FAR!! THERE'S NOTHING FUN ABOUT THIS FUN RIDE!
PLEASE RIDE WELL!
ZOOP
ZOOP
ZOOOP
GO, GO.
SAME AS EVERY YEAR. THEY GO AT A CRAZY PACE, SO DON'T EVEN THINK ABOUT KEEPING UP.
HUUUH?
EEEK! IT'S HAKONE ACADEMY! ♡
GOOD LUCK, BOYS—!!
AAAH, TOUDOU-KUN.
EEEEK! ♡

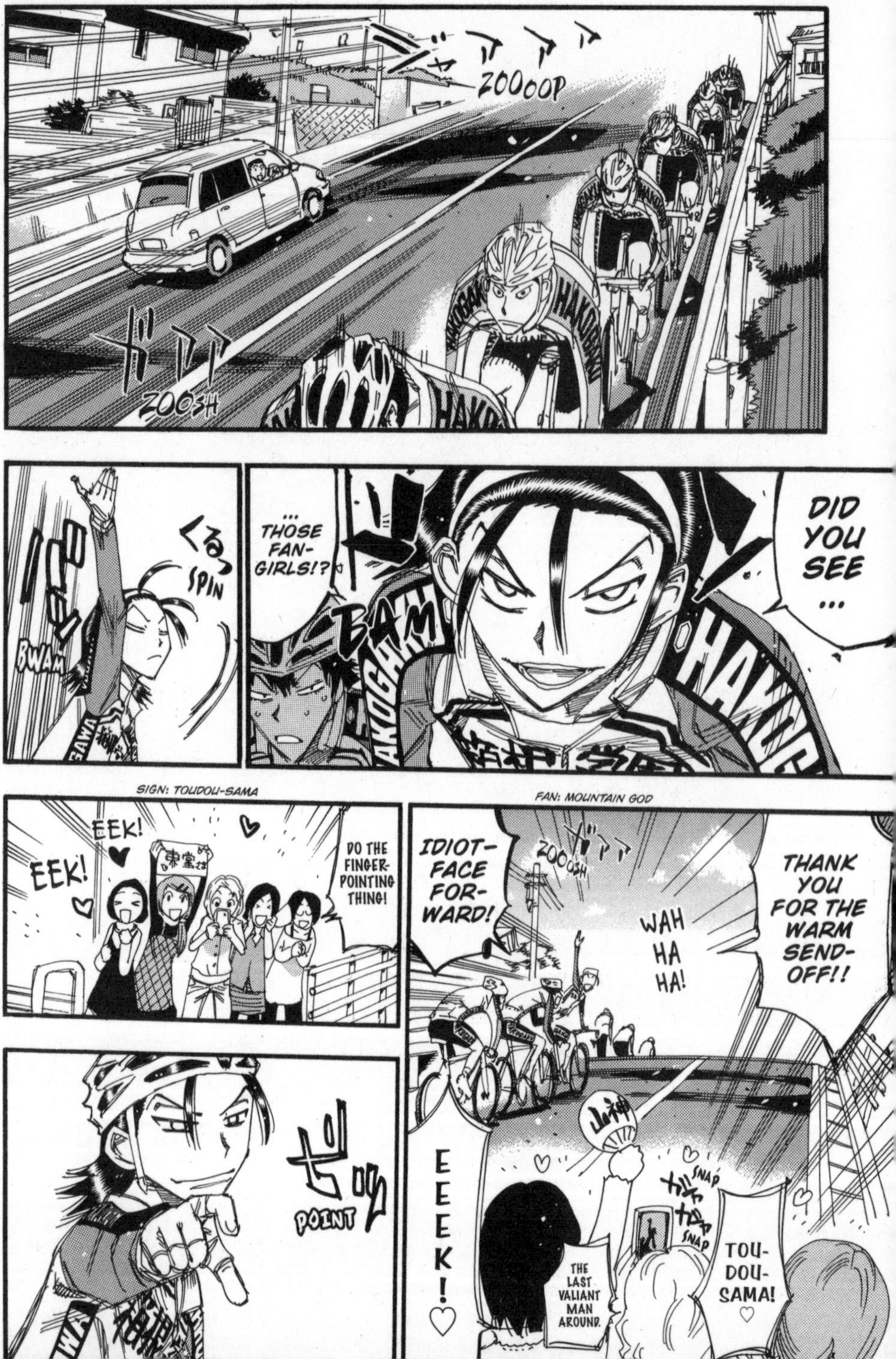
ZOOOOP
ZOOSH
DID YOU SEE ...
... THOSE FAN-GIRLS!?
BAM
くるっ
SPIN
BWAM
FAN: MOUNTAIN GOD
THANK YOU FOR THE WARM SEND-OFF!!
WAH HA HA!
IDIOT-FACE FORWARD!
ZOOOSH
TOU-DOU-SAMA!
SNAP
SNAP
THE LAST VALIANT MAN AROUND.
EEEEK!
SIGN: TOUDOU-SAMA
EEK!
EEK!
DO THE FINGER-POINTING THING!
POINT

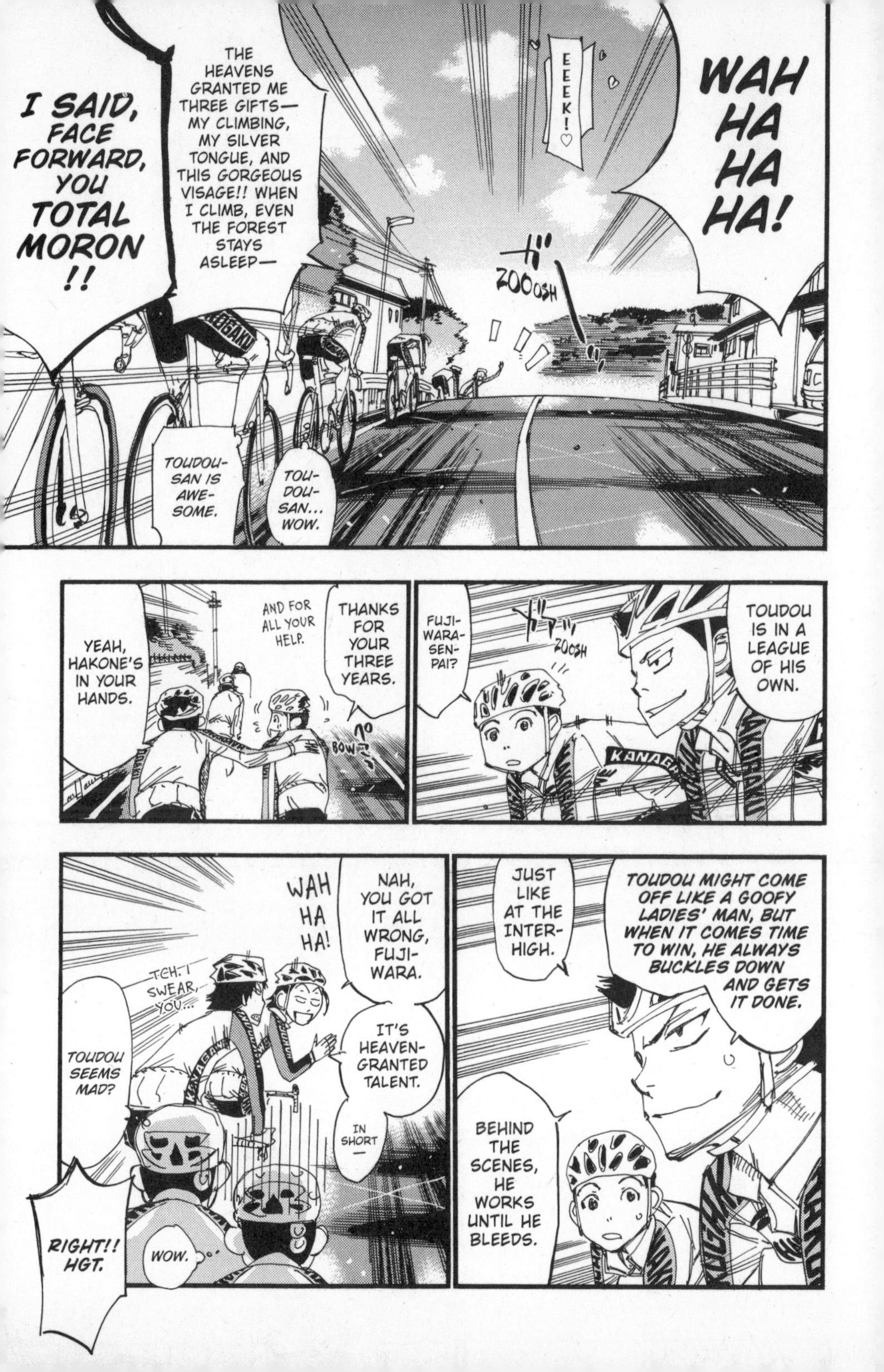
WAH HA HA HA!
EEEEK!♡
THE HEAVENS GRANTED ME THREE GIFTS—MY CLIMBING, MY SILVER TONGUE, AND THIS GORGEOUS VISAGE!! WHEN I CLIMB, EVEN THE FOREST STAYS ASLEEP—
I SAID, FACE FORWARD, YOU TOTAL MORON!!
ZOOOSH
TOU-DOU-SAN... WOW.
TOUDOU-SAN IS AWE-SOME.
TOUDOU IS IN A LEAGUE OF HIS OWN.
ZOOSH
FUJI-WARA-SEN-PAI?
THANKS FOR YOUR THREE YEARS.
AND FOR ALL YOUR HELP.
BOW
YEAH, HAKONE'S IN YOUR HANDS.
TOUDOU MIGHT COME OFF LIKE A GOOFY LADIES' MAN, BUT WHEN IT COMES TIME TO WIN, HE ALWAYS BUCKLES DOWN AND GETS IT DONE.
JUST LIKE AT THE INTER-HIGH.
BEHIND THE SCENES, HE WORKS UNTIL HE BLEEDS.
NAH, YOU GOT IT ALL WRONG, FUJI-WARA.
WAH HA HA!
IT'S HEAVEN-GRANTED TALENT.
IN SHORT—
TCH. I SWEAR, YOU...
TOUDOU SEEMS MAD?
WOW.
RIGHT!! HGT.

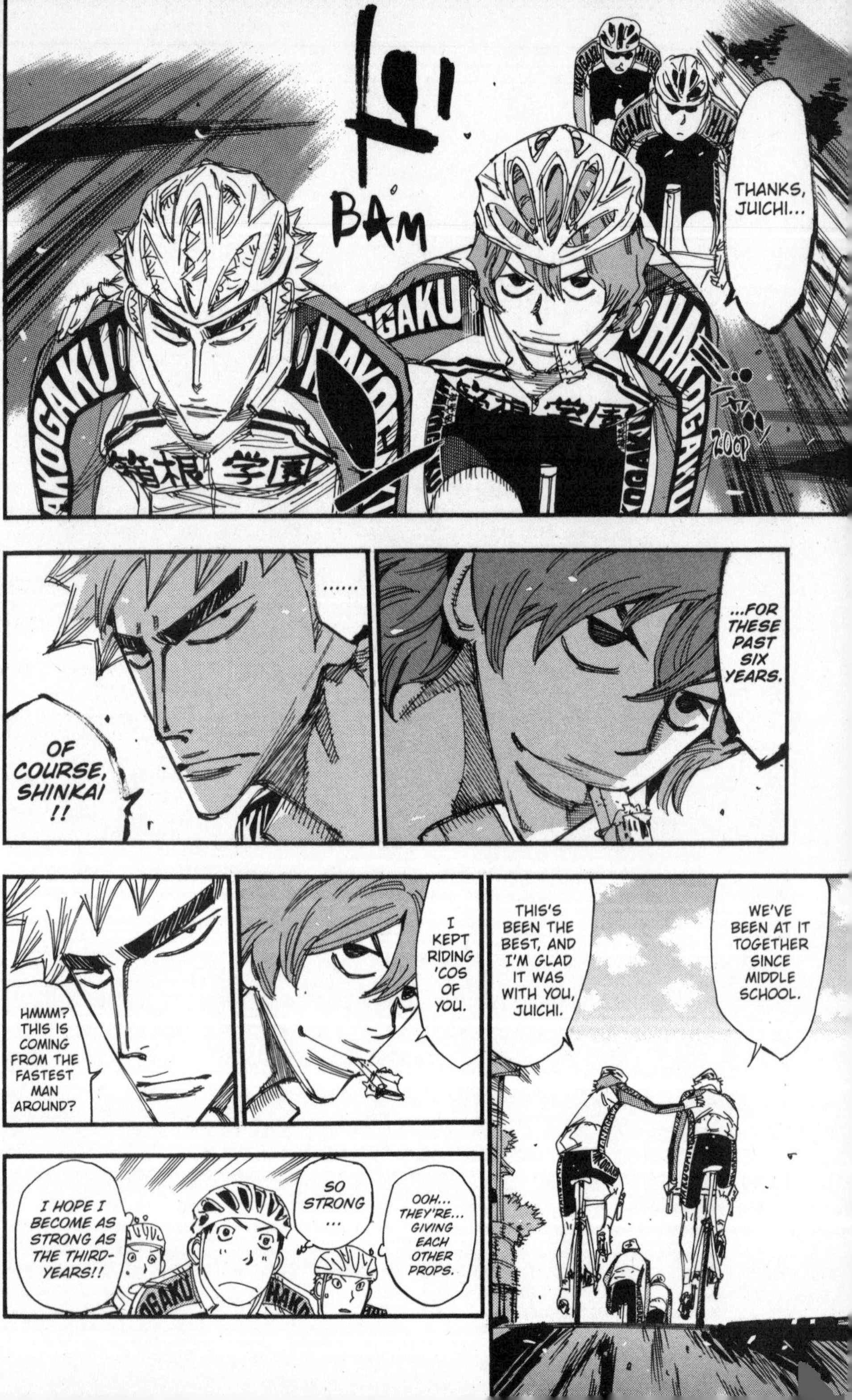
THANKS, JUICHI...
BAM
ZOOP
...FOR THESE PAST SIX YEARS.
......
OF COURSE, SHINKAI!!
WE'VE BEEN AT IT TOGETHER SINCE MIDDLE SCHOOL.
THIS'S BEEN THE BEST, AND I'M GLAD IT WAS WITH YOU, JUICHI.
I KEPT RIDING 'COS OF YOU.
HMMM? THIS IS COMING FROM THE FASTEST MAN AROUND?
OOH... THEY'RE... GIVING EACH OTHER PROPS.
SO STRONG ...
I HOPE I BECOME AS STRONG AS THE THIRD-YEARS!!

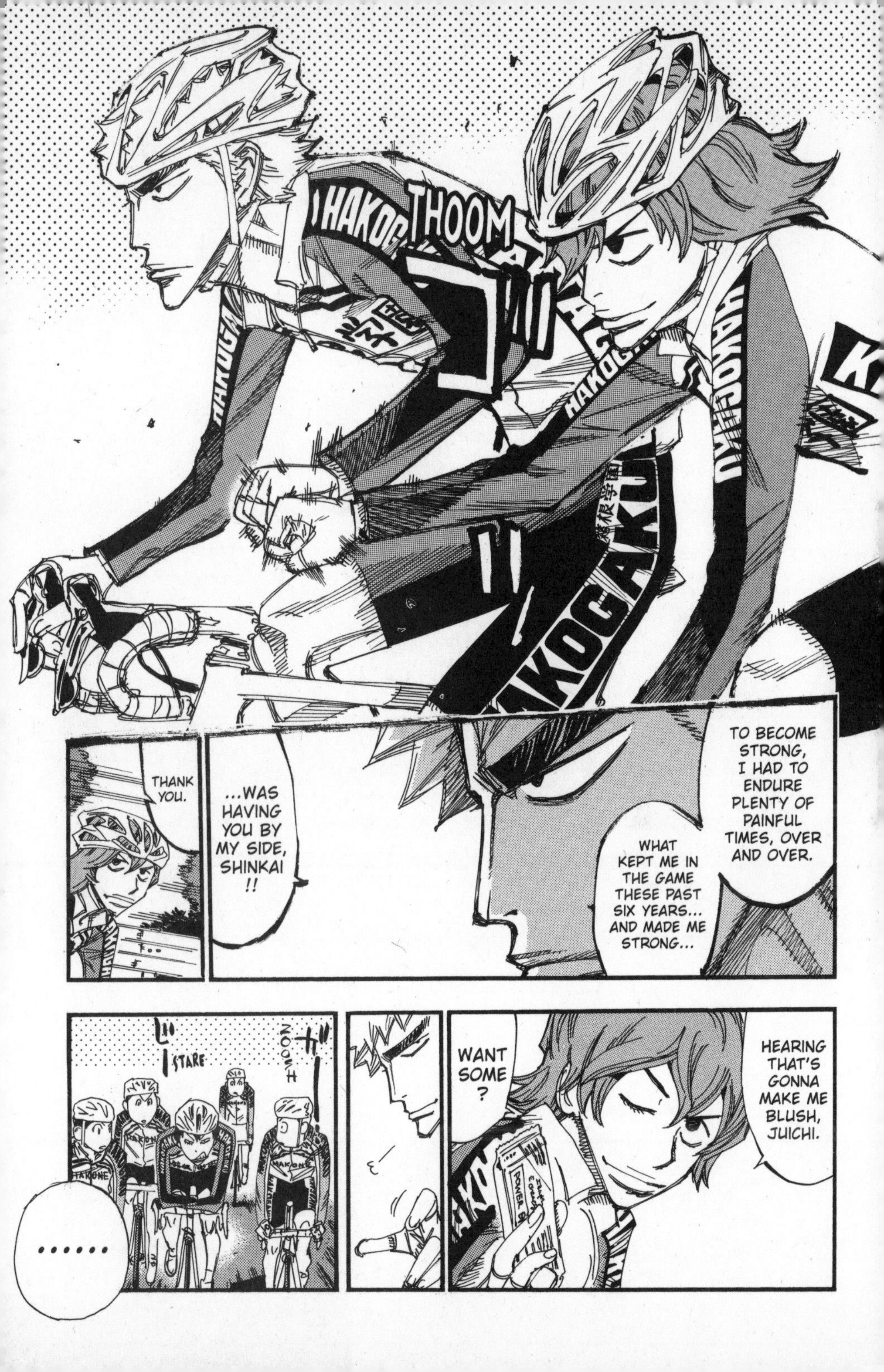
THOOM
TO BECOME STRONG, I HAD TO ENDURE PLENTY OF PAINFUL TIMES, OVER AND OVER.
WHAT KEPT ME IN THE GAME THESE PAST SIX YEARS... AND MADE ME STRONG...
...WAS HAVING YOU BY MY SIDE, SHINKAI !!
THANK YOU.
HEARING THAT'S GONNA MAKE ME BLUSH, JUICHI.
WANT SOME ?
STARE
......

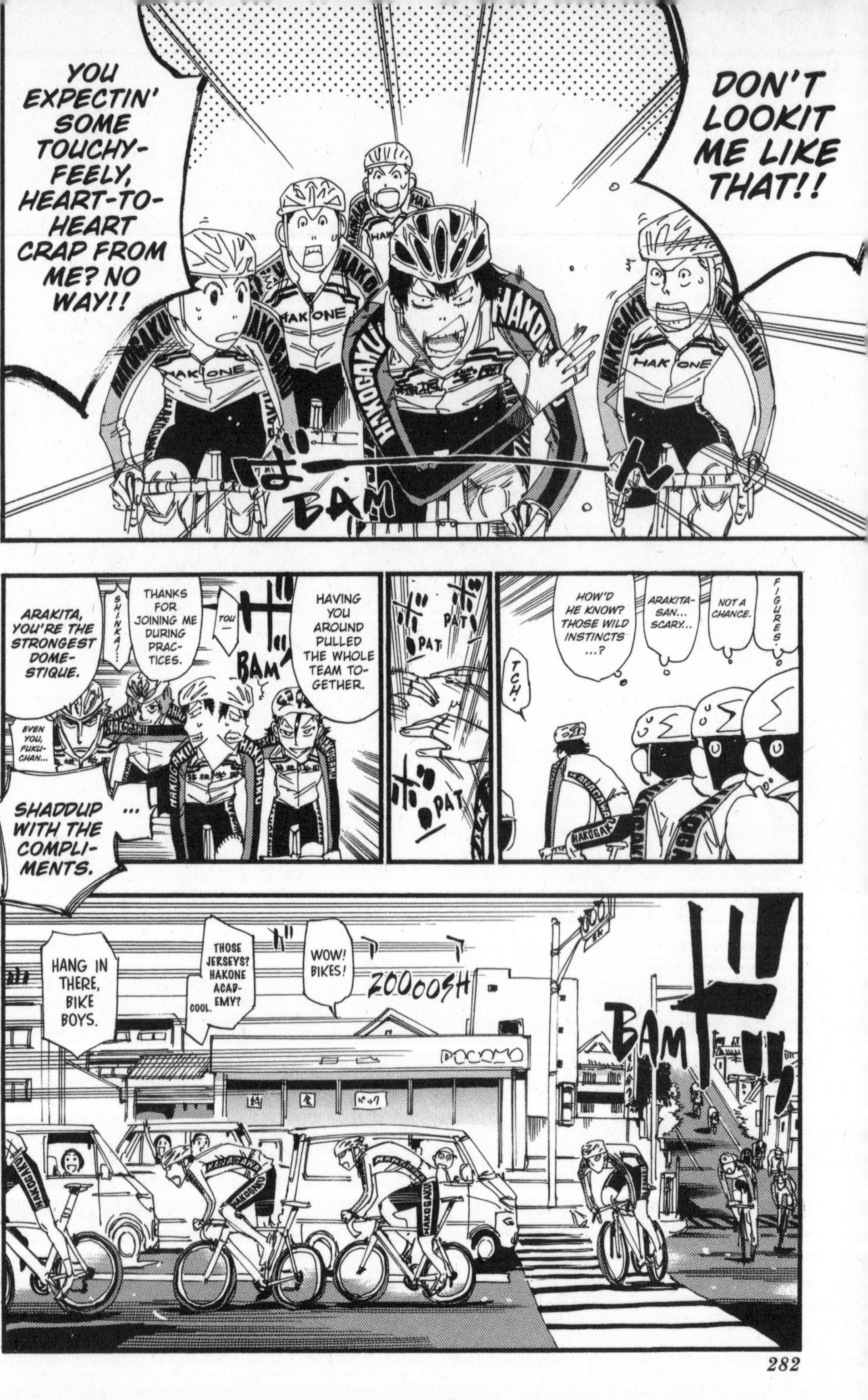
DON'T LOOKIT ME LIKE THAT!!
YOU EXPECTIN' SOME TOUCHY-FEELY, HEART-TO-HEART CRAP FROM ME? NO WAY!!
BAM
FIGURES.
NOT A CHANCE.
ARAKITA-SAN... SCARY...
HOW'D HE KNOW? THOSE WILD INSTINCTS...?
TCH.
PAT
PAT
PAT
HAVING YOU AROUND PULLED THE WHOLE TEAM TOGETHER.
TOU
BAM
THANKS FOR JOINING ME DURING PRACTICES.
SHINKAI?!
ARAKITA, YOU'RE THE STRONGEST DOMESTIQUE.
EVEN YOU, FUKU-CHAN...
...
SHADDUP WITH THE COMPLIMENTS.
BAM
ZOOOOSH
WOW! BIKES!
THOSE JERSEYS? HAKONE ACADEMY?
COOL.
HANG IN THERE, BIKE BOYS.

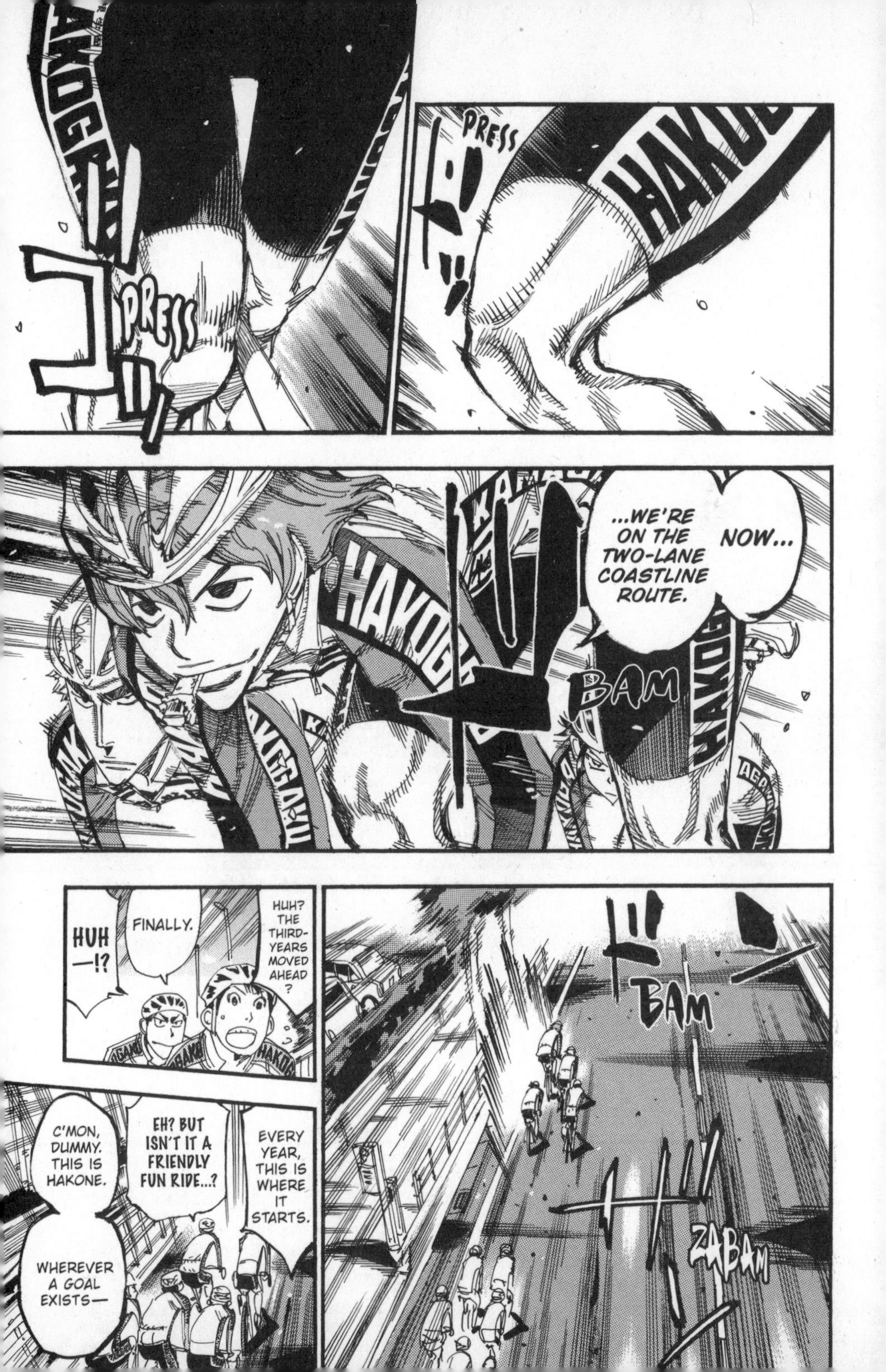
PRESS
PRESS
NOW...
...WE'RE ON THE TWO-LANE COASTLINE ROUTE.
BAM
BAM
ZABAM
HUH? THE THIRD-YEARS MOVED AHEAD?
FINALLY.
HUH—!?
EVERY YEAR, THIS IS WHERE IT STARTS.
EH? BUT ISN'T IT A FRIENDLY FUN RIDE...?
C'MON, DUMMY. THIS IS HAKONE.
WHEREVER A GOAL EXISTS—

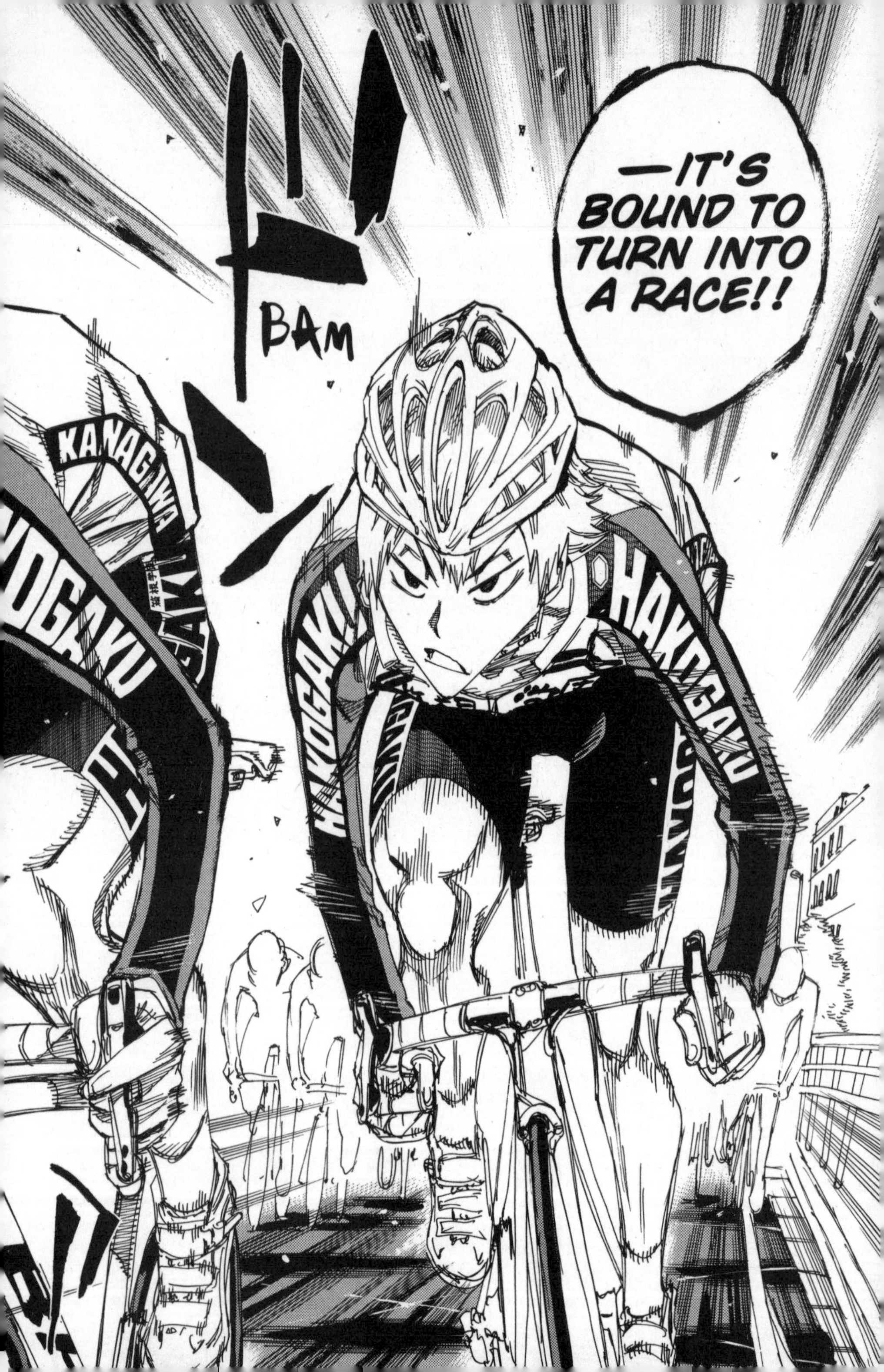
—IT'S BOUND TO TURN INTO A RACE!!
BAM
KANAGAWA
HAKOGAKU

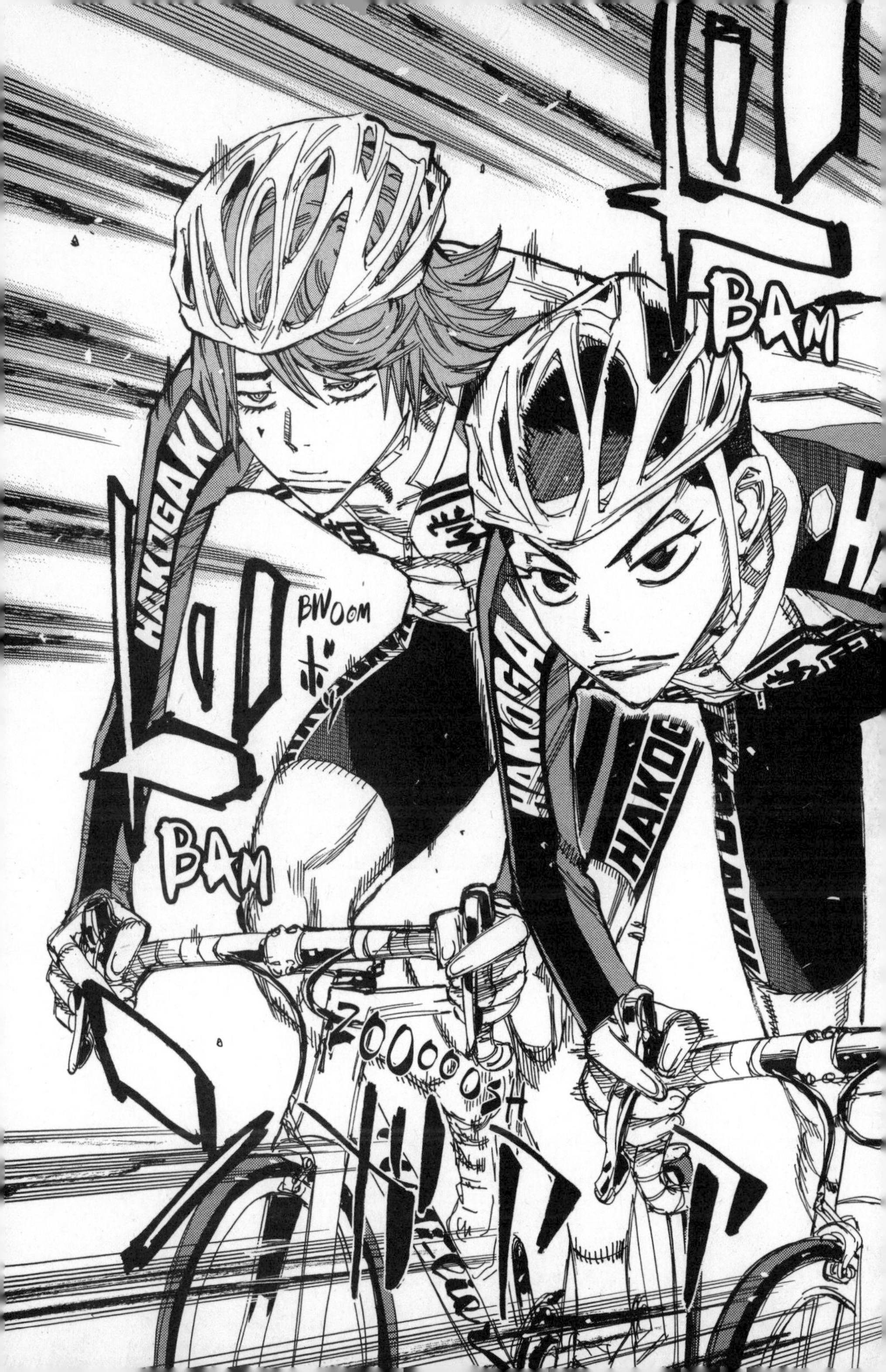
BAM
BWOOM
ボ
BAM
ZOOOOOSH

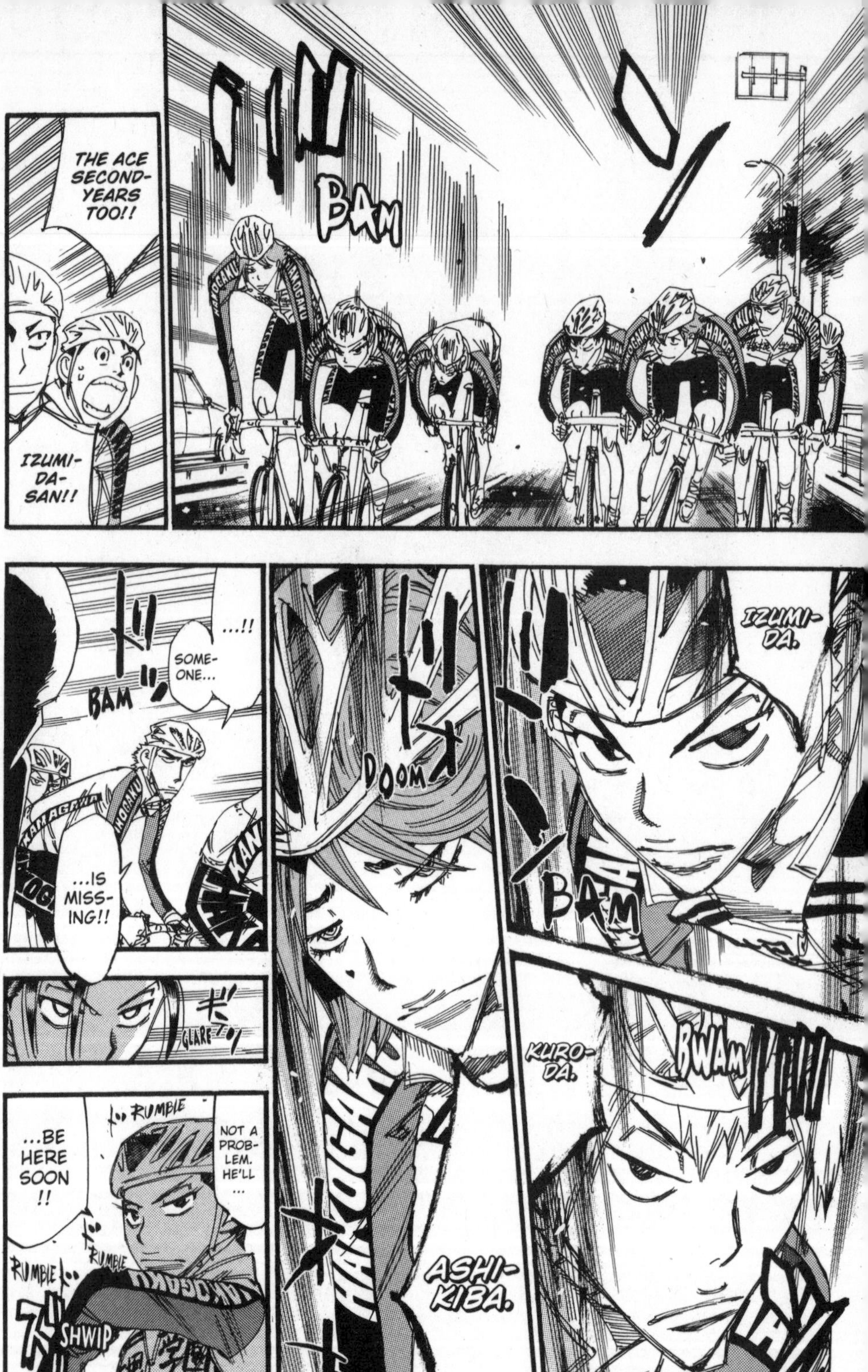
BAM
THE ACE SECOND-YEARS TOO!!
IZUMIDA-SAN!!
IZUMIDA.
BAM
KURODA.
BWAM
DOOM
ASHIKIBA.
...!!
SOMEONE...
BAM
...IS MISSING!!
GLARE
NOT A PROBLEM. HE'LL...
...BE HERE SOON!!
RUMBLE
RUMBLE
RUMBLE
SHWIP

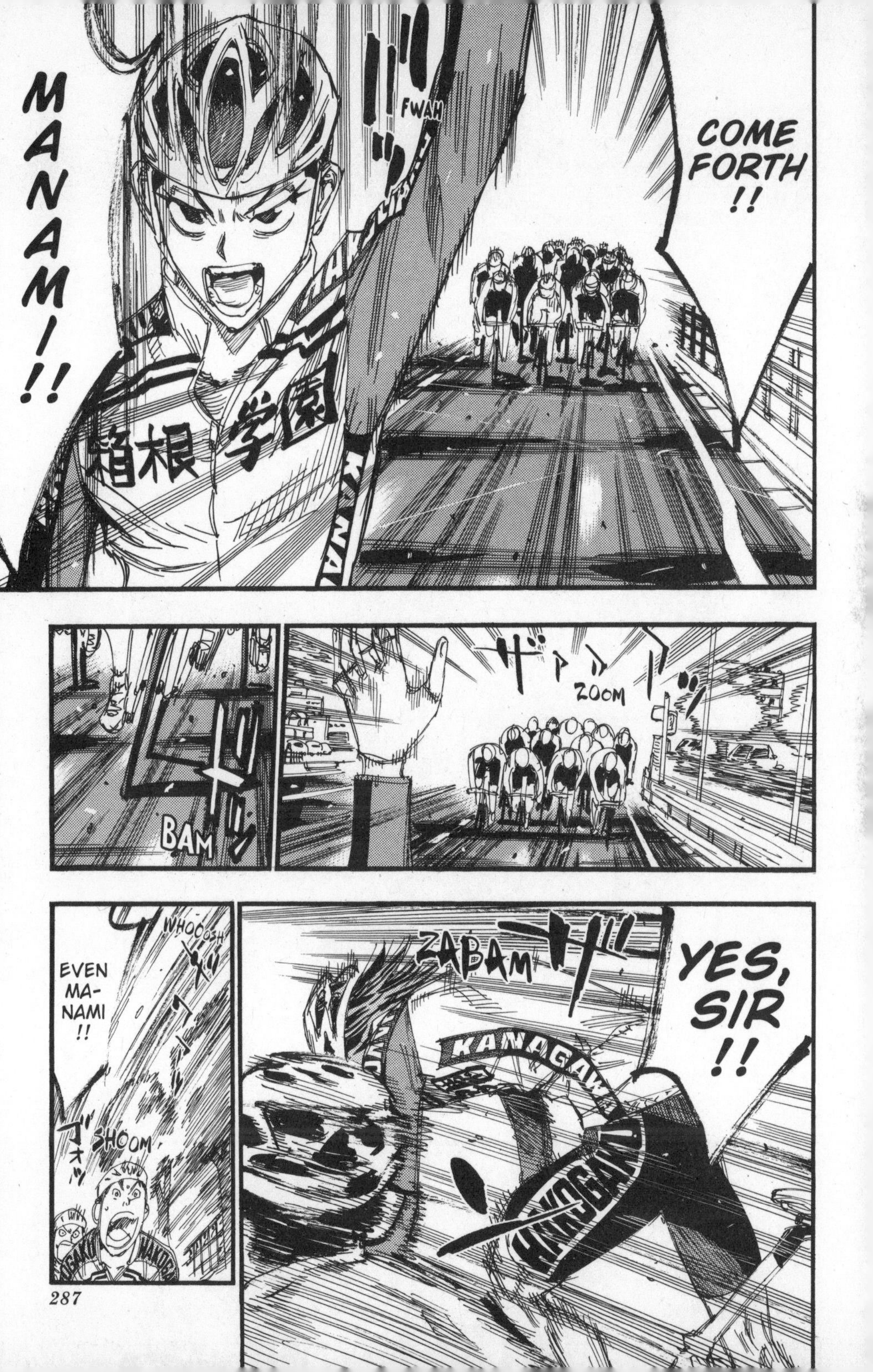
COME FORTH !!
FWAH
MANAMI!!
ZOOM
BAM
ZABAM
YES, SIR !!
WHOOOSH
EVEN MA-NAMI !!
SHOOM

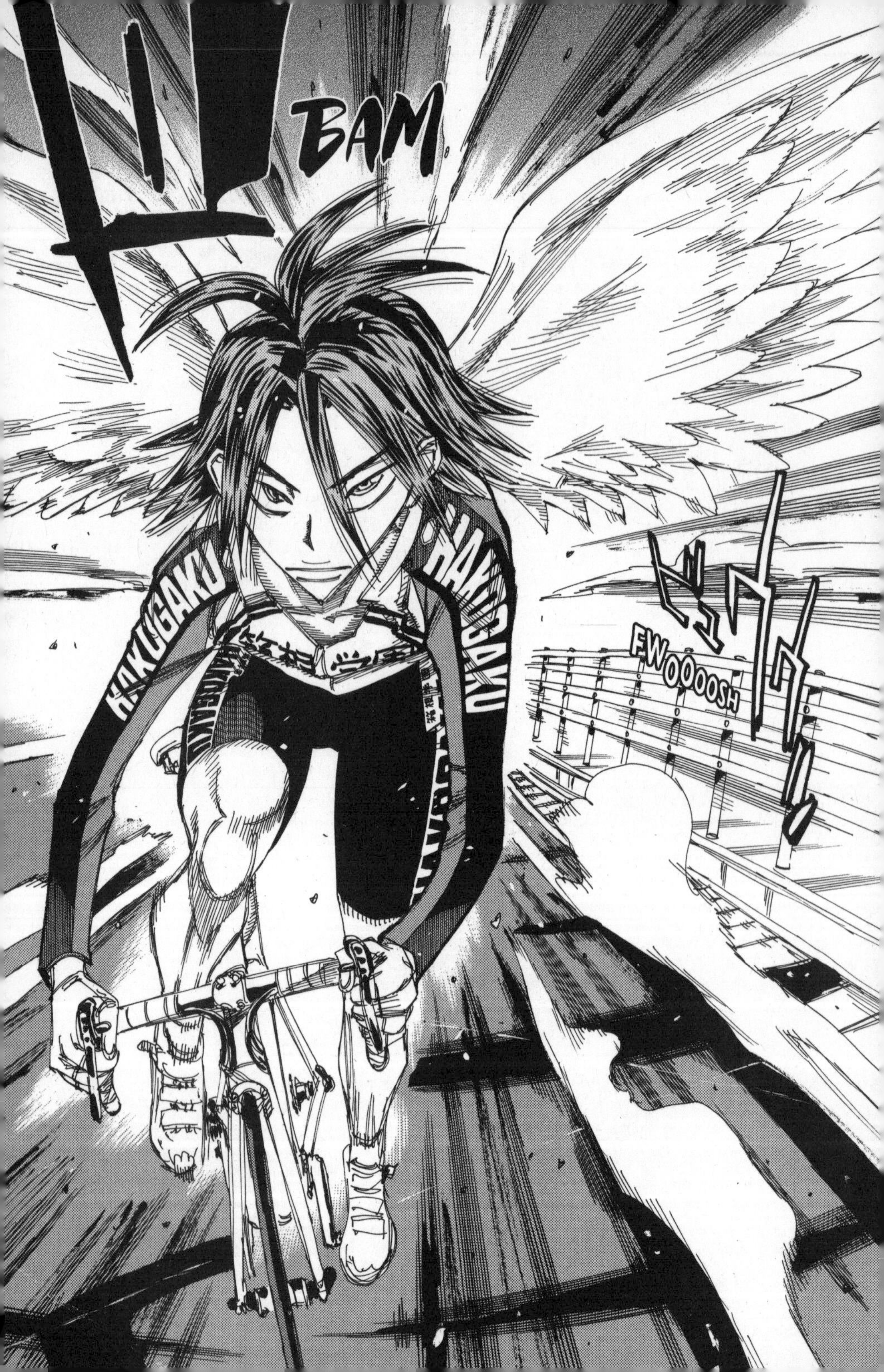
BAM
FWOOOOSH
HAKOGAKU
HAKOGAKU

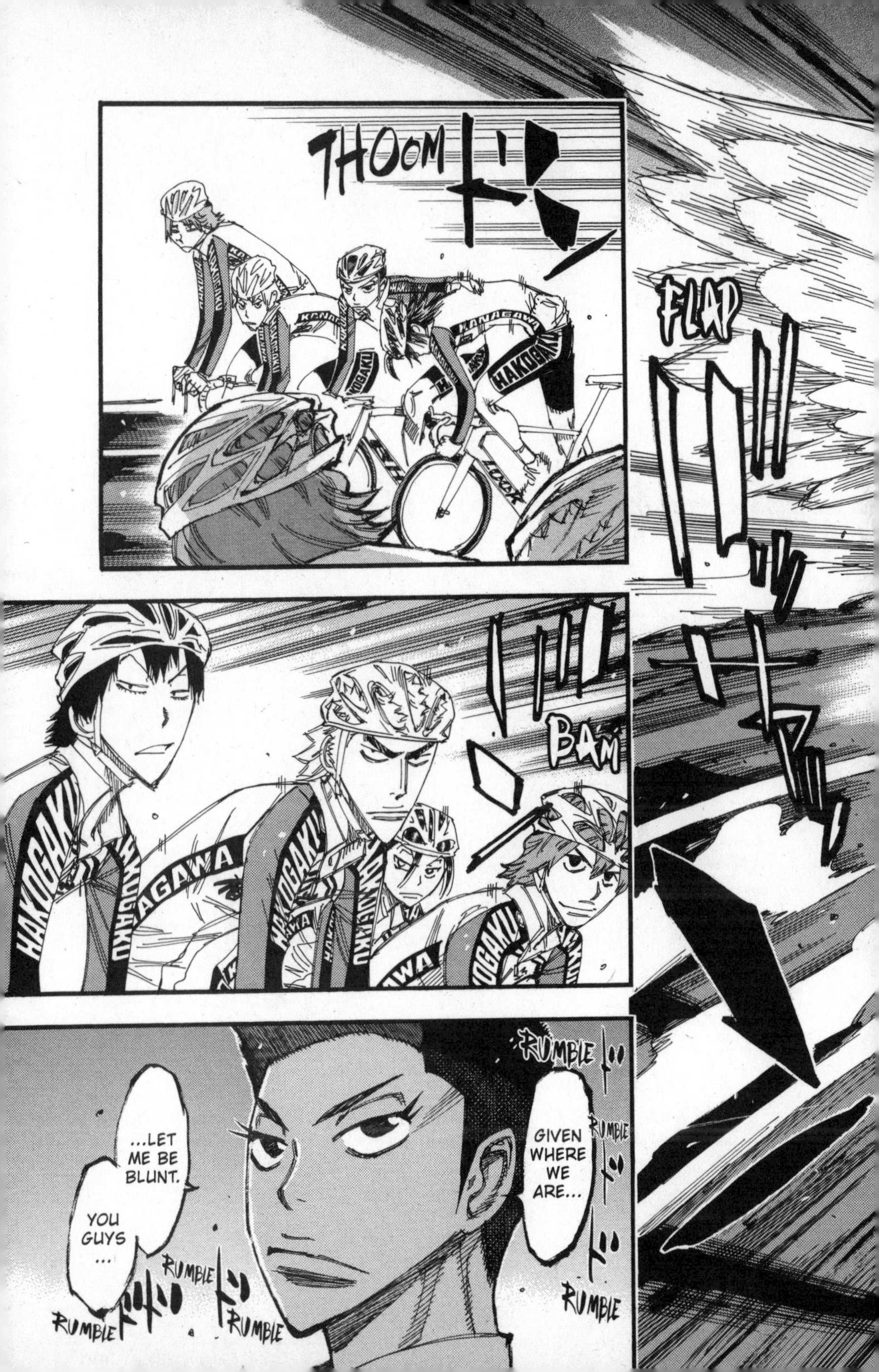
FLAP
THOOM
BAM
RUMBLE
GIVEN WHERE WE ARE...
RUMBLE
RUMBLE
...LET ME BE BLUNT.
YOU GUYS ...
RUMBLE
RUMBLE
RUMBLE

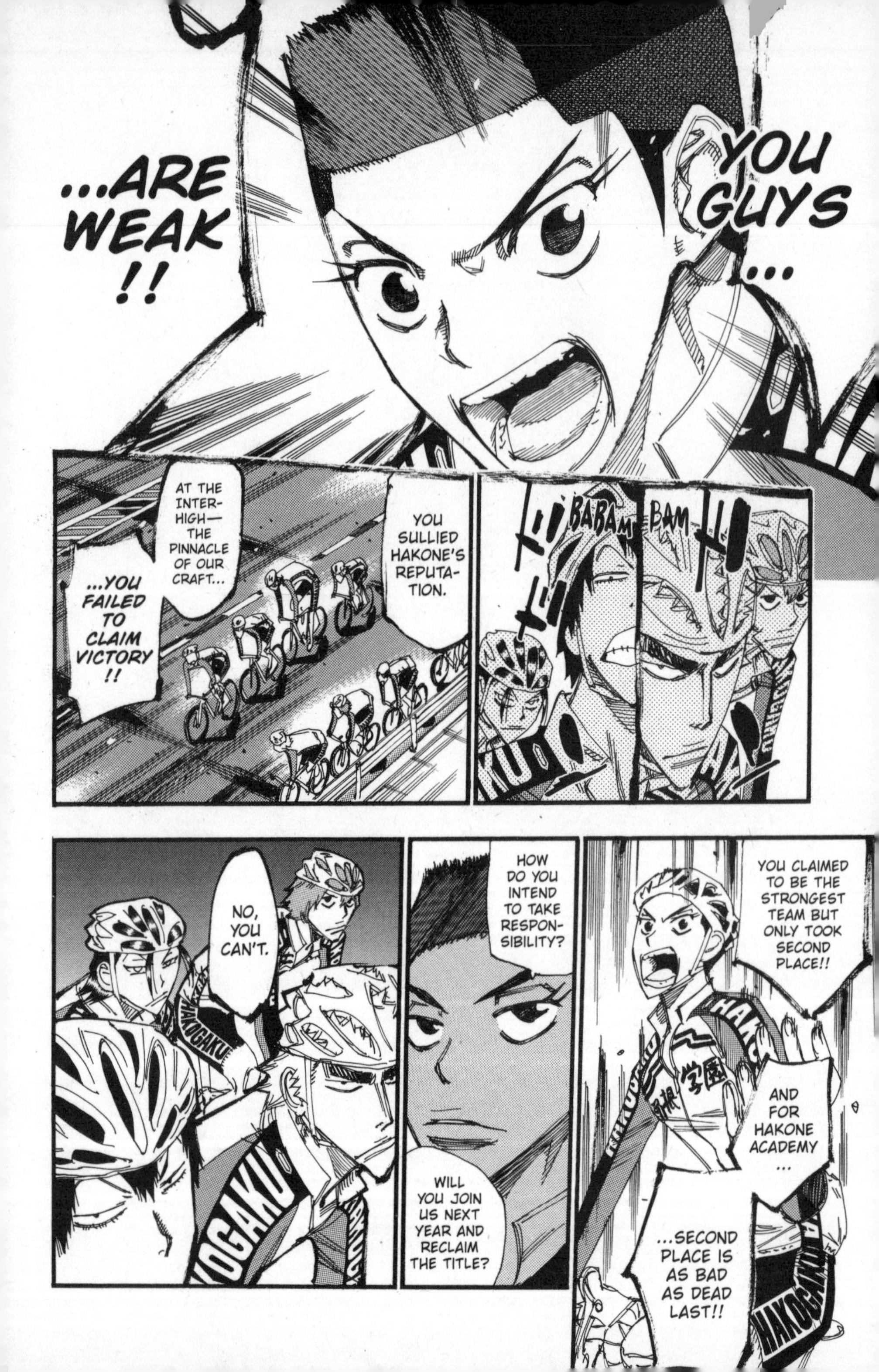
YOU GUYS ...
...ARE WEAK!!
BABAM BAM
YOU SULLIED HAKONE'S REPUTATION.
AT THE INTER-HIGH— THE PINNACLE OF OUR CRAFT...
...YOU FAILED TO CLAIM VICTORY!!
YOU CLAIMED TO BE THE STRONGEST TEAM BUT ONLY TOOK SECOND PLACE!!
AND FOR HAKONE ACADEMY ...
...SECOND PLACE IS AS BAD AS DEAD LAST!!
HOW DO YOU INTEND TO TAKE RESPON-SIBILITY?
WILL YOU JOIN US NEXT YEAR AND RECLAIM THE TITLE?
NO, YOU CAN'T.

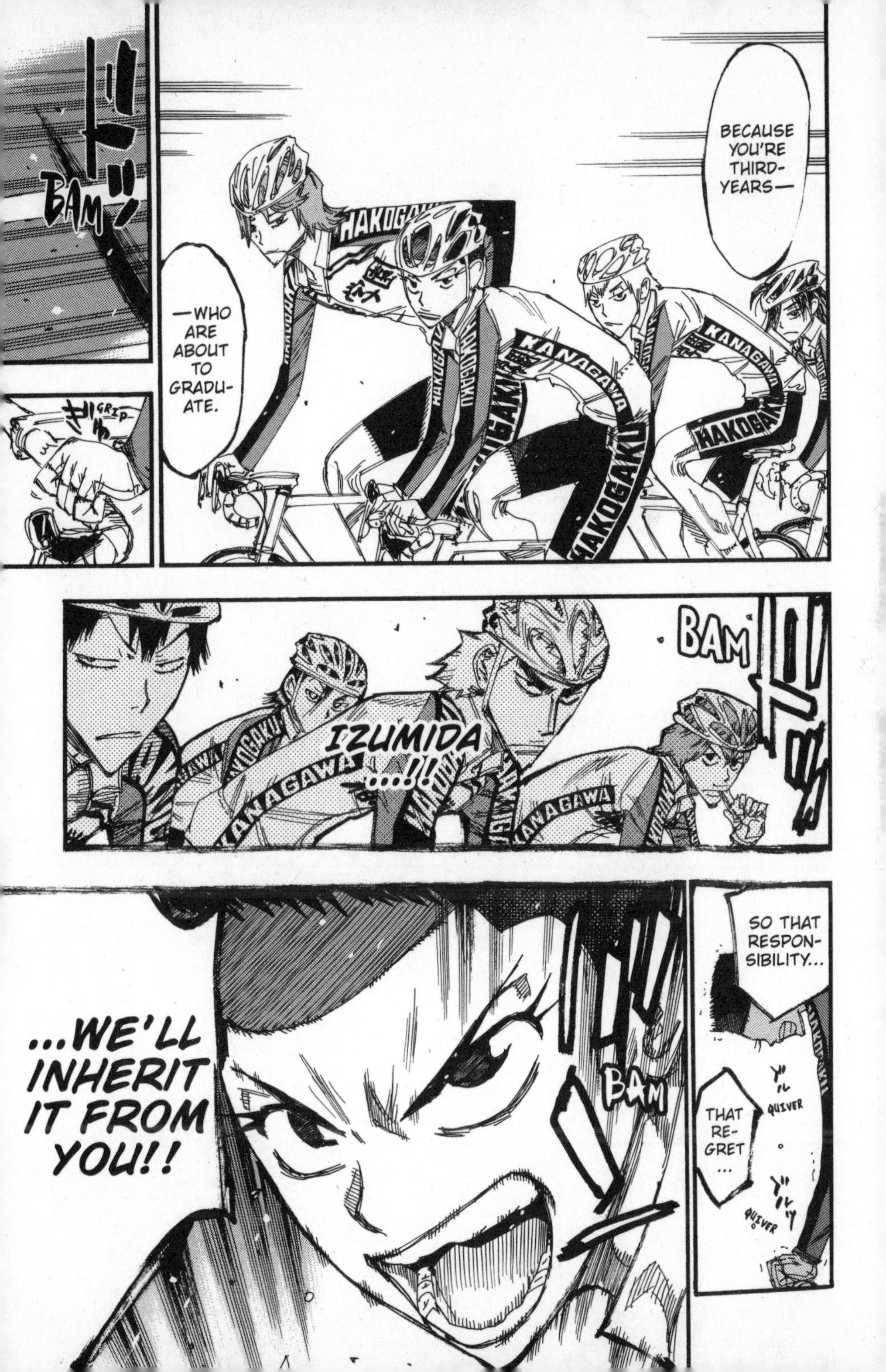

BECAUSE YOU'RE THIRD-YEARS—
—WHO ARE ABOUT TO GRADUATE.
BAM
GRIP
BAM
IZUMIDA ...!!
SO THAT RESPONSIBILITY...
QUIVER
THAT REGRET...
QUIVER
BAM
...WE'LL INHERIT IT FROM YOU!!

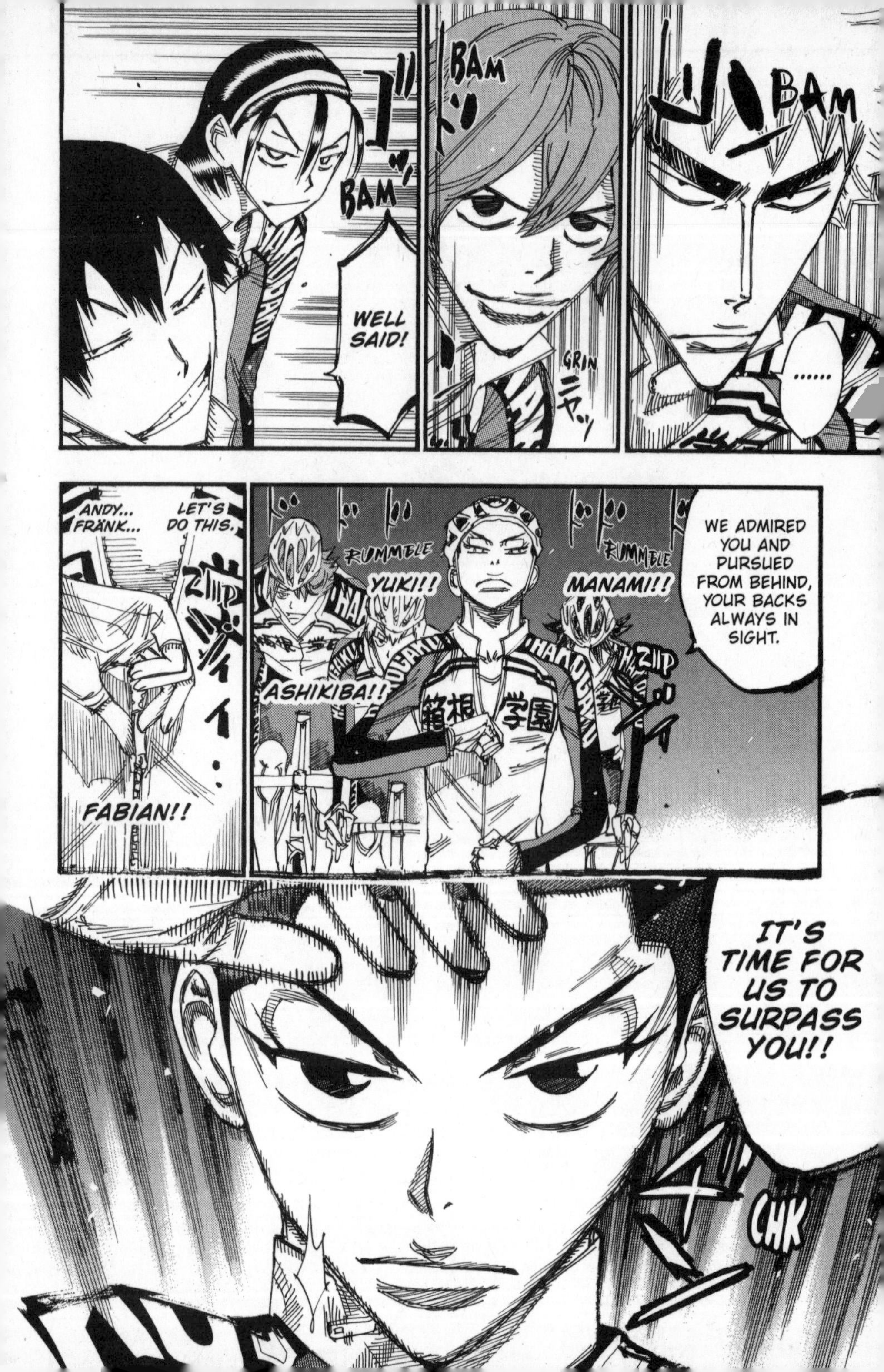
BAM
......
BAM
GRIN
BAM
WELL SAID!
WE ADMIRED YOU AND PURSUED FROM BEHIND, YOUR BACKS ALWAYS IN SIGHT.
RUMMBLE
MANAMI!!
ZIP
RUMMBLE
YUKI!!
ASHIKIBA!!
LET'S DO THIS.
ANDY... FRÄNK...
ZIP
FABIAN!!
IT'S TIME FOR US TO SURPASS YOU!!
CHK

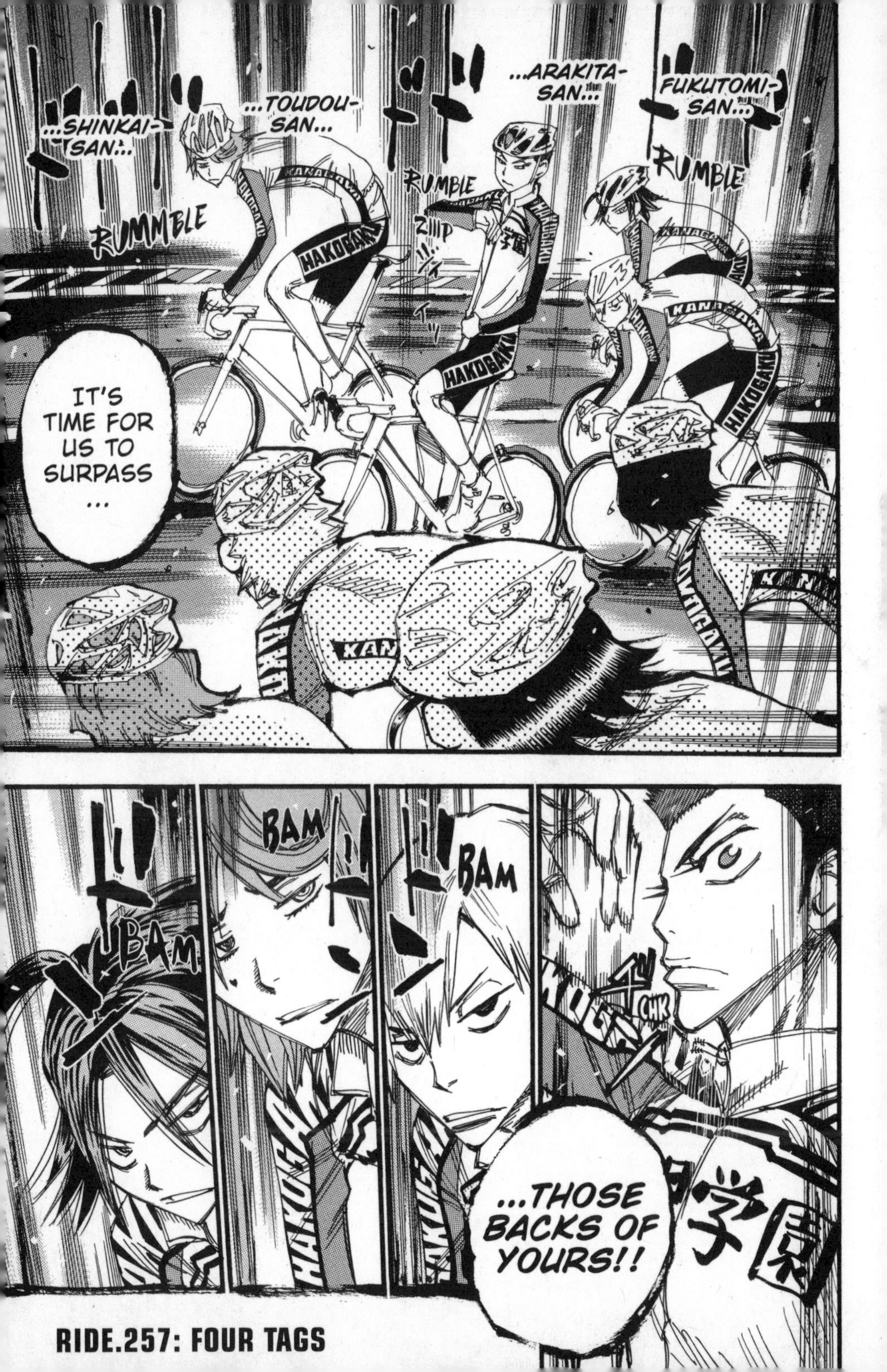
FUKUTOMI-SAN...
RUMBLE
...ARAKITA-SAN...
RUMBLE
ZIIIP
...TOUDOU-SAN...
...SHINKAI-SAN...
RUMMBLE
IT'S TIME FOR US TO SURPASS ...
CHK
BAM
BAM
BAM
...THOSE BACKS OF YOURS!!

RIDE.257: FOUR TAGS

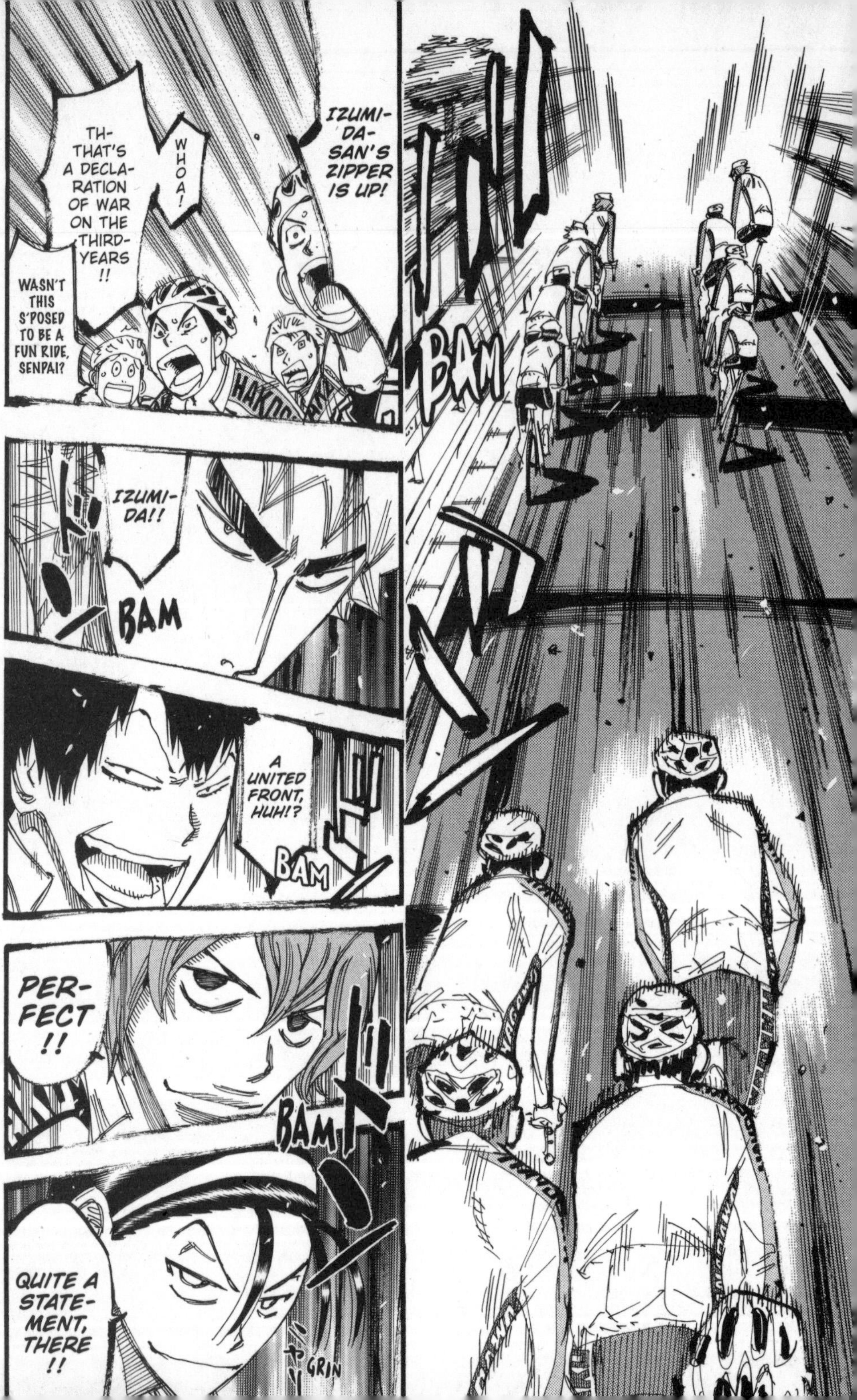
BAM
IZUMI-DA-SAN'S ZIPPER IS UP!
WHOA!
TH-THAT'S A DECLARATION OF WAR ON THE THIRD-YEARS!!
WASN'T THIS S'POSED TO BE A FUN RIDE, SENPAI?
IZUMI-DA!!
BAM
A UNITED FRONT, HUH!?
BAM
PERFECT!!
BAM
QUITE A STATEMENT, THERE!!
GRIN

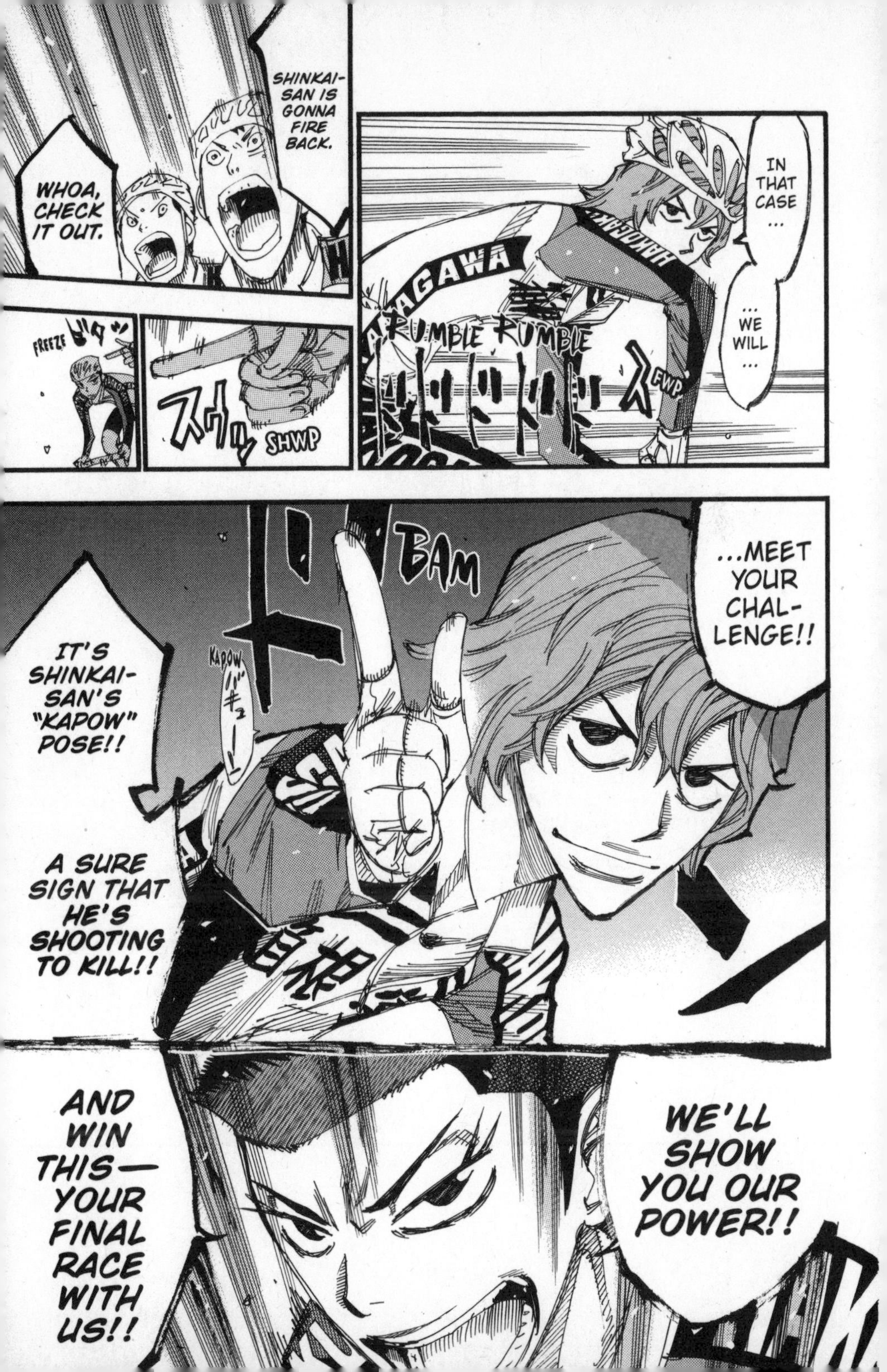
IN THAT CASE ...
... WE WILL ...
RUMBLE RUMBLE
FWP
SHINKAI-SAN IS GONNA FIRE BACK.
WHOA, CHECK IT OUT.
SHWP
FREEZE
...MEET YOUR CHAL-LENGE!!
BAM
KAPOW
IT'S SHINKAI-SAN'S "KAPOW" POSE!!
A SURE SIGN THAT HE'S SHOOTING TO KILL!!
WE'LL SHOW YOU OUR POWER!!
AND WIN THIS—YOUR FINAL RACE WITH US!!

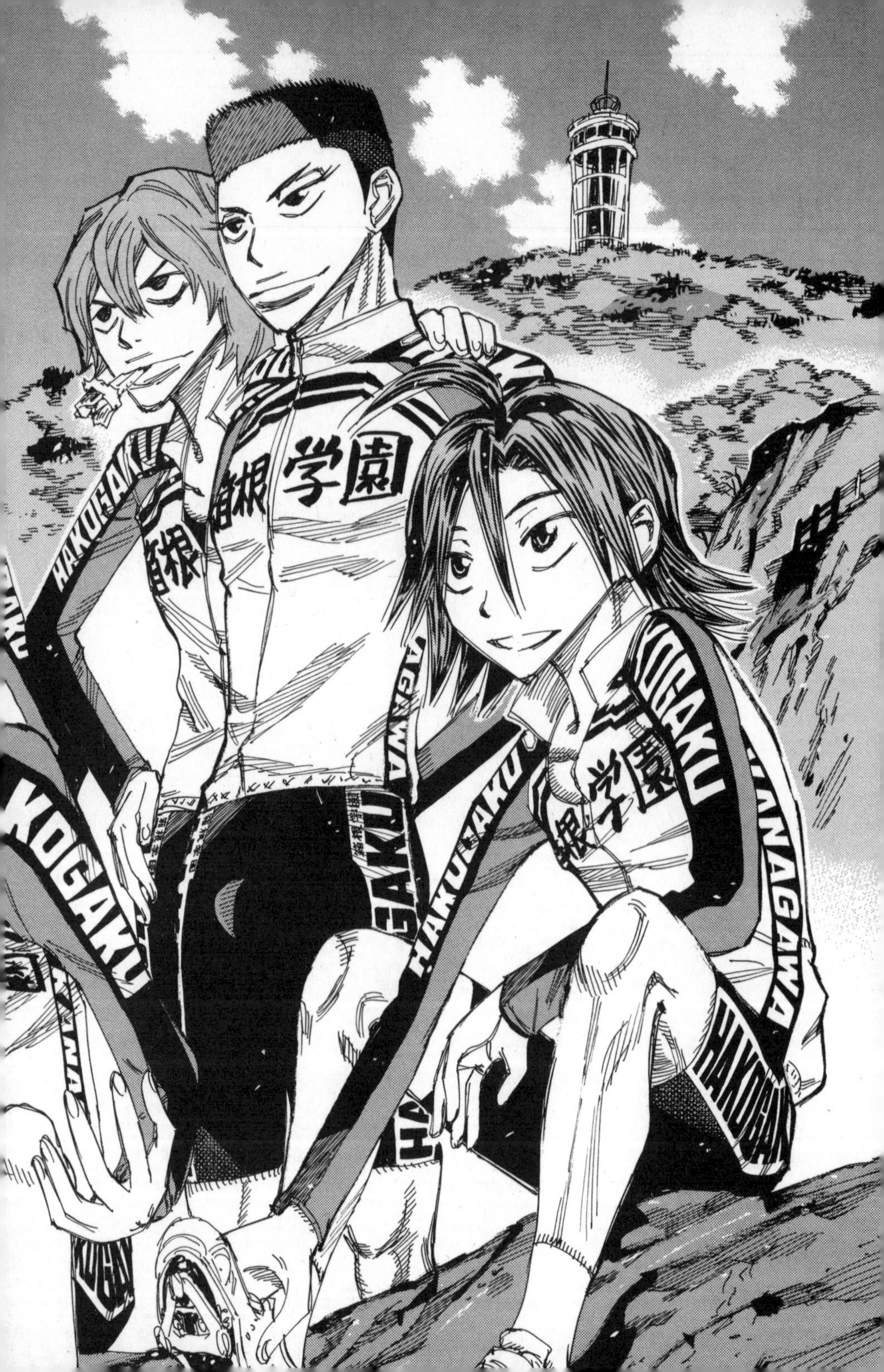
箱根学園
HAKOGAKU
KANAGAWA

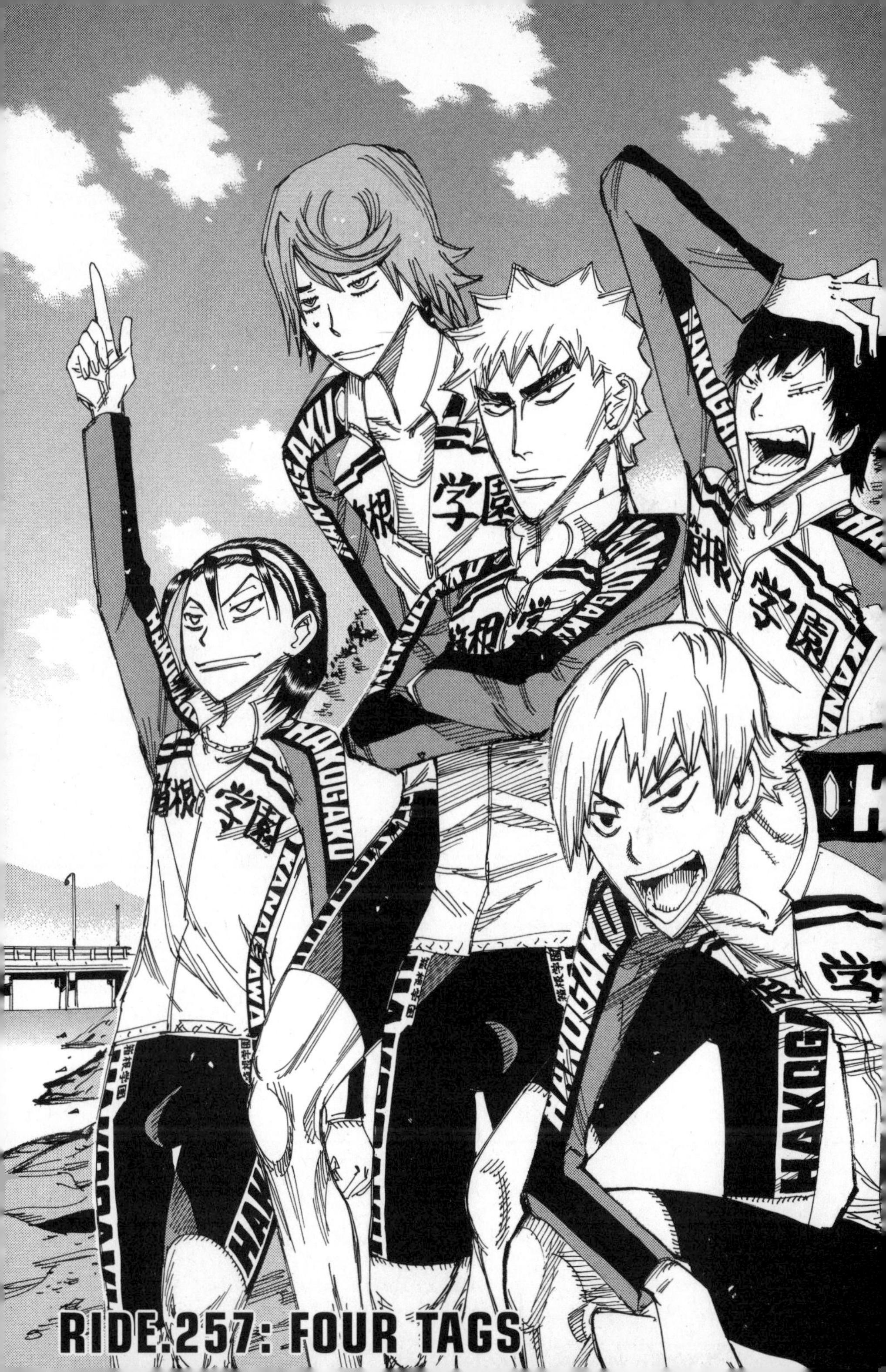

RIDE.257: FOUR TAGS

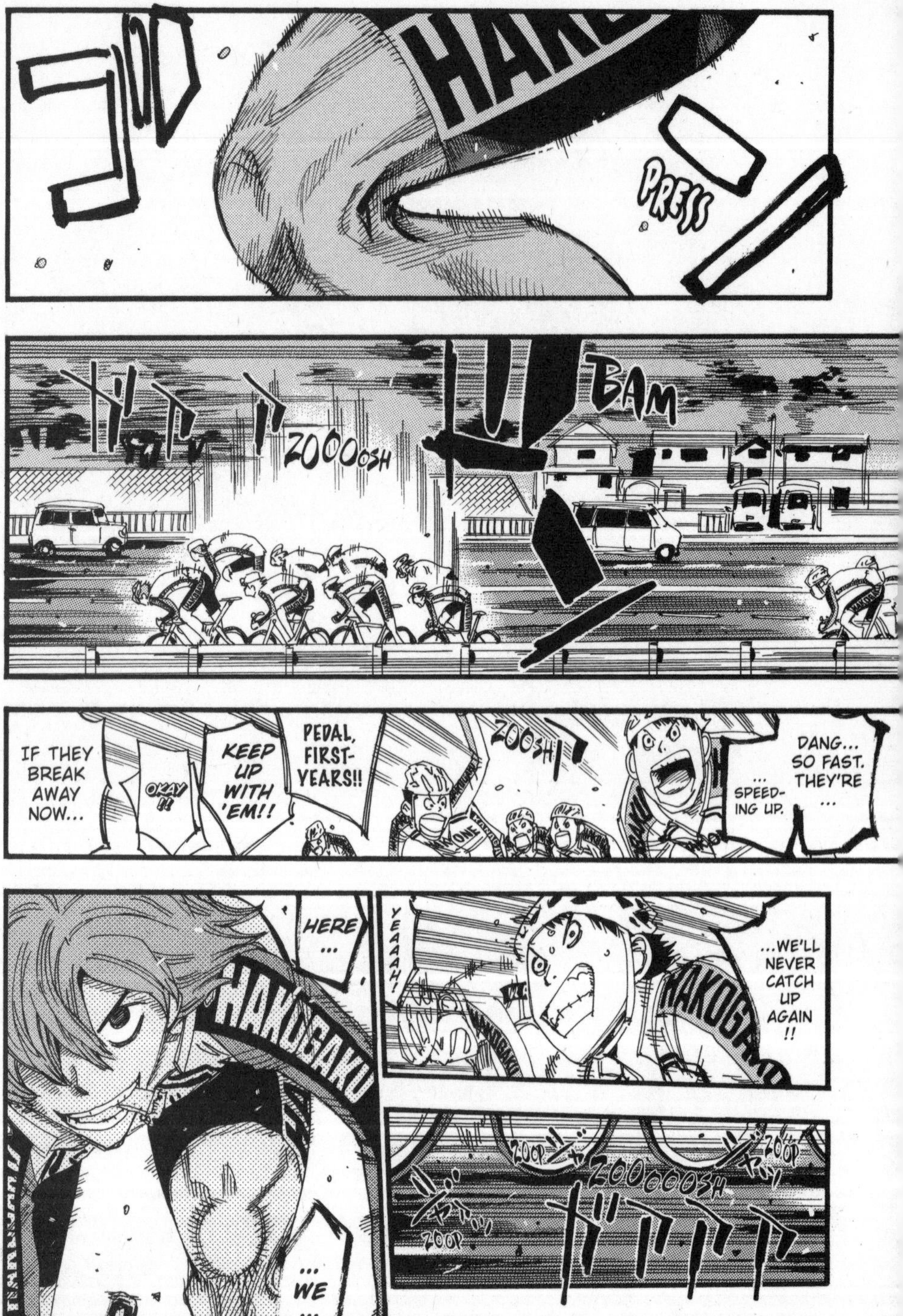
PRESS
BAM
ZOOOOSH
DANG... SO FAST. THEY'RE ...
... SPEEDING UP.
ZOOSH
PEDAL, FIRST-YEARS!!
KEEP UP WITH 'EM!!
OKAY!!
IF THEY BREAK AWAY NOW...
...WE'LL NEVER CATCH UP AGAIN!!
YEAAAH!
ZOOP
ZOOOOOSH
ZOOP
ZOOP
HERE ...
... WE ...

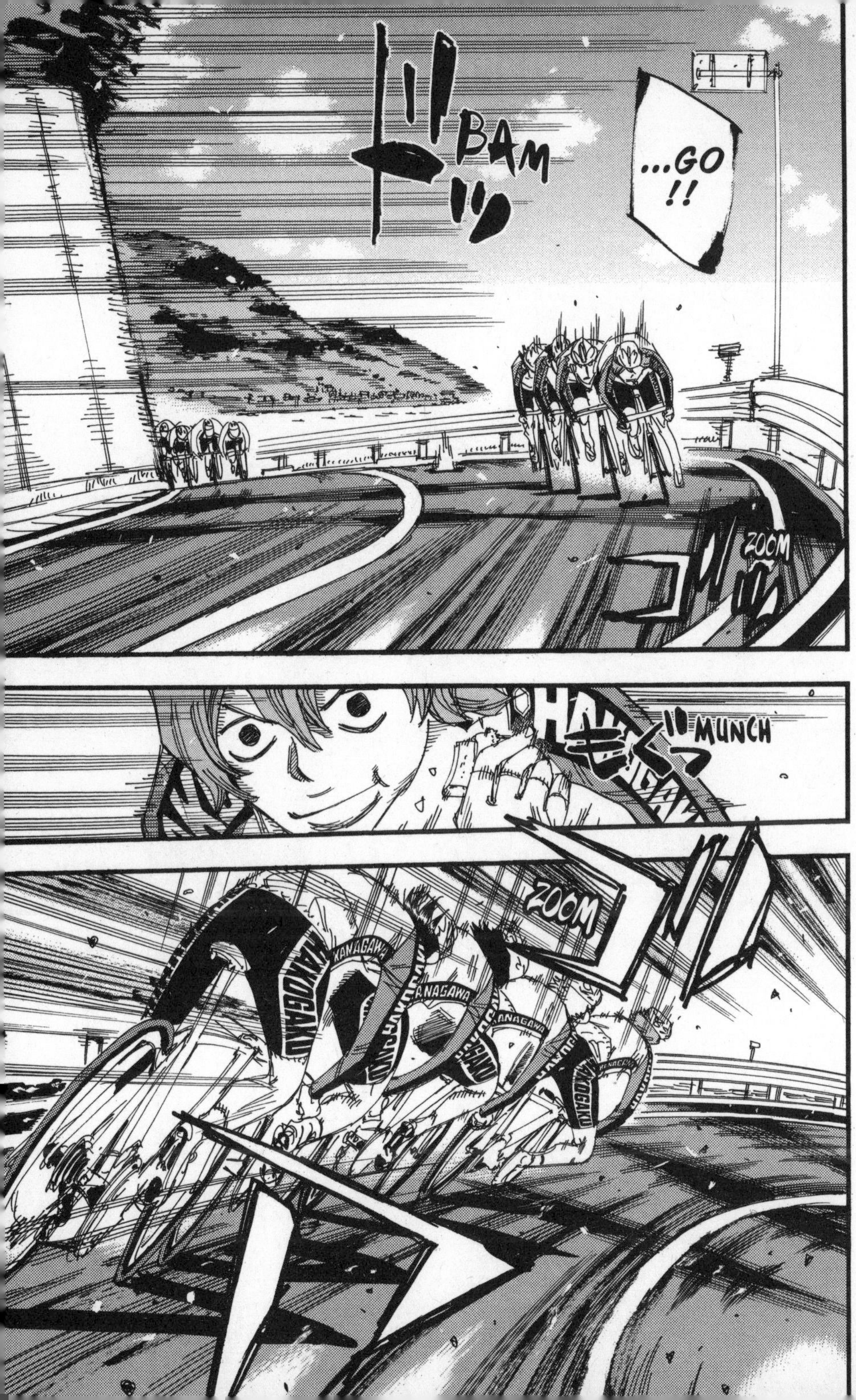
...GO !!
BAM
ZOOM
MUNCH
ZOOM

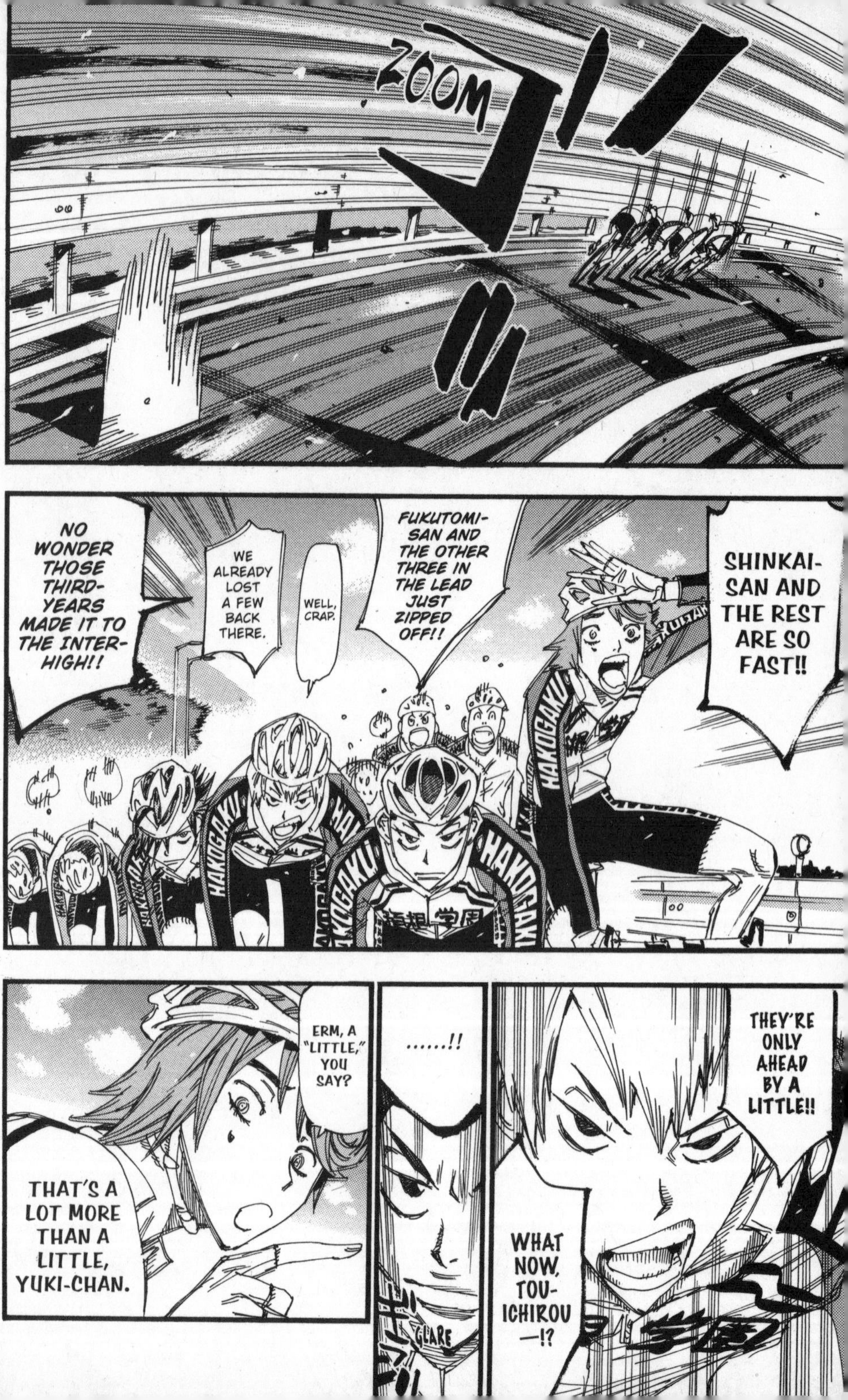
ZOOM
SHINKAI-SAN AND THE REST ARE SO FAST!!
FUKUTOMI-SAN AND THE OTHER THREE IN THE LEAD JUST ZIPPED OFF!!
WELL, CRAP.
WE ALREADY LOST A FEW BACK THERE.
NO WONDER THOSE THIRD-YEARS MADE IT TO THE INTER-HIGH!!
THEY'RE ONLY AHEAD BY A LITTLE!!
WHAT NOW, TOU-ICHIROU—!?
......!!
GLARE
ERM, A "LITTLE," YOU SAY?
THAT'S A LOT MORE THAN A LITTLE, YUKI-CHAN.

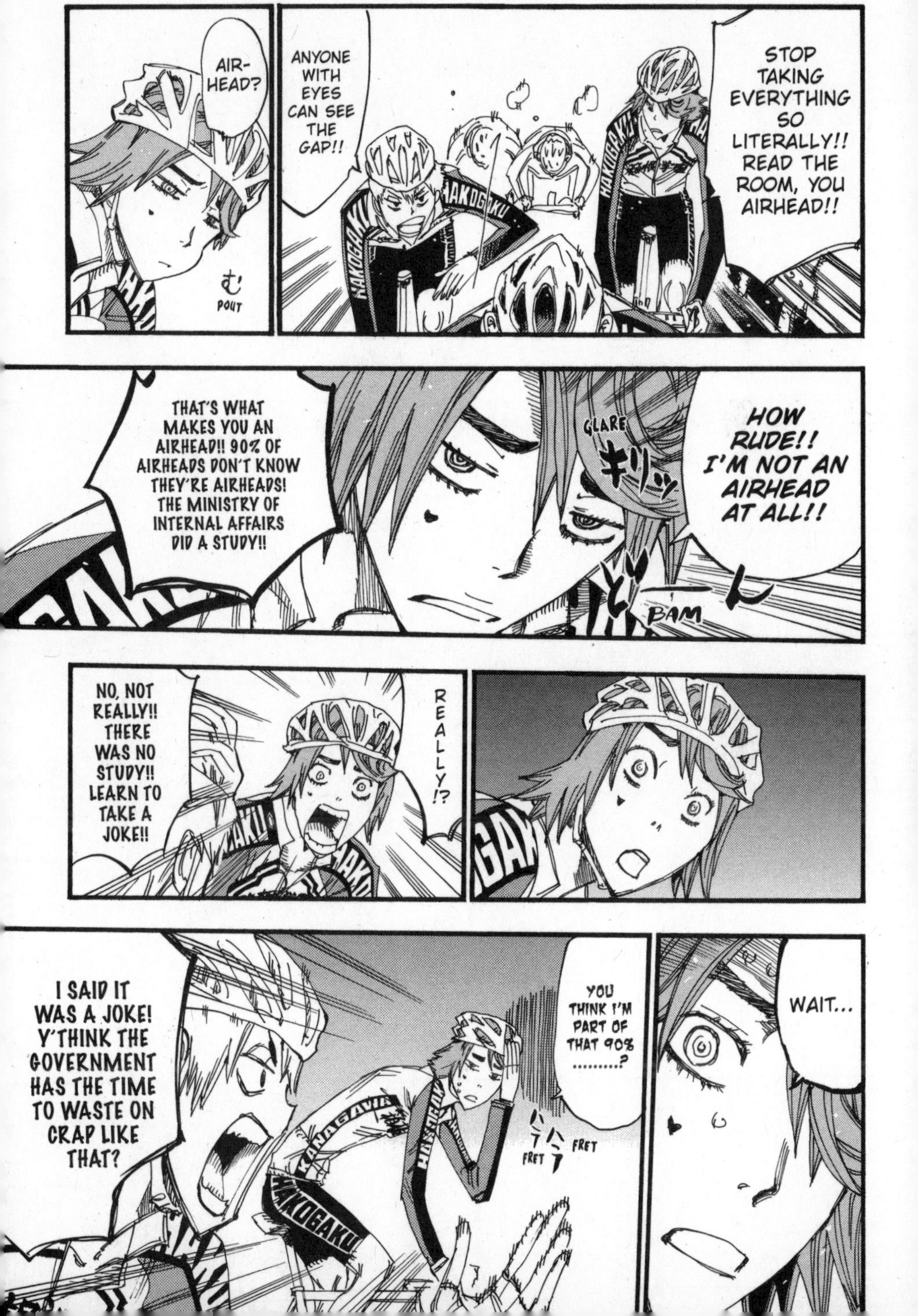
STOP TAKING EVERYTHING SO LITERALLY!! READ THE ROOM, YOU AIRHEAD!!
ANYONE WITH EYES CAN SEE THE GAP!!
AIR-HEAD?
POUT
HOW RUDE!! I'M NOT AN AIRHEAD AT ALL!!
GLARE
BAM
THAT'S WHAT MAKES YOU AN AIRHEAD!! 90% OF AIRHEADS DON'T KNOW THEY'RE AIRHEADS! THE MINISTRY OF INTERNAL AFFAIRS DID A STUDY!!
REALLY!?
NO, NOT REALLY!! THERE WAS NO STUDY!! LEARN TO TAKE A JOKE!!
WAIT...
YOU THINK I'M PART OF THAT 90% ....?
FRET FRET
I SAID IT WAS A JOKE! Y'THINK THE GOVERNMENT HAS THE TIME TO WASTE ON CRAP LIKE THAT?

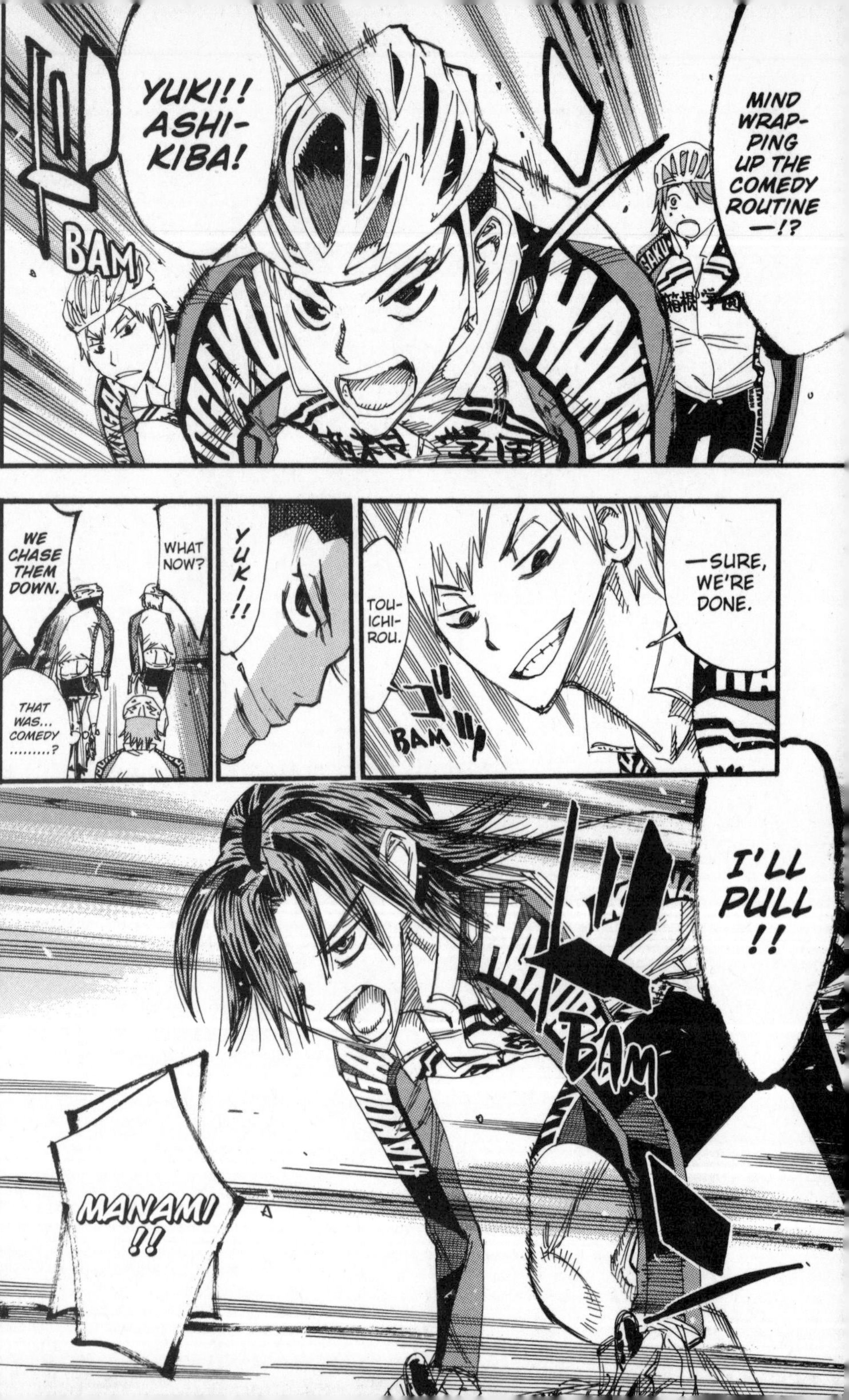
MIND WRAPPING UP THE COMEDY ROUTINE—!?
YUKI!! ASHIKIBA!
BAM
—SURE, WE'RE DONE.
TOUICHIROU.
BAM
YUKI!!
WHAT NOW?
WE CHASE THEM DOWN.
THAT WAS... COMEDY ....?
I'LL PULL!!
BAM
MANAMI!!

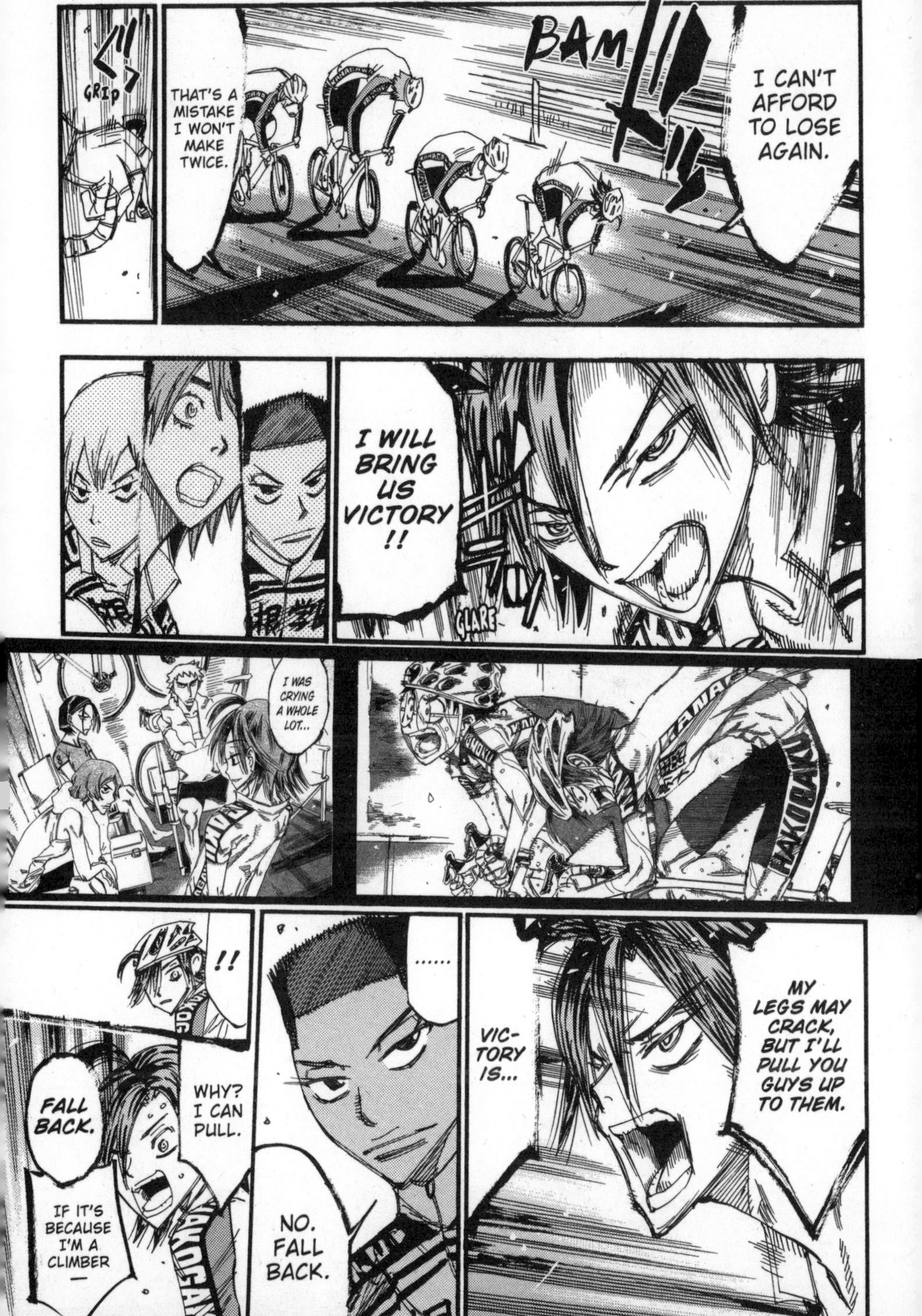
BAM
I CAN'T AFFORD TO LOSE AGAIN.
THAT'S A MISTAKE I WON'T MAKE TWICE.
GRIP
I WILL BRING US VICTORY!!
GLARE
I WAS CRYING A WHOLE LOT...
MY LEGS MAY CRACK, BUT I'LL PULL YOU GUYS UP TO THEM.
VIC-TORY IS...
......
NO. FALL BACK.
!!
FALL BACK.
WHY? I CAN PULL.
IF IT'S BECAUSE I'M A CLIMBER—

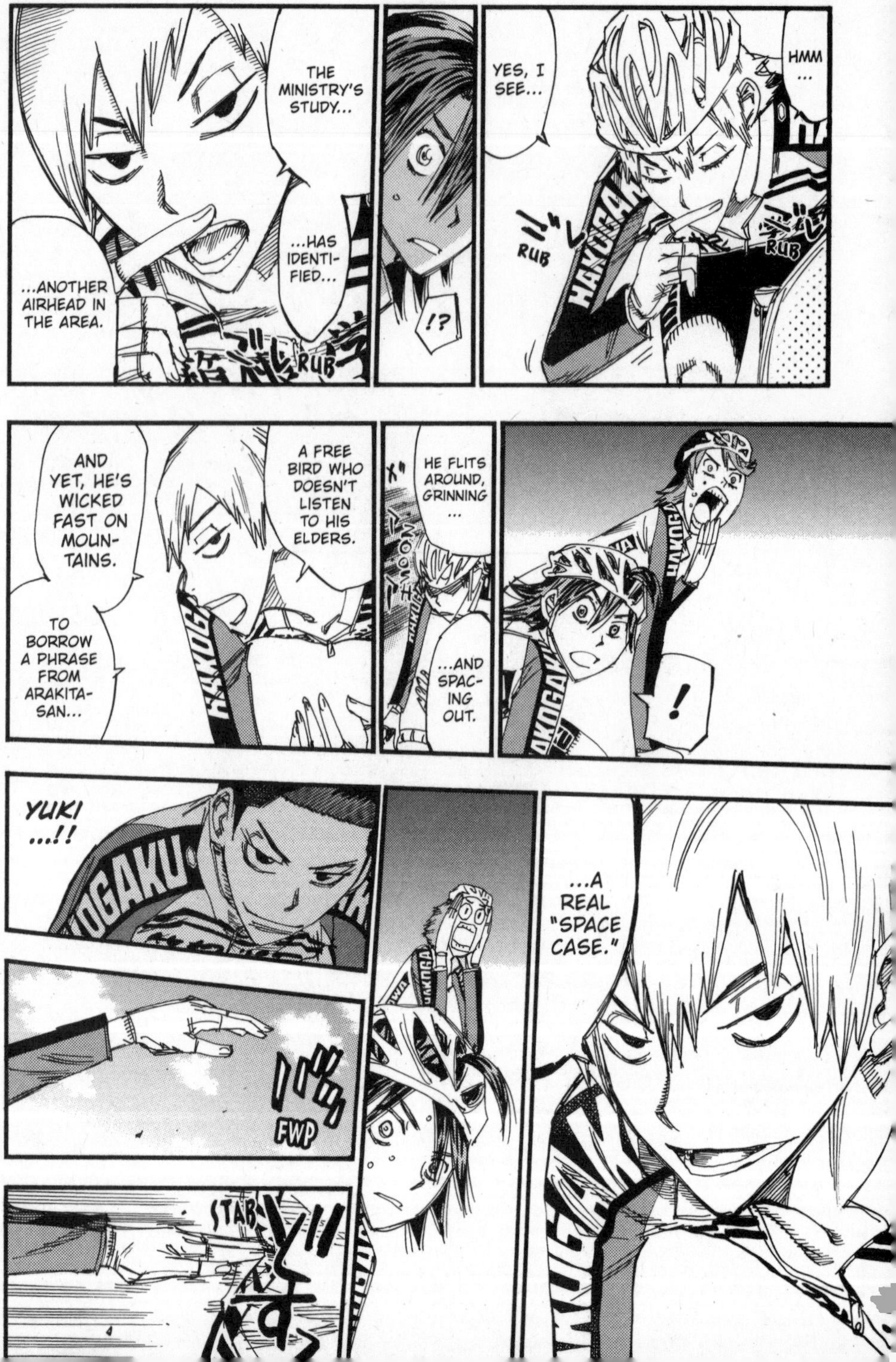
HMM ...
YES, I SEE...
RUB
RUB
!?
THE MINISTRY'S STUDY...
...HAS IDENTIFIED...
...ANOTHER AIRHEAD IN THE AREA.
RUB
!
HE FLITS AROUND, GRINNING ...
...AND SPACING OUT.
A FREE BIRD WHO DOESN'T LISTEN TO HIS ELDERS.
AND YET, HE'S WICKED FAST ON MOUNTAINS.
TO BORROW A PHRASE FROM ARAKITA-SAN...
...A REAL "SPACE CASE."
YUKI ...!!
FWP
STAB

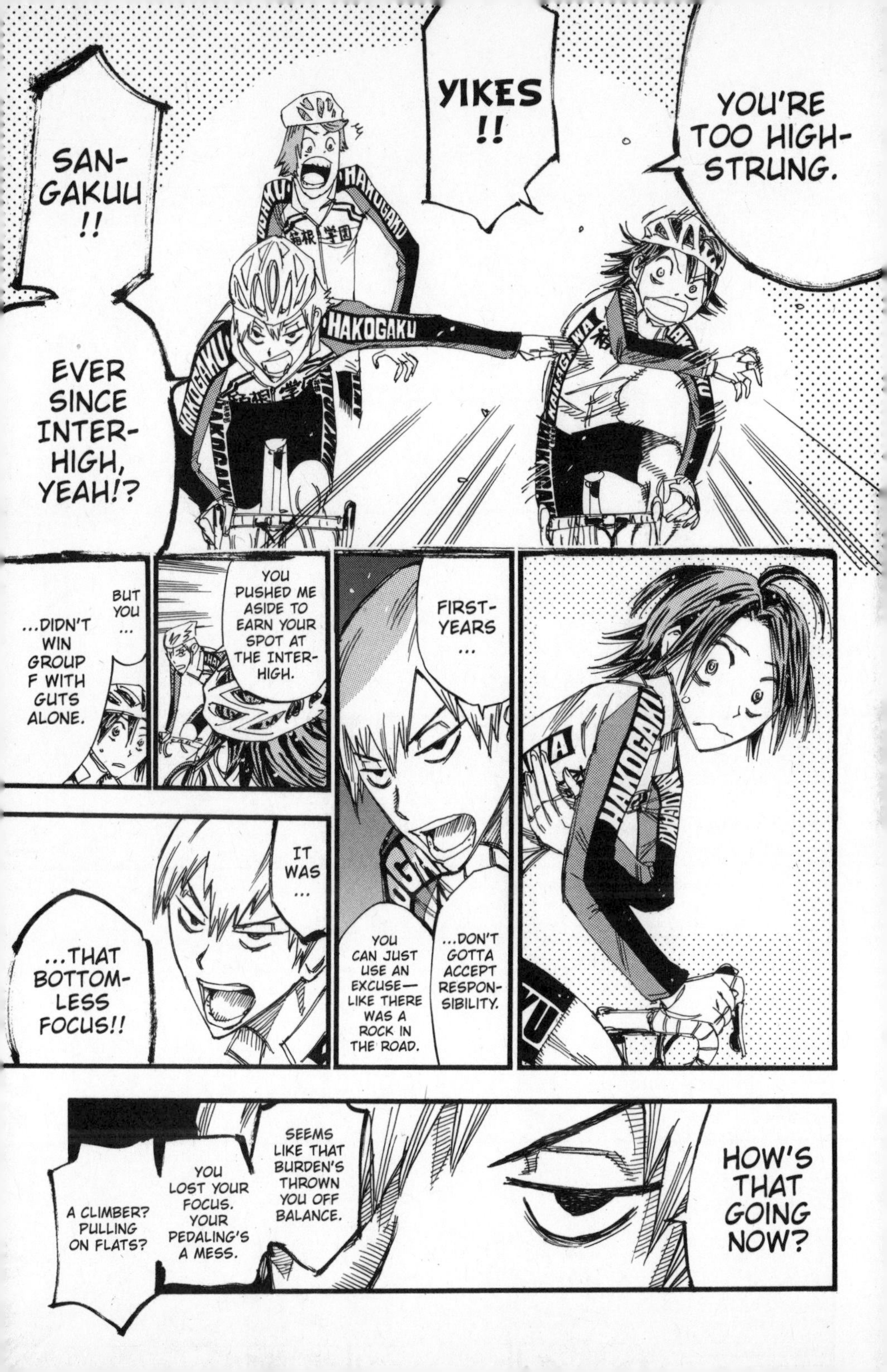
YOU'RE TOO HIGH-STRUNG.
YIKES!!
SAN-GAKUU!!
EVER SINCE INTER-HIGH, YEAH!?
FIRST-YEARS...
...DON'T GOTTA ACCEPT RESPONSIBILITY.
YOU CAN JUST USE AN EXCUSE—LIKE THERE WAS A ROCK IN THE ROAD.
YOU PUSHED ME ASIDE TO EARN YOUR SPOT AT THE INTER-HIGH.
BUT YOU...
...DIDN'T WIN GROUP F WITH GUTS ALONE.
IT WAS...
...THAT BOTTOMLESS FOCUS!!
HOW'S THAT GOING NOW?
SEEMS LIKE THAT BURDEN'S THROWN YOU OFF BALANCE.
YOU LOST YOUR FOCUS. YOUR PEDALING'S A MESS.
A CLIMBER? PULLING ON FLATS?

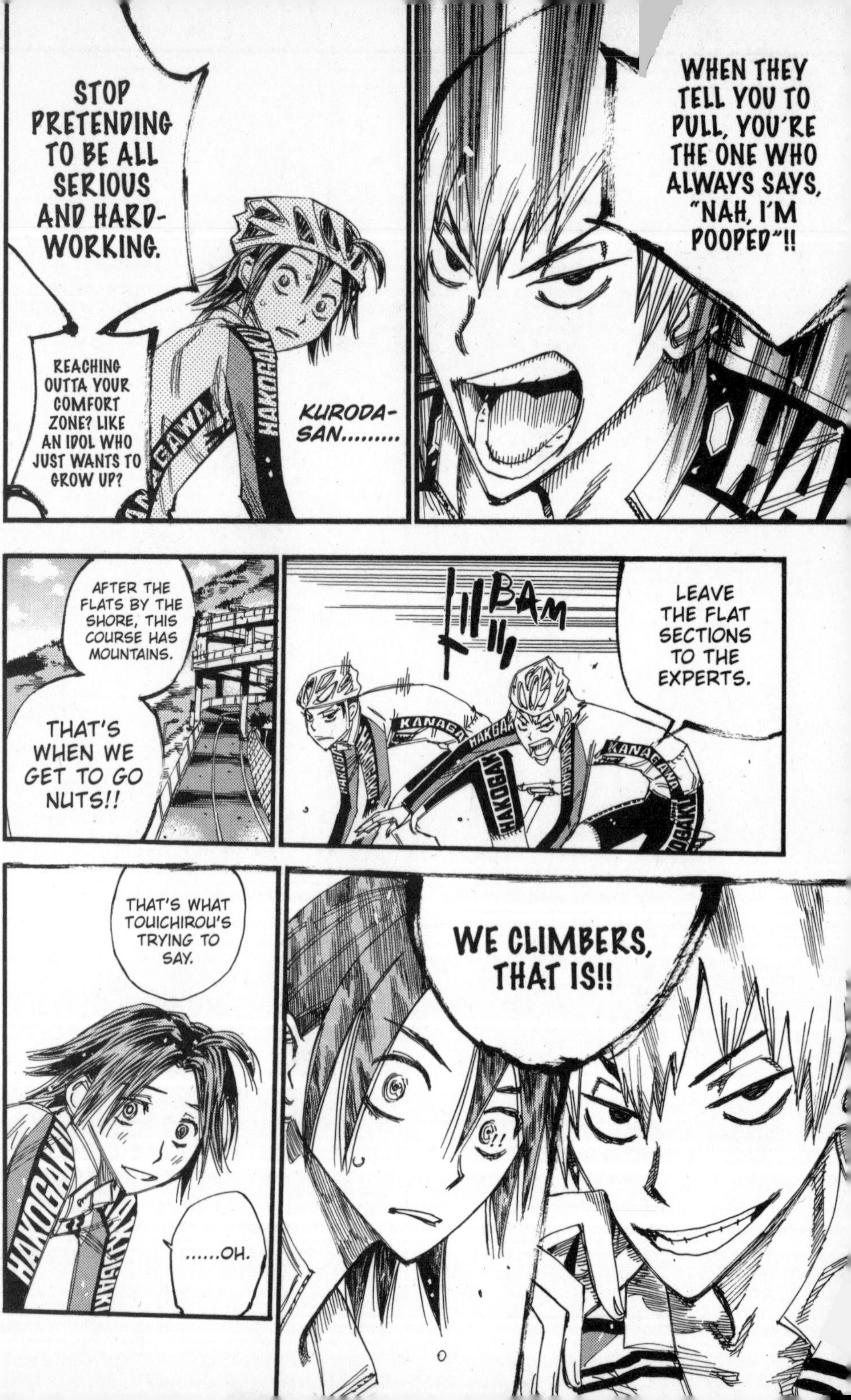
WHEN THEY TELL YOU TO PULL, YOU'RE THE ONE WHO ALWAYS SAYS, "NAH, I'M POOPED"!!
STOP PRETENDING TO BE ALL SERIOUS AND HARD-WORKING.
REACHING OUTTA YOUR COMFORT ZONE? LIKE AN IDOL WHO JUST WANTS TO GROW UP?
KURODA-SAN.........
BAM
LEAVE THE FLAT SECTIONS TO THE EXPERTS.
AFTER THE FLATS BY THE SHORE, THIS COURSE HAS MOUNTAINS.
THAT'S WHEN WE GET TO GO NUTS!!
WE CLIMBERS, THAT IS!!
THAT'S WHAT TOUICHIROU'S TRYING TO SAY.
......OH.

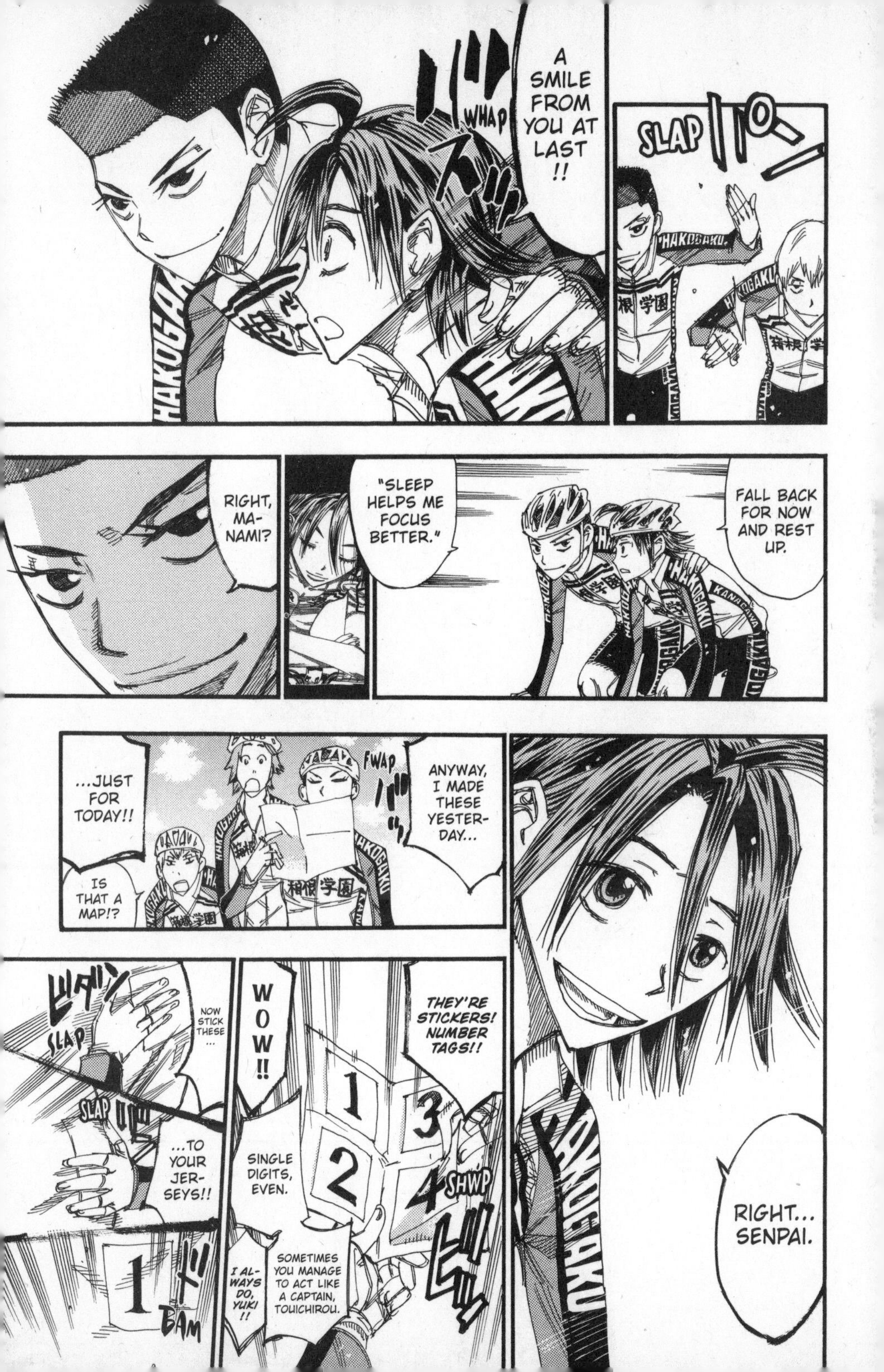
SLAP
A SMILE FROM YOU AT LAST!!
WHAP
FALL BACK FOR NOW AND REST UP.
"SLEEP HELPS ME FOCUS BETTER."
RIGHT, MA-NAMI?
RIGHT... SENPAI.
ANYWAY, I MADE THESE YESTER-DAY...
FWAP
...JUST FOR TODAY!!
IS THAT A MAP!?
THEY'RE STICKERS! NUMBER TAGS!!
WOW!!
SINGLE DIGITS, EVEN.
SHWP
SOMETIMES YOU MANAGE TO ACT LIKE A CAPTAIN, TOUICHIROU.
I ALWAYS DO, YUKI!!
NOW STICK THESE...
SLAP
SLAP
...TO YOUR JERSEYS!!
BAM

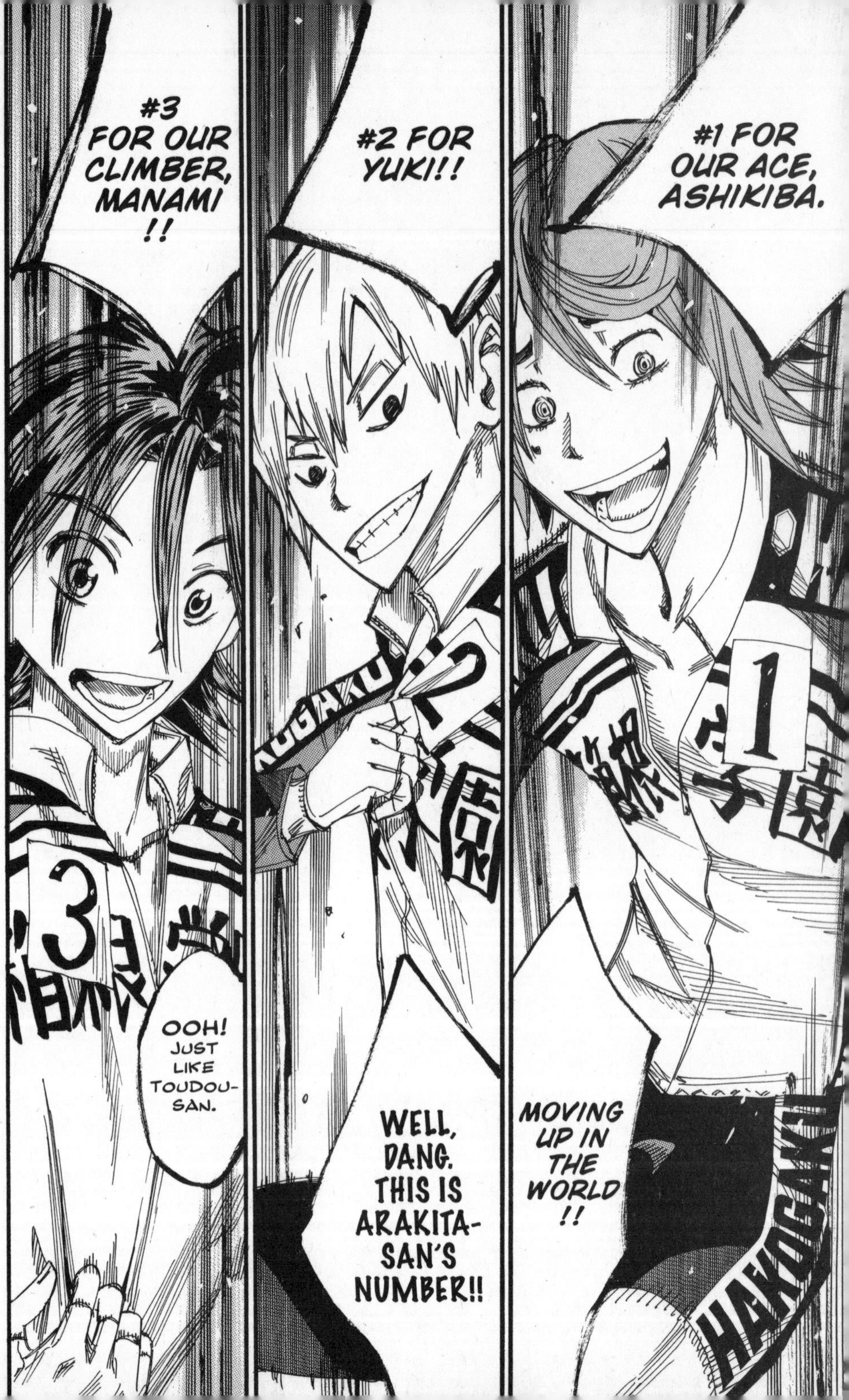
#1 FOR OUR ACE, ASHIKIBA.
MOVING UP IN THE WORLD!!
#2 FOR YUKI!!
WELL, DANG. THIS IS ARAKITA-SAN'S NUMBER!!
#3 FOR OUR CLIMBER, MANAMI!!
OOH! JUST LIKE TOUDOU-SAN.

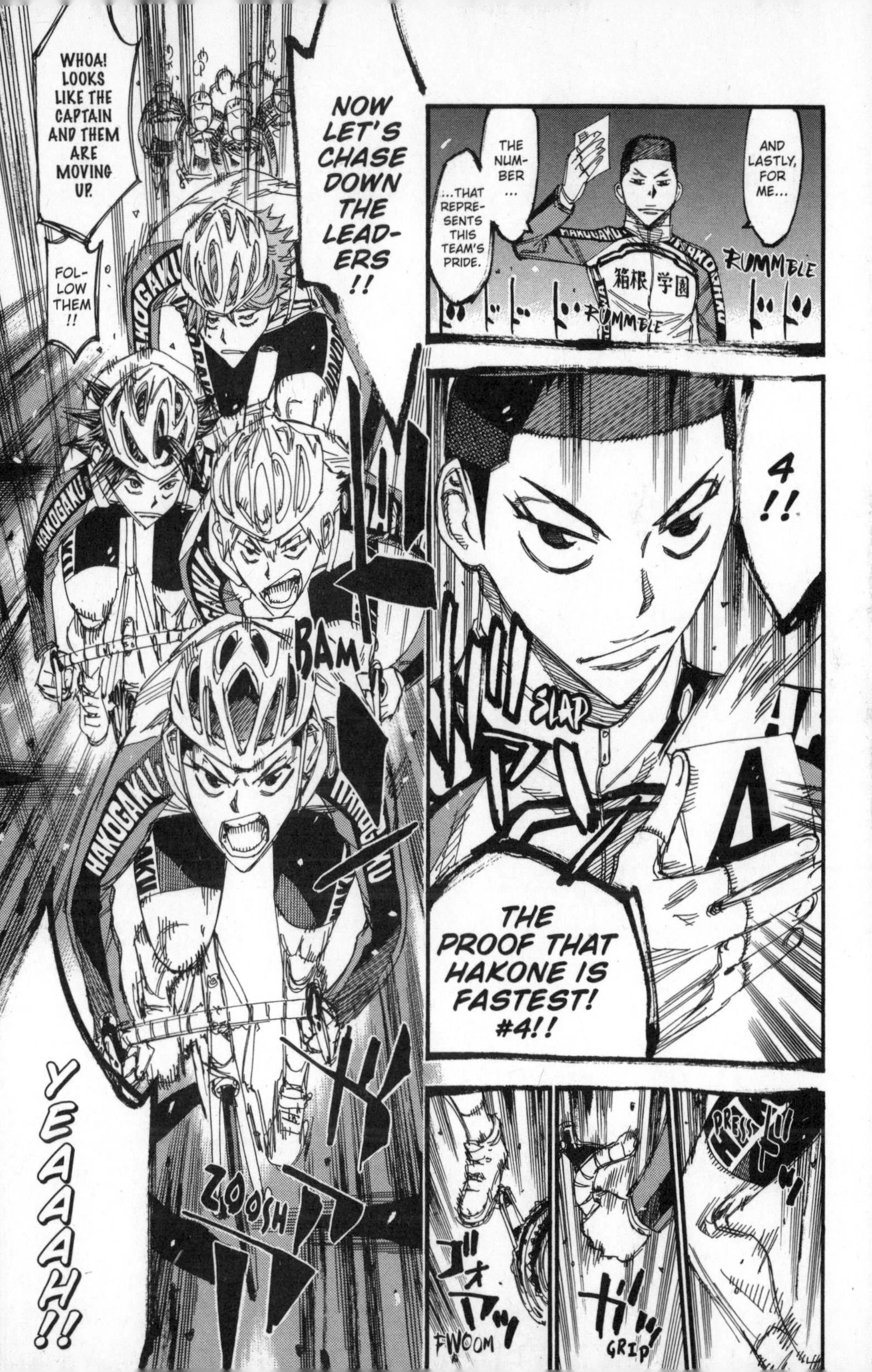
AND LASTLY, FOR ME...
THE NUMBER...
...THAT REPRESENTS THIS TEAM'S PRIDE.
RUMMBLE
RUMMBLE
4!!
SLAP
THE PROOF THAT HAKONE IS FASTEST! #4!!
PRESS
GRIP
FWOOM
NOW LET'S CHASE DOWN THE LEADERS!!
WHOA! LOOKS LIKE THE CAPTAIN AND THEM ARE MOVING UP.
FOLLOW THEM!!
BAM
ZOOSH
YEAAAAH!!

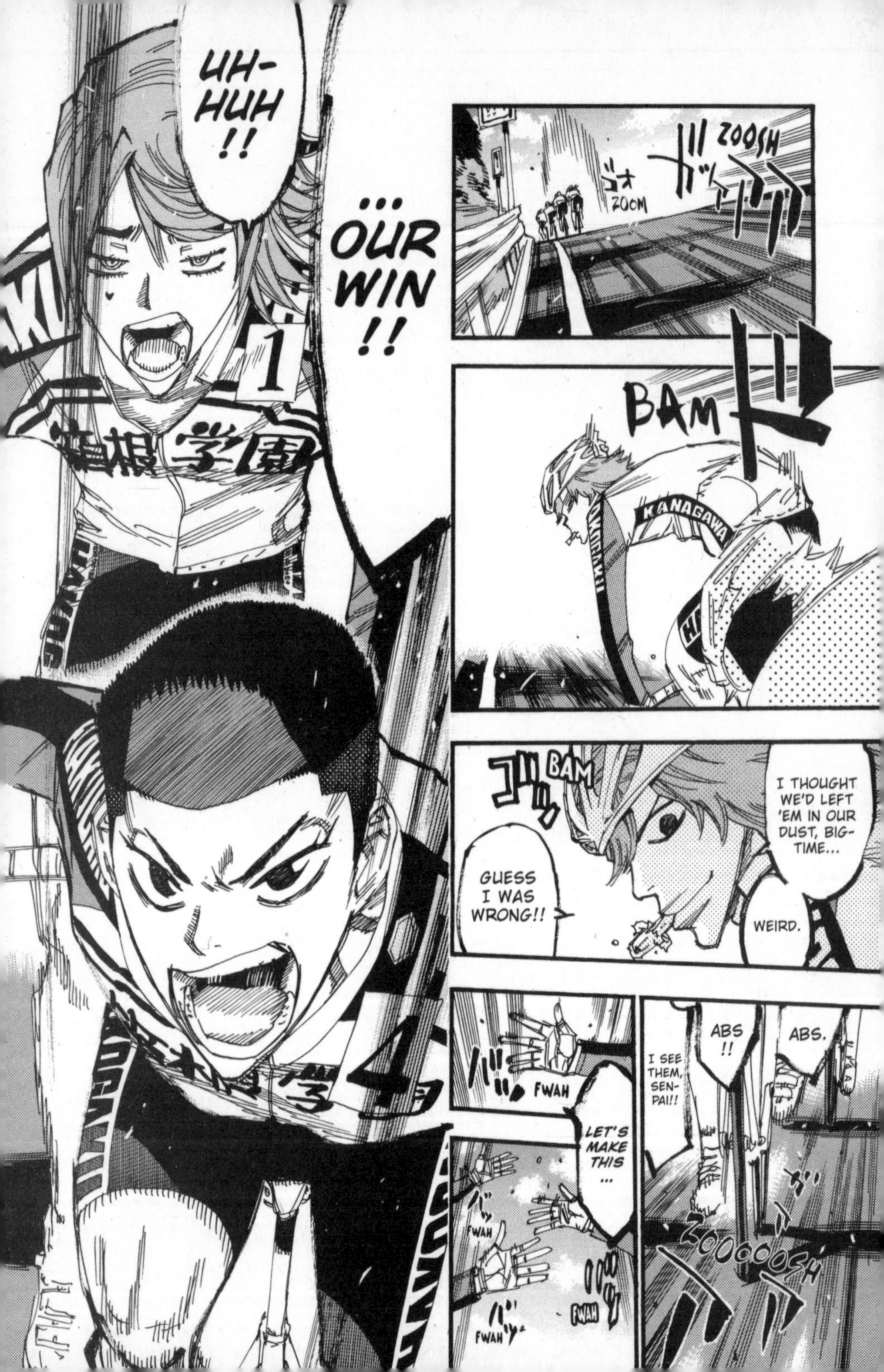
ZOOSH
ZOOM
BAM
KANAGAWA
BAM
I THOUGHT WE'D LEFT 'EM IN OUR DUST, BIG-TIME...
WEIRD.
GUESS I WAS WRONG!!
ABS.
ABS!!
I SEE THEM, SENPAI!!
ZOOOOOOSH
FWAH
LET'S MAKE THIS...
FWAH
FWAH
FWAH
UH-HUH!!
...OUR WIN!!

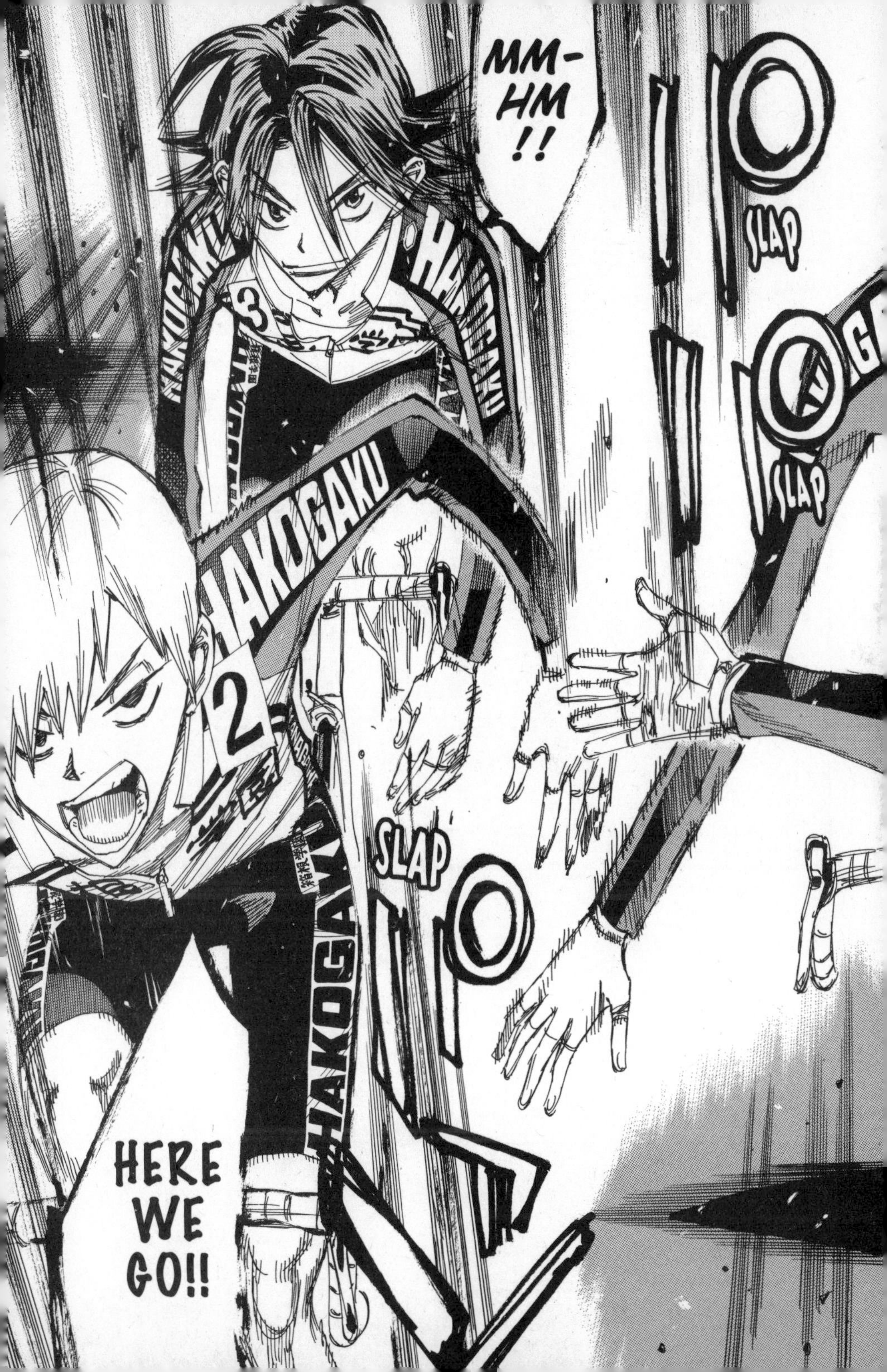
MM-HM!!
SLAP
SLAP
SLAP
HERE WE GO!!

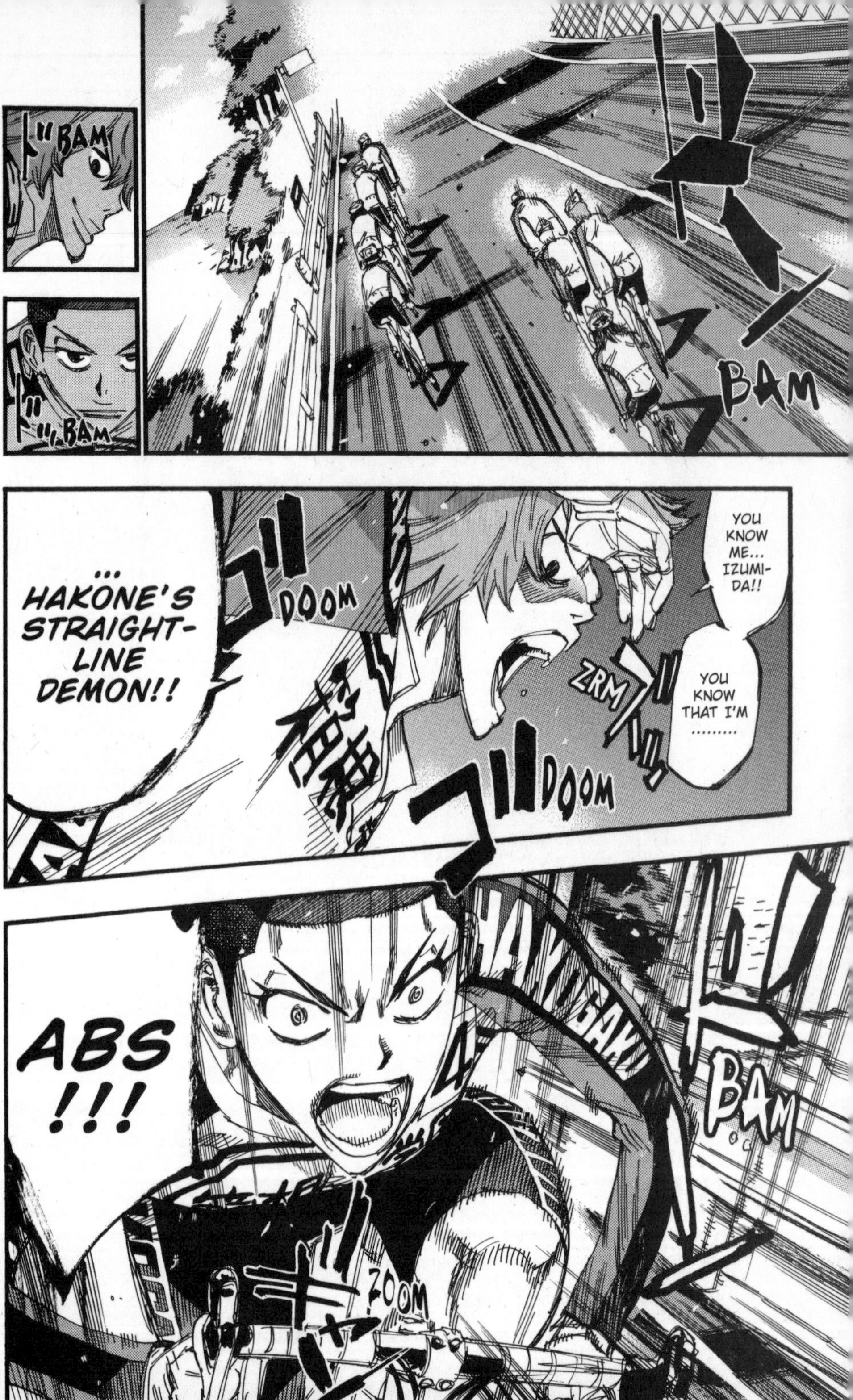
BAM
BAM
BAM
YOU KNOW ME... IZUMIDA!!
YOU KNOW THAT I'M ....
ZRM
DOOM
DOOM
... HAKONE'S STRAIGHT-LINE DEMON!!
BAM
ABS !!!
ZOOM

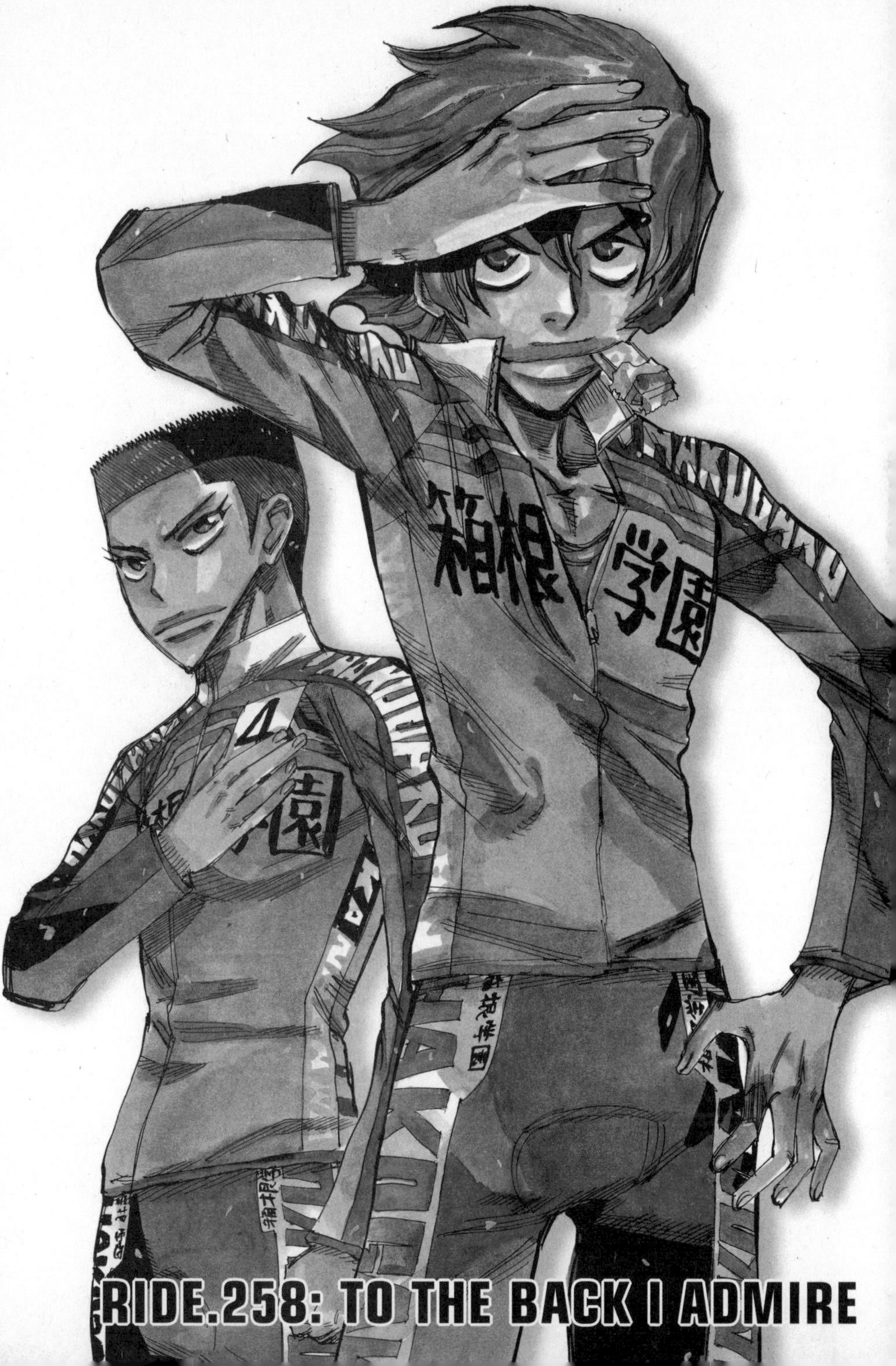
箱根学園

RIDE.258: TO THE BACK I ADMIRE

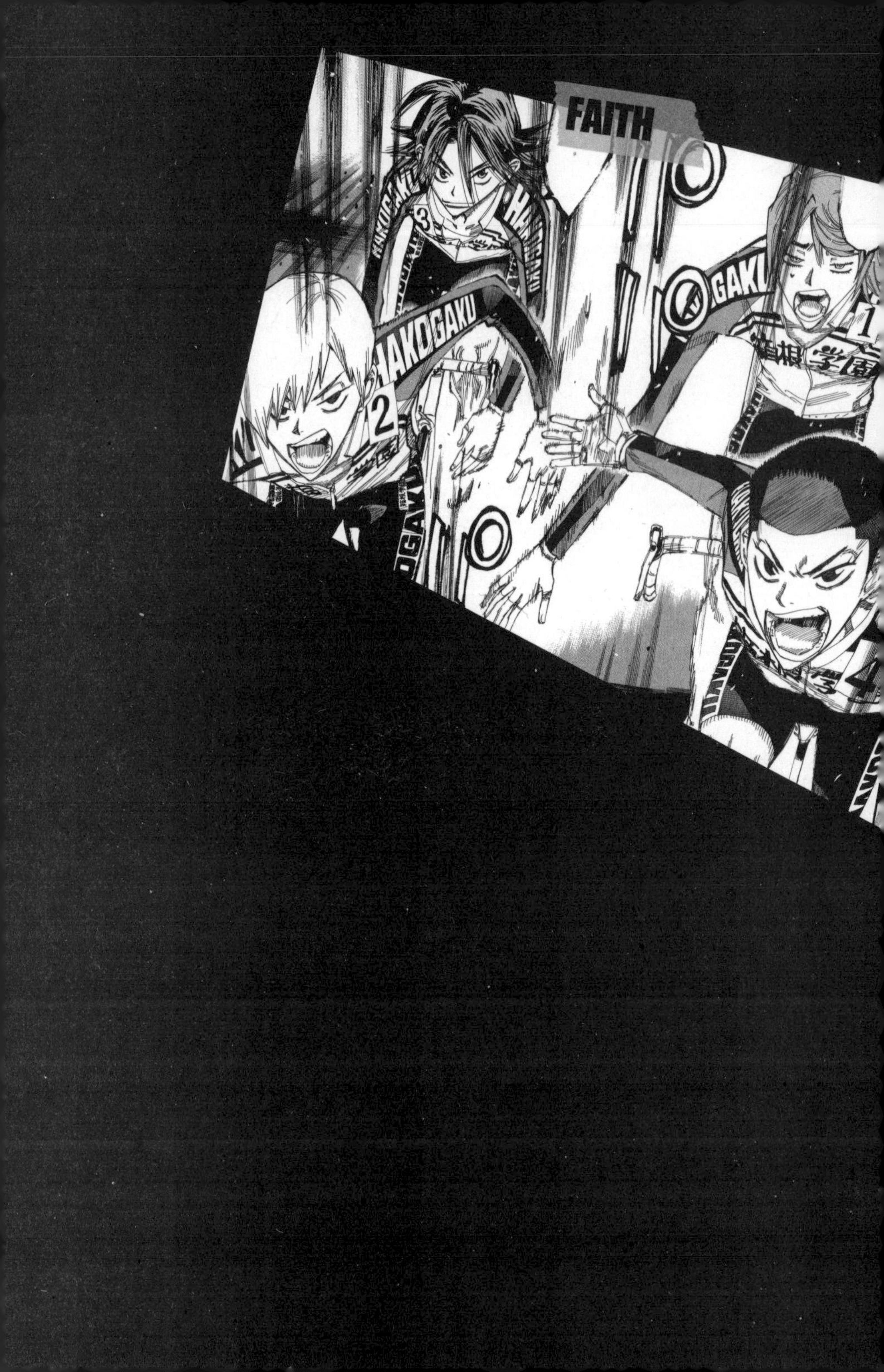
FAITH

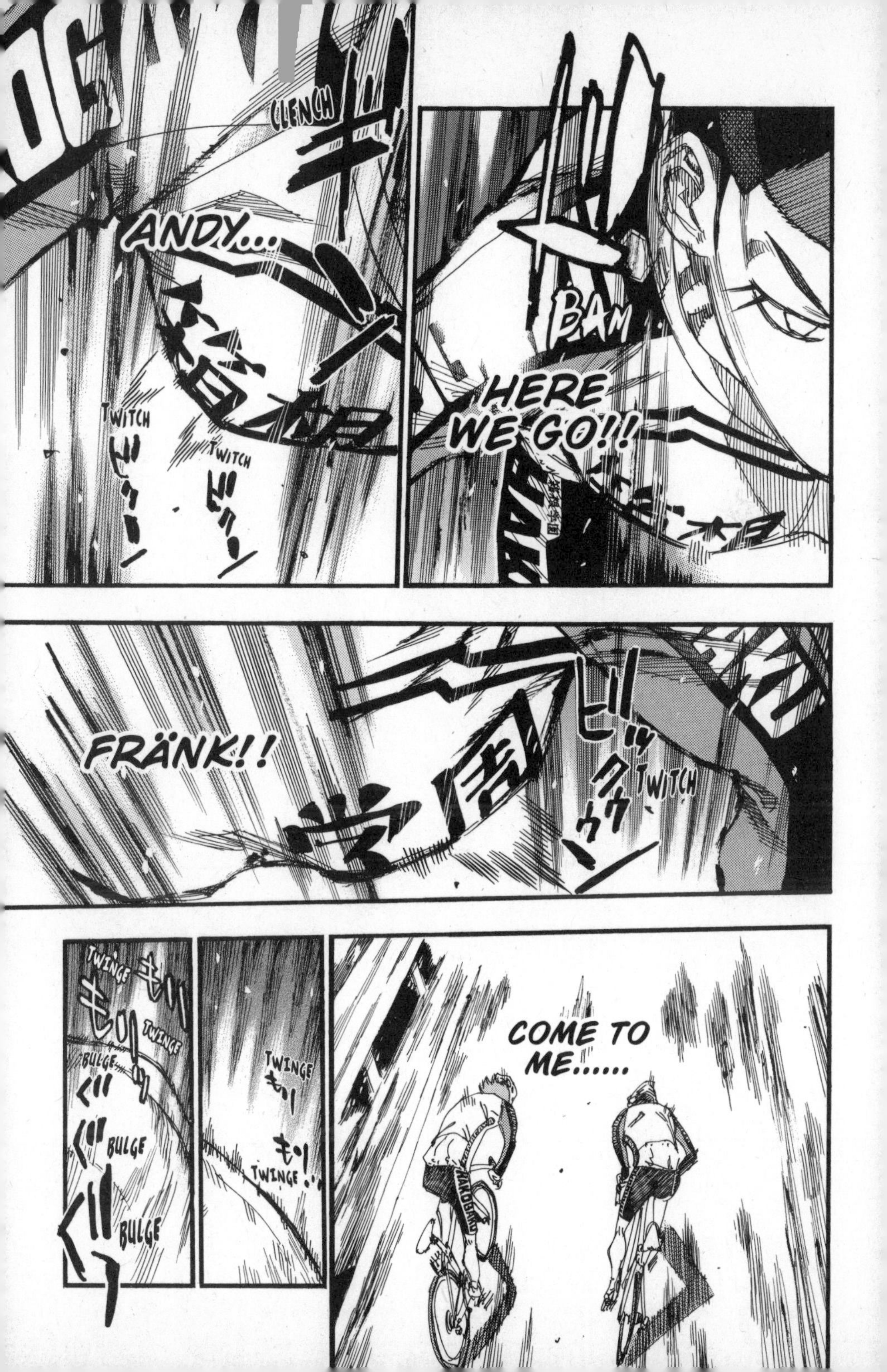
BAM
HERE WE GO!!
CLENCH
ANDY...
TWITCH
TWITCH
TWITCH
FRÄNK!!
COME TO ME......
TWINGE
TWINGE!!
TWINGE
TWINGE
BULGE
BULGE
BULGE

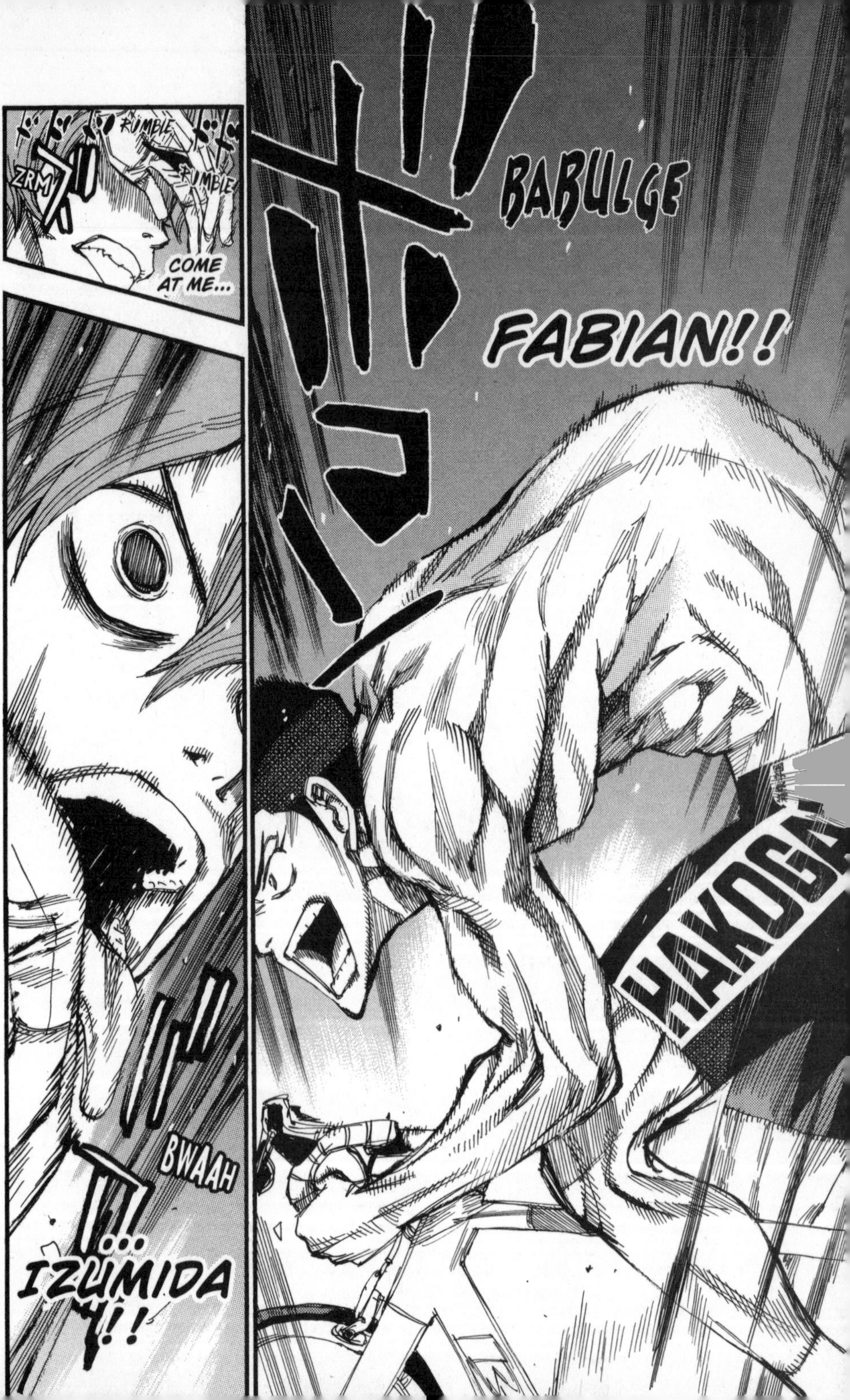
BABULGE
FABIAN!!
HAKOGA
RUMBLE
ZRM
RUMBLE
COME AT ME...
BWAAH
...IZUMIDA!!

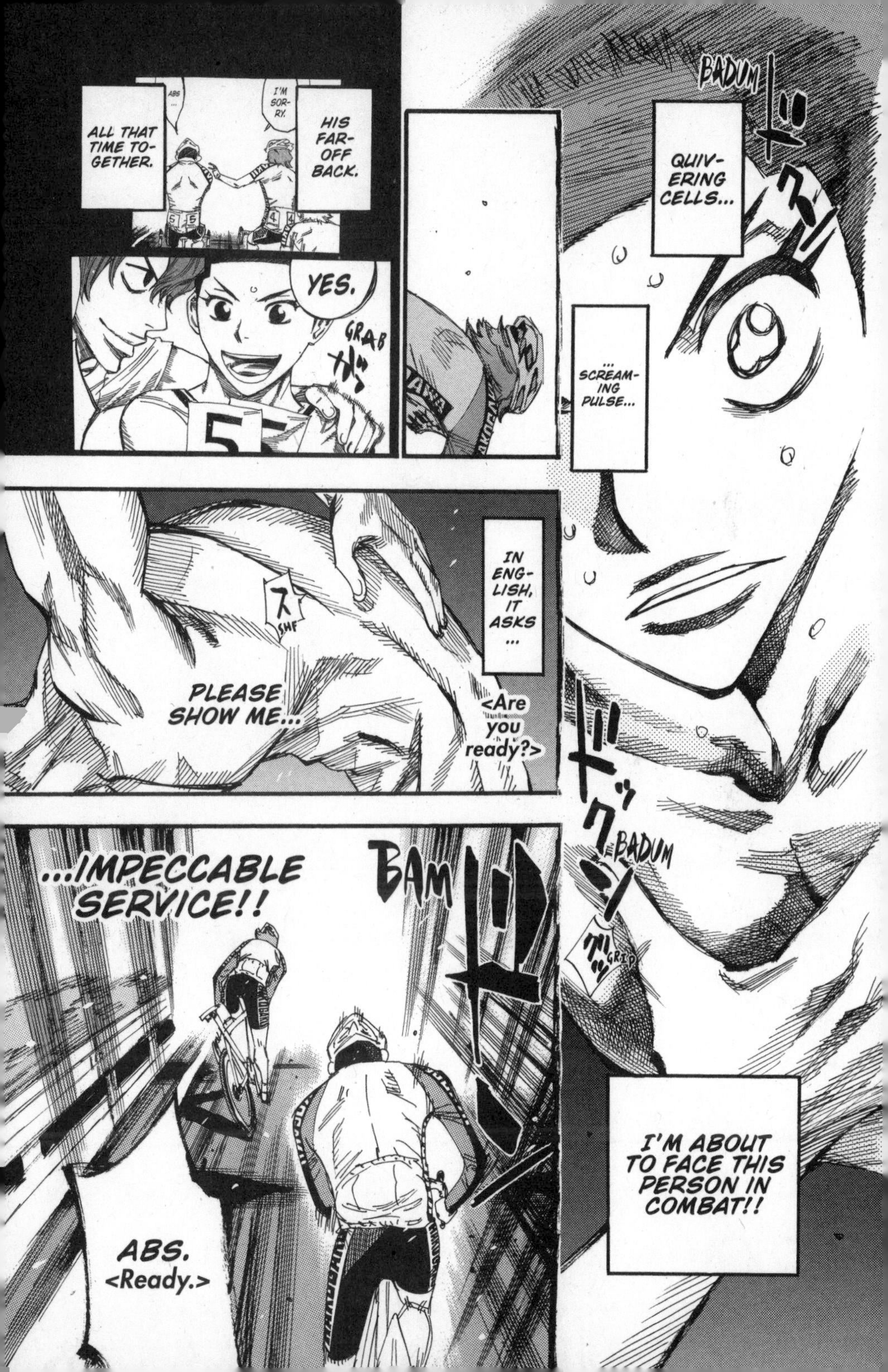
BADUM
QUIVERING CELLS...
...SCREAMING PULSE...
BADUM
GRIP
I'M ABOUT TO FACE THIS PERSON IN COMBAT!!
HIS FAR-OFF BACK.
I'M SORRY.
ABS...
ALL THAT TIME TOGETHER.
YES.
GRAB
IN ENGLISH, IT ASKS...
<Are you ready?>
SHF
PLEASE SHOW ME...
BAM
...IMPECCABLE SERVICE!!
ABS.
<Ready.>

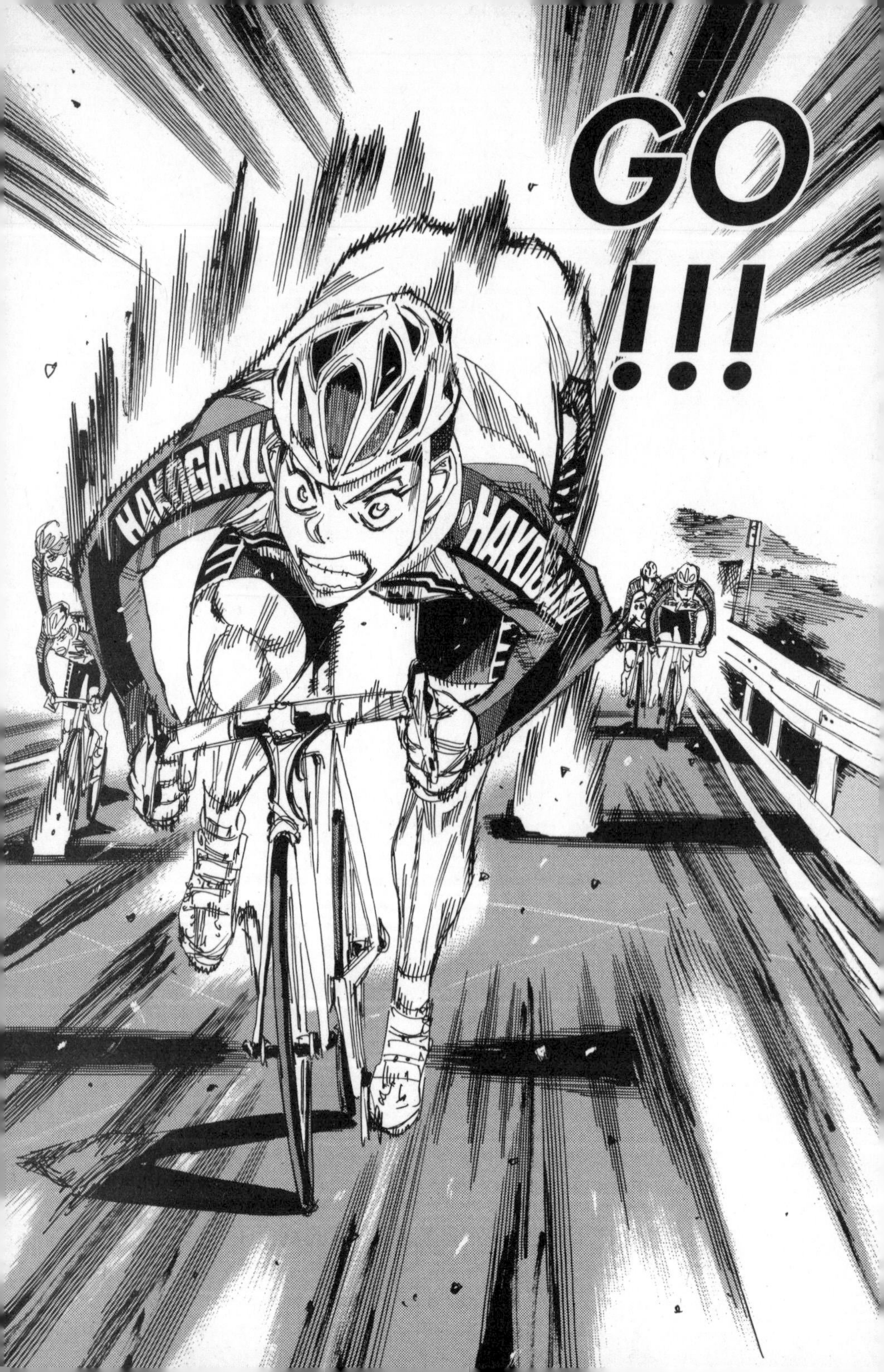
GO !!!
HAKOGAKU
HAKOGAKU

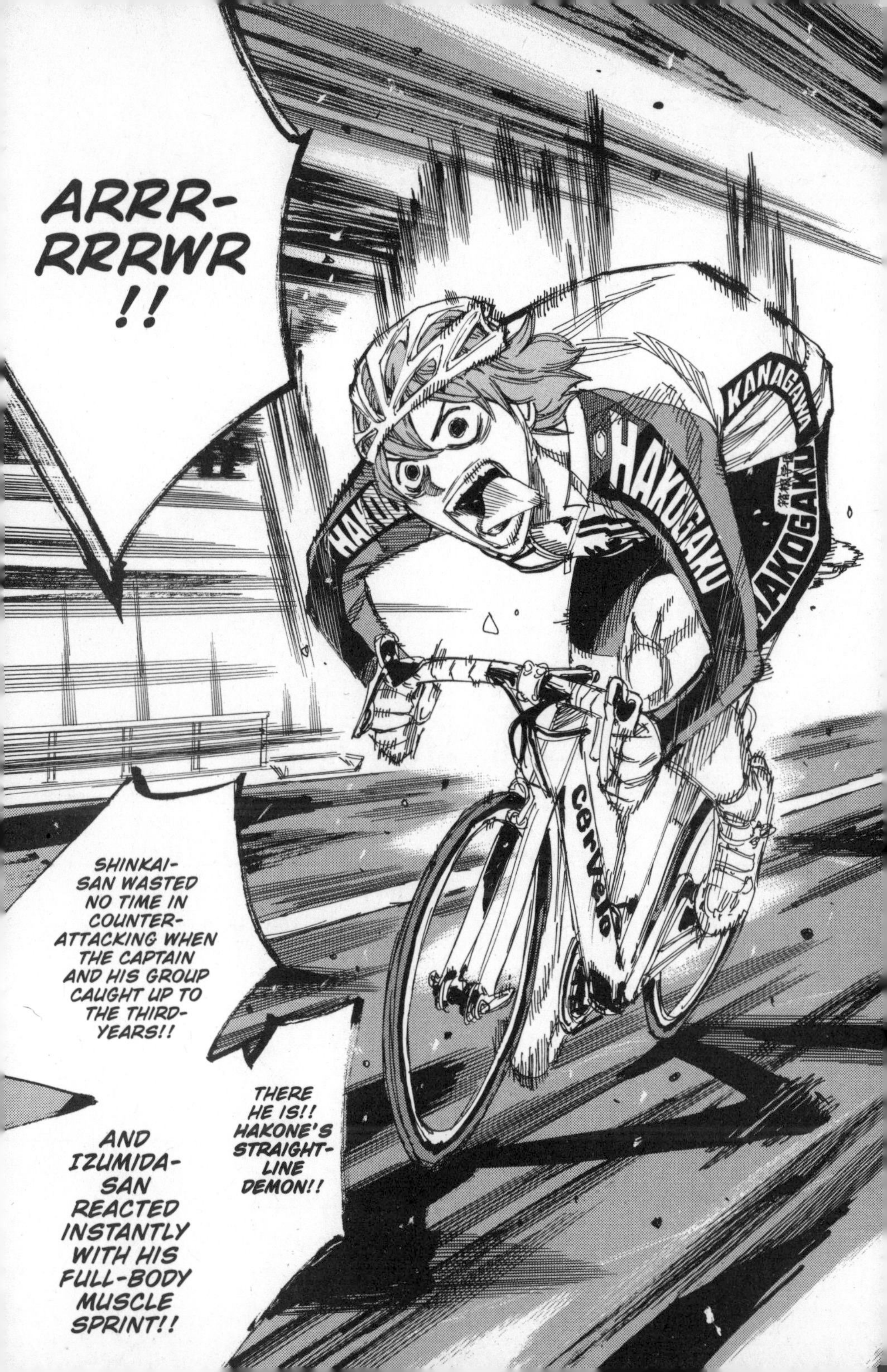
ARRRR-RRRRWR!!
SHINKAI-SAN WASTED NO TIME IN COUNTER-ATTACKING WHEN THE CAPTAIN AND HIS GROUP CAUGHT UP TO THE THIRD-YEARS!!
THERE HE IS!! HAKONE'S STRAIGHT-LINE DEMON!!
AND IZUMIDA-SAN REACTED INSTANTLY WITH HIS FULL-BODY MUSCLE SPRINT!!

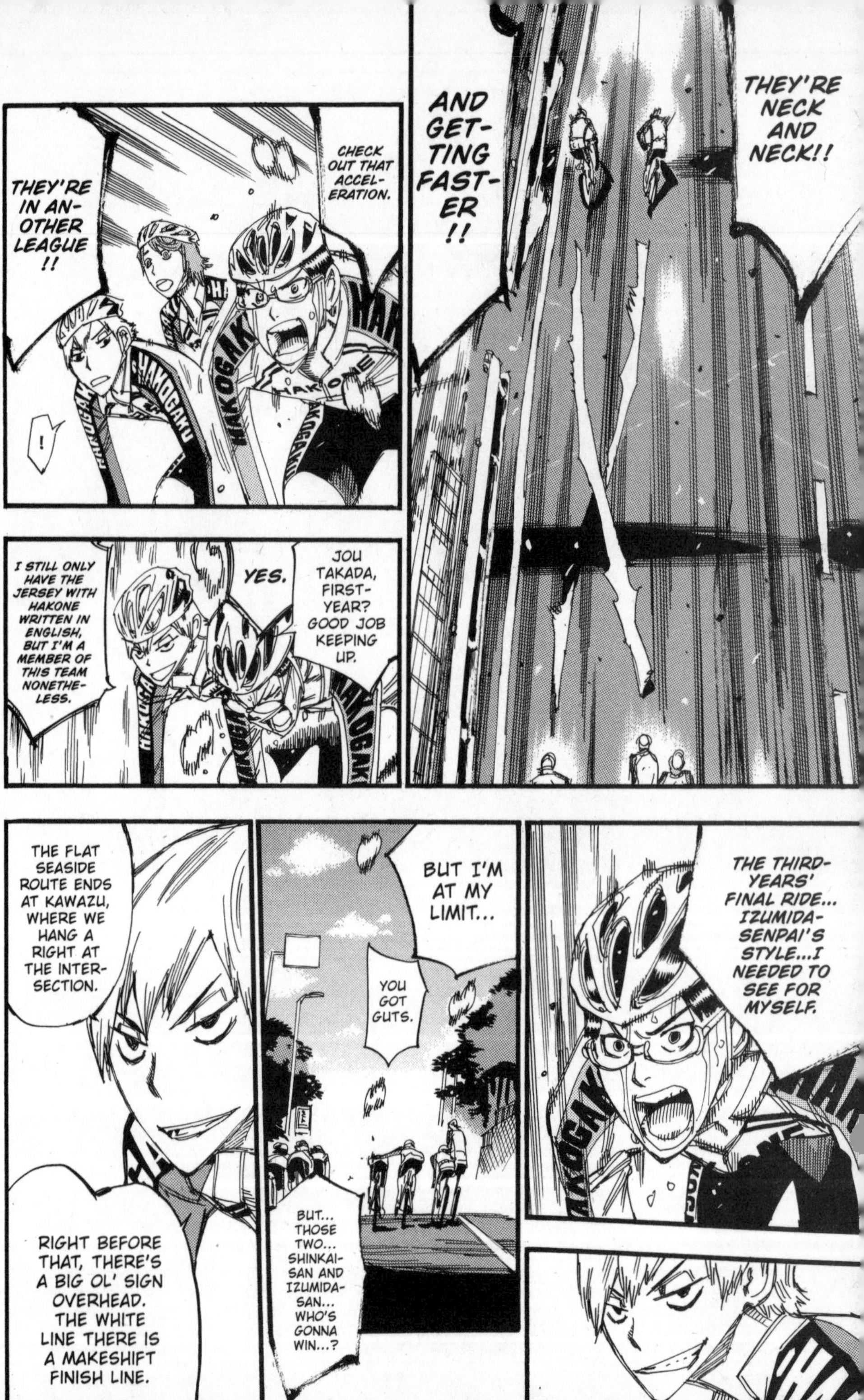
THEY'RE NECK AND NECK!!
AND GETTING FASTER!!
CHECK OUT THAT ACCELERATION.
THEY'RE IN ANOTHER LEAGUE!!
!
JOU TAKADA, FIRST-YEAR? GOOD JOB KEEPING UP.
YES.
I STILL ONLY HAVE THE JERSEY WITH HAKONE WRITTEN IN ENGLISH, BUT I'M A MEMBER OF THIS TEAM NONETHELESS.
THE THIRD-YEARS' FINAL RIDE... IZUMIDA-SENPAI'S STYLE...I NEEDED TO SEE FOR MYSELF.
BUT I'M AT MY LIMIT...
YOU GOT GUTS.
BUT... THOSE TWO... SHINKAI-SAN AND IZUMIDA-SAN... WHO'S GONNA WIN...?
THE FLAT SEASIDE ROUTE ENDS AT KAWAZU, WHERE WE HANG A RIGHT AT THE INTERSECTION.
RIGHT BEFORE THAT, THERE'S A BIG OL' SIGN OVERHEAD. THE WHITE LINE THERE IS A MAKESHIFT FINISH LINE.

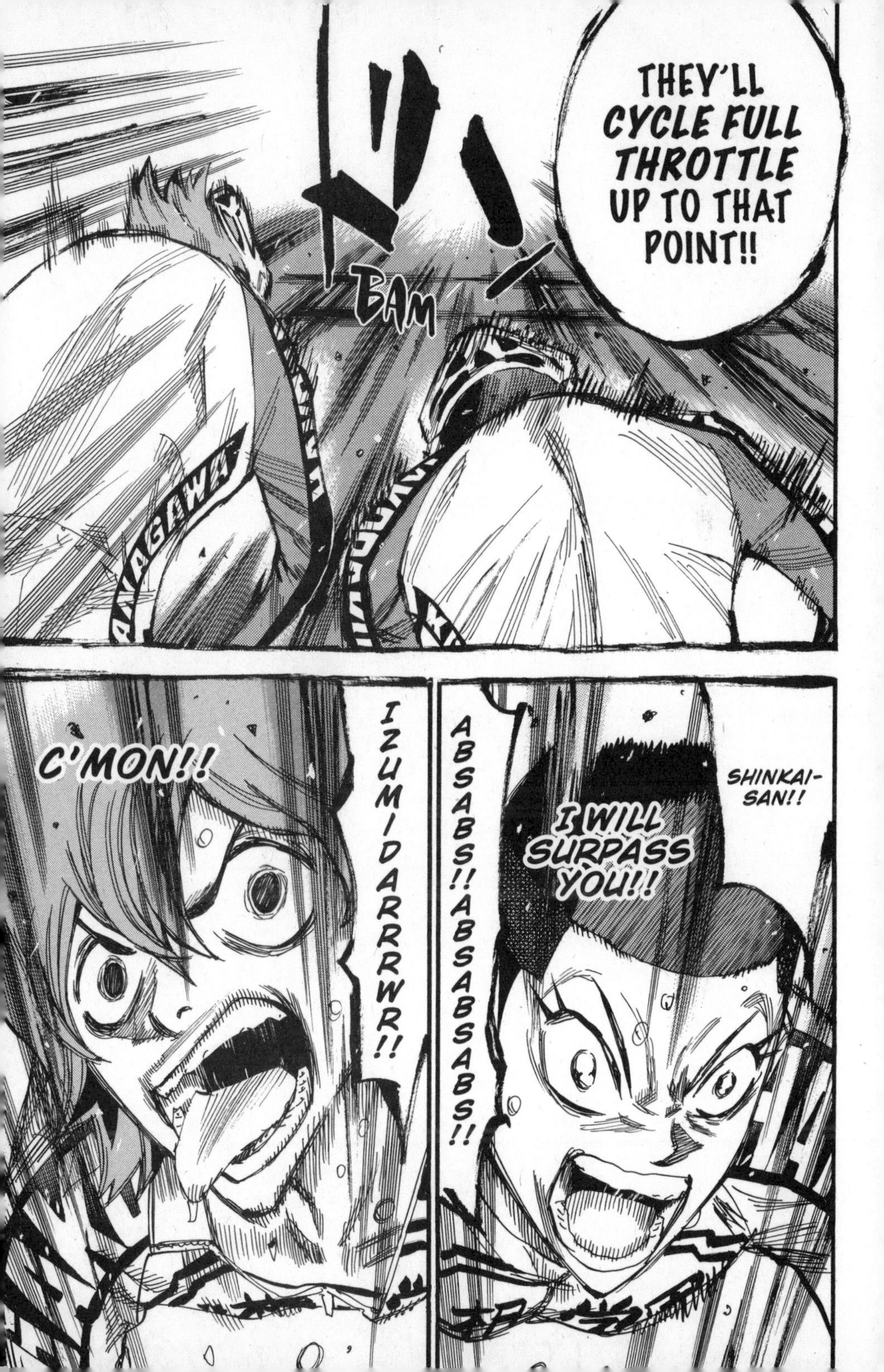
THEY'LL CYCLE FULL THROTTLE UP TO THAT POINT!!
BAM
SHINKAI-SAN!!
I WILL SURPASS YOU!!
ABSABS!!ABSABSABSABS!!
IZUMIDARRRRWR!!
C'MON!!

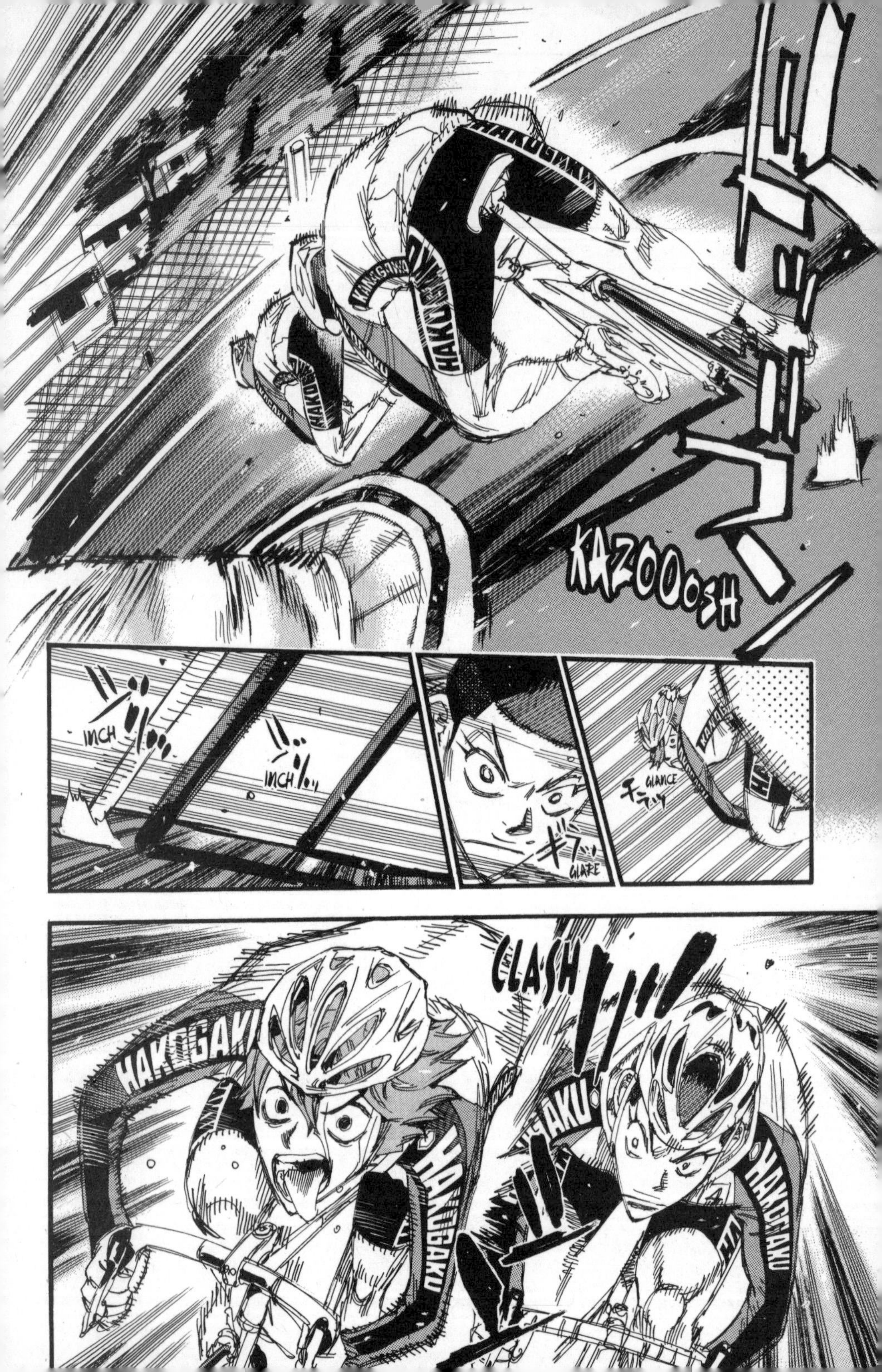
KAZOOOSH
GLANCE
GLARE
INCH
INCH
CLASH

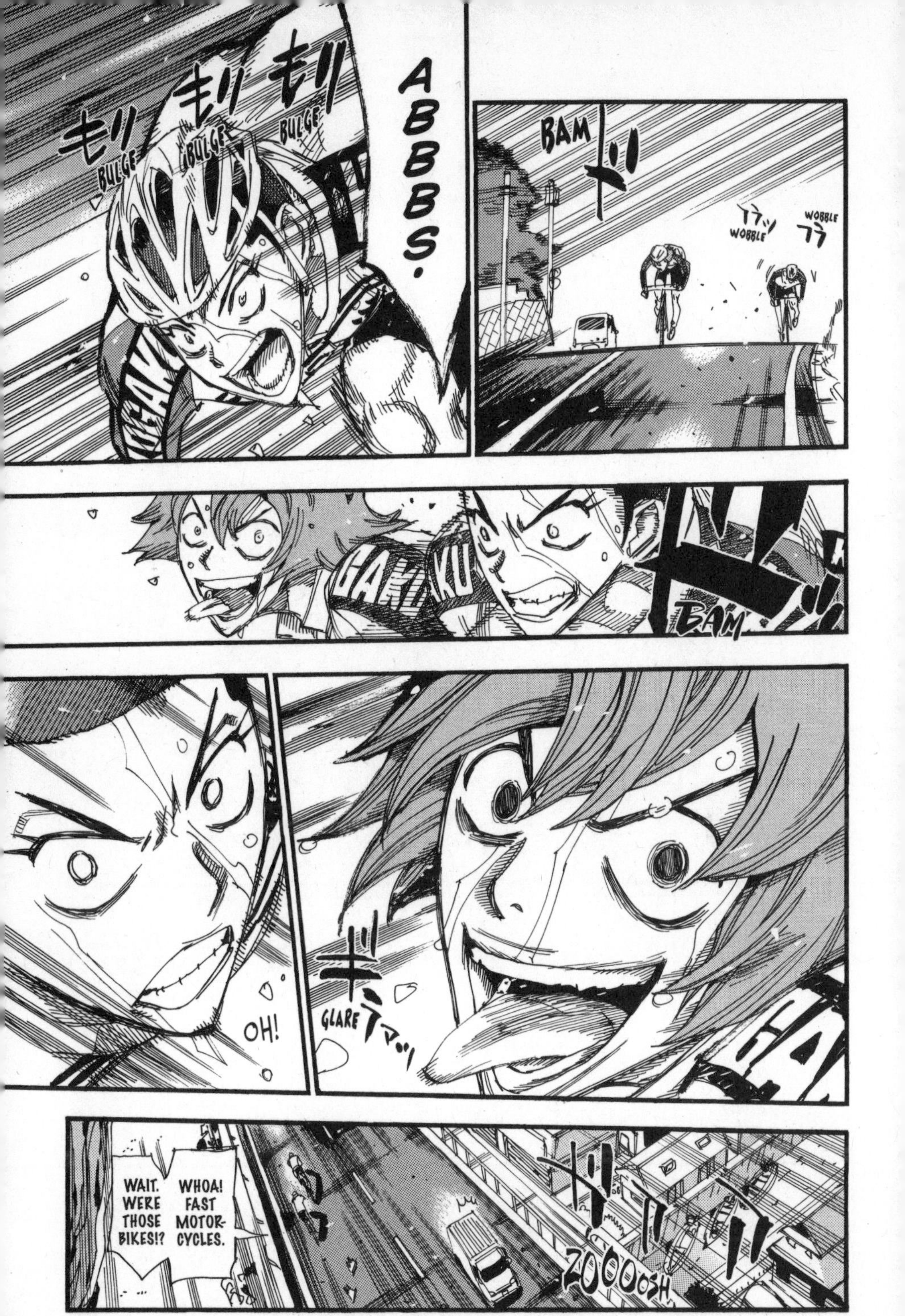
BAM
WOBBLE
WOBBLE
ABBBS.
BULGE
BULGE
BULGE
BAM
GLARE
OH!
ZOOOOSH
WHOA! FAST MOTOR-CYCLES.
WAIT. WERE THOSE BIKES!?

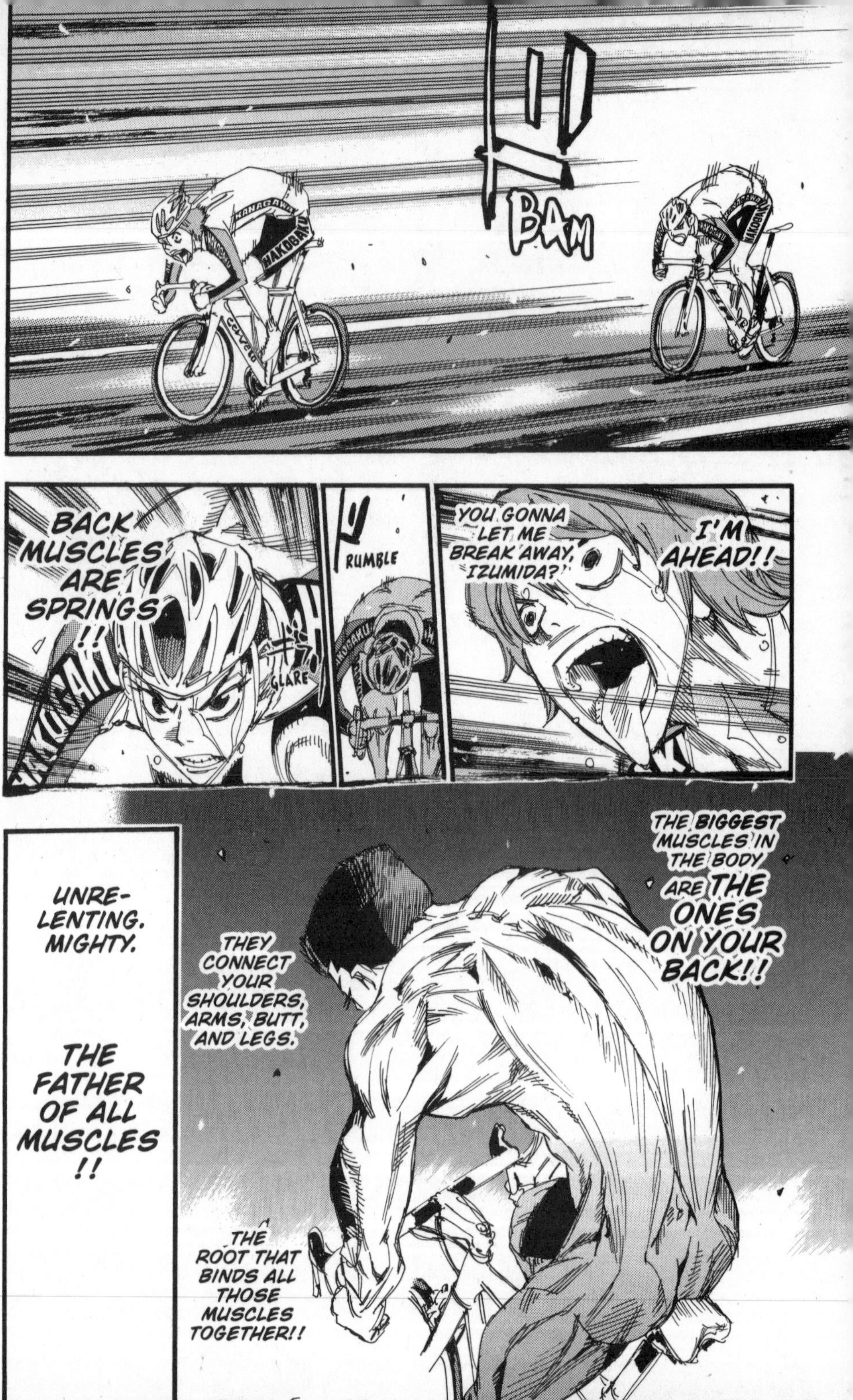
BAM
I'M AHEAD!!
YOU GONNA LET ME BREAK AWAY, IZUMIDA?
RUMBLE
BACK MUSCLES ARE SPRINGS!!
GLARE
THE BIGGEST MUSCLES IN THE BODY ARE THE ONES ON YOUR BACK!!
THEY CONNECT YOUR SHOULDERS, ARMS, BUTT, AND LEGS.
THE ROOT THAT BINDS ALL THOSE MUSCLES TOGETHER!!
UNRE-LENTING. MIGHTY.
THE FATHER OF ALL MUSCLES!!

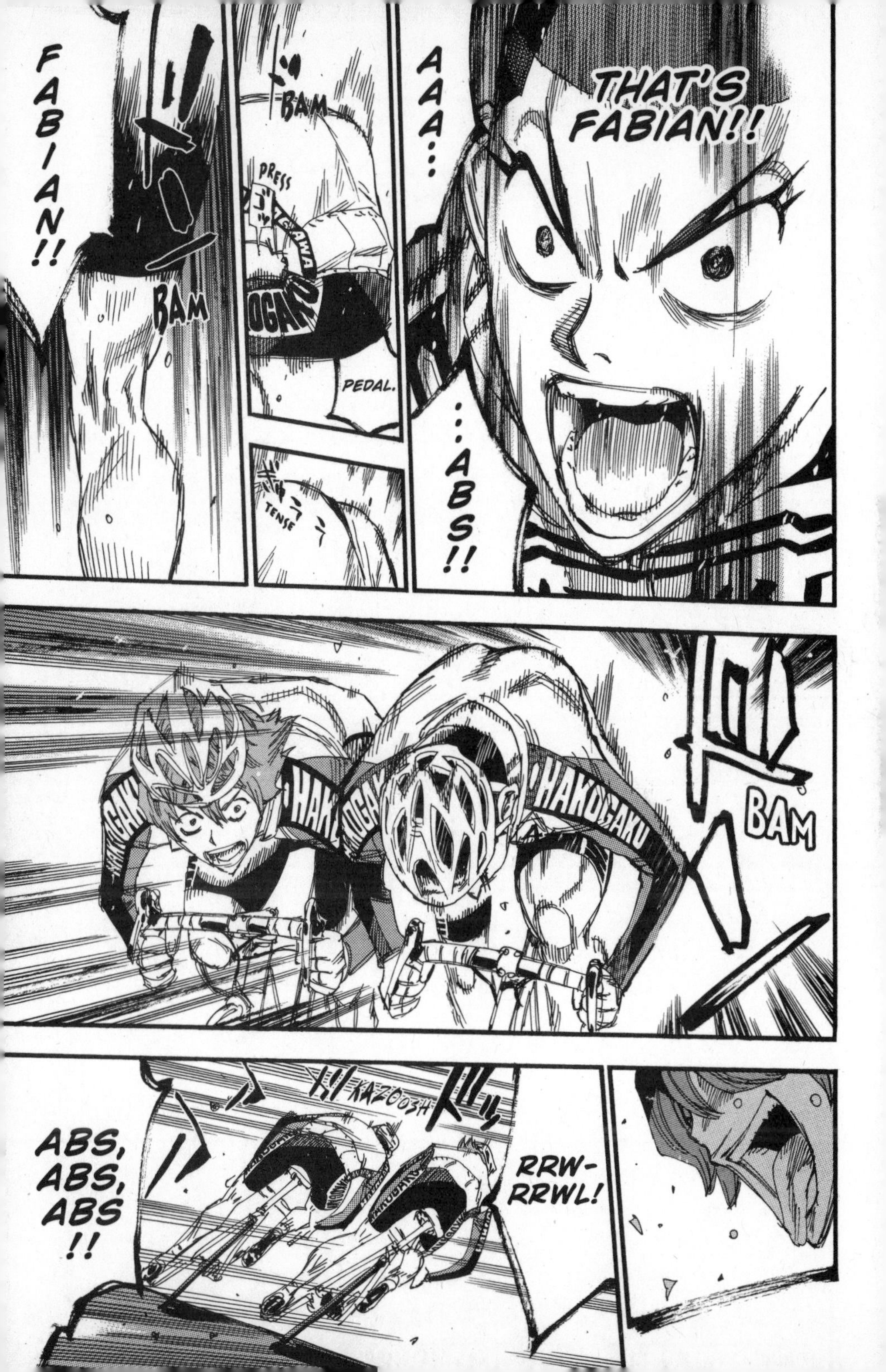
THAT'S FABIAN!!
AAAA... ...ABS!!
BAM
PRESS
PEDAL.
TENSE
FABIAN!!
BAM
BAM
KAZOOSH
RRW-RRWL!
ABS, ABS, ABS!!

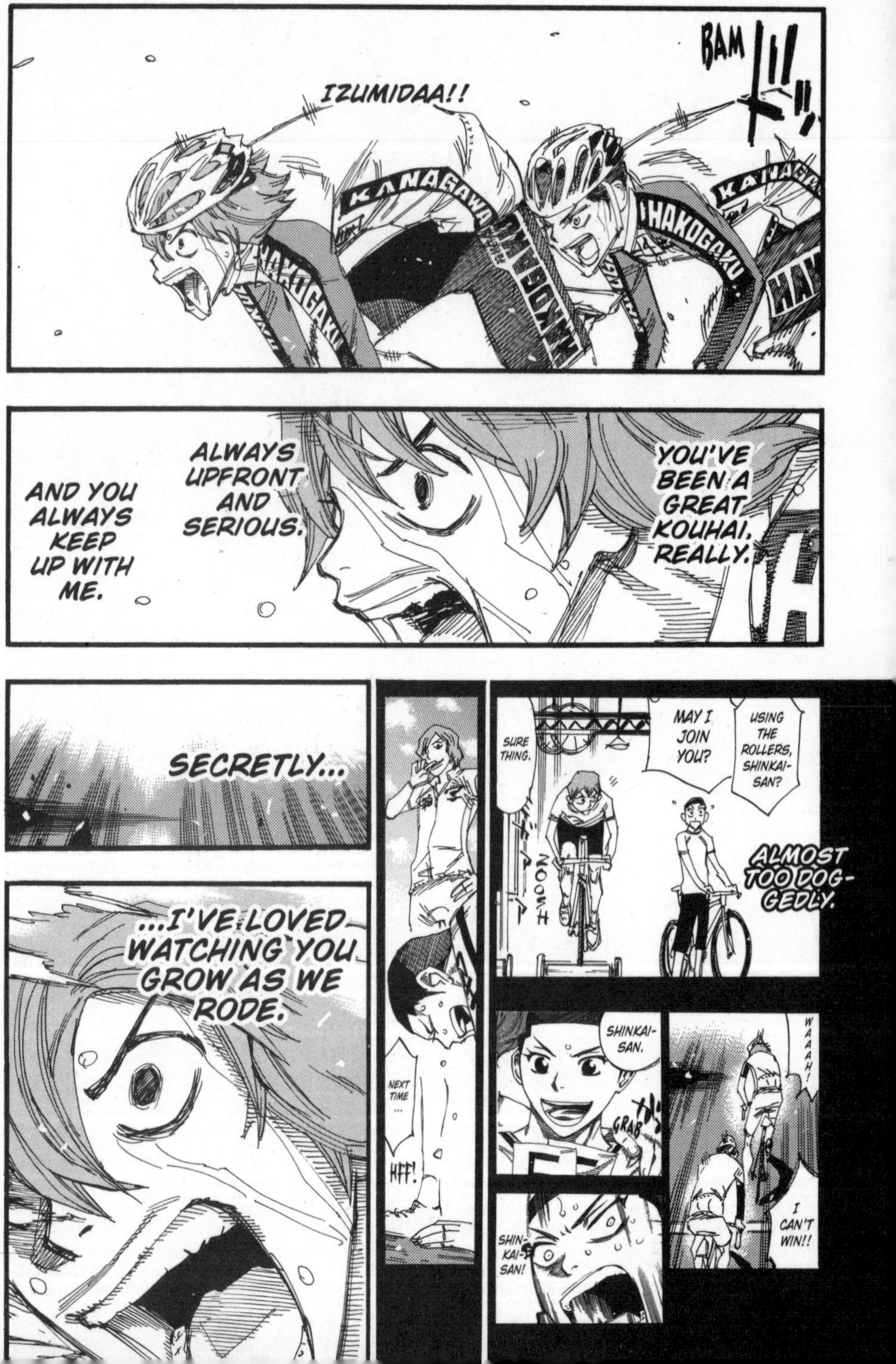
BAM
IZUMIDAA!!
YOU'VE BEEN A GREAT KOUHAI, REALLY.
ALWAYS UPFRONT AND SERIOUS.
AND YOU ALWAYS KEEP UP WITH ME.
USING THE ROLLERS, SHINKAI-SAN?
MAY I JOIN YOU?
SURE THING.
ALMOST TOO DOG-GEDLY.
WAAAH!
I CAN'T WIN!!
SHINKAI-SAN.
GRAB
SHIN-KAI-SAN!
NEXT TIME...
HFF!
SECRETLY...
...I'VE LOVED WATCHING YOU GROW AS WE RODE.

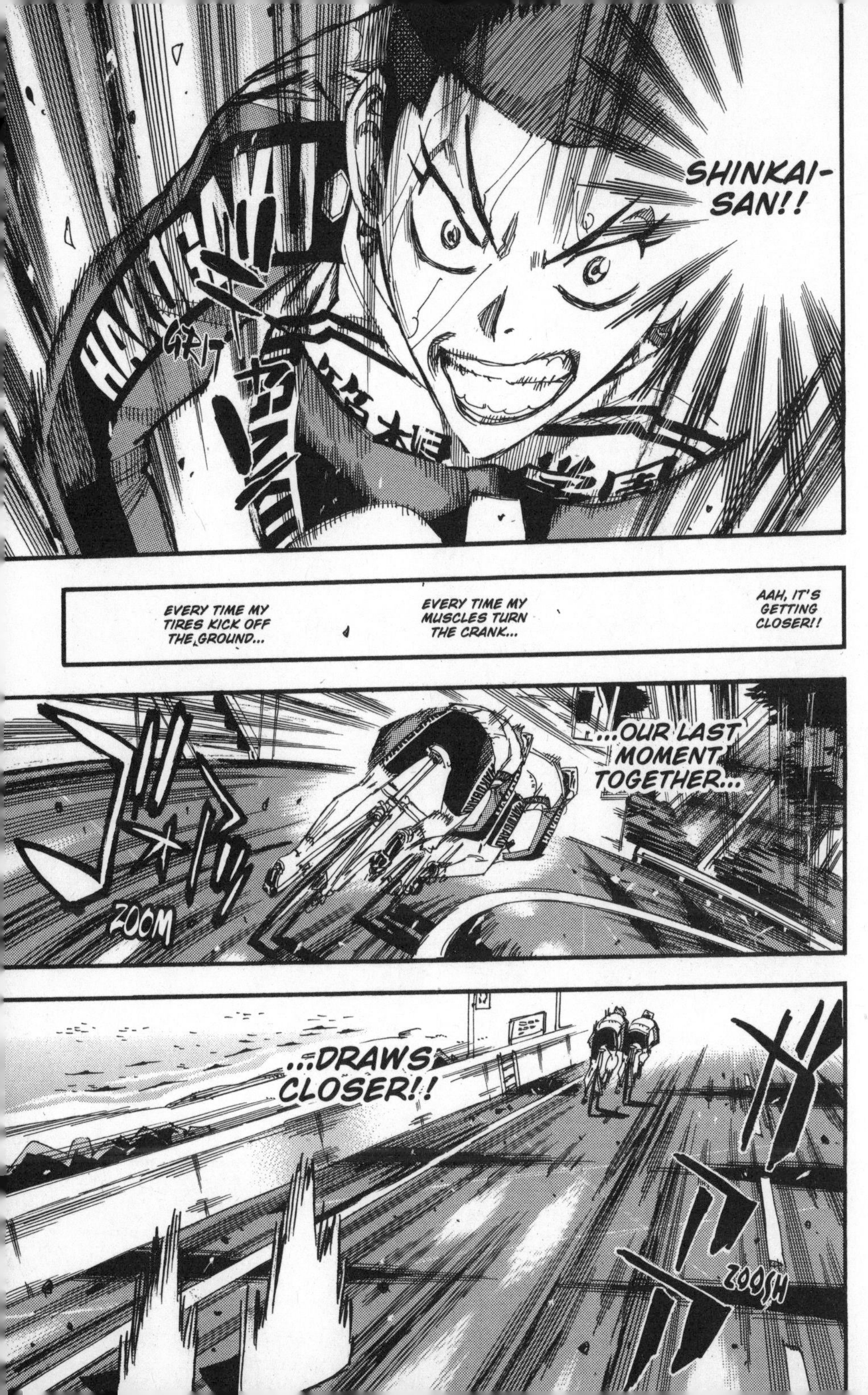
SHINKAI-SAN!!
GRIT
AAH, IT'S GETTING CLOSER!!
EVERY TIME MY MUSCLES TURN THE CRANK...
EVERY TIME MY TIRES KICK OFF THE GROUND...
...OUR LAST MOMENT TOGETHER...
ZOOM
ZOOSH
...DRAWS CLOSER!!

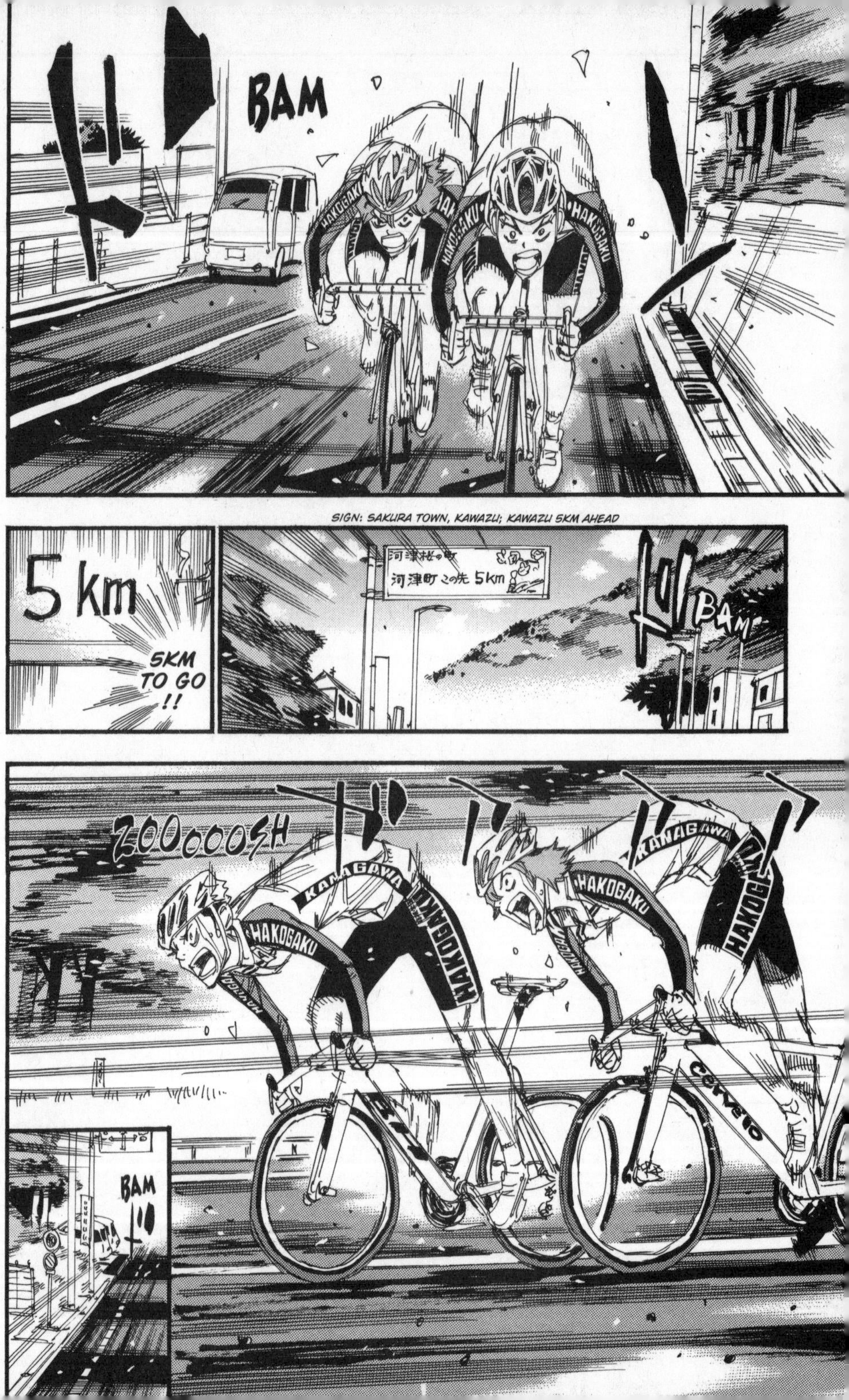
BAM
SIGN: SAKURA TOWN, KAWAZU; KAWAZU 5KM AHEAD
河津桜の町
河津町この先 5km
BAM
5 km
5KM TO GO !!
ZOOOOOSH
BAM

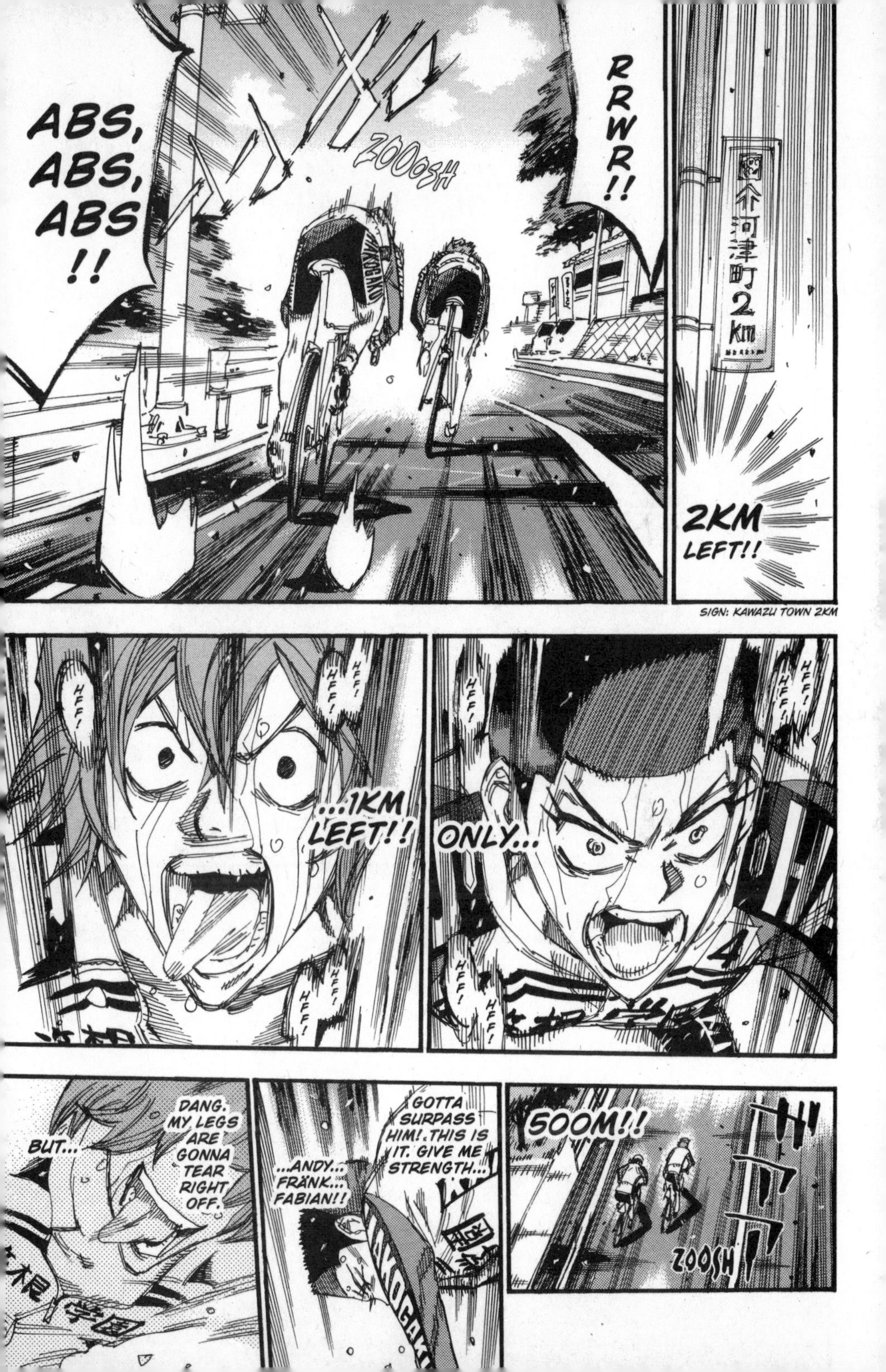
2KM LEFT!!
RRWR!!
ZOOOSH
ABS, ABS, ABS!!
SIGN: KAWAZU TOWN 2KM
HFF! HFF!
ONLY...
HFF! HFF!
...1KM LEFT!!
HFF! HFF!
HFF! HFF!
500M!!
ZOOSH
GOTTA SURPASS HIM! THIS IS IT. GIVE ME STRENGTH...
...ANDY... FRÄNK... FABIAN!!
DANG. MY LEGS ARE GONNA TEAR RIGHT OFF.
BUT...

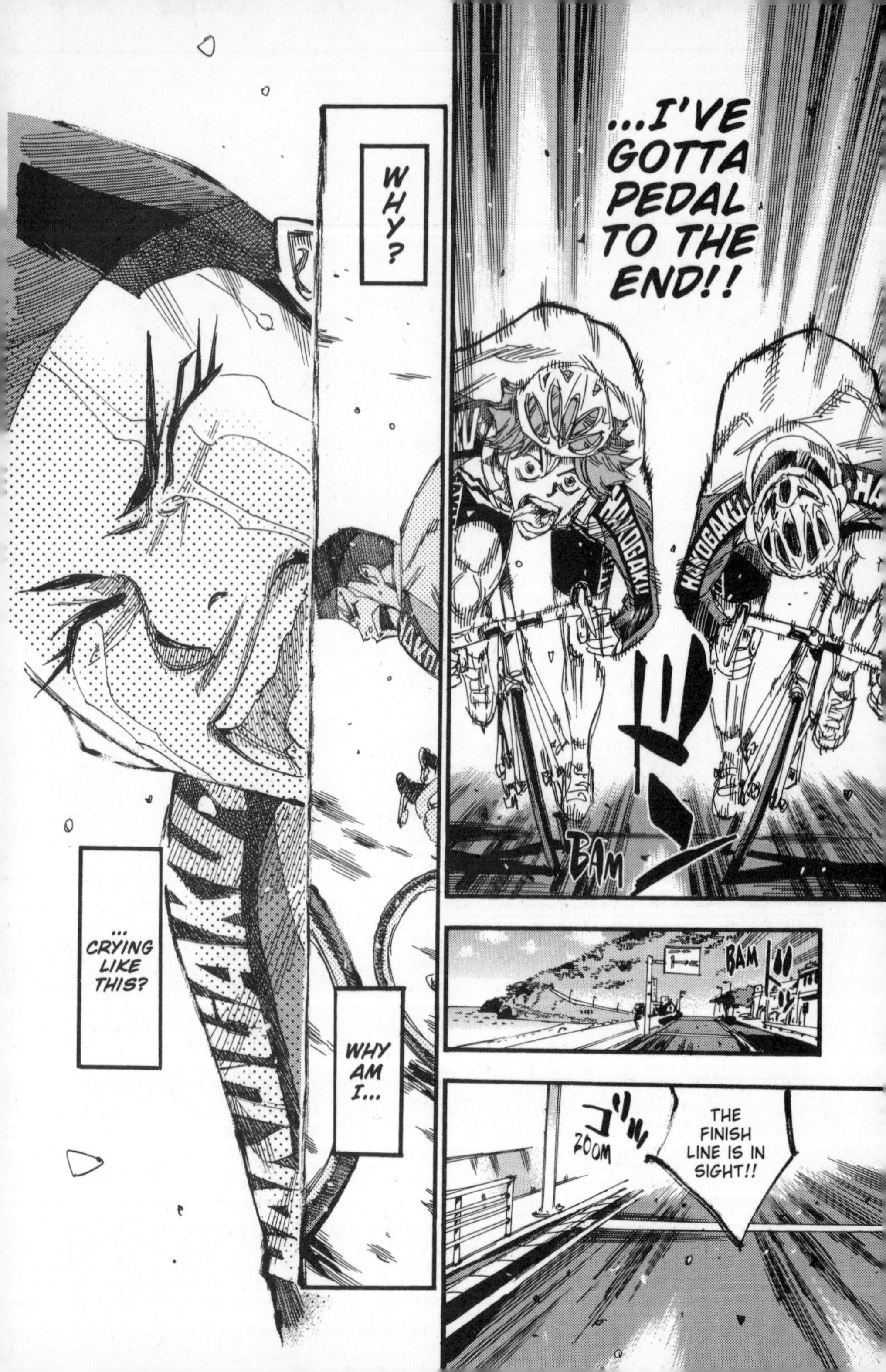
...I'VE GOTTA PEDAL TO THE END!!
BAM
BAM
ZOOM
THE FINISH LINE IS IN SIGHT!!
WHY?
WHY AM I...
...CRYING LIKE THIS?

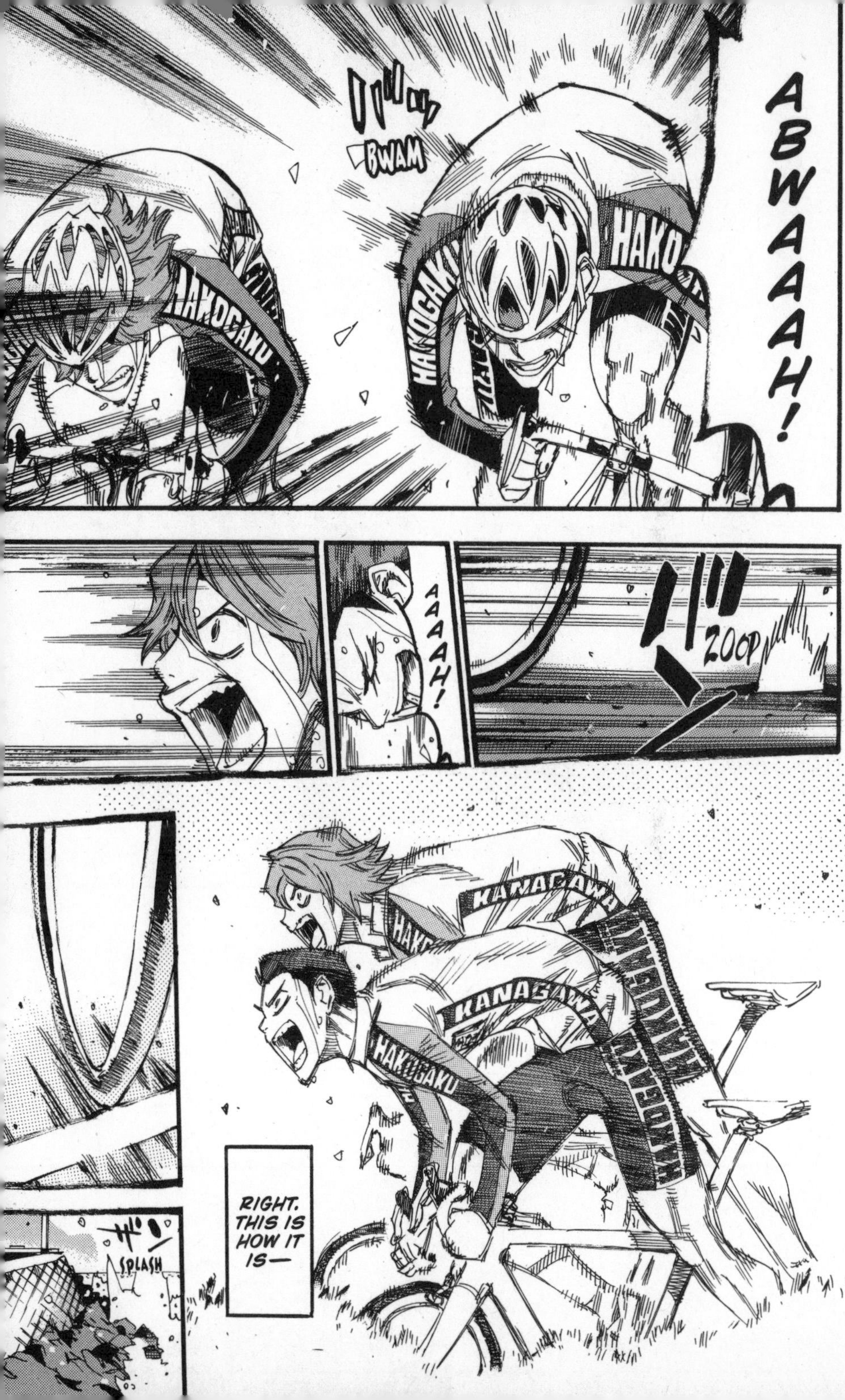
ABWAAAAAH!
BWAM
HAKOGAKU
ZOOP
AAAAAH!
KANAGAWA
HAKOGAKU
RIGHT. THIS IS HOW IT IS—
SPLASH

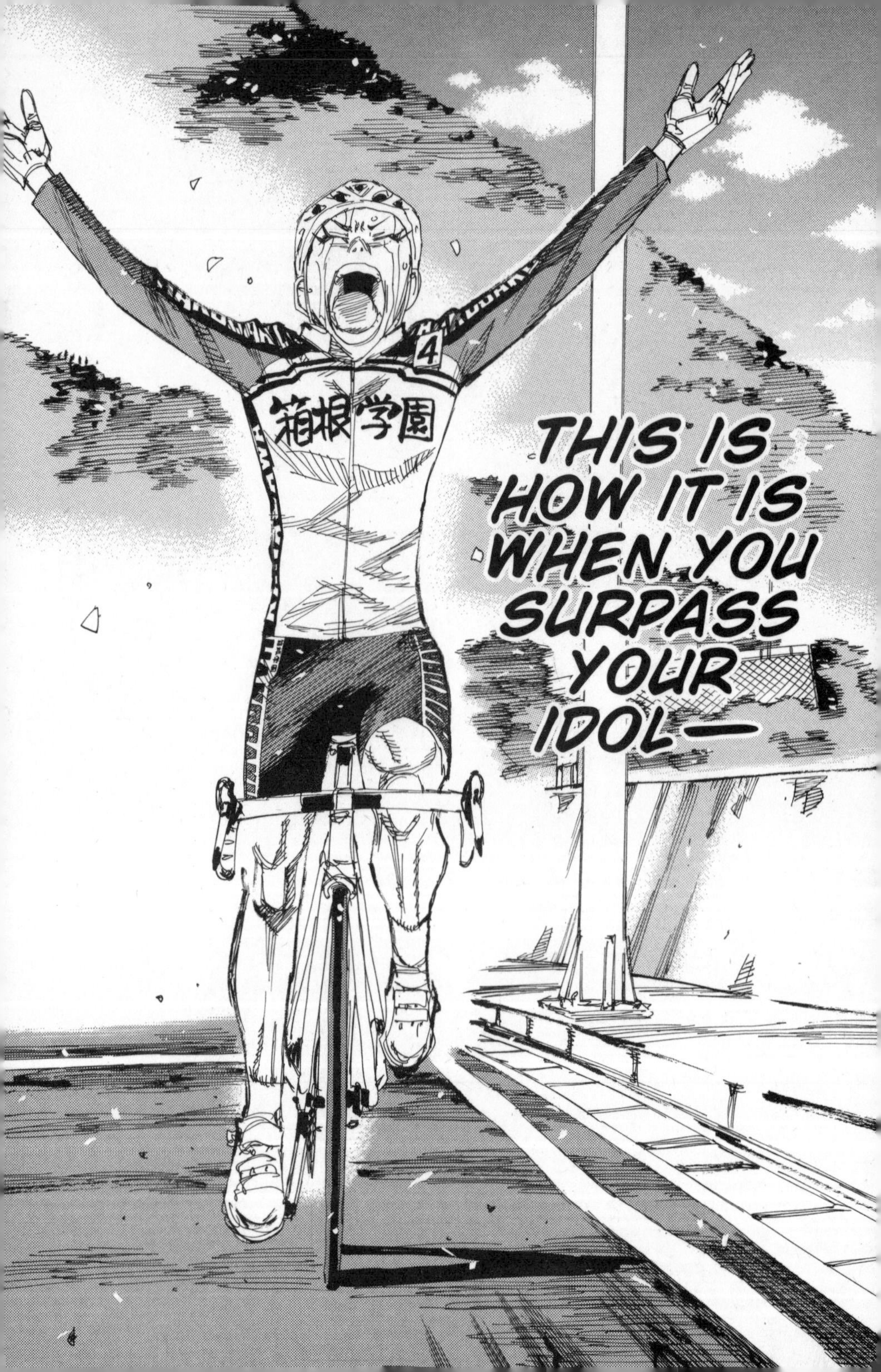
箱根学園
4
THIS IS HOW IT IS WHEN YOU SURPASS YOUR IDOL—

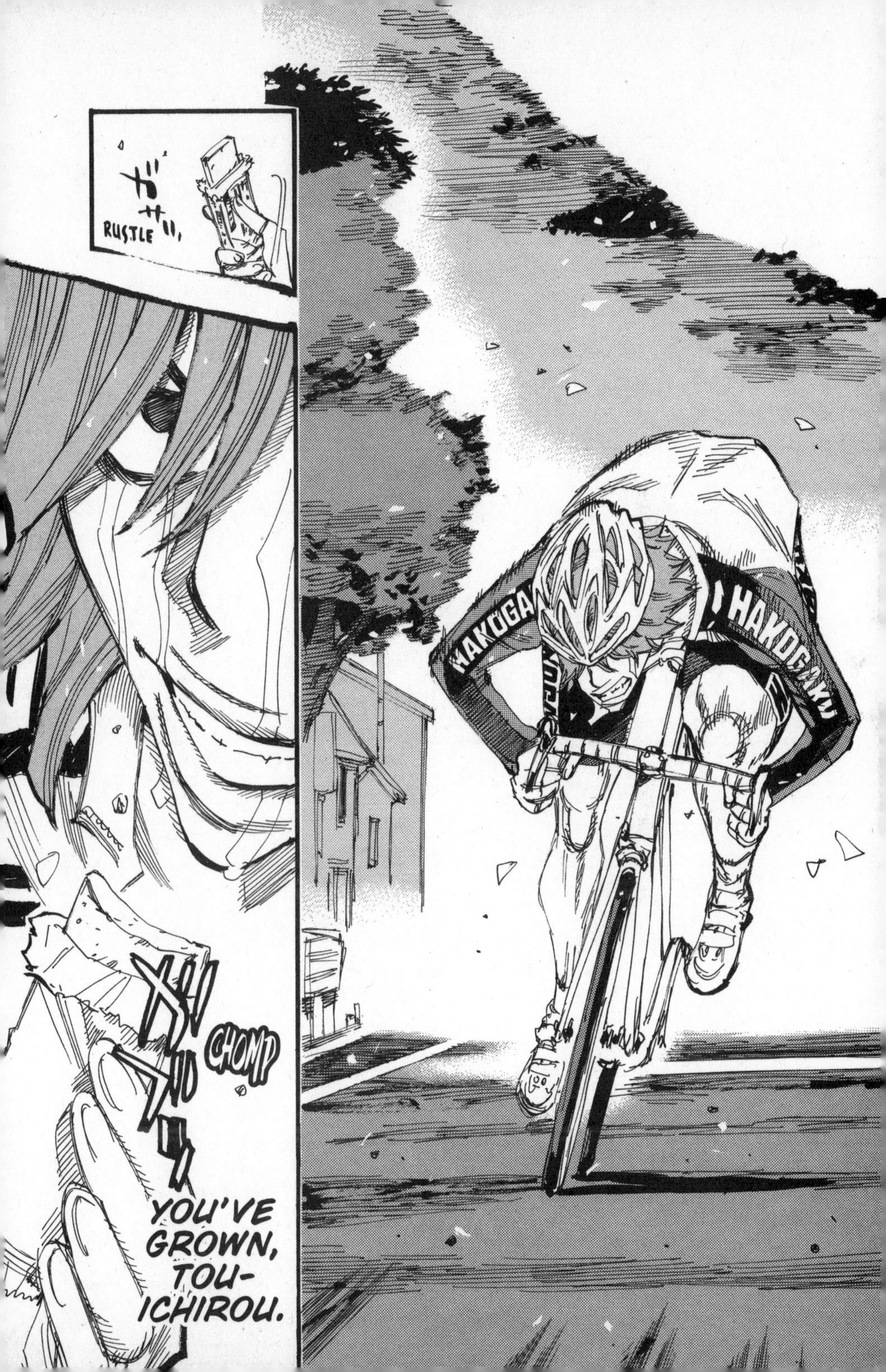
RUSTLE
CHOMP
YOU'VE GROWN, TOU-ICHIROU.

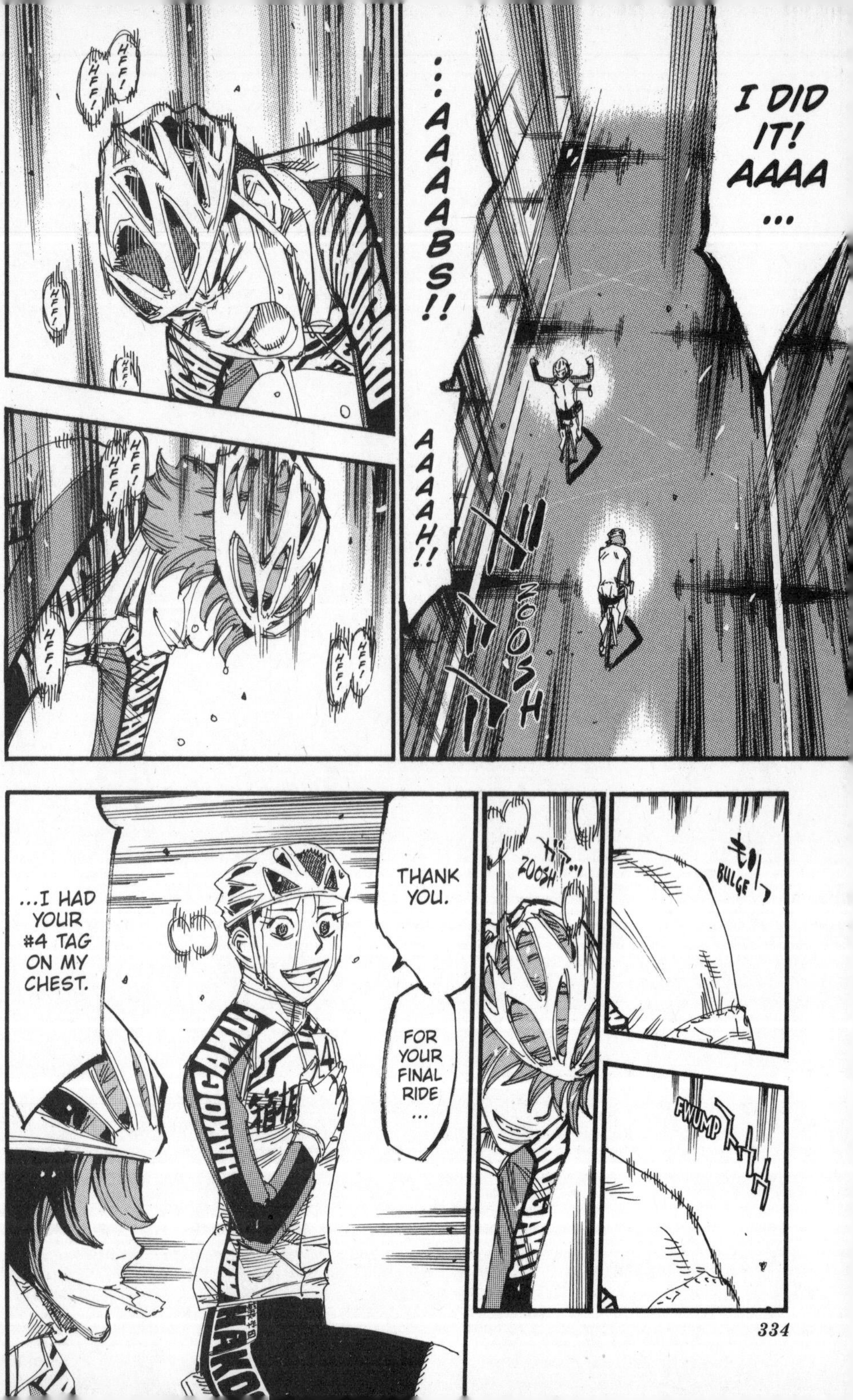
I DID IT! AAAA...
...AAAAABS!!
AAAAAH!!
ZOOSH
HFF! HFF!
HFF!
HFF!
HFF! HFF!
HFF!
HFF!
BULGE
FWUMP
ZOOSH
THANK YOU.
FOR YOUR FINAL RIDE...
...I HAD YOUR #4 TAG ON MY CHEST.

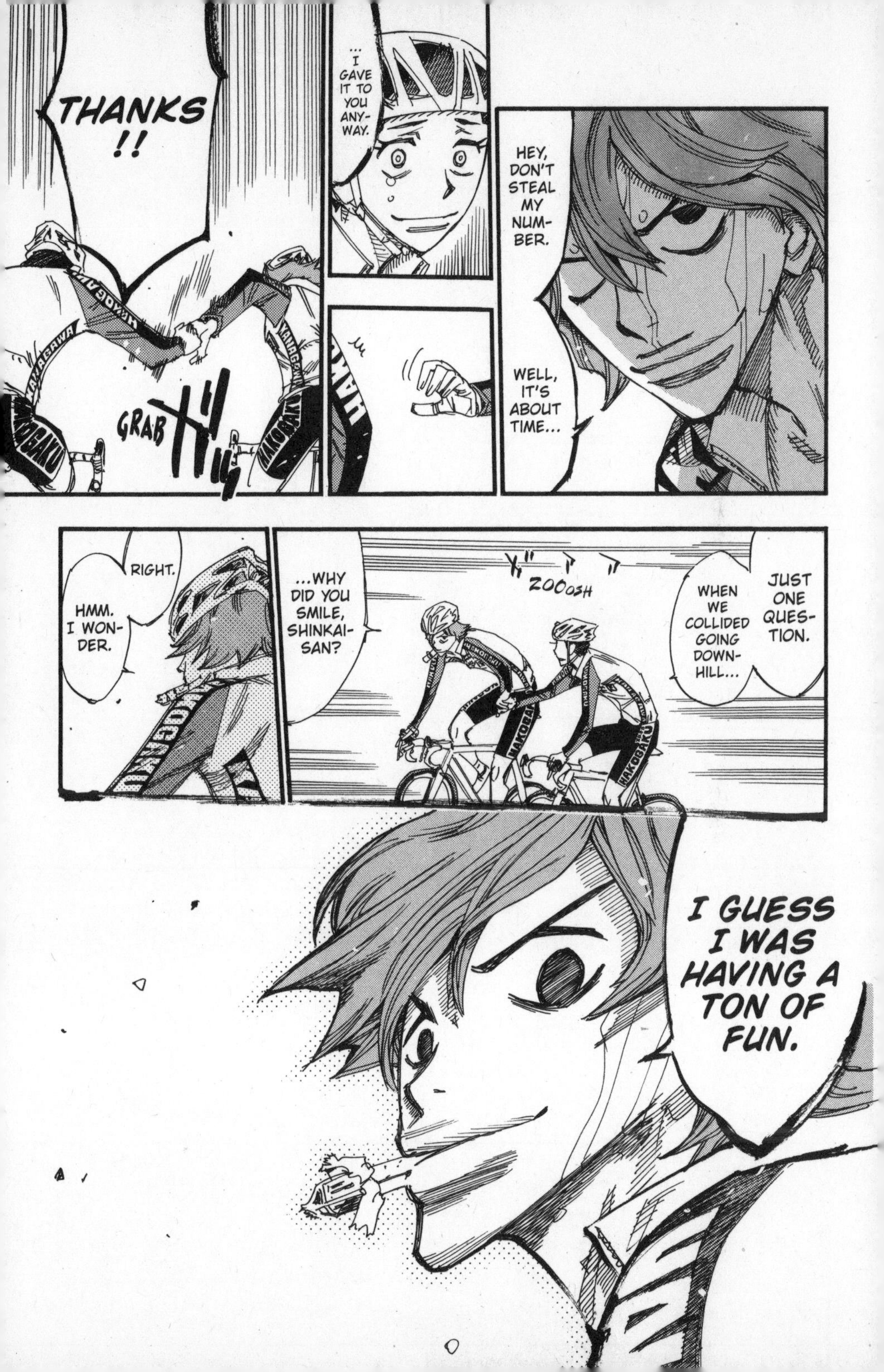
HEY, DON'T STEAL MY NUMBER.
WELL, IT'S ABOUT TIME...
...I GAVE IT TO YOU ANYWAY.
THANKS!!
GRAB
JUST ONE QUESTION.
WHEN WE COLLIDED GOING DOWNHILL...
ZOOOSH
...WHY DID YOU SMILE, SHINKAI-SAN?
RIGHT.
HMM. I WONDER.
I GUESS I WAS HAVING A TON OF FUN.

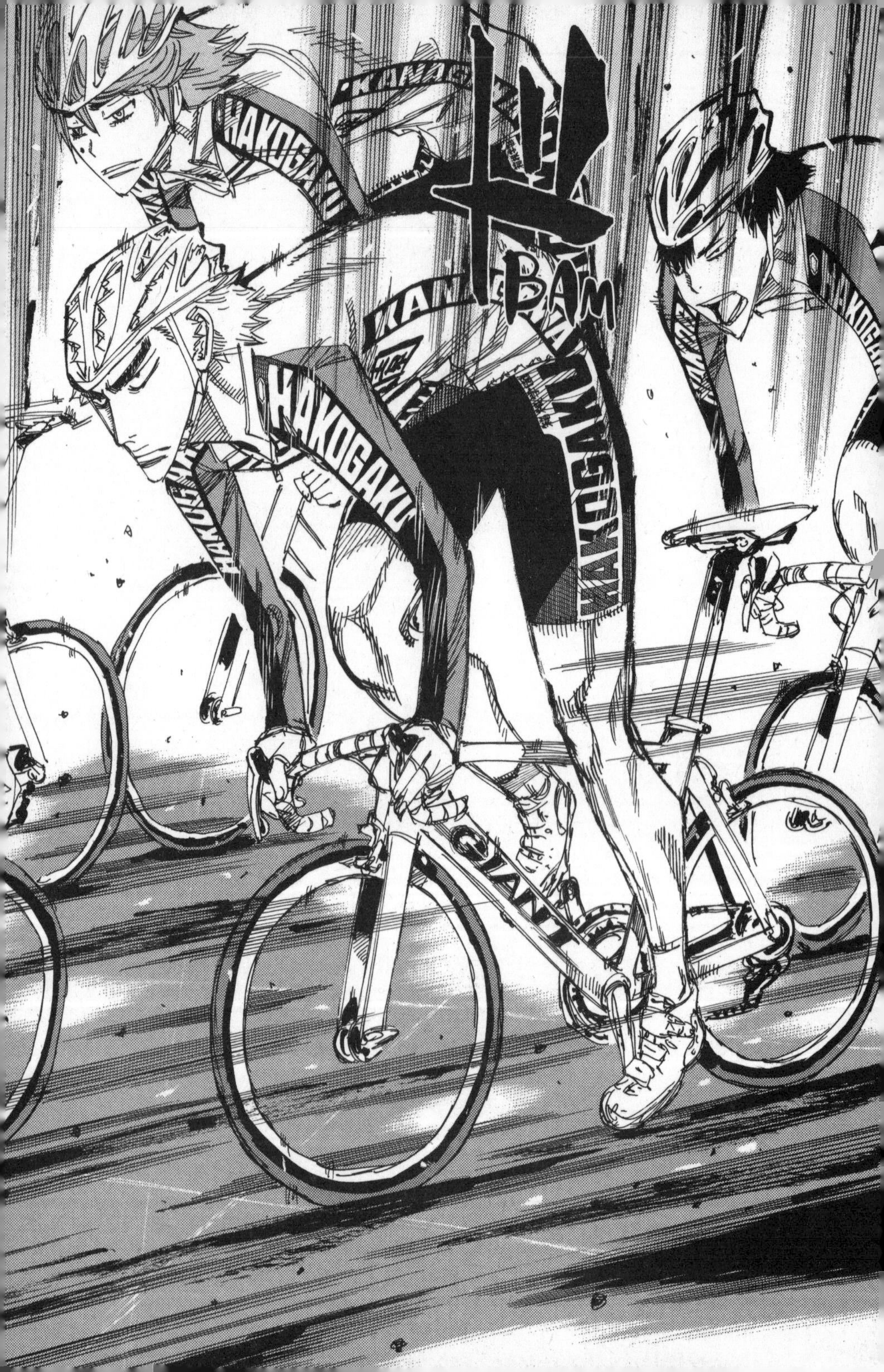
BAM
HAKOGAKU
HAKOGAKU
HAKOGAKU
GIANT

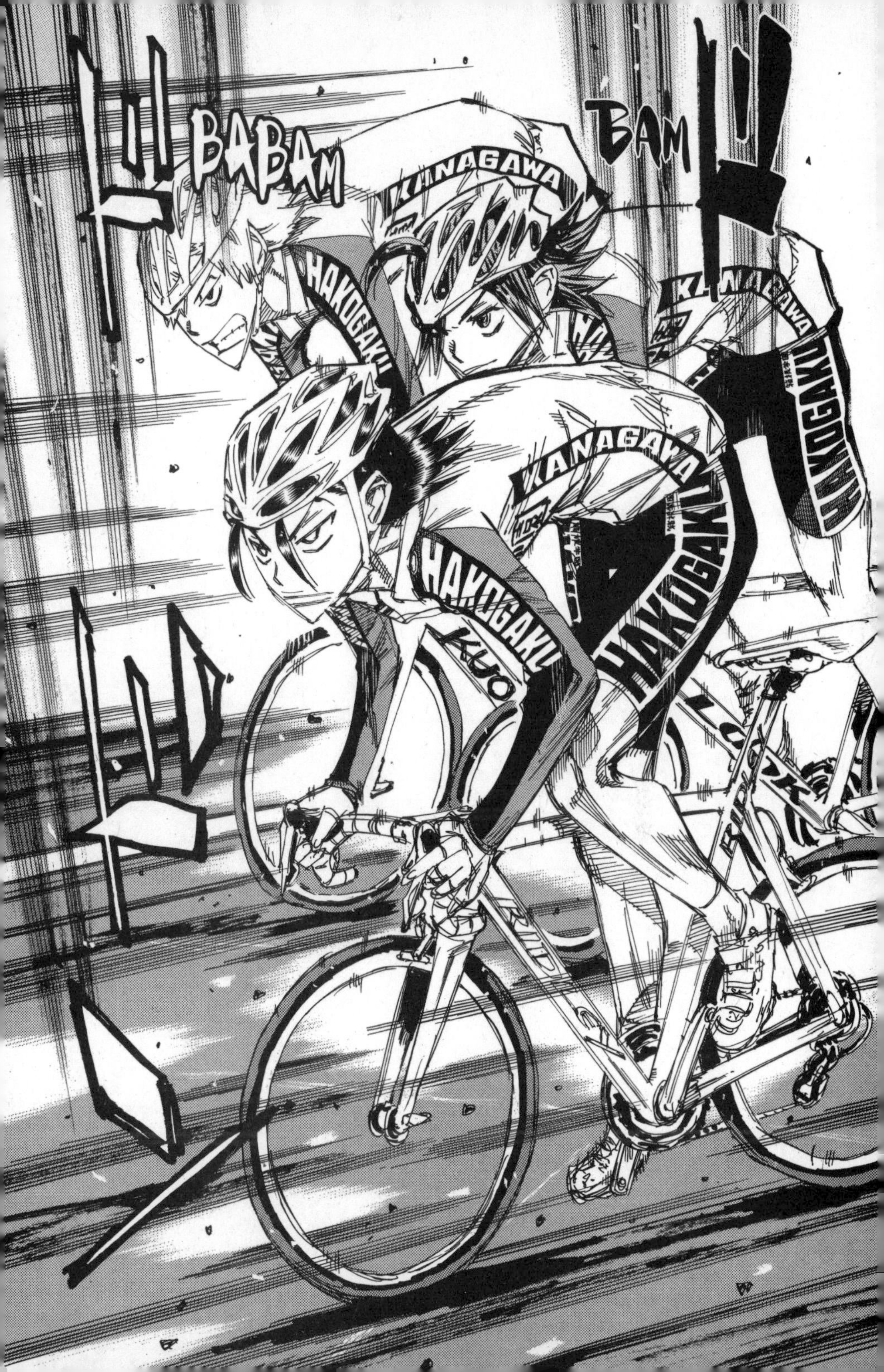
BAM
BABAM

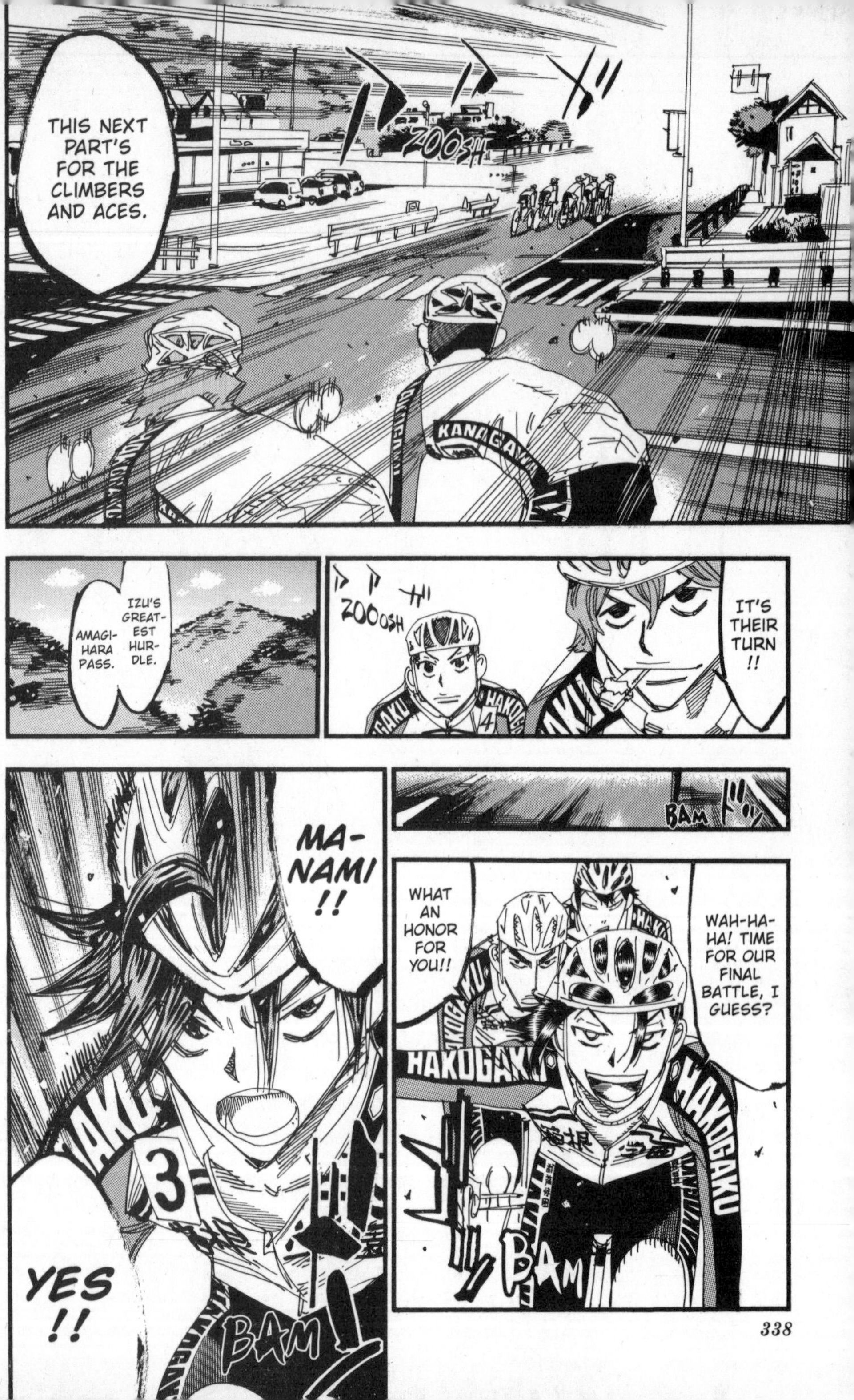
THIS NEXT PART'S FOR THE CLIMBERS AND ACES.
ZOOSH
ZOOOSH
IT'S THEIR TURN!!
IZU'S GREAT-EST HUR-DLE.
AMAGI-HARA PASS.
BAM
WAH-HA-HA! TIME FOR OUR FINAL BATTLE, I GUESS?
WHAT AN HONOR FOR YOU!!
BAM
MA-NAMI!!
YES!!
BAM

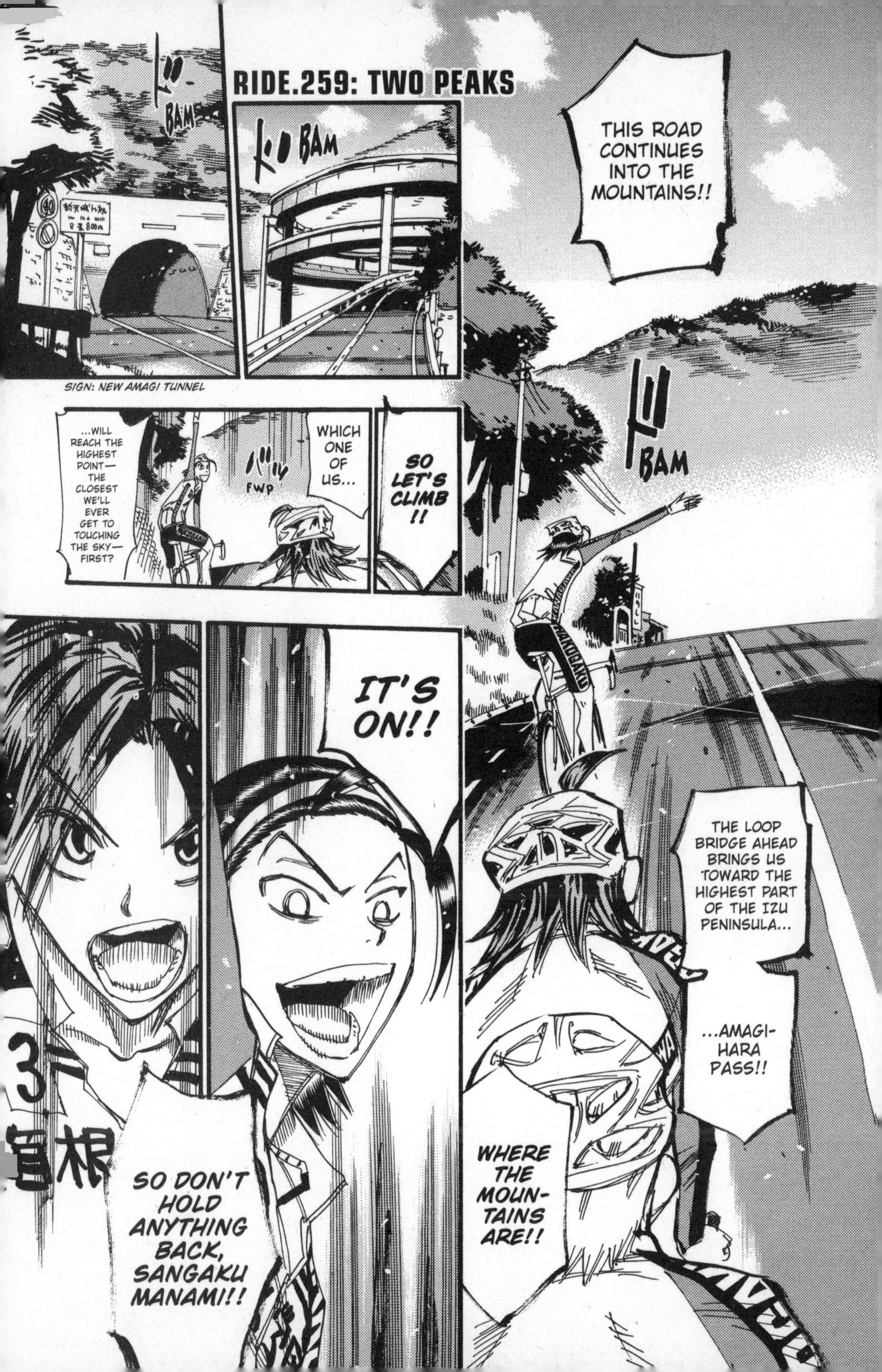

RIDE.259: TWO PEAKS
THIS ROAD CONTINUES INTO THE MOUNTAINS!!
BAM
THE LOOP BRIDGE AHEAD BRINGS US TOWARD THE HIGHEST PART OF THE IZU PENINSULA...
...AMAGI-HARA PASS!!
WHERE THE MOUN-TAINS ARE!!
BAM
BAM
SIGN: NEW AMAGI TUNNEL
SO LET'S CLIMB!!
WHICH ONE OF US...
FWP
...WILL REACH THE HIGHEST POINT—THE CLOSEST WE'LL EVER GET TO TOUCHING THE SKY—FIRST?
IT'S ON!!
SO DON'T HOLD ANYTHING BACK, SANGAKU MANAMI!!

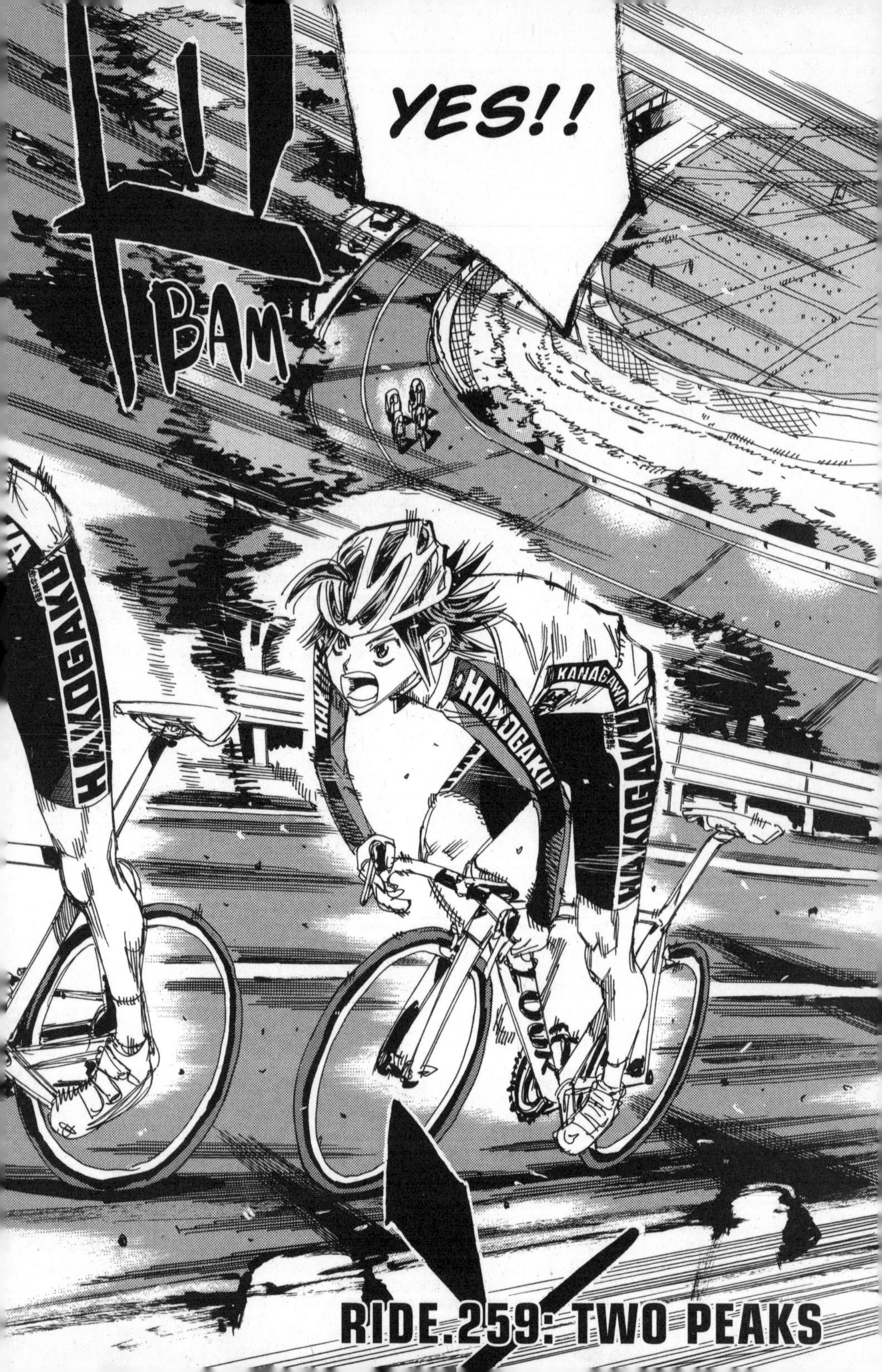
YES!!
BAM
HAKOGAKU
KANAGAWA
RIDE.259: TWO PEAKS

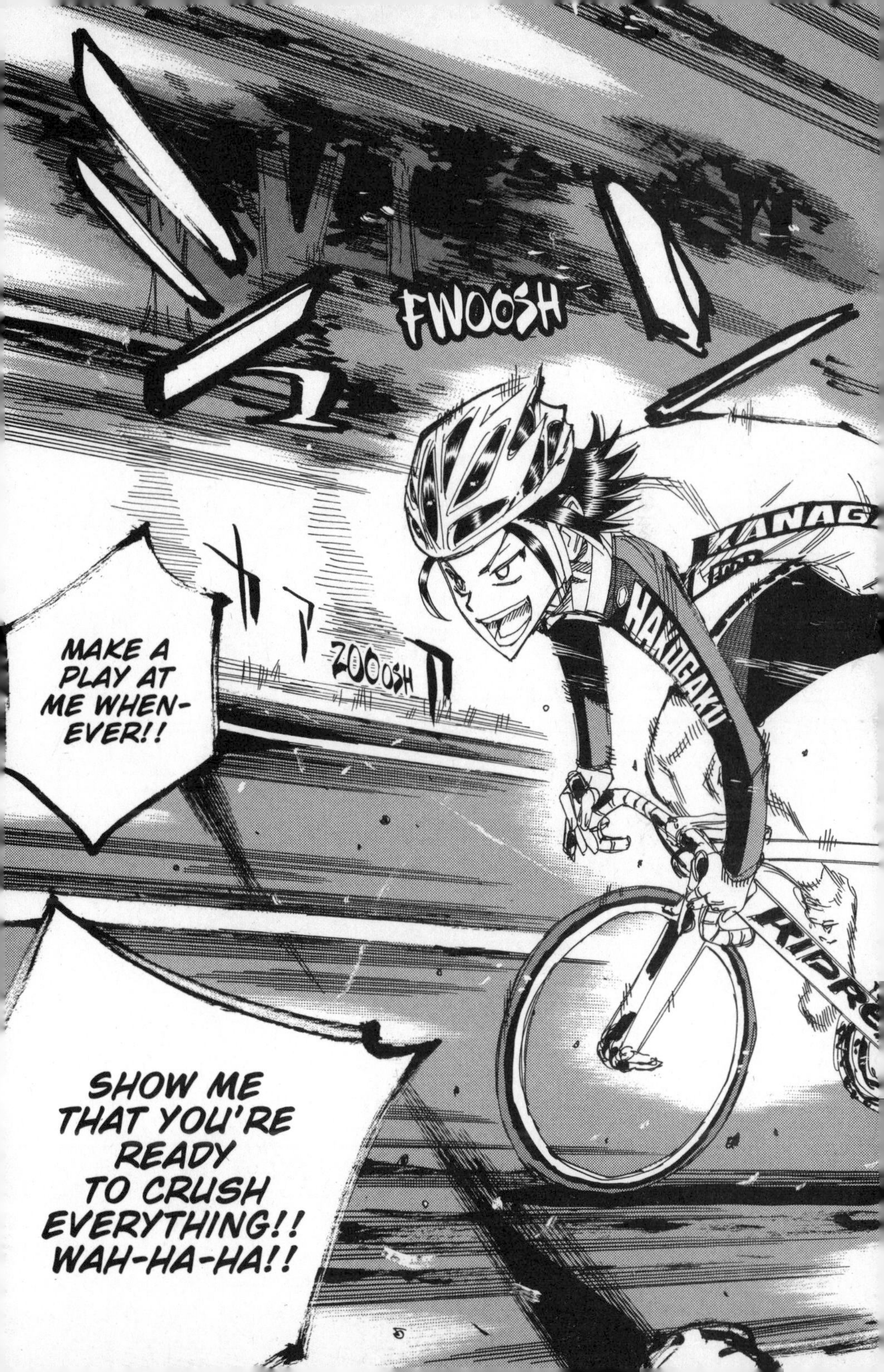
FWOOSH
MAKE A PLAY AT ME WHEN-EVER!!
ZOOOSH
SHOW ME THAT YOU'RE READY TO CRUSH EVERYTHING!! WAH-HA-HA!!
KANAG
HAKOGAKU
RIDRE

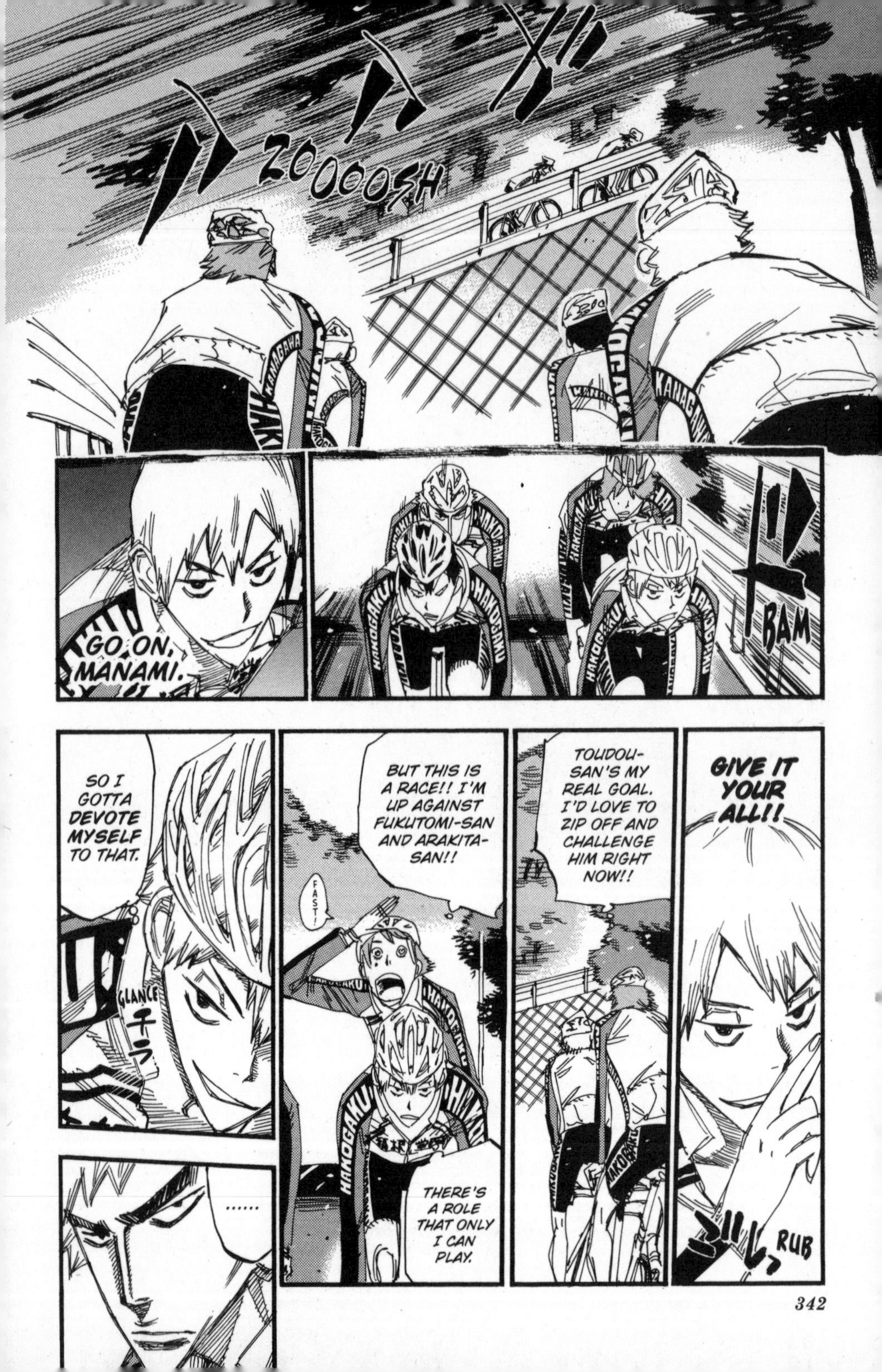
ZOOOOSH
BAM
GO ON, MANAMI.
GIVE IT YOUR ALL!!
RUB
TOUDOU-SAN'S MY REAL GOAL. I'D LOVE TO ZIP OFF AND CHALLENGE HIM RIGHT NOW!!
BUT THIS IS A RACE!! I'M UP AGAINST FUKUTOMI-SAN AND ARAKITA-SAN!!
FAST!
THERE'S A ROLE THAT ONLY I CAN PLAY.
SO I GOTTA DEVOTE MYSELF TO THAT.
GLANCE
......

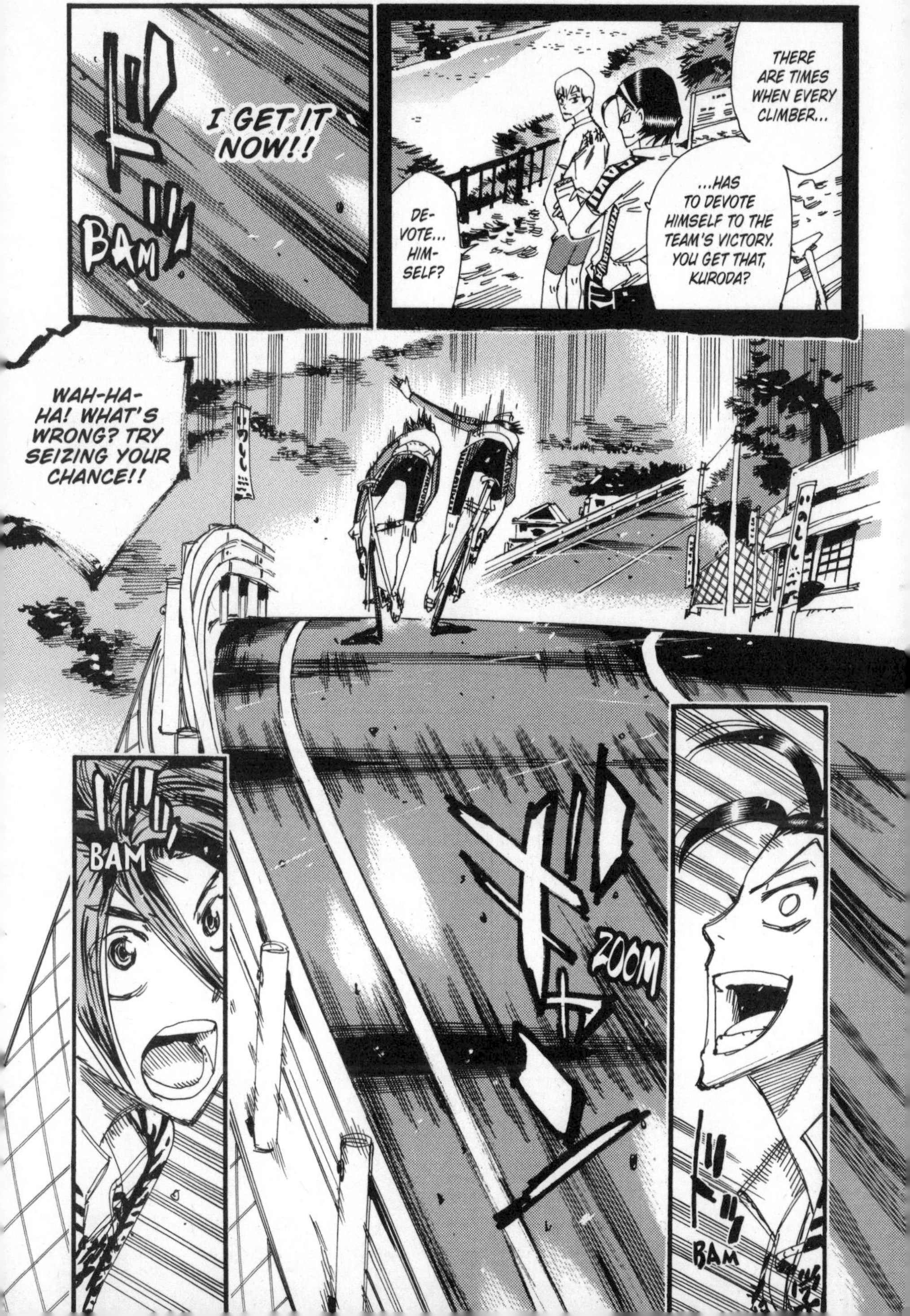
THERE ARE TIMES WHEN EVERY CLIMBER...
...HAS TO DEVOTE HIMSELF TO THE TEAM'S VICTORY. YOU GET THAT, KURODA?
DE-VOTE... HIM-SELF?
I GET IT NOW!!
BAM
WAH-HA-HA! WHAT'S WRONG? TRY SEIZING YOUR CHANCE!!
ZOOM
BAM
BAM

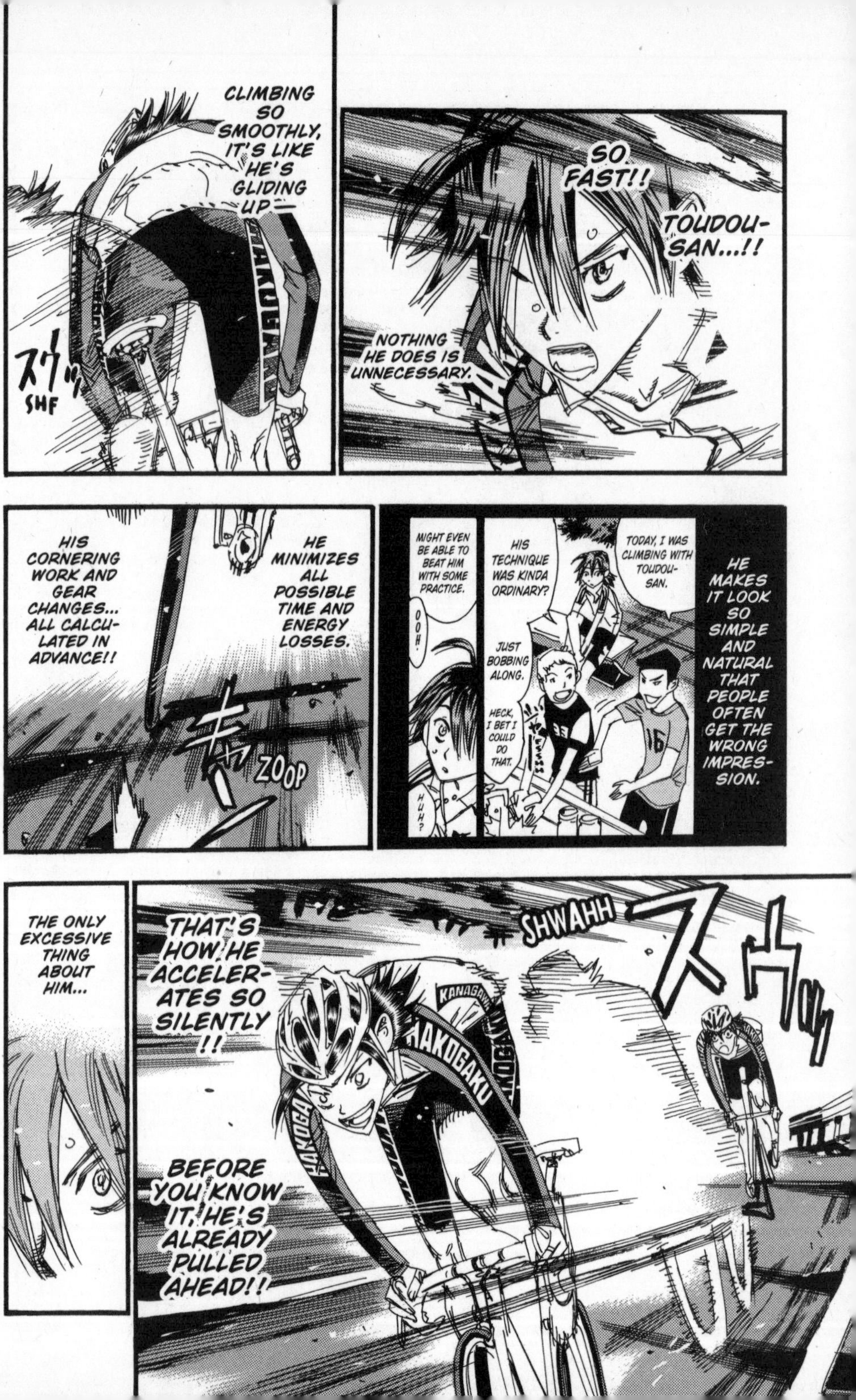
SO FAST!!
TOUDOU-SAN...!!
NOTHING HE DOES IS UNNECESSARY.
CLIMBING SO SMOOTHLY, IT'S LIKE HE'S GLIDING UP—
スゥッ
SHF
HE MAKES IT LOOK SO SIMPLE AND NATURAL THAT PEOPLE OFTEN GET THE WRONG IMPRESSION.
TODAY, I WAS CLIMBING WITH TOUDOU-SAN.
HIS TECHNIQUE WAS KINDA ORDINARY?
JUST BOBBING ALONG.
HECK, I BET I COULD DO THAT.
MIGHT EVEN BE ABLE TO BEAT HIM WITH SOME PRACTICE.
OOH!
HUH?
HE MINIMIZES ALL POSSIBLE TIME AND ENERGY LOSSES.
HIS CORNERING WORK AND GEAR CHANGES... ALL CALCULATED IN ADVANCE!!
ZOOP
SHWAHH
THAT'S HOW HE ACCELERATES SO SILENTLY!!
BEFORE YOU KNOW IT, HE'S ALREADY PULLED AHEAD!!
THE ONLY EXCESSIVE THING ABOUT HIM...

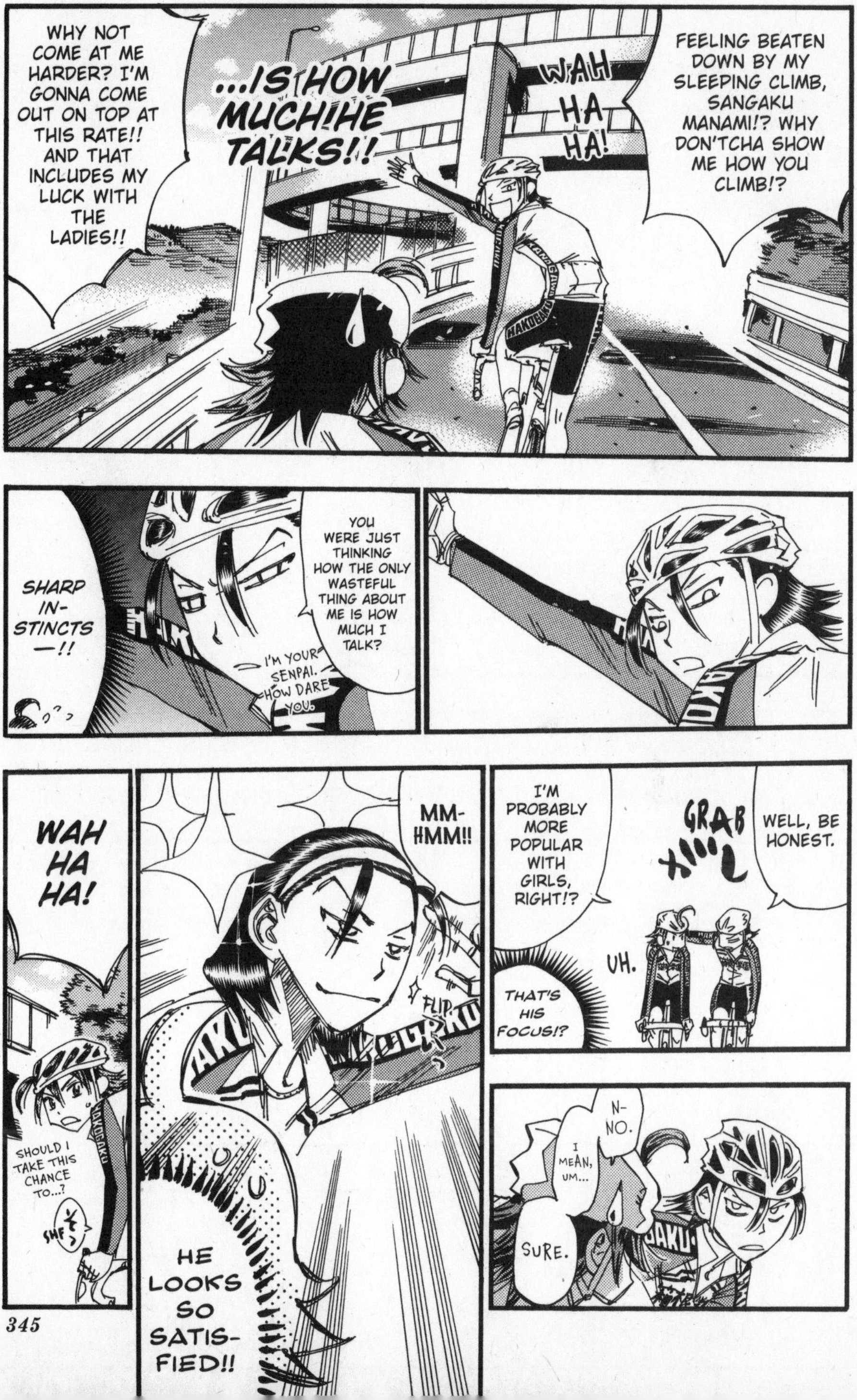
FEELING BEATEN DOWN BY MY SLEEPING CLIMB, SANGAKU MANAMI!? WHY DON'TCHA SHOW ME HOW YOU CLIMB!?
WAH HA HA!
...IS HOW MUCH HE TALKS!!
WHY NOT COME AT ME HARDER? I'M GONNA COME OUT ON TOP AT THIS RATE!! AND THAT INCLUDES MY LUCK WITH THE LADIES!!
YOU WERE JUST THINKING HOW THE ONLY WASTEFUL THING ABOUT ME IS HOW MUCH I TALK?
I'M YOUR SENPAI. HOW DARE YOU.
SHARP IN-STINCTS—!!
WELL, BE HONEST.
GRAB
I'M PROBABLY MORE POPULAR WITH GIRLS, RIGHT!?
UH.
THAT'S HIS FOCUS!?
N-NO.
I MEAN, UM...
SURE.
MM-HMM!!
FLIP
HE LOOKS SO SATIS-FIED!!
WAH HA HA!
SHOULD I TAKE THIS CHANCE TO...?
SHF

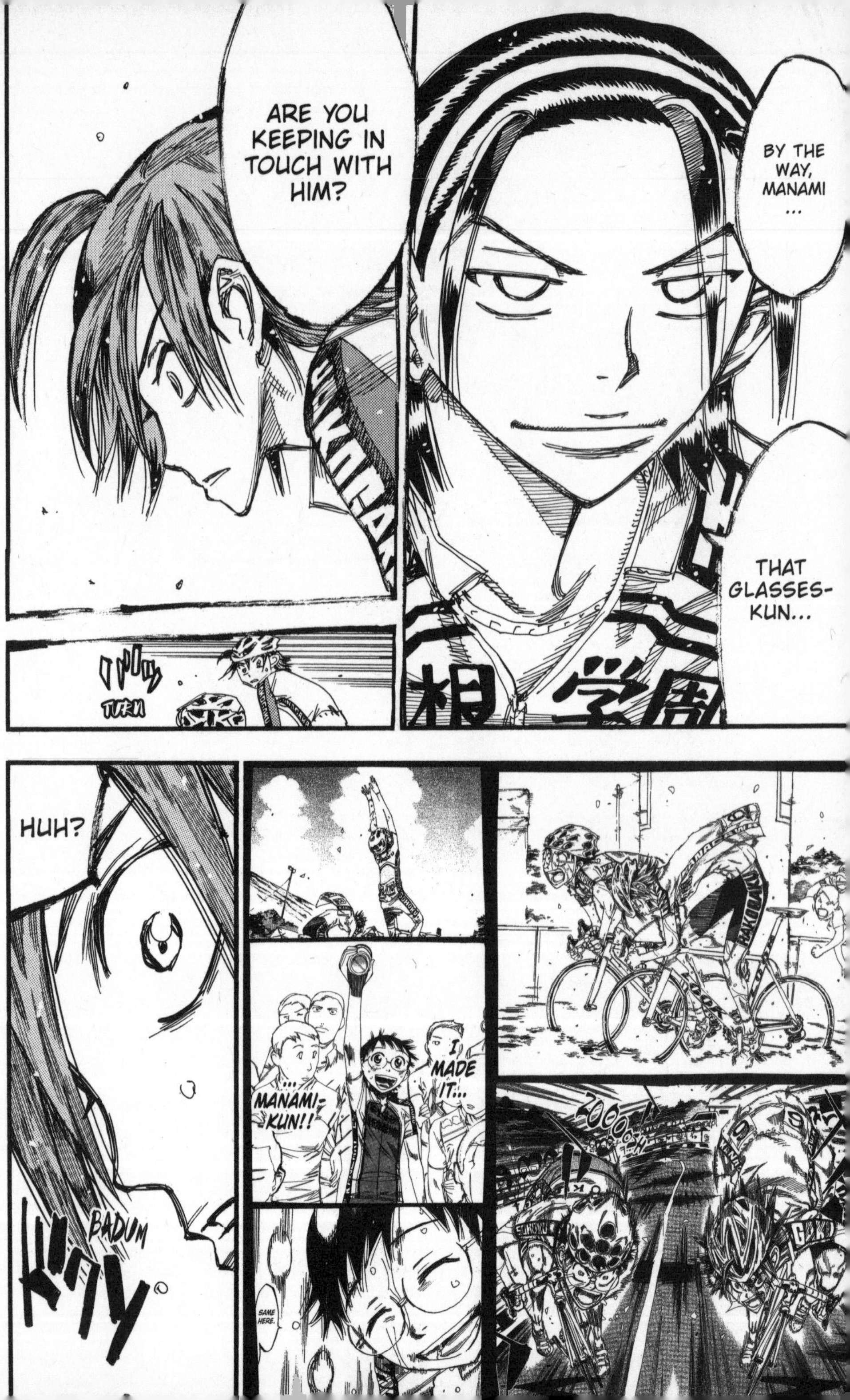
BY THE WAY, MANAMI...
THAT GLASSES-KUN...
ARE YOU KEEPING IN TOUCH WITH HIM?
TURN
I MADE IT...
...MANAMI-KUN!!
SAME HERE.
HUH?
BADUM

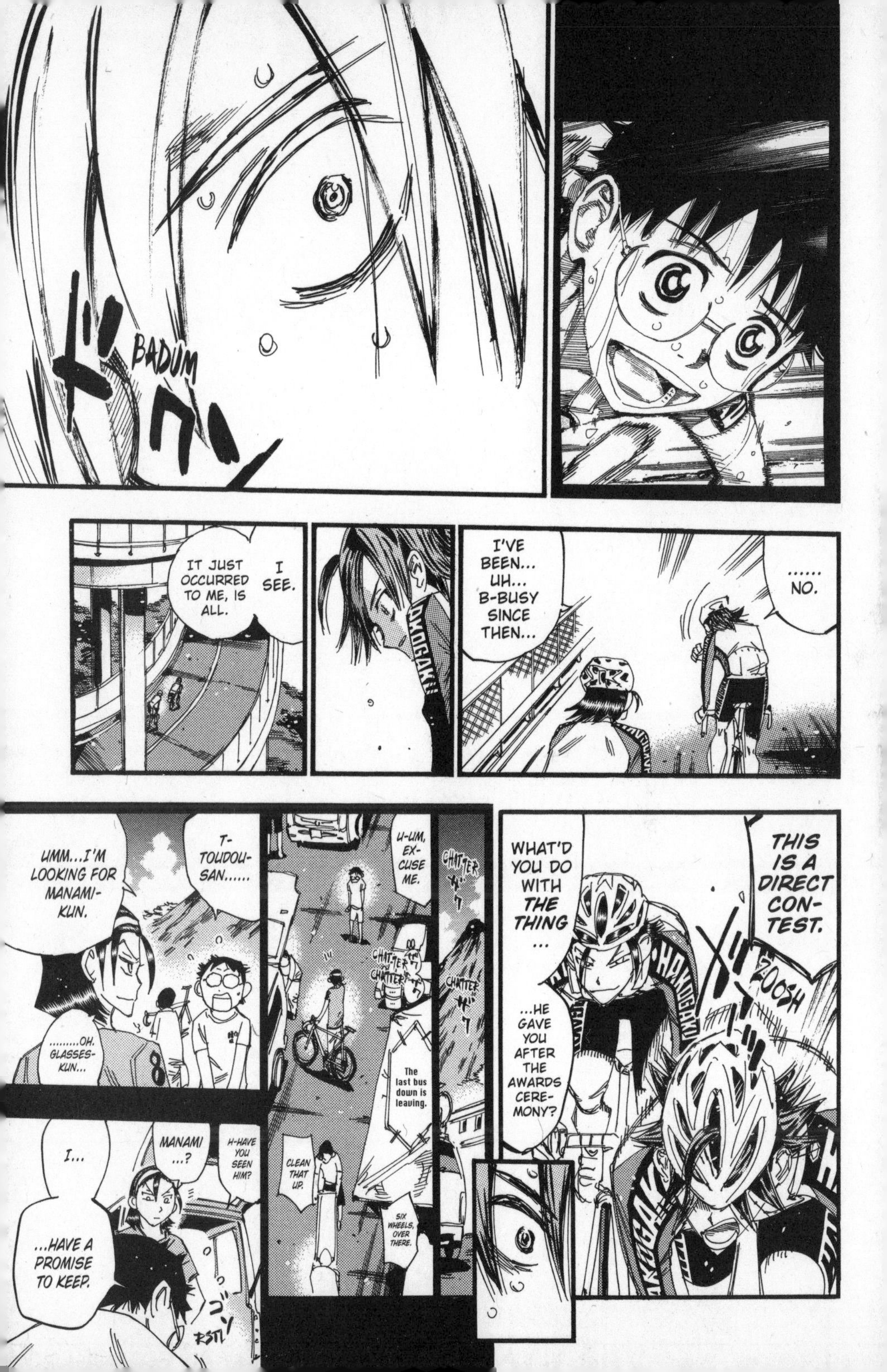
BADUM
......NO.
I'VE BEEN... UH... B-BUSY SINCE THEN...
I SEE.
IT JUST OCCURRED TO ME, IS ALL.
THIS IS A DIRECT CON-TEST.
ZOOSH
WHAT'D YOU DO WITH THE THING...
...HE GAVE YOU AFTER THE AWARDS CERE-MONY?
U-UM, EX-CUSE ME.
CHATTER
CHATTER CHATTER
CHATTER
The last bus down is leaving.
CLEAN THAT UP.
SIX WHEELS, OVER THERE.
T-TOUDOU-SAN......
UMM...I'M LOOKING FOR MANAMI-KUN.
........OH. GLASSES-KUN...
H-HAVE YOU SEEN HIM?
MANAMI...?
I...
...HAVE A PROMISE TO KEEP.
RSTL

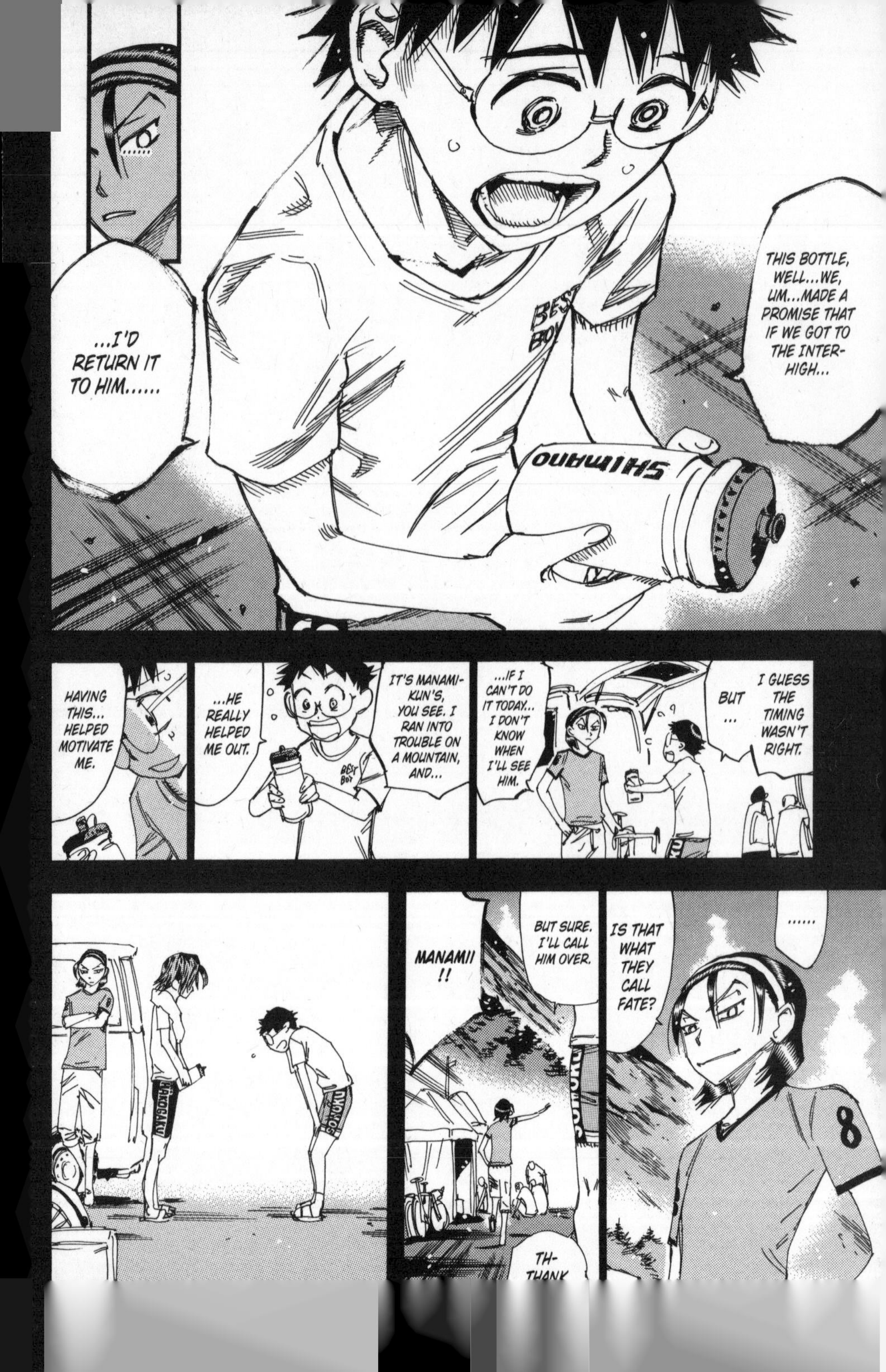
THIS BOTTLE, WELL...WE, UM...MADE A PROMISE THAT IF WE GOT TO THE INTER-HIGH...
...I'D RETURN IT TO HIM......
I GUESS THE TIMING WASN'T RIGHT.
BUT ...
...IF I CAN'T DO IT TODAY... I DON'T KNOW WHEN I'LL SEE HIM.
IT'S MANAMI-KUN'S, YOU SEE. I RAN INTO TROUBLE ON A MOUNTAIN, AND...
...HE REALLY HELPED ME OUT.
HAVING THIS... HELPED MOTIVATE ME.
......
IS THAT WHAT THEY CALL FATE?
BUT SURE. I'LL CALL HIM OVER.
MANAMI !!
TH- THANK

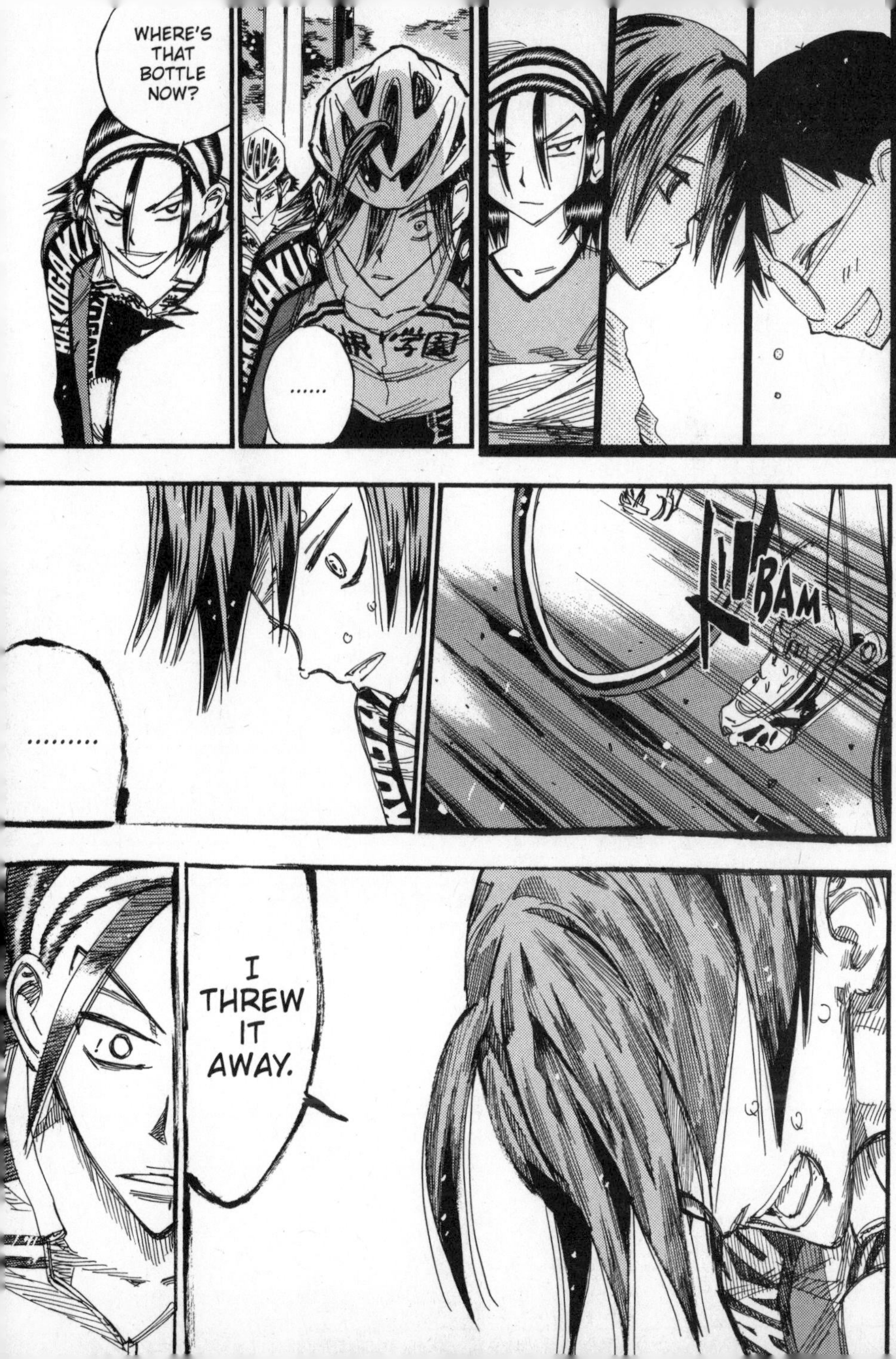
......
WHERE'S THAT BOTTLE NOW?
!! BAM
....
I THREW IT AWAY.

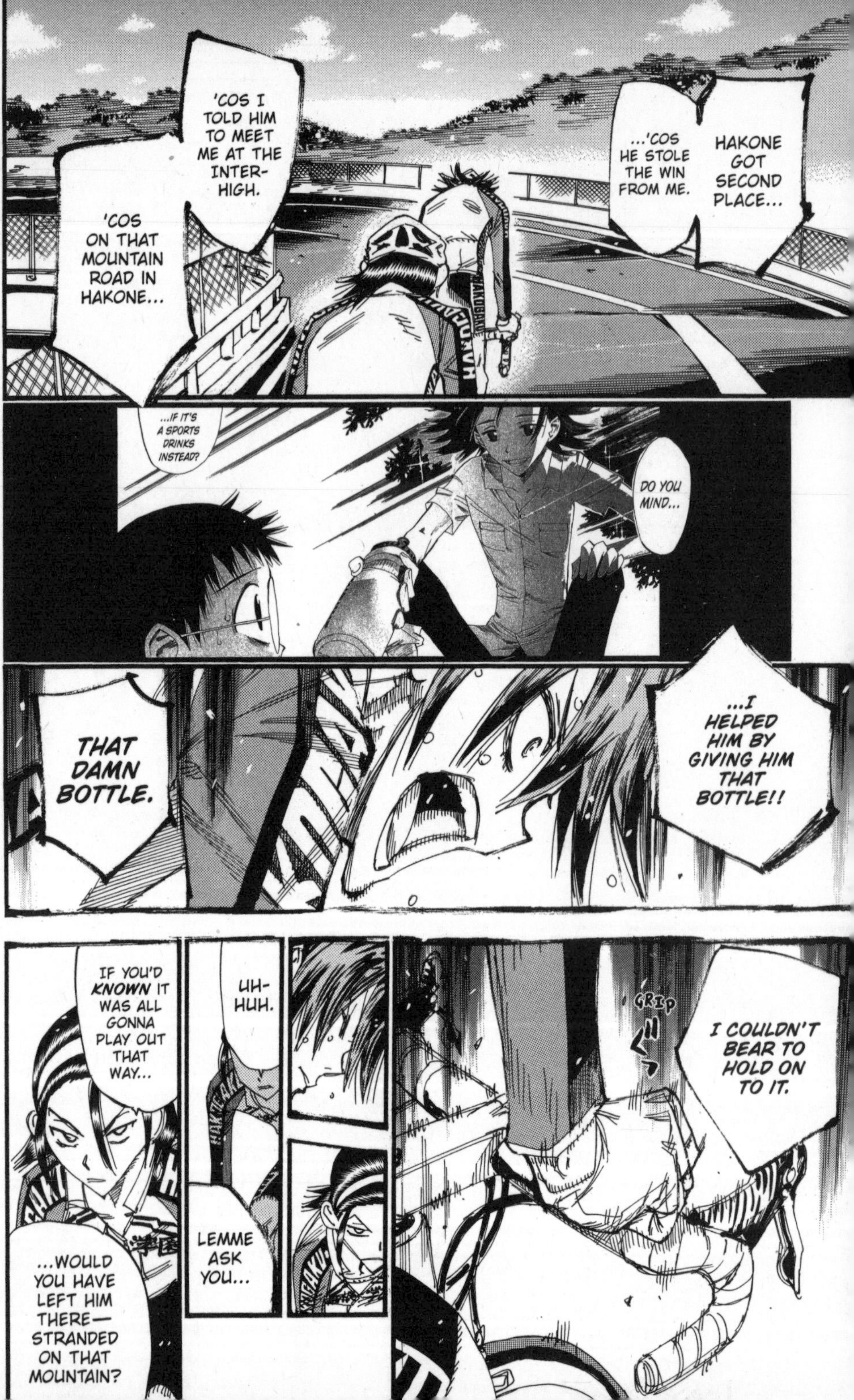
HAKONE GOT SECOND PLACE...
...'COS HE STOLE THE WIN FROM ME.
'COS I TOLD HIM TO MEET ME AT THE INTER-HIGH.
'COS ON THAT MOUNTAIN ROAD IN HAKONE...
DO YOU MIND...
...IF IT'S A SPORTS DRINKS INSTEAD?
...I HELPED HIM BY GIVING HIM THAT BOTTLE!!
THAT DAMN BOTTLE.
GRIP
I COULDN'T BEAR TO HOLD ON TO IT.
UH-HUH.
LEMME ASK YOU...
IF YOU'D KNOWN IT WAS ALL GONNA PLAY OUT THAT WAY...
...WOULD YOU HAVE LEFT HIM THERE—STRANDED ON THAT MOUNTAIN?

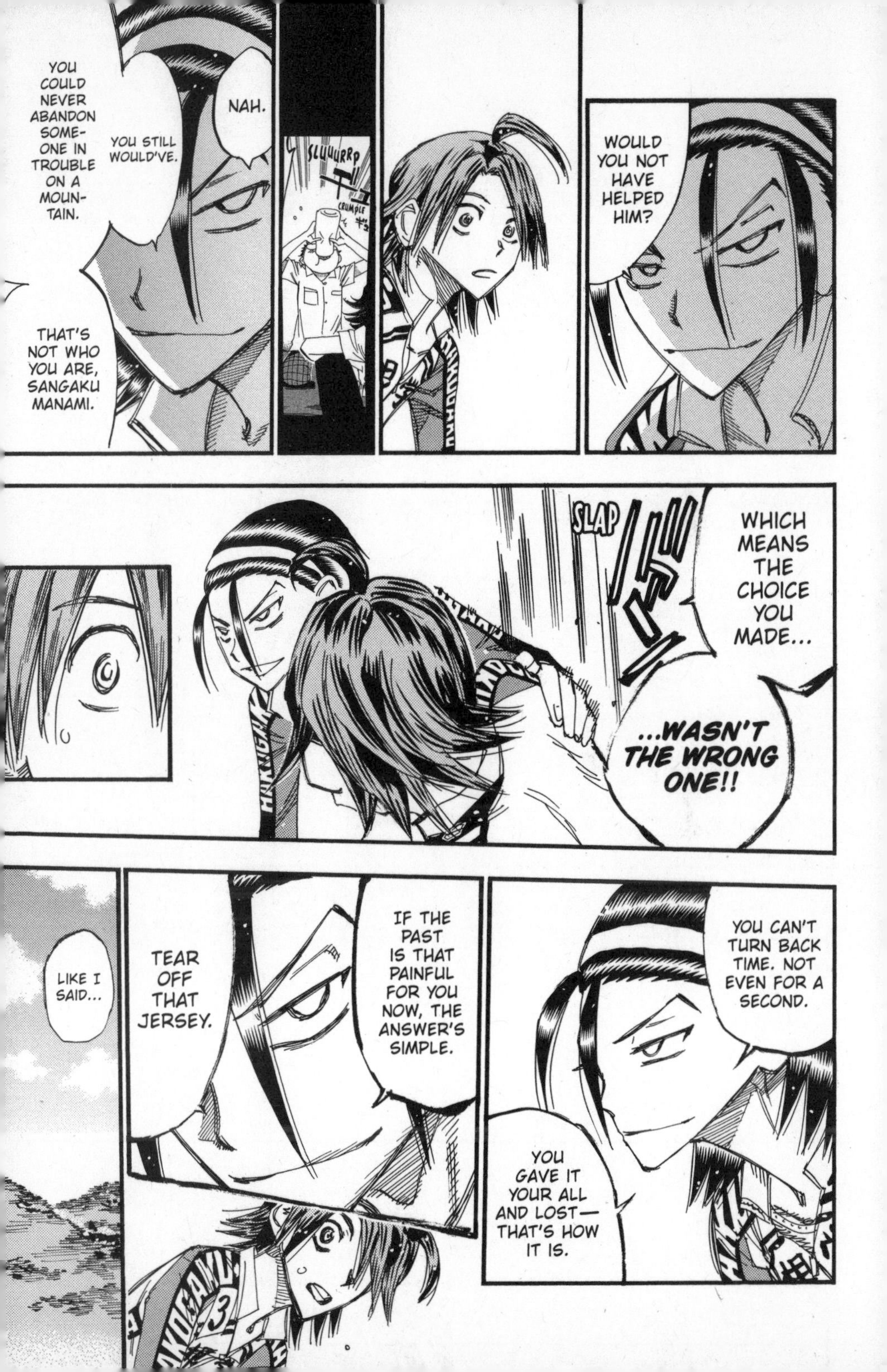
WOULD YOU NOT HAVE HELPED HIM?
SLUUURRP
CRUMPLE
NAH.
YOU STILL WOULD'VE.
YOU COULD NEVER ABANDON SOMEONE IN TROUBLE ON A MOUNTAIN.
THAT'S NOT WHO YOU ARE, SANGAKU MANAMI.
WHICH MEANS THE CHOICE YOU MADE...
SLAP
...WASN'T THE WRONG ONE!!
YOU CAN'T TURN BACK TIME. NOT EVEN FOR A SECOND.
YOU GAVE IT YOUR ALL AND LOST—THAT'S HOW IT IS.
IF THE PAST IS THAT PAINFUL FOR YOU NOW, THE ANSWER'S SIMPLE.
TEAR OFF THAT JERSEY.
LIKE I SAID...

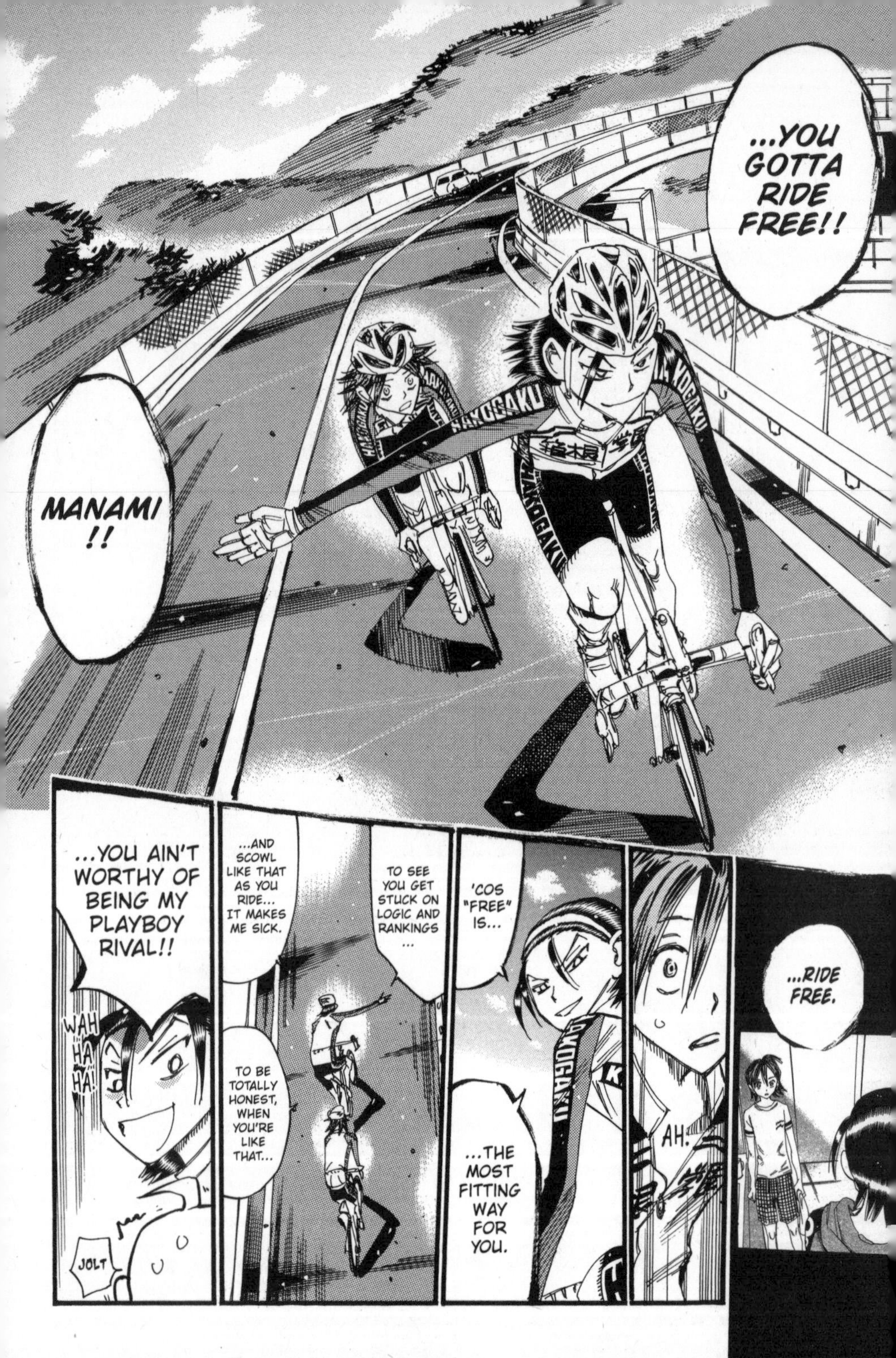
...YOU GOTTA RIDE FREE!!
MANAMI!!
...RIDE FREE.
AH.
'COS "FREE" IS...
...THE MOST FITTING WAY FOR YOU.
TO SEE YOU GET STUCK ON LOGIC AND RANKINGS...
...AND SCOWL LIKE THAT AS YOU RIDE... IT MAKES ME SICK.
TO BE TOTALLY HONEST, WHEN YOU'RE LIKE THAT...
...YOU AIN'T WORTHY OF BEING MY PLAYBOY RIVAL!!
WAH HA HA!
JOLT

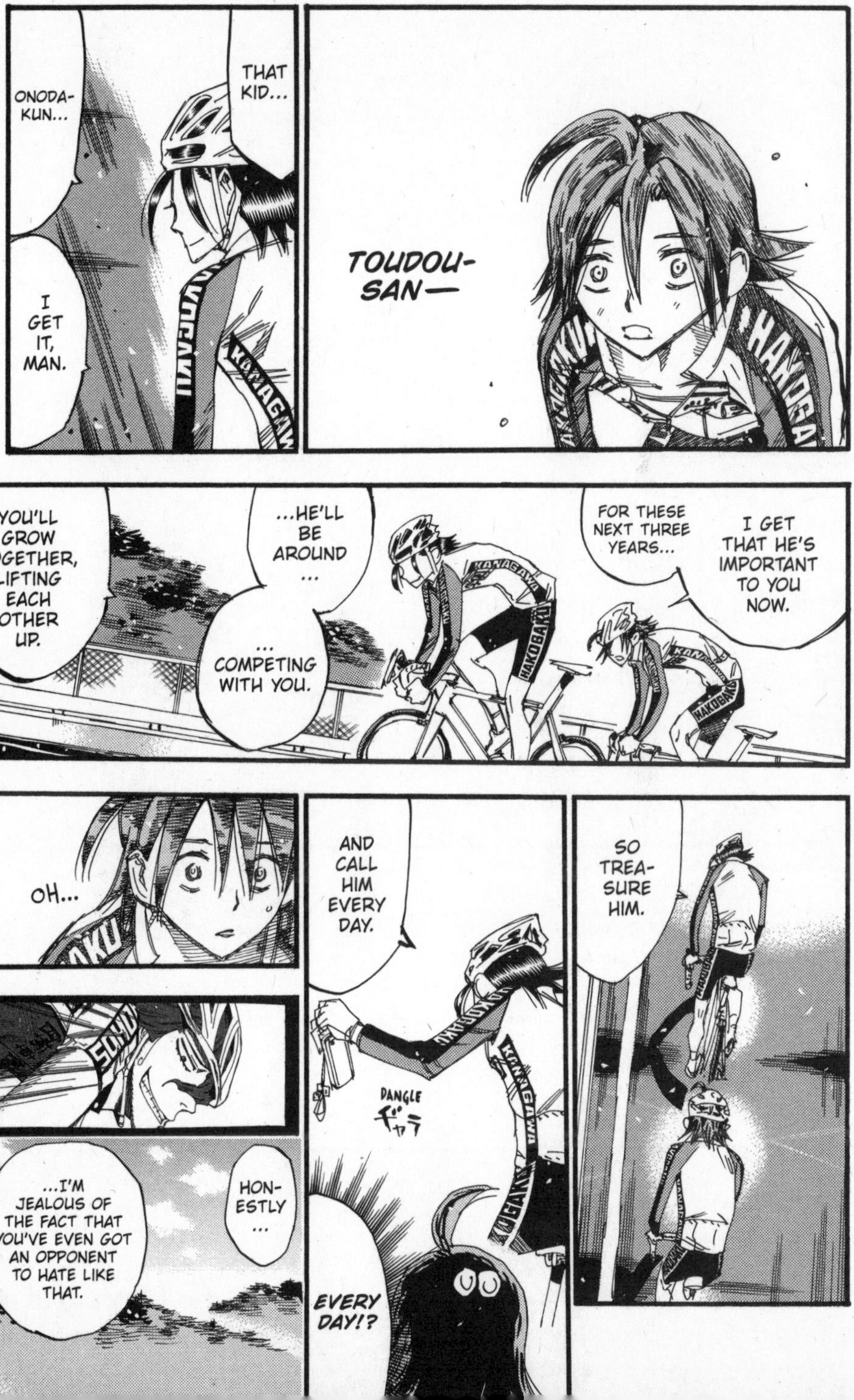
TOUDOU-SAN—
THAT KID...
ONODA-KUN...
I GET IT, MAN.
I GET THAT HE'S IMPORTANT TO YOU NOW.
FOR THESE NEXT THREE YEARS...
...HE'LL BE AROUND...
...COMPETING WITH YOU.
YOU'LL GROW TOGETHER, LIFTING EACH OTHER UP.
SO TREASURE HIM.
AND CALL HIM EVERY DAY.
DANGLE
EVERY DAY!?
OH...
HONESTLY...
...I'M JEALOUS OF THE FACT THAT YOU'VE EVEN GOT AN OPPONENT TO HATE LIKE THAT.

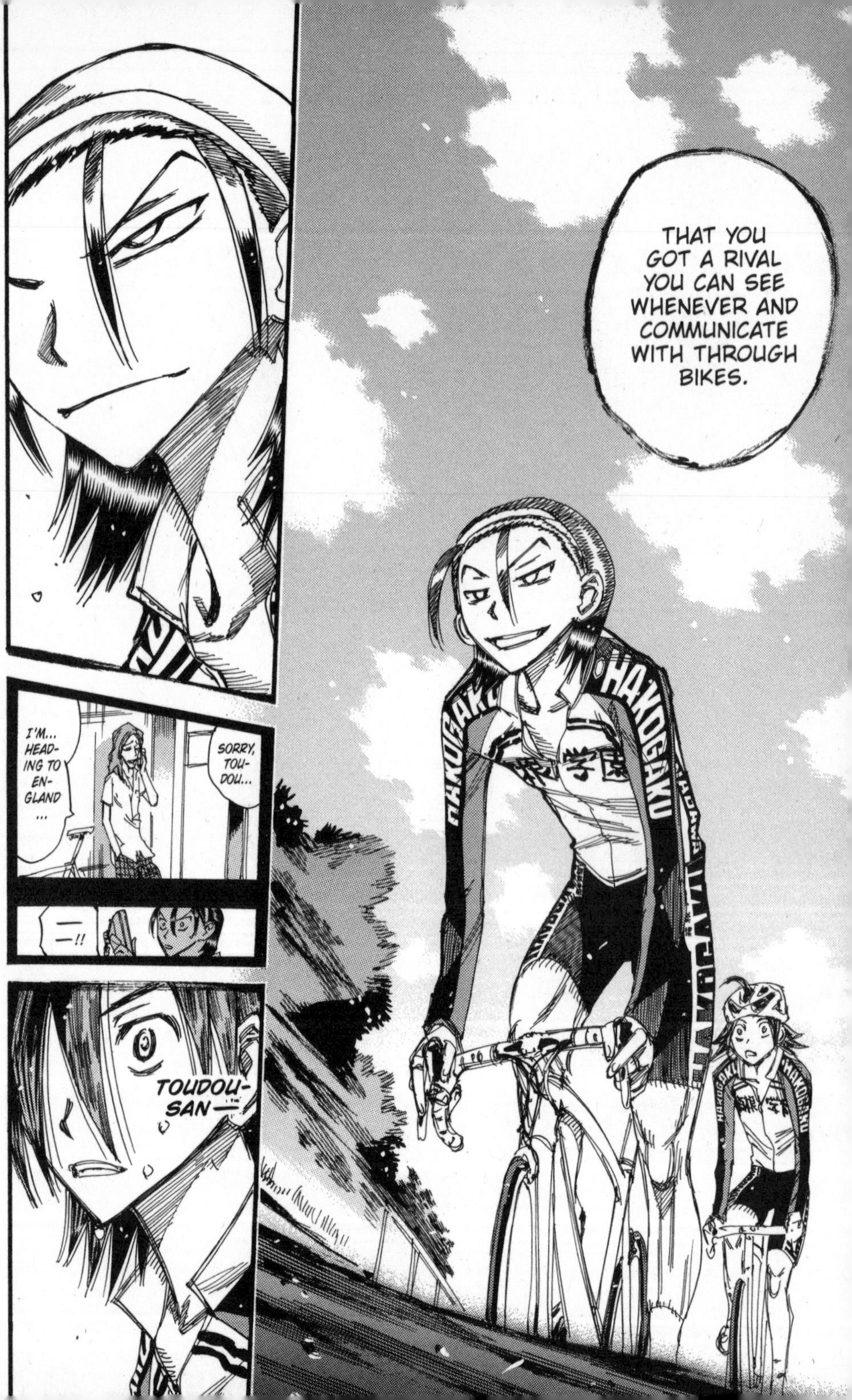
THAT YOU GOT A RIVAL YOU CAN SEE WHENEVER AND COMMUNICATE WITH THROUGH BIKES.
SORRY, TOUDOU...
I'M... HEADING TO ENGLAND...
—!!
TOUDOU-SAN—

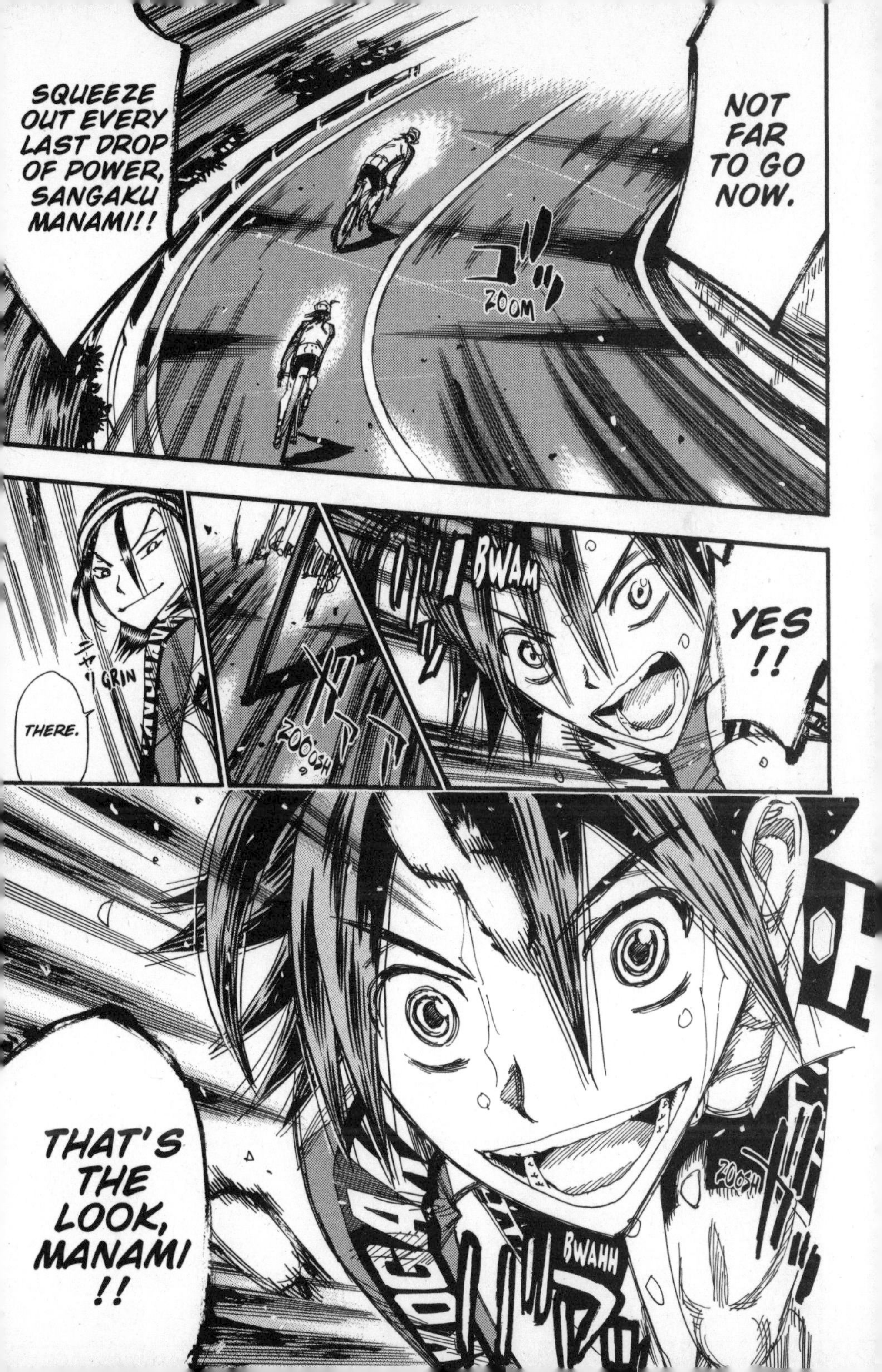
NOT FAR TO GO NOW.
SQUEEZE OUT EVERY LAST DROP OF POWER, SANGAKU MANAMI!!
ZOOM
BWAM
YES!!
ZOOOSH
GRIN
THERE.
ZOOSH
BWAHH
THAT'S THE LOOK, MANAMI!!

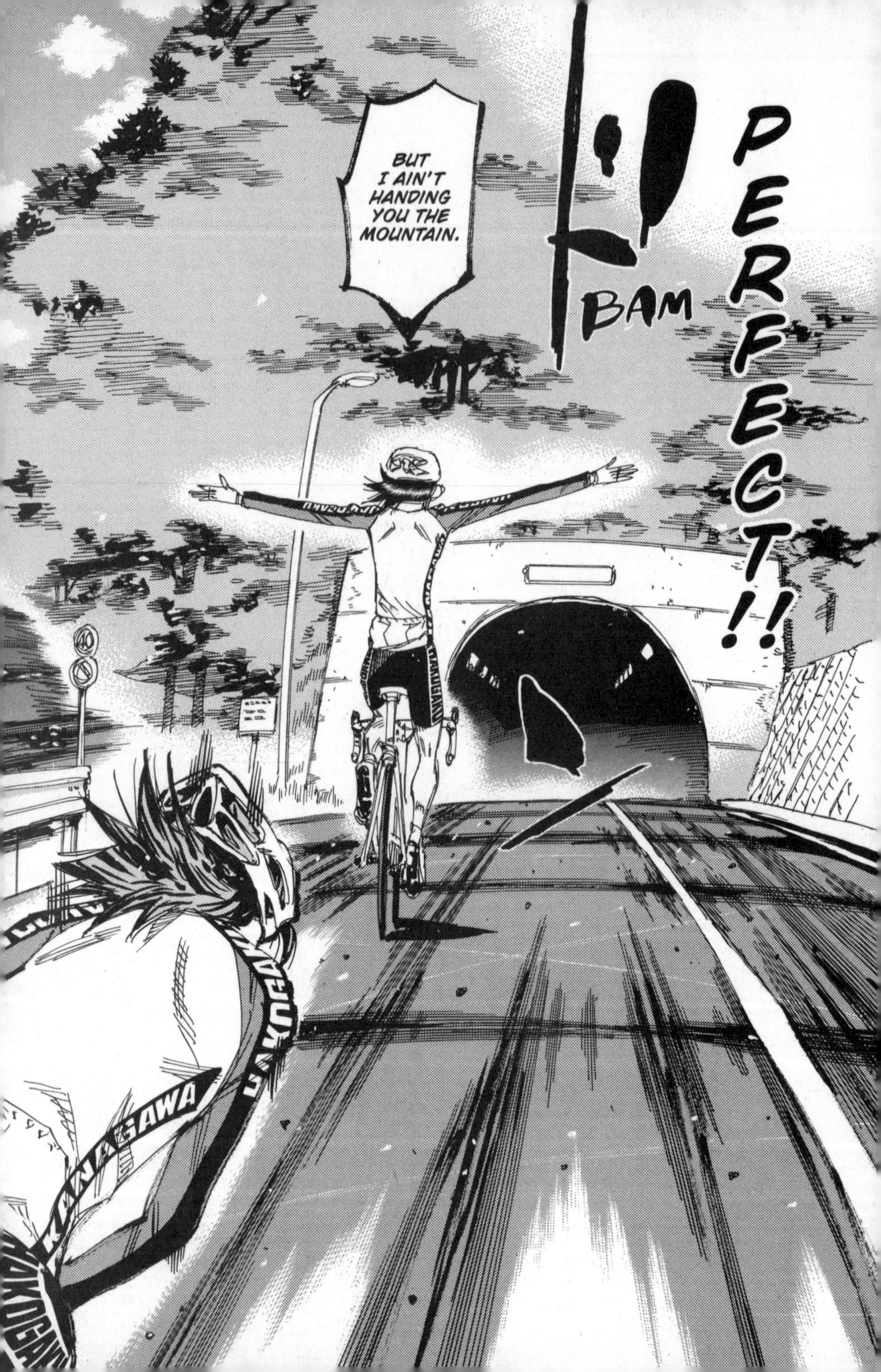
PERFECT!!
BAM
BUT I AIN'T HANDING YOU THE MOUNTAIN.
KANAGAWA

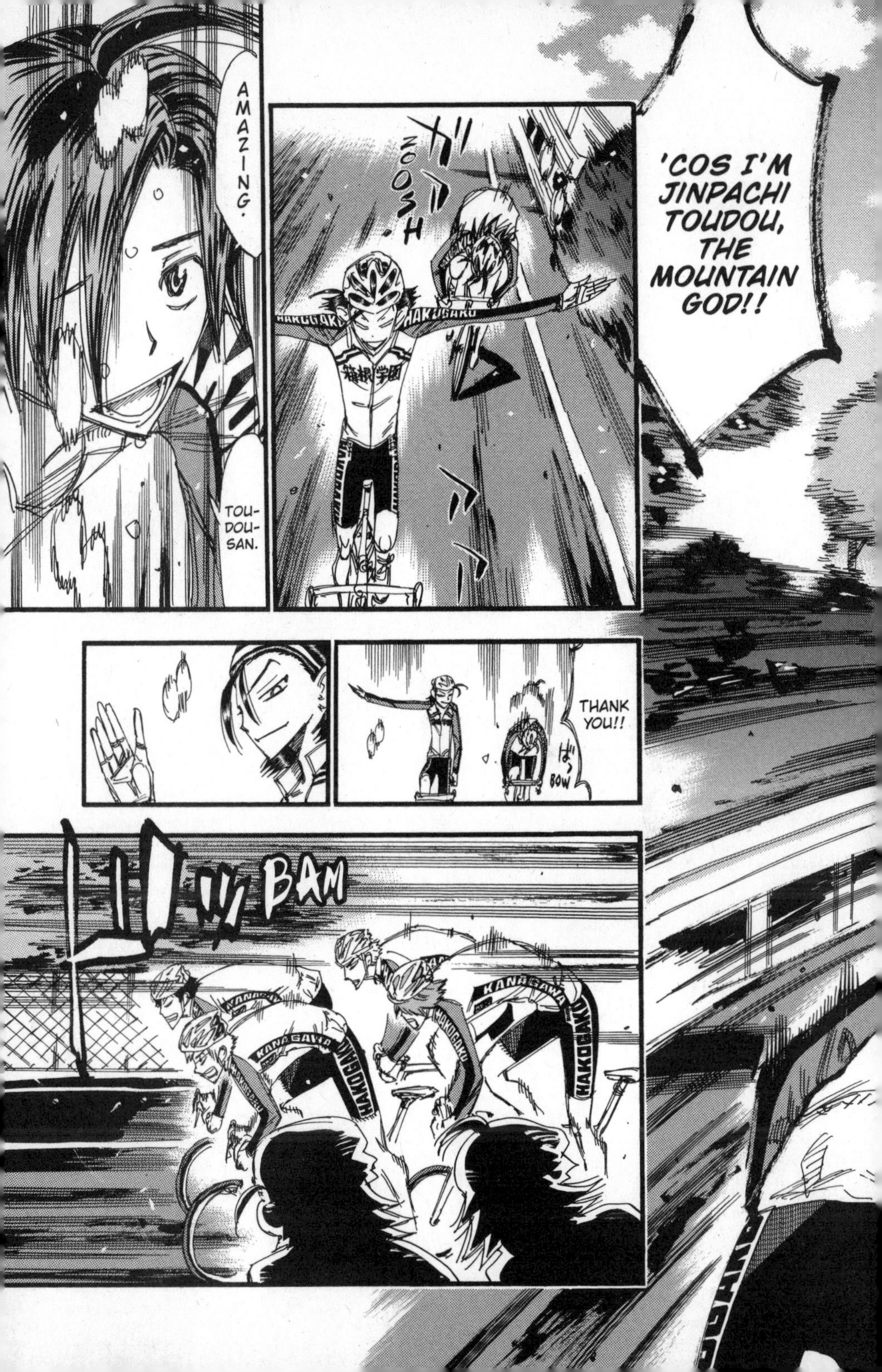
'COS I'M JINPACHI TOUDOU, THE MOUNTAIN GOD!!
ZOOOSH
AMAZING.
TOUDOU-SAN.
THANK YOU!!
BOW
BAM

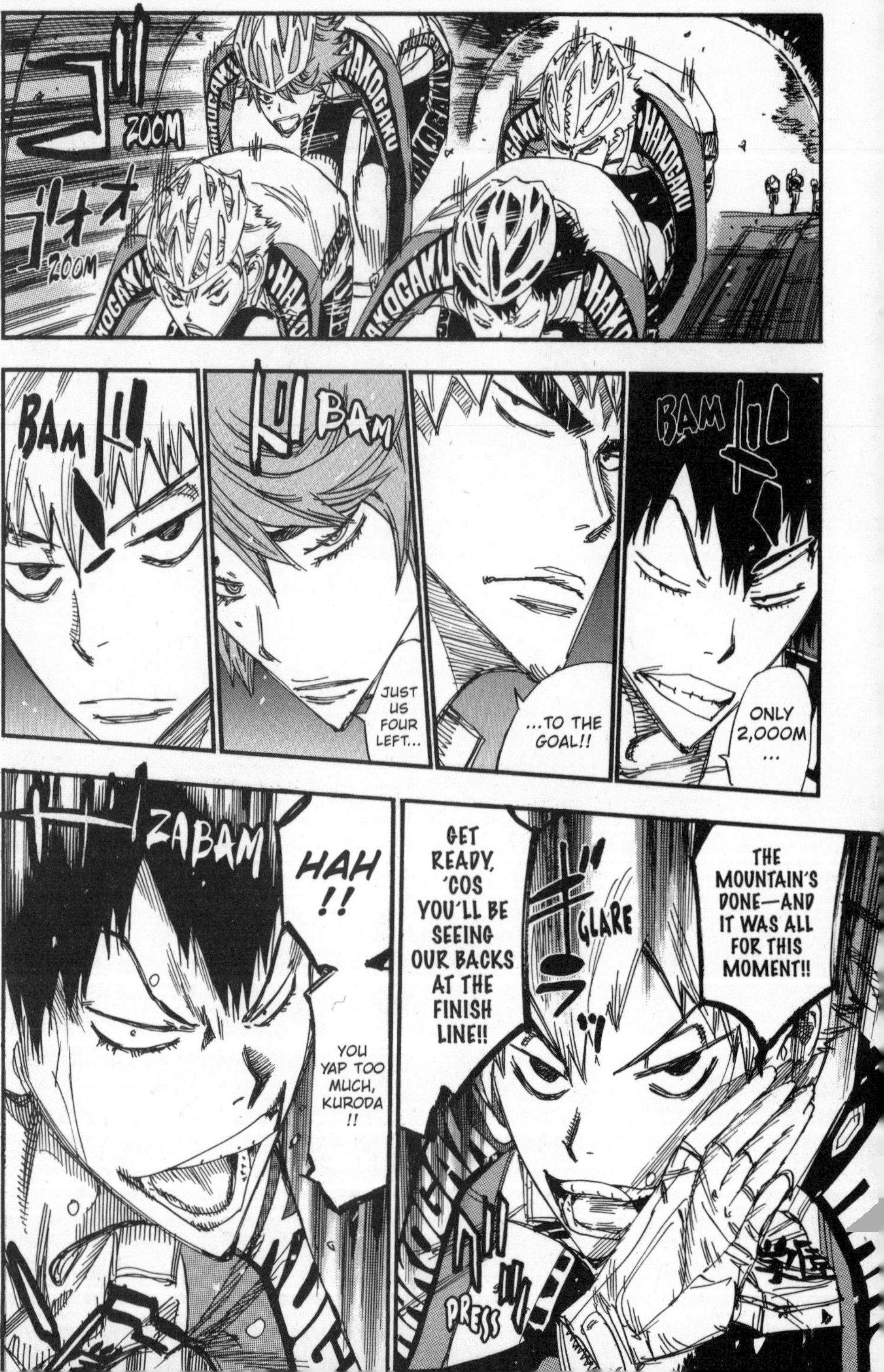
ZOOM
ZOOM
BAM
ONLY 2,000M ...
...TO THE GOAL!!
BAM
JUST US FOUR LEFT...
BAM
THE MOUNTAIN'S DONE—AND IT WAS ALL FOR THIS MOMENT!!
GLARE
GET READY, 'COS YOU'LL BE SEEING OUR BACKS AT THE FINISH LINE!!
PRESS
HAH !!
ZABAM
YOU YAP TOO MUCH, KURODA !!

RIDE.260: KURODA'S DEFIANCE

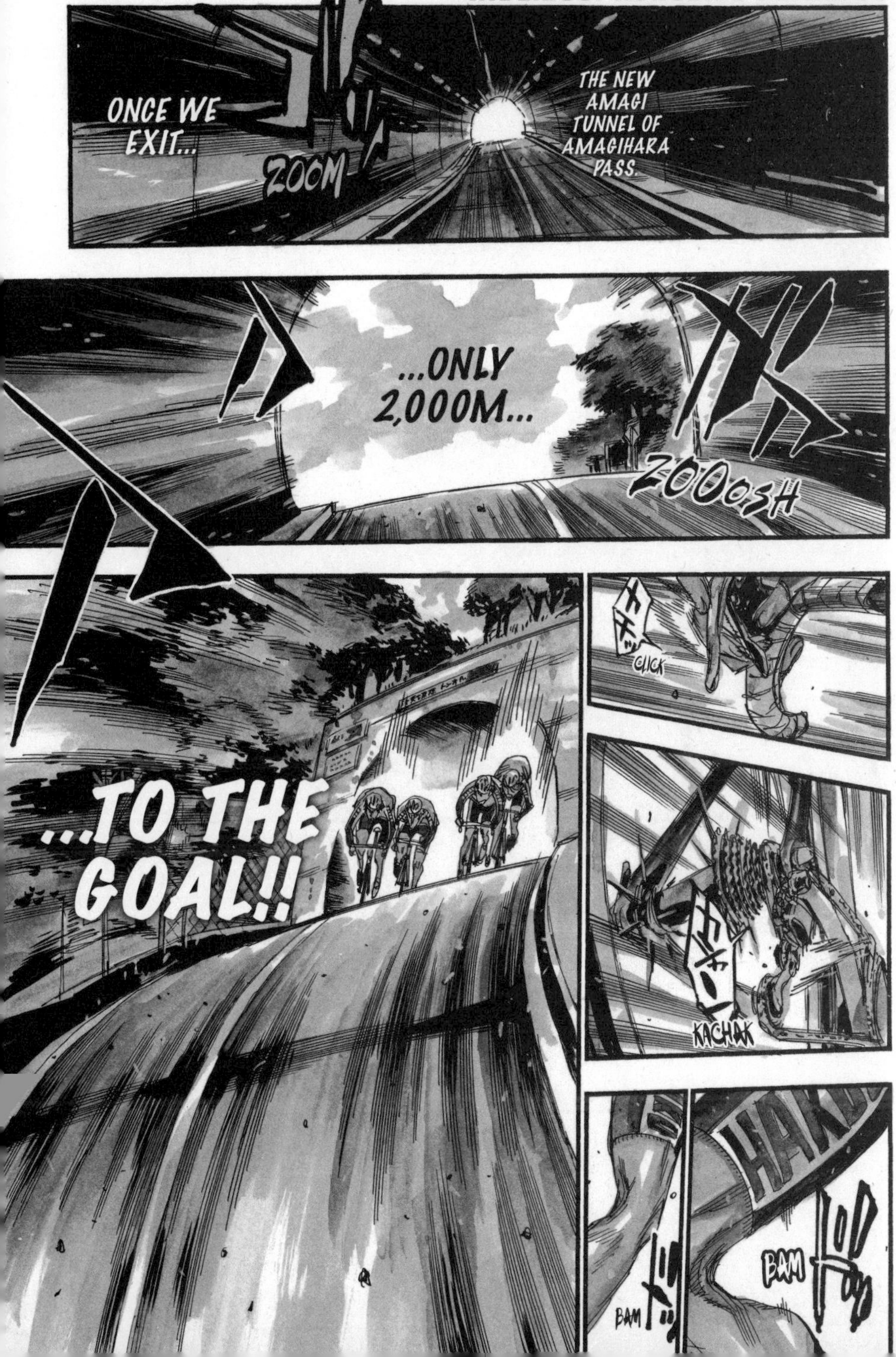
THE NEW AMAGI TUNNEL OF AMAGIHARA PASS.
ONCE WE EXIT...
ZOOM
ZOOOSH
...ONLY 2,000M...
CLICK
KACHAK
BAM
BAM
...TO THE GOAL!!

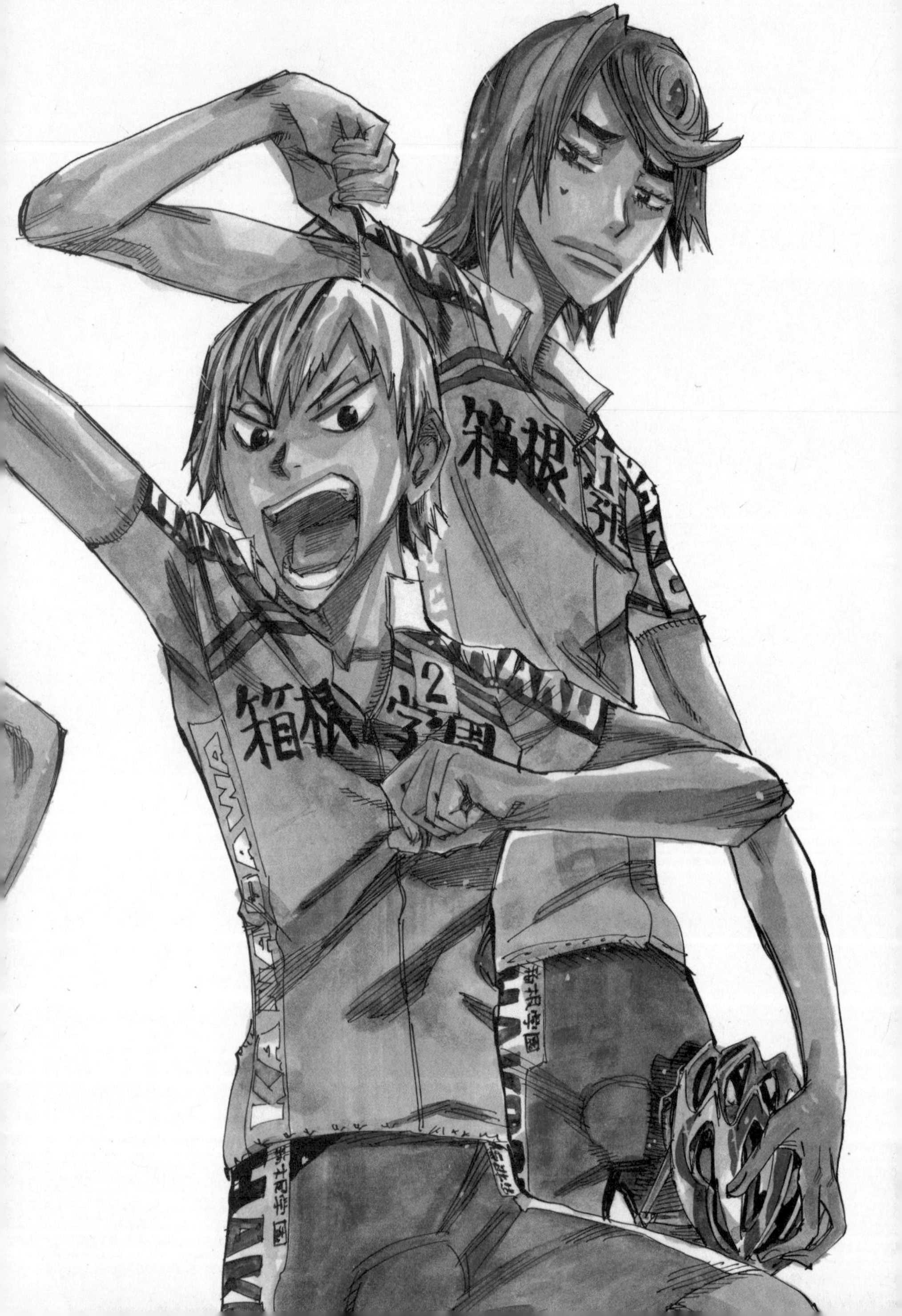
箱根
2
箱根学園

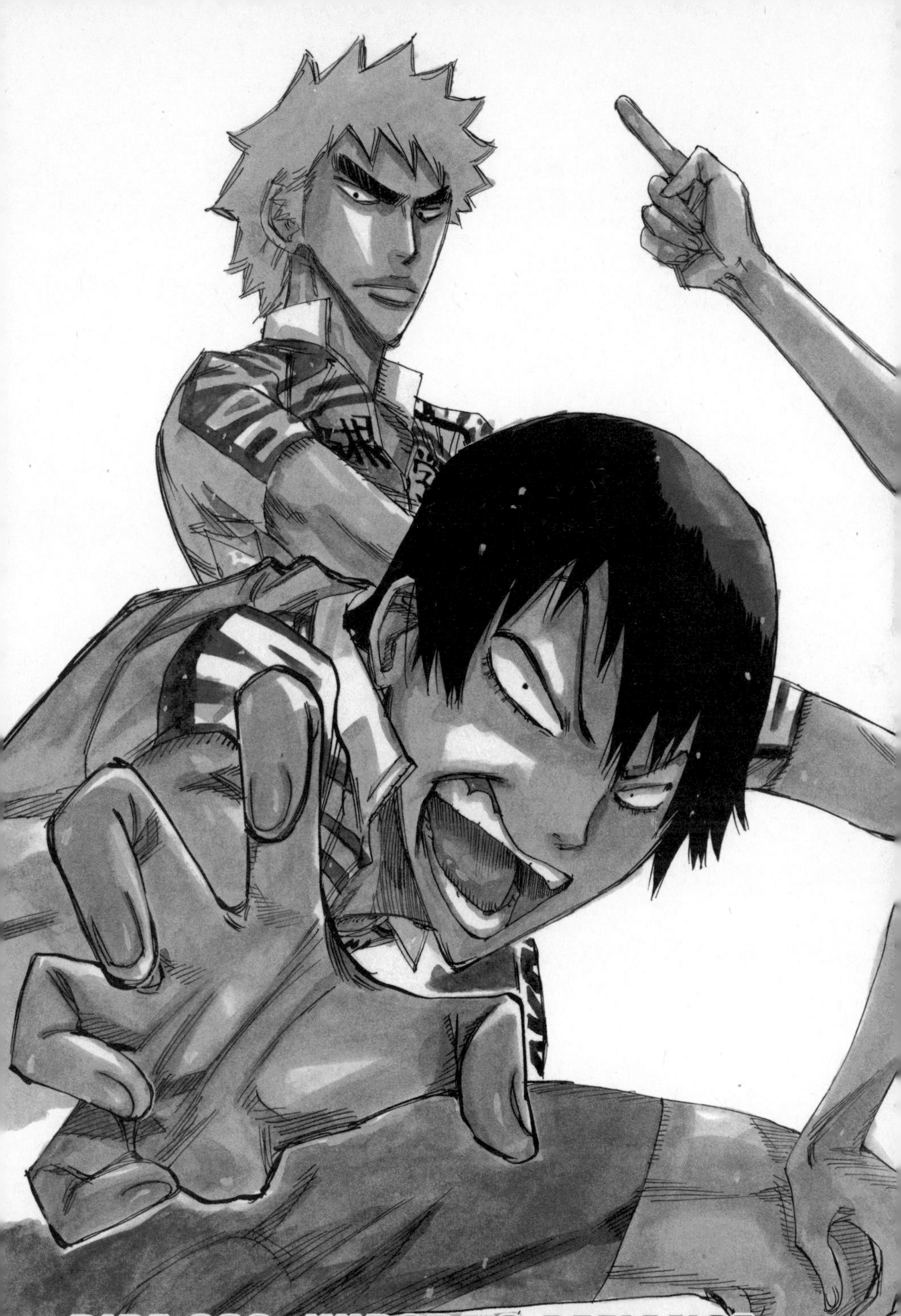

RIDE.260: KURODA'S DEFIANCE

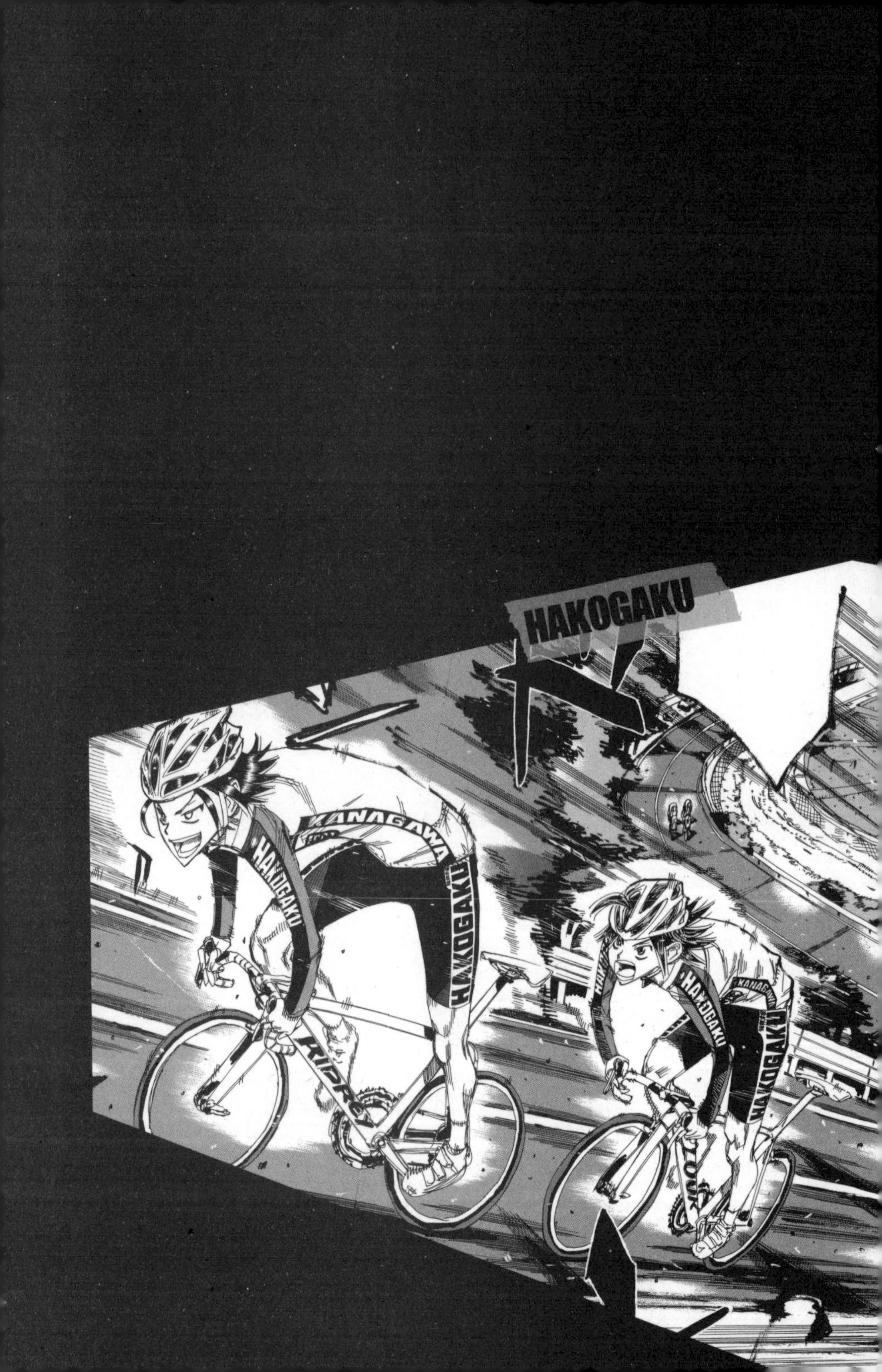
HAKOGAKU

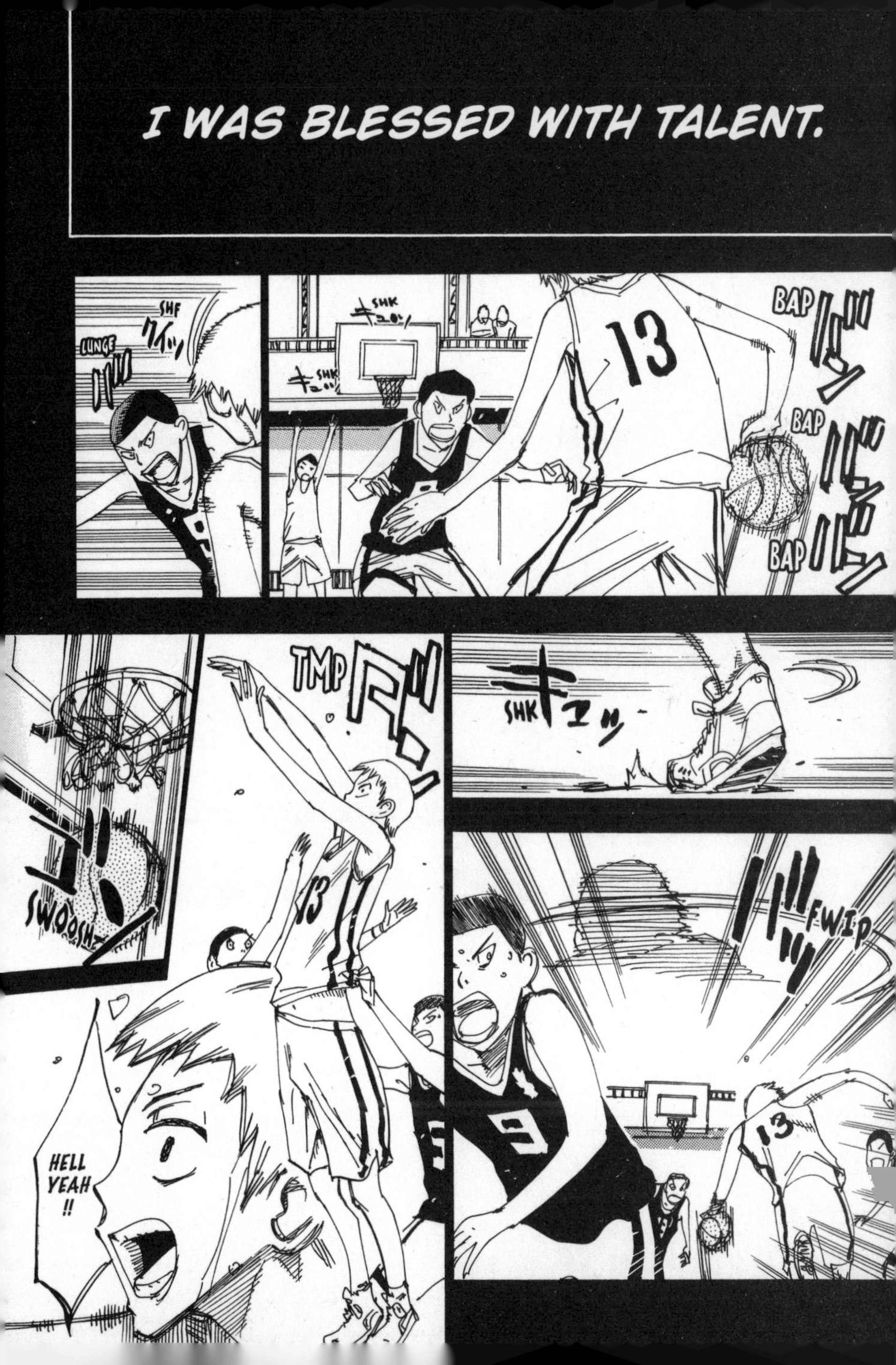
I WAS BLESSED WITH TALENT.
BAP
SHK
SHK
BAP
BAP
SHF
LUNGE
SHK
FWIP
TMP
SWOOSH
HELL YEAH !!

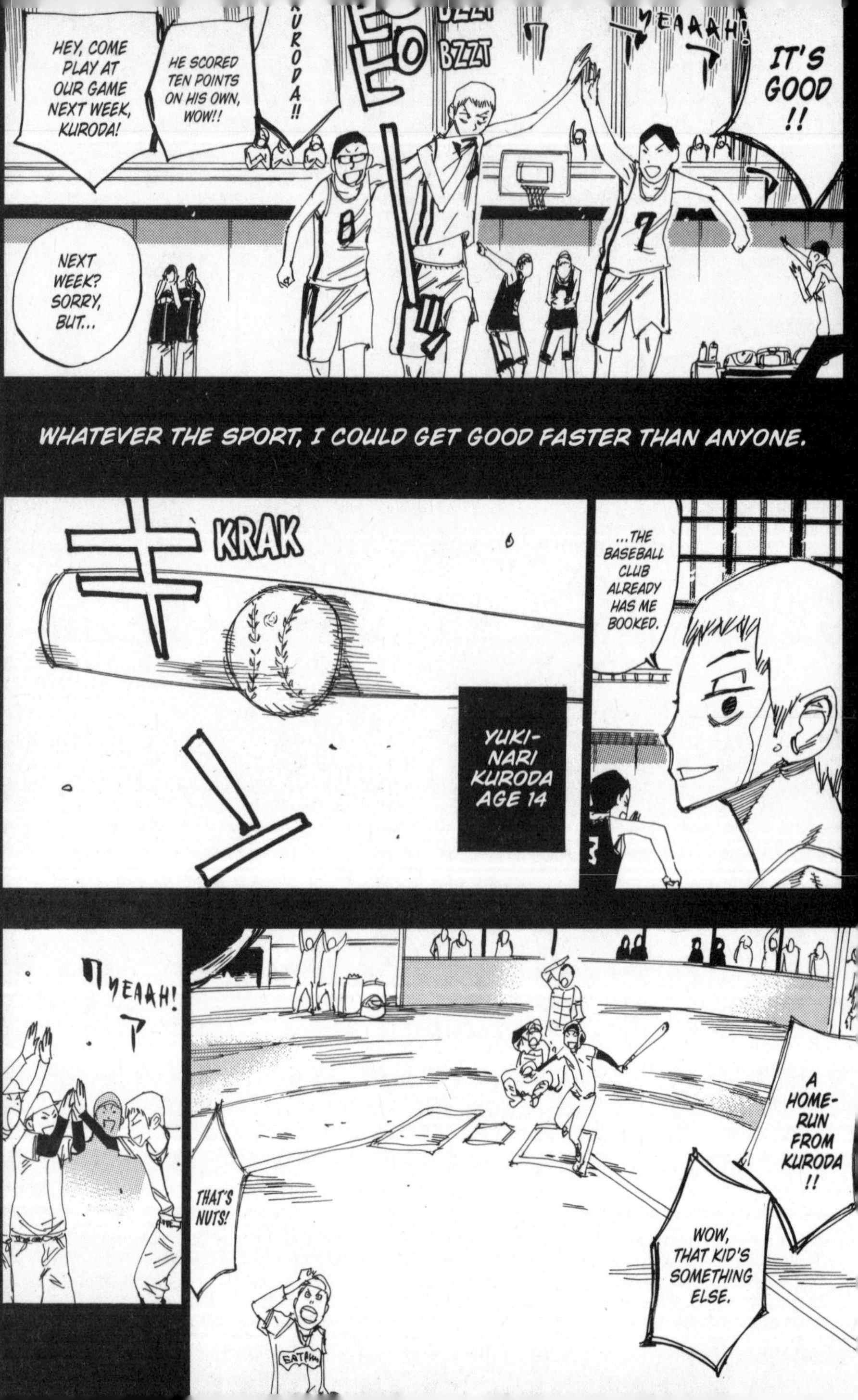
IT'S GOOD!!
YEAAAH!
BZZT
KURODA!!
HE SCORED TEN POINTS ON HIS OWN, WOW!!
HEY, COME PLAY AT OUR GAME NEXT WEEK, KURODA!
NEXT WEEK? SORRY, BUT...
WHATEVER THE SPORT, I COULD GET GOOD FASTER THAN ANYONE.
...THE BASEBALL CLUB ALREADY HAS ME BOOKED.
KRAK
YUKI-NARI KURODA AGE 14
A HOME-RUN FROM KURODA!!
WOW, THAT KID'S SOMETHING ELSE.
THAT'S NUTS!
YEAAH!

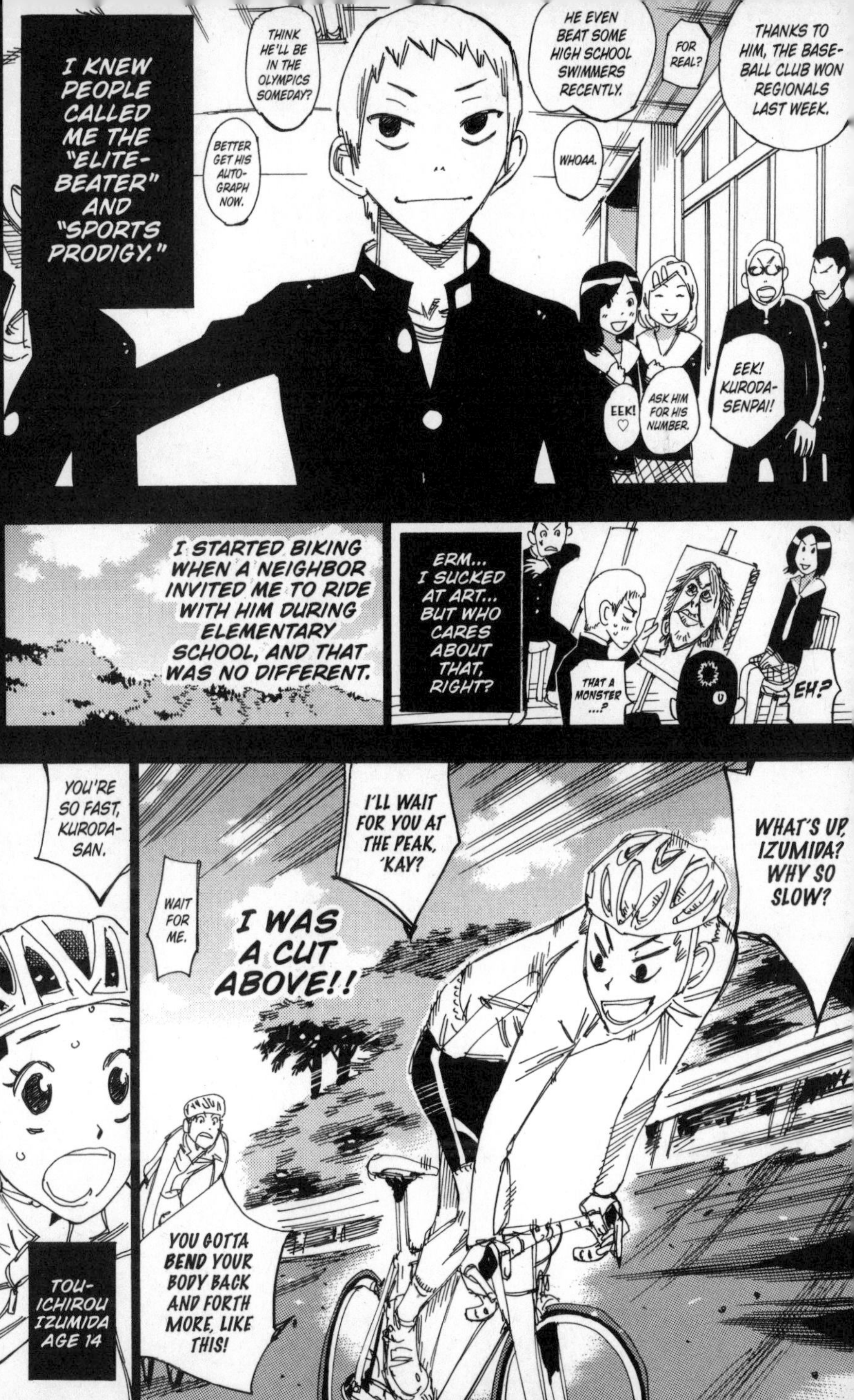
THANKS TO HIM, THE BASEBALL CLUB WON REGIONALS LAST WEEK.
FOR REAL?
HE EVEN BEAT SOME HIGH SCHOOL SWIMMERS RECENTLY.
WHOAA.
THINK HE'LL BE IN THE OLYMPICS SOMEDAY?
BETTER GET HIS AUTOGRAPH NOW.
I KNEW PEOPLE CALLED ME THE "ELITE-BEATER" AND "SPORTS PRODIGY."
EEK! KURODA-SENPAI!
ASK HIM FOR HIS NUMBER.
EEK! ♡
ERM... I SUCKED AT ART... BUT WHO CARES ABOUT THAT, RIGHT?
EH?
THAT A MONSTER ...?
I STARTED BIKING WHEN A NEIGHBOR INVITED ME TO RIDE WITH HIM DURING ELEMENTARY SCHOOL, AND THAT WAS NO DIFFERENT.
WHAT'S UP, IZUMIDA? WHY SO SLOW?
I'LL WAIT FOR YOU AT THE PEAK, 'KAY?
I WAS A CUT ABOVE!!
WAIT FOR ME.
YOU GOTTA BEND YOUR BODY BACK AND FORTH MORE, LIKE THIS!
YOU'RE SO FAST, KURODA-SAN.
TOUICHIROU IZUMIDA AGE 14

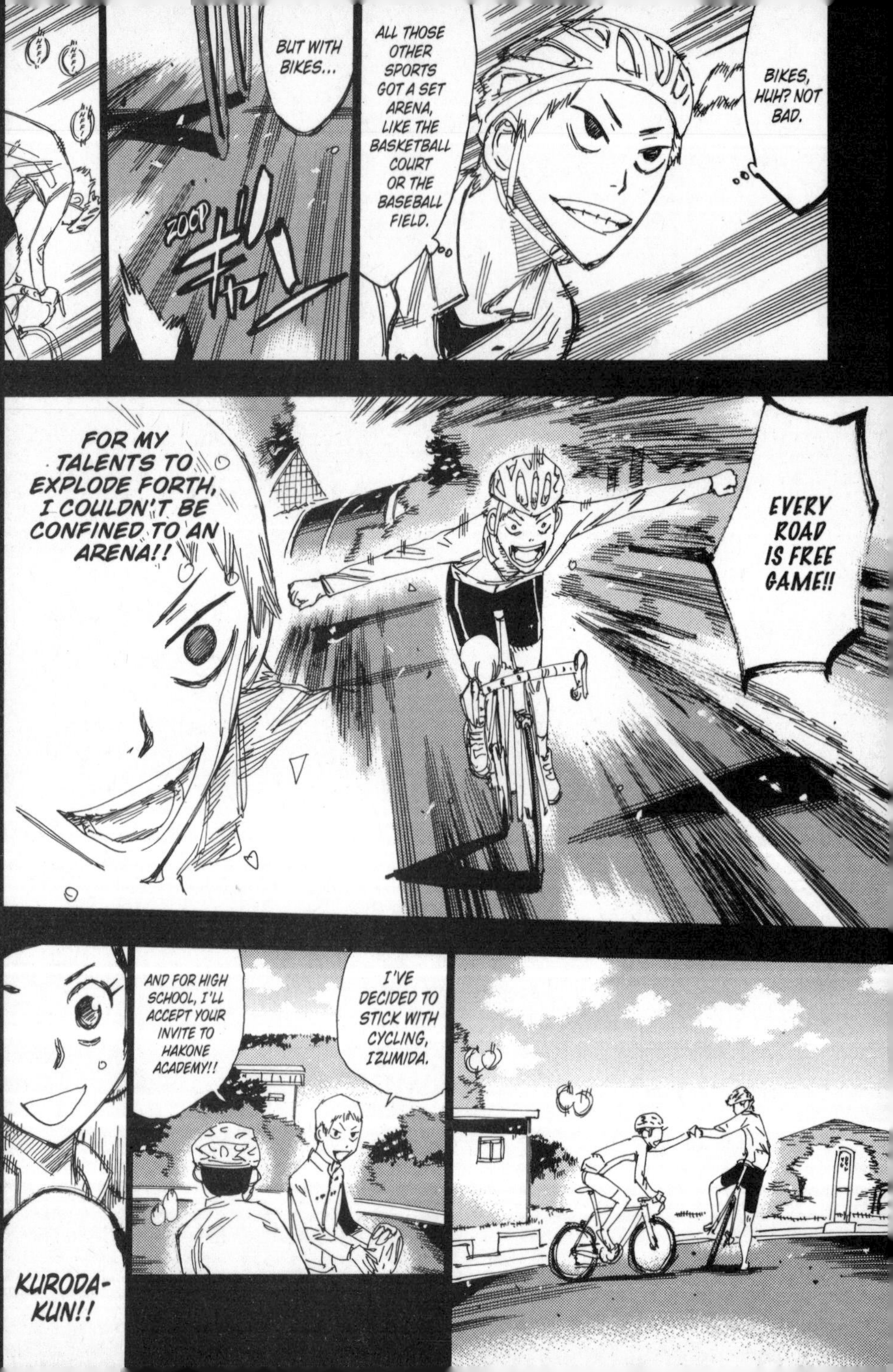
BIKES, HUH? NOT BAD.
ALL THOSE OTHER SPORTS GOT A SET ARENA, LIKE THE BASKETBALL COURT OR THE BASEBALL FIELD.
BUT WITH BIKES...
ZOOP
FOR MY TALENTS TO EXPLODE FORTH, I COULDN'T BE CONFINED TO AN ARENA!!
EVERY ROAD IS FREE GAME!!
I'VE DECIDED TO STICK WITH CYCLING, IZUMIDA.
AND FOR HIGH SCHOOL, I'LL ACCEPT YOUR INVITE TO HAKONE ACADEMY!!
KURODA-KUN!!

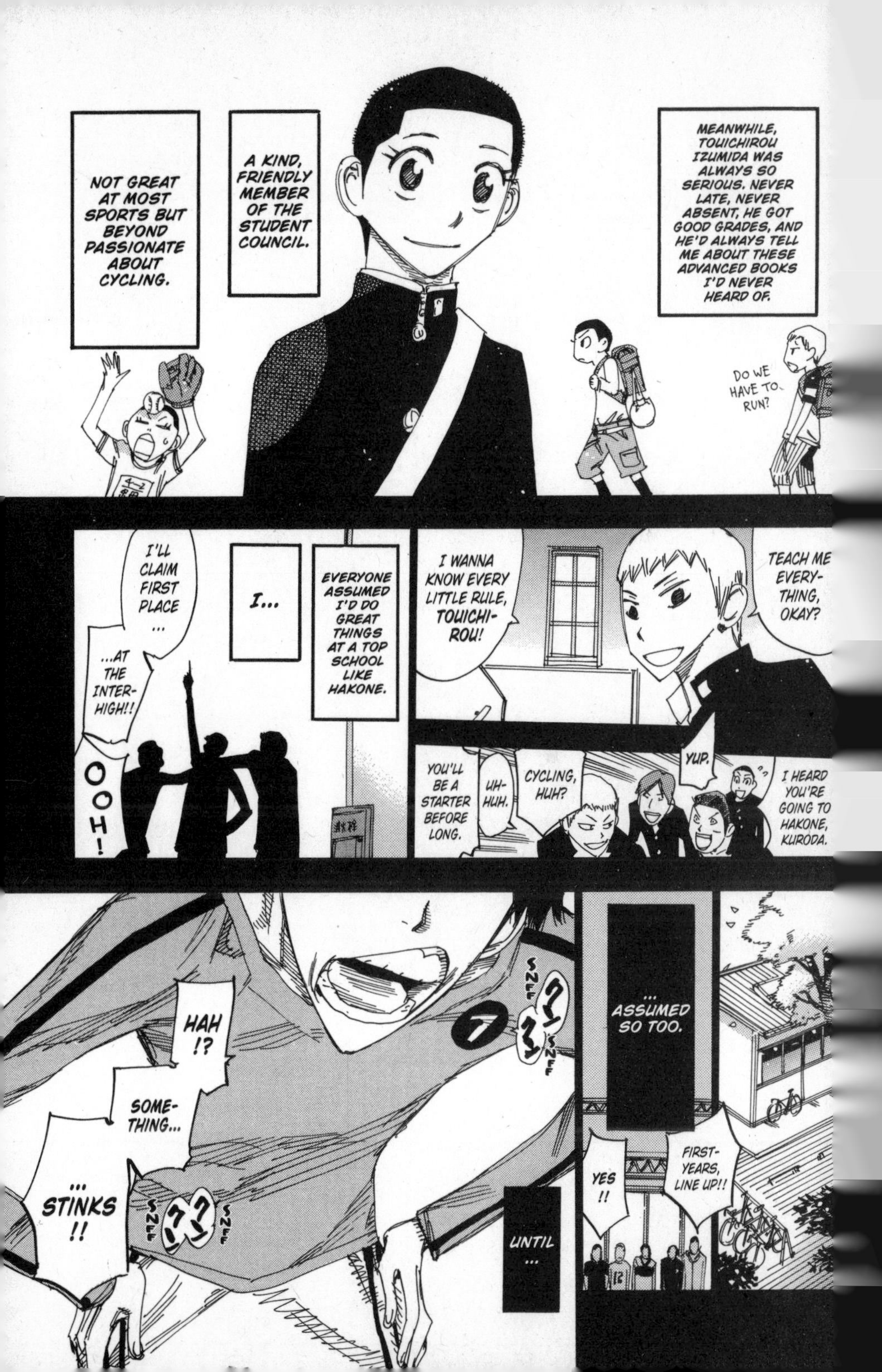
MEANWHILE, TOUICHIROU IZUMIDA WAS ALWAYS SO SERIOUS. NEVER LATE, NEVER ABSENT, HE GOT GOOD GRADES, AND HE'D ALWAYS TELL ME ABOUT THESE ADVANCED BOOKS I'D NEVER HEARD OF.
DO WE HAVE TO RUN?
A KIND, FRIENDLY MEMBER OF THE STUDENT COUNCIL.
NOT GREAT AT MOST SPORTS BUT BEYOND PASSIONATE ABOUT CYCLING.
I WANNA KNOW EVERY LITTLE RULE, TOUICHIROU!
TEACH ME EVERY-THING, OKAY?
I HEARD YOU'RE GOING TO HAKONE, KURODA.
YUP.
CYCLING, HUH?
UH-HUH.
YOU'LL BE A STARTER BEFORE LONG.
EVERYONE ASSUMED I'D DO GREAT THINGS AT A TOP SCHOOL LIKE HAKONE.
I...
I'LL CLAIM FIRST PLACE ...
...AT THE INTER-HIGH!!
OOH!
... ASSUMED SO TOO.
FIRST-YEARS, LINE UP!!
YES !!
UNTIL ...
SNFF
SNFF
HAH !?
SOME-THING...
... STINKS !!
SNFF
SNFF

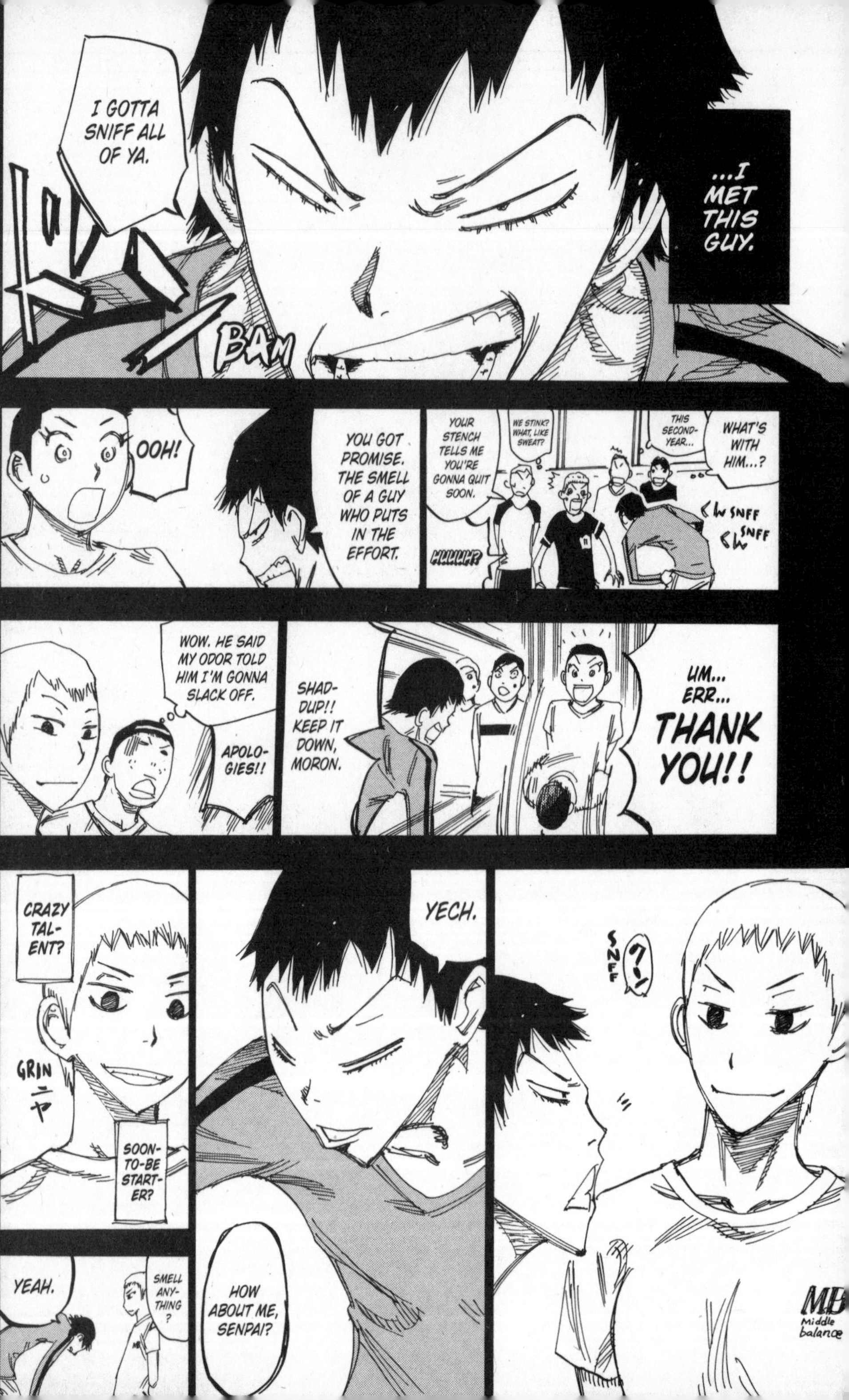
...I MET THIS GUY.
I GOTTA SNIFF ALL OF YA.
BAM
WHAT'S WITH HIM...?
THIS SECOND-YEAR...
WE STINK? WHAT, LIKE SWEAT?
YOUR STENCH TELLS ME YOU'RE GONNA QUIT SOON.
SNFF
SNFF
HUUUH?
YOU GOT PROMISE. THE SMELL OF A GUY WHO PUTS IN THE EFFORT.
OOH!
UM... ERR... THANK YOU!!
SHAD-DUP!! KEEP IT DOWN, MORON.
WOW. HE SAID MY ODOR TOLD HIM I'M GONNA SLACK OFF.
APOLO-GIES!!
SNFF
MB
Middle balance
YECH.
HOW ABOUT ME, SENPAI?
CRAZY TAL-ENT?
GRIN
SOON-TO-BE STARTER?
SMELL ANY-THING?
YEAH.

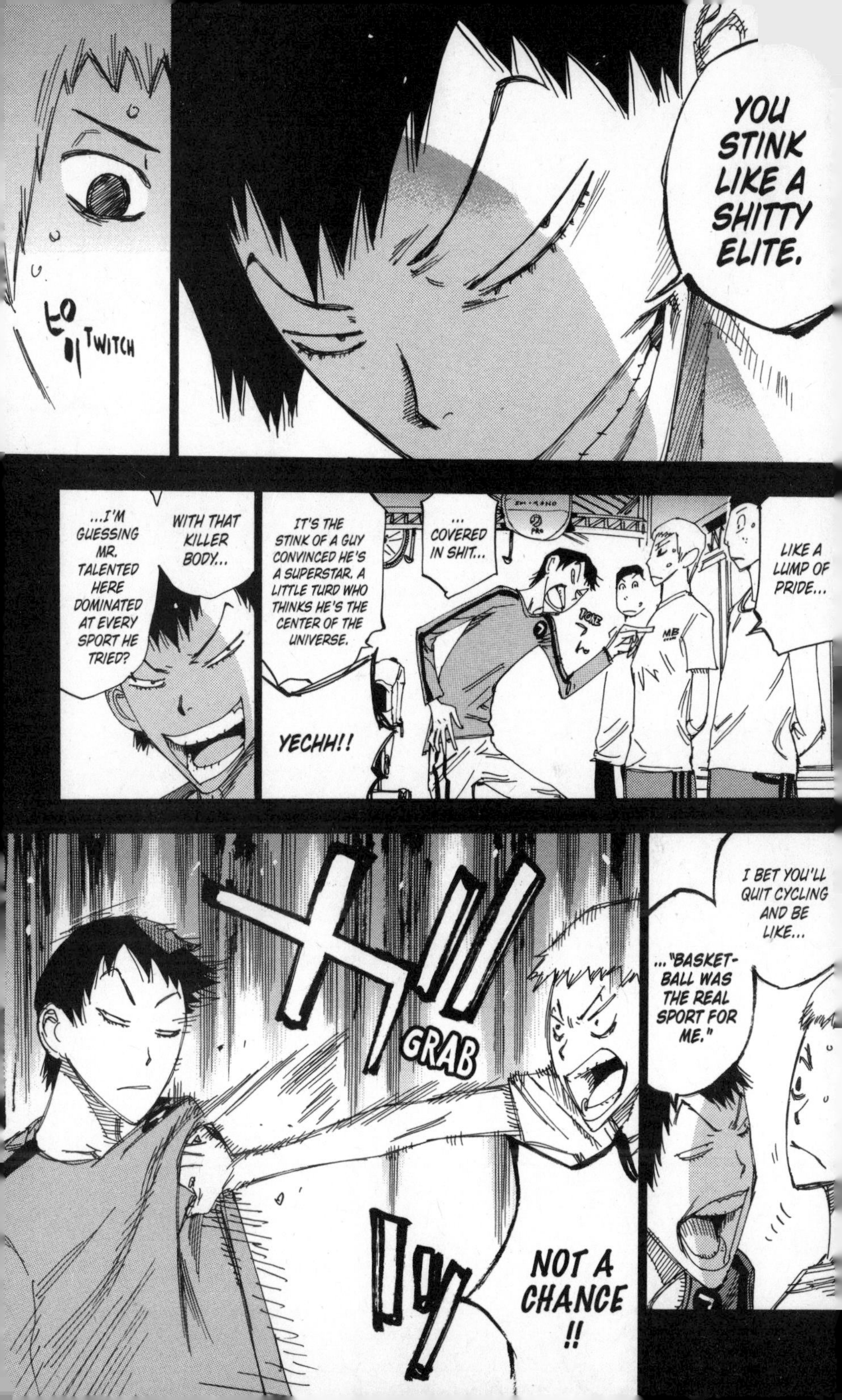
YOU STINK LIKE A SHITTY ELITE.
TWITCH
LIKE A LUMP OF PRIDE...
...COVERED IN SHIT...
IT'S THE STINK OF A GUY CONVINCED HE'S A SUPERSTAR. A LITTLE TURD WHO THINKS HE'S THE CENTER OF THE UNIVERSE.
POKE
YECHH!!
WITH THAT KILLER BODY...
...I'M GUESSING MR. TALENTED HERE DOMINATED AT EVERY SPORT HE TRIED?
I BET YOU'LL QUIT CYCLING AND BE LIKE...
..."BASKET-BALL WAS THE REAL SPORT FOR ME."
GRAB
NOT A CHANCE!!

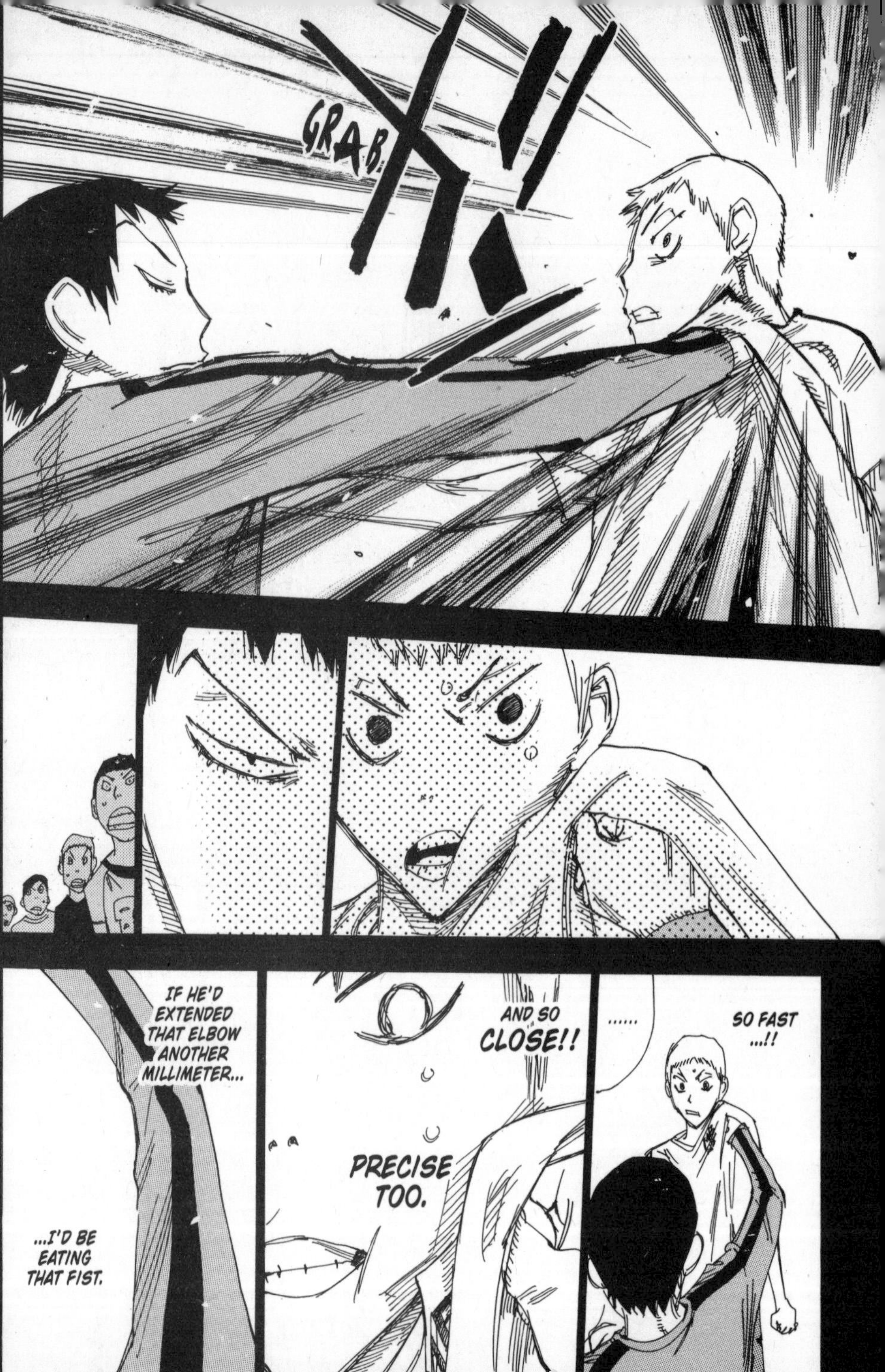
GRAB
SO FAST ...!!
......
AND SO CLOSE!!
PRECISE TOO.
IF HE'D EXTENDED THAT ELBOW ANOTHER MILLIMETER...
...I'D BE EATING THAT FIST.

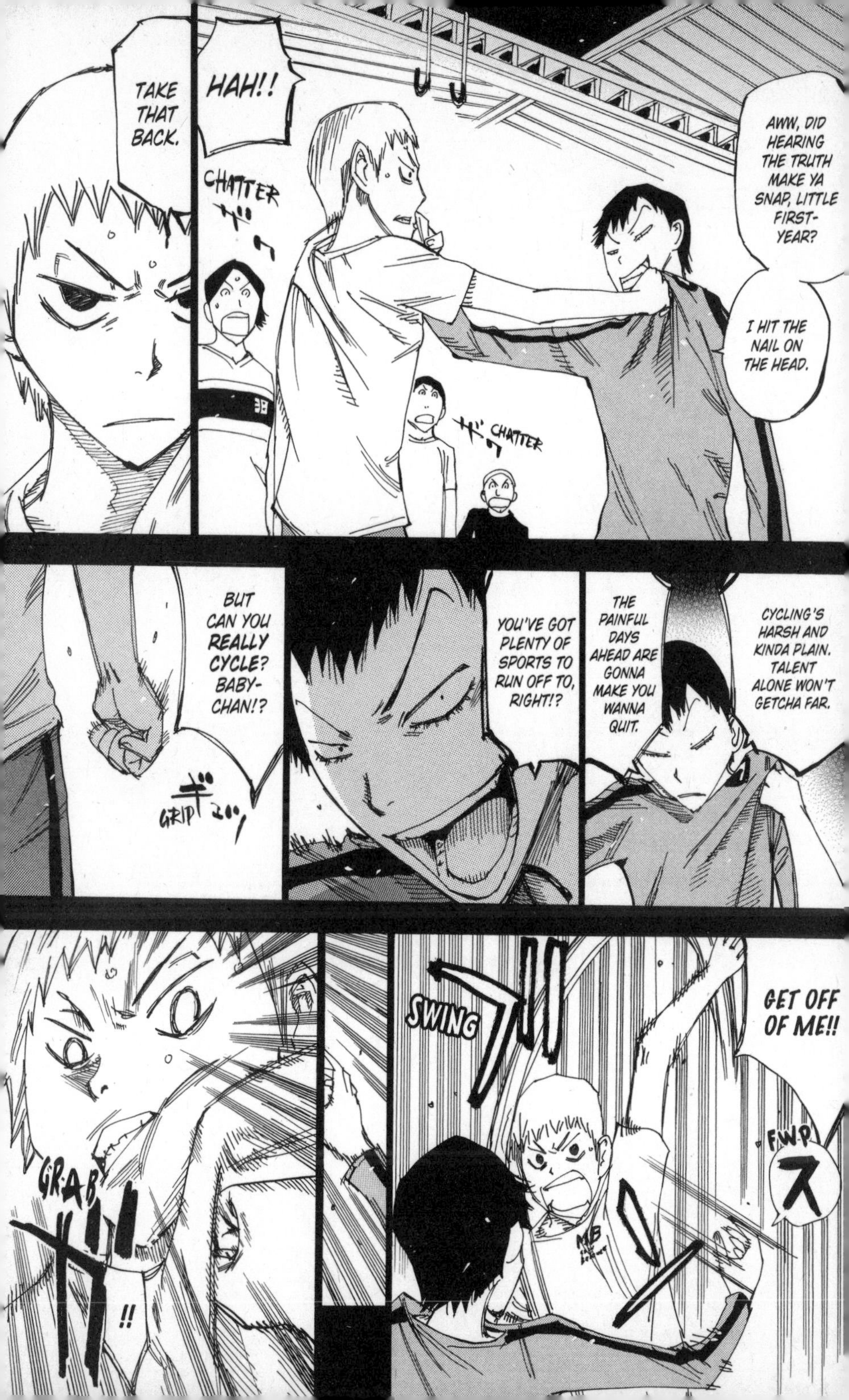
AWW, DID HEARING THE TRUTH MAKE YA SNAP, LITTLE FIRST-YEAR?
HAH!!
CHATTER
I HIT THE NAIL ON THE HEAD.
CHATTER
TAKE THAT BACK.
CYCLING'S HARSH AND KINDA PLAIN. TALENT ALONE WON'T GETCHA FAR.
THE PAINFUL DAYS AHEAD ARE GONNA MAKE YOU WANNA QUIT.
YOU'VE GOT PLENTY OF SPORTS TO RUN OFF TO, RIGHT!?
BUT CAN YOU REALLY CYCLE? BABY-CHAN!?
GRIP
GET OFF OF ME!!
SWING
FWP
GRAB
!!

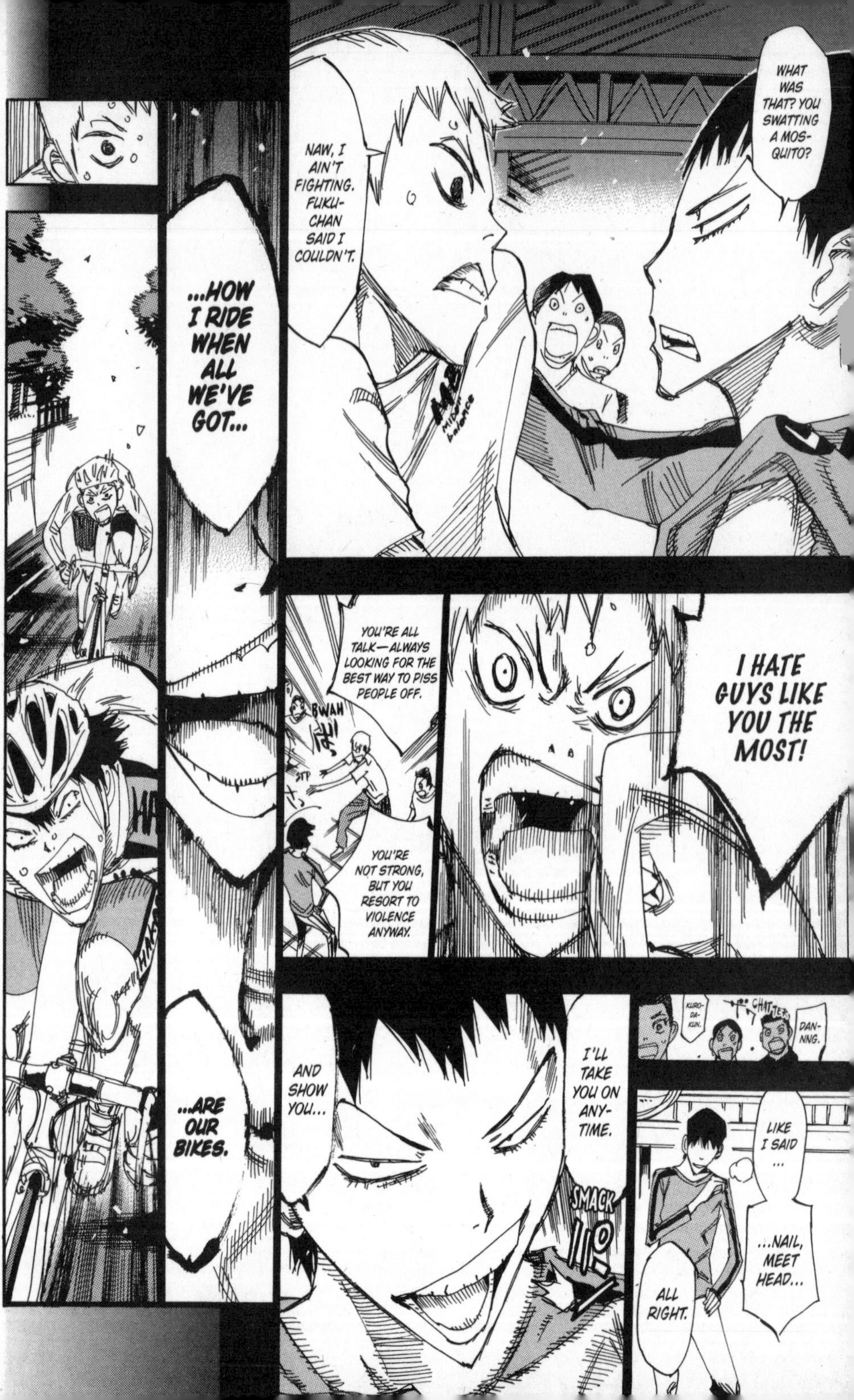
WHAT WAS THAT? YOU SWATTING A MOS-QUITO?
NAW, I AIN'T FIGHTING. FUKU-CHAN SAID I COULDN'T.
I HATE GUYS LIKE YOU THE MOST!
YOU'RE ALL TALK—ALWAYS LOOKING FOR THE BEST WAY TO PISS PEOPLE OFF.
BWAH
STP
YOU'RE NOT STRONG, BUT YOU RESORT TO VIOLENCE ANYWAY.
DANNNG.
CHATTER
KURO-DA-KUN.
LIKE I SAID...
...NAIL, MEET HEAD...
ALL RIGHT.
I'LL TAKE YOU ON ANYTIME.
SMACK
AND SHOW YOU...
...HOW I RIDE WHEN ALL WE'VE GOT...
...ARE OUR BIKES.

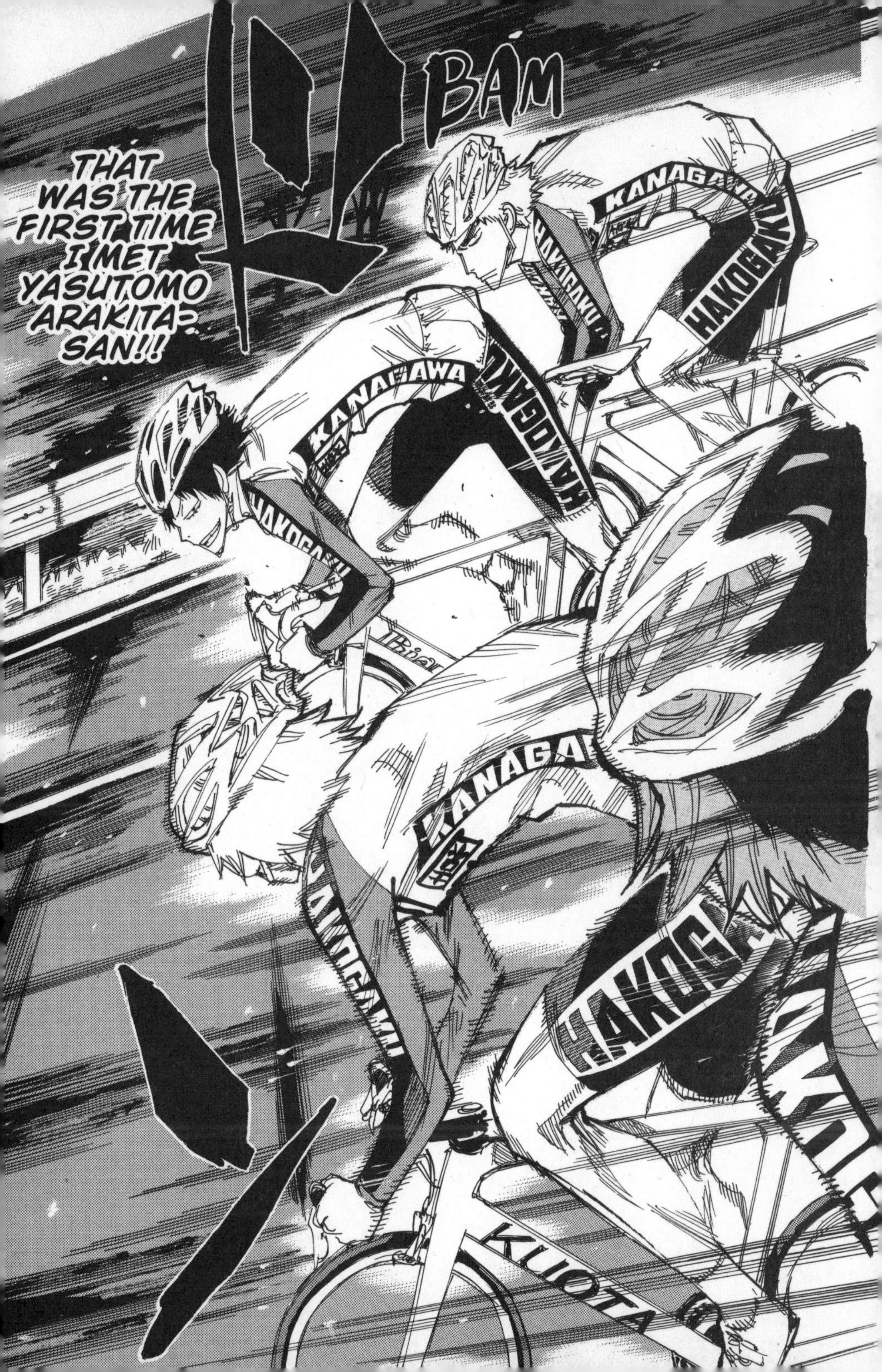
BAM
THAT WAS THE FIRST TIME I MET YASUTOMO ARAKITA-SAN!!
KANAGAWA
HAKOGAKU
KANAGAWA
HAKOGAKU
KANAGA
HAKOGAKU
KUOTA

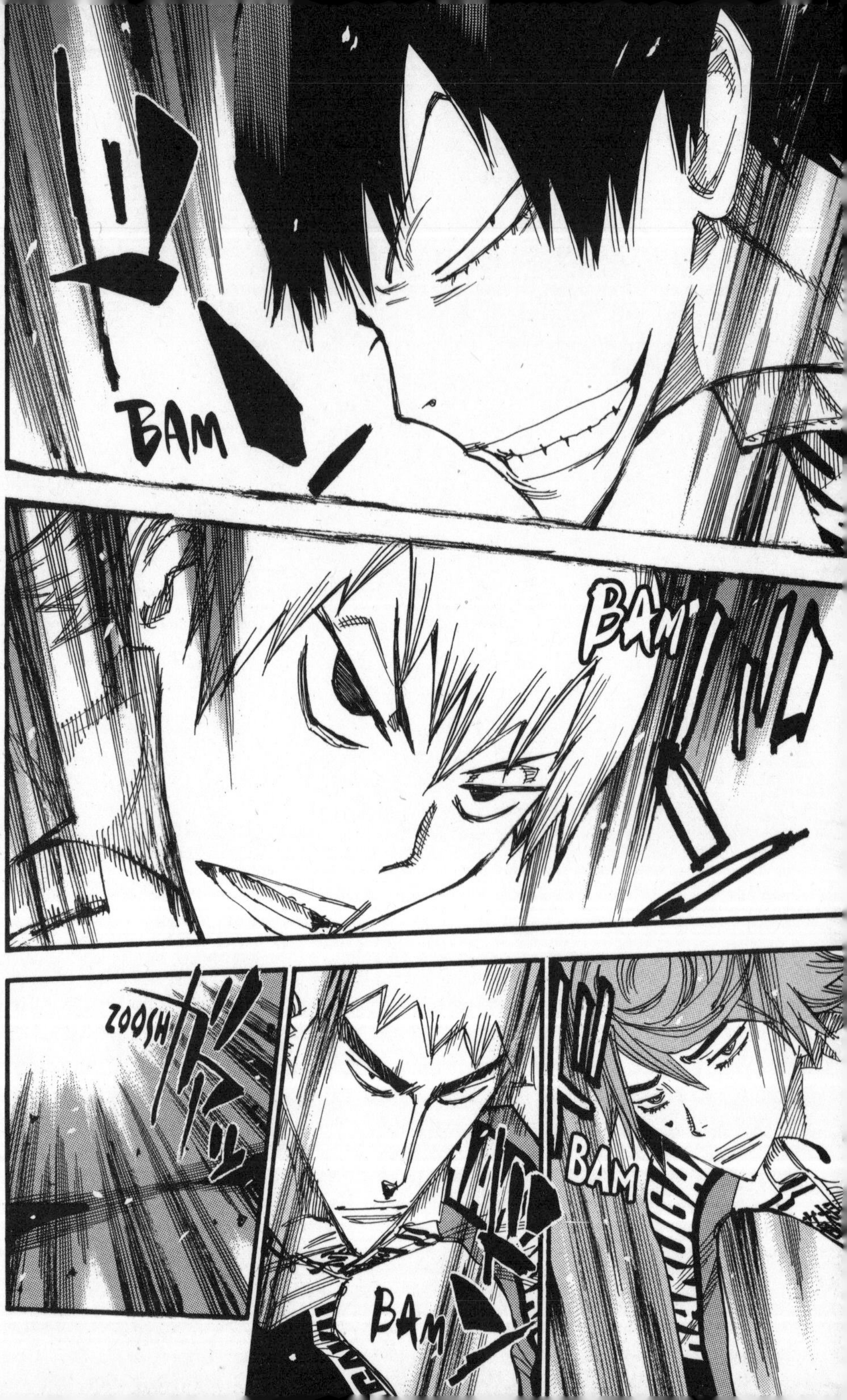
BAM
BAM
BAM
BAM
ZOOSH

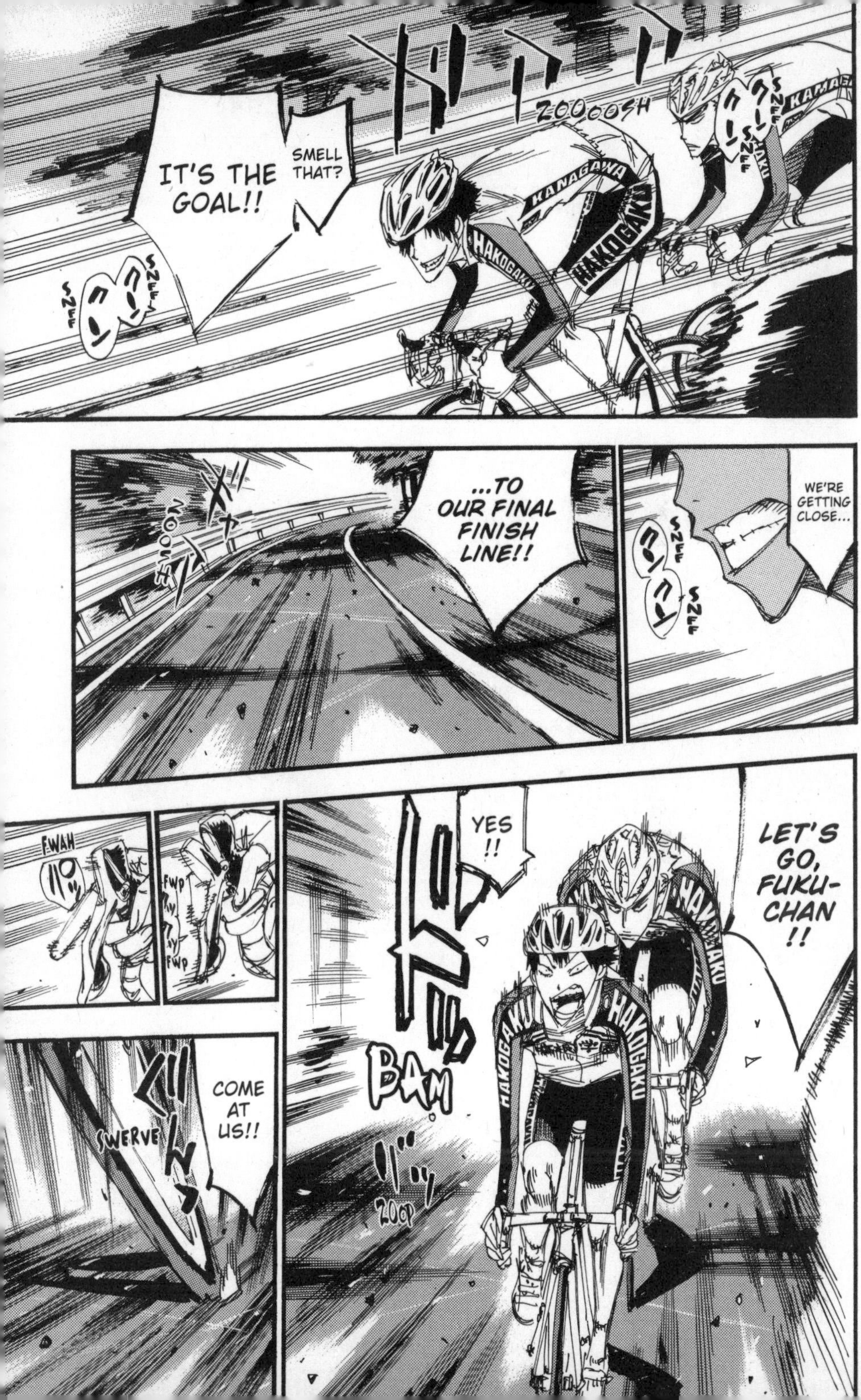
ZOOOOSH
SNFF
SNFF
SMELL THAT?
IT'S THE GOAL!!
SNFF
SNFF
WE'RE GETTING CLOSE...
SNFF
SNFF
...TO OUR FINAL FINISH LINE!!
ZOOOSH
LET'S GO, FUKU-CHAN!!
YES!!
BAM
ZOOP
FWP
FWP
FWAH
COME AT US!!
SWERVE

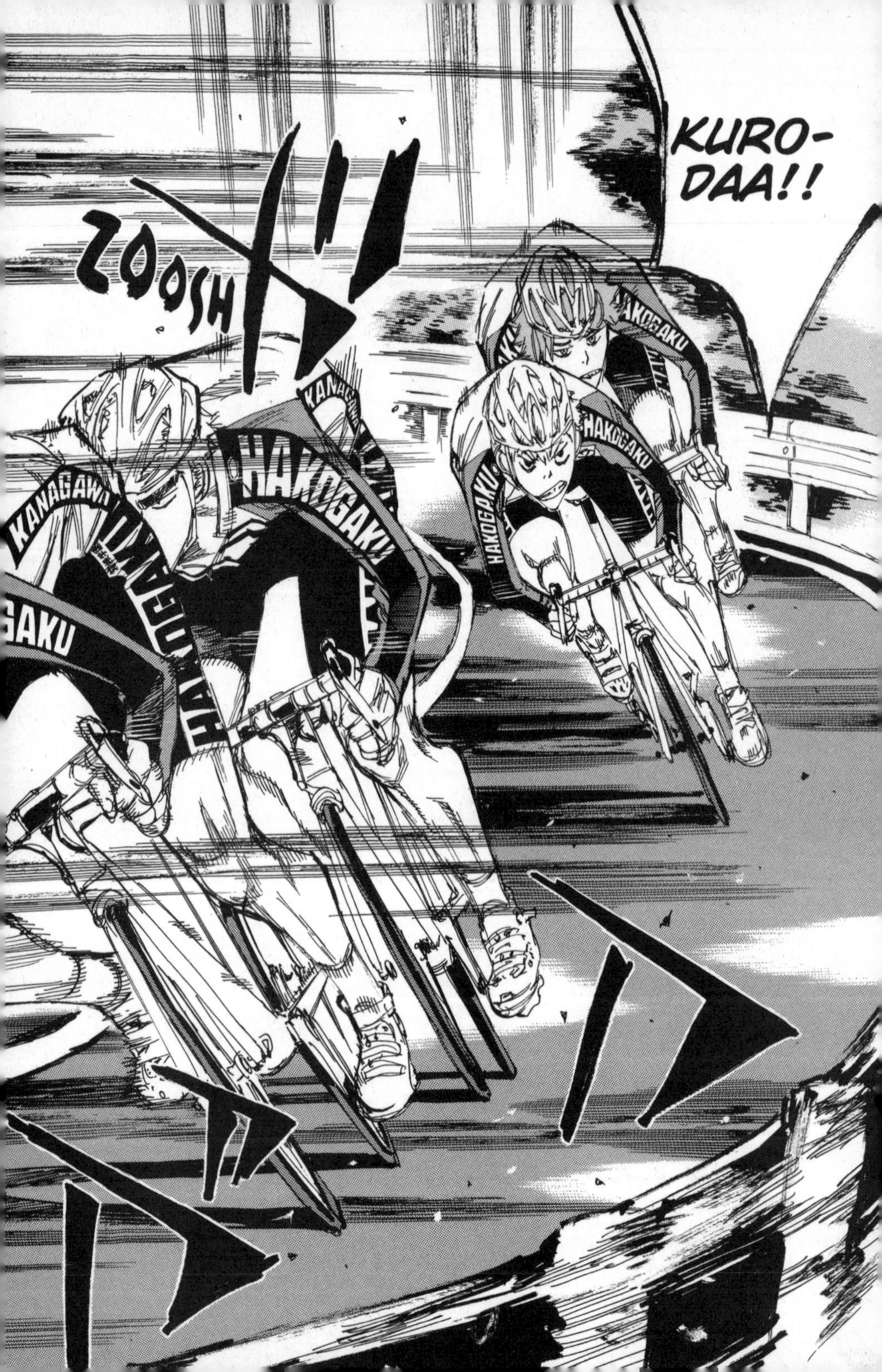
KURO-
DAA!!
ZOOSH
HAKOGAKU
KANAGAWA
HAKOGAKU
KANAGAWA
HAKOGAKU
HAKOGAKU
GAKU
HAKOGAKU
HAKOGAKU
HAKOGAKU

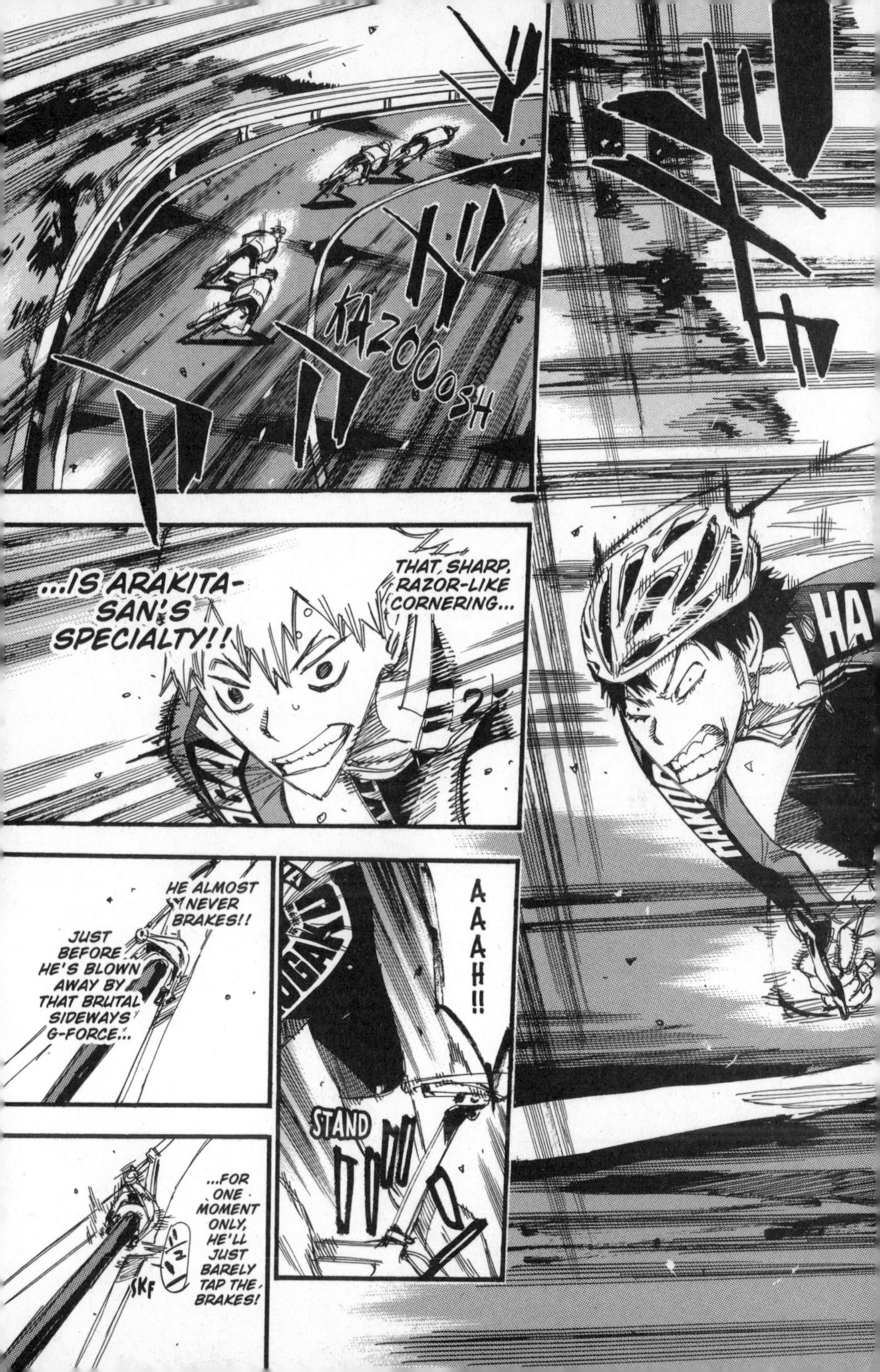
KAZOOOSH
THAT SHARP, RAZOR-LIKE CORNERING...
...IS ARAKITA-SAN'S SPECIALTY!!
AAAAH!!
STAND
HE ALMOST NEVER BRAKES!!
JUST BEFORE HE'S BLOWN AWAY BY THAT BRUTAL SIDEWAYS G-FORCE...
...FOR ONE MOMENT ONLY, HE'LL JUST BARELY TAP THE BRAKES!
SKF

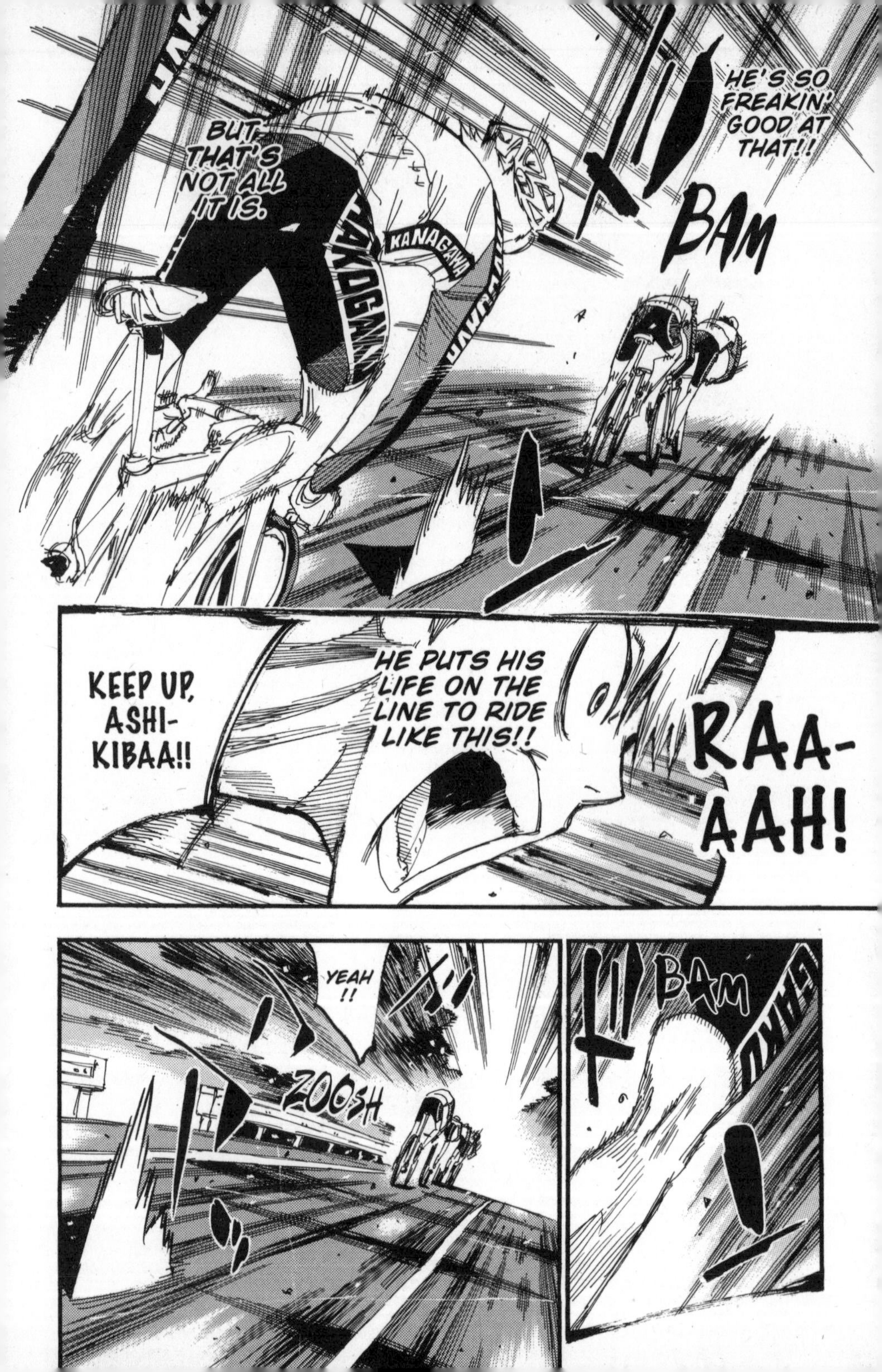
HE'S SO FREAKIN' GOOD AT THAT!!
BAM
BUT THAT'S NOT ALL IT IS.
RAA-AAH!
HE PUTS HIS LIFE ON THE LINE TO RIDE LIKE THIS!!
KEEP UP, ASHI-KIBAA!!
BAM
YEAH!!
ZOOSH

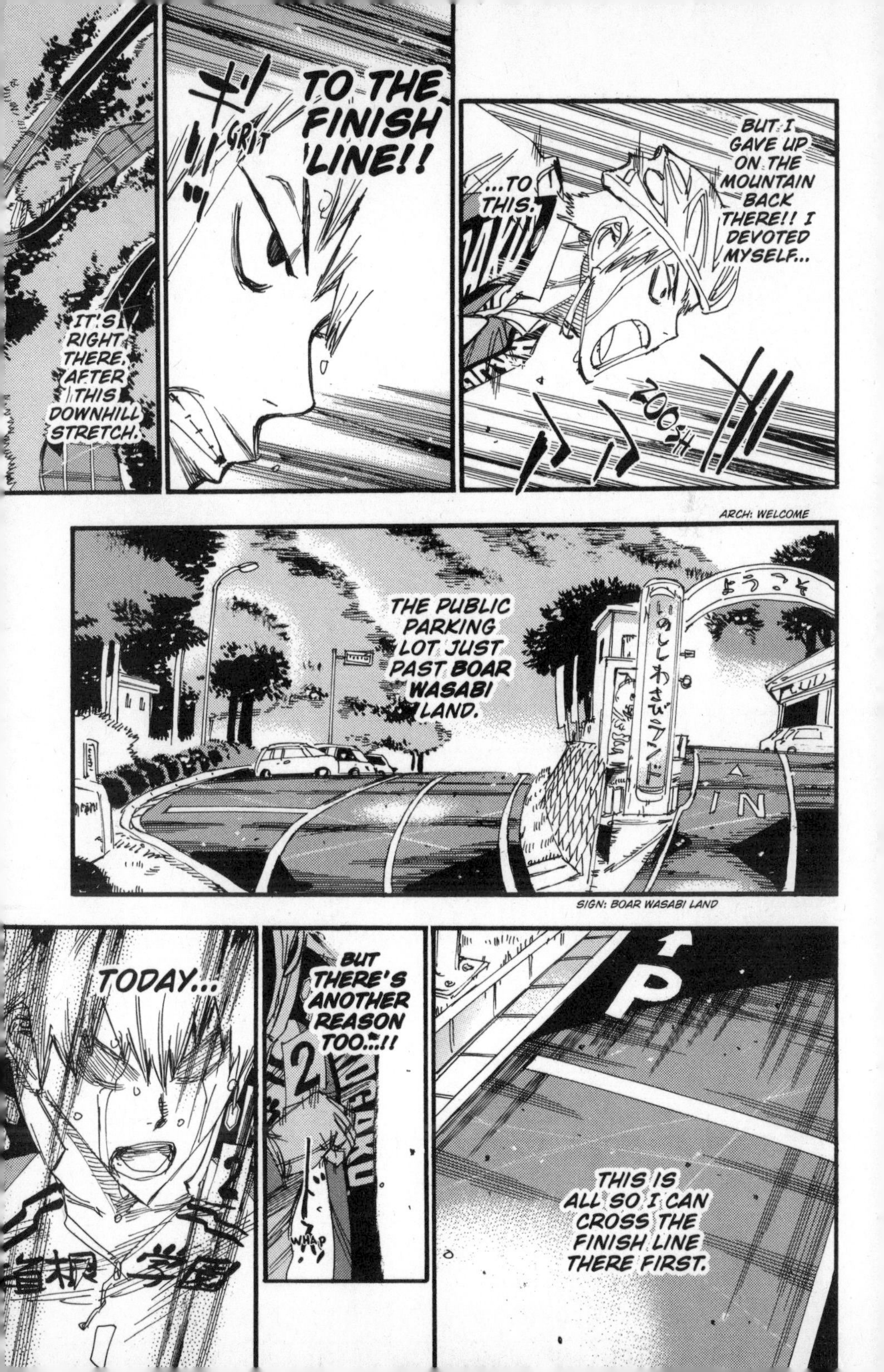
BUT I GAVE UP ON THE MOUNTAIN BACK THERE!! I DEVOTED MYSELF...
...TO THIS.
ZOOSH
TO THE FINISH LINE!!
GRIT
IT'S RIGHT THERE, AFTER THIS DOWNHILL STRETCH.
ARCH: WELCOME
ようこそ
いのししわさびランド
THE PUBLIC PARKING LOT JUST PAST BOAR WASABI LAND.
IN
SIGN: BOAR WASABI LAND
P
THIS IS ALL SO I CAN CROSS THE FINISH LINE THERE FIRST.
BUT THERE'S ANOTHER REASON TOO...!!
WHAP
TODAY...

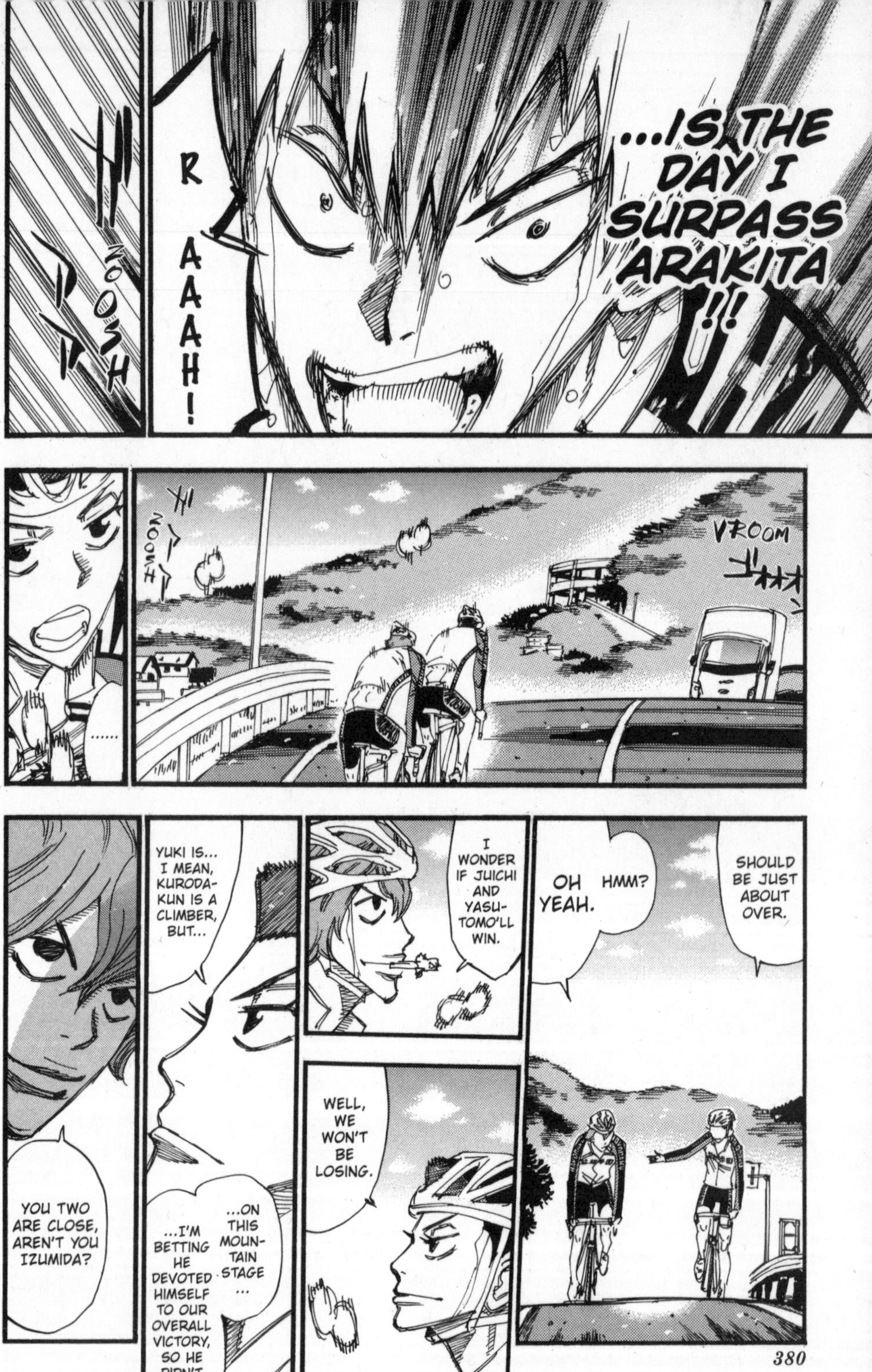
...IS THE DAY I SURPASS ARAKITA!!
RAAAAH!
WOOSH
VROOM
WOOSH
......
SHOULD BE JUST ABOUT OVER.
HMM?
OH YEAH.
I WONDER IF JUICHI AND YASUTOMO'LL WIN.
WELL, WE WON'T BE LOSING.
...ON THIS MOUNTAIN STAGE...
YUKI IS... I MEAN, KURODA-KUN IS A CLIMBER, BUT...
...I'M BETTING HE DEVOTED HIMSELF TO OUR OVERALL VICTORY, SO HE DIDN'T RACE AHEAD.
YOU TWO ARE CLOSE, AREN'T YOU IZUMIDA?

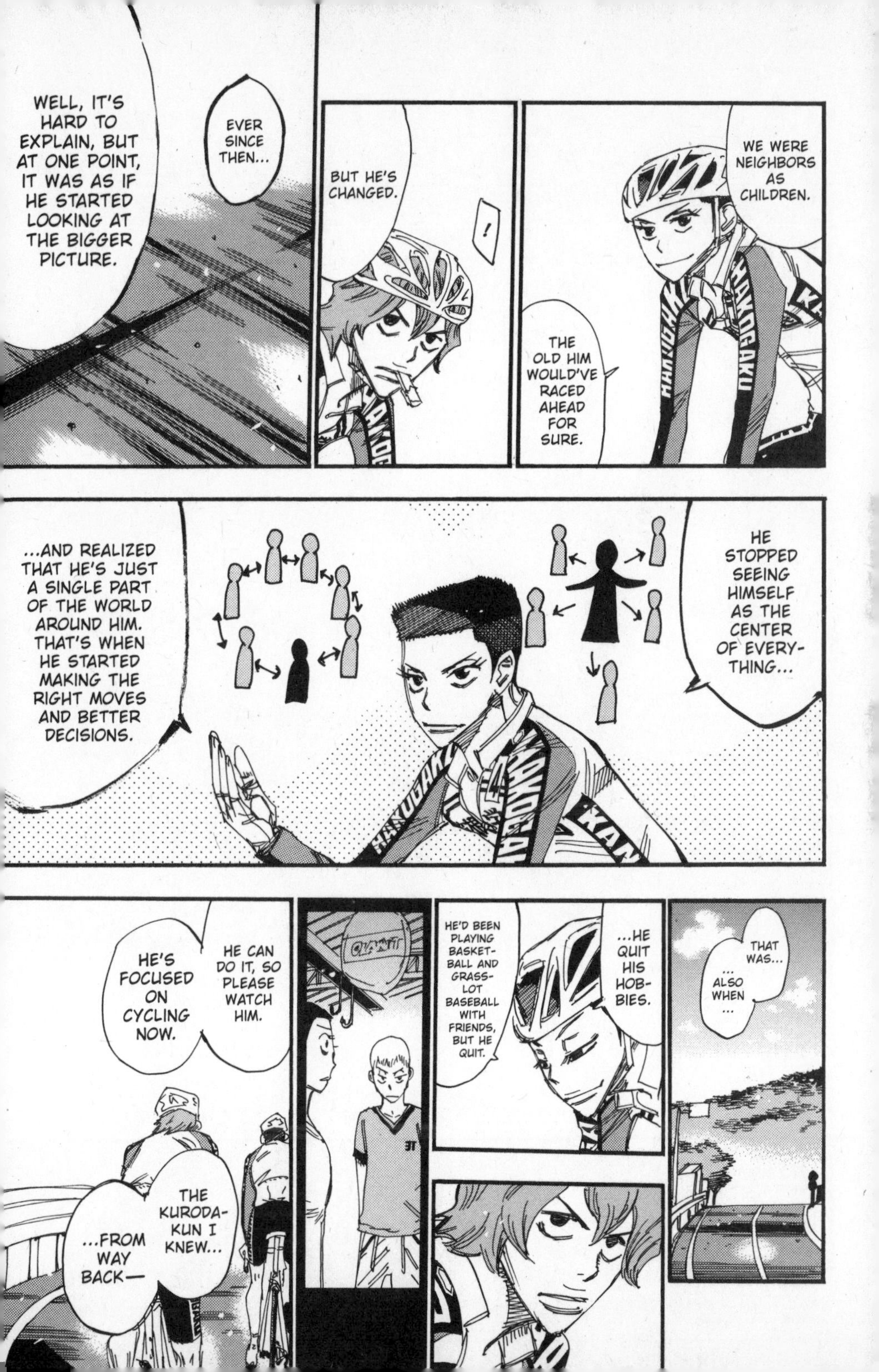

WE WERE NEIGHBORS AS CHILDREN.
THE OLD HIM WOULD'VE RACED AHEAD FOR SURE.
BUT HE'S CHANGED.
!
EVER SINCE THEN...
WELL, IT'S HARD TO EXPLAIN, BUT AT ONE POINT, IT WAS AS IF HE STARTED LOOKING AT THE BIGGER PICTURE.
HE STOPPED SEEING HIMSELF AS THE CENTER OF EVERY-THING...
...AND REALIZED THAT HE'S JUST A SINGLE PART OF THE WORLD AROUND HIM. THAT'S WHEN HE STARTED MAKING THE RIGHT MOVES AND BETTER DECISIONS.
THAT WAS...
...ALSO WHEN...
...HE QUIT HIS HOB-BIES.
HE'D BEEN PLAYING BASKET-BALL AND GRASS-LOT BASEBALL WITH FRIENDS, BUT HE QUIT.
HE CAN DO IT, SO PLEASE WATCH HIM.
HE'S FOCUSED ON CYCLING NOW.
THE KURODA-KUN I KNEW...
...FROM WAY BACK—

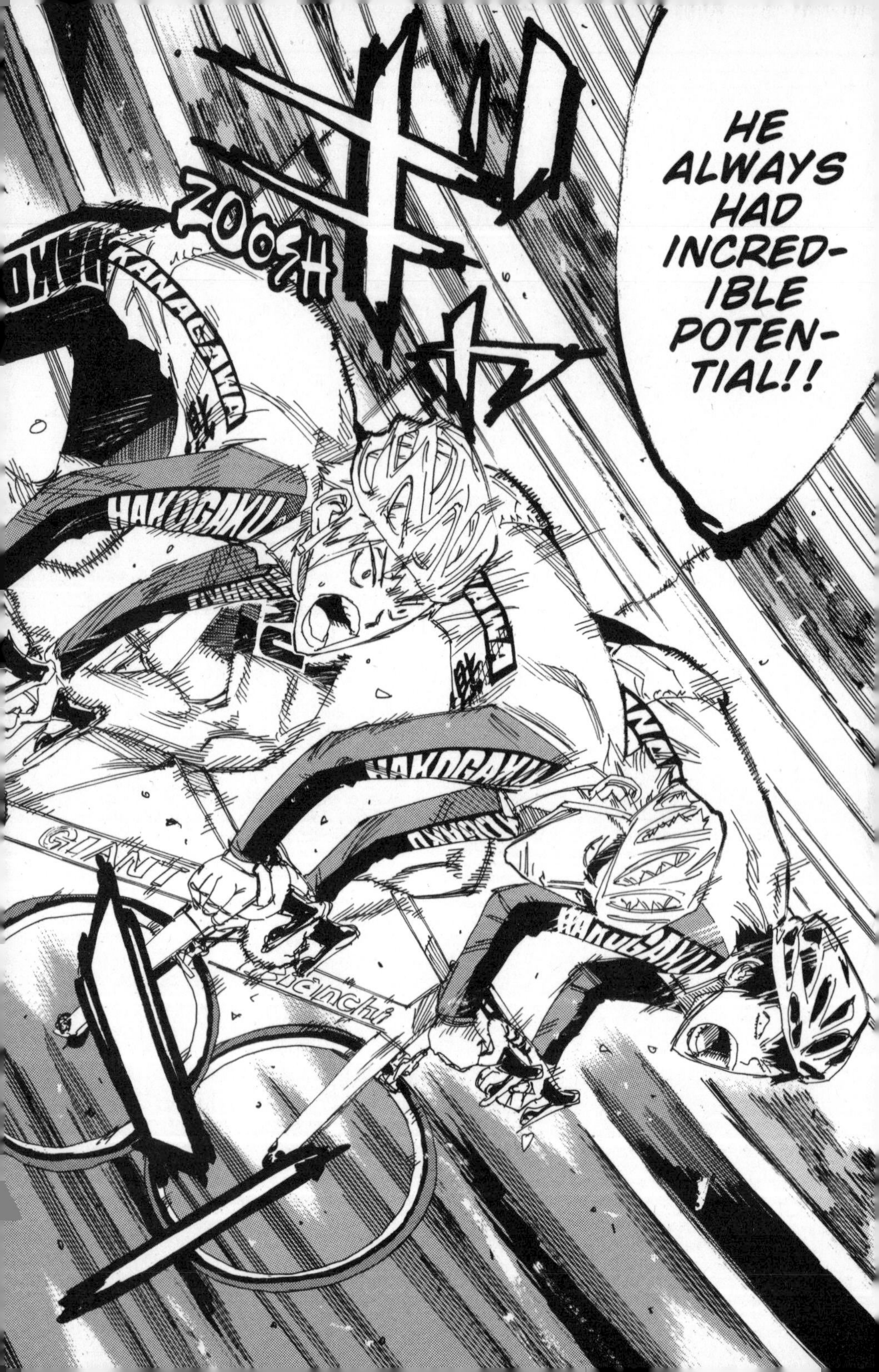
HE ALWAYS HAD INCRED-IBLE POTEN-TIAL!!
ZOOSH

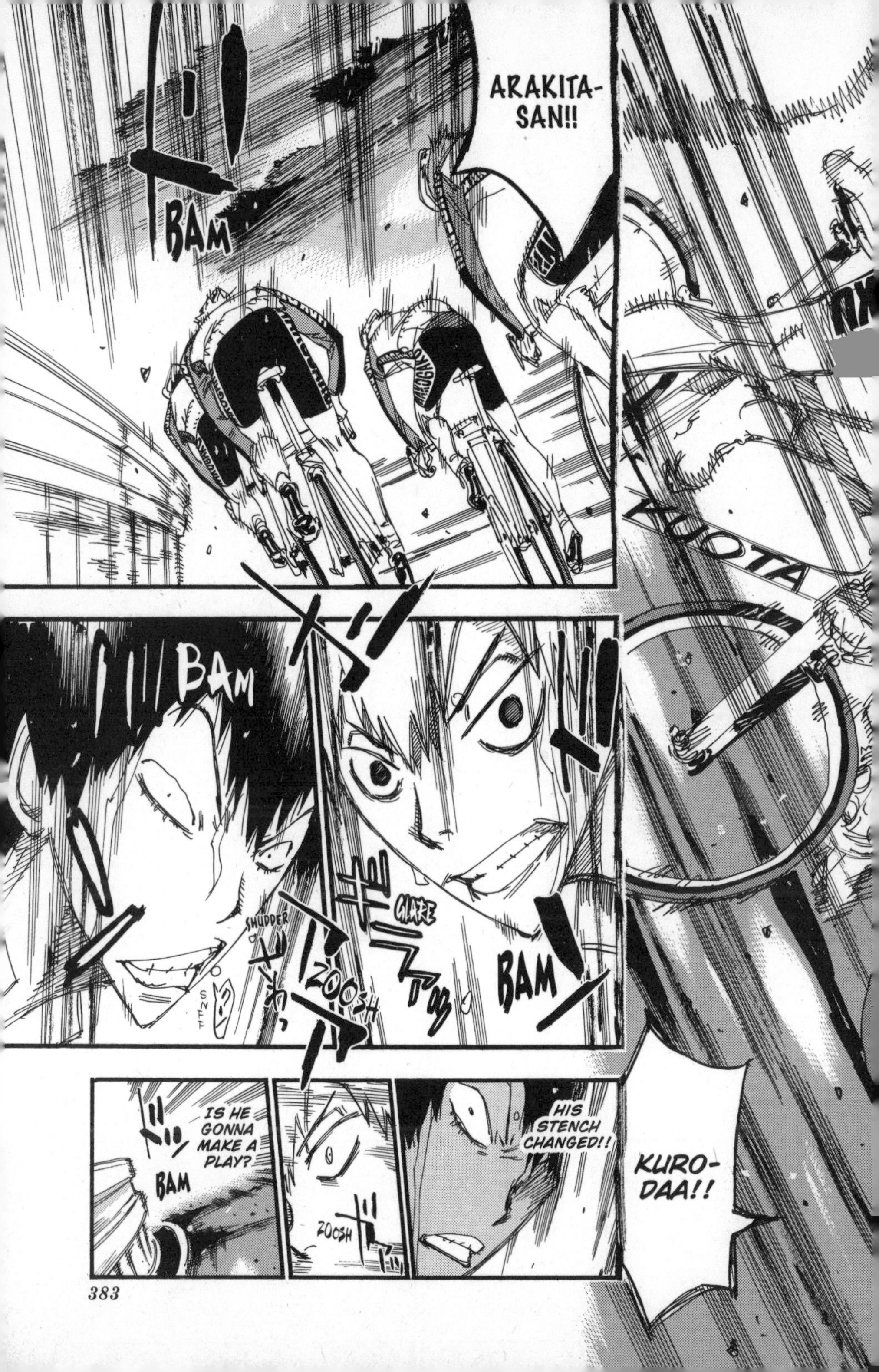
KURO-DAA!!
ARAKITA-SAN!!
BAM
BAM
GLARE
BAM
SHUDDER
ZOOSH
SNIFF
HIS STENCH CHANGED!!
ZOOSH
IS HE GONNA MAKE A PLAY?
BAM

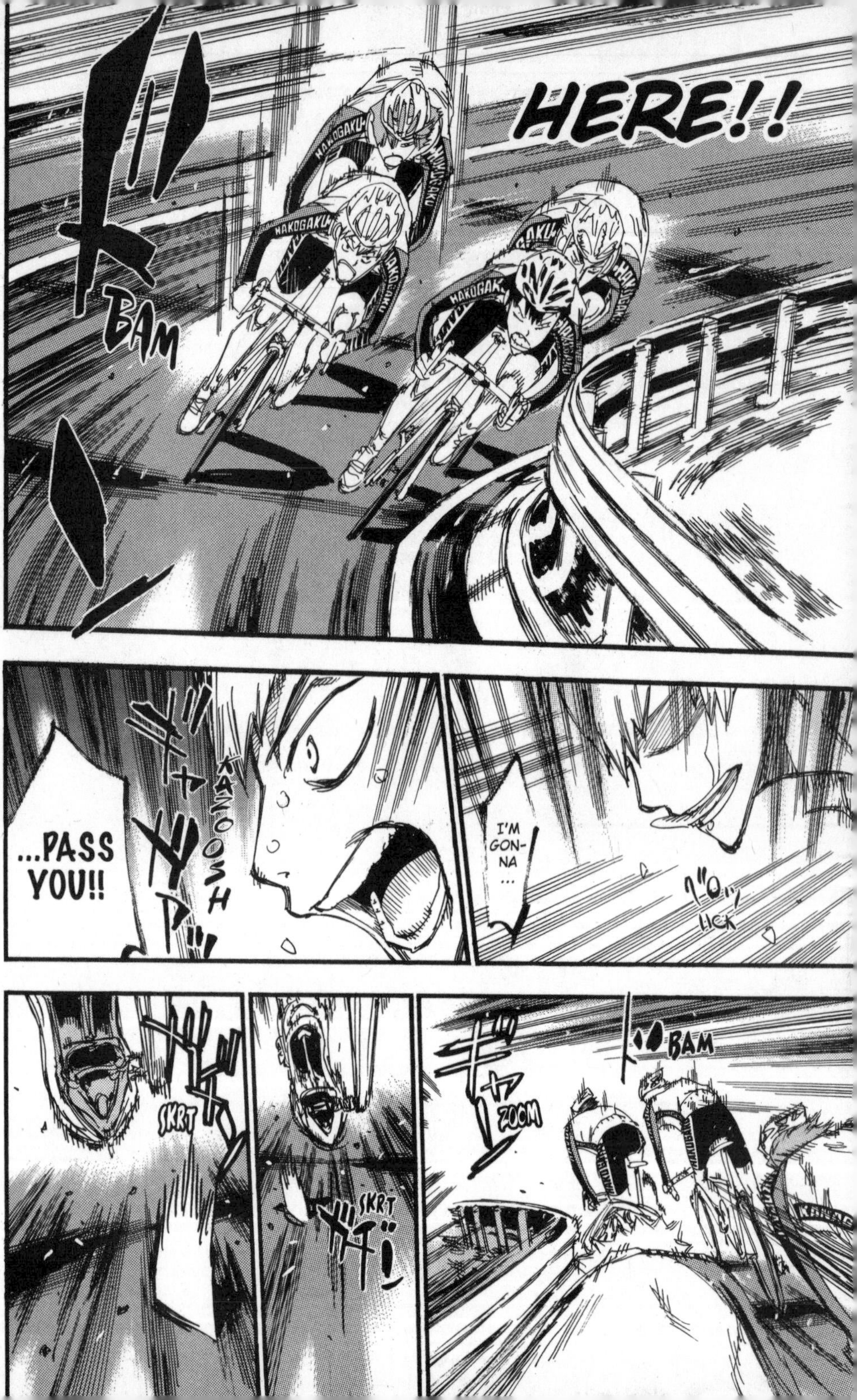
HERE!!
BAM
I'M GONNA...
LICK
...PASS YOU!!
KAZOOSH
BAM
ZOOM
SKRT
SKRT

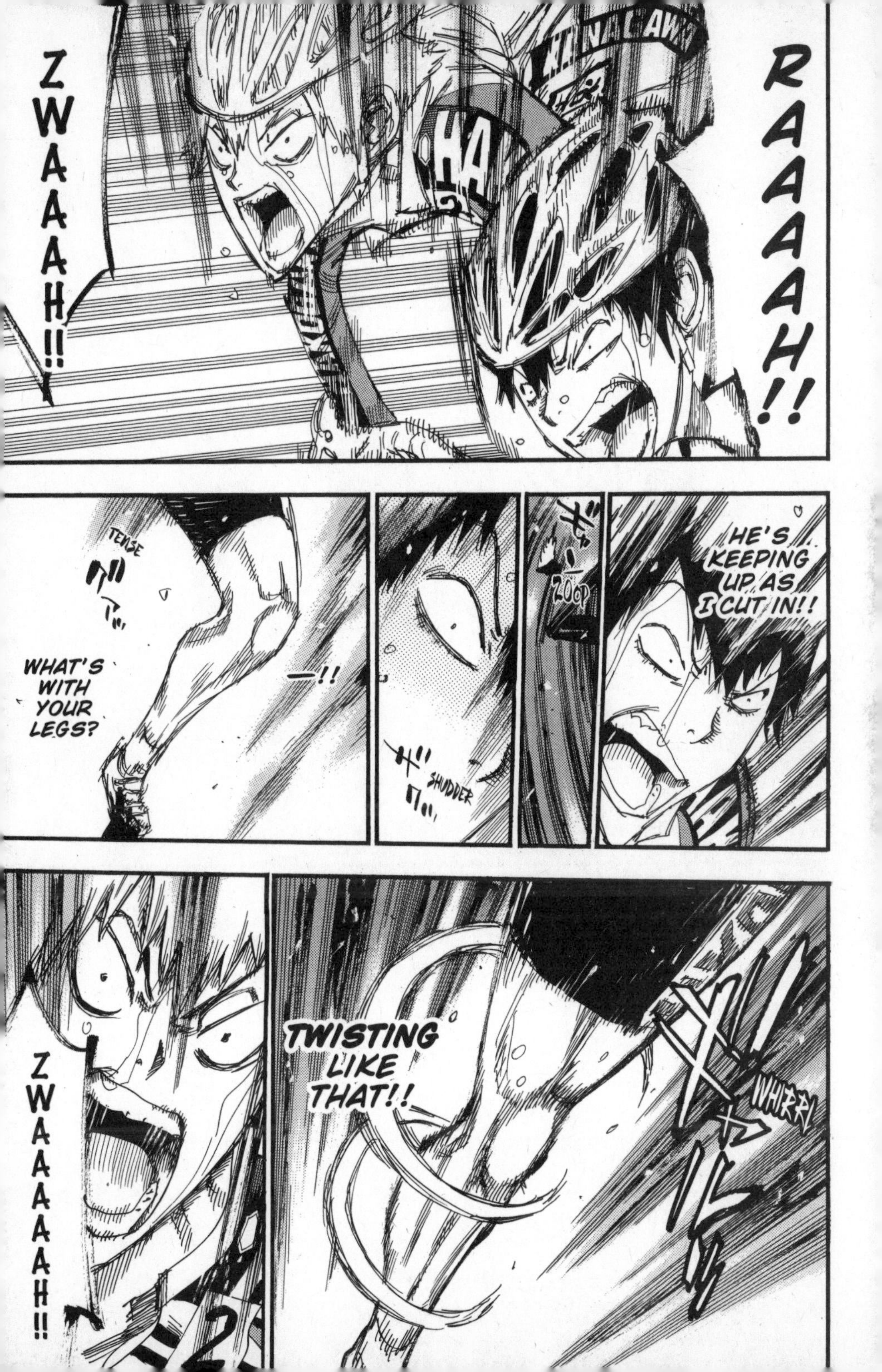
RAAAAAH!!
ZWAAAAH!!
HE'S KEEPING UP AS I CUT IN!!
ZOOP
—!!
SHUDDER
TENSE
WHAT'S WITH YOUR LEGS?
WHIRR
TWISTING LIKE THAT!!
ZWAAAAAAAH!!

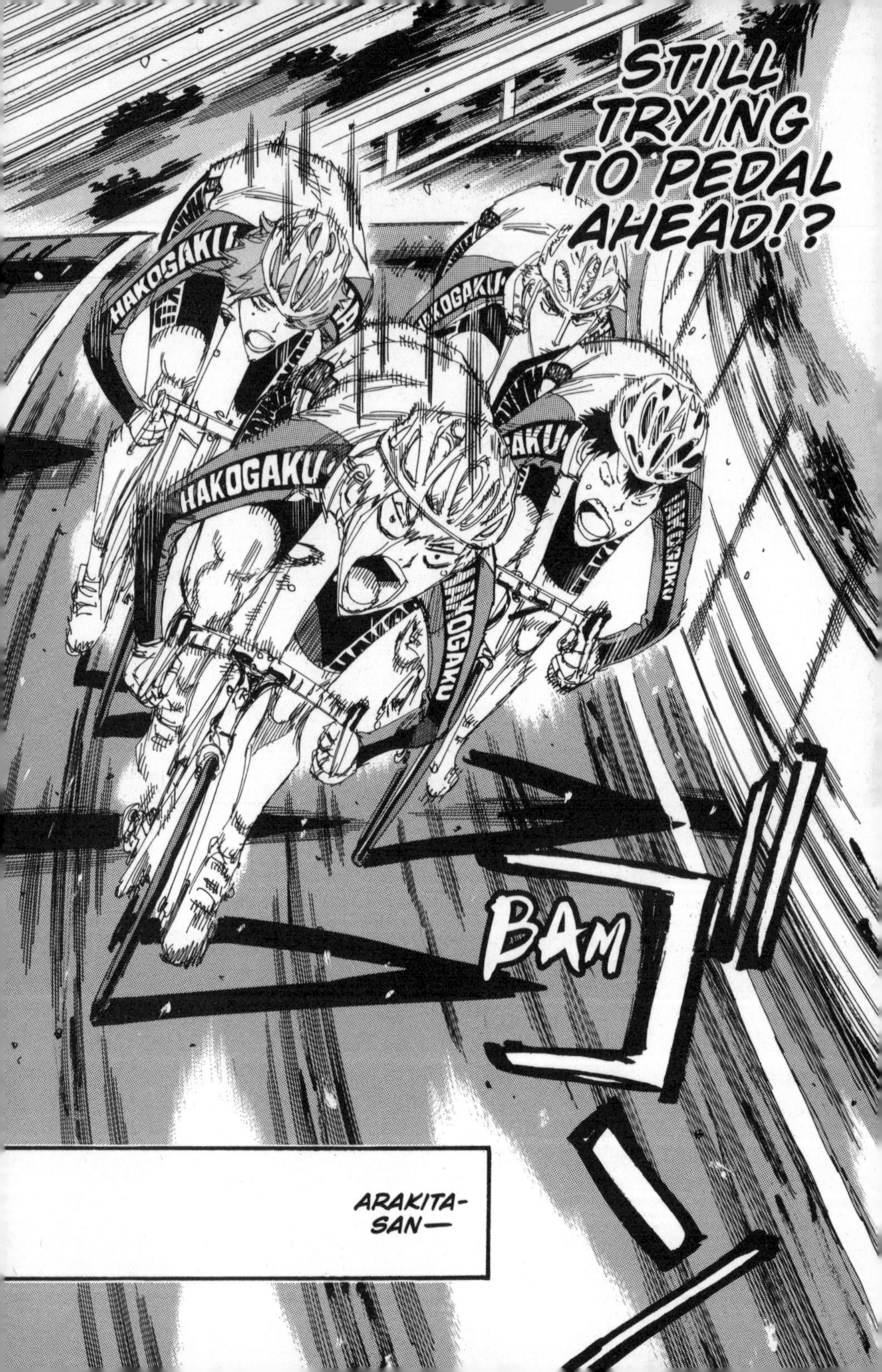
STILL TRYING TO PEDAL AHEAD!?
HAKOGAKU
HAKOGAKU
HAKOGAKU
BAM
ARAKITA-SAN—

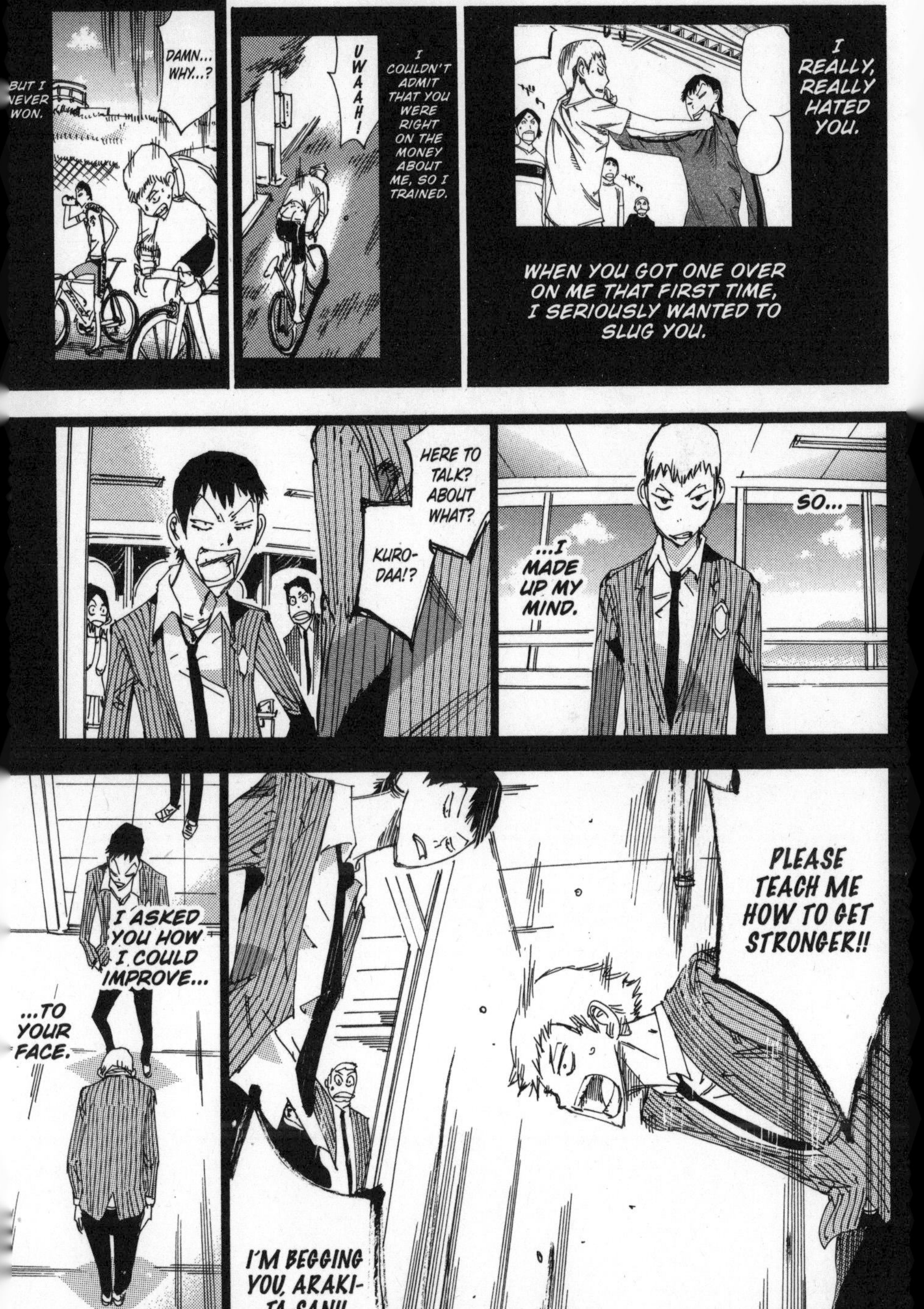
I REALLY, REALLY HATED YOU.
WHEN YOU GOT ONE OVER ON ME THAT FIRST TIME, I SERIOUSLY WANTED TO SLUG YOU.
UWAAH!
I COULDN'T ADMIT THAT YOU WERE RIGHT ON THE MONEY ABOUT ME, SO I TRAINED.
DAMN... WHY...?
BUT I NEVER WON.
SO...
...I MADE UP MY MIND.
HERE TO TALK? ABOUT WHAT?
KURO-DAA!?
PLEASE TEACH ME HOW TO GET STRONGER!!
I'M BEGGING YOU, ARAKITA-SAN!!
I ASKED YOU HOW I COULD IMPROVE...
...TO YOUR FACE.

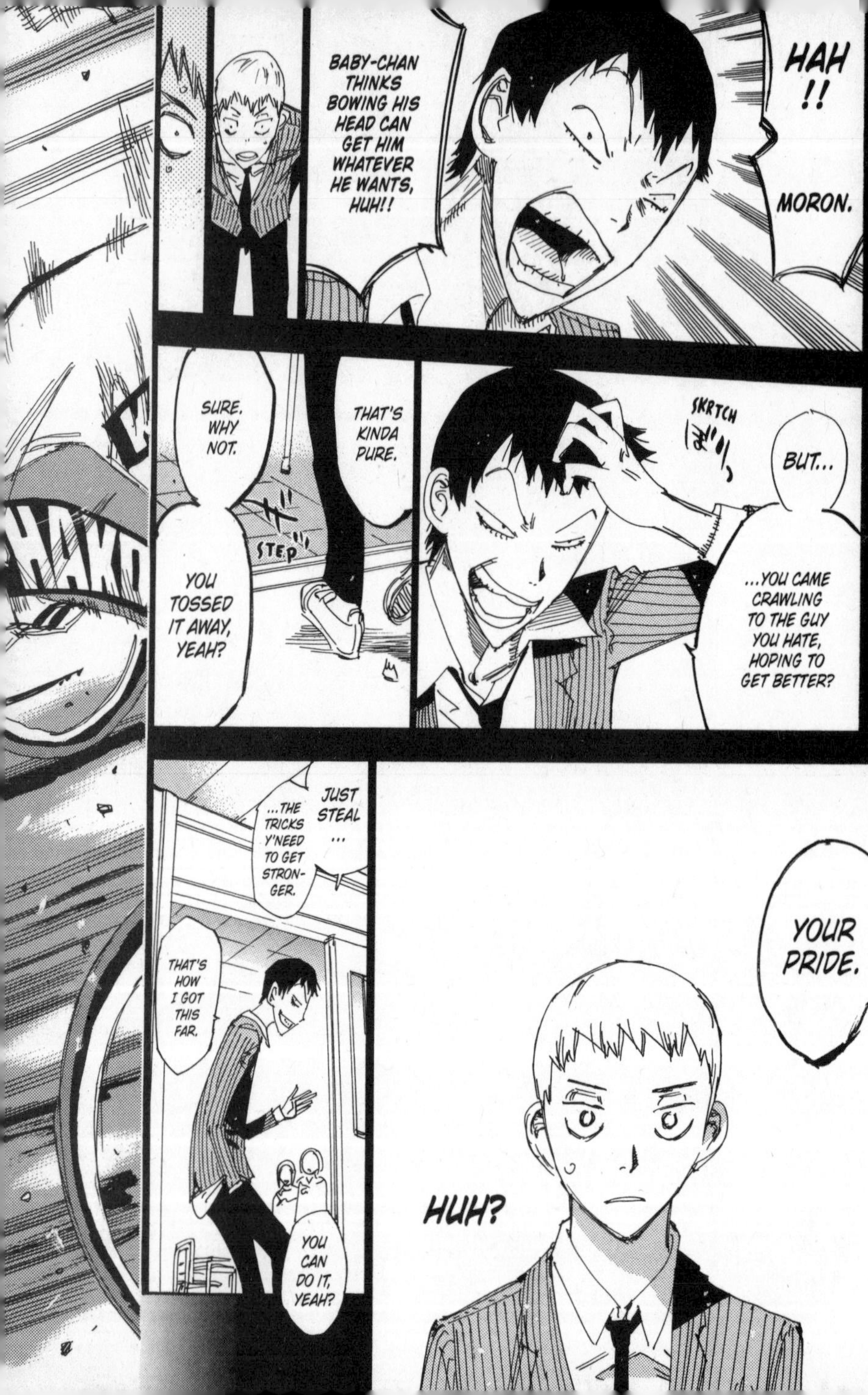
HAH!!
MORON.
BABY-CHAN THINKS BOWING HIS HEAD CAN GET HIM WHATEVER HE WANTS, HUH!!
SKRTCH
BUT...
...YOU CAME CRAWLING TO THE GUY YOU HATE, HOPING TO GET BETTER?
THAT'S KINDA PURE.
SURE. WHY NOT.
STEP
YOU TOSSED IT AWAY, YEAH?
YOUR PRIDE.
HUH?
JUST STEAL...
...THE TRICKS Y'NEED TO GET STRONGER.
THAT'S HOW I GOT THIS FAR.
YOU CAN DO IT, YEAH?

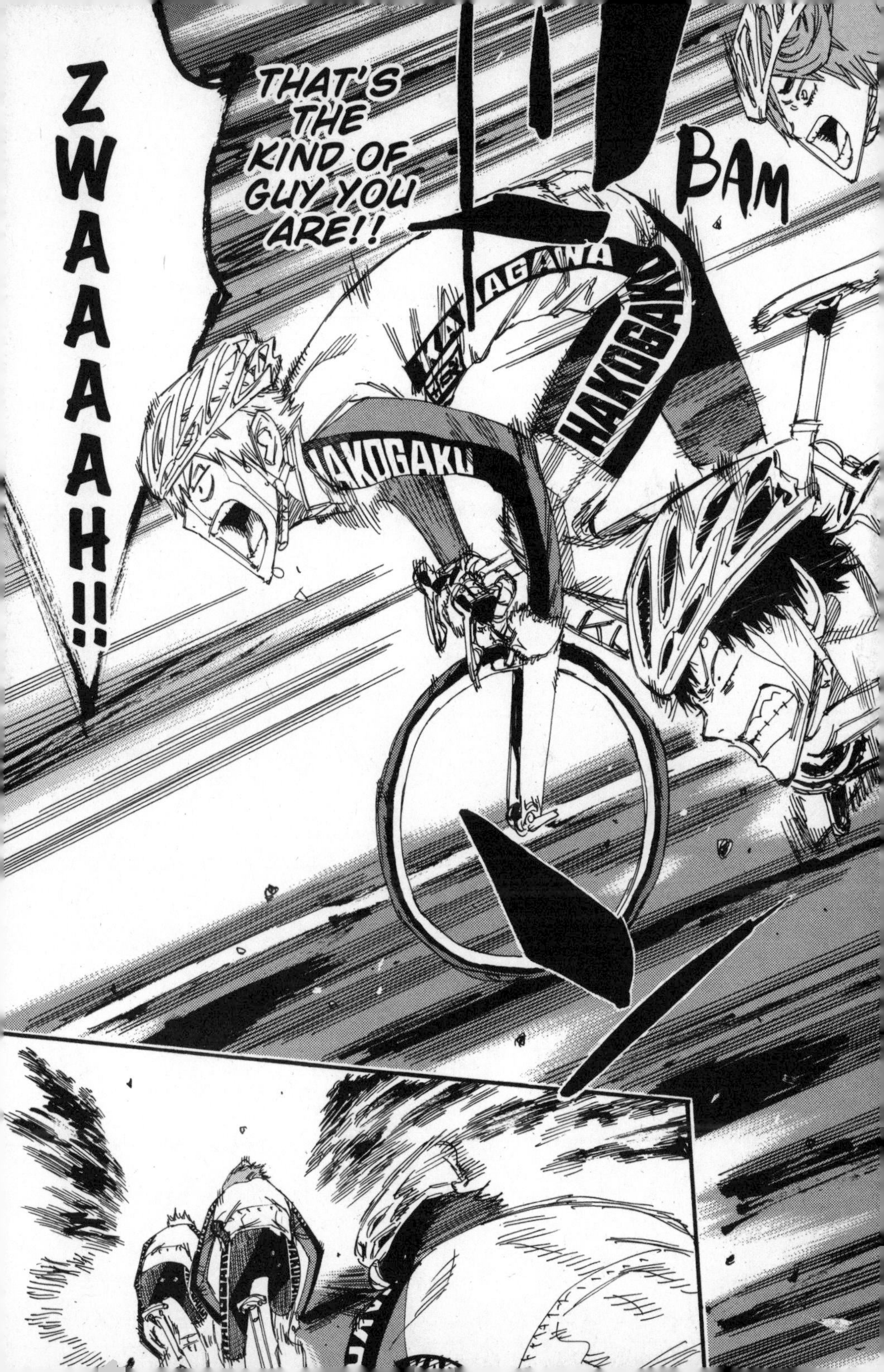
BAM
THAT'S THE KIND OF GUY YOU ARE!!
ZWAAAAAH!!

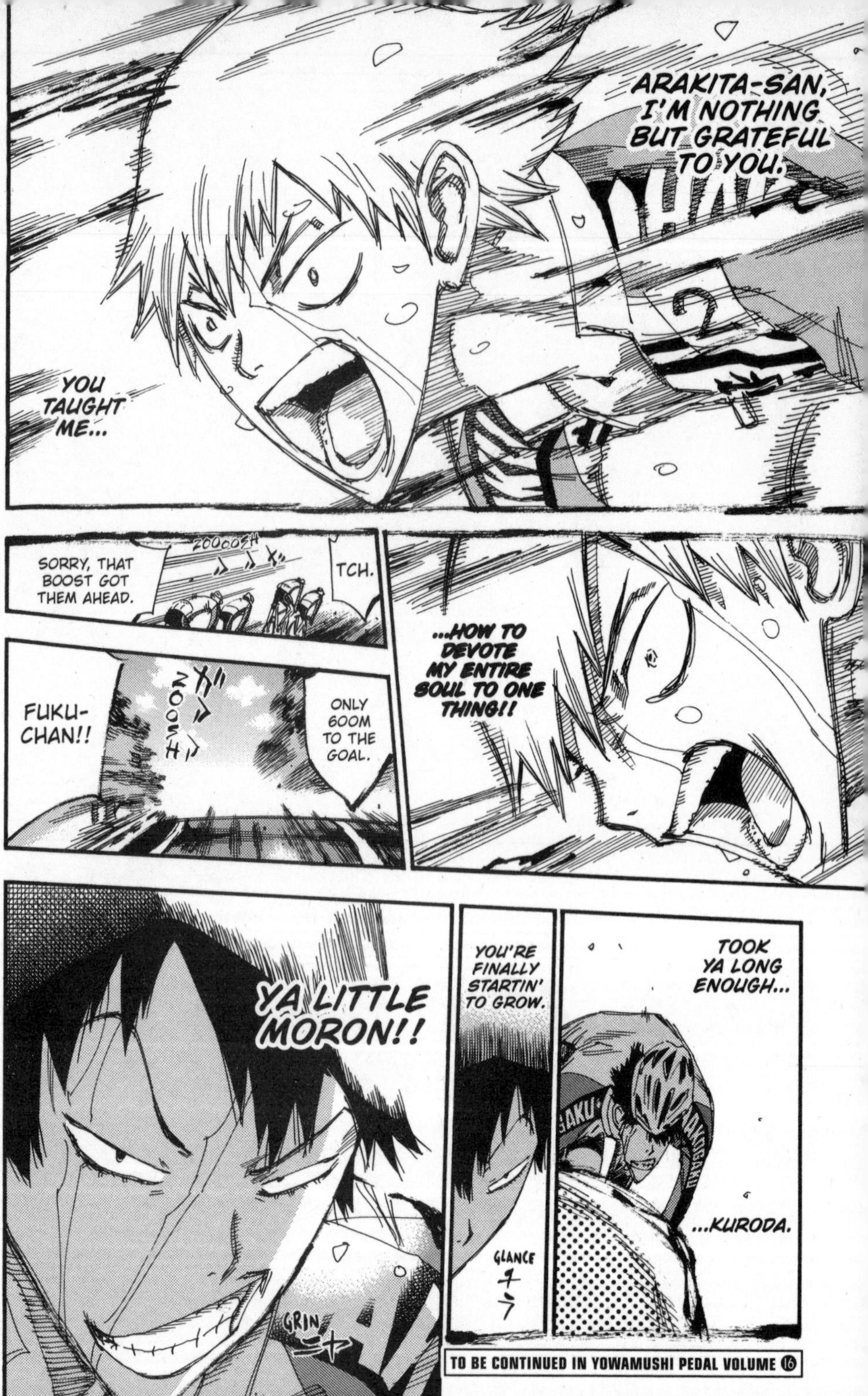
ARAKITA-SAN, I'M NOTHING BUT GRATEFUL TO YOU.
YOU TAUGHT ME...
...HOW TO DEVOTE MY ENTIRE SOUL TO ONE THING!!
TCH.
ZOOOOSH
SORRY, THAT BOOST GOT THEM AHEAD.
ONLY 600M TO THE GOAL.
WOOSH
FUKU-CHAN!!
TOOK YA LONG ENOUGH...
...KURODA.
YOU'RE FINALLY STARTIN' TO GROW.
GLANCE
YA LITTLE MORON!!
GRIN

TO BE CONTINUED IN YOWAMUSHI PEDAL VOLUME 16

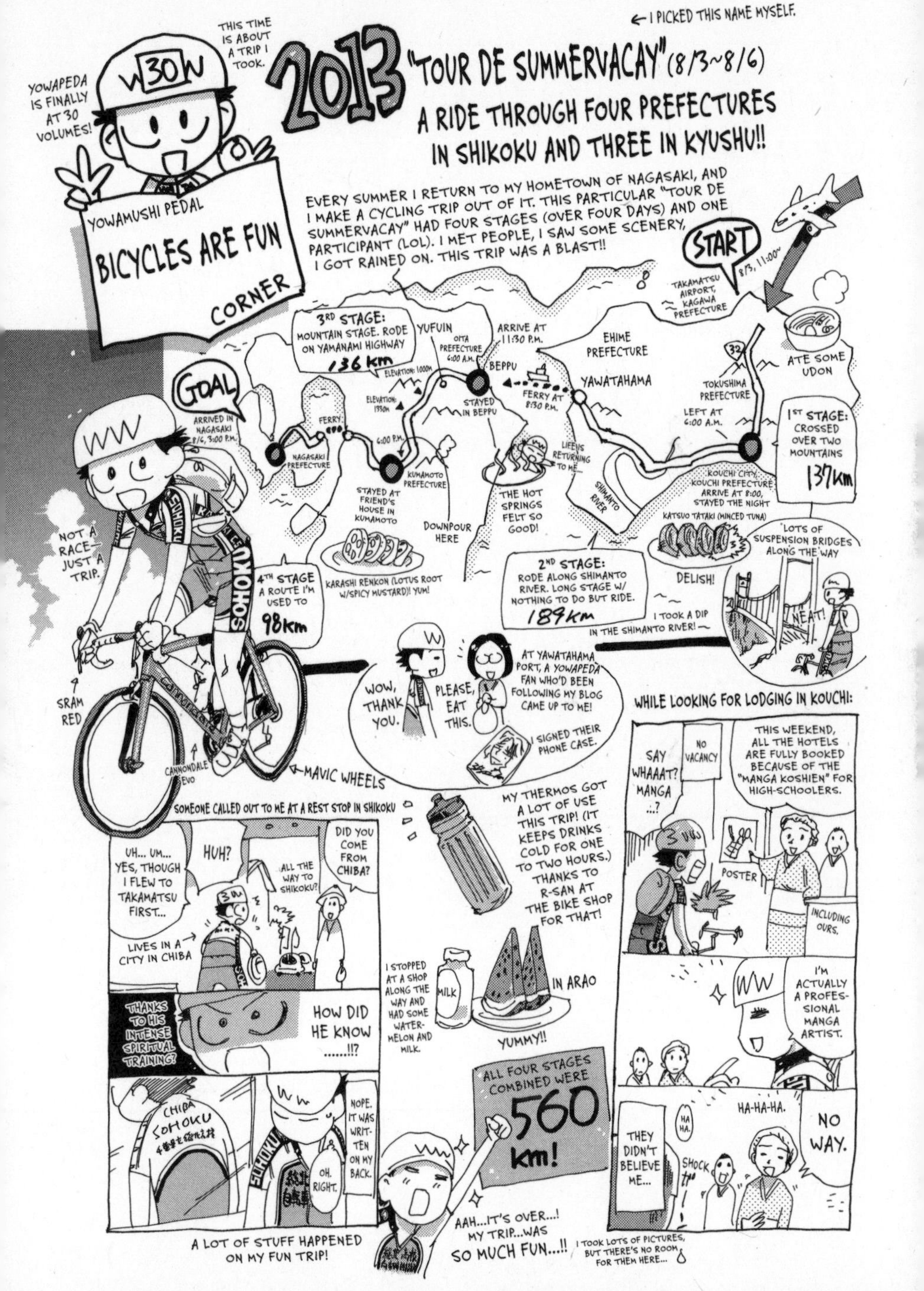
← I PICKED THIS NAME MYSELF.
2013 "TOUR DE SUMMERVACAY" (8/3~8/6)
A RIDE THROUGH FOUR PREFECTURES IN SHIKOKU AND THREE IN KYUSHU!!
THIS TIME IS ABOUT A TRIP I TOOK.
W30W
YOWAPEDA IS FINALLY AT 30 VOLUMES!
YOWAMUSHI PEDAL
BICYCLES ARE FUN
CORNER
EVERY SUMMER I RETURN TO MY HOMETOWN OF NAGASAKI, AND I MAKE A CYCLING TRIP OUT OF IT. THIS PARTICULAR "TOUR DE SUMMERVACAY" HAD FOUR STAGES (OVER FOUR DAYS) AND ONE PARTICIPANT (LOL). I MET PEOPLE, I SAW SOME SCENERY, I GOT RAINED ON. THIS TRIP WAS A BLAST!!
START
8/3, 11:00~
TAKAMATSU AIRPORT, KAGAWA PREFECTURE
ATE SOME UDON
32
TOKUSHIMA PREFECTURE
EHIME PREFECTURE
YAWATAHAMA
LEFT AT 6:00 A.M.
1ST STAGE: CROSSED OVER TWO MOUNTAINS
137km
KOUCHI CITY, KOUCHI PREFECTURE ARRIVE AT 8:00, STAYED THE NIGHT
SHIMANTO RIVER
KATSUO TATAKI (MINCED TUNA)
DELISH!
LOTS OF SUSPENSION BRIDGES ALONG THE WAY
NEAT!
I TOOK A DIP IN THE SHIMANTO RIVER!
2ND STAGE: RODE ALONG SHIMANTO RIVER. LONG STAGE W/ NOTHING TO DO BUT RIDE.
189km
FERRY AT 8:30 P.M.
ARRIVE AT 11:30 P.M.
BEPPU
STAYED IN BEPPU
OITA PREFECTURE 6:00 A.M.
LIFE IS RETURNING TO ME...
THE HOT SPRINGS FELT SO GOOD!
YUFUIN
3RD STAGE: MOUNTAIN STAGE. RODE ON YAMANAMI HIGHWAY
136km
ELEVATION: 1000M
ELEVATION: 1330M
6:00 P.M.
DOWNPOUR HERE
KUMAMOTO PREFECTURE
STAYED AT FRIEND'S HOUSE IN KUMAMOTO
KARASHI RENKON (LOTUS ROOT W/SPICY MUSTARD)! YUM!
FERRY
NAGASAKI PREFECTURE
GOAL
ARRIVED IN NAGASAKI 8/6, 3:00 P.M.
4TH STAGE A ROUTE I'M USED TO
98km
WW
SOHOKU
NOT A RACE JUST A TRIP.
SRAM RED
CANNONDALE EVO
MAVIC WHEELS
AT YAWATAHAMA PORT, A YOWAPEDA FAN WHO'D BEEN FOLLOWING MY BLOG CAME UP TO ME!
PLEASE, EAT THIS.
WOW, THANK YOU.
I SIGNED THEIR PHONE CASE.
WHILE LOOKING FOR LODGING IN KOUCHI:
THIS WEEKEND, ALL THE HOTELS ARE FULLY BOOKED BECAUSE OF THE "MANGA KOSHIEN" FOR HIGH-SCHOOLERS.
NO VACANCY
SAY WHAAAT? MANGA ...?
POSTER
INCLUDING OURS.
I'M ACTUALLY A PROFES-SIONAL MANGA ARTIST.
NO WAY.
HA-HA-HA.
HA HA.
SHOCK
THEY DIDN'T BELIEVE ME...
MY THERMOS GOT A LOT OF USE THIS TRIP! (IT KEEPS DRINKS COLD FOR ONE TO TWO HOURS.) THANKS TO R-SAN AT THE BIKE SHOP FOR THAT!
I STOPPED AT A SHOP ALONG THE WAY AND HAD SOME WATER-MELON AND MILK.
MILK
IN ARAO
YUMMY!!
ALL FOUR STAGES COMBINED WERE 560 km!
AAH...IT'S OVER...! MY TRIP...WAS SO MUCH FUN...!!
I TOOK LOTS OF PICTURES, BUT THERE'S NO ROOM FOR THEM HERE...
SOMEONE CALLED OUT TO ME AT A REST STOP IN SHIKOKU
DID YOU COME FROM CHIBA?
ALL THE WAY TO SHIKOKU?
HUH?
UH... UM... YES, THOUGH I FLEW TO TAKAMATSU FIRST...
LIVES IN A CITY IN CHIBA
HOW DID HE KNOW ......!!?
THANKS TO HIS INTENSE SPIRITUAL TRAINING?
NOPE. IT WAS WRIT-TEN ON MY BACK.
OH. RIGHT.
CHIBA SOHOKU
SOHOKU
A LOT OF STUFF HAPPENED ON MY FUN TRIP!

Translation Notes

Common Honorifics
-san: The Japanese equivalent of Mr./Mrs./Miss. If a situation calls for politeness, this is the fail-safe honorific.
-kun: Used most often when referring to boys, this indicates affection or familiarity. Occasionally used by older men among their peers, but it may also be used by anyone referring to a person of lower standing.
-chan: An affectionate honorific indicating familiarity used mostly in reference to girls; also used in reference to cute persons or animals of either gender.
-senpai: A suffix used to address upperclassmen or more experienced co-workers.
-shi: A more formal version of *san* common to written Japanese, it's the default honorific used in newspapers.
no honorific: Indicates familiarity or closeness; if used without permission or reason, addressing someone in this manner would constitute an insult.

A kilometer is approximately .6 of a mile.

PAGE 86
Peloton: A cycling term for the "pack," or the main group of riders in a race.

PAGE 162
Nobody's luck holds out forever: Takeshi Daitsubu's catchphrase is a well-known proverb in Japanese that states that even the forgiving Buddha will get annoyed if you touch his face three times. Or, even a saint's patience has its limits. It's no coincidence that "Daitsubu" is sort of an anagram of "*Daibutsu*," which means "Great Buddha."

PAGE 163
Vale Tudo: A full-contact combat sport that originated in Brazil, known for its no-holds-barred, anything-goes nature. It is also said to be the precursor of modern MMA.

PAGE 172
Piste: A bicycle specialized for track racing.

PAGE 174
Jumbo Pea: Naruko's nickname for Daitsubu in Japanese is "*oo-tsubu*," which uses the alternate pronunciation of Daitsubu's "*dai*" kanji. "*Oo-tsubu*" contrasts with Tadokoro's nickname for Naruko, "*akai mame-tsubu*," which is translated as "red pea."

PAGE 200
Yoshiko-chan: A Japanese comedian from the Osakan comedy group GAMBARERUYA.

PAGE 282
Domestique: The ace's helper on a cycling team.

YOWAMUSHI PEDAL VOLUME 16

Read on for a sneak peek of Volume 16!

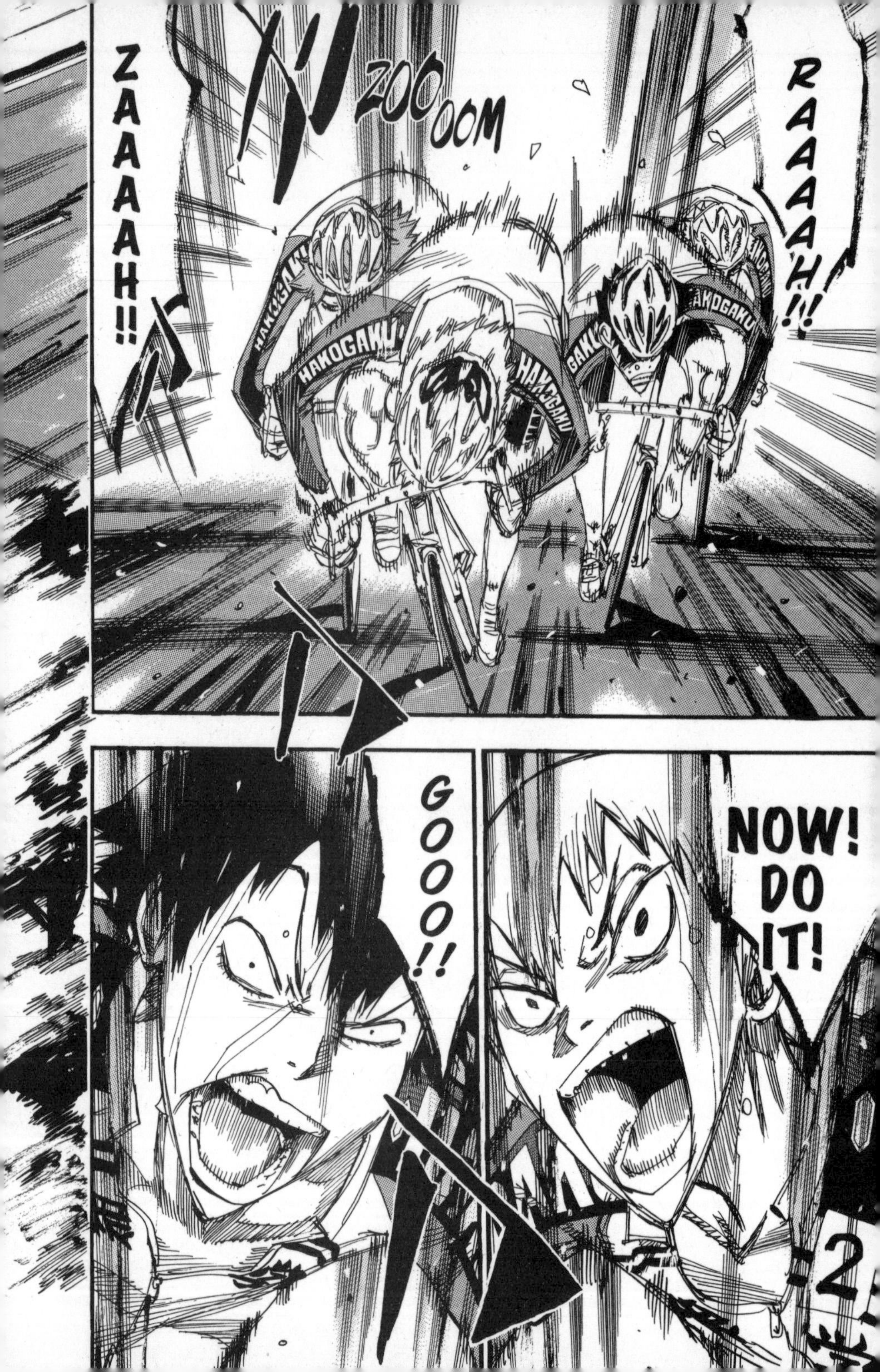
RAAAAH!!
ZOOOOM
ZAAAAH!!
NOW! DO IT!
GOOO!!

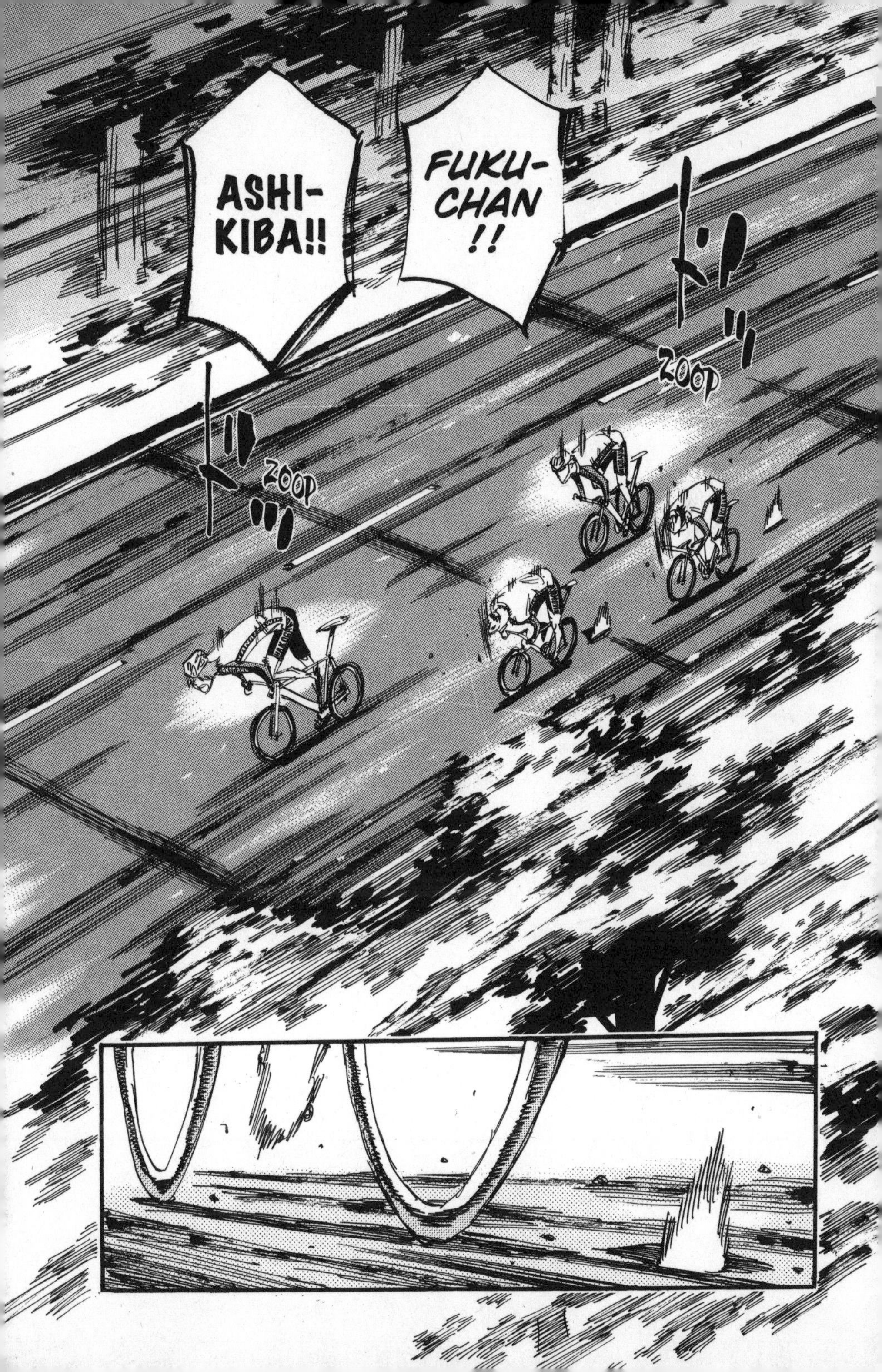
FUKU-CHAN!!
ZOOP
ASHI-KIBA!!
ZOOP

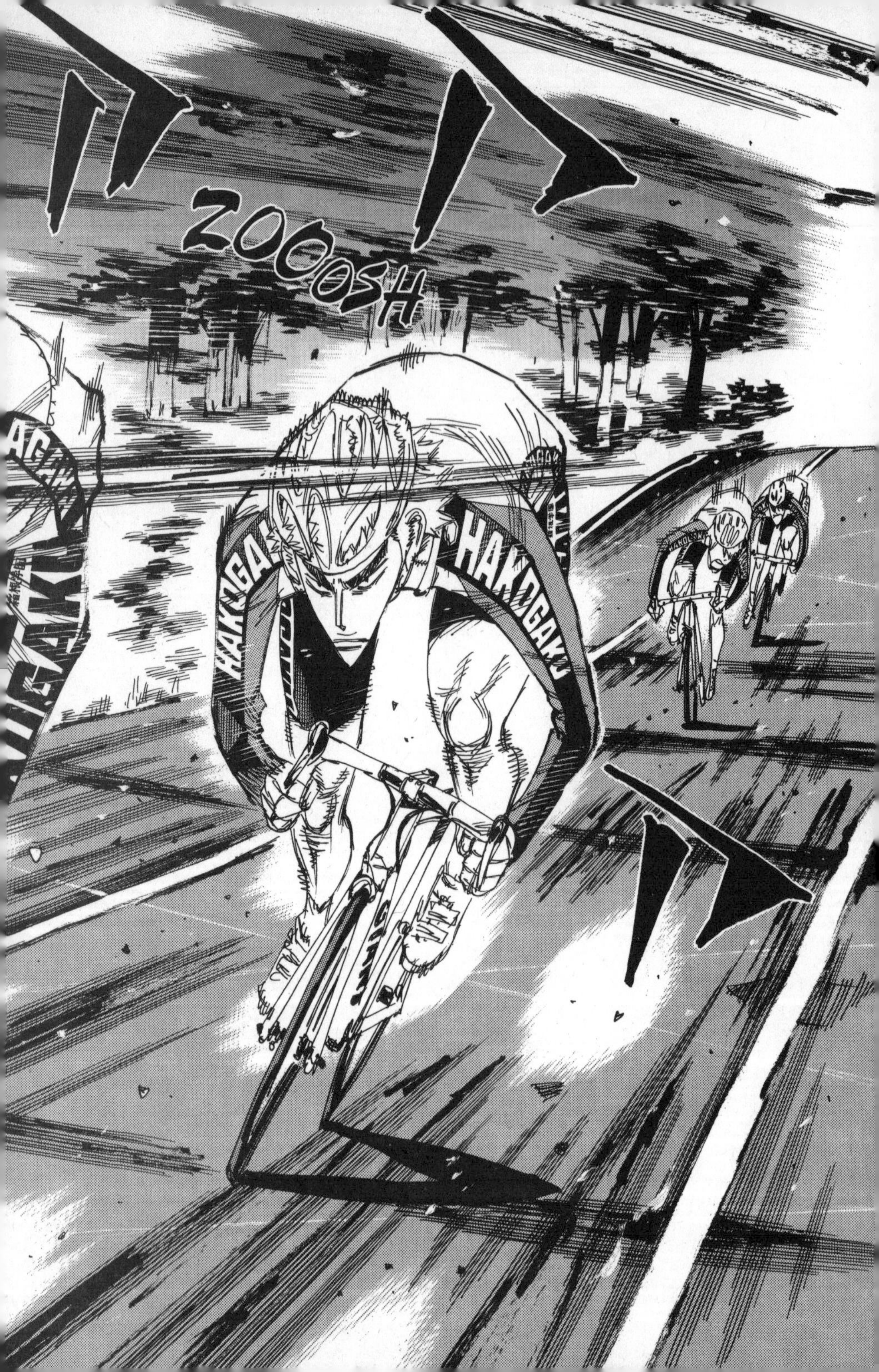
ZOOOSH
HAKOGAKU

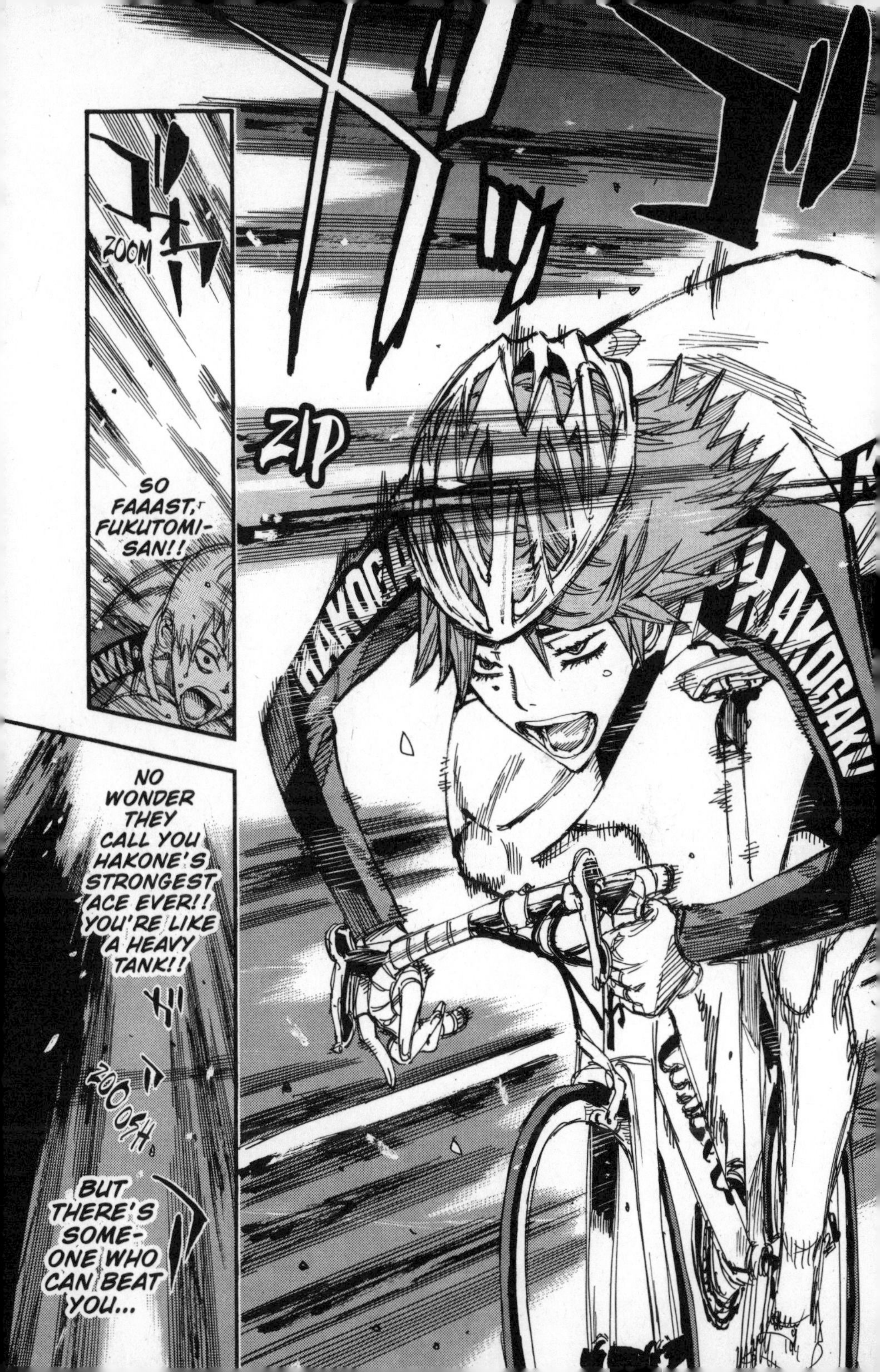
ZIP
ZOOM
SO FAAAST, FUKUTOMI-SAN!!
NO WONDER THEY CALL YOU HAKONE'S STRONGEST ACE EVER!! YOU'RE LIKE A HEAVY TANK!!
ZOOOSH
BUT THERE'S SOME-ONE WHO CAN BEAT YOU...

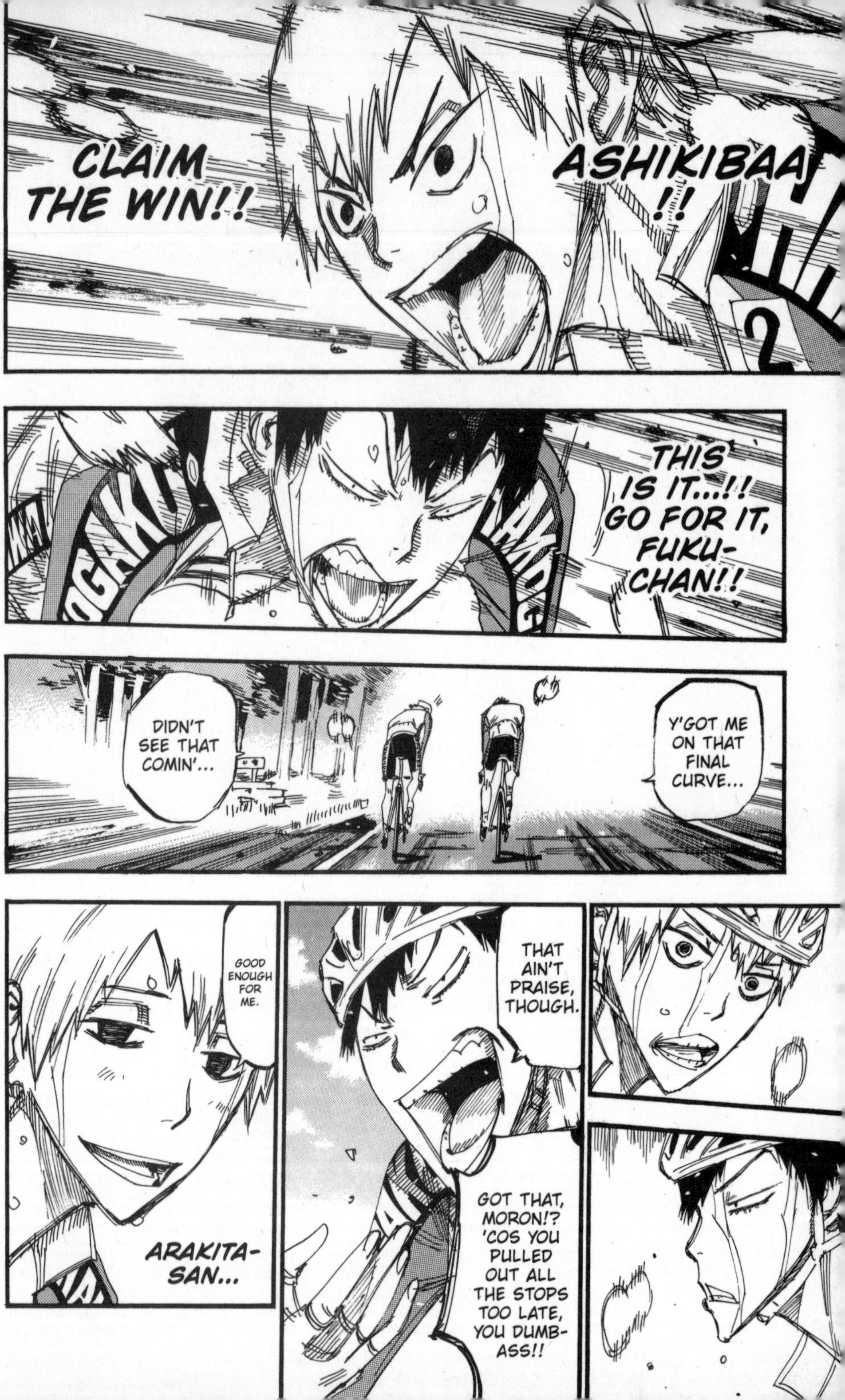
ASHIKIBAA !!
CLAIM THE WIN!!
THIS IS IT...!! GO FOR IT, FUKU-CHAN!!
Y'GOT ME ON THAT FINAL CURVE...
DIDN'T SEE THAT COMIN'...
THAT AIN'T PRAISE, THOUGH.
GOT THAT, MORON!? 'COS YOU PULLED OUT ALL THE STOPS TOO LATE, YOU DUMB-ASS!!
GOOD ENOUGH FOR ME.
ARAKITA-SAN...

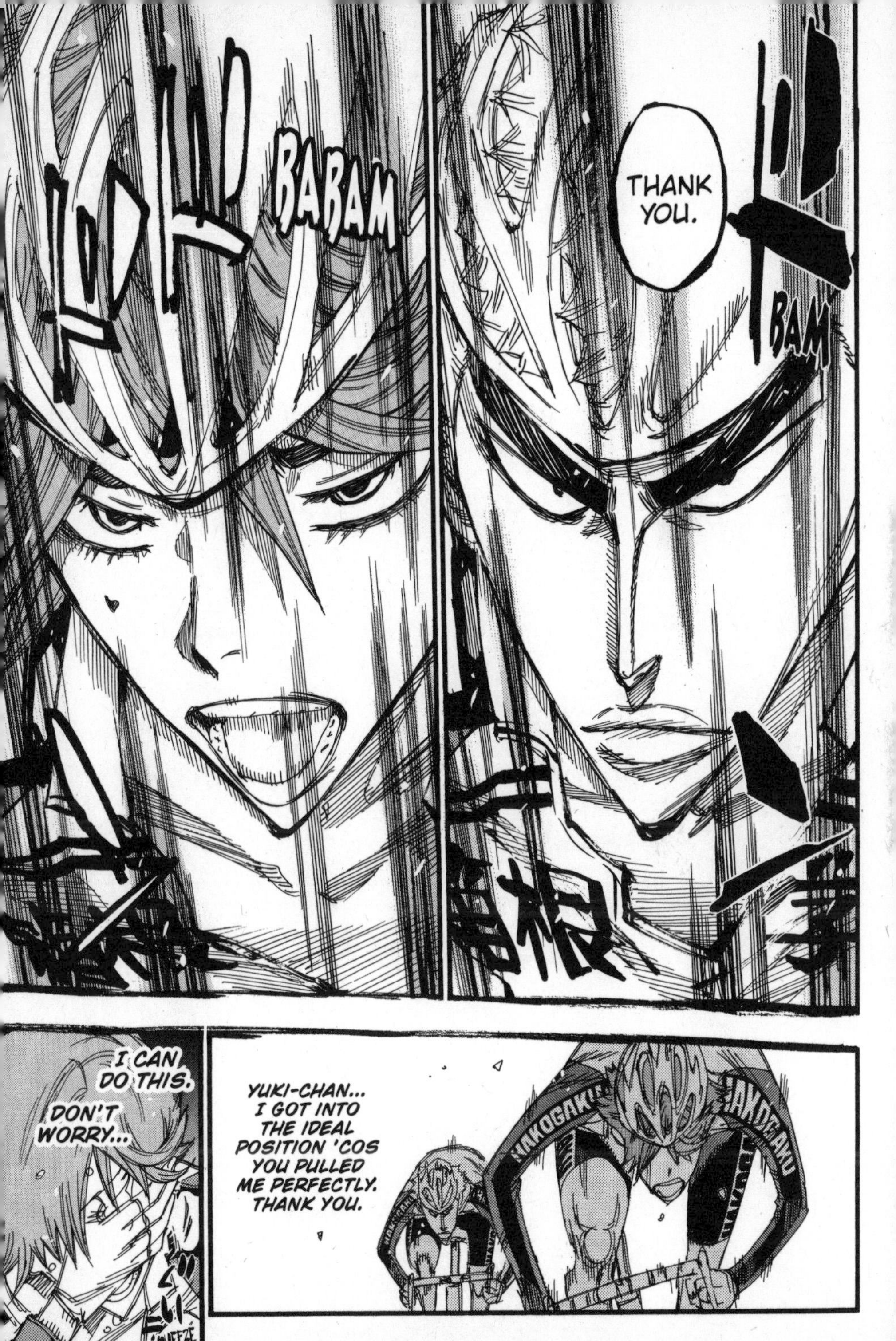
THANK YOU.
BAM
BABAM
YUKI-CHAN... I GOT INTO THE IDEAL POSITION 'COS YOU PULLED ME PERFECTLY. THANK YOU.
HAKOGAKU
I CAN DO THIS.
DON'T WORRY...
SQUEEZE

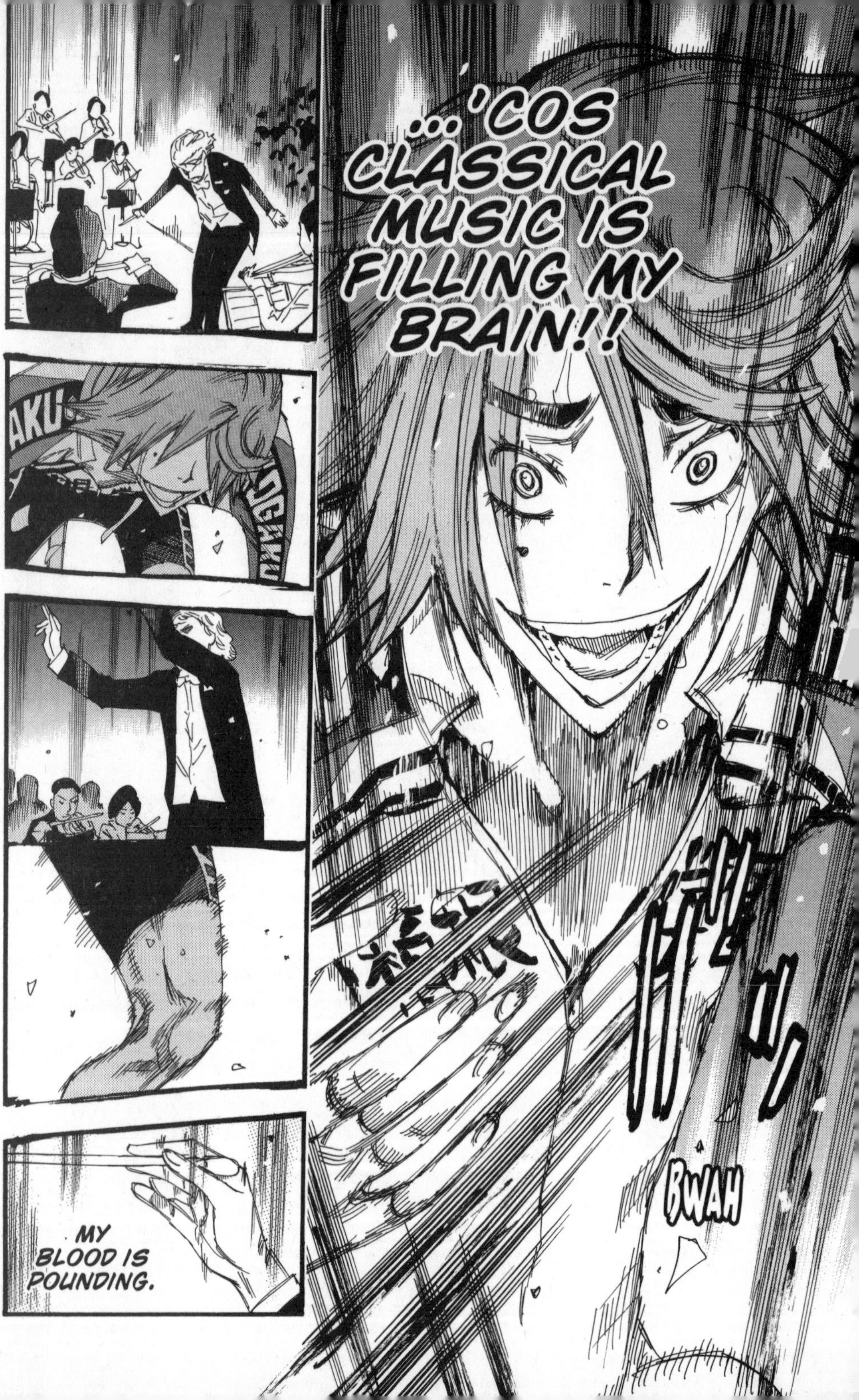
...'COS CLASSICAL MUSIC IS FILLING MY BRAIN!!
BWAH
MY BLOOD IS POUNDING.

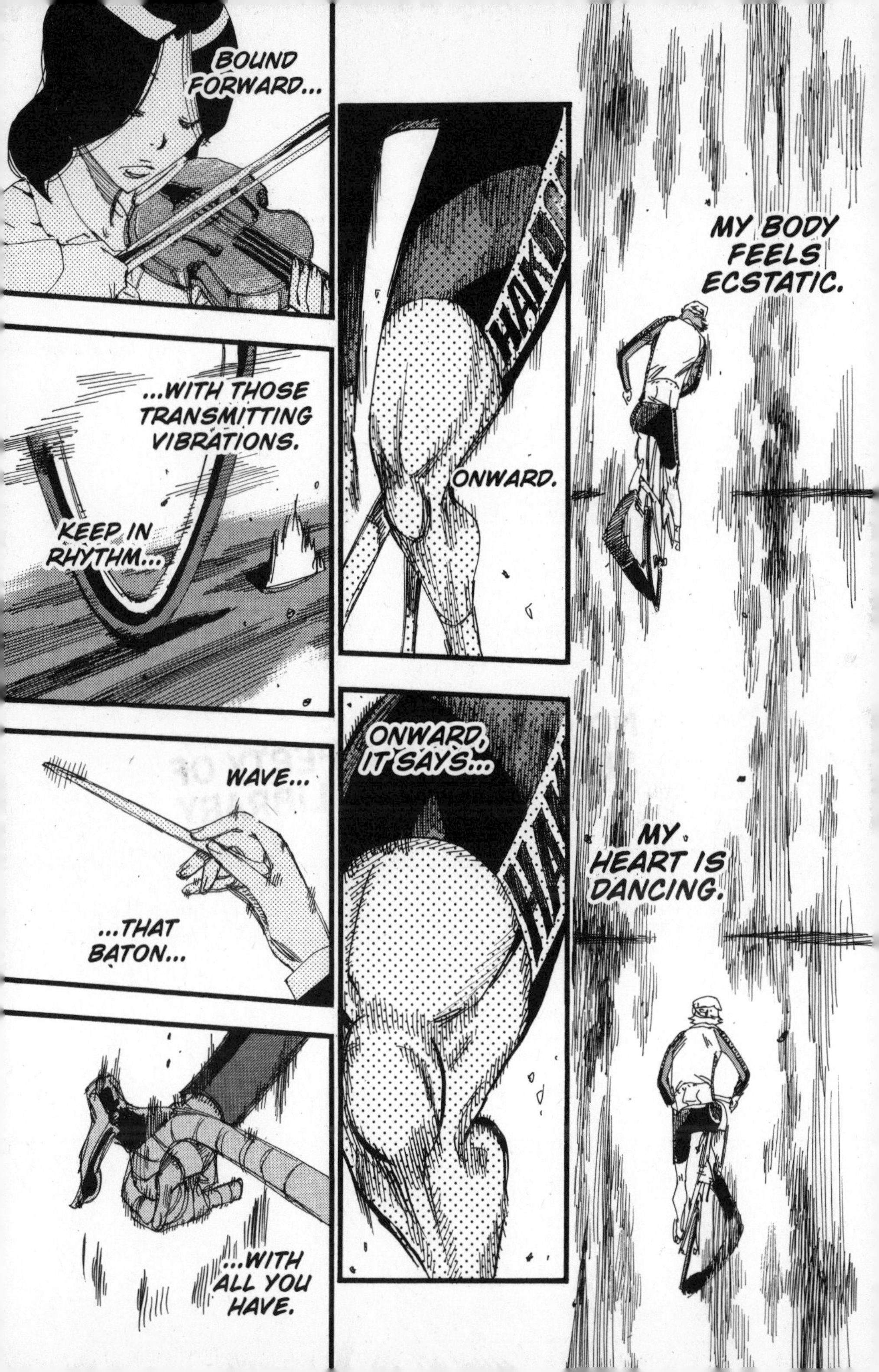
MY BODY FEELS ECSTATIC.
MY HEART IS DANCING.
ONWARD.
ONWARD, IT SAYS...
BOUND FORWARD...
...WITH THOSE TRANSMITTING VIBRATIONS.
KEEP IN RHYTHM...
WAVE...
...THAT BATON...
...WITH ALL YOU HAVE.

YOWAMUSHI PEDAL ⑮

WATARU WATANABE

Translation: Caleb D. Cook

Lettering: Lys Blakeslee, Rachel J. Pierce

This book is a work of fiction. Names, characters, places, and incidents are the product of the author's imagination or are used fictitiously. Any resemblance to actual events, locales, or persons, living or dead, is coincidental.

YOWAMUSHI PEDAL Volume 29, 30
© 2013 Wataru Watanabe
All rights reserved.
First published in Japan in 2013 by Akita Publishing Co., Ltd., Tokyo.
English translation rights arranged with Akita Publishing Co., Ltd. through Tuttle-Mori Agency, Inc., Tokyo.

English translation © 2020 by Yen Press, LLC

Yen Press
150 West 30th Street, 19th Floor
New York, NY 10001

Visit us at yenpress.com
facebook.com/yenpress
twitter.com/yenpress
yenpress.tumblr.com

First Yen Press Edition: September 2020

Yen Press is an imprint of Yen Press, LLC.
The Yen Press name and logo are trademarks of Yen Press, LLC.

Library of Congress Control Number: 2015960124

ISBNs: 978-1-9753-1057-8 (paperback)
      978-1-9753-1056-1 (ebook)

10 9 8 7 6 5 4 3 2 1

WOR

Printed in the United States of America